Introduction to Programming with Fortran

Ian Chivers · Jane Sleightholme

Introduction to Programming with Fortran

Fourth Edition

 Springer

Ian Chivers
Rhymney Consulting
London
UK

Jane Sleightholme
Fortranplus
London
UK

ISBN 978-3-030-09248-1   ISBN 978-3-319-75502-1   (eBook)
https://doi.org/10.1007/978-3-319-75502-1

The Yorkshire connection dedicates the book to Steve, Mark and Jonathan. The Welsh connection dedicates the book to Joan, Martin and Jenny.

Acknowledgements

The material in the book has evolved first

- from our combined experience of working in Computing Services within the University of London at

  - King's College, IDC (1986–2002) and JS (1985–2008)
  - Chelsea College, JS (1978–1985)
  - Imperial College, IDC (1978–1986)

in the teaching, advice and support of Fortran and related areas, and second
- in the provision of commercial training courses. The following are some of the organisations we've provided training for:

  - AMEC, Warrington
  - Aveva, Cambridge
  - AWE, Aldermaston
  - Centre for Ecology and Hydrology, Wallingford
  - DTU—Danish Technical University
  - Environment Agency, Worthing
  - Esso Petroleum, Fawley
  - JET—Joint European Torus
  - The Met Office, Bracknell and Exeter
  - National Nuclear Laboratory
  - Natural Resources Canada, Ottawa
  - Petroleum Geo-Services (PGS), Houston and Weybridge
  - QinetiQ, Farnborough
  - RAF Waddington
  - Ricardo Software
  - Risk Management Solutions
  - Rolls Royce, Derby
  - SHMU, Slovak Hydrometeorological Institute, Bratislava, Slovakia
  - University of Ulster, Jordanstown, Northern Ireland

– VCS, Germany
– Veritas DGC Ltd., Crawley
– Westland Helicopters, Yeovil.

Thanks are due to:

- The staff and students at King's College, Chelsea College and Imperial College.
- The people who have attended the commercial courses. It has been great fun teaching you and things have been very lively at times.
- The people on the Fortran 90 list and comp.lang.fortran. Access to the expertise of several hundred people involved in the use and development of Fortran on a daily basis across a wide range of disciplines is inestimable.
- The people at NAG for the provision of beta test versions of their Fortran compilers and technical help and support.
- The people at Intel for the provision of beta test versions of their Fortran compilers and technical help and support.
- The people running the Archer service for their help.
- The people at Oracle who helped with the C Interop examples.
- The staff and facilities at PTR Associates. It is a pleasure training there.
- Helmut Michels at the Max Planck Institute for permission to use the *dislin* library.
- The patience of our families during the time required to develop the courses upon which this book is based and whilst preparing the camera-ready copy.
- Helen Desmond and Nancy Wade-Jones at Springer for their enthusiasm and encouragement when things were going wrong!

Our Fortran home page is:

https://www.fortranplus.co.uk/

All of the programme examples can be found there.

If you would like to contact us, our email addresses are:
Ian Chivers: ian@rhymneyconsulting.co.uk
Jane Sleightholme: jane@fortranplus.co.uk

The manuscript was produced using Springer's LaTeX style sheet. We used proTeXt, MiKTeX and TeXnicCentre on the Windows platform. The graphs and plots were produced using the *dislin* graphics library. We started using TeX at Imperial College on several CDC systems in the 1980s. TeX and LaTeX have come a long way since then and plain TeX seems a distant memory.

Contents

List of Tables

Chapter 1
Overview

> *I don't know what the language of the year 2000 will look like,*
> *but it will be called Fortran*
>
> C.A.R. Hoare

Aims

The aims of the chapter are to provide a background to the organisation of the book.

1.1 Introduction

The book aims to provide coverage of a reasonable working subset of the Fortran programming language. The subset chosen should enable you to solve quite a wide range of frequently occurring problems.

This book has been written for three audiences:

- the complete beginner with little or no programming background
- an experienced Fortran programmer who wants to update their skills and move to a modern version of the language
- a programmer familiar with another language wanting to see what modern Fortran has to offer

Chapters 2 and 3 provide a coverage of problem solving and the history and development of programming languages. Chapter 2 is essential for the beginner as the concepts introduced there are used and expanded on throughout the rest of the book. Chapter 3 should be read at some point but can be omitted initially. Programming languages evolve and some understanding of where Fortran has come from and where it is going will prove valuable in the longer term.

- Chapter 2 looks at problem solving in some depth, and there is a coverage of the way we define problems, the role of algorithms, the use of both top-down and

© Springer International Publishing AG, part of Springer Nature 2018
I. Chivers and J. Sleightholme, *Introduction to Programming with Fortran*,
https://doi.org/10.1007/978-3-319-75502-1_1

bottom-up methods, and the requirement for formal systems analysis and design for more complex problems.

- Chapter 3 looks at the history and development of programming languages. This is essential as Fortran has evolved considerably from its origins in the mid-1950s, through the first standard in 1966, the Fortran 77 standard, the Fortran 90 standard, the Fortran 95 standard, TR 15580 and TR 15581, Fortran 2003, Fortran 2008 to Fortran 2018. It helps to put many of the current and proposed features of Fortran into context. Languages covered include Cobol, Algol, Lisp, Snobol, PL/1, Algol 68, Simula, Pascal, APL, Basic, C, Ada, Modula, Modula 2, Logo, Prolog, SQL, ICON, Oberon, Oberon 2, Smalltalk, C++, C#, Java and Python.

Chapters 4–8 cover the major features provided in Fortran for numeric programming in the first instance and for general purpose programming in the second. Each chapter has a set of problems. It is essential that a reasonable range of problems are attempted and completed, as it is impossible to learn any language without practice.

- Chapter 4 provides an introduction to programming with some simple Fortran examples. For people with a knowledge of programming this chapter can be covered fairly quickly.
- Chapter 5 looks at arithmetic in some depth, with a coverage of the various numeric data types, expressions and assignment of scalar variables. There is also a thorough coverage of the facilities provided in Fortran to help write programs that work on different hardware platforms.
- Chapter 6 is an introduction to arrays and do loops. The chapter starts with some examples of tabular structures that one should be familiar with. There is then an examination of what concepts we need in a programming language to support manipulation of tabular data.
- Chapter 7 takes the ideas introduced in Chap. 6 and extends them to higher-dimensioned arrays, additional forms of the dimension attribute and corresponding form of the do loop, and the use of looping for the control of repetition and manipulation of tabular information without the use of arrays.
- Chapter 8 looks at more of the facilities offered for the manipulation of whole arrays and array sections, ways in which we can initialise arrays using constructors, look more formally at the concepts we need to be able to accurately describe and understand arrays, and finally look at the differences between the way Fortran allows us to use arrays and the mathematical rules governing matrices.

Chapters 9, 10 and 11 look at input and output (I/O) and file handling in Fortran. An understanding of I/O is necessary for the development of so-called production, non interactive programs. These are essentially fully developed programs that are used repeatedly with a variety of data inputs and results.

- Chapter 9 looks at output of results and how to generate something that is more comprehensible and easy to read than what is available with free format output and also how to write the results to a file rather than the screen.
- Chapter 10 extends the ideas introduced in Chap. 9 to cover input of data, or reading data into a program and also considers file I/O.

- Chapter 11 provides a summary of input and output concepts introduced in Chaps. 9 and 10, and expands on them by introducing additional features of the read, write, open and close statements.

Chapter 12 introduces the first building block available in Fortran for the construction of programs for the solution of larger, more complex problems. It looks at the functions available in Fortran, the so-called intrinsic functions and procedures (over 100 of them) and covers how you can define and use your own functions.

It is essential to develop an understanding of the functions provided by the language and when it is necessary to write your own.

Chapter 13 introduces more formally the concept of control structures and their role in structured programming. Some of the control structures available in Fortran are introduced in earlier chapters, but there is a summary here of those already covered plus several new ones that complete our coverage of a minimal working set.

Chapters 14–16 complete our coverage of the intrinsic facilities in Fortran for data typing.

- Chapter 14 looks at the character data type in Fortran. There is a coverage of I/O again, with the operators available—only one in fact.
- Chapter 15 looks at the last numeric data type in Fortran, the complex data type. This data type is essential to the solution of a small class of problems in mathematics and engineering.
- Chapter 16 looks at the logical data type. The material covered here helps considerably in increasing the power and sophistication of the way we use and construct logical expressions in Fortran. This proves invaluable in the construction and use of logical expressions in control structures.

Chapter 17 introduces derived or user defined types with a small number of examples.

Chapter 18 looks at the dynamic data-structuring facilities now available in Fortran with the addition of pointers. This chapter looks at the basic syntax of pointers. They are used in range of examples in later chapters in the book.

The next two chapters look at the second major building block in Fortran — the subroutine. Chapter 19 provides a gentle introduction to some of the fundamental concepts of subroutine definition and use and Chapter 20 extends these ideas.

Chapter 21 introduces one of modern Fortran's major key features - the module. A Fortran module can be thought of as equivalent to a class in C++, Java and C#. This chapter looks at the basic syntax, with a couple of simple examples.

Chapter 22 looks at simple data structuring in Fortran, as we have now covered modules in a bit more depth.

Chapter 23 introduces algorithms and the big O notation.

Chapter 24 looks briefly at operator overloading, first introduced in Fortran 90.

Chapter 25 looks at generic programming.

Chapter 26 has a small set of mathematical examples.

Chapter 27 introduces parameterised derived types.

Chapter 28 introduces object oriented programming in Fortran.

Chapter 29 is the second chapter on object oriented programming

Chapters 30–34 look at parallel programming in Fortran with coverage of MPI, OpenMP and Coarray Fortran.

Chapter 35 looks at C interoperability.

Chapter 36 looks at IEEE Arithmetic support in Fortran.

Chapter 37 looks at derived type I/O in Fortran

Chapter 38 looks at a number examples of sorting and searching

Chapter 39 looks at handling missing data in calculations

Chapter 40 looks at converting from Fortran 77 to more modern Fortran.

Chapter 41 looks at using a graphics library for plotting

Chapter 42 has an example of abstract interfaces and procedure pointers in Fortran

Some of the chapters have annotated bibliographies. These often have pointers and directions for further reading. The coverage provided cannot be seen in isolation. The concepts introduced are by intention brief, and fuller coverage must be sought where necessary. References to the standard in the book are to the current Fortran 2018 revision unless otherwise stated. There are several appendices:

- Appendix A—This is a glossary which provides coverage of both the new concepts provided by Fortran and a range of computing terms and ideas.
- Appendix B—is a reference appendix on attribute declarations and specifications
- Appendix C—provides details of compatibility between standards
- Appendix D—Contains a list of some of the more commonly used intrinsic procedures in Fortran and includes an explanation of each procedure with a coverage of the rules and restrictions that apply and examples of use where appropriate. There also some tables summarising information about the procedures
- Appendix E—Contains the English and Latin text extracts used in one of the problems in the chapter on characters, and the coded text extract used in one of the problems in Chap. 14.
- Appendix F—Formal syntax.
- Appendix G—Sample compiler options

This book is not and cannot possibly be completely self-contained and exhaustive in its coverage of the Fortran language. Our first intention has been to produce a coverage of the features that will get you started with Fortran and enable you to solve a range of problems successfully. All in all Fortran is an exciting language, and it has caught up with language developments of the last 50 years.

1.2 Program Examples

All of the program examples are available on line at

```
https://www.fortranplus.co.uk/
```

All examples have been reformatted using the Nag compiler *polish* option. This makes the programs have a consistent style. The examples in the book have been formatted to have a line length of 48 characters to fit the printed page. They were then manually edited to improve where the lines broke. The examples on the web site have been formatted to have a line length of 132 characters.

1.3   Web Addresses

Web addresses are used throughout the book. As some of these are likely to change over the lifetime of the book our web site will have up to date addresses. We have organised them by chapter.

Chapter 2
Introduction to Problem Solving

They constructed ladders to reach to the top of the enemy's wall, and they did this by calculating the height of the wall from the number of layers of bricks at a point which was facing in their direction and had not been plastered. The layers were counted by a lot of people at the same time, and though some were likely to get the figure wrong the majority would get it right...Thus, guessing what the thickness of a single brick was, they calculated how long their ladder would have to be

Thucydides, The Peloponnesian War

'When I use a word,' Humpty Dumpty said, in a rather scornful tone, 'it means just what I choose it to mean — neither more nor less'
'The question is,' said Alice, 'whether you can make words mean so many different things'

Lewis Carroll, Through the Looking Glass and What Alice Found There

It is possible to invent a single machine which can be used to compute any computable sequence

Alan Turing

Aims

The aims of this chapter are:

- To examine some of the ideas and concepts involved in problem solving.
- To introduce the concept of an algorithm.
- To introduce two ways of approaching algorithmic problem solving.
- To introduce the ideas involved with systems analysis and design, i.e., to show the need for pencil and paper study before using a computer system.
- To introduce the Unified modelling Language - UML, a general purpose modelling language used in the field of software engineering.

© Springer International Publishing AG, part of Springer Nature 2018
I. Chivers and J. Sleightholme, *Introduction to Programming with Fortran*,
https://doi.org/10.1007/978-3-319-75502-1_2

2.1 Introduction

It is informative to consider some of the dictionary definitions of problem:

- A matter difficult of settlement or solution, Chambers.
- A question or puzzle propounded for solution, Chambers.
- A source of perplexity, Chambers.
- Doubtful or difficult question, Oxford.
- Proposition in which something has to be done, Oxford.
- A question raised for inquiry, consideration, or solution, Webster's.
- An intricate unsettled question, Webster's.

A common thread seems to be a question that we would like answered or solved. So one of the first things to consider in problem solving is how to pose the problem. This is often not as easy as is seems. Two of the most common methods to use here are:

- In natural language.
- In artificial or stylised language.

Both methods have their advantages and disadvantages.

2.2 Natural Language

Most people use natural language and are familiar with it, and the two most common forms are the written and spoken word. Consider the following language usage:

- The difference between a 3-year-old child and an adult describing the world.
- The difference between the way an engineer and a physicist would approach the design of a car engine.
- The difference between a manager and a worker considering the implications of the introduction of new technology.

Great care must be taken when using natural language to define a problem and a solution. It is possible that people use the same language to mean completely different things, and one must be aware of this when using natural language whilst problem solving.

Natural language can also be ambiguous: Old men and women eat cheese. Are both the men and women old?

2.3 Artificial Language

The two most common forms of artificial language are technical terminology and notations. Technical terminology generally includes both the use of new words and alternate use of existing words. Consider some of the concepts that are useful when examining the expansion of gases in both a theoretical and practical fashion:

- Temperature.
- Pressure.
- Mass.
- Isothermal expansion.
- Adiabatic expansion.

Now look at the following:

- A chef using a pressure cooker.
- A garage mechanic working on a car engine.
- A doctor monitoring blood pressure.
- An engineer designing a gas turbine.

Each has a particular problem to solve, and all will approach their problem in their own way; thus they will each use the same terminology in slightly different ways.

2.3.1 Notations

Some examples of notations are:

- Algebra.
- Calculus.
- Logic.

All of the above have been used as notations for describing both problems and their solutions.

2.4 Resume

We therefore have two ways of describing problems and they both have a learning phase until we achieve sufficient understanding to use them effectively. Having arrived at a satisfactory problem statement we next have to consider how we get the solution. It is here that the power of the algorithmic approach becomes useful.

2.5 Algorithms

An algorithm is a sequence of steps that will solve part or all of a problem. One of the most easily understood examples of an algorithm is a recipe. Most people have done some cooking, if only making toast and boiling an egg.

A recipe is made up of two parts:

- A check list of things you need.
- The sequence or order of steps.

Problems can occur at both stages, e.g., finding out halfway through the recipe that you do not have an ingredient or utensil; finding out that one stage will take an hour when the rest will be ready in ten minutes. Note that certain things can be done in any order — it may not make any difference if you prepare the potatoes before the carrots.

There are two ways of approaching problem solving when using a computer. They both involve algorithms, but are very different from one another. They are called top-down and bottom up.

The name algorithm is derived from the name of a ninth century Persian mathematician Abu Ja'far Mohammed ibn Musa al-Kuwarizmi (father of Ja'far Mohammed, son of Moses, native of Kuwarizmi), and has been corrupted in western culture as Al-Kuwarizmi.

2.5.1 Top-Down

In a top-down approach the problem is first specified at a high or general level: prepare a meal. It is then refined until each step in the solution is explicit and in the correct sequence, e.g., peel and slice the onions, then brown in a frying pan before adding the beef. One drawback to this approach is that it is very difficult to teach to beginners because they rarely have any idea of what primitive tools they have at their disposal. Another drawback is that they often get the sequencing wrong, e.g., now place in a moderately hot oven is frustrating because you may not have lit the oven (sequencing problem) and secondly because you may have no idea how hot moderately hot really is. However, as more and more problems are tackled, top-down becomes one of the most effective methods for programming.

2.5.2 Bottom-Up

Bottom-up is the reverse to top-down! As before you start by defining the problem at a high level, e.g., prepare a meal. However, now there is an examination of what tools, etc. you have available to solve the problem. This method lends itself to teaching since a repertoire of tools can be built up and more complicated problems can be tackled. Thinking back to the recipe there is not much point in trying to cook a six course meal if the only thing that you can do is boil an egg and open a tin of beans. The bottom-up approach thus has advantages for the beginner. However, there may be a problem when no suitable tool is available. A colleague and friend of the authors learned how to make Bechamel sauce, and was so pleased by his success that every other meal had a course with a Bechamel sauce. Try it on your eggs one morning. Here is a case of specifying a problem, prepare a meal, and using an inappropriate but plausible tool, Bechamel sauce.

The effort involved in tackling a realistic problem, introducing the constructs as and when they are needed and solving it is considerable. This approach may not lead to a reasonably comprehensive coverage of the language, or be particularly useful from a teaching point of view. case studies do have great value, but it helps if you know the elementary rules before you start on them. Imagine learning French by studying Balzac, before you even look at a French grammar book. You can learn this way but even when you have finished, you may not be able to speak to a Frenchman and be understood. A good example of the case study approach is given in the book Software Tools, by Kernighan and Plauger.

In this book our aim is to gradually introduce more and more tools until you know enough to approach the problem using the top-down method, and also realise from time to time that it will be necessary to develop some new tools.

2.5.3   Stepwise Refinement

Both of the above techniques can be combined with what is called stepwise refinement. The original ideas behind this approach are well expressed in a paper by Wirth, entitled "Program Development by Stepwise Refinement", published in 1971. It means that you start with a global problem statement and break the problem down in stages, into smaller and smaller sub problems that become more and more amenable to solution. When you first start programming the problems you can solve are quite simple, but as your experience grows you will find that you can handle more complex problems.

When you think of the way that you solve problems you will probably realise that unless the problem is so simple that you can answer it straight-away some thinking and pencil and paper work are required. An example that some may be familiar with is in practical work in a scientific discipline, where coming unprepared to the situation can be very frustrating and unrewarding. It is therefore appropriate to look at ways of doing analysis and design before using a computer.

2.6   Modular Programming

As the problems we try solving become more complex we need to look at ways of managing the construction of programs that comprise many parts. Modula 2 was one of the first languages to support this methodology and we will look at modular programming in more depth in a subsequent chapter.

2.7   Object Oriented Programming

There is a class of problems that are best solved by the treatment of the components of these problems as objects. We will look at the concepts involved in object oriented programming and object oriented languages in the next chapter.

2.8   Systems Analysis and Design

When one starts programming it is generally not apparent that one needs a methodology to follow to become successful as a programmer. This is usually because the problems are reasonably simple, and it is not necessary to be explicit about all of the stages one has gone through in arriving at a solution. As the problems become more complex it is necessary to become more rigorous and thorough in one's approach, to keep control in the face of the increasing complexity and to avoid making mistakes. It is then that the benefit of systems analysis and design becomes obvious. Broadly we have the following stages in systems analysis and design:

- Problem definition.
- Feasibility study and fact finding.
- Analysis.
- Initial system design.
- Detailed design.
- Implementation.
- Evaluation.
- Maintenance.

and each problem we address will entail slightly different time spent in each of these stages. Let us look at each stage in more detail.

2.8.1   Problem Definition

Here we are interested in defining what the problem really is. We should aim at providing some restriction on both the scope of the problem, and the objectives we set ourselves. We can use the methods mentioned earlier to help us out. It is essential that the objectives are:

- Clearly defined.
- Understood and agreed to by all people concerned, when more than one person is involved.
- Realistic.

2.8.2 Feasibility Study and Fact Finding

Here we look to see if there is a feasible solution. We would try and estimate the cost of solving the problem and see if the investment was warranted by the benefits, i.e., cost-benefit analysis.

2.8.3 Analysis

Here we look at what must be done to solve the problem. Note that we are interested in finding out what we need to do, but that we do not actually do it at this stage.

2.8.4 Design

Once the analysis is complete we know what must be done, and we can proceed to the design. We may find there are several alternatives, and we thus examine alternate ways in which the problem can be solved. It is here that we use the techniques of top-down and bottom-up problem solving, combined with stepwise refinement to generate an algorithm to solve the problem. We are now moving from the logical to the physical side of the solution. This stage ends with a choice among several alternatives. Note that there is generally not one ideal solution, but several, each with its own advantages and disadvantages.

2.8.5 Detailed Design

Here we move from the general to the specific, The end result of this stage should be a specification that is sufficiently tightly defined to generate actual program code.

It is at this stage that it is useful to generate pseudocode. This means writing out in detail the actions we want carried out at each stage of our overall algorithm. We gradually expand each stage (stepwise refinement) until it becomes Fortran — or whatever language we want.

2.8.6 Implementation

It is at this stage that we actually use a computer system to create the program(s) that will solve the problem. It is here that we actually need to know enough about a programming language to use it effectively to solve our problem. This is only one stage in the overall process, and mistakes at any of the stages can create serious difficulties.

2.8.7 *Evaluation and Testing*

Here we try to see if the program(s) we have produced will actually do what they are supposed to. We need to have data sets that enable us to say with confidence that the program really does work. This may not be an easy task, as quite often we only have numeric methods to solve the problem, which is why we are using the computer in the first place — hence we are relying on the computer to provide the proof; i.e., we have to use a computer to determine the veracity of the programs — and as Heller says, Catch 22.

2.8.8 *Maintenance*

It is rare that a program is run once and never used again. This means that there will be an ongoing task of maintaining the program, generally to make it work with different versions of the operating system or compiler, and to incorporate new features not included in the original design. It often seems odd when one starts programming that a program will need maintenance, as we are reluctant to regard a program in the same way as a mechanical object like a car that will eventually fall apart through use. Thus maintenance means keeping the program working at some tolerable level, often with a high level of investment in manpower and resources. Research in this area has shown that anything up to 80% of the manpower investment in a program can be in maintenance.

2.9   Unified Modelling Language - UML

UML is a general purpose modelling language used in the field of software engineering. It was developed by Grady Booch, Ivar Jacobson and James Rumbaugh whilst working at Rational Software in the 1990's. They were three of the leading exponents of object oriented software methodologies at the time and decided to unify the various approaches that each had developed.

UML combines techniques from data modelling (entity relationship diagrams), business modelling (work flows), object modelling, and component modelling. It can be used with all processes, throughout the software development life cycle, and across different implementation technologies.

It tends to be used more in business computing than scientific computing.

2.10 Conclusions

A drawback, inherent in all approaches to programming and to problem solving in general, is the assumption that a solution is indeed possible. There are problems which are simply insoluble — not only problems like balancing a national budget, weather forecasting for a year, or predicting which radioactive atom will decay, but also problems which are apparently computationally solvable.

Knuth gives the example of a chess problem — determining whether the game is a forced victory for white. Although there is an algorithm to achieve this, it requires an inordinately long time to complete. For practical purposes it is unsolvable.

Other problems can be shown mathematically to be undecidable. The work of Gödel in this area has been of enormous importance, and the bibliography contains a number of references for the more inquisitive and mathematically orientated reader. The Hofstader coverage is the easiest, and least mathematical.

As far as possible we will restrict ourselves to solvable problems, like learning a programming language.

Within the formal world of Computer Science our description of an algorithm would be considered a little lax. For our introductory needs it is sufficient, but a more rigorous approach is given by Hopcroft and Ullman in Introduction to Automata Theory, Languages and Computation, and by Beckman in Mathematical Foundations of programming.

2.11 Problems

2.1 What is an algorithm?

2.2 What distinguishes top-down from bottom-up approaches to problem solving? Illustrate your answer with reference to the problem of a car, motor-cycle or bicycle having a flat tire.

2.12 Bibliography

A.V. Aho A.V., Hopcroft J.E.,and J.D. Ullman J.D., The Design and Analysis of Computer Algorithms, Addison-Wesley, 1982.

- Theoretical coverage of the design and analysis of computer algorithms.

  Beckman F.S., Mathematical Foundations of Programming, Addison-Wesley, 1981.

- Good clear coverage of the theoretical basis of computing.

  Bulloff J.J., Holyoke T.C., Hahn S.W., Foundations of Mathematics — Symposium Papers Commemorating the 60th Birthday of Kurt Gödel, Springer-Verlag, 1969.

- The comment by John von Neumann highlights the importance of Gödel's work,.. Kurt Gödel's achievement in modern logic is singular and monumental — indeed it is more than a monument, it is a landmark which will remain visible far in space and time. Whether anything comparable to it has occurred in the logic of modern times may be debated. In any case, the conceivable proxima are very, very few. The subject of logic has certainly changed its nature and possibilities with Gödel's achievement.

  Dahl O.J., Dijkstra E.W., Hoare C.A.R., Structured programming, Academic Press, 1972.

- This is the seminal book on structured programming.

  Davis M., Computability and Unsolvability, Dover, 1982.

- The book is an introduction to the theory of computability and noncomputability — the theory of recursive functions in mathematics. Not for the mathematically faint hearted!

  Davis W.S., Systems Analysis and Design, Addison-Wesley, 1983.

- Good introduction to systems analysis and design, with a variety of case studies. Also looks at some of the tools available to the systems analyst.

  Edmonds D., Eidinow J., Wittgensteins Poker, Faber and Faber, 2001.

- The subtitle of the book provides a better understanding of the content - 'The story of a 10 minute argument between two great philosophers', which took place on Friday 25 October 1946 at the Cambridge Moral Science Club. The title of Poppers paper was 'Are there Philosophical problems?'. Ludwig Wittgenstein and Bertrand Russell were in the audience. Well worth a read.
- Here is an extract of a quote from the Times Literary Supplement. *A succinctly composed, informative, wonderfully readable and often funny account of a single impassioned encounter between the great overbearing philosopher Ludwig Wittgenstein and the younger, less great but equally overbearing philosopher Karl Popper... reads like an inspired collaboration between Iris Murdoch and Monty Python.*

  Fogelin R.J., Wittgenstein, Routledge and Kegan Paul, 1980.

- The book provides a gentle introduction to the work of the philosopher Wittgenstein, who examined some of the philosophical problems associated with logic and reason.

Gödel K., On Formally Undecidable Propositions of Principia Mathematica and Related Systems, Oliver and Boyd, 1962.

- An English translation of Gödel's original paper by Meltzer, with quite a lengthy introduction by R.B. Braithwaite, then Knightbridge Professor of Moral Philosophy at Cambridge University, England, and classified under philosophy at the library at King's, rather than mathematics.

Hofstadter D.,The Eternal Golden Braid, Harvester Press, 1979.

- A very readable coverage of paradox and contradiction in art, music and logic, looking at the work of Escher, Bach and Gödel, respectively.

Hopcroft J.E., Ullman J.D., Introduction to Automata Theory, Languages and Computation, Addison-Wesley, 1979.

- Coverage of the theoretical basis of computing.

Jacobson, Ivar, Grady Booch, James Rumbaugh, (1998). The Unified Software Development Process. Addison Wesley Longman. ISBN 0-201-57169-2.

- The original book on UML.

Kernighan B.W., Plauger P.J., Software Tools, Addison-Wesley, 1976.

- Interesting essays on the program development process, originally using a nonstandard variant of Fortran. Also available using Pascal.

Knuth D.E., The Art of Computer Programming, Addison-Wesley,

- Vol 1. Fundamental Algorithms, 1974
- Vol 2. Semi-numerical Algorithms, 1978
- Vol 3. Sorting and Searching, 1972

  – Contains interesting insights into many aspects of algorithm design. Good source of specialist algorithms, and Knuth writes with obvious and infectious enthusiasm (and erudition).

Millington D., Systems Analysis and Design for Computer Applications, Ellis Horwood, 1981.

- Short and readable introduction to systems analysis and design.

Popper K., The Logic of Scientific Discovery, 1934 (as Logik der Forschung, English translation 1959), Routledge, ISBN 0-415-27844-9.

• Popper argues that science should adopt a methodology based on falsifiability, because no number of experiments can ever prove a theory, but a single experiment can contradict one. A classic.

Salmon M.H., Logic and Critical Thinking, Harcourt Brace Jovanovich, 1984.

• Quite a good introduction to logic and critical thinking. Coverage of arguments, deductive and inductive arguments, causal arguments, probability and inductive logic, confirmation of hypotheses.

Wirth N., Algorithms + Data Structures = Programs, Prentice Hall, 1976.

• One of the seminal texts in computer science. Essential reading.

Wirth N., Program Development by Stepwise Refinement, Communications of the ACM, April 1971, Volume 14, Number 4, pp. 221–227.

• Clear and simple exposition of the ideas of stepwise refinement.

Chapter 3
Introduction to Programming Languages

We have to go to another language in order to think clearly about the problem

Samuel R. Delany, Babel-17

Aims

The primary aim of this chapter is to provide a short history of program language development and give some idea as to the concepts that have had an impact on Fortran. It concentrates on some but not all of the major milestones of the last 40 years, in roughly chronological order. The secondary aim is to show the breadth of languages available. The chapter concludes with coverage of a small number of more specialised languages.

3.1   Introduction

It is important to realise that programming languages are a recent invention. They have been developed over a relatively short period — 60 years — and are still undergoing improvement. Time spent gaining some historical perspective will help you understand and evaluate future changes. This chapter starts right at the beginning and takes you through some, but not all, of the developments during this 55 year span. The bulk of the chapter describes languages that are reasonably widely available commercially, and therefore ones that you are likely to meet. The chapter concludes with a coverage of some more specialised and/or recent developments.

© Springer International Publishing AG, part of Springer Nature 2018   19
I. Chivers and J. Sleightholme, *Introduction to Programming with Fortran*,
https://doi.org/10.1007/978-3-319-75502-1_3

3.2   Some Early Theoretical Work

Some of the most important early theoretical work in computing was that of Turing and von Neumann. Turing's work provided the base from which it could be shown that it was possible to get a machine to solve problems. The work of von Neumann added the concept of storage and combined with Turing's work to provide the basis for most computers designed to this day.

3.3   What Is a Programming Language?

For a large number of people a programming language provides the means of getting a digital computer to solve a problem. There is a wide range of problems and an equally wide range of programming languages, with particular languages being suited to a particular class of problems, all of which often appears bewildering to the beginner.

3.4   Program Language Development and Engineering

There is much in common between the development of programming languages and the development of anything from the engineering world. Consider the car: old cars offer much of the same functionality as more modern ones, but most people prefer driving newer models. The same is true of programming languages, where you can achieve much with the older languages, but the newer ones are easier to use.

3.5   The Early Days

A concept that proves very useful when discussing programming languages is that of the level of a machine. By this is meant how close a language is to the underlying machine that the program runs on. In the early days of programming (up to 1954) there were only two broad categories: machine languages and assemblers. The language that digital machines use is that of 0 and 1, i.e., they are binary devices. Writing a program in terms of patterns of 0 and 1 was not particularly satisfactory and the capability of using more meaningful mnemonics was soon introduced. Thus it was realised quite quickly that one of the most important aspects of programming languages is that they have to be read and understood by both machines and humans.

3.5.1 Fortran's Origins

The next stage was the development of higher-level languages. The first of these was Fortran and it was developed over a 3 year period from 1954 to 1957 by an IBM team led by John Backus. This group achieved considerable success, and helped to prove that the way forward lay with high-level languages for computer-based problem solving. Fortran stands for formula translation and was used mainly by people with a scientific background for solving problems that had a significant arithmetic content. It was thus relatively easy, for the time, to express this kind of problem in Fortran.

By 1966 and the first standard Fortran:

- Was widely available.
- Was easy to teach.
- Had demonstrated the benefits of subroutines and independent compilation.
- Was relatively machine independent.
- Often had very efficient implementations.

Possibly the single most important fact about Fortran was, and still is, its widespread usage in the scientific community.

3.5.2 Fortran 77

The next standard in 1977 (actually 1978, and thus out by one — a very common programming error, more of this later!) added a number of major improvements including

- Block IF and END IF statements, with optional ELSE and ELSE IF clauses, to provide improved language support for structured programming
- DO loop extensions, including parameter expressions, negative increments, and zero trip counts
- OPEN, CLOSE, and INQUIRE statements for improved I/O capability
- IMPLICIT statement, to override implicit conventions that undeclared variables are INTEGER if their name begins with I, J, K, L, M, or N (and REAL otherwise)
- CHARACTER data type, replacing Hollerith strings with vastly expanded facilities for character input and output and processing of character-based data
- PARAMETER statement for specifying constants
- SAVE statement for persistent local variables
- Generic names for intrinsic functions
- A set of intrinsics (LGE, LGT, LLE, LLT) for lexical comparison of strings

One important feature sometimes overlooked was backwards compatibility. This meant that the standard did not invalidate any standard conformant Fortran 66 program. This protected investment in old code.

3.5.3 Cobol

The business world also realised that computers were useful and several languages were developed, including FLOWMATIC, AIMACO, Commercial Translator and FACT, leading eventually to Cobol — COmmon Business Orientated Language. There is a need in commercial programming to describe data in a much more complex fashion than for scientific programming, and Cobol had far greater capability in this area than Fortran. The language was unique at the time in that a group of competitors worked together with the objective of developing a language that would be useful on machines used by other manufacturers.

The contributions made by Cobol include:

- Firstly the separation among:
- The task to be undertaken.
- The description of the data involved.
- The working environment in which the task is carried out.
- Secondly a data description mechanism that was largely machine independent.
- Thirdly its effectiveness for handling large files.
- Fourthly the benefit to be gained from a programming language that was easy to read.

Modern developments in computing — of report generators, file-handling software, fourth-generation development tools, and especially the increasing availability of commercial relational database management systems — are gradually replacing the use of Cobol, except where high efficiency and/or tight control are required.

3.5.4 Algol

Another important development of the 1950s was Algol. It had a history of development from Algol 58, the original Algol language, through Algol 60 eventually to the Revised Algol 60 Report. Some of the design criteria for Algol 58 were:

- The language should be as close as possible to standard mathematical notation and should be readable with little further explanation.
- It should be possible to use it for the description of computing processes in publications.
- The new language should be mechanically translatable into machine programs.

A sad feature of Algol 58 was the lack of any input/output facilities, and this meant that different implementations often had incompatible features in this area.

The next important step for Algol occurred at a UNESCO-sponsored conference in June 1959. There was an open discussion on Algol and the outcome was Algol 60, and eventually the Revised Algol 60 Report.

It was at this conference that John Backus gave his now famous paper on a method for defining the syntax of a language, called Backus Normal Form, or BNF. The full significance of the paper was not immediately recognised. However, BNF was to prove of enormous value in language definition, and helped provide an interface point with computational linguistics.

The contributions of Algol to program language development include:

- Block structure.
- Scope rules for variables because of block structure.
- The BNF definition by Backus — most languages now have a formal definition.
- The support of recursion.
- Its offspring.

Thus Algol was to prove to make a contribution to programming languages that was never reflected in the use of Algol 60 itself, in that it has been the parent of one of the main strands of program language development.

3.6 Chomsky and Program Language Development

Programming languages are of considerable linguistic interest, and the work of Chomsky in 1956 in this area was to prove of inestimable value. Chomsky's system of transformational grammar was developed in order to give a precise mathematical description to certain aspects of language. Simplistically, Chomsky describes grammars, and these grammars in turn can be used to define or generate corresponding kinds of languages. It can be shown that for each type of grammar and language there is a corresponding type of machine. It was quickly realised that there was a link with the earlier work of Turing.

This link helped provide a firm scientific base for programming language development, and modern compiler writing has come a long way from the early work of Backus and his team at IBM. It may seem unimportant when playing a video game at home or in an arcade, but for some it is very comforting that there is a firm theoretical basis behind all that fun.

3.7 Lisp

There were also developments in very specialized areas. List processing was proving to be of great interest in the 1950s and saw the development of IPLV between 1954 and 1958. This in turn led to the development of Lisp at the end of the 1950s. Lisp has proved to be of considerable use for programming in the areas of artificial intelligence, playing chess, automatic theorem proving and general problem solving. It was one of the first languages to be interpreted rather than compiled. Whilst interpreted languages are invariably slower and less efficient in their use of the underlying computer systems than compiled languages, they do provide great opportunities for the user to explore and try out ideas whilst sitting at a terminal. The power that this gives to the computational problem solver is considerable.

Possibly the greatest contribution to program language development made by Lisp was its functional notation. One of the major problems for the Lisp user has been the large number of Lisp flavours, and this has reduced the impact that the language has had and deserved.

3.8 Snobol

Snobol was developed to aid in string processing, which was seen as an important part of many computing tasks, e.g., parsing of a program. Probably the most important thing that Snobol demonstrated was the power of pattern matching in a programming language, e.g., it is possible to define a pattern for a title that would include Mr, Mrs, Ms, Miss, Rev, etc., and search for this pattern in a text using Snobol. Like Lisp it is generally available as an interpreter rather than a compiler, but compiled versions do exist, and are often called Spitbol. Pattern-matching capabilities are now to be found in many editors and this makes them very powerful and useful tools. It is in the area of text manipulation that Snobol's greatest contribution to program language development lies.

3.9 Second-Generation Languages

3.9.1 PL/1 and Algol 68

It is probably true that Fortran, Algol 60 and Cobol are the three main first-generation high-level languages. The 1960s saw the emergence of PL/1 and Algol 68. PL/1 was a synthesis of features of Fortran, Algol 60 and Cobol. It was soon realised that whilst PL/1 had great richness and power of expression this was in some ways offset by the greater difficulties involved in language definition and use.

These latter problems were also true of Algol 68. The report introduced its own syntactic and semantic conventions and thus forced another stage in the learning process on the prospective user. However, it has a small but very committed user population who like the very rich facilities provided by the language.

3.9.2 Simula

Another strand that makes up program language development is provided by Simula, a general purpose programming language developed by Dahl, Myhrhaug and

Nygaard of the Norwegian Computing Centre. The most important contribution that Simula makes is the provision of language constructs that aid the programming of complex, highly interactive problems. It is thus heavily used in the areas of simulation and modelling. It was effectively the first language to offer the opportunity of object orientated programming, and we will come back to this very important development in programming languages later in this chapter.

3.9.3   Pascal

The designer of Pascal, Niklaus Wirth, had participated in the early stages of the design of Algol 68 but considered that the generality and complexity of Algol 68 was a move in the wrong direction. Pascal (like Algol 68) had its roots in Algol 60 but aimed at providing expressive power through a small set of straightforward concepts. This set is relatively easy to learn and helps in producing readable and hence more comprehensible programs.

It became the language of first choice within the field of computer science during the 1970s and 1980s, and the comment by Wirth sums up the language very well: "although Pascal had no support from industry, professional societies, or government agencies, it became widely used. The important reason for this success was that many people capable of recognising its potential actively engaged themselves in its promotion. As crucial as the existence of good implementations is the availability of documentation. The conciseness of the original report made it attractive for many teachers to expand it into valuable textbooks. Innumerable books appeared between 1977 and 1985, effectively promoting Pascal to become the most widespread language used in introductory programming courses. Good course material and implementations are the indispensable prerequisites for such an evolution."

3.9.4   APL

APL is another interesting language of the early 1960s. It was developed by Iverson early in the decade and was available by the mid to late 1960s. It is an interpretive vector and matrix based language with an extensive set of operators for the manipulation of vectors, arrays, etc., of whatever data type. As with Algol 68 it has a small but dedicated user population. A possibly unfair comment about APL programs is that you do not debug them, but rewrite them!

3.9.5   Basic

Basic stands for Beginners All Purpose Symbolic Instruction Code, and was developed by Kemeny and Kurtz at Dartmouth during the 1960s. Its name gives a clue to its audience and it is very easy to learn. It is generally interpreted, though compiled versions do exist. It has proved to be well suited to the rapid development of small programs. It is much criticised because it lacks features that encourage or force the adoption of sound programming techniques.

3.9.6   C

There is a requirement in computing to be able to access the underlying machine directly or at least efficiently. It is therefore not surprising that computer professionals have developed high-level languages to do this. This may well seem a contradiction, but it can be done to quite a surprising degree. Some of the earliest published work was that of Martin Richards on the development of BCPL.

This language directly influenced the work of Ken Thompson and can be clearly seen in the programming languages B and C. The UNIX operating system is almost totally written in C and demonstrates very clearly the benefits of the use of high-level languages wherever possible.

With the widespread use of UNIX within the academic world C gained considerable ground during the 1970s and 1980s. UNIX systems also offered much to the professional software developer, and became widely used for large-scale software development and as Ritchie says: "C is quirky, flawed, and an enormous success. while accidents of history surely helped, it evidently satisfied a need for a system implementation language efficient enough to displace assembly language, yet sufficiently abstract and fluent to describe algorithms and interactions in a wide variety of environments."

There have been several versions of C. Before the language was standardised most people relied on an informal specification contained in the book by Dennis Ritchie and Brian Kernighan, and this version is called K&R C. In 1989 the American National Standards Institute published the ANSI C or C89 standard. It became an ISO standard a year later. The second edition of the K&R book covers the ANSI C standard. ISO later released an extension to the internationalization support of the standard in 1995, and a revised standard (C99) in 1999.

C99 introduced several new features, including inline functions, several new data types (including long long int and a complex type to represent complex numbers), variable-length arrays, improved support for IEEE 754 floating point, support for variadic macros (macros of variable arity), and support for one-line comments beginning with // which are part of C++. This increased the compatibility of C and C++. Many of these had already been implemented as extensions in several C compilers.

The current version of the standard - C11 was approved in December 2011.

The C11 standard adds several new features to C and the library, including type generic macros, anonymous structures, improved Unicode support, atomic operations, multithreading, and bounds-checked functions. It improved compatibility with C++.

3.10   Some Other Strands in Language Development

There are many strands that make up program language development and some of them are introduced here.

3.10.1   Abstraction, Stepwise Refinement and Modules

Abstraction has proved to be very important in programming. It enables a complex task to be broken down into smaller parts concentrating on what we want to happen rather than how we want it to happen. This leads almost automatically to the ideas of stepwise refinement and modules, with collections of modules to perform specific tasks or steps.

3.10.2   Structured Programming

Structured programming in its narrowest sense concerns itself with the development of programs using a small but sufficient set of statements and, in particular, control statements. It has had a great effect on program language design, and most languages now support the minimal set of control structures.

In a broader sense structured programming subsumes other objectives, including simplicity, comprehensibility, verifiability, modifiability and maintenance of programs.

3.10.3   Data Structuring and Procedural Programming

By the 1970's languages started to emerge that offered the ability to organise data logically - so called data structuring, and we will look at two of these in the coverage below - C and Pascal.

C provided this facility via structs and Pascal did it via records. These languages also offered two ways of processing the data - directly or via procedures. The terms concrete and abstract data type are sometimes also used in the literature.

An example may help here. Consider a date. This is typically made up of three components, a day, a month and a year. In C we can create a user defined type called a date using structs. We can then create variables of this type. This is done in Pascal in a similar way using records.

Access to the components of a date (day, month and year) can then either be direct - an example of a concrete data types, or indirect (via procedures) - an abstract data types.

Simplistically direct access (or concrete data types) offer the benefit of efficiency, and the possibility of lack of data integrity. In our date example we may set a day to the value 31 when the month is February.

Indirect access (or abstract data types) are slightly less efficient as we now have the overhead of a procedure call to access the data, but better opportunity for data integrity as we can provide hidden code within the procedures to ensure that the day, month and year combinations are valid.

Fortran did not provide this facility until the Fortran 90 standard.

3.10.4   Standardisation

The purposes of a standard are quite varied and include:

- Investment in people: by this we mean that the time spent in learning a standard language pays off in the long term, as what one learns is applicable on any hardware/software platform that has a standard conformant compiler.
- Portability: one can take the code one has written for one hardware/software platform and move it to any hardware/software platform that has a standard conformant compiler.
- Known reference point: when making comparisons one starts with reference to the standard first, and then between the additional functionality of the various implementations

These are some but not all of the reasons for the use of standards. Their importance is summed up beautifully by Ronald G. Ross in his introduction to the Cannan and Otten book on the SQL standard: "Anybody who has ever plugged in an electric cord into a wall outlet can readily appreciate the inestimable benefits of workable standards. Indeed, with respect to electrical power, the very fact that we seldom even think about such access (until something goes wrong) is a sure sign of just how fundamentally important a successful standard can be."

3.11   Ada

Ada represents the culmination of many years of work in program language development. It was a collective effort and the main aim was to produce a language suitable for programming large-scale and real-time systems. Work started in 1974 with the formulation of a series of documents by the American Department of Defence (DoD), which led to the Steelman documents. It is a modern algorithmic language with the usual control structures and facilities for the use of modules, and allows separate compilation with type checking across modules.

Ada is a powerful and well-engineered language. Its widespread use is certain as it has the backing of the DoD. However, it is a large and complex language and consequently requires some effort to learn.

The latest version of the language is Ada 2012. The following url

```
http://www.ada-europe.org/resources/online
```

provides a good starting point. Visit this site if you want up to date details about Ada. Another good source is

```
http://www.adaic.org/ada-resources/standards/ada12
```

Both sites have free electronic versions of the various Ada standards.

3.12   Modula

Modula was designed by Wirth during the 1970s at ETH, for the programming of embedded real-time systems. It has many of the features of Pascal, and can be taken for Pascal at a glance. The key new features that Modula introduced were those of processes and monitors.

As with Pascal it is relatively easy to learn and this makes it much more attractive than Ada for most people, achieving much of the capability without the complexity.

3.13   Modula 2

Wirth carried on developing his ideas about programming languages and the culmination of this can be seen in Modula 2. In his words: "In 1977, a research project with the goal to design a computer system (hardware and software) in an integrated approach, was launched at the Institut fur Informatik of ETH Zurich. This system (later to be called Lilith) was to be programmed in a single high level language, which therefore had to satisfy requirements of high level system design as well as those of low level programming of parts that closely interact with the given hardware. Modula 2 emerged from careful design deliberations as a language that includes all aspects of Pascal and extends them with the important module concept and those of multi-programming. Since its syntax was more in line with Modula than Pascal's the chosen name was Modula 2."

The language's main additions with regard to Pascal are:

• The module concept, and in particular the facility to split a module into a definition part and an implementation part.

- A more systematic syntax which facilitates the learning process. In particular, every structure starting with a keyword also ends with a keyword, i.e., is properly bracketed.
- The concept of process as the key to multiprogramming facilities.
- So-called low-level facilities, which make it possible to breach the rigid type consistency rules and allow one to map data with Modula 2 structure onto a store without inherent structure.
- The procedure type, which allows procedures to be dynamically assigned to variables.

A sad feature of Modula 2 was the long time taken to arrive at a standard for the language.

3.14 Other Language Developments

The following is a small selection of language developments that the authors find interesting — they may well not be included in other people's coverage.

3.14.1 Logo

Logo is a language that was developed by Papert and colleagues at the Artificial Intelligence Laboratory at MIT. Papert is a professor of both mathematics and education, and has been much influenced by the psychologist Piaget. The language is used to create learning environments in which children can communicate with a computer. The language is primarily used to demonstrate and help children develop fundamental concepts of mathematics. Probably the turtle and turtle geometry are known by educationalists outside of the context of Logo. Turtles have been incorporated into the Smalltalk computer system developed at Xerox Palo Alto Research Centre — Xerox PARC.

3.14.2 Postscript, T_EX and L^AT_EX

The 1980s saw a rapid spread in the use of computers for the production of printed material. The 3 languages are each used quite extensively in this area.

Postscript is a low-level interpretive programming language with good graphics capabilities. Its primary purpose is to enable the easy production of pages containing text, graphical shapes and images. It is rarely seen by most end users of modern desktop publishing systems, but underlies many of these systems. It is supported by an increasing number of laser printers and typesetters.

T_EX is a language designed for the production of mathematical texts, and was developed by Donald Knuth. It linearises the production of mathematics using a standard computer keyboard. It is widely used in the scientific community for the production of documents involving mathematical equations.

L^AT_EX is Leslie Lamport's version of T_EX, and is regarded by many as more friendly. It is basically a set of macros that hide raw T_EX from the end user. The T_EX ratio is probably 1–9 (or so I'm reliably informed by a T_EXie).

3.14.3 Prolog

Prolog was originally developed at Marseille by a group led by Colmerauer in 1972/73. It has since been extended and developed by several people, including Pereira (L.M.), Pereira (F), Warren and Kowalski. Prolog is unusual in that it is a vehicle for logic programming. Most of the languages described here are basically algorithmic languages and require a specification of how you want something done. Logic programming concentrates on the what rather than the how. The language appears strange at first, but has been taught by Kowalski and others to 10-year-old children at schools in London.

3.14.4 SQL

SQL stands for Structured Query Language, and was originally developed by people mainly working for IBM in the San Jose Research Laboratory. It is a relational database language, and enables programmers to define, manipulate and control data in a relational database. Simplistically, a relational database is seen by a user as a collection of tables, comprising rows and columns. It has become the most important language in the whole database field.

3.14.5 ICON

ICON is in the same family as Snobol, and is a high-level general purpose programming language that has most of the features necessary for efficient processing of nonnumeric data. Griswold (one of the original design team for Snobol) has learnt much since the design and implementation of Snobol, and the language is a joy to use in most areas of text manipulation.

It is available for most systems via anonymous FTP from a number of sites on the Internet.

3.15   Object Oriented Programming

Object oriented represents a major advance in program language development. The concepts that this introduces include:

- Classes.
- Objects.
- Messages.
- Methods.

These in turn draw on the ideas found in more conventional programming languages and correspond to

- Extensible data types.
- Instances of a class.
- Dynamically bound procedure calls.
- Procedures of a class.

Inheritance is a very powerful high-level concept introduced with object oriented programming. It enables an existing data type with its range of valid operations to form the basis for a new class, with more data types added with corresponding operations, and the new type is compatible with the original.

Fortran 2003 offered support for object oriented programming. This is achieved via the module facility rather than the class facility found in other languages like C++, Java and C#.

3.15.1   Simula

As was mentioned earlier, the first language to offer functionality in this area was Simula, and thus the ideas originated in the 1960s. The book Simula Begin by Birtwistle, Dahl, Myhrhaug and Nygaard is well worth a read as it represents one of the first books to introduce the concepts of object oriented programming.

3.15.2   Smalltalk

Language plus use of a computer system.

Smalltalk has been under development by the Xerox PARC Learning Research Group since the 1970s. In their words: "Smalltalk is a graphical, interactive programming environment. As suggested by the personal computer vision, Smalltalk is designed so that every component in the system is accessible to the user and can be presented in a meaningful way for observation and manipulation. The user interface issues in Smalltalk revolve around the attempt to create a visual language for each object. The preferred hardware system for Smalltalk includes a high resolution graphical display screen and a pointing device such as a graphics pen or mouse. With these devices the user can select information viewed on the screen and invoke messages in order to interact with the information." Thus Smalltalk represents a very different strand in program language development. The ease of use of a system like this has long been appreciated and was first demonstrated commercially in the Macintosh microcomputers.

Wirth has spent some time at Xerox PARC and has been influenced by their work. In his own words "the most elating sensation was that after sixteen years of working for computers the computer now seemed to work for me." This influence can be seen in the design of the Lilith machine, the original Modula 2 engine, and in the development of Oberon as both a language and an operating system.

3.15.3   Oberon and Oberon 2

As Wirth says: "The programming language Oberon is the result of a concentrated effort to increase the power of Modula-2 and simultaneously to reduce its complexity. Several features were eliminated, and a few were added in order to increase the expressive power and flexibility of the language."

Oberon and Oberon 2 are thus developments beyond Modula 2. The main new concept added to Oberon was that of type extension. This enables the construction of new data types based on existing types and allows one to take advantage of what has already been done for that existing type.

Language constructs removed included:

- Variant records.
- Opaque types.
- Enumeration types.
- Subrange types.
- Local modules.
- With statement.
- Type transfer functions.
- Concurrency.

The short paper by Wirth provides a fuller coverage. It is available at ETH via anonymous FTP.

3.15.4   Eiffel

Eiffel was originally developed by Interactive Software Engineering Inc. (ISE) founded by Bertrand Meyer. Meyer's book Object-Oriented Software Construction

contains a detailed treatment of the concepts and theory of the object technology that
led to Eiffel's design.

The language first became available in 1986, and the first edition of Meyer's book
was published in 1988. The following is a quote from the Wikipedia entry.

- The design goal behind the Eiffel language, libraries, and programming methods is to enable programmers to create reliable, reusable software modules. Eiffel
  supports multiple inheritance, genericity, polymorphism, encapsulation, type-safe
  conversions, and parameter covariance. Eiffel's most important contribution to
  software engineering is design by contract (DbC), in which assertions, precondi-
  tions, postconditions, and class invariants are employed to help ensure program
  correctness without sacrificing efficiency.

3.15.5 C++

Stroustrup did his PhD thesis at the Computing Laboratory, Cambridge University,
England, and worked with Simula. He had previously worked with Simula at the University of Aarhus in Denmark. His comments are illuminating: "but was pleasantly
surprised by the way the mechanisms of the Simula language became increasingly
helpful as the size of the program increased. The class and co-routine mechanisms
of Simula and the comprehensive type checking mechanisms ensured that problems
and errors did not (as I - and I guess most people - would have expected) grow linearly with the size of the program. Instead, the total program acted like a collection
of very small (and therefore easy to write, comprehend and debug) programs rather
than a single large program."

He designed C++ to provide Simula's functionality within the framework of C's
efficiency, and he succeeded in this goal as C++ is one of the most widely used object
oriented programming language.

The language began as enhancements to C, adding classes, virtual functions,
operator overloading, multiple inheritance, templates and exception handling by the
time of the first standard.

Its influence in the area of programming language design can be seen in Java and
C#.

Table 3.1 summarises the C++ standardisation history.

The following are some of the guidelines used by the standards committee in the
development of C++11.

Table 3.1 C++ standardisation history

Year	C++ standard	Informal name
1998	ISO/IEC 14882:1998	C++98
2003	ISO/IEC 14882:2003	C++03
2007	ISO/IEC TR 19768:2007	C++TR1
2011	ISO/IEC 14882:2011	C++11

- Maintain stability and compatibility with C++98 and possibly with C;
- Prefer introduction of new features through the standard library, rather than extending the core language;
- Prefer changes that can evolve programming technique;
- Improve C++ to facilitate systems and library design, rather than to introduce new features useful only to specific applications;
- Increase type safety by providing safer alternatives to earlier unsafe techniques;
- Increase performance and the ability to work directly with hardware;
- Provide proper solutions for real-world problems;
- Implement zero-overhead principle (additional support required by some utilities must be used only if the utility is used);
- Make C++ easy to teach and to learn without removing any utility needed by expert programmers.

C++14 was a small extension over C++11 and was published in December 2014. C++17 was a major update and was published in December 2017.

3.15.6 Java

Bill Joy (of Sun fame) had by the late 1980s decided that C++ was too complicated and that an object oriented environment based upon C++ would be of use. At around about the same time James Gosling (mister emacs) was starting to get frustrated with the implementation of an SGML editor in C++. Oak was the outcome of Gosling's frustration.

Sun over the next few years ended up developing Oak for a variety of projects. It wasn't until Sun developed their own web browser, Hotjava, that Java as a language hit the streets. And as the saying goes the rest is history.

Java is a relatively simple object oriented language. Whilst it has its origins in C++ it has dispensed with most of the dangerous features. It is OO throughout. Everything is a class.

It is interpreted and the intermediate byte code will run on any machine that has a Java virtual machine for it. This is portability at the object code level, unlike portability at the source code level — which is what we expect with most conventional languages. Some of the safe features of the language include:

- Built in garbage collection.
- Array subscript checking.
- No pointers — everything is passed by reference.

It is multithreaded, which makes it a delight for many applications. It has an extensive windows toolkit, the so called AWT that was in the original release of the language and Swing that came in later.

It is under continual development and at the time of writing was in its eighth major release.

Sun was acquired by Oracle in 2010.

3.15.7   C#

C# is a recent language from Microsoft and is a key part of their .NET framework. It is a modern, well-engineered language in the same family of programming languages in terms of syntax as C, C++ and Java. If you have a knowledge of one of these languages it will look very familiar.

One of the design goals was to produce a component oriented language, and to build on the work that Microsoft had done with OLE, ActiveX and COM:

- ActiveX is a set of technologies that enables software components to interact with one another in a networked environment, regardless of the language in which they were created. ActiveX was built on the Component Object Model (COM).
- COM is the object model on which ActiveX Controls and OLE are built. COM allows an object to expose its functionality to other components and to host applications. It defines both how the object exposes itself and how this exposure works across processes and networks. COM also defines the object's life cycle.
- OLE is a mechanism that allows users to create and edit documents containing items or objects created by multiple applications. OLE was originally an acronym for Object Linking and Embedding. However, it is now referred to simply as OLE. Parts of OLE not related to linking and embedding are now part of Active technology.

Other design goals included creating a language:

- Where everything is an object — C# also has a mechanism for going between objects and fundamental types (integers, reals, etc.).
- Which would enable the construction of robust and reliable software — it has garbage collection, exception handling and type safety.
- Which would use a C/C++/Java syntax which is already widely known and thus help programmers converting from one of these languages to C#.

It has been updated three times since its original release. Some of the more important features added in C# 2 were Generics, Iterators, Partial Classes, Nullable Types and Static Classes. The major feature that C# 3 added for most people was LINQ, a mechanism for data querying. C# 4 was released in 2010 and added a number of additional features.

3.15.8   Python

Python is an object-oriented, interpreted, and interactive programming language. Python was conceived in the late 1980s, and its implementation was started in December 1989 by Guido van Rossum at CWI in the Netherlands as a successor to the ABC language (itself inspired by SETL) capable of exception handling and interfacing with the Amoeba operating system. Van Rossum is Python's principal author, and his continuing central role in deciding the direction of Python is reflected in the title given to him by the Python community, (benevolent dictator for life - BDFL).

Heres a very brief summary of what started it all, written by Guido van Rossum:

> I had extensive experience with implementing an interpreted language in the ABC group at CWI, and from working with this group I had learned a lot about language design. This is the origin of many Python features, including the use of indentation for statement grouping and the inclusion of very-high-level data types (although the details are all different in Python). I had a number of gripes about the ABC language, but also liked many of its features. It was impossible to extend the ABC language (or its implementation) to remedy my complaints in fact its lack of extensibility was one of its biggest problems. I had some experience with using Modula−2+ and talked with the designers of Modula-3 and read the Modula−3 report. Modula−3 is the origin of the syntax and semantics used for exceptions, and some other Python features. I was working in the Amoeba distributed operating system group at CWI. We needed a better way to do system administration than by writing either C programs or Bourne shell scripts, since Amoeba had its own system call interface which wasnt easily accessible from the Bourne shell. My experience with error handling in Amoeba made me acutely aware of the importance of exceptions as a programming language feature. It occurred to me that a scripting language with a syntax like ABC but with access to the Amoeba system calls would fill the need. I realized that it would be foolish to write an Amoeba-specific language, so I decided that I needed a language that was generally extensible. During the 1989 Christmas holidays, I had a lot of time on my hand, so I decided to give it a try. During the next year, while still mostly working on it in my own time, Python was used in the Amoeba project with increasing success, and the feedback from colleagues made me add many early improvements. In February 1991, after just over a year of development, I decided to post to USENET. The rest is in the Misc/HISTORY file.

Python 2.0 was released on 16 October 2000 and had many major new features, including a cycle-detecting garbage collector and support for Unicode. With this release the development process was changed and became more transparent and community-backed.

Python 3.0 (also called Python 3000 or py3k), a major, backwards-incompatible release, was released on 3 December 2008 after a long period of testing. Many of its major features have been backported to the backwards-compatible Python 2.6 and 2.7.

Here is the main Python web site.

```
https://www.python.org/
```

It is quite widely used. Large organizations that make use of Python include Google, Yahoo!, CERN, and NASA.

Our involvement with Python started when we were asked about Python training by people working at the Atomic Weapons Establishment in Aldermaston. We put together a short 3 day intensive course for them.

Quite a fun language!

3.16   Back to Fortran!

We finish off with a coverage of the developments since the Fortran 77 standard. Practically all of the Fortran compilers available today fully support the Fortran 90 and 95 standards. Support for features from the Fortran 2003 and 2008 standards is improving on a regular basis. See the following document

```
https://www.fortranplus.co.uk/
fortran-information/
```

for up to date information on what each compiler offers in terms of standard support.

3.16.1   Fortran 90

Almost as soon as the Fortran 77 standard was complete and published, work began on the next version. The language drew on many of the ideas covered in this chapter and these help to make Fortran 90 a very promising language. Some of the new features included:

- New source form, with blanks being significant and names being up to 31 characters.
- Implicit none.
- Better control structures.
- Control of the precision of numerical computation.
- Array processing.
- Pointers.
- User defined data types and operators.
- Procedures.
- Modules.
- Recursion.
- Dynamic storage allocation.

This was the major update that the Fortran community had been waiting a long time for. Backwards compatibility was again a key aim. This standard did not invalidate any standard conformant Fortran 77 program.

3.16.2   Fortran 95

Fortran was next standardised in 1996 — yet again out by one! Firstly we have a clear up of some of the areas in the standard that had emerged as requiring clarification. Secondly Fortran 95 added the following major concepts:

- The `forall` construct.
- Pure and elemental procedures.
- Implicit initialisation of derived-type objects.
- Initial association status for pointers.

  The first two help considerably in parallelization of code.
  Minor features include amongst others:

- Automatic deallocation of allocatable arrays.
- Intrinsic `sign` function distinguishes between −0 and +0.
- Intrinsic function `null` returns disconnected pointer.
- Intrinsic function `cpu_time` returns the processor time.
- References to some pure functions are allowed in specification statements.
- Nested `where` constructs.
- Masked `elsewhere` construct.
- Small changes to the `ceiling`, `floor`, `maxloc` and `minloc` intrinsic functions

Some of these were added to keep Fortran in line with High Performance Fortran (HPF). More details are given later.

Part 2 of the standard (ISO/IEC 1539-2:1994) adds the functional specification for varying length character data type, and this extends the usefulness of Fortran for character applications very considerably.

3.16.3   ISO Technical Reports TR15580 and TR15581

There are two additional reports that have been published on Fortran. TR 15580 specifies three modules that provide access to IEEE floating point arithmetic and TR15581 allows the use of the allocatable attribute on dummy arguments, function results and structure components.

3.16.4   Fortran 2003

The language is known as Fortran 2003 even though the language did not make it through the standardisation process until 2004. It was a major revision.

- Derived type enhancements

  - parameterised derived types (allows the kind, length, or shape of a derived type's components to be chosen when the derived type is used)
  - mixed component accessibility (allows different components to have different accessibility)
  - public entities of private type
  - improved structure constructors
  - finalisers

- Object oriented programming support

  - enhanced data abstraction (allows one type to extend the definition of another type)
  - polymorphism (allows the type of a variable to vary at run time)
  - dynamic type allocation
  - select type construct (allows a choice of execution flow depending upon the type a polymorphic object currently has)
  - type-bound procedures

- The associate construct (allows a complex expression or object to be denoted by a simple symbol)
- Data manipulation enhancements

  - allocatable components
  - deferred-type parameters
  - volatile attribute
  - explicit type specification in array constructors
  - intent specification of pointer arguments
  - specified lower bounds of pointer assignment, and pointer rank remapping
  - extended initialisation expressions
  - `max` and `min` intrinsics for character type
  - enhanced complex constants

- Input/output enhancements

  - asynchronous transfer operations (allow a program to continue to process data while an input/output transfer occurs)
  - stream access (allows access to a file without reference to any record structure)
  - user specified transfer operations for derived types
  - user specified control of rounding during format conversions
  - the flush statement
  - named constants for preconnected units
  - regularisation of input/output keywords
  - access to input/output error messages

- Procedure pointers
- Scoping enhancements

  - the ability to rename defined operators (supports greater data abstraction)
  - control of host association into interface bodies

- Support for IEC 60559 (IEEE 754) exceptions and arithmetic (to the extent a processor's arithmetic supports the IEC standard)
- Interoperability with the C programming language (allows portable access to many libraries and the low-level facilities provided by C and allows the portable use of Fortran libraries by programs written in C)
- Support for international usage

  – ISO 10646
  – choice of decimal or comma in numeric formatted input/output

- Enhanced integration with the host operating system

  – access to command line arguments and environment variables
  – access to the processor's error messages (improves the ability to handle exceptional conditions)

The earlier web address has details of Fortran compiler conformance to this standard.

3.16.5 DTR 19767 Enhanced Module Facilities

The module system in Fortran has a number of shortcomings and this DTR addresses some of the issues.

One of the major issues was the so-called recompilation cascade. Changes to one part of a module forced recompilation of all code that used the module. Modula 2 addressed this issue by distinguishing between the definition or interface and implementation. This can now be achieved in Fortran via submodules.

3.16.6 Fortran 2008

The next standard, ISO/IEC 1539-1:2010, commonly known as Fortran 2008, was approved in September 2010. The new features include:

- Submodules
- Coarrays
- Performance enhancements

  – do concurrent
  – Contiguous attribute
  – Simply contiguous arrays

- Data declaration

  – Maximum rank
  – Long integers
  – Allocatable components of recursive type
  – Implied-shape array
  – Pointer initialization
  – Data statement restrictions lifted
  – Kind of a forall index
  – Type statement for intrinsic types
  – Declaring type-bound procedures

- Extensions to value attribute

- Data usage

  - Omitting an allocatable component in a structure constructor
  - Multiple allocations with source=
  - Copying the properties of an object in an allocate statement
  - Polymorphic assignment
  - Accessing real and imaginary parts
  - Pointer functions
  - Elemental dummy argument restrictions lifted

- Input/Output

  - Finding a unit when opening a file
  - g0 edit descriptor
  - Unlimited format item
  - Recursive input/output

- Execution control

  - The block construct
  - Exit statement
  - Stop code

- Intrinsic procedures and modules

  - Bit processsing
  - Storage size
  - Optional argument radix added to selected real kind
  - Extensions to trigonometric and hyperbolic intrinsic functions
  - Bessel functions
  - Error and gamma functions
  - Euclidean vector norms
  - Parity
  - Execute command line
  - Optional argument back added to maxloc and minloc
  - Find location in an array
  - String comparison
  - Constants
  - Compiler information
  - Function for C sizeof
  - Additional optional argument for ieee_selected_real_kind

- Programs and procedures

  - Save attribute for module and submodule data
  - Empty contains part
  - Form of the end statement for an internal or module procedure
  - Internal procedure as an actual argument or pointer target

– Null pointer or unallocated allocatable as an absent dummy argument
– Non-pointer actual for pointer dummy argument
– Generic resolution by pointer/allocatable or data/procedure
– Elemental procedures that are not pure
– Entry statement becomes obsolescent

- Source form

– Semicolon at line start

A more thorough coverage can be found in John Reid's paper.

```
https://wg5-fortran.org/N1851-N1900/N1891.pdf
```

3.16.7   TS 29113 Further Interoperability of Fortran with C

This TS was published in 2012.

3.16.8   Fortran 2018

According to the current WG5 work schedule it is expected that the Fortran 2018
standard will be published in August 2018.

Here is a short list of some of the changes introduced by this standard. It has been
taken from John Reid's paper on the new features of Fortran 2018. The first edition
of this paper is N2127 and was published in 2017. The second edition is N2145 and
was published in January 2018.

- Additional parallel features in Fortran

– Teams
– Image failure
– Form team statement
– Change team construct
– Coarrays allocated in teams
– Critical construct
– Lock and unlock statements
– Sync team statement
– Image selectors
– Intrinsic functions get team and team number
– Intrinsic function image index
– Intrinsic function num images
– Intrinsic function this image
– Intrinsic function move alloc

- Fail image statement
- Detecting failed and stopped images
- Collective subroutines
- New and enhanced atomic subroutines
- Failed images and stat=specifiers
- Events

- Conformance with ISO/IEC/IEEE 60559:2011

  - Subnormal values
  - Type for floating-point modes
  - Round away from zero
  - Decimal rounding mode
  - Rounded conversions
  - Fused multiply-add
  - Test sign
  - Conversion to integer type
  - Remainder function
  - Maximum and minimum values
  - Adjacent machine numbers
  - Comparisons

- Removal of deficiencies and discrepancies

  - Default accessibility for entities accessed from a module
  - Implicit none enhancement
  - Enhancements to inquire
  - d0.d, e0.d, es0.d, en0.d, g0.d and ew.d e0 edit descriptors
  - Formatted input error conditions
  - Rules for generic procedures
  - Enhancements to stop and error stop
  - Intrinsics that access the computing environment
  - New elemental intrinsic function out of range
  - New reduction intrinsic reduce
  - Intrinsic function coshape
  - Intrinsic subroutine random init
  - Intrinsic function sign
  - Intrinsic functions extends type of and same type as
  - Nonstandard procedure from a standard intrinsic module
  - Kind of the do variable in implied do
  - Locality clauses in do concurrent
  - Control of host association
  - Connect a file to more than one unit
  - Advancing input with size=
  - Extension to the generic statement
  - Removal of anomalies regarding pure procedures
  - Recursive and non-recursive procedures

- Simplification of calls of the intrinsic cmplx
- Removal of the restriction on argument dim of many intrinsic functions
- Kinds of arguments of intrinsic and IEEE procedures
- Hexadecimal input/output
- Deletions
    Arithmetic if
    Nonblock do construct
- New obsolescences
    common and equivalence
    Labelled do statements
    Specific names for intrinsic functions
    The forall construct and statement

Both N2127 and N2145 can be found on the WG5 site.

```
https://wg5-fortran.org/documents.html
```

Both versions can also be found at the ACM Fortran Forum site.

```
http://dl.acm.org/citation.cfm?id=J286
```

N2127 was published in the August 2017 edition, and N2145 can be found in the April 2018 edition.

Table 3.2 summarises the Fortran standardisation history.

Fortran 2018 is currently on schedule for a 2018 publication date.

Table 3.2 Fortran standardisation history

Year	Fortran standard	Informal name
1966	Ansi x3.9-1966	Fortran 66
1978	Ansi x3.9-1977	Fortran 77
1978	ISO 1539-1980	Fortran 77
1991	ISO/IEC 1539:1991	Fortran 90
1997	ISO/IEC 1539-1:1997	Fortran 95
1998	ISO/IEC TR 15580:1998	Floating-point exception handling
1998	ISO/IEC TR 15581:1998	Enhanced data type facilities
1999	ISO/IEC 1539-3:1999	Conditional compilation
2000	ISO/TEC 1539-2:2000	Part 2: varying length character strings
2001	ISO/TEC TR 15580:2001	Floating-point exception handling
2004	ISO/IEC 1539-1:2004	Fortran 2003
2009	ISO/IEC 1539-1	Module TSR
2010	1539-1:2010	Fortran 2008
2012	ISO/TEC TS 29113:2012 ISO/TEC NP TS 18508	Further interoperability of fortran with C Additional parallel features in fortran
201?	1539-1:2018	Fortran 2018

3.17   Fortran Discussion Lists

The first to look at is the Fortran 90 list. Details can be found at

```
http://www.jiscmail.ac.uk/lists/COMP-FORTRAN-90.html
```

If you subscribe you will have access to people involved in Fortran standardisation, language implementers for most of the hardware and software platforms, people using Fortran in many very specialised areas, people teaching Fortran, etc.

There is also a comp.lang.fortran list available via USENET news. This provides access to people worldwide with enormous combined expertise in all aspects of Fortran. Invariably someone will have encountered your problem or one very much like it and have one or more solutions.

Here is an extract from Wikipedia.

Usenet is a worldwide distributed Internet discussion system. It was developed from the general purpose UUCP dial-up network architecture. Tom Truscott and Jim Ellis conceived the idea in 1979 and it was established in 1980. Users read and post messages (called articles or posts, and collectively termed news) to one or more categories, known as newsgroups. Usenet resembles a bulletin board system (BBS) in many respects, and is the precursor to Internet forums that are widely used today. Usenet can be superficially regarded as a hybrid between email and web forums. Discussions are threaded, as with web forums and BBSes, though posts are stored on the server sequentially.

One notable difference between a BBS or web forum and Usenet is the absence of a central server and dedicated administrator. Usenet is distributed among a large, constantly changing conglomeration of servers that store and forward messages to one another in so-called news feeds. Individual users may read messages from and post messages to a local server operated by a commercial usenet provider, their Internet service provider, university, employer, or their own server.

Another to consider is the Fortran group on 'linkedin' The address is

```
https://www.linkedin.com/
```

3.18   ACM Fortran Forum

Ian Chivers is also Editor of Fortran Forum, the SIGPLAN Special Interest Publication on Fortran, ACM Press. Visit

```
http://portal.acm.org/citation.cfm?id=J286
```

for more information.

3.19   Other Sources

The following URLs are very useful:
Our Fortran web site.

```
https://www.fortranplus.co.uk
```

The Fortran Company, maintained by Walt Brainerd.

```
http://www.fortran.com/
```

3.20   Summary

It is hoped that you now have some idea about the wide variety of uses that programming languages are put to.

3.21   Bibliography

Fortran 2008 Standard, ISO/IEC 1539-1:2010, price CHF 338. Publication date: 2010-10-06.

```
http://www.iso.org/iso/home/store.htm
```

Fortran 2003 Standard, ISO/IEC DIS 1539-1:2004(E)
DTR 19767: Enhanced module Facilities: ISO/IEC TR 19767:2004(E)
The Fortran 77 and 66 standards are available from the WG5 site.

```
https://wg5-fortran.org/fearlier.html
```

The ISO home page is

```
http://www.iso.org/
```

The J3 home page is:

```
https://j3-fortran.org
```

The WG5 home page is:

```
https://wg5-fortran.org/
```

Both have copies of working documents.
Adobe Systems Incorporated, Postscript Language:
Tutorial and Cookbook, Addison-Wesley, 1985; Reference Manual, Addison-Wesley, 1985; Program Design, Addison-Wesley, 1985.

- The three books provide a comprehensive coverage of the facilities and capabilities of Postscript.

  They third edition of the reference manual is available online.

```
http://www.adobe.com/products/postscript/pdfs/PLRM.pdf
```

ACM SIG PLAN, History of programming Languages Conference — HOPL-II, ACM Press, 1993.

- One of the best sources of information on C++, CLU, Concurrent Pascal, Formac, Forth, Icon, Lisp, Pascal, Prolog, Smalltalk and Simulation Languages by the people involved in the original design and or implementation. Very highly recommended. This is the second in the HOPL series, and the first was edited by Wexelblat. Details are given later.

  Adams J.C., Brainerd W.S., Hendrickson R.A., Maine R.E., Martin J.T., Smith B.T., The Fortran 2003 Handbook, Springer, 2009.

- Their most recent version, and a complete coverage of the 2003 standard. As with the Metcalf, Reid and Cohen book some of the authors were on the J3 committee. Very thorough.

  Annals of the History of Computing, Special Issue: Fortran's 25 Anniversary, ACM, Article 6,1, 1984.

- Very interesting comments, some anecdotal, about the early work on Fortran.

  Barnes J., Programming in Ada 95, Addison-Wesley, 1996.

- One of the best Ada books. He was a member of the original design team.

  Bergin T.J., Gibson R.G., History of Programming Languages, Addison-Wesley, 1996.

- This is a formal book publication of the Conference Proceedings of HOPL II. The earlier work is based on preprints of the papers.

  Birtwistle G.M., Dahl O. J., Myhrhaug B., Nygaard K.,
  SIMULA BEGIN, Chartwell-Bratt Ltd, 1979.

- A number of chapters in the book will be of interest to programmers unfamiliar with some of the ideas involved in a variety of areas including systems and models, simulation, and co-routines. Also has some sound practical advice on problem solving.

Brinch-Hansen P., The Programming Language Concurrent Pascal, IEEE Transactions on Software Engineering, June 1975, 199-207.

- Looks at the extensions to Pascal necessary to support concurrent processes.

  Cannan S., Otten G., SQL — The Standard Handbook, McGraw-Hill, 1993.

- Very thorough coverage of the SQL standard, ISO 9075:1992(E).

  Chivers I.D., Clark M.W., History and Future of Fortran, data Processing, vol. 27 no 1, January/February 1985.

- Short article on an early draft of the standard, around version 90.

  Chivers Ian, Essential C# Fast, Springer, ISBN 1-85233-562-9.

- A quick introduction to the C# programming language.

  Chivers I.D., A Practical Introduction to Standard Pascal, Ellis Horwood, 1986.

- A short introduction to Pascal.

  Date C.J., A Guide to the SQL Standard, Addison-Wesley, 1997.

- Date has written extensively on the whole database field, and this book looks at the SQL language itself. As with many of Date's works quite easy to read.

  Deitel H.M., Deitel P.J., Java: How to program, 10th Edition Pearson Education

- A good introduction to Java and programming for people with little or no background in programming.

  Deitel H.M., Deitel P.J., Visual Basic How to Program, Pearson Education, 2014.

- Good practical introduction to VB .NET.

  Dyson G., Turing's Cathedral, The origins of the Digital Universe, Pantheon Books, 2012.

- The following is taken from the books blurb. ... *Dyson focuses on a small group of men and women, led by John von Neuman at the Institute of Advanced Study in Princeton, New Jersey, who build one of the first computers to realise Alan Turing's vision of a Universal Machine.*

  Eckstein R., Loy M., Wood D., Java Swing, O'Reilly, 1998.

- Comprehensive coverage of the visual interface features available in Java.

  Geissman L.B., Separate Compilation in Modula 2 and the Structure of the Modula 2 Compiler on the Personal Computer Lilith, Dissertation 7286, ETH Zurich.

- Fascinating background reading concerning Modula 2 and the Lilith architecture.

  Goldberg A., Robson D., Smalltalk 80: The Language and its Implementation, Addison-Wesley, 1983.

- Written by some of the Xerox PARC people who have been involved with the development of Smalltalk. Provides a good introduction (if that is possible with the written word) of the capabilities of Smalltalk.

Goos G., Hartmanis J. (Eds), The programming Language Ada — Reference Manual, Springer Verlag, 1981.

- The definition of the language.

Goossens M., Mittelbach F., Rahtz S., Roegel D., Voß H. The LATEX Graphics Companion, second edition, Addison Wesley, 2007.

- Another essential LATEX book.

Griswold R.E., Poage J.F., Polonsky I.P., The Snobol4 programming Language, Prentice-Hall, 1971.

- The original book on the language. Also provides some short historical material on the language.

Griswold R.E., Griswold M.T., The Icon programming Language, Prentice-Hall, 1983.

- The definition of the language with a lot of good examples. Also contains information on how to obtain public domain versions of the language for a variety of machines and operating systems.

Harbison S.P., Steele G.L., A C Reference Manual, Prentice-Hall, 2002.

- Very good coverage of the various flavours of C, including K&R C, Standard C 1989, Standard C 1995, Standard C 1999 and Standard C++

Hellman D., The Python Standard Library by Example, Addison-Wesley, 2011.

- Good introduction to the Python standard library.

Hoare C.A.R., Hints on programming Language Design, SIGACT/SIGPLAN Symposium on Principles of programming Languages, October 1973.

- The first sentence of the introduction sums it up beautifully: "I would like in this paper to present a philosophy of the design and evaluation of programming languages which I have adopted and developed over a number of years, namely that the primary purpose of a programming language is to help the programmer in the practice of his art."

Jacobi C., Code Generation and the Lilith Architecture, Dissertation 7195, ETH Zurich

- Fascinating background reading concerning Modula 2 and the Lilith architecture.

Jenson K., Wirth N., Pascal: User Manual and Report, Springer-Verlag, 1975.

- The original definition of the Pascal language. Understandably dated when one looks at more recent expositions on programming in Pascal.

Kemeny J.G., Kurtz T.E., Basic programming, Wiley, 1971.

- The original book on Basic by its designers.

Kernighan B.W., Ritchie D.M., The C programming Language, Prentice-Hall; first edition 1978; second edition 1988.

- The original work on the C language, and thus essential for serious work with C.

Kowalski R., Logic programming in the Fifth Generation, The Knowledge Engineering Review, The BCS Specialist Group on Expert Systems.

- A short paper providing a good background to Prolog and logic programming, with an extensive bibliography.

Knuth D. E., The TeXbook, Addison-Wesley, 1986.

- Knuth writes with an tremendous enthusiasm and perhaps this is understandable as he did design TeX. Has to be read from cover to cover for a full understanding of the capability of TeX.

Lamport L., LaTeX User's Guide and Reference Manual, 2005, Addison Wesley, ISBN 0201529831.

- The original LaTeX book. Essential reading.

Lyons J., Chomsky, Fontana/Collins, 1982.

- A good introduction to the work of Chomsky, with the added benefit that Chomsky himself read and commented on it for Lyons. Very readable.

Malpas J., Prolog: A Relational Language and its Applications, Prentice-Hall, 1987.

- A good introduction to Prolog for people with some programming background. Good bibliography. Looks at a variety of versions of Prolog.

Marcus C., Prolog programming: Applications for Database Systems, Expert Systems and Natural Language Systems, Addison-Wesley.

- Coverage of the use of Prolog in the above areas. As with the previous book aimed mainly at programmers, and hence not suitable as an introduction to Prolog as only two chapters are devoted to introducing Prolog.

Metcalf M. and Reid J., Cohen M., Modern Fortran Explained, Oxford University Press, 2011

- A clear compact coverage of the main features of Fortran. John Reid is Convener of the WG5 committee and Malcolm Cohen was the editor of Fortran 2008.

Mittelbach F., Goossens M., Braams J., Carlisle D., and Rowley C., The LaTeX Companion, 2005, Addison Wesley, ISBN 0201362996.

- The LaTeX book. It is required if you are setting a book using LaTeX.

Mossenbeck H., Object-Orientated programming in Oberon-2, Springer-Verlag, 1995.

- One of the best introductions to object oriented programming. Uses Oberon-2 as the implementation language. Highly recommended.

Papert S., Mindstorms - Children, Computers and Powerful Ideas, Harvester Press, 1980.

- Very personal vision of the uses of computers by children. It challenges many conventional ideas in this area.

Sammet J., programming Languages: History and Fundamentals, Prentice-Hall, 1969.

- Possibly the most comprehensive introduction to the history of program language development — ends unfortunately before the 1980s.

Sethi R., programming Languages: Concepts and Constructs, Addison-Wesley, 1989.

- The annotated bibliographic notes at the end of each chapter and the extensive bibliography make it a useful book.

Reiser M., Wirth N., programming in Oberon — Steps Beyond Pascal and Modula, Addison-Wesley, 1992.

- Good introduction to Oberon. Revealing history of the developments behind Oberon.

Reiser M., The Oberon System: User Guide and programmer's Manual, Addison-Wesley, 1991.

- How to use the Oberon system, rather than the language.

Stroustrup B., The C++ Programming Language, Addison-Wesley; third edition 1997; fourth edition 2014. 1997.

- The C++ book. Written by the designer of the language. The third edition is a massive improvement over the earlier editions. The fourth edition covers C++11. One of the best books on C++ and C++11 in particular.

Young S. J., An Introduction to Ada, 2nd Edition, Ellis Horwood, 1984.

- A readable introduction to Ada. Greater clarity than the first edition.

Wexelblat, History of programming Languages, HOPL I, ACM Monograph Series, Academic Press, 1978.

- Very thorough coverage of the development of programming languages up to June 1978. Sessions on Fortran, Algol, Lisp, Cobol, APT, Jovial, GPSS, Simula, JOSS, Basic, PL/I, Snobol and APL, with speakers involved in the original languages. Very highly recommended.

Wiener R., Software development using Eiffel, Prentice Hall, 1995.

- The book's subtitle is *There can be life other than* $C++$ The book gives a good introduction to object oriented analysis and design using the Booch 94 method using Eiffel.

Wirth N., An Assessment of the Programming Language Pascal, IEEE Transactions on Software Engineering, June 1975, 192-198.

- Short paper by Wirth on his experience with Pascal.

Wirth N., History and Goals of Modula 2, Byte, August 1984, 145-152.

- Straight from the horse's mouth!

Wirth N., On the Design of programming Languages, Proc. IFIP Congress 74, 386-393, North-Holland.

- Short paper given in 1974 on designing programming languages.

Wirth N., The programming Language Pascal, Acta Informatica 1, 35-63, 1971.

- Short paper on the development of Pascal from Algol 60.

Wirth N., Modula: a language for modular multiprogramming, Software Practice and Experience, 7, 3–35, 1977.

- Short paper on Modula, the precursor of Modula 2.

Wirth N., Programming in Modula 2, Springer-Verlag, 1983.

- The original definition of the language. Essential reading for anyone considering programming in Modula 2 on a long term basis.

Wirth N. Type Extensions, ACM Trans. on Prog. Languages and Systems, 10, 2 (April 1988), 2004-214

- Short paper on type extension.

Wirth N. From Modula 2 to Oberon, Software — Practice and Experience, 18,7 (July 1988), 661–670

- Brief paper on the move from Modula 2 to Oberon, looking at features that were removed and added.

Wirth N., Gutknecht J., Project Oberon: The Design of an Operating System and Compiler, Addison-Wesley, 1992.

- Fascinating background to the development of Oberon. Highly recommended for anyone involved in large scale program development, not only in the areas of programming languages and operating systems, but more generally.

Chapter 4
Introduction to Programming

Though this be madness, yet there is method in 't

Shakespeare

*Plenty of practice' he went on repeating, all the time that Alice
was getting him on his feet again. 'plenty of practice.*
The White Knight, Through the Looking Glass and What Alice
Found There, Lewis Carroll

Aims

The aims of the chapter are:

- To introduce the idea that there is a wide class of problems that can be solved with a computer and, further, that there is a relationship between the kind of problem to be solved and the choice of programming language that is used.
- To give some of the reasons for the choice of Fortran.
- To introduce the fundamental components or kinds of statements to be found in a general purpose programming language.
- To introduce the three concepts of name, type and value.
- To illustrate the above with sample programs based on three of the five intrinsic data types:
- character, integer and real.
- To introduce some of the formal syntactical rules of Fortran.

4.1 Introduction

We have seen that an algorithm is a sequence of steps that will solve a part or the whole of a problem. A program is the realisation of an algorithm in a programming language, and there are at first sight a surprisingly large number of programming languages. The reason for this is that there is a wide range of problems that are solved using a computer, e.g., the telephone company generating itemised bills or

© Springer International Publishing AG, part of Springer Nature 2018
I. Chivers and J. Sleightholme, *Introduction to Programming with Fortran*,
https://doi.org/10.1007/978-3-319-75502-1_4

the meteorological centre producing a weather forecast. These two problems make different demands on a programming language, and it is unlikely that the same language would be used to solve both.

The range of problems that you want to solve will therefore strongly influence your choice of programming language. Fortran stands for FORmula TRANslation, which gives a hint of the expected range of problems for which it is suitable.

4.2   Language Strengths and Weaknesses

Some of the reasons for choosing Fortran are:

- It is a modern and expressive language;
- The language is suitable for a wide class of both numeric and nonnumeric problems;
- The language is widely available on a range of hardware and operating system platforms;
- A lot of software already exists that has been written in Fortran. Some 15% of code worldwide is estimated to be in Fortran.

There are a few warts, however. Given that there has to be backwards compatibility with earlier versions some of the syntax is clumsy to say the least. However, a considerable range of problems can now be addressed quite cleanly, if one sticks to a subset of the language and adopts a consistent style.

4.3   Elements of a Programming Language

As with ordinary (so-called natural) languages, e.g., English, French, Gaelic, German, etc., programming languages have rules of syntax, grammar and spelling. The application of these rules in a programming language is more strict. A program has to be unambiguous, since it is a precise statement of the actions to be taken. Many everyday activities are rather vaguely defined — Buy some bread on your way home — but we are generally sufficiently adaptable to cope with the variations which occur as a result. if, in a program to calculate wages, we had an instruction deduct some money for tax and insurance we could have an awkward problem when the program calculated completely different wages for the same person for the same amount of work every time it was run. One of the implications of the strict syntax of a programming language for the novice is that apparently silly error messages will appear when one first starts writing programs. As with many other new subjects you will have to learn some of the jargon to understand these messages.

Programming languages are made up of statements. We will look at the various kinds of statements briefly below.

4.3.1 Data Description Statements

These are necessary to describe the kinds of data that are to be processed. In the wages program, for example, there is obviously a difference between people's names and the amount of money they earn, i.e., these two things are not the same, and it would not make any sense adding your name to your wages. The technical term for this is data type — a wage would be of a different data type (a number) to a surname (a sequence of characters).

4.3.2 Control Structures

A program can be regarded as a sequence of statements to solve a particular problem, and it is common to find that this sequence needs to be varied in practice. Consider again the wages program. It will need to select among a variety of circumstances (say married or single, paid weekly or monthly, etc), and also to repeat the program for everybody employed. So there is the need in a programming language for statements to vary and/or repeat a sequence of statements.

4.3.3 Data-Processing Statements

It is necessary in a programming language to be able to process data. The kind of processing required will depend on the kind or type of data. In the wages program, for example, you will need to distinguish between names and wages. Therefore there must be different kinds of statements to manipulate the different types of data, i.e., wages and names.

4.3.4 Input and Output (I/O) Statements

For flexibility, programs are generally written so that the data that they work on exist outside the program. In the wages example the details for each person employed would exist in a file somewhere, and there would be a record for each person in this file. This means that the program would not have to be modified each time a person left, was ill, etc., although the individual records might be updated. It is easier to modify data than to modify a program, and it is less likely to produce unexpected results. To be able to vary the action there must be some mechanism in a programming language for getting the data into and out of the program. This is done using input and output statements, sometimes shortened to I/O statements.

4.4   Example 1: Simple Text I/O

Let us now consider a simple program which will read in somebody's first name and print it out:

```
program ch0401
!
! This program reads in and prints out a name
!
  implicit none
  character *20 :: first_name

  print *, ' type in your first name.'
  print *, ' up to 20 characters'
  read *, first_name
  print *, first_name
end program ch0401
```

There are several very important points to be covered here, and they will be taken in turn:

- Each line is a statement.
- There is a sequence to the statements. The statements will be processed in the order that they are presented, so in this example the sequence is print, read, print.
- The first statement names the program. It makes sense to choose a name that conveys something about the purpose of the program.
- The next three lines are comment statements. They are identified by a !. Comments are inserted in a program to explain the purpose of the program. They should be regarded as an integral part of all programs. It is essential to get into the habit of inserting comments into your programs straight away.
- The implicit none statement means that there has to be explicit typing of each and every data item used in the program. It is good programming practice to include this statement in every program that you write, as it will trap many errors, some often very subtle in their effect. Using an analogy with a play, where there is always a list of the persona involved before the main text of the play we can say that this statement serves the same purpose.
- The character*20 statement is a type declaration. It was mentioned earlier that there are different kinds of data. There must be some way of telling the programming language that these data are of a certain type, and that therefore certain kinds of operations are allowed and others are banned or just plain stupid! It would not make sense to add a name to a number, e.g., what does Fred + 10 mean? So this statement defines that the variable first_name is to be of type character and only character operations are permitted. The concept of a variable is covered in the next section. character variables of this type can hold up to 20 characters.

- The `print` statements print out an informative message to the screen — in this case a guide as to what to type in. The use of informative messages like this throughout your programs is strongly recommended.
- The `read` statement is one of the I/O statements. It is an instruction to read from the terminal or keyboard; whatever is typed in from the keyboard will end up being associated with the variable `first_name`. Input/output statements will be explained in greater detail in later sections.
- The `print` statement is another I/O statement. This statement will print out what is associated with the variable `first_name` and, in this case, what you typed in.
- The `end program` statement terminates this program. It can be thought of as being similar to a full stop in natural language, in that it finishes the program in the same way that a period (.) ends a sentence. Note the use of the name given in the program statement at the start of the program.
- Note also the use of the asterisk in three different contexts.
- Indentation has been used to make the structure of the program easier to determine. Programs have to be read by human beings and we will look at this in more depth later.
- Lastly, when you do run this program, character input will terminate with the first blank character.

The above program illustrates the use of some of the statements in the Fortran language. Let us consider the action of the `read *` statement in more detail — in particular, what is meant by a variable and a value.

4.5 Variables — Name, Type and Value

The idea of a variable is one that you are likely to have met before, probably in a mathematical context. Consider the following:

$$circumference = 2\pi r \tag{4.1}$$

This is an equation for the calculation of the circumference of a circle. The following represents a translation of this into Fortran:

```
circumference = 2 * pi * radius
```

There are a number of things to note about this equation:

- Each of the variables on the right-hand side of the equals sign (`pi` and `radius`) will have a value, which will allow the evaluation of the expression.
- When the expression is fully evaluated the value is assigned to the variable on the left-hand side of the equals sign.
- In mathematics the multiplication is implied. In Fortran we have to use the `*` operator to indicate that we want to multiply 2 by pi by the radius.
- We do not have access to mathematical symbols like π in Fortran but have to use variable names based on letters from the Roman alphabet.

Variable name	Data type	Value stored
Temperature	Real	28.55
Number_of_people	Integer	100
First_name	Character	Jane

Table 4.1 Variable name, type and value

The whole line is an example of an arithmetic assignment statement in Fortran.

The following arithmetic assignment statement illustrates clearly the concepts of name and value, and the difference in the equals sign in mathematics and computing:

$$i = i + 1 \qquad\qquad (4.2)$$

In Fortran this reads as take the current value of the variable i and add one to it, store the new value back into the variable i, i.e., i takes the value i+1. Algebraically, $i = i + 1$ does not make any sense.

Variables can be of different types. Table 4.1 shows some of those available in Fortran.

Note the use of underscores to make the variable names easier to read.

The concept of data type seems a little strange at first, especially as we commonly think of integers and reals as numbers. However, the benefits to be gained from this distinction are considerable. This will become apparent after you have written several programs.

4.6   Example 2: Simple Numeric I/O and Arithmetic

Let us now consider another program, one that reads in three numbers, adds them up and prints out both the total and the average:

```
program ch0402
!
! This program reads in three numbers and sums
! and averages them
!
  implicit none
  real :: n1, n2, n3, average = 0.0, total = 0.0
  integer :: n = 3
  print *, ' type in three numbers.'
  print *, ' Separated by spaces or commas'
  read *, n1, n2, n3
  total = n1 + n2 + n3
  average = total/n
  print *, 'Total of numbers is ', total
  print *, 'Average of the numbers is ', average
end program ch0402
```

Here are some of the key points about this program.

- This program has declarations for numeric variables and Fortran (in common with most programming languages) discriminates between `real` and `integer` data types.
- The variables `average`, `total` and `n` are also given initial values within the type declaration.
  Variables are initially undefined in Fortran, so the variables `n1`, `n2`, `n3` fall into this category, as they have not been given values at the time that they are declared.
- The first `print` statement makes a text message (in this case what is between the apostrophes) appear at the screen. As was noted earlier, it is good practice to put out a message like this so that you have some idea of what you are supposed to type in.
- The `read` statement looks at the input from the keyboard (i.e., what you type) and in this instance associates these values with the three variables. These values can be separated by commas (,), spaces ( ), or even by pressing the carriage return key, i.e., they can appear on separate lines.
- The next statement actually does some data processing. It adds up the values of the three variables (`n1`, `n2`, and `n3`) and assigns the result to the variable `total`. This statement is called an arithmetic assignment statement.
  and is covered more fully in the next chapter.
- The next statement is another data-processing statement. It calculates the average of the numbers entered and assigns the result to average. We could have actually used the value 3 here instead, i.e., written `average = total/3` and have exactly the same effect. This would also have avoided the type declaration for n. However, the original example follows established programming practice of declaring all variables and establishing their meaning unambiguously. We will see further examples of this type throughout the book.
- Indentation has been used to make the structure of the program easier to determine.
- The `sum` and `average` are printed out with suitable captions or headings. Do not write programs without putting captions on the results. It is too easy to make mistakes when you do this, or even to forget what each number means.
- Finally we have the end of the program and again we have the use of the name in the program statement.

4.7 Some More Fortran Rules

There are certain things to learn about Fortran which have little immediate meaning and some which have no logical justification at all, other than historical precedence. Why is a cat called a cat? At the end of several chapters there will be a brief summary of these rules or regulations when necessary. Here are a few:

- Source is free format.
- Lower case letters are permitted, but not required to be recognised.
- Multiple statements may appear on one line and are separated by the semicolon character.
- There is an order to the statements in Fortran. Within the context of what you have covered so far, the order is:

  - Program statement.
  - Type declarations, e.g., implicit, integer, real or character.
  - Processing and I/O statements.
  - End program statement.

- Comments may appear anywhere in the program, after program and before end; they are introduced with a ! character, and can be in line.
- Names may be up to 63 characters in length and include the underscore character.
- Lines may be up to 132 characters.
- Up to 39 continuation lines are allowed (using the ampersand (&) as the continuation character).
- The syntax of the read and print statement introduced in these examples is

  - read format, input-item-list.
  - print format, output-item-list.
       where format is * in the examples and called list directed formatting.
       and input-item-list is a list of variable names separated by commas.
       and output-item-list is a list of variable
     names and/or a sequence of characters enclosed in either "or ", again separated by commas.

- If the implicit none statement is not used, variables that are not explicitly declared will default to real if the first letter of the variable name is A–H or O–Z, and to integer if the first letter of the variable name is I–N.

4.8   Fortran Character Set

Table 4.2 has details of the Fortran character set.

   The default character type shall support a character set that includes the Fortran character set. By supplying non-default character types, the processor may support additional character sets. The characters available in the ASCII and ISO 10646 character sets are specified by ISO/IEC 646:1991 (International Reference Version) and ISO/IEC 10646-1:2000 UCS-4, respectively; the characters available in other non default character types are not specified by the standard, except that one character in each non default character type shall be designated as a blank character to be used as a padding character.

Table 4.2 The Fortran character set

Graphic	Name of character	Graphic	Name of character
Alphanumeric characters			
A–Z	Uppercase letters	0–9	Digits
a–z	Lowercase letters	_	Underscore
Special characters			
	Blank	;	Semicolon
=	Equals	!	Exclamation mark
+	Plus	"	Quotation mark
−	Minus	%	Percent
⋆	Asterisk	&	Ampersand
/	Slash or oblique	~	Tilde
\	Backslash	<	Less than
(	Left parenthesis	>	Greater than
)	Right parenthesis	?	Question mark
[	Left square bracket	'	Apostrophe
]	Right square bracket	`	Grave accent
{	Left curly bracket	^	Circumflex accent
}	Right curly bracket	|	Vertical bar or line
,	Comma	$	Currency symbol
.	Period or decimal point	#	Number sign
:	Colon	@	Commercial at

Table 4.3 has details of the ASCII character set.

If you live and work outside of the USA and UK you may well have problems with your keyboard when programming. There is a very good entry in Wikipedia on keyboards, that is well worth a look at for the curious.

Table 4.3 ASCII character set

Decimal	Character	Decimal	Character	Decimal	Character	Decimal	Character
0	nul	32	&	64	@	96	'
1	soh	33	!	65	A	97	a
2	stx	34	"	66	B	98	b
3	etx	35	#	67	C	99	c
4	eot	36	$	68	D	100	d
5	enq	37	%	69	E	101	e
6	ack	38	&	70	F	102	f
7	bel	39	'	71	G	103	g
8	bs	40	(	72	H	104	h

(continued)

Table 4.3 (continued)

9	ht	41	)	73	I	105	i
10	lf	42	*	74	J	106	j
11	vt	43	+	75	K	107	k
12	ff	44	,	76	L	108	l
13	cr	45	-	77	M	109	m
14	so	46	.	78	N	110	n
15	si	47	/	79	O	111	o
16	dle	48	0	80	P	112	p
17	dc1	49	1	81	Q	113	q
18	dc2	50	2	82	R	114	r
19	dc3	51	3	83	S	115	s
20	dc4	52	4	84	T	116	t
21	nak	53	5	85	U	117	u
22	syn	54	6	86	V	118	v
23	etb	55	7	87	W	119	w
24	can	56	8	88	X	120	x
25	em	57	9	89	Y	121	y
26	sub	58	:	90	Z	122	z
27	esc	59	;	91	[	123	{
28	fs	60	<	92	\	124	|
29	gs	61	=	93	]	125	}
30	rs	62	>	94	^	126	~
31	us	63	?	95	_	127	del

4.9 Good Programming Guidelines

The following are guidelines, and do not form part of the Fortran language definition:

- Use comments to clarify the purpose of both sections of the program and the whole program.
- Choose meaningful names in your programs.
- Use indentation to highlight the structure of the program. Remember that the program has to be read and understood by both humans and a computer.
- Use `implicit none` in all programs you write to minimise errors.
- Do not rely on the rules for explicit typing, as this is a major source of errors in programming.

4.10   Compilers Used

A number of hardware platforms, operating systems and compilers have been used when writing this book and earlier books. The following have been used in the production of this edition of the book:

- NAG Fortran Builder 6.1 and 6.2 for Windows.
- NAG Fortran Compiler 6.1 and 6.2 for Windows.
- NAG Fortran Compiler 6.1 and 6.2 for Linux.
- Intel Fortran 16.x, 17.x, 18.x for Windows.
- Intel Fortran 16.x, 18.x for Linux.
- gnu gfortran 4.8.x, 4.9.x, 4.10.x, 5.4.x, 7.x, 8.0.x for Windows.
- gnu gfortran 4.8.x, 6.3.x for Linux.
- Cray Fortran: Version 8.x.x - Cray Archer service.
- Oracle Solaris Studio 12.6 for Linux.

Our recommendation is that you use at least two compilers in the development of your code. Moving code between compilers and platforms teaches you a lot.

The following were used in the production of the third edition of the book:

- NAG Fortran Builder 6.0 for Windows.
- NAG Fortran compiler 6.0 for Windows.
- NAG Fortran Compiler 6.0 for Linux.
- NAG Fortran Builder 5.3.1 for Windows.
- Nag Fortran compiler 5.3.1 and 5.3.2 for Windows.
- Intel Fortran 14.x, 15.x for Windows.
- Intel Fortran 15.x for Linux.
- gnu gfortran 4.8.x, 4.9.x, 4.10.x for Windows.
- gnu gfortran 4.8.x for Linux.
- Cray Fortran: Version 8.2.1 - Cray Archer service.
- Oracle Solaris Studio 12.4 for Linux.

The following were used in the production of earlier editions.

- NAG Fortran Builder 5.1, 5.2, 5.3 for Windows.
- NAG Fortran Compiler 5.1, 5.2, 5.3 for Linux.
- Intel Fortran 11.x, 12.x, 13.x for Windows.
- Intel Fortran 12.x for Linux.
- gnu gfortran 4.x for Windows.
- gnu gfortran 4.x for Linux.
- Cray Fortran: Version 7.3.1 - Cray Hector service.
- g95 for Linux.
- pgi 10.x - Cray Hector service.
- IBM XL Fortran for AIX, V13.1 (5724-X15), Version: 13.01.0000.0002.
- Oracle Solaris Studio 12.0, 12.1, 12.2 for Linux.

The following have been used with earlier books:

- DEC VAX under VMS and later OPEN VMS with the NAG Fortran 90 compiler.
- DEC Alpha under OPEN VMS using the DEC Fortran 90 compiler.
- Sun Ultra Sparc under Solaris:

  - NAGACE F90 compiler.
  - NAGWare F95 compiler.
  - Sun (Release 1.x) F90 compiler.
  - Sun (Release 2.x) F90 compiler.

- PCs under DOS and Windows:

  - DEC/Compaq Fortran 90 and Fortran 95 compilers.
  - Intel Compiler (7.x, 8.x).
  - Lahey Fujitsu Fortran 95 (5.7).
  - NAG Fortran 95 Compiler.
  - NAG Salford Fortran 90 Compiler.
  - Salford Fortran 95 Compiler.

- PCs under Linux:

  - Intel Compiler.
  - Lahey Fujitsu Fortran 95 Pro (6.1).
  - NAG Fortran 95 (4.x, 5.x).

It is very illuminating to use more than one compiler whilst developing programs.

4.11   Compiler Documentation

The compiler may come with documentation. Here are some details for a number of compilers.

4.11.1   gfortran

Manuals are available at

```
http://gcc.gnu.org/wiki/GFortran\#manuals
```

The following

```
http://gcc.gnu.org/onlinedocs/
gcc-4.5.2/gfortran.pdf
```

is a 236 page pdf.

4.11.2 IBM

Here is a starting point. The urls have been split as the lines are too long.

```
http://www-03.ibm.com/software/
products/en/fortcompfami/
```

Here is a starting point for the XLF for AIX system.

```
http://www-01.ibm.com/support/
docview.wss?uid=swg27036673
```

and the starting point for the pdf version of the documentation is.

```
http://www-01.ibm.com/support/
docview.wss?uid=swg27036673
```

They provide

- Getting Started with XL Fortran for AIX 15.1 This book introduces you to XL Fortran for Linux and its features, including features new for 15.1.
- Installation Guide - XL Fortran for AIX 15.1 This book contains information for installing XL Fortran and configuring your environment for basic compilation and program execution.
- Compiler Reference - XL Fortran for AIX 15.1 This book contains information about the many XL Fortran compiler options and environment variables that you can use to tailor the XL Fortran compiler to your application development needs.
- Language Reference - XL Fortran for AIX 15.1 This book contains information about the Fortran programming language as supported by IBM, including language extensions for portability and conformance to non-proprietary standards, compiler directives and intrinsic procedures.
- Optimization and Programming Guide - XL Fortran for AIX 15.1 This book contains information on advanced programming topics, such as application porting, inter language calls, floating-point operations, input/output, application optimization and parallelization, and the XL Fortran high-performance libraries.

4.11.3 Intel

Windows. The following will end up available after a complete install.

- Intel MKL

  - Release notes

- Reference Manual
- User Guide

- Parallel Debugger Extension

  - Release Notes

- Compiler

  - Reference Manual, Visual Studio Help files or html.
  - User Guide, Visual Studio Help files or html.

  Intel also provide the following

  ```
  https://software.intel.com/en-us/articles/
  intel-software-technical-documentation/
  ```

4.11.4 Nag

Windows

- Fortran Builder Help

  - Fortran Builder Tutorial - 44 pages
  - Fortran Builder Operation Guide - 67 pages
  - Fortran Language Guide - 115 pages
  - Compiler Manual - 149 pages
  - LAPACK Guide - 70 pages (440 MB as PDF!)
  - GTK+ Library - 201 pages
  - OpenGL/GLUT Library - 38 pages
  - SIMDEM Library - 78 pages

4.11.5 Oracle/Sun

Oracle make available a range of documentation. From within Oracle Solaris Studio

- Help

  - Help Contents
  - Online Docs and Support
  - ..
  - ..
  - Quick Start Guide

and you will get taken to the Oracle site by some of these entries.

You can also download a 300+ MB zip file which contains loads of Oracle documentation. You should be able to locate (after some rummaging around)

- Sun Studio 12: Fortran Programming Guide - 174 pages
- Sun Studio 12: Fortran User's Guide - 216 pages
- Sun Studio 12: Fortran Library Reference - 144 pages
- Fortran 95 Interval Arithmetic Programming Reference - 166 pages

   Happy reading :-)

4.12   Program Development

A number of ways of developing programs have been used, including:

- Using an integrated development environment, including

  - NAG Fortran Builder under Windows.
  - Microsoft Visual Studio with the Intel compiler under Windows.
  - Oracle Sunstudio under SuSe Linux.

- Using a DOS box and simple command line prompt under Windows.
- Using ssh to log in to the Archer service.
- Using a VPN, and SSH to log in to the IBM Power 7 system at Slovak Hydrometeorological Institute Jeseniova 17.
- Using a console or terminal window under SuSe Linux.
- Using X-Windows software to log into the SUN Ultra Sparc systems.
- Using terminal emulation software to log into the SUN Ultra Sparc.
- Using DEC terminals to log into the DEC VAX and DEC Alpha systems.
- Using PCs running terminal emulation software to log into the DEC VAX and DEC Alpha systems.

   It is likely that you will end up doing at least one of the above and probably more. The key stages involved are:

- Creating and making changes to the Fortran program source.
- Saving the file.
- Compiling the program:
- If there are errors you must go back to the Fortran source and make the changes indicated by the compiler error messages.
- Linking if successful to generate an executable:
- Automatic link. This happens behind the scenes and the executable is generated for you immediately.
- Manual link. You explicitly invoke the linker to generate the executable.
- Running the program.

- Determining whether the program actually works and gives the results expected.

These steps must be taken regardless of the hardware platform, operating system and compiler you use. Some people like working at the operating system prompt (e.g., DOS, Linux and UNIX), and others prefer working within a development environment. Both have their strengths and weaknesses.

4.13 Problems

4.1 Compile and run Example 1 in this chapter. Experiment with the following types of input.
   Ian
   Ian Chivers
   "Jane Margaret Sleightholme"

4.2 Compile and run Example 2 in this chapter.
   Think about the following points:

- Is there a difference between separating the input by spaces or commas?
- Do you need the decimal point?
- What happens when you type in too many data?
- What happens when you type in too few data?

If you have access to more than one compiler repeat the above and compare the results.

4.3 Write a program that will read in your name and address and print them out in reverse order.
   Think about the following points:

- How many lines are there in your name and address?
- What is the maximum number of characters in the longest line in your name and address?
- What happens at the first blank character of each input line?
- Which characters can be used in Fortran to enclose each line of text typed in and hence not stop at the first blank character?
- If you use one of the two special characters to enclose text what happens if you start on one line and then press the return key before terminating the text?

The action here will vary between Fortran implementations.

Chapter 5
Arithmetic

Taking Three as the subject to reason about — A convenient number to state — We add Seven, and Ten, and then multiply out By One Thousand diminished by Eight. The result we proceed to divide, as you see, By Nine Hundred and Ninety and Two: then subtract Seventeen, and the answer must be Exactly and perfectly true.

Lewis Carroll, The Hunting of the Snark

Round numbers are always false.

Samuel Johnson

Aims

The aims of this chapter are to introduce:

- The Fortran rules for the evaluation of arithmetic expressions to ensure that they are evaluated as you intend;
- The idea of truncation and rounding;
- The use of the parameter attribute to define or set up constants;
- The use of Fortran's kind types to determine and control the precision by which arithmetic in Fortran is carried out;
- The concept of numeric models and positional number systems for integer and real arithmetic and their implementation on binary devices.
- Testing the numerical representation of different integer kind types on a system – 8, 16, 32 and 64 bit integers
- Testing the numerical representation of different real kind types on a system – 32, 64, 80 and 128 bit reals
- Round off
- Relative error
- Absolute error

© Springer International Publishing AG, part of Springer Nature 2018
I. Chivers and J. Sleightholme, *Introduction to Programming with Fortran*,
https://doi.org/10.1007/978-3-319-75502-1_5

5.1   Introduction

Most problems in the academic and scientific communities require arithmetic evaluation as part of the algorithm. The arithmetic performed by computers is not the same as the arithmetic you are familiar with in conventional mathematics and algebra.

There are two areas that we need to address

- computation involving finite precision - so called computer arithmetic
- the rules that apply in a programming language - different programming languages have different rules for the evaluation of expressions

The outcome of the above means that $2 + 2$ is not necessarily 4 when using a computer!

5.2   The Fortran Operators and the Arithmetic Assignment Statement

In the previous chapter, we introduced the arithmetic assignment statement, emphasising the concepts of name, type and value. Here we will consider the way that arithmetic expressions are evaluated in Fortran.

Table 5.1 lists the five arithmetic operators available in Fortran.

Table 5.1 Fortran operators

Mathematical operation	Fortran symbol or operator
Addition	+
Subtraction	−
Division	/
Multiplication	*
Exponentiation	**

Exponentiation is raising a number to a power. Note that the exponentiation operator is the * character twice.

The following are some examples of valid arithmetic assignment statements in Fortran:

```
taxable_income = gross_wage - personal_allowance
cost = bill + vat + service
delta = deltax/deltay
area = pi * radius * radius
cube = big ** 3
```

These expressions are all simple, and there are no problems when it comes to evaluating them. However, now consider the following:

```
tax = gross_wage - personal_allowance * tax_rate
```

This is a poorly written arithmetic expression. There is a choice of doing the subtraction before or after the multiplication. Our everyday experience says that the subtraction should take place before the multiplication. However, if this expression were evaluated in Fortran the multiplication would be done before the subtraction.

5.3 Example 1: Simple Arithmetic Expressions in Fortran

A complete program to show the correct form in Fortran is as follow:

```
program ch0501
  implicit none
!
! Example of a Fortran program
! to calculate net pay
! given an employee's gross pay
!
! The UK personal allowance is
! correct as of 2014
!
  real :: gross_wage, net_wage, tax
  real :: tax_rate = 0.25
  integer :: personal_allowance = 10000
  character (len=60) :: their_name

  print *, 'Input employees name'
  read *, their_name
  print *, 'Input Gross wage'
  read *, gross_wage
  tax = (gross_wage-personal_allowance)*tax_rate
  net_wage = gross_wage - tax
  print *, 'Employee: ', their_name
  print *, 'Gross Pay: ', gross_wage
  print *, 'Tax: ', tax
  print *, 'Net Pay:', net_wage
end program ch0501
```

Let us look at some of the key points of this program.

- We have the `implicit none` statement which aids in detecting typing errors.
- We declare the variables `gross_wage`, `net_wage`, `tax` and `tax_rate` to be of type `real` as they will hold floating point values, i.e. numbers with a decimal point.
- The variable `their_name` is of type `character` and can hold up to 60 characters.
- The variable `personal_allowance` is of type `integer` as it holds integer values.
- We then have some i/o statements to prompt the user for input and read in their name and gross pay.
- We then calculate the tax payable and net income using two simple arithmetic assignment statements.
- We then print out the results.

This example illustrates some basic arithmetic in Fortran.

5.4   The Fortran Rules for Arithmetic

We need to look at three areas here:

- The rules for forming expressions — the syntax.
- The rules for interpreting expressions — the semantics.
- The rules for evaluating expressions — optimisation.

The syntax rules determine which expressions are valid. The semantics determine a valid interpretation, and once this has been done the compiler can replace the expression with any other one that is mathematically equivalent, generally in the interests of optimisation.

Here is the section of the Fortran 2018 standard on expression evaluation.

- 10.1.5.2.4 Evaluation of numeric intrinsic operations

  - 1 The execution of any numeric operation whose result is not defined by the arithmetic used by the processor is prohibited. Raising a negative real value to a real power is prohibited.
  - 2 Once the interpretation of a numeric intrinsic operation is established, the processor may evaluate any mathematically equivalent expression, provided that the integrity of parentheses is not violated.
  - 3 Two expressions of a numeric type are mathematically equivalent if, for all possible values of their primaries, their mathematical values are equal. However, mathematically equivalent expressions of numeric type may produce different computational results.

The rules for the evaluation of expressions in Fortran are as follows:

- Brackets are used to define priority in the evaluation of an expression.
- Operators have a hierarchy of priority — a precedence. The hierarchy of operators is:
- Exponentiation: when the expression has multiple exponentiation, the evaluation is from right to left. For example,

```
l = i ** j ** k
```

is evaluated by first raising j to the power k, and then using this result as the exponent for i; more explicitly,

```
l = i ** (j ** k)
```

Although this is similar to the way in which we might expect an algebraic expression to be evaluated, it is not consistent with the rules for multiplication and division, and may lead to some confusion. When in doubt, use brackets.

- Multiplication and division: within successive multiplications and divisions, the rules regarding any mathematically equivalent expression means that you must use brackets to ensure the evaluation you want. For example, with

```
a = b * c / d * e
```

for real and complex numeric types the compiler does not necessarily evaluate in a left to right manner, i.e., evaluate b times c, then divide the result by d and finally take that result and multiply by e.
- Addition and subtraction: as for multiplication and division the rules regarding any equivalent expression apply. However, it is seldom that the order of addition and subtraction is important, unless other operators are involved.

Table 5.2 summarises the hierarchy of the operators.

Table 5.2 Hierarachy or precedence of the Fortran operators

Mathematical operation	Fortran symbol or operator
Exponentiation	**
Division	/
Multiplication	*
Addition	+
Subtraction	−

The following are all examples of valid arithmetic expressions in Fortran:

```
slope = (y1-y2)/(x1-x2)
x1 = (-b+((b*b-4*a*c)**0.5))/(2*a)
q = mass_d/2*(mass_a*veloc_a/mass_d)**2 + &
((mass_a * veloc_a)**2)/2
```

Note that brackets have been used to make the order of evaluation more obvious. It is often possible to write involved expressions without brackets, but, for the sake of clarity, it is often best to leave the brackets in, even to the extent of inserting a few extra ones to ensure that the expression is evaluated correctly. The expression will be evaluated just as quickly with the brackets as without. Also note that none of the expressions is particularly complex. The last one is about as complex as you should try: with more complexity than this it is easy to make a mistake.

5.5   Expression Equivalence

The rule regarding any equivalent expression means if a, b and c are numeric then the following are true:

```
a + b = b + a
- a + b = b - a
a + b + c = a + (b + c)
```

The last is nominally evaluated left to right, as the additions are of equal precedence:

```
a * b = b * a
a * b * c = a * (b * c)
```

and again the last is nominally evaluated left to right, as the multiplications are of equal precedence:

```
a * b - a * c = a * (b - c)
a / b / c = a / (b * c)
```

The last is true for real and complex numeric types only.

Problems arise when the value that a faulty expression yields lies within the range of expected values and the error may well go undetected. This may appear strange at first, but a computer does exactly what it is instructed to do. If, through a misunderstanding on the part of a programmer, the program is syntactically correct but logically wrong from the point of view of the problem definition, then this will not be spotted by the compiler. If an expression is complex, break it down into successive statements with elements of the expression on each line, e.g.,

```
temp = b * b - 4 * a * c
x1 = ( - b + ( temp ** 0.5 )) / ( 2 * a )
```

and

```
Moment = Mass_A * Veloc_A
Q = Mass_D / 2 * ( Moment / Mass_D ) **2 + &
    ( Moment **2) / 2
```

5.6 Rounding and Truncation

Computer arithmetic can be subject to truncation and rounding.

- Truncation. This operation involves throwing away part of the number, e.g., with 14.6 truncating the number to two figures leaves 14.
- Rounding. Consider 14.6 again. This is rounded to 15. Basically, the number is changed to the nearest whole number. It is still a real number. What do you think will happen with 14.5; will this be rounded up or down?

You must be aware of these two operations. They may occasionally cause problems in division and in expressions with more than one data type.

5.7 Example 2: Type Conversion and Assignment

To see some of the problems that can occur consider the examples below:

```
program ch0502
  implicit none
  real :: a, b, c
  integer :: i

  a = 1.5
  b = 2.0
  c = a/b
  i = a/b
  print *, a, b
  print *, c
  print *, i
end program ch0502
```

After executing these statements c has the value 0.75, and i has the value zero! This is an example of type conversion across the = sign. The variables on the right are all real, but the last variable on the left is an integer. The value is therefore made into an integer by truncation. In this example, 0.75 is real, so i becomes zero when truncation takes place.

5.8   Example 3: Integer Division and Real Assignment

Consider now an example where we assign into a real variable (so that no truncation due to the assignment will take place), but where part of the expression on the right-hand side involves integer division:

```
program ch0503
  implicit none
  integer :: i, j, k
  real :: answer

  i = 5
  j = 2
  k = 4
  answer = i/j*k
  print *, i
  print *, j
  print *, k
  print *, answer
end program ch0503
```

The value of answer is 8, because the i/j term involves integer division. The expected answer of 10 is not that different from the actual one of 8, and it is cases like this that cause problems for the unwary, i.e., where the calculated result may be close to the actual one. In complicated expressions it would be easy to miss something like this.

To recap, truncation takes place in Fortran:

- Across an = sign, when a real is assigned to an integer.
- In integer division.

It is very important to be careful when attempting mixed mode arithmetic — that is, when mixing reals and integers. If a real and an integer are together in a division or multiplication, the result of that operation will be real; when addition or subtraction takes place in a similar situation, the result will also be real. The problem arises when some parts of an expression are calculated using integer arithmetic and other parts with real arithmetic:

```
c = a + b - i / j
```

The integer division is carried out before the addition and subtraction; hence the result of i/j is integer, although all the other parts of the expression will be carried out with real arithmetic.

5.9 Example 4: Time Taken for Light to Travel from the Sun to Earth

How long does it take for light to reach the Earth from the Sun? Light travels 9.46 10^{12} km in 1 year. We can take a year as being equivalent to 365.25 days. (As all school children know, the astronomical year is 365 days, 5 h, 48 min and 45.9747 s — hardly worth the extra effort.) The distance between the Earth and Sun is about 150,000,000 km. There is obviously a bit of imprecision involved in these figures, not least since the Earth moves in an elliptical orbit, not a circular one. One last point to note before presenting the program is that the elapsed time will be given in minutes and seconds. Few people readily grasp fractional parts of a year:

```
program ch0504
  implicit none
  real :: light_minute, distance, elapse
  integer :: minute, second
  real, parameter :: light_year = 9.46*10**12
! Light_year  : Distance travelled by light
! in one year in km
! Light_minute : Distance travelled by light
! in one minute in km
! Distance    : Distance from sun to earth in
! km
! Elapse      : Time taken to travel a
! distance (Distance) in minutes
! Minute      : integer number part of elapse
! Second      : integer number of seconds
! equivalent to fractional
! part of elapse
!
  light_minute = light_year/(365.25*24.0*60.0)
  distance = 150.0*10**6
  elapse = distance/light_minute
  minute = elapse
  second = (elapse-minute)*60
  print *, ' Light takes ', minute, ' Minutes'
```

```
  print *, ' ', second, ' Seconds'
  print *, ' To reach the earth from the sun'
end program ch0504
```

The calculation is straightforward; first we calculate the distance travelled by light in 1 min, and then use this value to find out how many minutes it takes for light to travel a set distance. Separating the time taken in minutes into whole-number minutes and seconds is accomplished by exploiting the way in which Fortran will truncate a real number to an integer on type conversion. The difference between these two values is the part of a minute which needs to be converted to seconds. Given the inaccuracies already inherent in the exercise, there seems little point in giving decimal parts of a second.

It is worth noting that some structure has been attempted by using comment lines to separate parts of the program into fairly distinct chunks. Note also that the comment lines describe the variables used in the program.

Can you see any problems with this example?

5.10   The Parameter Attribute

This attribute is used to provide a way of associating a meaningful name with a constant in a program. Consider a program where π was going to be used a lot. It would be silly to have to type in 3.14159265358 every time. There would be a lot to type and it is likely that a mistake could be made typing in the correct value. It therefore makes sense to set up pi once and then refer to it by name. However, if pi was just a variable then it would be possible to do the following:

```
real :: li,pi
  .
pi=4.0*atan(1.0)
  .
pi=4*alpha/beta
  .
```

The pi = 4*alpha/beta statement should have been li = 4*alpha/beta. What has happened is that, through a typing mistake (p and l are close together on a keyboard), an error has crept into the program. It will not be spotted by the compiler. Fortran provides a way of helping here with the parameter attribute, which should be added to or combined with a type declaration.

Table 5.3 has details of some commonly used physical constants.

Table 5.3 Some commonly used physical constants

Atomic mass constant	m_u	$1.660\ 538\ 921 \times 10^{-27}$ kg
Avogadro constant	N_A,L	$6.022\ 141\ 29 \times 10^{23}$ mol^{-1}
Boltzmann constant	k	$1.380\ 6488 \times 10^{-23}$ J K^{-1}
Electron mass	m_e	$9.109\ 382\ 91 \times 10^{-31}$ kg
Elementary charge	e	$1.602\ 176\ 565 \times 10^{-19}$ C
Proton mass	m_p	$1.672\ 621\ 777 \times 10^{-27}$ kg
Speed of light in vacuum	c, c_0	$299\ 792\ 458$ m s^{-1}
Newtonian constant of gravitation	G	$6.673\ 84 \times 10^{-11}$ m^3 kg^t -1 s^{-2}

The data has been taken from

```
http://physics.nist.gov/cuu/index.html
```

A type statement with a parameter attribute may contain an arithmetic expression, so that some relatively simple arithmetic may be performed in setting up these constants. The evaluation must be confined to addition, subtraction, multiplication, division and integer exponentiation.

The following are some examples of the parameter attribute for some of the physical constants.

```
real , parameter :: pi = &
   4.0*atan(1.0)
real , parameter :: c  = &
   299792458 * 10.0 ** (-1)
real , parameter :: e  = &
   1.602176565 * 10.0 ** (-19)
```

We have introduced the Fortran intrinsic function atan in this example, and for further details see Appendix D. We will also be covering intrinsic functions in a later chapter. The advantage of the parameter attribute is that you could not then assign another value to pi, c or charge. If you tried to do this, the compiler would generate an error message.

5.11 Round Off Errors and Computer Arithmetic

Precision is not the same as accuracy. In this age of digital timekeeping, it is easy to provide an extremely precise answer to the question What time is it? This answer need not be accurate, even though it is reported to tenths (or even hundredths!) of a second. Do not be fooled into believing that an answer reported to ten places of decimals must be accurate to ten places of decimals. The computer can only retain a limited precision. When calculations are performed, this limitation will tend to generate inaccuracies in the result. The estimation of such inaccuracies is the domain of the branch of mathematics known as Numerical Analysis.

To give some idea of the problems, consider an imaginary decimal computer which retains two significant digits in its calculations. For example, 1.2, 12.0, 120.0 and 0.12 are all given to two-digit precision. Note therefore that 1234.5 would be represented as 1200.0 in this device. When any arithmetic operation is carried out, the result (including any intermediate calculations) will have two significant digits. Thus:

```
130 + 12 = 140 (rounding down from 142)
```

and similarly:

```
17 / 3 = 5.7 (rounding up from 5.666666...)
```

and:

```
16 * 16 = 260
```

where there are more involved calculations, the results can become even less attractive. Assume we wish to evaluate

```
(16 * 16) / 0.14
```

We would like an answer in the region of 1828.5718, or, to two significant digits, 1800.0. if we evaluate the terms within the brackets first, the answer is 260/0.14, or 1857.1428; 1900.0 on the two-digit machine. Thinking that we could do better, we could rewrite the fraction as

```
(16 / 0.14) * 16
```

Which gives a result of 1800.0.

Algebra shows that all these evaluations are equivalent if unlimited precision is available.

A round-off error, also called rounding error, is the difference between the calculated approximation of a number and its exact mathematical value. We will look at this issue in more depth later in this chapter.

5.12   Relative and Absolute Errors

When we are calculating numerical approximations to a solution we often need to measure how accurate our estimated solution is. If we are using an iterative method we could look at the difference between successive calculations, or our algorithm may have an expression for estimating errors.

Either way there are two types of errors, absolute and relative.

Looking at relative errors is a better way of measuring accuracy than absolute errors because an absolute error depends on the size of the number being approximated.

If p' is an approximation to p then the relative error is $|p - p'|/|p|$ and the absolute error is $|p - p'|$.

Here is an example to illustrate the above.

5.13   Example 5: Relative and Absolute Error

```
program ch0505
  implicit none
  real :: p = 0.4e-4, papprox = 0.41e-4
  real :: abs_error, rel_error
  integer :: i

  do i = 1, 3
    abs_error = abs(p-papprox)
    rel_error = abs(p-papprox)/abs(p)
    print 100, p, papprox
100 format ('p        = ', e11.4, /, &
       'papprox  = ', e11.4)
    print 110, abs_error, rel_error
110 format ('abs error:', 12x, e11.4, /, &
       'rel error:', 12x, e11.4, /)
    p = p*1.0e5
    papprox = papprox*1.0e5
  end do
end program ch0505
```

This program introduces the intrinsic abs function   and a new statement, the format statement and the (e) edit descriptor. For the moment just concentrate on the output. We will look at the format statement and (e) edit descriptor in more depth in a later chapter. See Appendix D for more information on the abs intrinsic.

Here is the output from the Nag compiler.

```
p            =   0.4000E-04
approx to p =   0.4100E-04
abs error:                   0.1000E-05
rel error:                   0.2500E-01
```

```
p              =  0.4000E+01
approx to p =  0.4100E+01
abs error:                0.1000E+00
rel error:                0.2500E-01


p              =  0.4000E+06
approx to p =  0.4100E+06
abs error:                0.1000E+05
rel error:                0.2500E-01
```

This example shows that the same relative error of $0.25 * 10^{-1}$ occurs for widely varying absolute errors, therefore the absolute error can be misleading.

The relative error is more meaningful because it takes into consideration the size of the number.

5.14   Range, Precision and Size of Numbers

The range of integer numbers and the precision and the size of floating point numbers in computing are directly related to the number of bits allocated to their internal representation. Tables 5.4 and 5.5 summarise this information for the two most common bit sizes in use for integers and reals — 32 bits and 64 bits, as defined in the IEEE standard. Most hardware in use today supports these standards to a greater or lesser extent.

We will look at IEEE 754 in later sections and in a separate chapter.

Table 5.4 looks at integer numbers and Table 5.5 looks at real numbers.

For practical purposes all compilers support the information contained in these two tables.

Table 5.4 Word size and integer numbers

Number of bits	Power of 2	Power of 10	Maximum integer
32	(2**31)-1	O(10**9)	2, 147, 483, 647
64	(2**63)-1	O(10**18)	9, 223, 372, 036, 854, 774, 807

Table 5.5 Word size and real numbers

Number of bits	Precision	Smallest real	Largest real
32	6–9	≈0.3E-38	≈1.7E38
64	15–18	≈0.5E-308	≈0.8E+308

5.15   Overflow and Underflow

Care should also be taken when is one is near the numerical limits of the machine. Consider the following:

```
z = b * c / d
```

where b, c and d are all $O(10^{30})$ and we are using 32-bit floating point numbers where the maximum real is $O(10^{38})$. Here the product b * c generates a number of $O(10^{60})$ — beyond the limits of the machine. This is called overflow as the number is too large. Note that we could avoid this problem by retyping this as

```
z = b * (c / d)
```

where the bracketed expression c/d would now be $O(10^{30})/O(10^{30})$, and is within machine limits.

5.15.1   Example 6: Overflow

Here is a sample program that illustrates the above.

```
program ch0506
  implicit none
  real :: z = 0.0
  real :: b = 1.0e30
  real :: c = 1.0e30
  real :: d = 1.0e30

  z = b*c/d
  print *, z
  z = b*(c/d)
  print *, z
end program ch0506
```

Here is the output from the Intel compiler.

```
        Infinity
  1.0000000E+30
```

Here is the output from the Nag compiler.

```
nagfor ch0506.f90
NAG Fortran Compiler
```

```
Error: ch0506.f90, line 7:
Floating-point overflow in single-precision
multiplication
[NAG Fortran Compiler error termination, 1 error]
```

So the Nag compiler diagnoses the problem at compile time.

5.15.2 Example 7: Underflow

There is an inverse called underflow when the number is too small, which is illustrated below:

```
z = b * c * d
```

where b and c are $O(10^{-30})/O(10^{30})$. The intermediate result of $b * c$ is $O(10^{-60})$ — again beyond the limits of the machine. This problem could have been overcome by retyping as

```
z = b * (c * d)
```

Here is a simple program that illustrates underflow.

```
program ch0507
  implicit none
  real :: z = 0.0
  real :: b = 1.0e-30
  real :: c = 1.0e-30
  real :: d = 1.0e30

  z = b*c*d
  print *, z
  z = b*(c*d)
  print *, z
end program ch0507
```

Here is the output from running the program with the Nag and Intel compilers.

```
0.0000000E+00
1.0000000E-30
```

We will look at underflow in more detail in the chapter on IEEE arithmetic.

5.16   Health Warning: Optional Reading, Beginners Are Advised to Leave Until Later

Most people take arithmetic completely for granted and rarely think much about the subject. It is necessary to look at it in a bit more depth if we are to understand what the computer is doing in this area.

5.16.1   Positional Number Systems

Our way of working with numbers is essentially a positional one. When we look at the number 1024, for example, we rarely think of it in terms of 1 * 1000 + 0 * 100 + 2 * 10 + 4 * 1. Thus the normal decimal system we use in everyday life is a positional one, with a base of 10.

We are probably aware that we can use other number bases, and 2, 8 and 16 are fairly common alternate number bases. As the computer is a binary device it uses base 2.

We are also reasonably familiar with a mantissa exponent or floating point combination when the numbers get very large or very small, e.g., a parsec is commonly expressed as 3.08 * 10 ** 16, and here the mantissa is 3.08, and the exponent is 10 ** 16.

The above information will help in understanding the way in which integers and reals are represented on computer systems.

5.16.2   Fortran Representational Models

Fortran has three representational models for data

- the bit model
- the integer number system model
- the real number system model

and these models (and the corresponding intrinsic functions) return values related to the models. We look at each in turn below.

5.16.2.1   Bit Data Type and Representation Model

The model is only defined for positive integers (or cardinal numbers), where they are represented as a sequence of binary digits, and is based on the model:

$$i = \sum_{k=0}^{n-1} b_k 2^k$$

where i is the integer value, n is the number of bits, and b_k is a bit value of 0 or 1, with bit numbering starting at 0, and reading right to left. Thus the integer 43 and bit pattern 101011 is given by:

$$43 = (1 * 32) + (0 * 16) + (1 * 8) + (0 * 4) + (1 * 2) + (1 * 1)$$

or

$$43 = (1 * 2^5) + (0 * 2^4) + (1 * 2^3) + (0 * 2^2) + (1 * 2^1) + (1 * 2^0)$$

5.16.2.2 Integer Data Type and Representation Model

The integer data type is based on the model

$$i = s \sum_{k=1}^{q} l_k r^{k-1}$$

where i is the integer value, s is the sign, q is the number of digits (always positive), r is the radix or base (integer greater than 1), and l_k is a positive integer (less than r).

A base of 2 is typical so 1023 is

$$1023 = (1 * 2^9) + (1 * 2^8) + (1 * 2^7) + (1 * 2^6) + (1 * 2^5) + (1 * 2^4) + (1 * 2^3) + (1 * 2^2) + (1 * 2^1) + (1 * 2^0)$$

5.16.2.3 Real Data Type and Representation model

The real data type is based on the model

$$x = s b^e \sum_{k=1}^{m} f_k b^{-k}$$

where x is the real number, s is the sign, b is the radix or base (greater than 1), m is the number of bits in the mantissa, e is an integer in the range e_{min} to e_{max}, and f_k is a positive number less than b.

This means that with, for example, a 32-bit real there would be 8 bits allocated to the exponent and 24 to the mantissa. One of the bits in each part would be used to represent the sign and is called the sign bit. This reduces the number of bits that can actually be used to represent the mantissa and exponent to 31 and 7, respectively. There is also the concept of normalisation, where the exponent is adjusted so that the most significant bit is in position 22 — bits are typically numbered 0–22, rather than 1–23. This form of representation is not new, and is first documented around 1750 BC, when Babylonian mathematicians used a sexagesimal (radix 60) positional notation. It is interesting that the form they used omitted the exponent!

This is the theoretical basis of the representation of these three data types in Fortran.

This information together with the following provide a good basis for writing portable code across a range of hardware.

5.17 Kind Types

Fortran 90 introduced the concept of a `kind` parameter for the intrinsic types. Each of the intrinsic types has a `kind parameter` that selects a processor dependent representation of objects of that type and kind.

Each intrinsic type is classified as a numeric type or a nonnumeric type. The numeric types are integer, real, and complex. The nonnumeric intrinsic types are character and logical.

5.17.1 Example 8: Testing What Kind Types Are Available

The follow program shows what kind types are available for each intrinsic type.

```
program ch0508
  use iso_fortran_env

  print *, ' Real kinds      ', real_kinds
  print *, ' Integer kinds   ', integer_kinds
  print *, ' Character kinds ', character_kinds
  print *, ' Logical kinds   ', logical_kinds
end program ch0508
```

The intrinsic module ISO_FORTRAN_ENV provides public entities relating to the Fortran environment. The processor shall provide the named constants, derived types, and procedures described in sub-clause 16.10.2. of the Fortran 2018 standard.

Here is sample output from a number of compilers. In each case the numbers refer to the number of bytes.

```
gfortran
  Real kinds      4     8     10    16
  Integer kinds   1     2     4     8     16
  Character kinds 1     4


Intel
  Real kinds      4     8     16
  Integer kinds   1     2     4     8
  Character kinds 1
```

```
Nag
   Real kinds         4 8 16
   Integer kinds      1 2 4 8
   Character kinds    1 2 3 4
   Logical kinds      1 2 4 8
```

The Nag compiler has to be invoked with the -kind = byte flag to generate the above output.

```
Oracle
   Real kinds         4   8   16
   Integer kinds      1   2   4   8
   Character kinds    1
```

The gfortran compiler supports a 10 byte real kind. We will look at this in more depth later.

All four compilers support 1, 2, 4 and 8 byte integer types. The gfortran compiler also supports a 16 byte integer type.

All compilers support a 1 byte character type. gfortran also supports a 4 byte character type. Nag supports 2 and 3 byte character types.

All four compilers support a 1 byte logical type. Nag also supports 2, 3 and 4 byte logical types.

5.18   Testing the Numerical Representation of Different Kind Types on a System

Table 5.6 provides details of the kind query functions and Table 5.7 provides details of the numeric query functions.

The next set of programs test out the kinds of the intrinsic types supported by compilers.

Table 5.6 Kind inquiry functions

Function name	Simple explanation
kind	Kind parameter
selected_char_kind	Kind parameter of a specified character set
selected_int_kind	Kind parameter of an integer data type
selected_real_kind	Kind parameter of a real data type

Table 5.7   Numeric inquiry functions

Function name	Simple explanation
digits	Number of digits in the model number
epsilon	Smallest difference between two reals
huge	Returns the largest number
maxexponent	Maximum value for the model exponent
minexponent	Minimum value for the model exponent
precision	Returns the decimal precision
radix	Base of a model number
range	Decimal exponent range of a model number
tiny	Returns the smallest number

5.19   Example 9: Using the Numeric Inquiry Functions with Integer Types

This program looks at using the kind intrinsics with integer types.

```
program ch0509

  implicit none

! example of the use of the kind function
! and the numeric inquiry functions
! for integer kind types

! 8 bit              -128  to
! 127        10**2

! 16 bit            -32768 to
! 32767      10**4

! 32 bit      -2147483648 to
! 2147483647      10**9

! 64 bit
! -9223372036854775808 to
! 9223372036854775807    10**18

  integer :: i
  integer, parameter :: i8 = selected_int_kind(2 &
    )
```

```
integer, parameter :: i16 = selected_int_kind( &
  4)
integer, parameter :: i32 = selected_int_kind( &
  9)
integer, parameter :: i64 = selected_int_kind( &
  18)
integer (i8) :: i1
integer (i16) :: i2
integer (i32) :: i3
integer (i64) :: i4

print *, ' '
print *, ' integer kind support'
print *, ' kind              huge'
print *, ' '
print *, ' ', kind(i), ' ', huge(i)
print *, ' '
print *, ' ', kind(i1), ' ', huge(i1)
print *, ' ', kind(i2), ' ', huge(i2)
print *, ' ', kind(i3), ' ', huge(i3)
print *, ' ', kind(i4), ' ', huge(i4)
print *, ' '
end program ch0509
```

In this example we introduce parameters for each of the supported integer kind types.

Table 5.8 has details of the names we have given to the integer kind types.

Table 5.8 Integer kind type parameter name and integer value

Parameter	Integer type
i8	8 bit value
i16	16 bit value
i32	32 bit value
i64	64 bit value

As the kind type parameter has some information about the underlying representation.

Section 16.10.2.14 of the Fortran 2018 standard has details about these named constants:

- `int8`
- `int16`
- `int32`
- `int64`

where the values correspond to an integer type whose storage size expressed in bits is 8, 16, 32, and 64 respectively.

They are available via the `ISO_FORTRAN_ENV` intrinsic module.

They were introduced in the Fortran 2008 standard, and as only one compiler supports the whole of the Fortran 2008 standard at the time of writing the book we will use `i8`, `i16`, `i32` and `i64` in the examples.

Table 5.9 has details of `huge` for each of the integer types.

Table 5.9 Integer kind and huge comparision

gfortran		Intel		Nag	
Kind	Huge	Kind	Huge	Kind	Huge
4	2147483647	4	2147483647	3	2147483647
1	127	1	127	1	127
2	32767	2	32767	2	32767
4	2147483647	4	2147483647	3	2147483647
8	9223372036854775807	8	9223372036854775807	4	9223372036854775807

As can be seen from the output for these three compilers they all support the same 4 integer kind types, namely 8 bit, 16 bit, 32 bit and 64 bit.

Run this program on whatever system you have access to and compare the output with the above examples.

5.20   Example 10: Using the Numeric Inquiry Functions with Real Types

```
program ch0510
  implicit none
! real arithmetic
!
! 32 and 64 bit reals are normally available.
! The IEEE format is as described below.
!
! 32 bit reals  8 bit exponent, 24 bit mantissa
```

```fortran
! 64 bit reals 11 bit exponent, 53 bit mantissa
!
  real :: r
  integer, parameter :: sp = selected_real_kind( &
    6, 37)
  integer, parameter :: dp = selected_real_kind( &
    15, 307)
  integer, parameter :: qp = selected_real_kind( &
    30, 291)
  real (sp) :: rsp
  real (dp) :: rdp
  real (qp) :: rqp

  print *, '                =====================' 
  print *, '                Real kind information'
  print *, '                =====================' 
  print *, ' kind number'
  print *, '    ', kind(r), ' ', kind(rsp), ' ', &
    kind(rdp), ' ', kind(rqp)
  print *, ' digits details'
  print *, '    ', digits(r), ' ', digits(rsp), &
    ' ', digits(rdp), ' ', digits(rqp)
  print *, ' epsilon details'
  print *, '    ', epsilon(r)
  print *, '    ', epsilon(rsp)
  print *, '    ', epsilon(rdp)
  print *, '    ', epsilon(rqp)
  print *, ' huge value'
  print *, '    ', huge(r)
  print *, '    ', huge(rsp)
  print *, '    ', huge(rdp)
  print *, '    ', huge(rqp)
  print *, ' maxexponent value'
  print *, '    ', maxexponent(r)
  print *, '    ', maxexponent(rsp)
  print *, '    ', maxexponent(rdp)
  print *, '    ', maxexponent(rqp)
  print *, ' minexponent value'
  print *, '    ', minexponent(r)
  print *, '    ', minexponent(rsp)
  print *, '    ', minexponent(rdp)
  print *, '    ', minexponent(rqp)
  print *, ' precision details'
  print *, '    ', precision(r), ' ', &
    precision(rsp), ' ', precision(rdp), ' ', &
```

```
      precision(rqp)
    print *, ' radix details'
    print *, '      ', radix(r), ' ', radix(rsp), &
      ' ', radix(rdp), ' ', radix(rqp)
    print *, ' range details'
    print *, '      ', range(r), ' ', range(rsp), &
      ' ', range(rdp), ' ', range(rqp)
    print *, ' tiny details'
    print *, '      ', tiny(r)
    print *, '      ', tiny(rsp)
    print *, '      ', tiny(rdp)
    print *, '      ', tiny(rqp)
end program ch0510
```

In the above example we use a naming convention used by LAPACK95, which is a Fortran 95 interface to LAPACK.

For the real numeric kind types, where we have

- sp - single precision
- dp - double precision
- qp - quad precision

LAPACK is written in Fortran 90 and provides routines for solving systems of simultaneous linear equations, least-squares solutions of linear systems of equations, eigenvalue problems, and singular value problems. The associated matrix factorizations (LU, Cholesky, QR, SVD, Schur, generalized Schur) are also provided, as are related computations such as reordering of the Schur factorizations and estimating condition numbers. Dense and banded matrices are handled, but not general sparse matrices. In all areas, similar functionality is provided for real and complex matrices, in both single and double precision.

Their address is

```
http://www.netlib.org/lapack95/
```

Section 13.8.2.18 of the Fortran 2008 standard introduced real32, real64, and real128, where the values of these default integer scalar named constants shall be those of the kind type parameters that specify a real type whose storage size expressed in bits is 32, 64, and 128 respectively.

They are available via the ISO_FORTRAN_ENV intrinsic module.

As only one compiler supports the whole of the Fortran 2008 standard at the time of writing the book we will use sp, dp and qp in the examples.

Table 5.10 is a summary of the details of an extended type.

Table 5.10 Extended real type comparison

Function name	Cray	gfortran	Intel	Nag	Oracle
digits	113	113	113	106	113
maxexponent	16384	16384	16384	1023	16384
minexponent	−16381	−16381	−16381	−968	−16381
precision	33	33	33	31	33
radix	2	2	2	2	2
range	4931	4931	4931	291	4931

As can be seen all five compilers support the same 32 and 64 bit real types. They all support an extended 128 bit type, and Cray, gfortran, Intel and Oracle are the same, but Nag is different.

Here are the details for epsilon, huge and tiny for these compilers.

```
Epsilon
  Cray
    1.92592994438723585305597794258492732E-34
  gfortran
    1.92592994438723585305597794258492732E-0034
  Intel
    1.92592994438723585305597794258492732E-0034
  Nag
    2.46519032881566189191165177E-32
  Oracle (Sun)
    1.92592994438723585305597794258492732E-34
Huge
  Cray
    1.18973149535723176508575932662800702E+4932
  gfortran
    1.18973149535723176508575932662800702E+4932
  Intel
    1.18973149535723176508575932662800702E+4932
  Nag
    8.98846567431157953864652595E+307
  Oracle (Sun)
    1.18973149535723176508575932662800702E+4932
Tiny
  Cray
    3.36210314311209350626267781732175260E-4932
  gfortran
    3.36210314311209350626267781732175260E-4932
  Intel
```

```
  3.36210314311209350626267781732175 3E-4932
Nag
  2.00416836000897277799610805E-292
Oracle (Sun)
  3.36210314311209350626267781732175 26E-4932
```

Run this program on whatever system you have access to with your compiler(s) and compare the output with the above examples. Most compilers will offer support for 32, 64 and 128 bit reals.

5.21   gfortran Support for Intel Extended (80 bit) Precision

As was seen earlier the gfortran compiler also supports a 10 byte real. This is the Intel x86 extended precision format.

The x86 extended precision format is an 80-bit format first implemented in the Intel 8087 math coprocessor and is supported by all processors that are based on the x86 design which incorporate a floating-point unit (FPU). This 80-bit format uses one bit for the sign of the significand, 15 bits for the exponent field (i.e. the same range as the 128-bit quadruple precision IEEE 754 format) and 64 bits for the significand.

We will look at an example of using this kind type in a later chapter.

5.22   Example 11: Literal Real Constants in a Calculation

We have seen how to specify integer and real variables of different kind types but we also need to be able to do the same for literal constants. Examples of literal constants are 1.23, 5.643E-2 (default reals) and 400, -3 (default integers). To declare a literal constant to be of a different kind you need to specify the constant followed by an underscore and the kind type parameter. The following are two examples of 64 bit real literal constants: 1.23_dp, 5.643E-2_dp.

You should be careful when writing programs using variables that are not the default kind making sure that any literal constants are also of the same kind. For example if you are using 64 bit real variables then make sure all your real literal constants are 64 bit. Here is a program where the variables and constants pi, area and r are 32 bit reals and pid, aread and rd are 64 bit reals. Try compiling and running the program. Do you get the same results as us?

```
program ch0511
  implicit none
  integer, parameter :: dp = selected_real_kind( &
```

```
   15, 307)
 real, parameter :: pi = 3.1415926535897931
 real (dp), parameter :: pid = &
   3.1415926535897931_dp
 real :: area, r = 2.0
 real (dp) :: aread, rd = 2.0_dp

 area = pi*r*r
 aread = pid*rd*rd
 print 100, r, rd
100 format ('r       = ', f22.18, /, 'rd      = ', &
    f22.18)
 print 110, area, aread
110 format ('area  = ', f22.18, /, 'aread = ', &
    f22.18, /, 16x, '  ######')
end program ch0511
```

Here is the Nag compiler output.

```
C:\fortran\fortran_book_edition3\chapter5>a
r     =    2.000000000000000000
rd    =    2.000000000000000000
area  =   12.566370964050292969
aread =   12.566370614359172464
                ######
```

Now edit the program and remove the _dp from the literal constant assigned to pid. You will see that the results for area (32 bit real) and aread (64 bit real) are the same. This is because the literal constant for pid reverts to a default 32 bit real.

```
C:\fortran\fortran_book_edition3\chapter5>a
r     =    2.000000000000000000
rd    =    2.000000000000000000
area  =   12.566370964050292969
aread =   12.566370964050292969
                ######
```

5.23   Summation and Finite Precision

The next example look at some of the problems that occur with the summation of floating point numbers. We will look at more summation problems in later chapters.

5.23.1   Example 12: Rounding Problem

Consider the following program.

```
program ch0512
  implicit none
  real :: x1 = 1.0
  real :: x2 = 0.1
  integer i

  print *, ' x1 = ', x1
  print *, ' x2 = ', x2
  do i = 1, 990
    x1 = x1 + x2
  end do
  print *, ' x1 = ', x1
end program ch0512
```

Here is the output from the Intel compiler.

```
x1 =     1.000000
x2 =     0.1000000
x1 =    99.99905
```

Here is the output from the Nag compiler.

```
x1 =     1.0000000
x2 =     0.1000000
x1 =    99.9990463
```

In both cases the summation is inexact, due to rounding errors.

5.24   Example 13: Binary Representation of Different Integer Kind Type Numbers

For those who wish to look at the internal binary representation of integer numbers with a variety of kinds, we have included the following program

selected_int_kind(2) means provide at least an integer representation with numbers between -10^2 and $+10^2$.

selected_int_kind(4) means provide at least an integer representation with numbers between -10^4 and $+10^4$.

selected_int_kind(9) means provide at least an integer representation with numbers between -10^9 and $+10^9$.

We use the int function to convert from one integer representation to another.

We use the logical function btest to determine whether the binary value at that position within the number is a zero or a one, i.e., if the bit is set.

i_in_bits is a character string that holds a direct mapping from the internal binary form of the integer and a text string that prints as a sequence of zeros or ones:

```fortran
program ch0513
!
! use the bit functions in Fortran to write out
! a
! 32 bit integer number as a sequence of
! zeros and ones
!
  implicit none
  integer :: j
  integer :: i
  integer, parameter :: i8 = selected_int_kind(2 &
    )
  integer, parameter :: i16 = selected_int_kind( &
    4)
  integer, parameter :: i32 = selected_int_kind( &
    9)

  integer (i8) :: i1
  integer (i16) :: i2
  integer (i32) :: i3
  character (len=32) :: i_in_bits

  print *, ' type in an integer '
  read *, i
  i1 = int(i, kind(2))
  i2 = int(i, kind(4))
  i3 = int(i, kind(9))
  i_in_bits = ' '
  do j = 0, 7
    if (btest(i1,j)) then
      i_in_bits(8-j:8-j) = '1'
    else
      i_in_bits(8-j:8-j) = '0'
    end if
  end do
  print *, '            1            2            3'
```

```
    print *, '123456789012345678901234567890123456789012'
    print *, i1
    print *, i_in_bits
    do j = 0, 15
      if (btest(i2,j)) then
        i_in_bits(16-j:16-j) = '1'
      else
        i_in_bits(16-j:16-j) = '0'
      end if
    end do
    print *, i2
    print *, i_in_bits
    do j = 0, 31
      if (btest(i3,j)) then
        i_in_bits(32-j:32-j) = '1'
      else
        i_in_bits(32-j:32-j) = '0'
      end if
    end do
    print *, i3
    print *, i_in_bits
  end program ch0513
```

The do loop indices follow the convention of an 8-bit quantity starting at bit 0 and ending at bit 7, 16-bit quantities starting at 0 and ending at 15, etc.

The numbers written out follow the conventional mathematical notation of having the least significant quantity at the right-hand end of the digit sequence, i.e., with 127 in decimal we have $1 * 100$, $2 * 10$ and $7 * 1$, so 00100001 in binary means $1 * 32 + 1 * 1$ decimal.

Try running this program on the system you are using. Does it produce the results you expect? Experiment with a variety of numbers. Try at least the following 0, $+1$, -1, -128, 127, 128, -32768, 32767, 32768.

5.25   Example 14: Binary Representation of a Real Number

The following program is a simple variant of the previous one, but we now look at a floating point number:

```
program ch0514
!
! use the bit functions in Fortran to write out
! a
! 32 bit integer number equivalenced to a real
```

```
! using the transfer intrinsic as a sequence of
! zeros and ones
!

  implicit none
  integer :: i, j
  character (len=32) :: i_in_bits = ' '
  real :: x = 1.0

  print *, '           1             2             3'
  print *, '12345678901234567890123456789012'
  print *, i_in_bits
  i = transfer(x, i)
  do j = 0, 31
    if (btest(i,j)) then
      i_in_bits(32-j:32-j) = '1'
    else
      i_in_bits(32-j:32-j) = '0'
    end if
  end do
  print *, x
  print *, i_in_bits
end program ch0514
```

We use the intrinsic function `transfer` to help out here. The `btest` intrinsic takes an integer argument, so we need to copy the bit pattern of the real number into an integer variable.

5.26   Example 15: Initialisation of Physical Constants, Version 1

This is the first of three examples that uses the physical constant data in an earlier table to initialise parameters in a Fortran program.

```
program ch0515
  implicit none
  real, parameter :: atomic_mass_constant = &
    1.660538921*10**(-27)
  real, parameter :: avogadro_constant = &
    6.02214129*10**23
  real, parameter :: boltzmann_constant = &
    1.3806488*10**(-23)
  real, parameter :: electron_mass = 9.10938291* &
```

```
   10**(-31)
real, parameter :: elementary_charge = &
   1.602176565*10**(-19)
real, parameter :: proton_mass = 1.672621777* &
   10**(-27)
real, parameter :: speed_of_light_in_vacuum = &
   299792458
real, parameter :: &
   newtonian_constant_of_gravitation = 6.67384* &
   10**(-11)

print *, atomic_mass_constant
print *, avogadro_constant
print *, boltzmann_constant
print *, electron_mass
print *, elementary_charge
print *, proton_mass
print *, speed_of_light_in_vacuum
print *, newtonian_constant_of_gravitation
end program ch0515
```

Here is the output from the Intel compiler.

```
0.0000000E+00
1.2066952E+18
0.0000000E+00
0.0000000E+00
0.0000000E+00
0.0000000E+00
2.9979245E+08
0.0000000E+00
```

Here is the output from the Nag compiler.

```
nagfor ch0514.f90
NAG Fortran Compiler
Error: ch0514.f90, line 6:
Integer overflow for exponentiation 10**23
Errors in declarations,
no further processing for CH0514
[NAG Fortran Compiler error termination, 1 error]
```

5.27   Example 16: Initialisation of Physical Constants, Version 2

This is the second of three examples that uses the physical constant data in an earlier table to initialise parameters in a Fortran program.

```
program ch0516
  implicit none
  real, parameter :: atomic_mass_constant = &
    1.660538921e-27
  real, parameter :: avogadro_constant = &
    6.02214129e23
  real, parameter :: boltzmann_constant = &
    1.3806488e-23
  real, parameter :: electron_mass = &
    9.10938291e-31
  real, parameter :: elementary_charge = &
    1.602176565e-19
  real, parameter :: proton_mass = &
    1.672621777e-27
  real, parameter :: speed_of_light_in_vacuum = &
    299792458
  real, parameter :: &
    newtonian_constant_of_gravitation = &
    6.67384e-11

  print *, atomic_mass_constant
  print *, avogadro_constant
  print *, boltzmann_constant
  print *, electron_mass
  print *, elementary_charge
  print *, proton_mass
  print *, speed_of_light_in_vacuum
  print *, newtonian_constant_of_gravitation
end program ch0516
```

5.28   Example 17: Initialisation of Physical Constants, Version 3

This is the third of three examples that uses the physical constant data in an earlier table to initialise parameters in a Fortran program.

```
program ch0517
  implicit none
  real, parameter :: atomic_mass_constant = &
    1.660538921*10.0**(-27)
  real, parameter :: avogadro_constant = &
    6.02214129*10.0**23
  real, parameter :: boltzmann_constant = &
    1.3806488*10.0**(-23)
  real, parameter :: electron_mass = 9.10938291* &
    10.0**(-31)
  real, parameter :: elementary_charge = &
    1.602176565*10.0**(-19)
  real, parameter :: proton_mass = 1.672621777* &
    10.0**(-27)
  real, parameter :: speed_of_light_in_vacuum = &
    299792458
  real, parameter :: &
    newtonian_constant_of_gravitation = 6.67384* &
    10.0**(-11)

  print *, atomic_mass_constant
  print *, avogadro_constant
  print *, boltzmann_constant
  print *, electron_mass
  print *, elementary_charge
  print *, proton_mass
  print *, speed_of_light_in_vacuum
  print *, newtonian_constant_of_gravitation
end program ch0517
```

5.29 Summary of How to Select the Appropriate Kind Type

To write programs that will perform arithmetically in a similar fashion on a variety of hardware requires an understanding of:

- The integer data representation model and in practice the word size of the various integer kind types.
- The real data representation model and in practice the word size of the various real kind types and the number of bits in both the mantissa and exponent.

Armed with this information we can then choose a kind type that will ensure minimal problems when moving from one platform to another. End of health warning!

5.30   Variable Status

Fortran has two concepts regarding the status of a variable: defined and undefined. If a program does not provide an initial value (in a type statement) for a variable then its status is said to be undefined. Consider the following code segment taken from the earlier example that calculated the sum and average of three numbers:

```
real :: n1, n2, n3, average=0.0, total=0.0
integer :: n = 3
```

In the above the variables average, total and n all have a defined status. However, n1, n2 and n3 are said to be undefined. The use of undefined values is implementation dependent and therefore not portable. Care must be taken when writing programs to ensure that your variables have a defined status wherever possible. We will look at this area again in subsequent chapters.

5.31   Fortran and the IEEE 754 Standard

The ISO TR 15580 introduced IEEE Arithmetic support to Fortran.

IEEE 754-2008 governs binary floating-point arithmetic. It specifies number formats, basic operations, conversions, and exceptional conditions. The 2008 edition superseded both the

- 754-1985

standard and the related

- IEEE 854-1987

which generalized 754-1985 to cover decimal arithmetic as well as binary. The first standard IEEE 754: 1985 covered binary floating point arithmetic. The later IEEE 754: 1987 standard added decimal arithmetic.

The latest version of the standard is ISO/IEC/IEEE 60559:2011.

A considerable amount of hardware now offers support for the IEEE 754 standard. The standard can be purchased from

```
http://www.iso.org/
```

The following is a useful site.

```
http://grouper.ieee.org/groups/754/
```

There are quite a lot of good links.

There is a separate chapter in the book on IEEE arithmetic and Fortran.

5.32 Summary

The following are some practical rules and guidelines:

- Learn the rules for the evaluation of arithmetic expressions.
- Break expressions down where necessary to ensure that the expressions are evaluated in the way you want.
- Take care with truncation owing to integer division in an expression. Note that this will only be a problem where both parts of the division are integer.
- Take care with truncation owing to the assignment statement when there is an integer on the left-hand side of the statement, i.e., assigning a real into an integer variable.
- When you want to set up constants which will remain unchanged throughout the program, use the parameter attribute.
- Do not confuse precision and accuracy.
- Learn what the default kinds are for the numeric types you work with, what the maximum and minimum values and precision are for real data, and what the maximum and minimum are for integer data.
- You have been introduced to the use of several intrinsic functions.

5.33 Bibliography

Some understanding of floating point arithmetic and numerical analysis is essential for successful use of Fortran when programming. As Froberg says "numerical analysis is a science — computation is an art." The separate chapter on IEEE arithmetic also has several references.

The following are some of the more accessible books available.

Burden R.L., Faires J.D., Numerical Analysis, Brooks Cole, 2010.

- The first section of the book covers some of the mathematical preliminaries including a review of calculus, round-off errors and computer arithmetic, algorithms and convergence. They provide programs or software to solve the problems in C, Fortran, Maple, Mathematica, Matlab and Pascal.

Froberg C.E., Introduction to Numerical Analysis, Addison-Wesley, 1969.

- The short chapter on numerical computation is well worth a read; it covers some of the problems of conversion between number bases and some of the errors that are introduced when we compute numerically. The Samuel Johnson quote owes its inclusion to Froberg!

Goldberg D., What Every Computer Scientist Should Know About Floating-Point Arithmetic, Computing Surveys, March 1991.

- The paper is a very good introduction to floating point arithmetic. It is available on line.

Higham Nicholas J., Accuracy and Stability of Numerical Algorithms, SIAM, 2002.

• The first four chapters cover finite precision computation, floating point arithmetic, error analysis and summation methods.

Knuth D., Seminumerical Algorithms, Addison-Wesley, 1969.

• A more thorough and mathematical coverage than Wakerly. The chapter on positional number systems provides a very comprehensive historical coverage of the subject. As Knuth points out the floating point representation for numbers is very old, and is first documented around 1750 B.C. by Babylonian mathematicians. Very interesting and worthwhile reading.

Wakerly J.F., Microcomputer Architecture and programming, Wiley, 1981.

• The chapter on number systems and arithmetic is surprisingly easy. There is a coverage of positional number systems, octal and hexadecimal number system conversions, addition and subtraction of nondecimal numbers, representation of negative numbers, two's complement addition and subtraction, one's complement addition and subtraction, binary multiplication, binary division, bcd or binary coded decimal representation and fixed and floating point representations. There is also coverage of a number of specific hardware platforms, including DEC PDP-11, Motorola 68000, Zilog Z8000, TI 9900, Motorola 6809 and Intel 8086. A little old but quite interesting nevertheless.

5.34 Problems

5.1 Compile and run Examples 1–3 in this chapter.

5.2 Have another look at Example 4. Compile and run it. It will generate an error on some systems. Can you see where the error is?

5.3 Write a program to calculate the period of a pendulum. This is given mathematically as

$$t = 2\pi \sqrt{length/9.81}$$

use the following Fortran arithmetic assignment statement:

```
t = 2 * pi * (length / 9.81) ** .5
```

The length `length` is in metres, and the time `t` in seconds, and `pi` was given a value earlier in this chapter.

Repeat the above using two other methods. Try a hand-held calculator and a spreadsheet. Do you get the same answers?

5.4 Base conversion.

In this chapter you have seen a brief coverage of base conversion. The following program illustrates some of the problems that can occur when going from base 10 to base 2 and back again. Which numbers will convert without loss?

```
program base_conversion
  implicit none
  real :: x1 = 1.0
  real :: x2 = 0.1
  real :: x3 = 0.01
  real :: x4 = 0.001
  real :: x5 = 0.0001

  print *, ' ', x1
  print *, ' ', x2
  print *, ' ', x3
  print *, ' ', x4
  print *, ' ', x5
end program base_conversion
```

Which do you think will provide the same number as originally entered?

5.5 Simple subtraction. In this chapter we looked at representing floating point numbers in a finite number of bits.

Try the following program:

```
program subtract
  implicit none
  real :: a = 1.0002
  real :: b = 1.0001
  real :: c

  c = a - b
  print *, a
  print *, b
  print *, c
end program subtract
```

What are the absolute and relative errors in this calculation?

5.6 Expression equivalence. We introduced some of the rules that apply in Fortran for expression evaluation. In mathematics the following is true:
$$x^2 - y^2 = (x*x - y*y) = (x - y)*(x + y)$$
Try the following program:

```
program expression_equivalence
!
! simple evaluation of x*x-y*y
! when x and y are similar
!
! we will evaluate in three ways.
!
  implicit none
  real :: x = 1.002
  real :: y = 1.001
  real :: t1, t2, t3, t4, t5

  t1 = x - y
  t2 = x + y
  print *, t1
  print *, t2
  t3 = t1*t2
  t4 = x**2 - y**2
  t5 = x*x - y*y
  print *, t3
  print *, t4
  print *, t5
end program expression_equivalence
```

Solve the problem with pencil and paper, calculator and Excel.

The last three examples show that you must be careful when using a computer to solve problems.

5.7 The following is a simple variant of ch0504. In this case we initialise light year in an assignment statement. Do you think you will get the same results as from running the earlier example?

```
program ch0504p
  implicit none
  real :: light_minute, distance, elapse
  integer :: minute, second
  real :: light_year
! Light_year : Distance travelled by light
! in one year in km
! Light_minute : Distance travelled by light
! in one minute in km
! Distance : Distance from sun to earth in km
! Elapse : Time taken to travel a
! distance (Distance) in minutes
! Minute : integer number part of elapse
```

```
! Second : integer number of seconds
! equivalent to fractional part of elapse
!
  light_year = 9.46*10**12
  light_minute = light_year/(365.25*24.0*60.0)
  distance = 150.0*10**6
  elapse = distance/light_minute
  minute = elapse
  second = (elapse-minute)*60
  print *, ' Light takes ', minute, ' Minutes'
  print *, ' ', second, ' Seconds'
  print *, ' To reach the earth from sun'
end program ch0504p
```

5.8 Many communications satellites follow a geosynchronous orbit, some 35,870 km above the Earth s surface. What is the time lag incurred in using one such satellite for a telephone conversation?

This will also be the time delay for satellite based internet access.

You can use the above program as the basis for this problem. You will need to calculate the time in seconds (rather than minutes and seconds), as the distance is much smaller.

5.9 The Moon is about 384,400 km from the Earth on average What implications does this have for control of experiments on the Moon? What is the time lag?

5.10 The following table gives the distance in mkm from the Sun to the planets in the Solar system.

```
Mercury      57.9
Venus       108.9
Earth       149.6
Mars        227.9
Jupiter     778.3
Saturn     1427.0
Uranus     2869.6
Neptune    4496.6
Pluto      5900.0
```

Use this information to find the greatest and least time taken to send a message from the Earth to the other planets.

Assume that all orbits are in the same plane and circular. If it was good enough for Copernicus it's good enough for this example.

Chapter 6
Arrays 1: Some Fundamentals

Thy gifts, thy tables, are within my brain Full charactered with lasting memory.
William Shakespeare, The Sonnets
Here, take this book, and peruse it well: The iterating of these lines brings gold.
Christopher Marlowe, The Tragical History of Doctor Faustus

Aims

The aims of the chapter are to introduce the fundamental concepts of arrays and do loops, in particular:

- To introduce the idea of tables of data and some of the formal terms used to describe them:

  - Array.
  - Vector.
  - List and linear list.

- To discuss the array as a random access structure where any element can be accessed as readily as any other and to note that the data in an array are all of the same type.
- To introduce the twin concepts of data structure and corresponding control structure.
- To introduce the statements necessary in Fortran to support and manipulate these data structures.

6.1 Tables of Data

Consider the examples below.

© Springer International Publishing AG, part of Springer Nature 2018
I. Chivers and J. Sleightholme, *Introduction to Programming with Fortran*,
https://doi.org/10.1007/978-3-319-75502-1_6

6.1.1 Telephone Directory

A telephone directory consists of the following kinds of entries:

Name	Address	Number
Adcroft A.	61 Connaught Road, Roath, Cardiff	223309
Beale K.	14 Airedale Road, Balham	745 9870
Blunt R.U.	81 Stanlake Road, Shepherds Bush	674 4546
...		
...		
...		
Sims Tony	99 Andover Road,Twickenham	898 7330

This structure can be considered in a variety of ways, but perhaps the most common is to regard it as a table of data, where there are three columns and as many rows as there are entries in the telephone directory.

Consider now the way we extract information from this table. We would scan the name column looking for the name we are interested in, and then read along the row looking for either the address or telephone number, i.e., we are using the name to look up the item of interest.

6.1.2 Book Catalogue

A catalogue could contain:

Author(s)	Title	Publisher
Carroll L.	Alice through the Looking Glass	Penguin
Steinbeck J.	Sweet Thursday	Penguin
Wirth N.	Algorithms plus data Structures = programs	Prentice-Hall

Again, this can be regarded as a table of data, having three columns and many rows. We would follow the same procedure as with the telephone directory to extract the information. We would use the Author to look up what books are available.

6.1.3 Examination Marks or Results

This could consist of:

Name	Physics	Maths	Biology	History	English	French
Fowler L.	50	47	28	89	30	46
Barron L.W	37	67	34	65	68	98
Warren J.	25	45	26	48	10	36
Mallory D.	89	56	33	45	30	65
Codd S.	68	78	38	76	98	65

This can again be regarded as a table of data. This example has seven columns and five rows. We would again look up information by using the Name.

6.1.4 Monthly Rainfall

The following data are a sample of monthly average rainfall for London in inches:

Month	Rainfall
January	3.1
February	2.0
March	2.4
April	2.1
May	2.2
June	2.2
July	1.8
August	2.2
September	2.7
October	2.9
November	3.1
December	3.1

In this table there are two columns and twelve rows. To find out what the rainfall was in July, we scan the table for July in the Month column and locate the value in the same row, i.e., the rainfall figure for July.

These are just some of the many examples of problems where the data that are being considered have a tabular structure. Most general purpose languages therefore have mechanisms for dealing with this kind of structure. Some of the special names given to these structures include:

- Linear list.
- List.

- Vector.
- Array.

The term used most often here, and in the majority of books on Fortran programming, is array.

6.2   Arrays in Fortran

There are three key things to consider here:

- The ability to refer to a set or group of items by a single name.
- The ability to refer to individual items or members of this set, i.e., look them up.
- The choice of a control structure that allows easy manipulation of this set or array.

6.2.1   The Dimension Attribute

The dimension attribute defines a variable to be an array. This satisfies the first requirement of being able to refer to a set of items by a single name. Some examples are given below:

```
real , dimension(1:100) :: wages
integer , dimension(1:10000) ::    sample
```

For the variable `wages` it is of type `real` and an array of dimension or size 100, i.e., the variable array `wages` can hold up to 100 real items.

For the variable `sample` it is of type `integer` and an array of dimension or size 10,000, i.e., the variable `sample` can hold up to 10,000 integer items.

6.2.2   An Index

An index enables you to refer to or select individual elements of the array. In the telephone directory, book catalogue, exam marks table and monthly rainfall examples we used the name to index or look up the items of interest. We will give concrete Fortran code for this in the example of monthly rain fall.

6.2.3   Control Structure

The statement that is generally used to manipulate the elements of an array is the do statement. It is typical to have several statements controlled by the do statement, and the block of repeated statements is often called a do loop. Let us look at two complete programs that highlight the above.

6.3   Example 1: Monthly Rainfall

Let us look at this earlier example in more depth now. Consider the following:

Month	Associated integer representation	Array and index	Rainfall value
January	1	rainfall(1)	3.1
February	2	rainfall(2)	2.0
March	3	rainfall(3)	2.4
April	4	rainfall(4)	2.1
May	5	rainfall(5)	2.2
June	6	rainfall(6)	2.2
July	7	rainfall(7)	1.8
August	8	rainfall(8)	2.2
September	9	rainfall(9)	2.7
October	10	rainfall(10)	2.9
November	11	rainfall(11)	3.1
December	12	rainfall(12)	3.1

Most of you should be familiar with the idea of the use of an integer as an alternate way of representing a month, e.g., in a date expressed as 1/3/2000, for 1st March 2000 (Anglicised style) or January 3rd (Americanised style). Fortran, in common with other programming languages, only allows the use of integers as an index into an array. Thus when we write a program to use arrays we have to map between whatever construct we use in everyday life as our index (names in our examples of telephone directory, book catalogue, and exam marks) to an integer representation in Fortran. The following is an example of an assignment statement showing the use of an index:

```
rainfall(1)=3.1
```

We saw earlier that we could use the dimension attribute to indicate that a variable was an array. In the above example Fortran statement our array is called `rainfall`. In this statement we are assigning the value 3.1 to the first element of the array; i.e., the rainfall for the month of January is 3.1. We use the index 1 to represent the first month. Consider the following statement:

```
summeraverage = (rainfall(6) + rainfall(7) + &
                rainfall(8))/3
```

This statement says take the values of the rainfall for June, July and August, add them up and then divide by 3, and assign the result to the variable `summeraverage`, thus providing us with the rainfall average for the three summer months — Northern Hemisphere of course!

The following program reads in the 12 monthly values from the keyboard, computes the sum and average for the year, and prints the average out.

```
program ch0601
  implicit none
  real :: total = 0.0, average = 0.0
  real, dimension (1:12) :: rainfall
  integer :: month

  print *, ' type in the rainfall values'
  print *, ' one per line'
  do month = 1, 12
    read *, rainfall(month)
  end do
  do month = 1, 12
    total = total + rainfall(month)
  end do
  average = total/12
  print *, ' Average monthly rainfall was'
  print *, average
end program ch0601
```

`rainfall` is the array name. The variable `month` in brackets is the index. It takes on values from 1 to 12 inclusive, and is used to pick out or select elements of the array. The index is thus a variable and this permits dynamic manipulation of the array at run time. The general form of the do statement is

```
do counter = start, end, increment
```

The block of statements that form the loop is contained between the do statement, which marks the beginning of the block or loop, and the `enddo` statement, which marks the end of the block or loop.

In this program, the do loops take the form:

```
do month=1,12        start
    ...              body
enddo                end
```

The body of the loop in the program above has been indented. This is not required by Fortran. However it is good practice and will make programs easier to follow.

The number of times that the do loop is executed is governed by the last part of the do statement, i.e., by the

```
counter = start, end, increment
```

start as it implies, is the initial value which the counter (or index, or control variable) takes. Each time the loop is executed, the value of the counter will be increased by the value of increment, until the value of end is reached. If increment is omitted, it is assumed to be 1. No other element of the do statement may be omitted. In order to execute the statements within the loop (the body) it must be possible to reach end from start. Thus zero is an illegal value of increment. In the event that it is not possible to reach end, the loop will not be executed and control will pass to the statement after the end of the loop.

In the example above, both loops would be executed 12 times. In both cases, the first time around the loop the variable month would have the value 1, the second time around the loop the variable month would have the value 2, etc., and the last time around the loop month would have the value 12.

A summation:

$$\sum_{i=1}^{i=12} x_i$$

is often expressed in Fortran as a loop as in this example:

```
do month=1,12
  total = total + rainfall(month)
enddo
```

6.4 Possible Missing Data

The rainfall data in this example has been taken from the UK Met Office site. Visit

```
https://www.metoffice.gov.uk/public/weather/
climate-historic/#?tab=climateHistoric
```

to see where some of the stations are. One of us was born in Wales, the other in Yorkshire so we have chosen stations accordingly. The urls have been split over two lines when too long.

The following is one of the mid Wales stations:

```
https://www.metoffice.gov.uk/pub/data/weather/
uk/climate/stationdata/cwmystwythdata.txt
```

Here is a sample of data from this site for 1965.

yyyy	mm	tmax	tmin	af	rain	sun
		degC	degC	days	mm	hours
1965	1	4.8	-0.2	17	214.8	38.8
1965	2	4.4	-1.2	17	25.1	33.3
1965	3	7.7	0.5	11	93.7	114.6
1965	4	9.9	2.4	9	146.9	134.3
1965	5	13.5	5.8	3	108.7	120.8
1965	6	15.9	8.3	0	115.0	140.4
1965	7	15.3	8.6	0	105.0	106.4
1965	8	---	9.6	0	155.7	140.2
1965	9	---	6.6	0	245.7	70.6
1965	10	13.5	7.0	0	92.5	134.3
1965	11	6.2	0.8	11	115.7	73.8
1965	12	7.0	1.6	8	417.3	31.4

Wales is relatively wet for the UK!
The following station is Whitby:

```
https://www.metoffice.gov.uk/pub/data/weather/
uk/climate/stationdata/whitbydata.txt
```

Here is a sample of the Whitby data.

yyyy	mm	tmax	tmin	af	rain	sun
		degC	degC	days	mm	hours
1968	1	6.9	1.7	12	24.4	
1968	2	4.3	-0.7	16	45.1	
1968	3	9.4	3.4	2	34.5	
1968	4	10.8	1.6	9	28.8	
1968	5	10.6	2.8	2	37.1	
1968	6	16.7	6.8	0	58.5	
1968	7	15.0	8.1	0	81.4	
1968	8	16.3	9.6	0	28.0	
1968	9	15.7	---	---	66.0	
1968	10	14.7	---	---	35.2	
1968	11	8.5	5.1	1	35.1	
1968	12	5.7	1.5	9	---	

Bram Stoker found some of his inspiration for Dracula after staying in the town.
If you look at the data for some of these stations you will notice that data is missing
for some months.

How do you think you could cope with missing data in Fortran?

The SQL standard has the concept of nulls or missing values, and missing data in a statistics package is commonly flagged by an exceptional value e.g. −999.

We will look at using this data in Chap. 10.

6.5   Example 2: People's Weights and Setting the Array Size With a Parameter

In the table   below we have ten people, with their names as shown. We associate each name with a number — in this case we have ordered the names alphabetically, and the numbers therefore reflect their ordering. weight is the array name. The number in brackets is called the index and it is used to pick out or select elements of the array. The table is read as the first element of the array weight has the value 85, the second element has the value 76, etc.

Person	Associated integer representation	Array and index	Associated value
Andy	1	Weight(1)	85
Barry	2	Weight(2)	76
Cathy	3	Weight(3)	85
Dawn	4	Weight(4)	90
Elaine	5	Weight(5)	69
Frank	6	Weight(6)	83
Gordon	7	Weight(7)	64
Hannah	8	Weight(8)	57
Ian	9	Weight(9)	65
Jatinda	10	Weight(10)	76

In the first example we so-called hard coded the number 12, which is the number of months, into the program. It occurred four times. Modifying the program to work with a different number of months would obviously be tedious and potentially error prone.

In this example we parameterise the size of the array and reduce the effort involved in modifying the program to work with a different number of people:

```
program ch0602
! The program reads up to number_of_people
! weights into the array Weight
! Variables used
! Weight, holds the weight of the people
! Person, an index into the array
! Total, total weight
! Average, average weight of the people
```

```
! Parameters used
! NumberOfPeople ,10 in this case.
! The weights are written out so that
! they can be checked
!
  implicit none
  integer, parameter :: number_of_people = 10
  real :: total = 0.0, average = 0.0
  integer :: person
  real, dimension (1:number_of_people) :: weight

  do person = 1, number_of_people
    print *, ' type in the weight for person ', &
      person
    read *, weight(person)
    total = total + weight(person)
  end do
  average = total/number_of_people
  print *, ' The total of the weights is ', &
    total
  print *, ' Average Weight is ', average
  print *, ' ', number_of_people, &
    ' Weights were '
  do person = 1, number_of_people
    print *, weight(person)
  end do
end program ch0602
```

6.6 Summary

The dimension attribute declares a variable to be an array, and must come at
the start of a program unit, with other declarative statements. It has two forms and
examples of both of them are given below. In the first case we explicitly specify the
upper and lower bounds.

```
real , dimension(1:number_of_people) :: weight
```

In the second case the lower limit defaults to 1

```
real , dimension(number_of_people) :: weight
```

The latter form will be seen in legacy code, especially Fortran 77 code suites.

The `parameter` attribute declares a variable to have a fixed value that cannot be changed during the execution of a program. In our example above note that this statement occurs before the other declarative statements that depend on it. Table 6.1 summarises Fortran's statement ordering.

Table 6.1 Fortran statement ordering

Program	First statement	
Integer		In any order and the dimension and parameter attributes are added here
Real	Declarative	
Character		
Arithmetic assignment		In any order
Print *		
Read *	Executable	
Do		
Enddo		
End program	Last statement	

We choose individual members using an index, and these are always of `integer` type in Fortran.

The do loop is a very convenient control structure for manipulating arrays, and we use indentation to clearly identify loops.

6.7 Problems

6.1 Compile and run example 1 from this chapter. If you live in the UK visit the Met Office site mentioned earlier and choose a site near you, and a year of interest, making sure that the data set is complete for that year.

If you don't live in the UK is there a site similar to the Met Office site that has data for the country your are from?

6.2 Compile and run program 2.

6.3 Using a do loop and an array rewrite the program which calculated the average of three numbers to ten.

6.4 Modify the program that calculates the total and average of people's weights to additionally read in their heights and calculate the total and average of their heights. Use the data given below, which have been taken from a group of first year undergraduates:

```
Height          Weight
1.85               85
1.80               76
1.85               85
1.70               90
1.75               69
1.67               83
1.55               64
1.63               57
1.79               65
1.78               76
```

6.5 Your body mass index is given by your weight (in kilos) divided by your height (in metres) squared. Calculate and print out the BMI for each person.

Grades of obesity according to Garrow as follows:

- Grade 0 (desirable) 20–24.9
- Grade 1 (overweight) 25–29.9
- Grade 2 (obese) 30–40
- Grade 3 (morbidly obese) >40
- Ideal BMI range,
- Men, Range 20.1–25 kg/m^2
- Women, Range 18.7–23.8 kg/m^2

6.6 When working on either a UNIX system or a PC in a DOS box it is possible to use the following characters to enable you to read data from a file or write output to a file when running your program:

```
character       Meaning
<               read from file
>               write to file
```

On a typical UNIX system we could use

```
a.out < data.txt > results.txt
```

to read the data from the file called data.txt and write the output to a file called results.txt.

On a PC in a DOS box the equivalent would be

```
program.exe < data.txt > results.txt
```

This is a quick and dirty way of developing programs that do simple I/O; we don't have to keep typing in the data and we also have a record of the behaviour of the program. Rerun the program that prints out the BMI values to write the output to a file called results.txt. Examine this file in an editor.

6.7 Modify the program that read in your name to read in ten names. Use an array and a do loop. When you have read the names into the array write them out in reverse order on separate lines.

Hint: Look at the formal syntax of the do statement.

6.8 Modify the rainfall program (which assumes that the measurement is in inches) to convert the values to centimetres. One inch equals 2.54 cm. Print out the two sets of values as a table.

Hint: use a second array to hold the metric measurements.

6.9 Combine the programs that read in and calculate the average weight with the one that reads in peoples names. The program should read the weights into one array and the names into another. Allow 20 characters for the length of a name. print out a table linking names and weights.

6.10 In an earlier chapter we used the following formula to calculate the period of a pendulum:

```
t = 2 * pi * (length / 9.81) ** .5
```

write a program that uses a do loop to make the length go from 1 to 10 m in 1-m increments.

Produce a table with two columns, the first of lengths and the second of periods.

Chapter 7
Arrays 2: Further Examples

Sir, In your otherwise beautiful poem (The Vision of Sin) there is a verse which reads Every moment dies a man, every moment one is born. Obviously this cannot be true and I suggest that in the next edition you have it read Every moment dies a man, every moment 1 1/16 is born. Even this value is slightly in error but should be sufficiently accurate for poetry.

Charles Babbage in a letter to Lord Tennyson

Aims

The aims of the chapter are to extend the concepts introduced in the previous chapter and in particular:

- To set an array size at run time - allocatable arrays.
- To introduce the idea of an array with more than one dimension and the corresponding control structure to permit easy manipulation of higher-dimensioned arrays.
- To introduce an extended form of the dimension attribute declaration, and the corresponding alternative form to the do statement, to manipulate the array in this new form.
- To introduce the do loop as a mechanism for the control of repetition in general, not just for manipulating arrays.
- To formally define the block do syntax.

© Springer International Publishing AG, part of Springer Nature 2018
I. Chivers and J. Sleightholme, *Introduction to Programming with Fortran*,
https://doi.org/10.1007/978-3-319-75502-1_7

7.1 Varying the Array Size at Run Time

The earlier examples set the array size in the following two ways:

- Explicitly using a numeric constant
- Implicitly using a parameterised variable

In both cases we knew the size of the array at the time we compiled the program. We may not know the size of the array at compile time and Fortran provides the allocatable attribute to accommodate this kind of problem.

7.1.1 Example 1: Allocatable Arrays

Consider the following example.

```fortran
program ch0701
!
! This program is a simple variant of ch0602.
! The array is now allocatable
! and the user is prompted for the
! number of people at run time.
!
  implicit none
  integer :: number_of_people
  real :: total = 0.0, average = 0.0
  integer :: person
  real, dimension (:), allocatable :: weight

  print *, ' How many people?'
  read *, number_of_people
  allocate (weight(1:number_of_people))
  do person = 1, number_of_people
    print *, ' type in the weight for person ', &
      person
    read *, weight(person)
    total = total + weight(person)
  end do
  average = total/number_of_people
  print *, ' The total of the weights is ', &
    total
  print *, ' Average Weight is ', average
  print *, ' ', number_of_people, &
    ' Weights were '
```

```
   do person = 1, number_of_people
     print *, weight(person)
   end do
end program ch0701
```

The first statement of interest is the type declaration with the `dimension` and `allocatable` attributes, e.g.,

```
real , dimension(:) , allocatable :: weight
```

The second is the `allocate` statement

```
allocate(weight(1:number_of_people))
```

where the value of the variable `number_of_people` is not known until run time. This is known in Fortran as a deferred shape array.

7.2 Higher-Dimension Arrays

There are many instances where it is necessary to have arrays with more than one dimension. Consider the examples below.

7.2.1 Example 2: Two Dimensional Arrays and a Map

Consider the representation of the height of an area of land expressed as a two dimensional table of numbers e.g., we may have some information represented in a simple table as follows:

```
          Longitude
          1       2       3
Latitude
  1       10.0    40.0    70.0
  2       20.0    50.0    80.0
  3       30.0    60.0    90.0
```

The values in the array are the heights above sea level. The example is obviously artificial, but it does highlight the concepts involved. For those who have forgotten their geography, lines of latitude run east–west (the equator is a line of latitude) and lines of longitude run north–south (they go through the poles and are all of the same length). In the above table therefore the latitude values are ordered by row and the longitude values are ordered by column.

A program to manipulate this data structure would involve something like the following:

```
program ch0702
! Variables used
! Height - used to hold the heights above sea
! level
! Long - used to represent the longitude
! Lat - used to represent the latitude
! both restricted to integer values.
! Correct - holds the correction factor
  implicit none
  integer, parameter :: n = 3
  integer :: lat, long
  real, dimension (1:n, 1:n) :: height
  real, parameter :: correct = 10.0

  do lat = 1, n
    do long = 1, n
      print *, ' type in value at ', lat, ' ', &
        long
      read *, height(lat, long)
    end do
  end do
  do lat = 1, n
    do long = 1, n
      height(lat, long) = height(lat, long) + &
        correct
    end do
  end do
  print *, ' Corrected data is '
  do lat = 1, n
    do long = 1, n
      print *, height(lat, long)
    end do
  end do
end program ch0702
```

Note the way in which indentation has been used to highlight the structure in this example. Note also the use of a textual prompt to highlight which data value is expected. Running the program highlights some of the problems with the simple i/o used in the example above. We will address this issue in the next example.

The inner loop is said to be nested within the outer one. It is very common to encounter problems where nesting is a natural way to express the solution. Nesting is permitted to any depth. Here is an example of a valid nested do loop:

```
do          ! Start of outer loop
   do              ! Start of inner loop
      .
      .

   enddo           ! End of inner loop
enddo          ! End of outer loop
```

This example introduces the concept of two indices, and can be thought of as a row and column data structure.

7.2.2 Example 3: Sensible Tabular Output

The first example had the values printed in a format that wasn't very easy to work with. In this example we introduce a so-called implied do loop, which enables us to produce neat and humanly comprehensible output:

```
program ch0703
! Variables used
! Height - used to hold the heights above sea
! level
! Long - used to represent the longitude
! Lat - used to represent the latitude
! both restricted to integer values.
  implicit none
  integer, parameter :: n = 3
  integer :: lat, long
  real, dimension (1:n, 1:n) :: height
  real, parameter :: correct = 10.0

  do lat = 1, n
    do long = 1, n
      read *, height(lat, long)
      height(lat, long) = height(lat, long) + &
        correct
    end do
  end do
  do lat = 1, n
    print *, (height(lat,long), long=1, n)
```

```
   end do
end program ch0703
```

The key statement in this example is

```
print * , (height(lat,long),long=1,n)
```

This is called an implied do loop, as the longitude variable takes on values from 1 through 3 and will write out all three values on one line.

We will see other examples of this statement as we go on.

7.2.3   Example 4: Average of Three Sets of Values

This example extends the previous one. Now we have three sets of measurements and we are interested in calculating the average of these three sets. The two new data sets are:

```
    9.5      39.5      69.5
   19.5      49.5      79.5
   29.5      59.5      89.5
```

and

```
   10.5      40.5      70.5
   20.5      50.5      80.5
   30.5      60.5      90.5
```

and we have chosen the values to enable us to quickly check that the calculations for the averages are correct.

This program also uses implied do loops to read the data, as data in files are generally tabular:

```
program ch0704
! Variables used
! h1,h2,h3
! used to hold the heights above sea level
! h4
! used to hold the average of the above
! Long - used to represent the longitude
! Lat - used to represent the latitude
! both restricted to integer values.
  implicit none
```

```
integer, parameter :: n = 3
integer :: lat, long
real, dimension (1:n, 1:n) :: h1, h2, h3, h4

do lat = 1, n
  read *, (h1(lat,long), long=1, n)
end do
do lat = 1, n
  read *, (h2(lat,long), long=1, n)
end do
do lat = 1, n
  read *, (h3(lat,long), long=1, n)
end do
do lat = 1, n
  do long = 1, n
    h4(lat, long) = (h1(lat,long)+h2(lat,long) &
      +h3(lat,long))/n
  end do
end do
do lat = 1, n
  print *, (h4(lat,long), long=1, n)
end do
end program ch0704
```

The original data was accurate to three significant figures. The output from the above has spurious additional accuracy. We will look at how to correct this in the later chapter on output.

7.2.4 Example 5: Booking Arrangements in a Theatre or Cinema

A theatre or cinema consists of rows and columns of seats. In a large cinema or a typical theatre there would also be more than one level or storey. Thus, a program to represent and manipulate this structure would probably have a 2-d or 3-d array. Consider the following program extract:

```
program ch0705
  implicit none
  integer, parameter :: nr = 5
  integer, parameter :: nc = 10
  integer, parameter :: nf = 3
  integer :: row, column, floor
```

```
   character *1, dimension (1:nr, 1:nc, 1:nf) :: &
     seats = ' '

   do floor = 1, nf
     do row = 1, nr
       read *, (seats(row,column,floor), column=1 &
         , nc)
     end do
   end do
   print *, ' Seat plan is'
   do floor = 1, nf
     print *, ' Floor = ', floor
     do row = 1, nr
       print *, (seats(row,column,floor), column= &
         1, nc)
     end do
   end do
end program ch0705
```

Note here the use of the term `parameter` in conjunction with the integer declaration. This is called an entity orientated declaration. An alternative to this is an
attribute-orientated declaration, e.g.,

```
integer :: nr,nc,nf
parameter :: nr=5,nc=10,nf=3
```

and we will be using the entity-orientated declaration method throughout the rest of
the book. This is our recommended method as you only have to look in one place to
determine everything that you need to know about an entity.

7.3   Additional Forms of the Dimension Attribute and Do
Loop Statement

7.3.1   Example 6: Voltage from −20 to +20 Volts

Consider the problem of an experiment where the independent variable voltage varies
from −20 to +20 volts and the current is measured at 1-volt intervals. Fortran has a
mechanism for handling this type of problem:

```
program ch0706
  implicit none
  real, dimension (-20:20) :: current
```

```
   real :: resistance
   integer :: voltage

   print *, ' type in the resistance'
   read *, resistance
   do voltage = -20, 20
     current(voltage) = voltage/resistance
     print *, voltage, ' ', current(voltage)
   end do
end program ch0706
```

We appreciate that, due to experimental error, the voltage will not have exact integer values. However, we are interested in representing and manipulating a set of values, and thus from the point of view of the problem solution and the program this is a reasonable assumption. There are several things to note.

This form of the dimension attribute

```
dimension(first:last)
```

is of considerable use when the problem has an effective index which does not start at 1.

There is a corresponding form of the do statement which allows processing of problems of this nature. This is shown in the above program. The general form of the do statement statement is therefore:

```
do counter=start, end, increment
```

where start, end and increment can be positive or negative. Note that zero is a legitimate value of the dimension limits and of a do loop index.

7.3.2   Example 7: Longitude from −180 to +180

Consider the problem of the production of a table linking time difference with longitude. The values of longitude will vary from −180 to +180 degrees, and the time will vary from +12 hours to −12 hours. A possible program segment is:

```
program ch0707
   implicit none
   real, dimension (-180:180) :: time = 0
   integer :: degree, strip
   real :: value

   do degree = -180, 165, 15
```

```
      value = degree/15.
      do strip = 0, 14
        time(degree+strip) = value
      end do
    end do
    do degree = -180, 180
      print *, degree, ' ', time(degree)
    end do
  end program ch0707
```

7.3.3 Notes

The values of the time are not being calculated at every degree interval.

The variable `time` is a real variable. It would be possible to arrange for the time to be an integer by expressing it in either minutes or seconds.

This example takes no account of all the wiggly bits separating time zones or of British Summer Time or Daylight Saving Time.

What changes would you make to the program to accommodate +180? What is the time at −180 and +180?

7.4   The Do Loop and Straight Repetition

7.4.1   Example 8: Table of Liquid Conversion Measurements

Consider the production of a table of liquid measurements. The independent variable is the litre value; the gallon and US gallon are the dependent variables. Strictly speaking, a program to do this does not have to have an array, i.e., the do loop can be used to control the repetition of a set of statements that make no reference to an array. The following shows a complete but simple conversion program:

```
program ch0708
  implicit none
!
! 1 us gallon = 3.7854118 litres
! 1 uk gallon = 4.545 litres
!
  integer :: litre
  real :: gallon, usgallon

  do litre = 1, 10
```

```
      gallon = litre/4.545
      usgallon = litre/3.7854118
      print *, litre, ' ', gallon, ' ', usgallon
   end do
end program ch0708
```

Note here that the do statement has been used only to control the repetition of a block of statements — there are no arrays at all in this program.

This is the other use of the do statement. The do loop thus has two functions — its use with arrays as a control structure and its use solely for the repetition of a block of statements.

7.4.2   Example 9: Means and Standard Deviations

In the calculation of the mean and standard deviation of a list of numbers, we can use the following formulae. It is not actually necessary to store the values, nor to accumulate the sum of the values and their squares. In the first case, we would possibly require a large array, whereas in the second, it is conceivable that the accumulated values (especially of the squares) might be too large for the machine. The following example uses an updating technique which avoids these problems, but is still accurate. The do loop is simply a control structure to ensure that all the values are read in, with the index being used in the calculation of the updates:

```
program ch0709
! variables used are
! mean - for the running mean
! ssq - the running corrected sum of squares
! x - input values for
which
! mean and sd required
! w - local work variable
! sd - standard deviation
! r - another work variable
   implicit none
   real :: mean = 0.0, ssq = 0.0, x, w, sd, r
   integer :: i, n

   print *, ' enter the number of readings'
   read *, n
   print *, ' enter the ', n, &
      ' values, one per line'
   do i = 1, n
     read *, x
```

```
    w = x - mean
    r = i - 1
    mean = (r*mean+x)/i
    ssq = ssq + w*w*r/i
  end do
  sd = (ssq/r)**0.5
  print *, ' mean is ', mean
  print *, ' standard deviation is ', sd
end program ch0709
```

7.5   Summary

Arrays can have up to fifteen dimensions.

Do loops may be nested, but they must not overlap.

The dimension attribute allows limits to be specified for a block of information which is to be treated in a common way. The limits must be integer, and the second limit must exceed the first, e.g.,

```
real , dimension(-123:-10) :: list
real , dimension(0:100,0:100) :: surface
real , dimension(1:100) :: value
```

The last example could equally be written

```
real , dimension(100) :: value
```

where the first limit is omitted and is given the default value 1. The array list would contain 114 values, while surface would contain 10201.

A do statement and its corresponding enddo statement define a loop. The do statement provides a starting value, terminal value, and optionally, an increment for its index or counter.

The increment may be negative, but should never be zero. If it is not present, the default value is 1. It must be possible for the terminating value to be reached from the starting value.

The counter in a do loop is ideally suited for indexing an array, but it may be used anywhere that repetition is needed, and of course the index or counter need not be used explicitly.

The formal syntax of the block do construct is

```
[ do-construct-name : ] do [label] [ loop-control ]
  [execution-part-construct ]
[ label ] end-do
```

where the forms of the loop control are

```
[ , ] scalar-variable-name =
scalar-numeric-expression ,
scalar-numeric-expression
[ , scalar-numeric-expression ]
```

and the forms of the end-do are

```
end do [ do-construct-name ]
continue
```

and [] identify optional components of the block do construct. This statement is looked at in much greater depth in Chap. 13.

We have introduced the concept of a deferred-shape array. Arrays do not need to have their shape specified at compile time, only their rank. Their actual shape is deferred until runtime. We achieve this by the combined use of the allocatable attribute on the variable declaration and the allocate statement, which makes Fortran a very flexible language for array manipulation.

7.6 Problems

7.1 Compile and run all the examples in this chapter, except example 5. This is covered in Problem 7.8.

7.2 Modify the first example to convert the height in feet to height in metres. The conversion factor is one 1 foot equals 0.305 m.

Hint: You can either overwrite the height array or introduce a second array.

7.3 The following are two equations for temperature conversion

```
c =  5 /9 *  (t-32)
f = 32 + 9 /5 * t
```

Write a complete program where t is an integer do loop variable and loop from −50 to 250. Print out the values of c, t and f on one line. What do you notice about the c and f values?

7.4 Write a program to print out the 12 times table. Typical output would be of the form:

```
1   *   12   =   12
2   *   12   =   24
3   *   12   =   36
```

etc.

Hint: You don't need to use an array here.

7.5 Write a program to read the following data into a two-dimensional array:

```
1   2   3
4   5   6
7   8   9
```

Calculate totals for each row and column and produce output similar to that shown below:

```
 1    2    3   6
 4    5    6  15
 7    8    9  24
12   15   18
```

Hint 1: Example ch0602 shows how to sum over a loop.

Hint 2: You need to introduce two one-dimensional arrays to hold the row and column totals. You need to index over the rows to get the column totals and over the columns to get the row totals.

7.6 Modify the above to produce averages for each row and column as well as the totals.

7.7 Using the following data from Problem 6.4 in Chap. 6:

```
1.85      85
1.80      76
1.85      85
1.70      90
1.75      69
1.67      83
1.55      64
1.63      57
1.79      65
1.78      76
```

Use the program that evaluated the mean and standard deviation to do so for these heights and weights.

In the first case use the program as is and run it twice, first with the heights then with the weights.

What changes would you need to make to the program to read a height and a weight in a pair?

Hint: You could introduce separate scalar variables for the heights and weights.

7.8 Example 5 looked at seat bookings in a cinema or theatre. Here is an example of a sample data file for this program

```
P P P P P P P P P P
P P P C C C C P P P
C C C E E P P P P P
C C C C C C C C C C
E E E P P P P P P P
C C E E P P C C E E
P P P P P P P P P P
P P P C C C C P P P
C C C E E P P P P P
C C C C C C C C C C
E E E P P P P P P P
C C E E P P C C E E
P P P P P P P P P P
P P P C C C C P P P
C C C E E P P P P P
```

The key for this is as follows:

```
C = Confirmed Booking
P = Provisional Booking
E = Seat Empty
```

Compile and run the program. The output would benefit from adding row and column numbers to the information displayed. We will come back to this issue in a subsequent chapter on output formatting.

The data are in a file on the web and the address is given below.

```
https://www.fortranplus.co.uk
```

Problem 6.6 in the last chapter shows how to read data from a file.

Chapter 8
Whole Array and Additional Array Features

A good notation has a subtlety and suggestiveness which at times make it seem almost like a live teacher.

Bertrand Russell

Aims

The aims of the chapter are:

- To look more formally at the terminology required to precisely describe arrays.
- To introduce ways in which we can manipulate whole arrays and parts of arrays (sections).
- To introduce the concept of array element ordering and physical and virtual memory.
- To introduce ways in which we can initialise arrays using array constructors.
- To introduce the `where` statement and array masking.
- To introduce the `forall` statement and construct.
- Physical and virtual memory
- Type declaration statement summary.

8.1 Terminology

Fortran supports an abundance of array handling features. In order to make the description of these features more precise a number of additional terms have to be covered and these are introduced and explained below.

- Rank - The number of dimensions of an array is called its rank. A one dimensional array has rank 1, a two dimensional array has rank 2 and so on.

© Springer International Publishing AG, part of Springer Nature 2018
I. Chivers and J. Sleightholme, *Introduction to Programming with Fortran*,
https://doi.org/10.1007/978-3-319-75502-1_8

- Bounds - An array's bounds are the upper and lower limits of the index in each dimension.
- Extent - The number of elements along a dimension of an array is called the extent.

```
integer, dimension(-10:15):: current
```

has bounds −10 and 15 and an extent of 26.
- Size - The total number of elements in an array is its size.
- Shape - The shape of an array is determined by its rank and its extents in each dimension.
- Conformable - Two arrays are said to be conformable if they have the same shape, that is, they have the same rank and the same extent in each dimension.

8.2   Array Element Ordering

Array element ordering states that the elements of an array, regardless of rank, form a linear sequence. The sequence is such that the subscripts along the first dimension vary most rapidly, and those along the last dimension vary most slowly. This is best illustrated by considering, for example, a rank 2 array a defined by

```
real , dimension(1:4,1:2) :: a
```

a has 8 real elements whose array element order is a(1, 1), a(2, 1), a(3, 1), a(4, 1), a(1, 2), a(2, 2), a(3, 2), a(4, 2) i.e., mathematically by column and not row. We will look more formally at this later in this chapter.

8.3   Whole Array Manipulation

The examples of arrays so far have shown operations on arrays via array elements. One of the significant features of modern Fortran is its ability to manipulate arrays as whole objects. This allows arrays to be referenced not just as single elements but also as groups of elements. Along with this ability comes a whole host of intrinsic procedures for array processing. These procedures are mentioned in Chap. 12, and listed in alphabetical order with examples in Appendix D.

8.4   Assignment

An array name without any indices can appear on both sides of assignment and input and output statements. For example, values can be assigned to all the elements of an array in one statement:

```
real, dimension(1:12):: rainfall
rainfall=0.0
```

The elements of one array can be assigned to another:

```
integer, dimension(1:50) :: a,b
.

.

a=b
```

Arrays a and b must be conformable in order to do this.

The following example is illegal since x is rank 1 and extent 20, whilst z is rank 1 and extent 41.

```
real, dimension(1:20) :: x
real, dimension(1:41) :: z
x=50.0
z=x
```

But the following is legal because both arrays are now conformable, i.e., they are both of rank 1 and extent 41:

```
real , dimension (-20:20) :: x
real , dimension (1:41) :: y
x=50.0
y=x
```

8.5 Expressions

All the arithmetic operators available to scalars are available to arrays, but care must be taken because mathematically they may not make sense.

```
real , dimension (1:50) :: a,b,c,d,e
c=a+b
```

adds each element of a to the corresponding element of b and assigns the result to c.

```
e=c*d
```

multiplies each element of c by the corresponding element of d. This is not vector multiplication. To perform a vector dot product there is an intrinsic procedure `dot_product`, and an example of this is given in a subsequent section on array constructors.

For higher dimensions

```
real ,dimension (1:10,1:10) :: f,g,h
f=f**0.5
```

takes the square root of every element of `f`.

```
h=f+g
```

adds each element of `f` to the corresponding element of `g`.

```
h=f*g
```

multiplies each element of `f` by the corresponding element of `g`. The last statement is not matrix multiplication. An intrinsic procedure `matmul` performs matrix multiplication; further details are given in Appendix D.

8.6   Example 1: Rank 1 Whole Arrays in Fortran

Consider the following example, which is a solution to a problem set earlier, but is now addressed using some of the whole array features of Fortran

```
program ch0801
  implicit none
  integer, parameter :: n = 12
  real, dimension (1:n) :: rainfall_ins = 0.0
  real, dimension (1:n) :: rainfall_cms = 0.0
  integer :: month

  print *, &
    ' Input the rainfall values in inches'
  read *, rainfall_ins
  rainfall_cms = rainfall_ins*2.54
  do month = 1, n
    print *, ' ', month, ' ', rainfall_ins(month &
      ), ' ', rainfall_cms(month)
  end do
end program ch0801
```

The statements

```
real , dimension(1:n) :: rainfall_ins=0.0
real , dimension(1:n) :: rainfall_cms=0.0
```

are examples of whole array initialisation. Each element of the arrays is set to 0.0.
The statement

```
read *, rainfall_ins
```

is an example of whole array i/o, where we no longer have to use a do loop to read
each element in.

Finally, we have the statement

```
rainfall_cms = rainfall_ins * 2.54
```

which is an example of whole array arithmetic and assignment.

8.7 Example 2: Rank 2 Whole Arrays in Fortran

Here is a two-dimensional example:

```
program ch0802
! This program reads in a grid of temperatures
! (degrees Fahrenheit) at 25 grid references
! and converts them to degrees Celsius
  implicit none
  integer, parameter :: n = 5
  real, dimension (1:n, 1:n) :: fahrenheit, &
    celsius
  integer :: long, lat
!
! read in the temperatures
!
  do lat = 1, n
    print *, ' For Latitude= ', lat
    do long = 1, n
      print *, ' For Longitude', long
      read *, fahrenheit(lat, long)
    end do
  end do
!
! Conversion applied to all values
!
```

```
   celsius = 5.0/9.0*(fahrenheit-32.0)
   print *, celsius
   print *, fahrenheit
end program ch0802
```

Note the use of whole arrays in the print statements. The output does look rather messy though, and also illustrates array element ordering.

8.8   Array Sections

Often it is necessary to access part of an array rather than the whole, and this is possible with Fortran's powerful array manipulation features.

8.8.1   Example 3: Rank 1 Array Sections

Consider the following:

```
program ch0803
  implicit none
  integer, dimension (-5:5) :: x
  integer :: i

  x(-5:-1) = -1
  x(0) = 0
  x(1:5) = 1
  do i = -5, 5
    print *, ' ', i, ' ', x(i)
  end do
end program ch0803
```

The statement

```
   x(-5:-1) = -1
```

is working with a section of an array. It assigns the value –1 to elements x(-5) through x(-1).

The statement

```
   x(1:5)   = 1
```

is also working with an array section. It assigns the value 1 to elements x(1) through
x(5).

8.8.2 Example 4: Rank 2 Array Sections

In Chap. 6 we gave an example of a table of examination marks, and this is given
again below:

Name	Physics	Maths	Biology	History	English	French
Fowler L.	50	47	28	89	30	46
Barron L.W	37	67	34	65	68	98
Warren J.	25	45	26	48	10	36
Mallory D.	89	56	33	45	30	65
Codd S.	68	78	38	76	98	65

The following program reads the data in, scales column 3 by 2.5 as the Biology
marks were out of 40 (the rest are out of 100), calculates the averages for each subject
and for each person and prints out the results.

```
program ch0804
  implicit none
  integer, parameter :: nrow = 5
  integer, parameter :: ncol = 6
  real, dimension (1:nrow, 1:ncol) :: &
    exam_results = 0.0
  real, dimension (1:nrow) :: people_average = &
    0.0
  real, dimension (1:ncol) :: subject_average = &
    0.0
  integer :: r, c

  do r = 1, nrow
    read *, exam_results(r, 1:ncol)
  end do
  exam_results(1:nrow, 3) = 2.5* &
    exam_results(1:nrow, 3)
  do r = 1, nrow
    do c = 1, ncol
      people_average(r) = people_average(r) + &
        exam_results(r, c)
    end do
  end do
```

```
    people_average = people_average/ncol
    do c = 1, ncol
      do r = 1, nrow
        subject_average(c) = subject_average(c) + &
          exam_results(r, c)
      end do
    end do
    subject_average = subject_average/nrow
    print *, ' People averages'
    print *, people_average
    print *, ' Subject averages'
    print *, subject_average
  end program ch0804
```

The statement

```
    read *, exam_results(r,1:ncol)
```

uses sections to replace the implied do loop in the earlier example, takes column 3 of the two dimensional array `exam_results`, multiplies it by 2.5 (as a whole array) and overwrites the original values.

The statement

```
    exam_results(1:nrow,3) = &
      2.5 * exam_results(1:nrow,3)
```

uses array sections in the arithmetic and the assignment.

8.9   Array Constructors

Arrays can be given initial values in Fortran using array constructors. Some examples are given below.

8.9.1   Example 5: Rank 1 Array Initialisation — Explicit Values

```
  program ch0805
    implicit none
    integer, parameter :: n = 12
    real :: total = 0.0, average = 0.0
```

```
    real, dimension (1:n) :: rainfall = (/ 3.1, &
      2.0, 2.4, 2.1, 2.2, 2.2, 1.8, 2.2, 2.7, 2.9, &
      3.1, 3.1 /)
    integer :: month

    do month = 1, n
      total = total + rainfall(month)
    end do
    average = total/n
    print *, ' Average monthly rainfall was'
    print *, average
  end program ch0805
```

The statement

```
real , dimension(1:n) :: rainfall = &
(/3.1,2.0,2.4,2.1,2.2,2.2,1.8,2.2,2.7,2.9,3.1,3.1/)
```

provides initial values to the elements of the array rainfall.

8.9.2 Example 6: Rank 1 Array Initialisation Using an Implied Do Loop

The next example uses a simple variant:

```
program ch0806
  implicit none
!
! 1 us gallon = 3.7854118 litres
! 1 uk gallon = 4.545 litres
!
  integer, parameter :: n = 10
  real, parameter :: us = 3.7854118
  real, parameter :: uk = 4.545
  integer :: i
  integer, dimension (1:n) :: litre = [ (i,i=1,n &
    ) ]
  real, dimension (1:n) :: gallon, usgallon

  gallon = litre/uk
  usgallon = litre/us
  print *, ' Litres Imperial USA'
```

```
    print *, ' Gallon Gallon'
    do i = 1, n
      print *, litre(i), ' ', gallon(i), ' ', &
        usgallon(i)
    end do
  end program ch0806
```

The statement

```
integer , dimension(1:n) :: litre=[(i,i=1,n)]
```

initialises the 10 elements of the litre array to the values 1,2,3,4,5,6,7,8,9,10
respectively.

8.9.3   Example 7: Rank 1 Arrays and the dot_product Intrinsic

This example uses an array constructor and the intrinsic procedure dot_product.

```
program ch0807
  implicit none
  integer, dimension (1:3) :: x, y
  integer :: result

  x = [ 1, 3, 5 ]
  y = [ 2, 4, 6 ]
  result = dot_product(x, y)
  print *, result
end program ch0807
```

and result has the value 44, which is obtained by the normal mathematical dot product
operation, $1*2 + 3*4 + 5*6$.

The general form of the array constructor is [list of expressions] or
(/ a list of expressions /) where each expression is of the same type.

8.9.4   Initialising Rank 2 Arrays

To construct arrays of higher rank than one the intrinsic function reshape must be
used. An introduction to intrinsic functions is given in Chap. 12, and an alphabetic

list with a full explanation of each function is given in Appendix D. To use it in its simplest form:

```
matrix = reshape ( source, shape)
```

where `source` is a rank 1 array containing the values of the elements required in the new array, `matrix`, and `shape` is a rank 1 array containing the shape of the new array `matrix`.

We consider the rank 1 array b= (1,3,5,7,9,11), and we wish to store these values in a rank 2 array a, such that a is the matrix:

$$a = \begin{pmatrix} 1 & 7 \\ 3 & 9 \\ 5 & 11 \end{pmatrix}$$

The following code extract is needed:

```
integer, dimension(1:6) :: b
integer, dimension(1:3, 1:2) :: a
  b = (/1,3,5,7,9,11/)
  a = reshape(b,(/3,2/))
```

Note that the elements of the source array b must be stored in the array element order of the required array a.

8.9.5   Example 8: Initialising a Rank 2 Array

The following example illustrates the additional forms of the `reshape` function that are used when the number of elements in the source array is less than the number of elements in the destination. The complete form is

```
reshape(source, shape, pad, order)
```

`pad` and `order` are optional. See Appendix D for a complete explanation of `pad` and `order`:

```
program ch0808
  implicit none
  integer, dimension (1:2, 1:4) :: x
  integer, dimension (1:8) :: y = (/ 1, 2, 3, 4, &
    5, 6, 7, 8 /)
  integer, dimension (1:6) :: z = (/ 1, 2, 3, 4, &
```

```
   5, 6 /)
integer :: r, c

print *, ' Source array y'
print *, y
print *, ' Source array z'
print *, z
print *, ' Simple reshape sizes match'
x = reshape(y, (/2,4/) )
do r = 1, 2
  print *, (x(r,c), c=1, 4)
end do
print *, &
  ' Source 2 elements smaller pad with 0'
x = reshape(z, (/2,4/), (/0,0/) )
do r = 1, 2
  print *, (x(r,c), c=1, 4)
end do
print *, &
  ' As previous now specify order as 1*2'
x = reshape(z, (/2,4/), (/0,0/), (/1,2/) )
do r = 1, 2
  print *, (x(r,c), c=1, 4)
end do
print *, &
  ' As previous now specify order as 2*1'
x = reshape(z, (/2,4/), (/0,0/), (/2,1/) )
do r = 1, 2
  print *, (x(r,c), c=1, 4)
end do
end program ch0808
```

8.10   Miscellaneous Array Examples

The following are examples of some of the flexibility of arrays in Fortran.

8.10.1   Example 9: Rank 1 Arrays and a Stride of 2

Consider the following example:

```
program ch0809
  implicit none
  integer :: i
  integer, dimension (1:10) :: x = (/ (i,i=1,10) &
    /)
  integer, dimension (1:5) :: odd = (/ (i,i=1,10 &
    ,2) /)
  integer, dimension (1:5) :: even

  even = x(2:10:2)
  print *, ' x'
  print *, x
  print *, ' odd'
  print *, odd
  print *, ' even'
  print *, even
end program ch0809
```

The statement

```
integer , dimension(1:5)   :: odd=(/(i,i=1,10,2)/)
```

steps through the array 2 at a time.
The statement

```
even=x(2:10:2)
```

shows an array section where we go from elements two through ten in steps of two.
The 2:10:2 is an example of a subscript triplet in Fortran, and the first 2 is the lower
bound, the 10 is the upper bound, and the last 2 is the increment. Fortran uses the
term stride to mean the increment in a subscript triplet.

8.10.2 Example 10: Rank 1 Array and the Sum Intrinsic Function

The following example is based on ch0805. It uses the sum intrinsic to calculate the
sum of all the values in the rainfall array.

```
program ch0810
  implicit none
  real :: total = 0.0, average = 0.0
  real, dimension (12) :: rainfall = (/ 3.1, 2.0 &
```

```
     , 2.4, 2.1, 2.2, 2.2, 1.8, 2.2, 2.7, 2.9, &
       3.1, 3.1 /)

    total = sum(rainfall)
    average = total/12
    print *, ' Average monthly rainfall was'
    print *, average
  end program ch0810
```

The statement

```
    total = sum(rainfall)
```

replaces the statements below from the earlier example.

```
    do month=1,n
      total = total + rainfall(month)
    enddo
```

In this example the `sum` intrinsic function adds up all of the elements of the array `rainfall`.

So we have three ways of processing arrays:

- Element by element.
- Using sections.
- On a whole array basis.

The ability to use sections and whole arrays when programming is a major advance of the element by element processing supported by Fortran 77.

8.10.3   *Example 11: Rank 2 Arrays and the Sum Intrinsic Function*

This example is based on the earlier exam results program:

```
program ch0811
  implicit none
  integer, parameter :: nrow = 5
  integer, parameter :: ncol = 6
  real, dimension (1:nrow*ncol) :: results = (/ &
    50, 47, 28, 89, 30, 46, 37, 67, 34, 65, 68, &
    98, 25, 45, 26, 48, 10, 36, 89, 56, 33, 45, &
    30, 65, 68, 78, 38, 76, 98, 65 /)
  real, dimension (1:nrow, 1:ncol) :: &
```

```
      exam_results = 0.0
   real, dimension (1:nrow) :: people_average = &
      0.0
   real, dimension (1:ncol) :: subject_average = &
      0.0

   exam_results = reshape(results, (/nrow,ncol/), &
      (/0.0,0.0/), (/2,1/) )
   exam_results(1:nrow, 3) = 2.5* &
      exam_results(1:nrow, 3)
   subject_average = sum(exam_results, dim=1)
   people_average = sum(exam_results, dim=2)
   people_average = people_average/ncol
   subject_average = subject_average/nrow
   print *, ' People averages'
   print *, people_average
   print *, ' Subject averages'
   print *, subject_average
end program ch0811
```

This example has several interesting array features:

- We initialise a rank 1 array with the values we want in our exam marks array. The data are laid out in the program as they would be in an external file in rows and columns.
- We use reshape to initialise our exam marks array. We use the fourth parameter (/2,1/) to populate the rank 2 array with the data in row order.
- We use sum with a dim of 1 to compute the sums for the subjects.
- We use sum with a dim of 2 to compute the sums for the people.

8.10.4 Example 12: Masked Array Assignment and the where Statement

Fortran has array assignment both on an element by element basis and on a whole array basis. There is an additional form of assignment based on the concept of a logical mask.

Consider the example of time zones given in Chap. 7. The time array will have values that are both negative and positive. We can then associate the positive values with the concept of east of the Greenwich meridian, and the negative values with the concept of west of the Greenwich meridian e.g.:

```
program ch0812
   implicit none
```

```
real, dimension (-180:180) :: time = 0
integer :: degree, strip
real :: value
character (len=1), dimension (-180:180) :: &
  direction = ' '

do degree = -180, 165, 15
  value = degree/15.
  do strip = 0, 14
    time(degree+strip) = value
  end do
end do
do degree = -180, 180
  print *, degree, ' ', time(degree)
end do
where (time>0.0)
  direction = 'E'
elsewhere (time<0.0)
  direction = 'W'
end where
print *, direction
end program ch0812
```

8.10.5   Notes

The arrays must be conformable, i.e., in our example time and direction are the same shape.

The selective assignment is achieved through the where construct.

Both the where and elsewhere blocks can be executed.

The formal syntax is:

```
where (array logical expression)
  . . .
elsewhere (array logical expression)
  . . .
end where
```

The first array assignment is executed where time is positive and the second is executed where time is negative. For further coverage of logical expressions see Chaps. 13 and 16.

8.11 Array Element Ordering in More Detail

Fortran compilers will store arrays in memory according to the array element ordering scheme. Section 9.5.3.2 of the Fortran 2018 standard provides details of this. Table 8.1 summarises the information for rank 1, 2 and 3 arrays.

Table 8.1 Array element ordering in Fortran

Rank	Subscript bounds	Subscript list	Subscript order value
1	j1:k1	s1	$1 + (s1 - j1)$
2	j1:k1, j2:k2	s1, s2	$1 + (s1 - j1)$ $+ (s2 - j2)*d1$
3	j1:k1, j2:k2, j3 − k3	s1, s2, s3	$1 + (s1 - j1)$ $+ (s2 - j2)*d1$ $+ (s3 - j3)*d2*d1$

8.11.1 Example 13: Array Element Ordering

Here is a short program illustrating the above for a 2*5 array.

```
program ch0813
   implicit none
   integer :: j1 = 1
   integer :: k1 = 2
   integer :: j2 = 1
   integer :: k2 = 5
   integer :: s1
   integer :: s2
   integer :: d1
   integer :: position

   d1 = k1 - j1 + 1
   print *, ' Row   Column     Position'
   do s1 = j1, k1
     do s2 = j2, k2
       position = 1 + (s1-j1) + (s2-j2)*d1
       print 100, s1, s2, position
100    format (3x, i2, 6x, i2, 10x, i2)
     end do
   end do

end program ch0813
```

and here is the output.

```
Row   Column     Position
  1       1            1
  1       2            3
  1       3            5
  1       4            7
  1       5            9
  2       1            2
  2       2            4
  2       3            6
  2       4            8
  2       5           10
```

So for rank 2 arrays the array element ordering is by column, not row.

8.12   Physical and Virtual Memory

There will be a limit to the amount of physical memory available on any computer
system. To enable problems that require more than the amount of physical memory
available to be solved, most implementations will provide access to virtual memory,
which in reality means access to a portion of a physical disk.

Access to virtual memory is commonly provided by a paging mechanism of some
description. Paging is a technique whereby fixed-sized blocks of data are swapped
between real memory and disk as required.

In order to minimise paging (and hence reduce execution time) array operations
should be performed according to the array element order.

Page sizes, past and present, include:

- Sun UltraSparc – 4 Kb, 8 Kb.
- DEC Alpha – 8 Kb, 16 Kb, 32 Kb, 64 Kb.
- Intel 80 × 86 – 4 Kb.
- Intel Pentium PIII – 4 Kb, 2 Mb, 4 Mb.
- AMD64 – 4 Kb, 2 Mb, 4 Mb - legacy mode
- AMD64 – 4 Kb, 2 Mb, 1 Gb - 64 bit mode
- Intel 64 and IA-32 – 4 Kb, 2 Mb, 1 Gb - depending on mode.

See the references at the end of the chapter for more details.

8.13 Type Declaration Statement Summary

It is a convenient time to introduce a summary of the syntax of type declarations. You have already seen some of these, and we will cover the rest in later chapters.

A type declaration statement normally has three components

- a type declaration
- optional attributes
- variable list

Here are details of the type declaration.

- intrinsic type specifier
- type (derived type specification)
- class (derived type specification)
- class (*)

The attribute specification is one of

- allocatable
- asynchronous
- bind
- dimension
- external
- intent
- intrinsic
- optional
- parameter
- pointer
- private
- protected
- public
- save
- target
- value
- volatile

8.14 Summary

We can now perform operations on whole arrays and partial arrays (array sections) without having to refer to individual elements. This shortens program development time and greatly clarifies the meaning of programs.

Array constructors can be used to assign values to rank 1 arrays within a program unit. The `reshape` function allows us to assign values to a two or higher rank array when used in conjunction with an array constructor.

8.15   Problems

8.1 Compile and run all the examples.

8.2 Give the rank, bounds, extent and size of the following arrays:

```
real , dimension(1:15) :: a
integer , dimension(1:3,0:4) :: b
real , dimension(-2:2,0:1,1:4) :: c
integer , dimension(0:2,1:5) :: d
```

Which two of these arrays are conformable?

8.3 Write a program to read in five rank 1 arrays, a, b, c, d, e and then store them as five columns in a rank 2 array `table`.

8.4 Take the first part of Problem 7.5 in Chap. 7 and rewrite it using the `sum` intrinsic function.

8.16   Bibliography

8.16.1   DEC Alpha

Bhandarkar D.P., Alpha Implementation and Architecture: Complete Reference and Guide, Digital Press,1995.

8.16.2   AMD

Visit

```
http://support.amd.com/en-us/search/tech-docs
```

for details of the AMD manuals. The following five manuals are available for download as pdf's from the above site.

- AMD64 Architecture Programmer's Manual Volume 1: Application Programming
- AMD64 Architecture Programmer's Manual Volume 2: System Programming
- AMD64 Architecture Programmer's Manual Volume 3: General Purpose and System Instructions
- AMD64 Architecture Programmer's Manual Volume 4: 128-bit and 256 bit media instructions

- AMD64 Architecture Programmer's Manual Volume 5: 64-Bit Media and x87 Floating-Point Instructions

8.16.3   Intel

Visit

```
https://software.intel.com/en-us/articles/intel-sdm
```

for a list of manuals. The following three manuals are available for download as pdf's from the above site.

- Intel 64 and IA-32 Architectures Software Developer's Manual. Volume 1: Basic Architecture
- Intel 64 and IA-32 Architectures Software Developer's Manual. Combined Volumes 2A and 2B: Instruction Set Reference, A-Z.
- Intel 64 and IA-32 Architectures Software Developer's Manual. Combined Volumes 3A and 3B: System Programming Guide, Parts 1 and 2.

Chapter 9
Output of Results

"Why, sometimes I've believed as many as six impossible things before breakfast"

Lewis Carroll, Through the Looking-Glass and What Alice Found There

Aims

The aims here are to introduce some of the facilities for producing neat output using edit descriptors. There is also coverage of how to write the results to a file, rather than to the screen.

There are examples which will illustrate the use of

- The i edit descriptor for integer data
- The f edit descriptor for real data
- The e edit descriptor for real data
- The g edit descriptor for real data
- The x edit descriptor for spaces
- The a edit descriptor for character data
- Repetition of edit descriptors
- New lines
- Output using array sections
- Output using whole arrays
- The open, write, and close statements.

We will also provide a brief summary of the rest of the control and data edit descriptors, as people may see them in existing code.

© Springer International Publishing AG, part of Springer Nature 2018

I. Chivers and J. Sleightholme, *Introduction to Programming with Fortran*,

https://doi.org/10.1007/978-3-319-75502-1_9

9.1   Introduction

When you have used `print` `*` a few times it becomes apparent that it is not always as useful as it might be. The data are written out in a way which makes some sense, but may not be especially easy to read. Real numbers are generally written out with all their significant places, which is very often rather too many, and it is often difficult to line up the columns for data which are notionally tabular. It is possible to be much more precise in describing the way in which information is presented by the program. To do this, we use `format` statements. Through the use of the `format` we can:

- Specify how many columns a number should take up.
- Specify where a decimal point should lie.
- Specify where there should be white space.
- Specify titles.

The `format` statement has a label associated with it; through this label, the `print` statement associates the data to be written with the form in which to write them.

9.2   Integers and the **i** Format or Edit Descriptor

Integer format (or edit descriptor) is reasonably straightforward, and offers clues for formats used in describing other numbers. `i3` is an integer taking three columns. The number is right justified, a bit of jargon meaning that it is written as far to the right as it will go, so that there are no trailing or following blanks. Consider the following example:

9.2.1   *Example 1: Twelve Times Table*

```
program ch0901
  implicit none
  integer :: t

  print *, ' '
  print *, ' Twelve times table'
  print *, ' '
  do t = 1, 12
    print 100, t, t*12
  end do
100 format (' ', i3, ' * 12 = ', i3)
end program ch0901
```

The first statement of interest is

```
print 100, t,t*12
```

The 100 is a statement label. There must be a format statement with this label in the program. The variables to be written out are t and t*12.

The second statement of interest is

```
100 format(' ',i3,' *  12 = ',i3)
```

Inside the brackets we have ' ' print out what occurs between the quote marks, in this case one space.

, the comma separates items in the format statement.

i3 print out the first variable in the print statement right justified in three columns
, item separator.

' * 12 = ' print out what occurs between the quote characters.
, item separator

i3 print out the second variable (in this case an expression) right justified in three columns.

All of the output will appear on one line.

9.2.1.1   Notes

The numbers are right justified in the field width.

If the edit descriptor has too few columns for the data we will get asterisks * displayed.

If the number to be displayed is negative we must allow one column for the minus sign.

9.2.2   Example 2: Integer Overflow and the i Edit Descriptor

Now consider the following example:

```
program ch0902
  implicit none
  integer :: big = 10
  integer :: i

  do i = 1, 40
    print 100, i, big
    big = big*10
  end do
100 format (' ', i3, '  ', i12)
end program ch0902
```

This program will loop and the variable `big` will overflow, i.e., go beyond the range of valid values for a 32-bit integer (2, 147, 483, 647). Does the program crash or generate a run time error? This is the output from the NAG and Intel compilers.

```
 1                10
 2               100
 3              1000
 4             10000
 5            100000
 6           1000000
 7          10000000
 8         100000000
 9        1000000000
10        1410065408
11        1215752192
12        -727379968
. . .
31      -2147483648
32                 0
. . .
40                 0
```

Is there a compiler switch to trap this kind of error?

9.3 Reals and the f Edit Descriptor

The f edit descriptor can be seen as an extension of the integer format, but here we have to deal with the decimal point. The general form is

- `fw.d`
- where w is the total width
- The `.` is decimal point
- d is the number of digits after the decimal point.
- as with the integer edit descriptor the number is right justified in the field width.

Let us look at some examples to illustrate the use of the f edit descriptor.

9.3.1 Example 3: Imperial Pints and US Pints

```
program ch0903
  implicit none
```

```
   integer :: fluid
   real :: imperial_pint
   real :: us_pint

   print *, ' US                Imperial'
   print *, ' pint(s)           pint(s)'
   do fluid = 1, 10
     imperial_pint = fluid*1.20095
     us_pint = fluid/1.20095
     print 100, imperial_pint, fluid, us_pint
100 format (' ', f5.2, '      ', i3, '      ', f5.2)
   end do
end program ch0903
```

The first two `print` statements are a heading for the subsequent output. Some experimentation is normally required to get a reasonable looking table. Note that is this example we used the `f5.2` edit descriptor to print out both `imperial_pint` variable and the `us_pint` variable. That is an overall width of 5 spaces with 2 digits after the decimal point.

Note also that rounding has occurred, i.e. the real values are rounded to 2 digits after the decimal point.

9.3.2 Example 4: Imperial Pints and Litres

```
program ch0904
   implicit none
   integer :: fluid
   real :: litres
   real :: pints

   print *, ' Imperial     Litre(s)'
   print *, ' pint(s)              '
   do fluid = 1, 10
     litres = fluid/1.75
     pints = fluid*1.75
     print 100, pints, fluid, litres
   end do
100 format (' ', f6.2, '     ', i3, '     ', f5.2)
end program ch0904
```

Note that in this example we are using `f6.2` to print out the `pints` variable, and `f5.2` to print out the `litres` variable.

Note again that rounding is taking place, i.e. both variables are rounded to 2 digits after the decimal point.

9.3.3   Example 5: Narrow Field Widths and the f Edit Descriptor

Consider the following example.

```
program ch0905
  implicit none
  integer :: i
  real :: r1 = 9.9
  real :: r2 = 9.9
  real :: r3 = -9.9
  real :: r4 = -9.9

  do i = 1, 10
    print 100, i, r1, r2, r3, r4
100 format (' ', i3, '  ', f7.3, '  ', f7.3, &
      '  ', f7.3, '  ', f7.3)
    r1 = r1/10.0
    r2 = r2*10.0
    r3 = r3/10.0
    r4 = r4*10.0
  end do
end program ch0905
```

Here is the output.

```
 1     9.900     9.900    -9.900    -9.900
 2     0.990    99.000    -0.990   -99.000
 3     0.099   990.000    -0.099   *******
 4     0.010   *******    -0.010   *******
 5     0.001   *******    -0.001   *******
 6     0.000   *******    -0.000   *******
 7     0.000   *******    -0.000   *******
 8     0.000   *******    -0.000   *******
 9     0.000   *******    -0.000   *******
10     0.000   *******    -0.000   *******
```

When the number is too large for the field width asterisks are printed. Note also that space has to be allowed for the sign of the variable.

9.3.4 Example 6: Overflow and the f Edit Descriptor

Consider the following program:

```
program ch0906
  implicit none
  integer :: i
  real :: small = 1.0
  real :: big = 1.0

  do i = 1, 50
    print 100, i, small, big
100 format (' ', i3, ' ', f7.3, ' ', f7.3)
    small = small/10.0
    big = big*10.0
  end do
end program ch0906
```

In this program the variable small will underflow and big will overflow. The output from the Intel compiler is:

```
  1   1.000   1.000
  2   0.100  10.000
  3   0.010 100.000
  4   0.001 *******
...
 39   0.000 *******
 40   0.000  Infini
...
 50   0.000  Infini
```

When the number is too small for the format, the printout is what you would probably expect. When the number is too large, you get asterisks. When the number actually overflows the Intel compiler tells you that the number is too big and has overflowed. However the program ran to completion and did not generate a run time error.

9.4 Reals and the e Edit Descriptor

The exponential or scientific notation is useful in cases where we need to provide a format which may encompass a wide range of values. If likely results lie in a very wide range, we can ensure that the most significant part is given. This takes a form such as

```
e12.4
```

The 12 refers to the total width and the 4 to the number of significant digits.

9.4.1 Example 7: Simple e Edit Descriptor Example

Let's look at a simple example to see what the output is like and then go over some more about the rules that apply.

```
program ch0907
  implicit none
  integer :: i
  real :: r1 = 1.23456
  real :: r2 = 1.23456

  do i = 1, 10
    print 100, i, r1, r2
    r1 = r1/10.0
    r2 = r2*10.0
  end do
100 format (' ', i3, ' ', e12.4, ' ', e12.4)
end program ch0907
```

Here is the output

```
 1       0.1235E+01       0.1235E+01
 2       0.1235E+00       0.1235E+02
 3       0.1235E-01       0.1235E+03
 4       0.1235E-02       0.1235E+04
 5       0.1235E-03       0.1235E+05
 6       0.1235E-04       0.1235E+06
 7       0.1235E-05       0.1235E+07
 8       0.1235E-06       0.1235E+08
 9       0.1235E-07       0.1235E+09
10       0.1235E-08       0.1235E+10
```

There are a number of things to note here

- all exponent format numbers are written so that the number is between 0.1 and 0.9999..., with the exponent taking care of scale shifts, this implies that the first four significant digits are to be printed out.
- rounding is taking place
- the numbers are right justified

There is a minimum size for an exponential format. Because of all the extra bits and pieces it requires:

- The decimal point.
- The sign of the entire number.
- The sign of the exponent.
- The magnitude of the exponent.
- The e.

The width of the number less the number of significant places should not be less than 6. In the example given above, e12.4 meets this requirement. When the exponent is in the range 0 to 99, the e will be printed as part of the number; when the exponent is greater, the e is dropped, and its place is taken by a larger value; however, the sign of the exponent is always given, whether it is positive or negative. The sign of the whole number will usually only be given when it is negative. This means that if the numbers are always positive, the rule of six given above can be modified to a rule of five. It is safer to allow six places over, since, if the format is insufficient, all you will get are asterisks.

The most common mistake with an e format is to make the edit descriptor too small, so that there is insufficient room for all the padding to be printed.

9.5 Reals and the g Edit Descriptor

This edit descriptor combines both the f and e edit descriptors, depending on the size of the number.

9.5.1 Example 8: Simple g Edit Descriptor Example

Here is a variant of the previous examples with the g edit descriptor replacing the e edit descriptor.

```
program ch0908
  implicit none
  integer :: i
  real :: r1 = 1.23456
  real :: r2 = 1.23456

  print 100
100 format (' ', &
    '12345678901234567890123456789012345678901')
  print 110
```

```
110 format ('  i3   g12.4              g12.4')
  do i = 1, 10
    print 120, i, r1, r2
    r1 = r1/10.0
    r2 = r2*10.0
  end do
120 format (' ', i3, ' ', g12.4, ' ', g12.4)
end program ch0908
```

Here is the output

```
12345678901234567890123456789 01
 i3   g12.4              g12.4
  1      1.235               1.235
  2      0.1235             12.35
  3      0.1235E-01        123.5
  4      0.1235E-02       1235.
  5      0.1235E-03          0.1235E+05
  6      0.1235E-04          0.1235E+06
  7      0.1235E-05          0.1235E+07
  8      0.1235E-06          0.1235E+08
  9      0.1235E-07          0.1235E+09
 10      0.1235E-08          0.1235E+10
```

Fortran provides quite a useful set of edit descriptors for real numbers. The `print` `*` is very useful when developing programs.

9.6   Spaces

Fortran provides a variety of ways of generating spaces in a format statement and these include using quotes ('), double quotes (") and the x edit descriptor.

9.6.1   Example 9: Three Ways of Generating Spaces

```
program ch0909
  implicit none
  integer :: i

  do i = 1, 4
    print 100, i, i*i
```

```
    print 110, i, i*i
    print 120, i, i*i
100 format (' ', i2, ' ', i4)
110 format (' ', i2, ' ', i4)
120
format (1x, i2, 2x, i4)
  end do
end program ch0909
```

The output is the same from each format statement.

9.7   Characters — a Format or Edit Descriptor

This is perhaps the simplest output of all. Since you will already have declared the length of a character variable in your declarations,

```
character (10) :: b
```

when you come to write out b, the length is known — thus you need only specify that a character string is to be output:

```
print 100,b
100 format(1x,a)
```

If you feel you need a little extra control, you can append an integer value to the a, like a10 (a9 or a1), and so on. if you do this, only the first 10 (9 or 1) characters are written out; the remainder are ignored. Do note that 10a1 and a10 are not the same thing. 10a1 would be used to print out the first character of ten character variables, while a10 would write out the first 10 characters of a single character variable. The general form is therefore just a, but if more control is required, this may be followed by a positive integer.

9.7.1   Example 10: Character Output and the a Edit Descriptor

The following program is a simple rewrite of one of the programs from Chap. 4.

```
program ch0910
! This program reads in and prints out
! your
```

```
first name
   implicit none
   character (20) :: first_name

   print *, ' Type in your first name.'
   print *, ' up to 20 characters'
   read *, first_name
   print 100, first_name
100 format (1x, a) end program ch0910
```

9.7.2 Example 11: Character, Integer and Real Output in a Format Statement

The following example shows how to mix and match character, integer and real output in one format statement:

```
program ch0911
   implicit none
   character (len=15) :: firstname
   integer :: age
   real :: weight
   character (len=1) :: gender

   print *, ' type in your first name '
   read *, firstname
   print *, ' type in your age in years'
   read *, age
   print *, ' type in your weight in kilos'
   read *, weight
   print *, ' type in your gender (f/m)'
   read *, gender
   print *, ' your personal details are'
   print *
   print 100
   print 110, firstname, age, weight, gender
100 format (4x, 'first name', 4x, 'age', 1x, &
      'weight', 2x, 'gender')
110 format (1x, a, 2x, i3, 2x, f5.2, 2x, a)
end program ch0911
```

Take care to match up the variables with the appropriate edit descriptors. You also need to count the number of characters and spaces when lining up the heading.

9.8   Common Mistakes

It must be stressed that an integer can only be printed out with an i format, and a real with an f (or e) format. You cannot use integer variables or expressions with f, e or g edit descriptors or real variables and expressions with i edit descriptors. If you do, unpredictable results will follow. There are (at least) two other sorts of errors you might make in writing out a value. You might try to write out something which has never actually been assigned a value; this is termed an indefinite value. You might find that the letter i is written out. In passing, note that many loaders and link editors will preset all values to zero — i.e., unset (indefinite) values are actually set to zero. On better systems there is generally some way of turning this facility off, so that undefined is really indefinite. More often than not, indefinite values are the result of mistyping rather than of never setting values. It is not uncommon to type O for 0, or 1 for either I or l. The other likely error is to try to print out a value greater than the machine can calculate — out of range values. Some machines will print out such values as R, but some will actually print out something which looks right, and such overflow and underflow conditions can go unnoticed. Be wary.

9.9   Files in Fortran

One of the particularly powerful features of Fortran is the way it allows you to manipulate files. Up to now, most of the discussion has centred on reading from the keyboard and writing to the screen. It is also possible to read and write to one or more files. This is achieved using the open, write, read and close statements. In a later chapter we will consider reading from files but here we will concentrate on writing.

9.9.1   The open Statement

This statement sets up a file for either reading or writing. A typical form is

```
open (unit=1,file='data.txt')
```

The file will be known to the operating system as data.txt and can be written to by using the unit number. This statement should come before you first read data from or write data to to the file.

You can also use a character variable to hold the filename. This is shown in the code segment below.

```
character*60 :: filename
...
...
filename='data.txt'
...
...
open (unit=1,file=filename)
```

It is not possible to write to the file data.txt directly; it must be referenced through its unit number. Within the Fortran program you write to this file using a statement such as

```
write(unit=1,fmt=100) x,y
```

or

```
write(1,100) x,y
```

These two statements are equivalent.

9.9.2 The close Statement

Besides opening a file, we really ought to close it when we have finished writing to it:

```
close(unit=1)
```

In fact, on many systems it is not obligatory to open and close all your files. Almost certainly, the terminal will not require this, since INPUT and OUTPUT units will be there by default. At the end of the job, the system will close all your files. Nevertheless, explicit open and close cannot hurt, and the added clarity generally assists in understanding the program.

9.9.3 Example 12: Open and Close Usage

The following program contains all of the above statements:

```
program ch0912
  implicit none
  integer :: fluid
  real :: litres
```

```
  real :: pints

  open (unit=1, file='ch0912.txt')
  write (unit=1, fmt=100)
  do fluid = 1, 10
    litres = fluid/1.75
    pints = fluid*1.75
    write (unit=1, fmt=110) pints, fluid, litres
  end do
  close (1)
100 format (' Pints  Litres')
110 format (' ', f7.3, ' ', i3, ' ', f7.3)
end program ch0912
```

In this example the file will be created in the directory that the program executable runs in.

Using the following open statement

```
open (unit=1, file=&
  'c:\document\fortran\ch0912.txt')
```

creates the file in the

```
c:\document\fortran
```

directory under the Windows operating system.

Using the following open statement

```
open (unit=1, file=&
  '/home/ian/document/fortran/ch0912.txt')
```

creates the file in the

```
/home/ian/document/fortran
```

directory under a Linux operating system.

9.9.4 Example 13: Timing of Writing Formatted Files

The following example looks at the amount of time spent in different sections of a program with the main emphasis on formatted output:

```fortran
program ch0913
  implicit none
  integer, parameter :: n = 10000000
  integer, dimension (1:n) :: x = 0
  real, dimension (1:n) :: y = 0.0
  integer :: i
  real :: t, t1, t2, t3, t4, t5
  character *30 :: comment

  open (unit=10, file='ch0913.txt')
  call cpu_time(t)
  t1 = t
  comment = ' Program starts '
  print 120, comment, t1
  do i = 1, n
    x(i) = i
  end do
  call cpu_time(t)
  t2 = t - t1
  comment = ' Integer array initialised'
  print 120, comment, t2
  y = real(x)
  call cpu_time(t)
  t3 = t - t1 - t2
  comment = ' Real    array initialised'
  print 120, comment, t2
  do i = 1, n
    write (10, 100) x(i)
  end do
  call cpu_time(t)
  t4 = t - t1 - t2 - t3
  comment = ' Integer write '
  print 120, comment, t4
  do i = 1, n
    write (10, 110) y(i)
  end do
  call cpu_time(t)
  t5 = t - t1 - t2 - t3 - t4
  comment = ' Real    write '
  print 120, comment, t5
100 format (1x, i10)
110 format (1x, f10.0)
120 format (1x, a, 2x, f7.3)
end program ch0913
```

There is a call to the built-in intrinsic `cpu_time` to obtain timing information. Try this example out with your compiler. Formatted output takes up a lot of time, as we are converting from an internal binary representation to an external decimal form.

```
Program starts                    0.016
Integer array initialised         0.094
Real     array initialised        0.094
Integer write                     2.262
Real     write                    8.408
```

9.9.5   Example 14: Timing of Writing Unformatted Files

The following program is a variant of the above but now the output is in unformatted or binary form:

```fortran
program ch0914
  implicit none
  integer, parameter :: n = 10000000
  integer, dimension (1:n) :: x = 0
  real, dimension (1:n) :: y = 0
  integer :: i
  real :: t, t1, t2, t3, t4, t5
  character *30 :: comment

  open (unit=10, file='ch0914.dat', &
    form='unformatted')
  call cpu_time(t)
  t1 = t
  comment = ' Program starts '
  print 100, comment, t1
  do i = 1, n
    x(i) = i
  end do
  call cpu_time(t)
  t2 = t - t1
  comment = ' Integer assignment '
  print 100, comment, t2
  y = real(x)
  call cpu_time(t)
  t3 = t - t1 - t2
  comment = ' Real    assignment '
```

```
   print 100, comment, t2
   write (10) x
   call cpu_time(t)
   t4 = t - t1 - t2 - t3
   comment = ' Integer write '
   print 100, comment, t4
   write (10) y
   call cpu_time(t)
   t5 = t - t1 - t2 - t3 - t4
   comment = ' Real    write '
   print 100, comment, t5
100 format (1x, a, 2x, f7.3)
end program ch0914
```

Try this example out with your compiler. Unformatted is very efficient in terms of time. It also has the benefit for real or floating point numbers of no information loss.

```
Program starts              0.016
Integer assignment          0.078
Real    assignment          0.078
Integer write               0.078
Real    write               0.031
```

Note that binary or unformatted files are not necessarily portable between different compilers and different hardware platforms. You should consult your compiler documentation for help in this area.

9.10   Example 15: Implied Do Loops and Array Sections for Array Output

The following program shows how to use both implied do loops and array sections to output an array in a neat fashion:

```
program ch0915
  implicit none
  integer, parameter :: nrow = 5
  integer, parameter :: ncol = 6
  real, dimension (1:nrow*ncol) :: results = (/ &
    50, 47, 28, 89, 30, 46, 37, 67, 34, 65, 68, &
    98, 25, 45, 26, 48, 10, 36, 89, 56, 33, 45, &
    30, 65, 68, 78, 38, 76, 98, 65 /)
```

```
real, dimension (1:nrow, 1:ncol) :: &
  exam_results = 0.0
real, dimension (1:nrow) :: people_average = &
  0.0
real, dimension (1:ncol) :: subject_average = &
  0.0
integer :: r, c

exam_results = reshape(results, (/nrow,ncol/), &
  (/0.0,0.0/), (/2,1/) )
exam_results(1:nrow, 3) = 2.5* &
  exam_results(1:nrow, 3)
subject_average = sum(exam_results, dim=1)
people_average = sum(exam_results, dim=2)
people_average = people_average/ncol
subject_average = subject_average/nrow
do r = 1, nrow
  print 100, (exam_results(r,c), c=1, ncol), &
    people_average(r)
end do
print *, &
  '  ====  ====  ====  ====  ====  ===='
print 110, subject_average(1:ncol)
100 format (1x,6(1x,f5.1), ' = ', f6.2)
110 format (1x,  6(1x,f5.1))
end program ch0915
```

The print 100 uses an implied do loop and the print 110 uses an array section. Here is the output.

```
50.0  47.0  70.0  89.0  30.0  46.0 =  55.33
37.0  67.0  85.0  65.0  68.0  98.0 =  70.00
25.0  45.0  65.0  48.0  10.0  36.0 =  38.17
89.0  56.0  82.5  45.0  30.0  65.0 =  61.25
68.0  78.0  95.0  76.0  98.0  65.0 =  80.00
====  ====  ====  ====  ====  ====
53.8  58.6  79.5  64.6  47.2  62.0
```

We are using repeat factors in this example in the format statement to repeat the use of one or more edit descriptors, e.g. 6(1x,f5.1).

We have also added a print statement to make the output a bit more understandable.

9.11   Example 16: Repetition and Whole Array Output

Take care when using whole arrays. Consider the following program:

```
program ch0916
   real, dimension (10, 10) :: y
   integer :: nrows = 6
   integer :: ncols = 7
   integer :: i, j
   integer :: k = 0

   do i = 1, nrows
     do j = 1, ncols
       k = k + 1
       y(i, j) = k
     end do
   end do
   write (unit=*, fmt=100) y
100 format (1x, 10f10.4)
end program ch0916
```

There are several points to note with this example. Firstly, this is a whole array reference, and so the entire contents of the array will be written; there is no scope for fine control. Secondly, the order in which the array elements are written is according to Fortran's array element ordering, i.e., the first subscript varying 1 to 10 (the array bound), with the second subscript as 1, then 1 to 10 with the second subscript as 2 and so on; the sequence is

```
Y(1,1)Y(2,1)Y(3,1)Y(10,1)
Y(1,2)Y(2,2)Y(3,2)Y(10,2)
 .

 .
Y(1,10)Y(2,10)Y(10,10)
```

Thirdly we have defined values for part of the array.

Finally we have used write(unit=*,fmt=100) and this will print to the screen.

9.12   Example 17: Choosing the Decimal Symbol

Fortran provides a mechanism to choose the decimal symbol. The dc edit descriptor sets the decimal symbol to a comma. The dp edit descriptor sets the decimal symbol to a full stop or period.

The following example

```
program ch0917
  implicit none
  integer :: fluid
  real :: litres
  real :: pints

  open (unit=1, file='ch0917.txt')
  write (unit=1, fmt=100)
  do fluid = 1, 10
    litres = fluid/1.75
    pints = fluid*1.75
    write (unit=1, fmt=110) pints, fluid, litres
  end do
  close (1)
100 format (' Pints    Litres')
110 format (dc, ' ', f7.3, ' ', i3, ' ', f7.3)
end program ch0917
```

produces the following output.

```
   Pints        Litres
   1,750     1    0,571
   3,500     2    1,143
   5,250     3    1,714
   7,000     4    2,286
   8,750     5    2,857
  10,500     6    3,429
  12,250     7    4,000
  14,000     8    4,571
  15,750     9    5,143
  17,500    10    5,714
```

9.13 Example 18: Alternative Format Specification Using a String

Here is an example of an alternate format specification using a string.

```
program ch0918
  implicit none
  integer :: t
```

```
   print *, ' '
   print *, ' Twelve times table'
   print *, ' '
   do t = 1, 12
     print '('' '', i3, '' * 12 = '', i3)', t, &
       t*12
   end do
end program ch0918
```

9.14   Example 19: Alternative Format Specification Using a Character Variable

Here is an example of using a character variable in a format specification.

```
program ch0919
   implicit none
   integer :: t
   character *30 :: fmt_100 = &
     '('' '', i3, '' * 12 = '', i3)'

   print *, ' '
   print *, ' Twelve times table'
   print *, ' '
   do t = 1, 12
     write (unit=*, fmt=fmt_100) t, t*12
   end do
end program ch0919
```

9.15   The Remaining Control and Data Edit Descriptors

Tables 9.1 and 9.2 summarise details of the control and data edit descriptors available in Fortran.

Table 9.1   Summary of data edit descriptors

Descriptor	Description: data conversion
A w	character
B w[.m]	integer to/from binary
D w.d	real
DT [character literal constant][(v-list)]	derived type
E w.d[Ee]	real with exponent
EN w.d[Ee]	real to engineering
ES w.d[Ee]	real to scientific
F w.d	real with no exponent
G w.d[Ee]	any intrinsic type
I w[.m]	integer
L w	logical
O	octal
Z	hexadecimal
Symbol	Explanation
w	width of the field
m	number of digits in the field
d	number of digits after the decimal symbol
e	number of digits in the exponent field
v	signed integer literal constant
	interpretation depends on the user
	supplied derived type i/o subroutine

Table 9.2   Text edit descriptors

Descriptor	Description: data conversion
'text'	transfer of a character literal constant to output record
"text"	transfer of a character literal constant to output record

9.16   Summary

You have been introduced in this chapter to the use of format or layout descriptors which will give you greater control over output.

The main features are:

- The i format for integer variables.
- The e, f and g formats for real numbers.
- The a format for characters.
- The x, which allows insertion of spaces.

Output can be directed to files as well as to the terminal through the write statement.

The write, together with the open and close statements, also introduces the class of Fortran statements which use equated keywords, as well as positionally dependent parameters.

The format statement and its associated layout or edit descriptor are powerful and allow repetition of patterns of output (both explicitly and implicitly).

9.17 Problems

9.1 Rewrite the temperature conversion program which was Problem 7.3 in Chap. 7 to produce neat tabular output. Pay attention to the number of significant decimal places.

9.2 Information on car fuel consumption is usually given in miles per gallon in Britain and the United States and in l/100 km in Europe. Just to add an extra problem US gallons are 0.8 imperial gallons.

Prepare a table which allows conversion from either US or imperial fuel consumption figures to the metric equivalent. Use the parameter statement where appropriate:

```
1 imperial gallon = 4.54596 litres
1 mile = 1.60934 kilometres
```

9.3 The two most commonly used operating systems for Fortran programming are UNIX and DOS. It is possible to use the operating system file redirection symbols

```
< >
```

to read from a file and write to a file, respectively. Rerun the program in Problem 1 to write to a file using the open statement. Examine the file using an editor.

9.4 Modify any of the above to write to a file rather than the screen or terminal.

9.5 What features of Fortran reveal its evolution from punched card input?

9.6 Try to create a real number greater than the maximum possible on your computer — write it out. Try to repeat this for an integer. You may have to exercise some ingenuity.

9.7 Check what a number too large for the output format will be printed as on your local system — is it all asterisks?

9.8 Write a program which stores litres and corresponding pints in arrays. You should now be able to control the output of the table (excluding headings — although this could be done too) in a single write or print statement. If you don't like litres and pints, try some other conversion (sterling to US dollars, leagues to fathoms, Scots miles to Betelgeusian pfnings). The principle remains the same.

9.9 Fortran is an old programming language and the text formatting functionality discussed in this chapter assumes very dumb printing devices.

The primary assumption is that we are dealing with so-called monospace fonts, i.e., that digits, alphabetic characters, punctuation, etc., all have the same width.

If you are using a PC try using:

- Notepad

  and

- Word

To open your programs and some of the files created in this chapter. What happens to the layout?

If you are using Notepad look at the Word wrap and set Font options under the edit menu.

What fonts are available? What happens to the layout when you choose another font?

If you are using Word what fonts are available? What happens when you make changes to your file and exit Word? Is it sensible to save a Fortran source file as a Word document?

Chapter 10
Reading in Data

Winnie-the-Pooh read the two notices very carefully, first from left to right, and afterwards, in case he had missed some of it, from right to left

A A Milne, Winnie-the-Pooh

Aims

The aims of this chapter are to introduce some of the ideas involved in reading data into a program. In particular, using the following:

- Reading from files
- Reading integer data
- Reading real data
- Skipping columns of data in a file
- Skipping lines in a file
- Reading from several files consecutively
- Reading using internal files
- Timing of formatted and unformatted reads

10.1 Reading from Files

In the examples so far we have been reading from the keyboard using what Fortran calls list directed input. In this chapter we will look at reading data from files where the data is generally in tabular form.

© Springer International Publishing AG, part of Springer Nature 2018   191
I. Chivers and J. Sleightholme, *Introduction to Programming with Fortran*,
https://doi.org/10.1007/978-3-319-75502-1_10

10.2   Example 1: Reading Integer Data

In this example we are interested in reading in people's heights and weights in imperial measurements (feet and inches and stones and pounds) from a file and converting to their metric equivalent (metres and kilograms). The data is taken from an undergraduate class of Mechanical Engineering students.

Here is the data.

```
6    1   13    5
5   11   11   13
6    1   13    5
5    7   14    2
5    9   10   12
5    6   13    1
5    1   10    1
5    4    8   13
5   10   10    3
5   10   11   13
```

The first two columns are the heights in feet and inches, and the second two columns are the weights in stones and pounds.

Here is the program.

```fortran
program ch1001
  implicit none
  integer, parameter :: npeople = 10
  integer, dimension (1:npeople) :: height_feet, &
    height_inch, weight_stone, weight_pound
  real, dimension (1:npeople) :: weight_kg, &
    height_m
  integer :: i

  open (unit=10, file='ch1001.txt',status='old')
  open (unit=20, file='ch1001.out',status='new')

  do i = 1, npeople
    read (10, fmt=100) height_feet(i), &
      height_inch(i), weight_stone(i), &
      weight_pound(i)
    100 format (i2, 2x, i2, 2x, i2, 2x, i2)
    weight_kg(i) = (weight_stone(i)*14+ &
      weight_pound(i))/2.2
    height_m(i) = (height_feet(i)*12+height_inch &
      (i))*2.54/100
    write (unit=20, fmt=110) height_m(i), &
```

```
       weight_kg(i)
   110 format (1x, f5.2, 2x, f4.1)
   end do
   close (10)
   close (20)
end program ch1001
```

Here is the output.

```
1.85   85.0
1.80   75.9
1.85   85.0
1.70   90.0
1.75   69.1
1.68   83.2
1.55   64.1
1.63   56.8
1.78   65.0
1.78   75.9
```

The first statements of interest are

```
open (unit=10, file='ch1001.txt',status='old')
open (unit=20, file='ch1001.out',status='new')
```

which links the Fortran unit number 10 with a file called ch1001.txt, and links the Fortran unit number 20 with a file called ch1001.out.

The next statements of interest are

```
read(10,fmt=100)height_feet(i) ,height_inch(i), &
                weight_stone(i),weight_pound(i)
100 format(i2,2x,i2,2x,i2,2x,i2)
```

which reads 4 integer values from a line with integer data in columns 1–2, 5–6, 9–10 and 13–14 with 2 spaces between each value.

At the end of the program we close the files.

```
close(10)
close(20)
```

We write out the metric versions of the height and weight with the following statement.

```
write(unit=20,fmt=200) height_m(i),weight_kg(i)
200 format(1x,f5.2,2x,f4.1)
```

to the file called ch1001.out.

We recommend that when working with formatted files you use a text editor that displays the column and line details.

Notepad under Windows has a status bar option under the View menu. Gvim under Windows has line and column information available. Under Redhat, vim and gedit both display line and column information. Under SuSe Linux kedit and vim display line and column information. There should be an editor available on your system that has this option.

10.3   Example 2: Reading Real Data

This example reads in the height and weight data created by the previous program and calculates their BMI values. BMI stands for Body Mass Index and is calculated as *Weight/Height^2*

Here is the program.

```
program ch1002
   implicit none
   integer, parameter :: n = 10
   real, dimension (1:n) :: h
   real, dimension (1:n) :: w
   real, dimension (1:n) :: bmi
   integer :: i

   open (unit=100, file='ch1001.out',status='old')
   do i = 1, n
     read (100, fmt='(1x,f5.2, 2x, f4.1)') h(i), &
       w(i)
   end do
   close (100)
   bmi = w/(h*h)
   do i = 1, n
     write (unit=*, fmt='(1x,f4.1)') bmi(i)
   end do
end program ch1002
```

The following statement

```
open(unit=100,file='ch1001.out',status='old')
```

links the Fortran unit number 100 with the file ch1001.out.

The following statement

```
read (100,fmt='(1x,f5.2, 2x, f4.1)') h(i), w(i)
```

reads the height and weight data from the file. We skip the first space then read the
height from the next 5 columns in f5.1 format. We skip two spaces and then read
the weight from the next 4 columns in f4.1 format.

The following statement

```
close(100)
```

closes the file.

The following statement

```
write(unit=*,fmt='(1x,f4.1)') bmi(i)
```

writes out the BMI values in f4.1 format.

Here is the output.

```
24.8
23.4
24.8
31.1
22.6
29.5
26.7
21.4
20.5
24.0
```

10.4   Met Office Historic Station Data

The UK Met Office makes historic station data available.
Visit

```
http://www.metoffice.gov.uk/public/weather/
climate-historic/#?tab=climateHistoric
```

to see the data. The line has been broken to fit the page width.

The data consists of

- Mean daily maximum temperature (tmax)
- Mean daily minimum temperature (tmin)
- Days of air frost (af)
- Total rainfall (rain)
- Total sunshine duration (sun)

Here is a sample of the Nairn data. Nairn is a town in Scotland on the North Sea.
The first seven lines have had to be formatted to fit the page width.

```
Nairn    there is a site change in 1998
Location before 1998 2869E 8568N 8m amsl
  after 1998 2912E 8573N 23 m amsl
Estimated data is marked with a * after the value.
Missing data (more than 2 days missing in month)
  is marked by   ---.
Sunshine data taken from an automatic Kipp &
  Zonen sensor marked with a #, otherwise
  sunshine data taken from a
   Campbell Stokes recorder.
```

yyyy	mm	tmax	tmin	af	rain	sun
		degC	degC	days	mm	hours
1931	1	5.0	0.6	11	78.4	43.4
1931	2	6.7	0.7	7	48.9	63.6
1931	3	6.2	-1.5	19	37.6	145.4
1931	4	10.4	3.1	3	44.6	110.1
1931	5	13.2	6.1	1	63.7	167.4
1931	6	15.4	8.0	0	87.8	150.3
1931	7	17.3	10.6	0	121.4	111.2
1931	8	15.6	9.1	0	57.2	127.5
1931	9	15.0	8.4	0	38.1	122.3
1931	10	12.1	5.5	2	59.4	95.8
1931	11	10.3	3.9	3	43.7	61.5
1931	12	8.9	3.2	7	33.6	36.5

In the examples that follow we will be using this station's data.

10.5   Example 3: Reading One Column of Data from a File

Here is the file we will be reading the rainfall values from.

```
         1931   1    5.0     0.6     11    78.4    43.4
         1931   2    6.7     0.7      7    48.9    63.6
         1931   3    6.2    -1.5     19    37.6   145.4
         1931   4   10.4     3.1      3    44.6   110.1
         1931   5   13.2     6.1      1    63.7   167.4
         1931   6   15.4     8.0      0    87.8   150.3
         1931   7   17.3    10.6      0   121.4   111.2
         1931   8   15.6     9.1      0    57.2   127.5
         1931   9   15.0     8.4      0    38.1   122.3
         1931  10   12.1     5.5      2    59.4    95.8
         1931  11   10.3     3.9      3    43.7    61.5
         1931  12    8.9     3.2      7    33.6    36.5
1234567890123456789012345678901234567890123456789012345678901234567890
         1            2            3            4            5
```

We have added two additional lines at the end to indicate the columns where the data is. These lines are not read by the program.

Here is the program.

```
program ch1003
  implicit none
  character *20 :: file_name = &
    'nairndata_01.txt'
  integer, parameter :: nmonths = 12
  real, dimension (1:nmonths) :: rainfall
  real :: rain_sum
  real :: rain_average
  integer :: i

  open (unit=10, file=file_name)
  do i = 1, nmonths
    read (unit=10, fmt=100) rainfall(i)
100 format (37x, f5.1)
  end do
  close (10)
  rain_sum = sum(rainfall)/25.4
  rain_average = rain_sum/nmonths
  write (unit=*, fmt=110)
    110 format (19x, 'Yearly   Monthly', /, 19x, &
    'Sum      Average')
  write (unit=*, fmt=120) rain_sum, rain_average
    120 format ('Rainfall (inches) ', f7.2, 2x, &
    f7.2)
end program ch1003
```

The data file is called nairndata_01.txt and we open the file at the start of the program and associate the file with unit 100.

The following statements read the 12 monthly values from the file skipping the first 37 characters.

```
do i=1,nmonths
  read(unit=10,fmt=100) rainfall(i)
  100 format(37x,f5.1)
end do
```

We then close the file and calculate the rainfall sums and average and print out the results. Here is the output.

```
                    Yearly    Monthly
                    Sum       Average
    Rainfall (inches)   28.13     2.34
```

The format statement 110 uses a / to move to the next line, so that the headings line up.

10.6   Example 4: Skipping Lines in a File

This program is a simple variant of the last one.

Now we are reading from the original Met Office Nairn data file, which has seven header lines.

```fortran
program ch1004
  implicit none
  character *20 :: file_name = 'nairndata.txt'
  integer, parameter :: nmonths = 12
  real, dimension (1:nmonths) :: rainfall
  real :: rain_sum
  real :: rain_average
  integer :: i

  open (unit=10, file=file_name,status='old')
  do i = 1, 8
    read (unit=10, fmt=*)
  end do
  do i = 1, nmonths
    read (unit=10, fmt=100) rainfall(i)
100 format (37x, f5.1)
  end do
  close (100)
  rain_sum = sum(rainfall)/25.4
  rain_average = rain_sum/nmonths
  write (unit=*, fmt=110)
110 format (19x, ' Yearly   Monthly', /, 19x, &
    ' Sum       Average')
  write (unit=*, fmt=120) rain_sum, rain_average
120 format ('Rainfall  (inches) ', f7.2, 2x, &
    f7.2)
end program ch1004
```

The key statements are

```
do i=1,8
  read(unit=10,fmt=*)
end do
```

which skips the data on these lines. Fortran reads a record at a time in this example.
The output is as before.

10.7   Example 5: Reading from Several Files Consecutively

In this example we read from eight of the Met Office data files for Cardiff, Eastbourne,
Lerwick, Leuchars, Nairn, Paisley, Ross On Wye and Valley.

We skip the first seven lines, then read year, month rainfall and sunshine data,
skipping the other columns.

We then calculate rainfall and sunshine yearly totals and averages for these eight
stations.

We use a character array to hold the station file names.

Here is the program.

```
program ch1005
  implicit none
  character *20, dimension (8) :: file_name = (/ &
    'cardiffdata.txt      ', 'eastbournedata.txt ' &
    , 'lerwickdata.txt      ', &
    'leucharsdata.txt     ', 'nairndata.txt        ' &
    , 'paisleydata.txt      ', &
    'rossonwyedata.txt    ', 'valleydata.txt       ' &
    /)

  integer, parameter :: nmonths = 12
  integer, dimension (1:nmonths) :: year, month
  real, dimension (1:nmonths) :: rainfall, &
    sunshine
  real :: rain_sum
  real :: rain_average
  real :: sun_sum
  real :: sun_average
  integer :: i, j
  character *80 :: fmt1 = '(3x,i4,2x,i2,3x,4x,4x,&
    &4x,4x,4x,3x,f5.1,3x,f5.1)'
```

```
  do j = 1, 8
    open (unit=100, file=file_name(j),status='old')
    do i = 1, 7
      read (unit=100, fmt='(a)')
    end do
    if (j==5) then
      read (unit=100, fmt='(a)')
    end if
    do i = 1, nmonths
      read (unit=100, fmt=fmt1) year(i), &
        month(i), rainfall(i), sunshine(i)
    end do
    close (100)
    rain_sum = sum(rainfall)/25.4
    sun_sum = sum(sunshine)
    rain_average = rain_sum/nmonths
    sun_average = sun_sum/nmonths
    write (unit=*, fmt='(//,"Station = ",a,/)') &
      file_name(j)
    write (unit=*, fmt= &
      '(2x,''Start '',i4,2x,i2)') year(1), &
      month(1)
    write (unit=*, fmt= &
      '(2x,''End   '',i4,2x,i2)') year(12), &
      month(12)
    write (unit=*, fmt=100)
100 format (19x, ' Yearly   Monthly', /, 19x, &
      ' Sum       Average')
    write (unit=*, fmt=110) rain_sum, &
      rain_average
110 format ('Rainfall  (inches) ', f7.2, 2x, &
      f7.2)
    write (unit=*, fmt=120) sun_sum, sun_average
120 format ('Sunshine           ', f7.2, 2x, &
      f7.2)
  end do

end program ch1005
```

Each time round the loop we open one of the data files.

```
    open(unit=100,file=file_name(j),status='old')
```

We then skip the next seven lines.

```
do i=1,8
  read(unit=100,fmt='(a)')
end do
```

We then read the data.

```
do i=1,nmonths
  read(unit=100,fmt=fmt1) &
  year(i),month(i),&
  rainfall(i),sunshine(i)
end do
```

We then close the file.

```
close(100)
```

We then do the calculations and print out the sum and average data for each site. The format statement uses // to generate a blank line.

Programs that will download the latest versions of the Met Office station data files are available on our web site. The programs are available for both Windows and Linux.

10.8   Example 6: Reading Using Array Sections

Consider the following output, which is the exam results data from an earlier chapter after scaling.

```
50.0   47.0   70.0   89.0   30.0   46.0
37.0   67.0   85.0   65.0   68.0   98.0
25.0   45.0   65.0   48.0   10.0   36.0
89.0   56.0   82.5   45.0   30.0   65.0
68.0   78.0   95.0   76.0   98.0   65.0
```

A program to read this file using array sections is as follows:

```
program ch1006
  implicit none
  integer, parameter :: nrow = 5
  integer, parameter :: ncol = 6
  real, dimension (1:nrow, 1:ncol) :: &
    exam_results = 0.0
```

```
real, dimension (1:nrow) :: people_average = &
  0.0
real, dimension (1:ncol) :: subject_average = &
  0.0
integer :: r, c

open (unit=100, file='ch1006.txt',status='old')
do r = 1, nrow
  read (unit=100, fmt=100) exam_results(r, &
    1:ncol)
  people_average(r) = sum(exam_results(r,1: &
    ncol))
end do
close (100)
people_average = people_average/ncol
do c = 1, ncol
  subject_average(c) = sum(exam_results(1:nrow &
    ,c))
end do
subject_average = subject_average/nrow
do r = 1, nrow
  print 110, (exam_results(r,c), c=1, ncol), &
    people_average(r)
end do
print *, &
  ' ====  ====  ====  ====  ====  ===='
print 120, subject_average(1:ncol)

100 format (1x,  6(1x,f5.1))
110 format (1x,  6(1x,f5.1),  ' = ',  f6.2)
120 format (1x,  6(1x,f5.1))
end program ch1006
```

Here is the output.

```
50.0  47.0  70.0  89.0  30.0  46.0 =  55.33
37.0  67.0  85.0  65.0  68.0  98.0 =  70.00
25.0  45.0  65.0  48.0  10.0  36.0 =  38.17
89.0  56.0  82.5  45.0  30.0  65.0 =  61.25
68.0  78.0  95.0  76.0  98.0  65.0 =  80.00
====  ====  ====  ====  ====  ====
53.8  58.6  79.5  64.6  47.2  62.0
```

10.9   Example 7: Reading Using Internal Files

Sometimes external data does not have a regular structure and it is not possible to use the standard mechanisms we have covered so far in this chapter. Fortran provides something called internal file that allow us to solve this problem. The following example is based on a problem encountered whilst working at the following site

```
http://www.shmu.sk/sk/?page=1
```

They have data that is in the following format

```
#xxxxxxxxxx yyyyyyyyyy
```

where x and y can vary between 1 and 10 digits. The key here is to read the whole line (a maximum of 22 characters) and then scan the line for the blank character between the x and y digits.

We then use the `index` intrinsic to locate the position of the blank character. We now have enough information to be able to read the x and y integer data into the variables `n1` and `n2`.

```fortran
program ch1007
   implicit none
   integer :: ib1, ib2
   integer :: n1, n2
   character (len=22) :: buffer, buff1, buff2
! program to read a record of the form
! #xxxxxxxxxx yyyyyyyyyy
! so that integers n1 = xxxxxxxxxx n2 =
! yyyyyyyyyy
! where the number of digits varies from 1 to 10
!
! use internal files
   print *, 'input micael''s numbers'
   read (*, '(a)') buffer
   ib1 = index(buffer, ' ')
   ib2 = len_trim(buffer)
   buff1 = buffer(2:ib1-1)
   buff2 = buffer(ib1+1:ib2)
   read (buff1, '(i10)') n1
   read (buff2, '(i10)') n2
   print *, 'n1 = ', n1
   print *, 'n2 = ', n2
end program ch1007
```

The statement

```
read(buff1,'(i10)')n1
```

reads from the string buff1 and extracts the x number into the variable n1, and the statement

```
read(buff2,'(i10)')n2
```

reads from the string buff2 and extracts the y number into the variable n2.

This is a very powerful feature and allows you to manage quite widely varying external data formats in files. buff1 and buff2 are called internal files in Fortran terminology.

10.10   Example 8: Timing of Reading Formatted Files

A program to read a formatted file is shown below:

```
program ch1008
  implicit none
  integer, parameter :: n = 10000000
  integer, dimension (1:n) :: x
  real, dimension (1:n) :: y
  integer :: i
  real :: t, t1, t2, t3
  character *15 :: comment

  call cpu_time(t)
  t1 = t
  comment = ' Program starts '
  print 120, comment, t1
  open (unit=10, file='ch0913.txt', &
    status='old')
  do i = 1, n
    read (10, 100) x(i)
  end do
  call cpu_time(t)
  t2 = t - t1
  comment = ' Integer read '
  print 120, comment, t2
  do i = 1, n
    read (10, 110) y(i)
```

```
    end do
    call cpu_time(t)
    t3 = t - t1 - t2
    comment = ' Real read '
    print 120, comment, t3
    do i = 1, 10
      print 130, x(i), y(i)
    end do
100 format (1x, i10)
110 format (1x, f10.0)
120 format (1x, a, 2x, f7.3)
130 format (1x, i4, 2x, f10.7)

end program ch1008
```

Here is some sample timing.

```
Program starts    0.016
Integer read      2.964
Real read         4.072
    1    1.0000000
    2    2.0000000
   ...
   ...
    9    9.0000000
   10   10.0000000
```

10.11   Example 9: Timing of Reading Unformatted Files

The following is a program to read from an unformatted file:

```
program ch1009
  implicit none
  integer, parameter :: n = 10000000
  integer, dimension (1:n) :: x
  real, dimension (1:n) :: y
  integer :: i
  real :: t, t1, t2, t3
  character *15 :: comment

  call cpu_time(t)
  t1 = t
  comment = ' Program starts '
```

```
      print 100, comment, t1
      open (unit=10, file='ch0914.dat', &
        form='unformatted',status='old')
      read (10) x
      call cpu_time(t)
      t2 = t - t1
      comment = ' Integer read '
      print 100, comment, t2
      read (10) y
      call cpu_time(t)
      t3 = t - t1 - t2
      comment = ' Real read '
      print 100, comment, t3
      do i = 1, 10
        print 110, x(i), y(i)
      end do
100 format (1x, a, 2x, f7.3)
110 format (1x, i10, 2x, f10.6)
end program ch1009
```

Here is some sample timing.

```
   Program starts      0.031
   Integer read        0.016
   Real read           0.031
            1     1.000000
            2     2.000000
           ...
            9     9.000000
           10    10.000000
```

10.12   Summary

This chapter has provided a coverage of some of the basics of reading data into a program in Fortran. We have seen examples that have

- Read integer data
- Read real data
- Skipped lines in a file
- Skipped columns of data in a file
- Read from files
- Used the open and close statements
- Associated unit numbers with files

- Read using fixed format data files
- Shown the time difference between using formatted files and unformatted files
- Used internal files

The above coverage should enable you make effective use of reading data in Fortran.

We would recommend not using edit descriptors when reading numeric data entered via the keyboard as it is difficult to see if the data matches what the edit descriptors expect.

10.13 Problems

10.1 Compile and run the examples in this chapter. Note that you will have to run ch0913.f90 and ch0914.f90 to create the data files that are needed by ch1008.f90 and ch1009.f90

10.2 Write a program to read in and write out a real number using the following:

```
format(f7.2)
```

What is the largest number that you can read in and write out with this format? What is the largest negative number that you can read in and write out with this format? What is the smallest number, other than zero, that can be read in and written out?

10.3 Rewrite two of the earlier programs that used read, * and print, * to use format statements.

10.4 Write a program to read the file created by either the temperature conversion program or the litres and pints conversion program. Make sure that the programs ignore any header and title information. This kind of problem is very common in programming (writing a program to read and possibly manipulate data created by another program).

10.5 Demonstrate that input and output formats are not symmetric — i.e., what goes in does not necessarily come out.

10.6 What happens at your computer when you enter faulty data, inappropriate for the formats specified? We will look at how we address this problem in Chap. 18.

Chapter 11
Summary of I/O Concepts

It is a capital mistake to theorise before one has data
Sir Arthur Conan Doyle

Aims

This chapter covers more formally some of the concepts introduced in Chaps. 9 and 10. There is a coverage of

- I/O concepts and I/O statements
- Files, records and streams
- Sequential, direct and stream access
- Options or specifiers on the `open` statement
- Options or specifiers on the `close` statement
- Options or specifiers on the `write` statement
- Options or specifiers on the `read` statement

11.1 I/O Concepts and Statements

Fortran input and output statements provide the means of transferring data from external media to internal storage or from an internal file to internal storage and vice versa.

The input/output statements are the `open`, `close`, `read`, `write`, `print`, `backspace`, `endfile`, `rewind`, `flush`, `wait`, and `inquire` statements.

The `inquire` statement is a file inquiry statement.

The `backspace`, `endfile`, and `rewind` statements are file positioning statements.

© Springer International Publishing AG, part of Springer Nature 2018
I. Chivers and J. Sleightholme, *Introduction to Programming with Fortran*,
https://doi.org/10.1007/978-3-319-75502-1_11

Data is commonly organised in either record files or stream files. In a record type file transfers are done a record at a time. In a stream type file transfers are done in file storage units.

11.2   Records

A record is a sequence of values or a sequence of characters. There are three kinds of records:

- formatted
- unformatted
- end of file

A record in Fortran is commonly called a logical record.

A formatted record is typically a sequence of printable characters. You have seen examples in earlier chapters.

You saw examples of unformatted i/o in the previous chapters.

11.3   File Access

The three file access methods are:

- sequential
- direct
- stream

The examples so far have shown sequential access.

Direct access is a method of accessing the records of an external record file in arbitrary order.

Stream access is a method of accessing the file storage units of an external stream file. The properties of an external file connected for stream access depend on whether the connection is for unformatted or formatted access.

11.4   The open Statement

An open statement initiates or modifies the connection between an external file and a specified unit. The open statement can do a number of things including

- connect an existing file to a unit;
- create a file that is preconnected;

- create a file and connect it to a unit;
- change certain modes of a connection between a file and a unit.

The only keyword option that can be omitted is the unit specifier. This is assumed to be the first parameter of the open statement.

Table 11.1 summarises the open statement options.

Table 11.1 Open statement options

unit =	file-unit-number
access =	sequential, direct or stream
action =	read, write or readwrite
asynchronous =	yes or no
blank =	null or zero
decimal =	comma or point
delim =	apostrophe, quote or none
encoding =	utf8 or default
err =	statement label
file =	file name
form =	formatted or unformatted
iomsg =	iomsg-variable
iostat =	scalar-int-variable
newunit =	scalar-int-variable
pad =	yes or no
position =	asis, rewind, append
recl =	record length, positive integer
round =	up, down, zero, neareset, compatible or processor defined
sign =	plus, suppress or processor defined
status =	old, new, scratch, replace or unknown

11.5 Data Transfer Statements

The read, write and print statements are used to transfer data to and from files.

Table 11.2 summarises the options of the data transfer statements.

Table 11.2 Data transer statement options

unit =	io-unit
fmt =	format
nml =	namelist-group-name
advance =	yes or no
asynchronous =	yes or no
blank =	null or zero
decimal =	comma or point
delim =	apostrophe, quote or none
end =	label
eor =	label
err =	label
id =	scalar-int-variable
iomsg =	iomsg-variable
iostat =	scalar-int-variable
pad =	yes or no
pos =	file position in file storage units
rec =	record number to be read or written
round =	up, down, zero, neareset, compatible or processor defined
sign =	plus, suppress or processor defined
size =	scalar-int-variable

11.6   The `inquire` Statement

Table 11.3 summarises the options on the `inquire` statement.

Table 11.3 Inquire statement options

unit =	file-unit-number
file =	file name
access =	sequential, direct, stream
action =	read, write, readwrite, undefined
asynchronous =	yes, no
blank =	zero, null
decimal =	comma, point
delim =	apostrophe, quote, none
direct =	yes, no, unknown

Table 11.4   (continued)

encoding =	utf8, default
err =	label
exist =	true, false
form =	formatted, unformatted, undefined
formatted =	yes, no, unknown
id =	scalar-int-expr
iomsg =	iomsg-variable
iostat =	scalar-int-variable
name =	file name
named =	scalar-logical-variable
nextrec =	scalar-int-variable
number =	unit number, -1 if unassigned
opened =	true, false
pad =	yes, no
pending =	scalar-logical-variable
pos =	scalar-int-variable
position =	scalar-default-char-variable
read =	yes, no, unknown
readwrite =	yes, no, unknown
recl =	scalar-int-variable
round =	up, down, zero, neareset, compatible or processor defined
sequential =	yes, no, unknown
sign =	plus, suppress, processor defined
size =	scalar-int-variable
stream =	yes, no, unknown
unformatted =	yes, no, unknown
write =	yes, no, unknown

11.7   Error, End of Record and End of File

The set of input/output error conditions is processor dependent.

An end-of-record condition occurs when a non-advancing input statement attempts to transfer data from a position beyond the end of the current record, unless the file is a stream file and the current record is at the end of the file (an end-of-file condition occurs instead). An end-of-file condition occurs when

- an endfile record is encountered during the reading of a file connected for sequential access,
- an attempt is made to read a record beyond the end of an internal file, or
- an attempt is made to read beyond the end of a stream file.

An end-of-file condition may occur at the beginning of execution of an input statement. An end-of-file condition also may occur during execution of a formatted input statement when more than one record is required by the interaction of the input list and the format. An end-of-file condition also may occur during execution of a stream input statement.

11.7.1 Error Conditions and the *err=* Specifier

The set of error conditions which are detected is processor dependent. The standard does not specify any i/o errors. Compilers will vary in the errors they detect and how they treat them. The err= option provides one way of catching errors and taking the appropriate action.

11.7.2 End-of-File Condition and the *end=* Specifier

An end of file may occur during an input transfer. The end= option provides a way of handling the end of file in a program.

11.7.3 End-of-Record Condition and the *eor=* Specifier

An end of record may occur during an input transfer. The eor= option provides a way of handling this in a program.

11.7.4 *iostat=* Specifier

Execution of an input/output statement containing the iostat= specifier causes the scalar-int-variable in the iostat= specifier to become defined with one of a set of values. Normally

- 0 if no errors occur
- a processor dependent negative value if end-of-file occurs
- a processor dependent negative value if an end-of-record occurs

If you use iostat_inquire_internal_unit from the intrinsic module iso_fortran_env you will get a processor-dependent positive integer value if a unit number in an inquire statement identifies an internal file.

When using `iostat_inquire_internal_unit` you will get a processor-dependent positive integer value which is different from the above if any other error condition occurs,

11.7.5 `iomsg=` *Specifier*

If an error, end-of-file, or end-of-record condition occurs during execution of an input/output statement, the processor shall assign an explanatory message to `iomsg-variable`. If no such condition occurs, the processor shall not change the value of `iomsg-variable`.

11.8 Examples

Here are three examples using the `iostat=` option. Examples illustrating some of the other options can be found throughout the rest of the book.

11.8.1 *Example 1: Simple Use of the* `read`, `write`, `open`, `close`, `unit` *Features*

This example shows the use of several of the i/o features including

- the `write` statement
- the `read` statement
- the use of `unit=6` on a write statement
- the use of `unit=5` on a read statement
- several `fmt=` variations
- the `open` statement
- the `file=` option on the `open` statement
- the `iostat=` option on the `open` statement
- the `close` statement

```
program ch1101
   implicit none
   integer :: filestat
   real :: x
   character (len=20) :: which

   do
```

```
    write (unit=6, fmt= &
      '("data file name,or end")')
    read (unit=5, fmt='(a)') which
    if (which=='end') exit
    open (unit=1, file=which, iostat=filestat, &
      status='old')
    if (filestat>0) then
      print *, &
        'error opening file, please check'
      stop
    end if
    read (unit=1, fmt=100) x
    write (unit=6, fmt=110) which, x
    close (unit=1)

  end do


100 format (f6.0)
110 format ('from file ', a, ' x = ', f8.2)
end program ch1101
```

It is common for compilers to associate units 5 and 6 with the keyboard and screen.

11.8.2   Example 2: Using *iostat* to Test for Errors

```
program ch1102
  implicit none
  integer :: io_stat_number = -1
  integer :: i

  do
    print *, 'input integer i:'
    read (unit=*, fmt=100, iostat=io_stat_number &
      ) i
    print *, ' iostat=', io_stat_number
    if (io_stat_number==0) exit
  end do
  print *, 'i = ', i, ' read successfully'
100 format (i3)
end program ch1102
```

11.8.3 Example 3: Use of newunit and lentrim

This example illustrates the use of the following:

- the len_trim function
- the newunit option on the read statement to get an unused unit number
- the use of iostat= to test whether a file was opened correctly
- the use of the cycle control statement to go back to the start of the do and try reading the file name again
- the use of the iostat option to test if the read was successful

```fortran
program ch1103
  implicit none
  character (len=20) :: station, file_name
  integer :: i, io_stat_number, filestat, flen, &
    uno
  integer, parameter :: nmonths = 12
  integer, dimension (1:nmonths) :: year, month
  real, dimension (1:nmonths) :: rainfall, &
    sunshine
  real :: rain_sum
  real :: rain_average
  real :: sun_sum
  real :: sun_average

  do
    print *, 'input weather station'
    print *, ' or "end" to stop program'
    read '(a)', station
    if (station=='end') exit
    flen = len_trim(station)
    file_name = station(1:flen) // 'data.txt'
    open (newunit=uno, file=file_name, &
      iostat=filestat, status='old')
    if (filestat/=0) then
      print *, 'error opening file ', file_name
      print *, 'Retype the file name'
      cycle
    end if
    do i = 1, 7
      read (unit=uno, fmt='(a)')
    end do
    do i = 1, nmonths
      read (unit=uno, fmt=100, iostat= &
```

```
         io_stat_number) year(i), month(i), &
         rainfall(i), sunshine(i)
100    format (3x, i4, 2x, i2, 27x, f4.1, 3x, &
         f5.1)
       if (io_stat_number/=0) then
         print *, ' error reading record ', &
           i + 8, &
           ' so following results incorrect:'
         exit
       end if
     end do
     close (unit=uno)
     rain_sum = sum(rainfall)/25.4
     sun_sum = sum(sunshine)
     rain_average = rain_sum/nmonths
     sun_average = sun_sum/nmonths
     write (unit=*, fmt=110) station
110 format (/, /, 'Station = ', a, /)
     write (unit=*, fmt=120) year(1), month(1)
120 format (2x, 'Start ', i4, 2x, i2)
     write (unit=*, fmt=130) year(12), month(12)
130 format (2x, 'End   ', i4, 2x, i2)
     write (unit=*, fmt=140)
140 format (19x, ' Yearly Monthly', /, 19x, &
       ' Sum Average')
     write (unit=*, fmt=150) rain_sum, &
       rain_average
150 format ('Rainfall (inches) ', f7.2, 2x, &
       f7.2)
     write (unit=*, fmt=160) sun_sum, sun_average
160 format ('Sunshine ', f7.2, 2x, f7.2)
   end do
end program ch1103
```

In this program based on an earlier example in Chap. 10, we have use of the newunit option on the open statement. A unique negative number is returned, which cannot clash with any user specified unit number, which are always positive.We are also using the character intrinsic function len_trim and the character operator

//

We also introduce the do end do and cycle statements. These are covered in more detail in Chap. 13.

11.9   Unit Numbering

Care must be taken with unit numbering as firstly they must always be positive, and secondly many compilers have conventions that apply, for example unit 5 is often associated with the `read` * statement and unit 6 is often associated with the `print` * statement.

11.10   Summary

This chapter has listed most of the i/o options available in Fortran. There are a small number of examples that illustrate some of their use.

Later chapters provide additional examples.

11.11   Problems

The Whitby data and Cardiff data are on our web pages.

11.1 Compile and run the examples in this chapter.

11.2 With the Whitby or Cardiff data make a mistake, e.g. a non-numeric character in the last column. Test program `ch1103.f90` to see that it picks this up.

Chapter 12
Functions

I can call spirits from the vasty deep. Why so can I, or so can any man; but will they come when you do call for them?
William Shakespeare, King Henry IV, part 1

Aims

The aims of this chapter are:

- To consider some of the reasons for the inclusion of functions in a programming language.
- To introduce, with examples, some of the predefined functions available in Fortran.
- To introduce a classification of intrinsic functions, generic, elemental, transformational.
- To introduce the concept of a user defined function.
- To introduce the concept of a recursive function.
- To introduce the concept of user defined elemental and pure functions.
- To briefly look at scope rules in Fortran for variables and functions.
- To look at internal user defined functions.

12.1 Introduction

The role of functions in a programming language and in the problem-solving process is considerable and includes:

- Allowing us to refer to an action using a meaningful name, e.g., sine(x) a very concrete use of abstraction.

© Springer International Publishing AG, part of Springer Nature 2018
I. Chivers and J. Sleightholme, *Introduction to Programming with Fortran*,
https://doi.org/10.1007/978-3-319-75502-1_12

- Providing a mechanism that allows us to break a problem down into parts, giving us the opportunity to structure our problem solution.
- Providing us with the ability to concentrate on one part of a problem at a time and ignore the others.
- Allowing us to avoid the replication of the same or very similar sections of code when solving the same or a similar sub-problem which has the secondary effect of reducing the memory requirements of the final program.
- Allowing us to build up a library of functions or modules for solving particular sub-problems, both saving considerable development time and increasing our effectiveness and productivity.

Some of the underlying attributes of functions are:

- They take parameters or arguments.
- The parameter(s) can be an expression.
- A function will normally return a value and the value returned is normally dependent on the parameter(s).
- They can sometimes take arguments of a variety of types.

Most languages provide both a range of predefined functions and the facility to define our own. We will look at the predefined functions first.

12.2   An Introduction to Predefined Functions and Their Use

Fortran provides over a hundred intrinsic functions and subroutines. For the purposes of this chapter a subroutine can be regarded as a variation on a function. Subroutines are covered in more depth in a later chapter. They are used in a straightforward way. If we take the common trigonometric functions, sine, cosine and tangent, the appropriate values can be calculated quite simply by:

```
x=sin(y)
z=cos(y)
a=tan(y)
```

This is in rather the same way that we might say that x is a function of y, or x is sine y. Note that the argument, y, is in radians not degrees.

12.2.1 Example 1: Simple Function Usage

A complete example is given below:

```
program ch1201
  implicit none
  real :: x

  print *, ' type in an angle (in radians)'
  read *, x
  print *, ' Sine of ', x, ' = ', sin(x)
end program ch1201
```

These functions are called intrinsic functions. Table 12.1 has details of some of the intrinsic functions available in Fortran.

Table 12.1 Some of the intrinsic functions available in Fortran

Function	Action	Example
int	conversion to integer	j=int(x)
real	conversion to real	x=real(j)
abs	absolute value	x=abs(x)
mod	remaindering remainder when i divided by j	k=mod(i,j)
sqrt	square root	x=sqrt(y)
exp	exponentiation	y=exp(x)
log	natural logarithm	x=log(y)
log10	common logarithm	x=log10(y)
sin	sine	x=sin(y)
cos	cosine	x=cos(y)
tan	tangent	x=tan(y)
asin	arcsine	y=asin(x)
acos	arccosine	y=acos(x)
atan	arctangent	y=atan(x)
atan2	arctangent(a/b)	y=atan2(a,b)

A more complete list is given in Appendix D.

12.3   Generic Functions

All but four of the intrinsic functions and procedures are generic, i.e., they can be
called with arguments of one of a number of kind types.

12.3.1   Example 2: The abs Generic Function

The following short program illustrates this with the abs intrinsic function:

```
program ch1202
  implicit none
  complex :: c = cmplx(1.0, 1.0)
  real :: r = 10.9
  integer :: i = -27

  print *, abs(c)
  print *, abs(r)
  print *, abs(i)
end program ch1202
```

Type this program in and run it on the system you use.

It is now possible with Fortran for the arguments to the intrinsic functions to be
arrays. It is convenient to categorise the functions into either elemental or transformational, depending on the action performed on the array elements.

12.4   Elemental Functions

These functions work with both scalar and array arguments, i.e., with arguments
that are either single or multiple valued.

12.4.1   Example 3: Elemental Function Use

Taking the earlier example with the evaluation of sine as a basis,   we have:

```
program ch1203
  implicit none
  real, dimension (5) :: x = (/ 1.0, 2.0, 3.0, &
    4.0, 5.0 /)
```

```
  print *, ' sine of ', x, ' = ', sin(x)
end program ch1203
```

In the above example the sine function of each element of the array x is calculated and printed.

12.5 Transformational Functions

Transformational functions are those whose arguments are arrays, and work on these arrays to transform them in some way.

12.5.1 Example 4: Simple Transformational Use

To highlight the difference between an element-by-element function and a transformational function consider the following examples:

```
program ch1204
  implicit none
  real, dimension (5) :: x = (/ 1.0, 2.0, 3.0, &
    4.0, 5.0 /)
! elemental function
  print *, ' sine of ', x, ' = ', sin(x)
! transformational function
  print *, ' sum of ', x, ' = ', sum(x)
end program ch1204
```

The sum function adds each element of the array and returns the sum as a scalar, i.e., the result is single valued and not an array.

12.5.2 Example 5: Intrinsic dot_product Use

The following program uses the transformational function dot_product:

```
program ch1205
  implicit none
  real, dimension (5) :: x = (/ 1.0, 2.0, 3.0, &
    4.0, 5.0 /)
```

```
  print *, ' dot product of x with x is'
  print *, ' ', dot_product(x, x)
end program ch1205
```

Try typing these examples in and running them to highlight the differences between elemental and transformational functions.

12.6   Notes on Function Usage

You should not use variables which have the same name as the intrinsic functions; e.g., what does sin(x) mean when you have declared sin to be a real array?

When a function has multiple arguments care must be taken to ensure that the arguments are in the correct position and of the appropriate kind type.

You may also replace arguments for functions by expressions, e.g.,

```
x = log(2.0)
or
x = log(abs(y))
or
x = log(abs(y)+z/2.0)
```

12.7   Example 6: Easter

This example uses only one function, the mod (or modulus). It is used several times, helping to emphasise the usefulness of a convenient, easily referenced function. The program calculates the date of Easter for a given year. It is derived from an algorithm by Knuth, who also gives a fuller discussion of the importance of its algorithm. He concludes that the calculation of Easter was a key factor in keeping arithmetic alive during the Middle Ages in Europe. Note that determination of the Eastern churches' Easter requires a different algorithm:

```
program ch1206
  implicit none
  integer :: year, metcyc, century, error1, &
    error2, day
  integer :: epact, luna, temp
! a program to calculate the date of easter
  print *, ' input the year for which easter'
  print *, ' is to be calculated'
```

```fortran
  print *, ' enter the whole year, e.g. 1978 '
  read *, year
! calculating the year in the 19 year
! metonic cycle using
variable metcyc
  metcyc = mod(year, 19) + 1
  if (year<=1582) then
    day = (5*year)/4
    epact = mod(11*metcyc-4, 30) + 1
  else
!   calculating the century-century
    century = (year/100) + 1
!   accounting for arithmetic inaccuracies
!    ignores leap
years etc.
    error1 = (3*century/4) - 12
    error2 = ((8*century+5)/25) - 5
!   locating Sunday
    day = (5*year/4) - error1 - 10
!   locating the epact(full moon)
    temp = 11*metcyc + 20 + error2 - error1
    epact = mod(temp, 30)
    if (epact<=0) then
      epact = 30 + epact
    end if
    if ((epact==25 .and. metcyc>11) .or. &
      epact==24) then
      epact = epact + 1
    end if
  end if
! finding the full moon
  luna = 44 - epact
  if (luna<21) then
    luna = luna + 30
  end if
! locating easter Sunday
  luna = luna + 7 - (mod(day+luna,7))
! locating the correct month
  if (luna>31) then
    luna = luna - 31
    print *, ' for the year ', year
    print *, ' easter falls on April ', luna
  else
    print *, ' for the year ', year
    print *, ' easter falls on march ', luna
```

```
   end if
end program ch1206
```

We have introduced a new statement here, the `if then endif`, and a variant the `if then else endif`. A more complete coverage is given in the chapter on control structures. The main point of interest is that the normal sequential flow from top to bottom can be varied. In the following case,

```
if (expression) then
  block of statements
endif
```

If the expression is true the block of statements between the `if then` and the `endif` is executed. If the expression is false then this block is skipped, and execution proceeds with the statements immediately after the `endif`.

In the following case,

```
if (expression) then
  block 1
else
  block 2
endif
```

if the expression is true block 1 is executed and block 2 is skipped. If the expression is false then block 2 is executed and block 1 is skipped. Execution then proceeds normally with the statement immediately after the `endif`.

As well as noting the use of the `mod` generic function in this program, it is also worth noting the structure of the decisions. They are nested, rather like the nested do loops we met earlier.

12.8   Intrinsic Procedures

An alphabetical list of all intrinsic functions and subroutines is given in Appendix D. This list provides the following information:

- Function name.
- Description.
- Argument name and type.
- Result type.
- Classification.
- Examples of use.

This appendix should be consulted for a more complete and thorough understanding of intrinsic procedures and their use in Fortran.

12.9   Supplying Your Own Functions

There are two stages here: firstly, to define the function and, secondly, to reference or use it. Consider the calculation of the greatest common divisor of two integers.

12.9.1   Example 7: Simple User Defined Function

The following defines a function to achieve this:

```
module gcd_module

contains

  integer function gcd(a, b)
    implicit none
    integer, intent (in) :: a, b
    integer :: temp

    if (a<b) then
      temp = a
    else
      temp = b
    end if
    do while ((mod(a,temp)/=0) .or. (mod(b, &
      temp)/=0))
      temp = temp - 1
    end do
    gcd = temp
  end function gcd

end module gcd_module
```

To use this function, you reference or call it with a form like:

```
program ch1207

  use gcd_module

  implicit none
  integer :: i, j, result

  print *, ' type in two integers'
```

```
read *, i, j
result = gcd(i, j)
print *, ' gcd is ', result

end program ch1207
```

We will start by talking about the actual function and then cover the following statements

```
module gcd_module
contains
 . .

 . .
end module gcd_module
```

later in the chapter on modules.

The first line of the function

```
integer function gcd(a,b)
```

has a number of items of interest:

- Firstly the function has a type, and in this case the function is of type integer, i.e., it will return an integer value.
- The function has a name, in this case gcd.
- The function takes arguments or parameters, in this case a and b.

The structure of the rest of the function is the same as that of a program, i.e., we have declarations, followed by the executable part. This is because both a program and a function can be regarded as a program unit in Fortran terminology. We will look into this more fully in later chapters.

In the declaration we also have a new attribute for the integer declaration. The two parameters a and b are of type integer, and the intent(in) attribute means that these parameters will NOT be altered by the function. It is good programming practice for functions not to have side effects, i.e not modify their arguments, and do no i/o.

The value calculated is returned through the function name somewhere in the body of the executable part of the function. In this case gcd appears on the left-hand side of an arithmetic assignment statement at the bottom of the function. The end of the function is signified in the same way as the end of a program:

```
end function gcd
```

We then have the program which actually uses the function gcd. In the program the function is called or invoked with i and j as arguments. The variables are called a and b in the function, and references to a and b in the function will use the values that i and j have respectively in the main program. We cover the area of argument association in the next section.

Note also a new control statement, the do while enddo. In the following case,

```
do while (expression)
  block of statements
enddo
```

the block of statements between the do while and the enddo is executed whilst the expression is true. There is a more complete coverage in Chap. 13.

We have two options here regarding compilation. Firstly, to make the function and the program into one file, and invoke the compiler once. Secondly, to make the function and program into separate files, and invoke the compiler twice, once for each file. With large programs comprising one program and several functions it is probably worthwhile to keep the component parts in different files and compile individually, whereas if it consists of a simple program and one function then keeping things together in one file makes sense.

12.10   An Introduction to the Scope of Variables, Local Variables and Interface Checking

One of the major strengths of Fortran is the ability to work on parts of a problem at a time. This is achieved by the use of program units (a main program, one or more functions and one or more subroutines) to solve discrete sub-problems. Interaction between them is limited and can be isolated, for example, to the arguments of the function. Thus variables in the main program can have the same name as variables in the function and they are completely separate variables, even though they have the same name. Thus we have the concept of a local variable in a program unit.

In the example above i, j, result, are local to the main program. The declaration of gcd is to tell the compiler that it is an integer, and in this case it is an external function.

a and b in the function gcd do not exist in any real sense; rather they will be replaced by the actual variable values from the calling routine, in this case by whatever values i and j have. temp is local to gcd.

A common programming error in Fortran 66 and 77 was mismatches between actual and dummy arguments. Problems caused by this were often very subtle and hard to find.

Fortran 90 introduced a solution to the problem via the use of modules and contains statements. We have added

```
module gcd_module
contains
..
end module gcd_module
```

around the function definition, which contains the function in a module and the following statement in the main program

```
use gcd_module
```

provides an explicit interface (in Fortran terminology) that requires the compiler to check at compile time that the call is correct, i.e. that there are the correct number of parameters, they are of the correct type and in this case that the function return type is correct. We will cover this area in greater depth in later chapters.

12.11   Recursive Functions

There is an additional form of the function header that was required when recursive function support was introduced in Fortran 90. The Fortran 2018 standard makes this form optional. Recursion means the breaking down of a problem into a simpler but identical sub-problem. The concept is best explained with reference to an actual example. Consider the evaluation of a factorial, e.g., 5!. From simple mathematics we know that the following is true:

```
5!=5*4!
4!=4*3!
3!=3*2!
2!=2*1!
1!=1
```

and thus $5! = 5 * 4 * 3 * 2 * 1$ or 120.

12.11.1   Example 8: Recursive Factorial Evaluation

Let us look at a program with recursive function to solve the evaluation of factorials.

```
module factorial_module
  implicit none

contains
  recursive integer function factorial(i) &
    result (answer)
    implicit none
    integer, intent (in) :: i
```

```
      if (i==0) then
        answer = 1
      else
        answer = i*factorial(i-1)
      end if
    end function factorial
  end module factorial_module

  program ch1208
    use factorial_module
    implicit none
    integer :: i, f

    print *, ' type in the number, integer only'
    read *, i
    do while (i<0)
      print *, ' factorial only defined for '
      print *, ' positive integers: re-input'
      read *, i
    end do
    f = factorial(i)
    print *, ' answer is', f
  end program ch1208
```

What additional information is there? Firstly, we have an additional attribute on the function header that declares the function to be recursive. Secondly, we must return the result in a variable, in this case answer. Let us look now at what happens when we compile and run the whole program (both function and main program). If we type in the number 5 the following will happen:

- The function is first invoked with argument 5. The else block is then taken and the function is invoked again.
- The function now exists a second time with argument 4. The else block is then taken and the function is invoked again.
- The function now exists a third time with argument 3. The else block is then taken and the function is invoked again.
- The function now exists a fourth time with argument 2. The else block is then taken and the function is invoked again.
- The function now exists a fifth time with argument 1. The else block is then taken and the function is invoked again.
- The function now exists a sixth time with argument 0. The if block is executed and answer=1. This invocation ends and we return to the previous level, with answer=1*1.
- We return to the previous invocation and now answer=2*1.
- We return to the previous invocation and now answer=3*2.

- We return to the previous invocation and now `answer=4*6`.
- We return to the previous invocation and now `answer=5*24`.

The function now terminates and we return to the main program or calling routine. The answer 120 is the printed out.

Add a `print *,i` statement to the function after the last declaration and type the program in and run it. Try it out with 5 as the input value to verify the above statements.

Recursion is a very powerful tool in programming, and remarkably simple solutions to quite complex problems are possible using recursive techniques. We will look at recursion in much more depth in the later chapters on dynamic data types, and subroutines and modules.

12.12   Example 9: Recursive Version of gcd

The following is another example of the earlier gcd function but with the algorithm in the function replaced with an alternate recursive solution:

```
module gcd_module
  implicit none

contains
  recursive integer function gcd(i, j) &
    result (answer)
    implicit none
    integer, intent (in) :: i, j

    if (j==0) then
      answer = i
    else
      answer = gcd(j, mod(i,j))
    end if
  end function gcd
end module gcd_module

program ch1209
  use gcd_module
  implicit none
  integer :: i, j, result

  print *, ' type in two integers'
  read *, i, j
  result = gcd(i, j)
```

```
print *, ' gcd is ', result
end program ch1209
```

Try this program out on the system you work with, look at the timing information provided, and compare the timing with the previous example. The algorithm is a much more efficient algorithm than in the original example, and hence should be much faster. On one system there was a twentyfold decrease in execution time between the two versions.

Recursion is sometimes said to be inefficient, and the following example looks at a non-recursive version of the second algorithm.

12.13 Example 10: gcd After Removing Recursion

The following is a variant of the above, with the same algorithm, but with the recursion removed:

```
module gcd_module
  implicit none

contains
  integer function gcd(i, j)
    implicit none
    integer, intent (inout) :: i, j
    integer :: temp

    do while (j/=0)
      temp = mod(i, j)
      i = j
      j = temp
    end do
    gcd = i
  end function gcd
end module gcd_module

program ch1210
  use gcd_module
  implicit none
  integer :: i, j, result

  print *, ' type in two integers'
  read *, i, j
  result = gcd(i, j)
  print *, ' gcd is ', result
end program ch1210
```

12.14   Internal Functions

An internal function is a more restricted and hidden form of the normal function definition.

Since the internal function is specified within a program segment, it may only be used within that segment and cannot be referenced from any other functions or subroutines, unlike the intrinsic or other user defined functions.

12.14.1   Example 11: Stirling's Approximation

In this example we use Stirling's approximation for large n,

$$n! = \sqrt{2\pi n}(n/e)^n$$

and a complete program to use this internal function is given below:

```
program ch1211
  implicit none
  real :: result, n, r

  print *, ' type in n and r'
  read *, n, r
! number of possible combinations that can ! be formed when ! r
objects are selected out of a group of n ! n!/r!(n-r)!
  result = stirling(n)/(stirling(r)*stirling(n-r &
    ))
  print *, result
  print *, n, r
contains
  real function stirling(x)
    real, intent (in) :: x
    real, parameter :: pi = 3.1415927, &
      e = 2.7182828

    stirling = sqrt(2.*pi*x)*(x/e)**x
  end function stirling
end program ch1211
```

The difference between this example and the earlier ones lies in the `contains` statement. The function is now an integral part of the program and could not, for example, be used elsewhere in another function. This provides us with a very powerful way of information hiding and making the construction of larger programs more secure and bug free.

12.15   Pure Functions

We mentioned earlier that functions should not have side effects. If your functions do have side effects and are running the code on parallel systems we have the additional problem that it may not actually work! We would also like to be able to take advantage of automatic parallelisation if possible. In the following example we show how to do this using the pure prefix specification.

```
module gcd_module
  implicit none

contains
  pure integer function gcd(a, b)
    implicit none
    integer, intent (in) :: a, b
    integer :: temp

    if (a<b) then
      temp = a
    else
      temp = b
    end if
    do while ((mod(a,temp)/=0) .or. (mod(b, &
      temp)/=0))
      temp = temp - 1
    end do
    gcd = temp
  end function gcd
end module gcd_module

program ch1212
  use gcd_module
  implicit none
  integer :: i, j, result

  print *, ' type in two integers'
  read *, i, j
  result = gcd(i, j)
  print *, ' gcd is ', result
end program ch1212
```

Subroutines can also be made pure.

12.15.1   Pure Constraints

The following are some of the constraints on pure procedures

- a dummy argument must be intent(in)
- local variables may not have the save attribute
- no i/o must be done in the procedure
- any procedures referenced must be pure
- you cannot have a stop statement in a pure procedure

The above information should be enough to write simple pure functions.

12.16   Elemental Functions

Fortran 77 introduced the concept of generic intrinsic functions. Fortran 90 added
elemental intrinsic functions and the ability to write generic user defined functions.
Fortran 95 squared the circle and enabled us to write elemental user defined functions.
 Here is an example to illustrate this.

```
module reciprocal_module

contains
  real elemental function reciprocal(a)
    implicit none
    real, intent (in) :: a

    reciprocal = 1.0/a
  end function reciprocal
end module reciprocal_module

program ch1213
  use reciprocal_module
  implicit none
  real :: x = 10.0
  real, dimension (5) :: y = [ 1.0, 2.0, 3.0, &
    4.0, 5.0 ]

  print *, ' reciprocal of x is ', reciprocal(x)
  print *, ' reciprocal of y is ', reciprocal(y)
end program ch1213
```

Here is the output from one compiler.

```
reciprocal of x is    0.1000000
reciprocal of y is    0.9999999
0.5000000        0.3333333
0.2500000        0.2000000
```

Hence we can call our own elemental functions with both scalar and array arguments.

Elemental functions require the use of explicit interfaces, and we have therefore used modules to achieve this.

12.17   Resume

There are a large number of Fortran supplied functions and subroutines (intrinsic functions) which extend the power and scope of the language. Some of these functions are of generic type, and can take several different types of arguments. Others are restricted to a particular type of argument. Appendix D should be consulted for a fuller coverage concerning the rules that govern the use of the intrinsic functions and procedures.

When the intrinsic functions are inadequate, it is possible to write user defined functions. Besides expanding the scope of computation, such functions aid in problem visualisation and logical subdivision, may reduce duplication, and generally help in avoiding programming errors.

In addition to separately defined user functions, internal functions may be employed. These are functions which are used within a program segment.

Although the normal exit from a user defined function is through the end statement, other, abnormal, exits may be defined through the return statement.

Communication with non-recursive functions is through the function name and the function arguments. The function must contain a reference to the function name on the left-hand side of an assignment. Results may also be returned through the argument list.

We have also covered briefly the concept of scope for a variable, local variables, and argument association. This area warrants a much fuller coverage and we will do this after we have covered subroutines and modules.

12.18   Formal Syntax

The syntax of a function is:

```
{[function prefix] function_statement &
[result (result_name) ]
```

```
[specification part]
[execution_part]
[internal sub program part]
end [function [function name]]
```

and prefix is:

```
[type specification] recursive
```

or

```
[recursive] type specification
```

and the function_statement is:

```
function function_name ([dummy argument name list])
```

[ ] represent optional parts to the specification.
The simple syntax for a module as we have used them in this chapter is

```
module module_name
...
end module_name
```

and

```
use module_name
```

in the calling routine.

12.19   Rules and Restrictions

The type of the function must only be specified once, either in the function statement
or in a type declaration.

The names must match between the function header and end function function
name statement.

If there is a result clause, that name must be used as the result variable, so all
references to the function name are recursive calls.

The function name must be used to return a result when there is no result
clause.

We will look at additional rules and restrictions in later chapters.

12.20 Problems

12.1 Find out the action of the `mod` function function when one of the arguments is negative. Write your own modulus function to return only a positive remainder. Don't call it mod!

12.2 Create a table which gives the sines, cosines and tangents for -1 to $91°$ in $1°$ intervals. Remember that the arguments have to be in radians. What value will you give *pi*? One possibility is `pi=4*atan(1.0)`. Pay particular attention to the following angle ranges:

```
-1, 0,+1
29,30,31
44,45,46
59,60,61
89,90,91
```

What do you notice about sine and cosine at 0 and $90°$? What do you notice about the tangent of $90°$? Why do you think this is?

Use a calculator to evaluate the sine, cosine at 0 and $90°$. do the same for the tangent at $90°$. Does this surprise you?

Repeat using a spreadsheet, e.g., Excel.

Are you surprised?

Repeat the Fortran program using one or more real kind types.

12.3 Write a program that will read in the lengths a and b of a right-angled triangle and calculate the hypotenuse c. Use the Fortran `sqrt` intrinsic.

12.4 Write a program that will read in the lengths a and b of two sides of a triangle and the angle between them θ (in degrees). Calculate the length of the third side c using the cosine rule: $c^2 = a^2 + b^2 - 2abcos(\theta)$

12.5 Write a function to convert an integer to a binary character representation. It should take an integer argument and return a character string that is a sequence of zeros and ones. Use the program in Chap. 5 as a basis for the solution.

12.21 Bibliography

Abramowitz M., Stegun I., Handbook of Mathematical Functions, Dover, 1968.

- This book contains a fairly comprehensive collection of numerical algorithms for many mathematical functions of varying degrees of obscurity.
  It is a widely used source.

Association of Computing Machinery (ACM)

- Collected Algorithms, 1960–1974
- Transactions on Mathematical Software, 1975 —

A good source of more specialised algorithms. Early algorithms tended to be in Algol, Fortran now predominates.

12.21.1   Recursion and Problem Solving

The following are a number of books that look at the role of recursion in problem solving and algorithms.

Hofstader D. R., Gödel, Escher, Bach — an Eternal Golden Braid, Harvester Press.

- The book provides a stimulating coverage of the problems of paradox and contradiction in art, music and mathematics using the works of Escher, Bach and Gödel, and hence the title. There is a whole chapter on recursive structures and processes. The book also covers the work of Church and Turing, both of whom have made significant contributions to the theory of computing.

Kruse R.L., Data Structures and Program Design, Prentice-Hall, 1994.

- Quite a gentle introduction to the use of recursion and its role in problem solving. Good choice of case studies with explanations of solutions. Pascal is used.

Sedgewick R., Algorithms in Modula 3, Addison-Wesley, 1993.

- Good source of algorithms. Well written. The gcd algorithm was taken from this source.

Vowels R.A., Algorithms and data Structures in F and Fortran, Unicomp, 1998.

- The only book currently that uses Fortran 90/95 and F. Visit the Fortran web site for more details. They are the publishers. Sadly no longer available. We found one at over 100 on Abebooks!

```
http://www.fortran.com/fortran/market.html
```

Wirth N., Algorithms + Data Structures = Programs, Prentice-Hall, 1976.

- In the context of this chapter the section on recursive algorithms is a very worthwhile investment in time.

Wood D., Paradigms and Programming in Pascal, Computer Science Press.

- contains a number of examples of the use of recursion in problem solving. Also provides a number of useful case studies in problem solving.

Chapter 13
Control Structures and Execution Control

Summarizing: as a slow-witted human being I have a very small head and I had better learn to live with it and to respect my limitations and give them full credit, rather than try to ignore them, for the latter vain effort will be punished by failure
Edsger W. Dijkstra, Structured Programming

Aims

The aims of this chapter are to introduce:

- Selection among various courses of action as part of the algorithm.
- The concepts and statements in Fortran needed to support the above:
  - execution control.
  - executable constructs containing blocks.
    the associate construct.
    the block construct.
    the do construct.
    the if construct.
    the select case construct.
    the select rank construct.
    the select type construct.
  - Logical expressions and logical operators.
  - One or more blocks of statements.

© Springer International Publishing AG, part of Springer Nature 2018
I. Chivers and J. Sleightholme, *Introduction to Programming with Fortran*,
https://doi.org/10.1007/978-3-319-75502-1_13

13.1   Introduction

When we look at this area it is useful to gain some historical perspective concerning the control structures that are available in a programming language.

At the time of the development of Fortran in the 1950s there was little theoretical work around and the control structures provided were very primitive and closely related to the capability of the hardware.

At the time of the first standard in 1966 there was still little published work regarding structured programming and control structures. The seminal work by Dahl, Dijkstra and Hoare was not published until 1972.

By the time of the second standard there was a major controversy regarding languages with poor control structures like Fortran which essentially were limited to the `goto` statement. The facilities in the language had led to the development and continued existence of major code suites that were unintelligible, and the pejorative term spaghetti was applied to these programs. Developing an understanding of what a program did became an almost impossible task in many cases.

Fortran missed out in 1977 on incorporating some of the more modern and intelligible control structures that had emerged as being of major use in making code easier to understand and modify.

It was not until the 1990 standard that a reasonable set of control structures had emerged and became an accepted part of the language. The more inquisitive reader is urged to read at least the work by Dahl, Dijkstra and Hoare to develop some understanding of the importance of control structures and the role of structured programming.The paper by Knuth is also highly recommended as it provides a very balanced coverage of the controversy of earlier times over the `goto` statement.

13.2   Selection Among Courses of Action

In most problems you need to choose among various courses of action, e.g.,

- if overdrawn, then do not draw money out of the bank.
- if Monday, Tuesday, Wednesday, Thursday or Friday, then go to work.
- if Saturday, then go to watch Queens Park Rangers.
- if Sunday, then lie in bed for another two hours.

As most problems involve selection between two or more courses of action it is necessary to have the concepts to support this in a programming language. Fortran has a variety of selection mechanisms, some of which are introduced below.

13.3 The Block If Statement

The following short example illustrates the main ideas:

```
. wake up
.
. check the date and time
if (Today = = Sunday) then
  .
  . lie in bed for another two hours
  .
endif
.
. get up
. make breakfast
```

If today is Sunday then the block of statements between the `if` and the `endif` is executed. After this block has been executed the program continues with the statements after the `endif`. If today is not Sunday the program continues with the statements after the `endif` immediately. This means that the statements after the `endif` are executed whether or not the expression is true. The general form is:

```
if (logical expression) then
  .
  block of statements
  .
endif
```

The logical expression is an expression that will be either true or false; hence its name. Some examples of logical expressions are given below:

```
(alpha >= 10.1)
  test if alpha is greater than or equal to 10.1
(balance <= 0.0)
  test if overdrawn
(( today == saturday).or.( today == sunday))
  test if today is saturday or sunday
((actual - calculated) <= 1.0e-6)
  test if actual minus calculated
    is less than or equal to 1.0e-6
```

Table 13.1 lists the Fortran logical and relational operators.

Table 13.1 Fortran logical and relational operators

Operator	Meaning	Type
==	Equal	Relational
/=	Not equal	Relational
>=	Greater than or equal	Relational
<=	Less than or equal	Relational
<	Less than	Relational
>	Greater than	Relational
.AND.	and	Logical
.OR.	or	Logical
.NOT.	not	Logical

The first six should be self-explanatory. They enable expressions or variables to be compared and tested. The last three enable the construction of quite complex comparisons, involving more than one test; in the example given earlier there was a test to see whether `today` was Saturday or Sunday.

Use of logical expressions and logical variables (something not mentioned so far) is covered again in a later chapter on logical data types.

The `if expression then statements endif` is called a block if construct. There is a simple extension to this provided by the `else` statement. Consider the following example:

```
if (balance > 0.0) then
  . draw money out of the bank
else
  . borrow money from a friend
endif
buy a round of drinks.
```

In this instance, one or other of the blocks will be executed. Then execution will continue with the statements after the `endif` statement (in this case buy a round).

There is yet another extension to the block if which allows an `elseif` statement. Consider the following example:

```
if (today == monday) then

   .

elseif (today == tuesday) then

   .

elseif (today == wednesday) then

   .
```

```
elseif (today == thursday) then
    .
elseif (today == friday) then
    .
elseif (today == saturday) then
    .
elseif (today == sunday) then
    .
else
    there has been an error.
    the variable today has
    taken on an illegal value.
endif
```

Note that as soon as one of the logical expressions is true, the rest of the test is skipped, and execution continues with the statements after the `endif`. This implies that a construction like

```
if(i < 2)then
    ...
elseif(i < 1)then
    ...
else
    ...
endif
```

is inappropriate. If i is less than 2, the latter condition will never be tested. The `else` statement has been used here to aid in trapping errors or exceptions. This is recommended practice. A very common error in programming is to assume that the data are in certain well-specified ranges. The program then fails when the data go outside this range. It makes no sense to have a day other than Monday, Tuesday, Wednesday, Thursday, Friday, Saturday or Sunday.

13.3.1 Example 1: Quadratic Roots

A quadratic equation is:

$$ax^2 + bx + c = 0$$

This program has a simple structure. The roots of the quadratic are either real, equal and real, or complex depending on the magnitude of the term `b ** 2 - 4 * a * c`. The program tests for this term being greater than or less than zero: it assumes that the only other case is equality to zero (from the mechanics of a computer, floating point equality is rare, but we are safe in this instance):

```
program ch1301
  implicit none
  real :: a, b, c, term, a2, root1, root2

! a b and c are the coefficients of the terms
! a*x**2+b*x+c
! find the roots of the quadratic, root1 and
! root2

  print *, ' give the coefficients a, b and c'
  read *, a, b, c
  term = b*b - 4.*a*c
  a2 = a*2.
! if term < 0, roots are complex
! if term = 0, roots are equal
! if term > 0, roots are real and different
  if (term<0.0) then
    print *, ' roots are complex'
  else if (term>0.0) then
    term = sqrt(term)
    root1 = (-b+term)/a2
    root2 = (-b-term)/a2
    print *, ' roots are ', root1, ' and ', &
      root2
  else
    root1 = -b/a2
    print *, ' roots are equal, at ', root1
  end if
end program ch1301
```

Given the understanding you now have about real arithmetic and finite precision will the else block above ever be executed?

13.3.2   Example 2: Date Calculation

This next example is also straightforward. It demonstrates that, even if the conditions on the if statement are involved, the overall structure is easy to determine. The comments and the names given to variables should make the program self-explanatory. Note the use of integer division to identify leap years:

```
program ch1302
  implicit none
  integer :: year, n, month, day, t

! calculates day and month from year and
! day-within-year
! t is an offset to account for leap years.
! Note that the first criteria is division by 4
! but that centuries are only
! leap years if divisible by 400
! not 100 (4 * 25) alone.

  print *, ' year, followed by day within year'
  read *, year, n
! checking for leap years
  if ((year/4)*4==year) then
    t = 1
    if ((year/400)*400==year) then
      t = 1
    else if ((year/100)*100==year) then
      t = 0
    end if
  else
    t = 0
  end if
! accounting for February
  if (n>(59+t)) then
    day = n + 2 - t
  else
    day = n
  end if
  month = (day+91)*100/3055
  day = (day+91) - (month*3055)/100
  month = month - 2
  print *, ' calendar date is ', day, month, &
    year
end program ch1302
```

13.4 The Case Statement

The case statement provides a very clear and expressive selection mechanism between two or more courses of action. Strictly speaking it could be constructed from the if then else if endif statement, but with considerable loss of clarity. Remember that programs have to be read and understood by both humans and compilers!

13.4.1   Example 3: Simple Calculator

```
program ch1303
  implicit none
! Simple case statement example
  integer :: i, j, k
  character :: operator

  do
    print *, ' type in two integers'
    read *, i, j
    print *, ' type in operator'
    read '(a)', operator

calculator: select case (operator)
    case ('+') calculator
      k = i + j
      print *, ' Sum of numbers is ', k
    case ('-') calculator
      k = i - j
      print *, ' Difference is ', k
    case ('/') calculator
      k = i/j
      print *, ' Division is ', k
    case ('*') calculator
      k = i*j
      print *, ' Multiplication is ', k
    case default calculator
      exit
    end select calculator

  end do
end program ch1303
```

The user is prompted to type in two integers and the operation that they would like carried out on those two integers. The case statement then ensures that the appropriate arithmetic operation is carried out. The program terminates when the user types in any character other than +, −, * or /.

The case default option introduces the `exit` statement. This statement is used in conjunction with the `do` statement. When this statement is executed control passes to the statement immediately after the matching `end do` statement. In the example above the program terminates, as there are no executable statements after the `end do`.

13.4.2 Example 4: Counting Vowels, Consonants, etc.

This example is more complex, but again is quite easy to understand. The user types in a line of text and the program produces a summary of the frequency of the characters typed in:

```
program ch1304
  implicit none

! Simple counting of vowels, consonants,
! digits, blanks and the rest

  integer :: vowels = 0, consonants = 0, &
    digits = 0
  integer :: blank = 0, other = 0, i
  character :: letter
  character (len=80) :: line

  read '(a)', line
  do i = 1, 80
    letter = line(i:i)
!   the above extracts one character
!   at position i
    select case (letter)
    case ('A', 'E', 'I', 'O', 'U', 'a', 'e', &
        'i', 'o', 'u')
      vowels = vowels + 1
    case ('B', 'C', 'D', 'F', 'G', 'H', 'J', &
        'K', 'L', 'M', 'N', 'P', 'Q', 'R', 'S', &
        'T', 'V', 'W', 'X', 'Y', 'Z', 'b', 'c', &
        'd', 'f', 'g', 'h', 'j', 'k', 'l', 'm', &
        'n', 'p', 'q', 'r', 's', 't', 'v', 'w', &
        'x', 'y', 'z')
      consonants = consonants + 1
    case ('1', '2', '3', '4', '5', '6', '7', &
        '8', '9', '0')
```

```
      digits = digits + 1
    case (' ')
      blank = blank + 1
    case default
      other = other + 1
    end select
  end do
  print *, ' Vowels = ', vowels
  print *, ' Consonants = ', consonants
  print *, ' Digits = ', digits
  print *, ' Blanks = ', blank
  print *, ' Other characters = ', other
end program ch1304
```

13.5   The Various Forms of the Do Statement

You have already been introduced in the chapters on arrays to the iterative form of
the do loop, i.e.,

```
do variable = start, end, increment
  block of statements
end do
```

A complete coverage of this form is given in the three chapters on arrays.

There are a number of additional forms of the block do that complete our requirements:

```
do while (logical expression)
  block of statements
enddo

do concurrent
  block of statements
enddo

do
  block of statements
   if (logical expression) exit
end do
```

The first form is often called a while loop as the block of statements executes
whilst the logical expression is true, and the second form is often called a repeat until
loop as the block of statements executes until the statement is true.

Note that the while block of statements may never be executed, and the repeat until block will always be executed at least once.

13.5.1 *Example 5: Sentinel Usage*

The following example shows a complete program using this construct:

```
program ch1305
  implicit none
! this program picks up the first occurrence
! of a number in a list.
! a sentinel is used, and the array is 1 more
! than the max size of the list.
  integer, allocatable, dimension (:) :: a
  integer :: mark
  integer :: i, howmany

  open (unit=1, file='data.txt',status='old')
  print *, ' What number are you looking for?'
  read *, mark
  print *, ' How many numbers to search?'
  read *, howmany
  allocate (a(1:howmany+1))
  read (unit=1, fmt=*)(a(i), i=1, howmany)
  i = 1
  a(howmany+1) = mark
  do while (mark/=a(i))
    i = i + 1
  end do
  if (i==(howmany+1)) then
    print *, ' item not in list'
  else
    print *, ' item is at position ', i
  end if
end program ch1305
```

The repeat until construct is written in Fortran as:

```
do
  ...
  ...
  if (logical expression) exit
```

```
end do
```

There are problems in most disciplines that require a numerical solution. The two main reasons for this are either that the problem can only be solved numerically or that an analytic solution involves too much work. Solutions to this type of problem often require the use of the repeat until construct. The problem will typically require the repetition of a calculation until the answers from successive evaluations differ by some small amount, decided generally by the nature of the problem. A program extract to illustrate this follows:

```
real , parameter :: tol=1.0e-6
  .
do
   ...
   change=
   ...
   if (change <= tol) exit
end do
```

Here the value of the tolerance is set to 1.0E–6. Note again the use of the exit statement. The do end do block is terminated and control passes to the statement immediately after the matching end do.

13.5.2   Cycle and Exit

These two statements are used in conjunction with the block do statement. You have seen examples above of the use of the exit statement to terminate the block do, and pass control to the statement immediately after the corresponding end do statement.

The cycle statement can appear anywhere in a block do and will immediately pass control to the start of the block do. Examples of cycle and exit are given in the next two examples, and later chapters in the book.

13.5.3   Example 6: The Evaluation of e**x

The function etox illustrates one use of the repeat until construct. The function evaluates e^x This may be written as

$$1 + x/1! + x^2/2! + x^3/3! \ldots$$

or

$$1 + \sum_{n=1}^{\infty} \frac{x^{n-1}}{(n-1)!} x/n$$

Every succeeding term is just the previous term multiplied by x/n. At some point the term x/n becomes very small, so that it is not sensibly different from zero, and successive terms add little to the value. The function therefore repeats the loop until x/n is smaller than the tolerance. The number of evaluations is not known beforehand, since this is dependent on x:

```fortran
module etox_module
   implicit none

contains
   real function etox(x)
      implicit none
      real :: term
      real, intent (in) :: x
      integer :: nterm
      real, parameter :: tol = 1.0e-6

      etox = 1.0
      term = 1.0
      nterm = 0
      do
         nterm = nterm + 1
         term = (x/nterm)*term
         etox = etox + term
         if (abs(term)<=tol) exit
      end do
   end function etox
end module etox_module

program ch1306
   use etox_module
   implicit none
   real, parameter :: x = 1.0
   real :: y

   print *, ' Fortran intrinsic ', exp(x)
   y = etox(x)
   print *, ' User defined etox ', y
end program ch1306
```

The whole program compares the user defined function with the Fortran intrinsic exp function.

13.5.4   Example 7: Wave Breaking on an Offshore Reef

This example is drawn from a situation where a wave breaks on an offshore reef or sand bar, and then reforms in the near-shore zone before breaking again on the coast. It is easier to observe the heights of the reformed waves reaching the coast than those incident to the terrace edge.

Both types of loops are combined in this example. The algorithm employed here finds the zero of a function. Essentially, it finds an interval in which the zero must lie; the evaluations on either side are of different signs. The while loop ensures that the evaluations are of different signs, by exploiting the knowledge that the incident wave height must be greater than the reformed wave height (to give the lower bound). The upper bound is found by experiment, making the interval bigger and bigger. Once the interval is found, its mean is used as a new potential bound. The zero must lie on one side or the other; in this fashion, the interval containing the zero becomes smaller and smaller, until it lies within some tolerance. This approach is rather plodding and unexciting, but is suitable for a wide range of problems

Here is the program:

```
program ch1307
  implicit none
  real :: hi, hr, hlow, high, half, xl
  real :: xh, xm, d
  real, parameter :: tol = 1.0e-6
! problem - find hi from expression given
! in function f
! F=A*(1.0-0.8*EXP(-0.6*C/A))-B
! The above is a Fortran 77
! statement function.
! hi is incident wave height (c)
! hr is reformed wave height (b)
! d is water depth at terrace edge (a)
  print *, ' Give reformed wave height, &
    &and water depth'
  read *, hr, d

! for hlow - let hlow=hr
! for high - let high=hlow*2.0

! check that signs of function
```

```
! results are different

  hlow = hr
  high = hlow*2.0
  xl = f(hlow, hr, d)
  xh = f(high, hr, d)

  do while ((xl*xh)>=0.0)
    high = high*2.0
    xh = f(high, hr, d)
  end do

  do
    half = (hlow+high)*0.5
    xm = f(half, hr, d)
    if ((xl*xm)<0.0) then
      xh = xm
      high = half
    else
      xl = xm
      hlow = half
    end if
    if (abs(high-hlow)<=tol) exit
  end do
  print *, ' Incident Wave Height Lies Between'
  print *, hlow, ' and ', high, ' metres'
contains
  real function f(a, b, c)
    implicit none
    real, intent (in) :: a
    real, intent (in) :: b
    real, intent (in) :: c

    f = a*(1.0-0.8*exp(-0.6*c/a)) - b
  end function f
end program ch1307
```

13.6 Do Concurrent

Here is some of the formal syntax of do loops taken from the standard.

```
loop-control is [ , ] do-variable =
```

```
    scalar-int-expr,
    scalar-int-expr
    [ , scalar-int-expr ]

or [ , ] WHILE ( scalar-logical-expr )

or [ , ] CONCURRENT
      concurrent-header
      concurrent-locality

do-variable is scalar-int-variable-name

The do-variable shall be a variable of type integer.

concurrent-header is ( [ integer-type-spec :: ]
    concurrent-control-list
    [ , scalar-mask-expr ] )

concurrent-control is index-name =
    concurrent-limit :
    concurrent-limit [ : concurrent-step ]

concurrent-limit is scalar-int-expr
```

Here are the rules that apply to the do concurrent loop control.

- The concurrent-limit and concurrent-step expressions in the concurrent-control-list are evaluated. These expressions may be evaluated in any order. The set of values that a particular index-name variable assumes is determined as follows.

  - The lower bound m1, the upper bound m2, and the step m3 are of type integer with the same kind type parameter as the index-name. Their values are established by evaluating the first concurrent-limit, the second concurrent-limit, and the concurrent-step expressions, respectively, including, if necessary, conversion to the kind type parameter of the index-name according to the rules for numeric conversion (Table 10.9 from the current standard). If concurrent-step does not appear, m3 has the value 1. The value m3 shall not be zero.
  - Let the value of max be (m2 m1 + m3)/m3. If max 0 for some index-name, the execution of the construct is complete. Otherwise, the set of values for the index-name is m1 + (k 1) m3 where k = 1, 2, …, max.

- The set of combinations of index-name values is the Cartesian product of the sets defined by each triplet specification. An index-name becomes defined when this set is evaluated.

- The scalar-mask-expr, if any, is evaluated for each combination of index-name values. If there is no scalar-mask-expr, it is as if it appeared with the value true. The index-name variables may be primaries in the scalar-mask-expr.
- The set of active combinations of index-name values is the subset of all possible combinations for which the scalar-mask-expr has the value true.

Note that the index-name variables can appear in the mask, for example

```
DO CONCURRENT (I=1:10, J=1:10, &
  A(I) > 0.0 .AND. B(J) < 1.0)
. . .
```

The following example illustrates a case in which the user knows that there are no repeated values in the index array IND. The DO CONCURRENT construct makes it easier for the processor to generate vector gather/scatter code, unroll the loop, or parallelize the code for this loop, potentially improving performance.

```
INTEGER :: A(N),IND(N)
DO CONCURRENT (I=1:M)
  A(IND(I)) = I
END DO
```

The following code demonstrates the use of the LOCAL clause so that the X inside the DO CONCURRENT construct is a temporary variable, and will not affect the X outside the construct.

```
X = 1.0
DO CONCURRENT (I=1:10) LOCAL (X)
  IF (A (I) > 0) THEN
    X = SQRT (A (I))
    A (I) = A (I) - X**2
  END IF
  B (I) = B (I) - A (I)
END DO
PRINT *, X ! Always prints 1.0.
```

A complete example of the do concurrent statement can be found in the chapter on OpenMP programming. FThe examples compares the performance of four ways of solving the same problem in Fortran using whole array syntax, a traditional simple do loop, a do concurrent solution and a solution base on OpenMP usage.

13.7   Summary

You have been introduced in this chapter to several control structures and these include:

- The `block if`.
- The `if then else if`.
- The `case` construct.
- The block do in three forms:
- The iterative do or `do variable=start, end, increment` ...`end do`.
- The while construct, or `do while` ...`end do`.
- The repeat until construct, or `do` ...`if then exit end do`.
- The `cycle` and `exit` statements, which can be used with the `do` statement
- The `do concurrent` statement.

These constructs are sufficient for solving a wide class of problems. There are other control statements available in Fortran, especially those inherited from Fortran 66 and Fortran 77, but those covered here are the ones preferred. We will look in Chap. 35 at one more control statement, the so-called goto statement, with recommendations as to where its use is appropriate.

13.7.1   Control Structure Formal Syntax

```
case
select case ( case variable )
  [ case case selector
    [executable construct ] ... ] ...
  [ case default
  [executable construct ]
end select
do
do [ label ]
  [executable construct ] ...
do termination
do [ label ] [ , ] loop variable =
  initial value , final value , [
increment ]
  [executable construct ] ...
do termination
do [ label ] [ , ] while
  (scalar logical expression )
  [executable construct ] ...
do termination
```

```
if
if ( scalar logical expression ) then
   [executable construct ] ...
   [ else if ( scalar logical expression    then
      [executable construct ] ... ] ...]
   [ else
         [executable construct ] ...]
   end if
```

13.8 Problems

13.1 Rewrite the program for the period of a pendulum. The new program should print out the length of the pendulum and period, for pendulum lengths from 0 to 100 cm in steps of 0.5 cm. The program should incorporate a function for the evaluation of the period.

13.2 Write a program to read an integer that must be positive.
Hint. use a do while to make the user re-enter the value.

13.3 Using functions, do the following:

- Evaluate $n!$ from $n = 0$ to $n = 10$
- Calculate 76!
- Now calculate $(x^n)/n!$, with $x = 13.2$ and $n = 20$.
- Now do it another way.

13.4 The program ch1307 is taken from a real example. In the particular problem, the reformed wave height was 1 m, and the water depth at the reef edge was 2 m. What was the incident wave height? Rather than using an absolute value for the tolerance, it might be more realistic to use some value related to the reformed wave height. These heights are unlikely to be reported to better than about 5% accuracy. Wave energy may be taken as proportional to wave height squared for this example. What is the reduction in wave energy as a result of breaking on the reef or bar for this particular case.

13.5 What is the effect of using int on negative real numbers? Write a program to demonstrate this.

13.6 How would you find the nearest integer to a real number? Now do it another way. Write a program to illustrate both methods. Make sure you test it for negative as well as positive values.

13.7 The function etox has been given in this chapter. The standard Fortran function exp does the same job. Do they give the same answers? Curiously the Fortran standard does not specify how a standard function should be evaluated, or even how accurate it should be.

The physical world has many examples in which processes require that some threshold be overcome before they begin operation: critical mass in nuclear reactions, a given slope to be exceeded before friction is overcome, and so on. Unfortunately, most of these sorts of calculations become rather complex and not really appropriate here. The following problem tries to restrict the range of calculation, whilst illustrating the possibilities of decision making.

13.8 If a cubic equation is expressed as

$$ax^3 + bx^2 + cx + d = 0$$

and we let

$$\Delta = 18abcd - 4b^3d + b^2c^2 - 4ac^3 - 27a^2d^2$$

We can determine the nature of the roots as follows
$\Delta > 0$: three distinct real roots
$\Delta = 0$: has a multiple root and all roots are real
$\Delta < 0$: 1 real root and 2 non real complex conjugate roots
Incorporate this into a program, to determine the nature of the roots of a cubic from suitable input.

13.9 The form of breaking waves on beaches is a continuum, but for convenience we commonly recognise three major types: surging, plunging and spilling. These may be classified empirically by reference to the wave period, T (seconds), the breaker wave height, H_b (metres), and the beach slope, m. These three variables are combined into a single parameter, B, where

$$B = H_b/(gmT^2)$$

g is the gravitational constant ($981\,\mathrm{cm\,s^{-2}}$). If B is less than 0.003, the breakers are surging; if B is greater than 0.068, they are spilling, and between these values, plunging breakers are observed.

(i) On the east coast of New Zealand, the normal pattern is swell waves, with wave heights of 1 to 2 m and wave periods of 10 to 15 s. During storms, the wave period is generally shorter, say 6 to 8 s, and the wave heights higher, 3 to 5 m. The beach slope may be taken as about 0.1. What changes occur in breaker characteristics as a storm builds up?

(ii) Similarly, many beaches have a concave profile. The lower beach generally has a very low slope, say less than 1° (m = 0.018), but towards the high-tide mark, the slope increases dramatically, to say 10° or more (m = 0.18). What changes in wave type will be observed as the tide comes in?

13.9 Bibliography

Dahl O.J., Dijkstra E.W., Hoare C.A.R., Structured programming, Academic Press, 1972.

- This is the original text, and a must. The quote at the start of the chapter by Dijkstra summarises beautifully our limitations when programming and the discipline we must have to master programming successfully.

Knuth D.E., Structured programming with goto Statements, in Current Trends in programming Methodology, Volume 1, Prentice-Hall, 1977.

- The chapter by Knuth provides a very succinct coverage of the arguments for the adoption of structured programming, and dispels many of the myths concerning the use of the goto statement. Highly recommended.

ISO/IEC DIS 1539-1 Information technology – Programming languages – Fortran – Part 1: Base language

- Fortran 2018 draft standard.

```
https://www.iso.org/standard/72320.html
```

Chapter 14
Characters

These metaphysics of magicians, And necromantic books are heavenly; Lines, circles, letters and characters.
Christopher Marlowe, The Tragical History of Doctor Faustus

Aims

The aims of this chapter are:

- To extend the ideas about characters introduced in earlier chapters.
- To demonstrate that this enables us to solve a whole new range of problems in a satisfactory way.

14.1 Introduction

For each type in a programming language there are the following concepts:

- Values are drawn from a finite domain.
- There are a restricted number of operations defined for each type.

For the character data type the basic unit is an individual character The complete Fortran character set is given in Sect. 4.8 in Chap. 4. This provides us with 95 printing characters. Other characters may be available. The Wikipedia entry

```
http://en.wikipedia.org/wiki/Character_encoding
```

has quite detailed information on how complex this area actually is.

As the most common current internal representation for the character data type uses 8 bits this should provide access to 256 characters. However, there is little

© Springer International Publishing AG, part of Springer Nature 2018
I. Chivers and J. Sleightholme, *Introduction to Programming with Fortran*,
https://doi.org/10.1007/978-3-319-75502-1_14

agreement over the encoding of these 256 possible characters, and the best you can normally assume is access to the ASCII character set, which is given in Chap. 4. One of the problems at the end of this chapter looks at determining what characters one has available.

The only operations defined are concatenation (joining character strings together) and comparison.

We will look into the area of character sets in more depth later in this chapter.

We can declare our character variables:

```
character :: a, string, line
```

Note that there is no default typing of the character variable (unlike integer and real data types), and we can use any convenient name within the normal Fortran conventions. In the declaration above, each character variable would have been permitted to store one character. This is limiting, and, to allow character strings which are several units long, we have to add one item of information:

```
character (10) :: a
character (16) :: string
character (80) :: line
```

This indicates that a holds 10 characters, `string` holds 16, and `line` holds 80. if all the character variables in a single declaration contain the same number of characters, we can abbreviate the declaration to

```
character(80) :: list, string, line
```

But we cannot mix both forms in the one declaration. We can now assign data to these variables, as follows:

```
a='first one '
string='a longer one'
line='the quick brown fox jumps over the lazy dog'
```

The delimiter apostrophe (') or quotation mark (") is needed to indicate that this is a character string (otherwise the assignments would have looked like invalid variable names).

14.2 Character Input

In an earlier chapter we saw how we could use the `read` * and `print` * statements to do both numeric and character input and output or I/O. When we use this form of the statement we have to include any characters we type within delimiters (either the apostrophe ' or the quotation mark "). This is a little restricting and there is a slightly more complex form of the read statement that allows one to just type the string on its own.

14.2.1 Example 1: The * Edit Descriptor

The following two programs illustrate the differences:

```
program ch1401
!
! Simple character i/o
!
  character (80) :: line

  read *, line
  print *, line
end program ch1401
```

This form requires enclosing the string with delimiters.

14.2.2 Example 2: The a Edit Descriptor

Consider the next form:

```
program ch1402
!
! Simple character i/o
!
  character (80) :: line

  read '(a)', line
  print *, line
end program ch1402
```

With this form one can just type the string in and input terminates with the carriage return key. The additional syntax ' (a) ' where ' (a) ' is a character edit descriptor. The simple examples we have used so far have used implied format specifiers and edit descriptors. For each data type we have one or more edit descriptors to choose from. For the character data type only the a edit descriptor is available.

14.3   Character Operators

The first manipulator is a new operator — the concatenation operator //. With this operator we can join two character variables to form a third, as in

```
character (5) :: first, second
character (10) :: third
first='three'
second='blind'
...
third=first//second
.
third=first//'mice'
```

where there is a discrepancy between the created length of the concatenated string and the declared lengths of the character strings, truncation will occur. For example,

```
third=first//' blind mice'
```

will only append the first five characters of the string 'blind mice' i.e., 'blin', and third will therefore contain 'three blin'.

What would happen if we assigned a character variable of length 'n' a string which was shorter than n? For example,

```
character (4) :: c2
c2='ab'
```

The remaining two characters are considered to be blank, that is, it is equivalent to saying

```
c2='ab    '
```

However, while the strings 'ab' and 'ab 'are equivalent, 'ab' and 'ab' are not. In the jargon, the character strings are always left justified, and the unset characters are trailing blanks.

If we concatenate strings which have 'trailing blanks', the blanks, or spaces, are considered to be legitimate characters, and the concatenation begins after the end of the first string. Thus

```
character (4) :: c2,c3
character (8) :: jj
c2='a'
c3='man'
jj=c2//c3
```

```
print*, 'the concatenation of ',c2,' and ',c3,' is'
print*,jj
```

would appear as

```
the concatenation of a    man gives
a    man
```

at the terminal.

14.4   Character Substrings

Sometimes we need to be able to extract parts of character variables — substrings. The actual notation for doing this is a little strange at first, but it is very powerful. To extract a substring we must provide two items:

- The position in the string at which the substring begins.
- The position at which it ends.

In the examples that follow we will use the following

```
string='share and enjoy'
```

```
Substring                Characters
string(3:3 )             a
string(3:5 )             are
string(:3  )             sha
string(11:  )            enjoy
```

Character variables may also form arrays:

```
character (10) , dimension(20) :: a
```

sets up a character array of twenty elements, where each element contains ten characters. In order to extract substrings from these array elements, we need to know where the array reference and the substring reference are placed. The array reference comes first, so that

```
do i=1,20
  first=a(i)(1:1)
end do
```

places the first character of each element of the array into the variable first. The syntax is therefore 'position in array, followed by position within string'.

Any argument can be replaced by an integer variable or expression:

```
string(i:j)
```

14.4.1 Example 3: Stripping Blanks from a String

This offers interesting possibilities, since we can, for example, strip blanks out of a string:

```
program ch1403
  implicit none
  character (80) :: string, strip
  integer :: ipos, i, length = 80

  ipos = 0
  print *, ' type in a string'
  read '(a)', string
  do i = 1, length
    if (string(i:i)/=' ') then
      ipos = ipos + 1
      strip(ipos:ipos) = string(i:i)
    end if
  end do
  print *, string
  print *, strip
end program ch1403
```

14.5 Character Functions

There are special functions available for use with character variables: index will give the starting position of a string within another string.

14.5.1 Example 4: The *index* Character Function

If, for example, we were looking for all occurrences of the string 'Geology' in a file, we could construct something like:

```
program ch1404
  implicit none
  character (80) :: line
  integer :: i

  do
    read '(a)', line
    i = index(line, 'Geology')
    if (i/=0) then
      print *, &
        ' String Geology found at position ', i
      print *, ' in line ', line
      exit
    end if
  end do
end program ch1404
```

There are two things to note about this program. Firstly the `index` function will only report the first occurrence of the string in the line; any later occurrences in any particular line will go unnoticed, unless you account for them in some way. Secondly, if the string does not occur, the result of the `index` function is zero, and given the infinite loop (do enddo) the program will crash at run time with an end of file error message. This isn't good programming practice.

14.5.2   The `len` and `len_trim` Functions

The `len` function provides the length of a character string. This function is not immediately useful, since you really ought to know how many characters there are in the string. However, as later examples will show, there are some cases where it can be useful. Remember that trailing blanks do count as part of the character string, and contribute to the length.

14.5.3   Example 5: Using `len` and `len_trim`

The following example illustrates the use of both `len` and `len_trim`:

```
program ch1405
  implicit none
  character (len=20) :: name
  integer :: name_length
```

```
    print *, ' type in your name'
    read '(a)', name
! show len first
    name_length = len(name)
    print *, ' name length is ', name_length
    print *, ' ', name(1:name_length), &
      '<-end is here'
    name_length = len_trim(name)
    print *, ' name length is ', name_length
    print *, ' ', name(1:name_length), &
      '<-end is here'
end program ch1405
```

14.6   Collating Sequence

The next group of functions need to be considered together. They revolve around
the concept of a collating sequence. In other words, each character used in Fortran
is ordered as a list and given a corresponding weight. No two weights are equal.
Although Fortran has only 63 defined characters, the machine you use will generally
have more; 95 printing characters is a typical minimum number. On this type of
machine the weights would vary from 0 to 94. There is a defined collating sequence,
 the ASCII sequence, which is likely to be the default. The parts of the collating sequence which are of most interest are fairly standard throughout all collating
sequences.

In general, we are interested in the numerals (0–9), the alphabetic characters
(A–Z, a–z) and a few odds and ends like the arithmetic operators (+ − / *), some
punctuation (. and ,) and perhaps the prime ('). As you might expect, 0–9 carry
successively higher weights (though not the weights 0 to 9), as do A to Z and a to z.
The other odds and ends are a little more problematic, but we can find out the weights
through the function ichar. This function takes a single character as argument and
returns an integer value. The ASCII weights for the alphanumerics are as follows:

```
    0--9    48--57
    A--Z    65--90
```

One of the exercises is to determine the weights for other characters. The reverse of
this procedure is to determine the character from its weighting, which can be achieved
through the function char. char takes an integer argument and returns a single
character. Using the ASCII collating sequence, the alphabet would be generated
from

```
do i=65,90
  print*,char(i)
enddo
```

This idea of a weighting can then be used in four other functions:

```
function      Action
 lle     lexically less than or equal to
 lge     lexically greater than or equal to
 lgt     lexically greater than
 llt     lexically less than
```

In the sequence we have seen before, A is lexically less than B, i.e., its weight is less. Clearly, we can use ichar and get the same result. For example,

```
if(lgt('a','b')) then
```

is equivalent to

```
if(ichar('a') > ichar('b')) then
```

but these functions can take character string arguments of any length. They are not restricted to single characters.

These functions provide very powerful tools for the manipulation of characters, and open up wide areas of non-numerical computing through Fortran. Text formatting and word processing applications may now be tackled (conveniently ignoring the fact that lower-case characters may not be available).

There are many problems that require the use of character variables. These range from the ability to provide simple titles on reports, or graphical output, to the provision of a natural language interface to one of your programs, i.e., the provision of an English-like command language. Software Tools by Kernighan and Plauger contains many interesting uses of characters in Fortran.

14.7   Example 6: Finding Out About the Character Set Available

The following program prints out the characters between 32 and 127.

```
program ch1406
  implicit none
  integer :: i
```

```
  do i = 32, 62
    print *, i, char(i), i + 32, char(i+32), &
      i + 64, char(i+64)
  end do
  i = 63
  print *, i, char(i), i + 32, char(i+32), &
    i + 64, 'del'
end program ch1406
```

This is the output from the Intel compiler under Windows.

32		64 @	96 `
33 !		65 A	97 a
34 "		66 B	98 b
35 #		67 C	99 c
36 $		68 D	100 d
37 %		69 E	101 e
38 &		70 F	102 f
39 '		71 G	103 g
40 (		72 H	104 h
41)		73 I	105 I
42 *		74 J	106 j
43 +		75 K	107 k
44 ,		76 L	108 l
45 -		77 M	109 m
46 .		78 N	110 n
47 /		79 O	111 o
48 0		80 P	112 p
49 1		81 Q	113 q
50 2		82 R	114 r
51 3		83 S	115 s
52 4		84 T	116 t
53 5		85 U	117 u
54 6		86 V	118 v
55 7		87 W	119 w
56 8		88 X	120 x
57 9		89 Y	121 y
58 :		90 Z	122 z
59 ;		91 [	123 {
60 <		92 \	124	
61 =		93]	125 }
62 >		94 ^	126 ~
63 ?		95 _	127 del

Try this program out on the system you use. Do the character sets match?

14.8 The `scan` Function

The scan functions scans a string for characters from a set of characters. The syntax is given below.

- scan(string, set) - Scans a string for any one of the characters in a set of characters.

14.8.1 *Example 7: Using the scan Function*

```
program ch1407
  implicit none
  character (1024) :: string01
  character (1) :: set = ' '
  integer :: i
  integer :: l
  integer :: start, end

  string01 = 'The important issue about &
    &a language, is not so'
  string01 = trim(string01) // ' ' // 'much &
    &what features the language possesses, &
    &but'
  string01 = trim(string01) // ' ' // 'the &
    &features it does possess, are sufficient, &
    &to'
  string01 = trim(string01) // ' ' // 'support &
    &the desired programming styles, in &
    &the'
  string01 = trim(string01) // ' ' // &
    'desired application areas.'
  l = len(trim(string01))
  print *, ' Length of string is = ', l
  print *, ' String is'
  print *, trim(string01)
  start = 1
  end = l
  print *, ' Blanks at positions '
  do
    i = scan(string01(start:end), set)
    start = start + i
    if (i==0) exit
    write (*, 100, advance='no') start - 1
```

```
  end do
100 format (i5)
end program ch1407
```

Note the use of the `trim` function when using the concatenation operator to initialise the string to the text we want.

The output from one compiler is given below. The text has been wrapped to fit the page

```
Length of string is =              217
String is
The important issue about a language, is not so much
what features the language    possesses,
but the features it does possess, are sufficient,
to support the desired programming styles,
in the desired application areas.
Blanks at positions
    4    14    20    26    28    38    41    45    48    53   58
   67    71    80    91    95    99   108   111   116   125  129
  141   144   152   156   164   176   184   187   191   199  211
```

The text in this program is used in two problems at the end of this chapter.

14.9 Summary

Characters represent a different data type to any other in Fortran, and as a consequence there is a restricted range of operations which may be carried out on them.

A character variable has a length which must be assigned in a character declaration statement.

Character strings are delimited by apostrophes (') or quotation marks ("). Within a character string, the blank is a significant character.

Character strings may be joined together (concatenated) with the // operator.

Substrings occurring within character strings may be also be manipulated.

Table 14.1 has details of a number of functions especially for use with characters.

Table 14.1 String functions in Fortran

Function name	Explanation
achar	Return the character in the ASCII character set
adjustl	Adjust left, remove leading blanks, add trailing blanks
adjustr	Adjust right, remove trailing blanks, insert leading blanks
char	Return the character in the processor collating sequence
iachar	As above but in the ASCII character set
index	Locate one string in another
len	Character length including trailing blanks
len_trim	Character length without the trailing blanks
lle	Lexically less than or equal to
lge	Lexically greater than or equal to
lgt	Lexically greater than
llt	Lexically less than
repeat	Concatenate several copies of a string
scan	Scans a string for anyone of the characters in the set
trim	Remove the trailing blanks
verify	Verify that a set of characters contains all the characters in a string

A detailed explanation is given in appendix D.

14.10 Problems

14.1 Suggest some circumstances where PRIME="" might be useful. What other alternative is there and why do you think we use that instead?

14.2 Write a program to write out the weights for the Fortran character set. Modify this program to print out the weights of the complete implementation defined character set for your version of Fortran. Is it ASCII? if not, how does it differ?

14.3 Write a program that produces the following output.

```
!
" \ #
$ \ % &
```

```
'()*
+,-./
012345
6789:;<<
=>>?@ABCD
EFGHIJKLM
NOPQRSTUVW
XYZ[\]^\_'ab
cdefghijklmn
opqrstuvwxyz\{
|\}\~
```

We assume the ASCII character set in this example.

14.4 Modify the above program to produce the following output.

```
        !
       "\#$
      \%&'()
     *+,-./0
    123456789
   :;<>?@ABCD
  EFGHIJKLMNOPQ
 RSTUVWXYZ[\]^\_'
abcdefghijklmnopq
rstuvwxyz\{|\}\~
```

Again we assume the ASCII character set.

14.5 Modify program ch1407 to break the text into phrases, using the comma and full stop as breaking characters. The output expected is given below.

```
The important issue about a language
is not so much what features the language possesses
but the features it does possess
are sufficient
to support the desired programming styles
in the desired application areas
```

Modify the above to break the text into words and count the frequency of occurrence of words by length. The output should be similar to that given below.

```
1    a                                          1
2    is so it to in                             5
3    The not the but the are the the            8
```

```
4    much what does                                3
5    issue about areas                             3
6    styles                                        1
7    possess support desired desired               4
8    language features language features           4
9    important possesses                           2
10   sufficient                                    1
11   programming application                       2
```

14.6 Use the `index` function in order to find the location of all the strings 'is' in the following data:

If a programmer is found to be indispensable, the best thing to do is to get rid of him as quickly as possible.

14.7 Find the 'middle' character in the following strings. Do you include blanks as characters? What about punctuation?

Practice is the best of all instructors. experience is a dear teacher, but fools will learn at no other.

14.8 In English, the order of occurrence of the letters, from most frequent to least is

```
E, T, A, O, N, R, I, S, H, D, L,
F, C, M, U, G, Y, P, W, B, V, K,
X, J, Q, Z
```

Use this information to examine the two files given in appendix E (one is a translation of the other) to see if this is true for these two extracts of text. The second text is in medieval Latin (c. 1320). Note that a fair amount of compression has been achieved by expressing the passage in Latin rather than modern English. Does this provide a possible model for information compression?

14.9 A very common cypher is the substitution cypher, where, for example, every letter A is replaced by (say) an M, every B is replaced by (say) a Y, and so on. These enciphered messages can be broken by reference to the frequency of occurrence of the letters (given in the previous question).

Since we know that (in English) E is the most commonly occurring letter, we can assume that the most commonly occurring letter in the enciphered message represents an E; we then repeat the process for the next most common and so on. Of course, these correspondences may not be exact, since the message may not be long enough to develop the frequencies fully.

However, it may provide sufficient information to break the cypher.

The file given in appendix E contains an encoded message. Break it.

Clue — Pg +Fybdujuvef jo Tdjfodf, Jorge Luis Borges.

14.10 Write a program that counts the total number of vowels in a sentence or text. Output the frequency of occurrence of each vowel.

Chapter 15
Complex

Aims

The aims of this chapter are:

- To introduce the last predefined numeric data type in Fortran.
- To illustrate with examples how to use this type.

15.1 Introduction

This variable type reflects an extension of the real data type available in Fortran — the complex data type, where we can store and manipulate complex variables. Problems that require this data type are restricted to certain branches of mathematics, physics and engineering. Complex numbers are defined as having a real and imaginary part, i.e., $a = x + iy$ where i is the square root of -1.

They are not supported in many programming languages as a base type which makes Fortran the language of first choice for many people.

To use this variable type we have to write the number as two parts, the real and imaginary elements of the number, for example,

```
complex :: u
u=cmplx(1.0,2.0)
```

represents the complex number $1 + i2$. Note that the complex number is enclosed in brackets. We can do arithmetic on variables like this, and most of the intrinsic functions such as `log`, `sin`, `cos`, etc., accept a complex data type as argument.

© Springer International Publishing AG, part of Springer Nature 2018   281
I. Chivers and J. Sleightholme, *Introduction to Programming with Fortran*,
https://doi.org/10.1007/978-3-319-75502-1_15

All the usual rules about mixing different variable types, like reals and integers, also apply to complex. Complex numbers are read in and written out in a similar way to real numbers, but with the provision that, for each single complex value, two format descriptors must be given. You may use either E or F formats (or indeed, mix them), as long as there are enough of them. Although you use brackets around the pairs of numbers in a program, these must not appear in any input, nor will they appear on the output.

15.2   Example 1: Use of **cmplx**, **aimag** and **conjg**

There are a number of intrinsic functions to enable complex calculations to be performed. The program below uses some of them:

```
program ch1501
  implicit none
  complex :: z, z1, z2, z3, zbar
  real :: x, y, zmod
  real :: x2 = 3.0, y2 = 4.0
  real :: x3 = -2.0, y3 = -3.0

  z1 = cmplx(1.0, 2.0) !            1 + i 2
  z2 = cmplx(x2, y2)    !           x2 + i y2
  z3 = cmplx(x3, y3)    !           x3 + i y3
  z = z1*z2/z3
  x = real(z)           !           real part of
!                                   z
  y = aimag(z)          !           imaginary
!                                   part of z
  zmod = abs(z)         !           modulus of z
  zbar = conjg(z)       !           complex
!                                   conjugate of
!                                   z
  print 100, z1, z2, z3
100 format (3(1x,f4.1,' + i ',f4.1,/))
  print 110, z, zmod, zbar
110 format (1x, f4.1, ' + i ', f4.1, /, 1x, &
      f4.1, /, 1x, f4.1, ' + i ', f4.1)
  print 120, x, y
120 format (2(1x,f4.1,/)) end program ch1501
```

15.3   Example 2: Polar Coordinate Example

The second order differential equation:

$$\frac{d^2y}{dt^2} + 2\frac{dy}{dt} + y = x(t)$$

could describe the behaviour of an electrical system, where $x(t)$ is the input voltage and $y(t)$ is the output voltage and dy/dt is the current. The complex ratio

$$\frac{y(w)}{x(w)} = 1/(-w^2 + 2jw + 1)$$

is called the frequency response of the system because it describes the relationship between input and output for sinusoidal excitation at a frequency of w and where j is $\sqrt{(-1)}$ The following program reads in a value of w and evaluates the frequency response for this value of w together with its polar form (magnitude and phase):

```
program ch1502
   implicit none

! program to calculate frequency
! response of a system
! for a given omega
! and its polar form (magnitude and phase).

   real :: omega, real_part, imag_part, &
     magnitude, phase
   complex :: frequency_response

! Input frequency omega

   print *, 'Input frequency'
   read *, omega

   frequency_response = 1.0/cmplx(-omega*omega+ &
     1.0, 2.0*omega)
   real_part = real(frequency_response)
   imag_part = aimag(frequency_response)

! Calculate polar coordinates
! (magnitude and phase)

   magnitude = abs(frequency_response)
   phase = atan2(imag_part, real_part)
```

```
   print *, ' at frequency ', omega
   print *, 'response = ', real_part, ' + i ', &
      imag_part
   print *, 'in polar form'
   print *, ' magnitude = ', magnitude
   print *, ' phase = ', phase
end program ch1502
```

15.4   Complex and Kind Type

The standard requires that there be a minimum of two kind types for real numbers and this is also true of the complex data type. Chapter 5 must be consulted for a full coverage of real kind types. We would therefore use something like the following to select a complex kind type other than the default:

```
integer , parameter :: &
   dp = selected_real_kind(15,307)
complex (dp) :: z
```

Chapter 21 includes a good example of how to use modules to define and use precision throughout a program and subprogram units.

15.5   Summary

Complex is used to store and manipulate complex numbers: those with a real and an imaginary part. There are standard functions which allow conversion between the numerical data types — cmplx, real and int.

15.6   Problem

15.1 The program used in Chap. 13 which calculated the roots of a quadratic had to abandon the calculation if the roots were complex. You should now be able to remedy this, remembering that it is necessary to declare any complex variables. Instead of raising the expression to the power 0.5 in order to take its square root, use the function sqrt. The formulae for the complex roots are

$$\frac{-b}{2a} \pm i \frac{\sqrt{-(b^2 - 4ac)}}{2a}$$

If you manage this to your satisfaction, try your skills on the roots of a cubic (see the problems in Chap. 13).

Chapter 16
Logical

A messenger yes/no semaphore her black/white keys in/out whirl
of morse hoopooe signals salvation deviously

Nathaniel Tarn, The Laurel Tree

Aims

The aims of this chapter are:

- To examine the last predefined type available in Fortran: logical.
- To introduce the concepts necessary to use logical expressions effectively:

  - Logical variables.
  - Logical operators.
  - The hierarchy of operations.
  - Truth tables.

16.1 Introduction

Often we have situations where we need on or off, true or false, yes or no switches, and in such circumstances we can use logical type variables, e.g.,

```
logical :: flag
```

Logicals may take only two possible values, as shown in the following:

```
flag=.true.
or
flag=.false.
```

© Springer International Publishing AG, part of Springer Nature 2018
I. Chivers and J. Sleightholme, *Introduction to Programming with Fortran*,
https://doi.org/10.1007/978-3-319-75502-1_16

Note the full stops, which are essential. With a little thought you can see why they are needed. You will already have met some of the ideas associated with logical variables from if statements:

```
if(a == b) then
       .
else
       .
endif
```

The logical expression (a == b) returns a value true or false, which then determines the route to be followed; if the quantity is true, then we execute the next statement, else we take the other route.

Similarly, the following example is also legitimate:

```
logical :: answer
answer=.true.
...
if (answer) then
    ...
else
    ...
endif
```

Again the expression if (answer) is evaluated; here the variable answer has been set to .true., and therefore the statements following the then are executed. Clearly, conventional arithmetic is inappropriate with logicals. What does 2 times true mean? (very true?). There are a number of special operators for logicals:

- .not. which negates a logical value (i.e., changes true to false or vice versa).
- .and. logical intersection.
- .or. logical union.

To illustrate the use of these operators, consider the following program extract:

```
logical :: a,b,c
a=.true.
b=.not.a          !(b now has the value 'false')
c=a.or.b          !(c has the value 'true')
c=a.and.b         !(c now has the value 'false')
```

Table 16.1 shows the effect of these operators on logicals in a simple case.

Table 16.1 Simple truth table

x1	x2	.not.x1	x1.and.x2	x1.or.x2
true	true	false	true	true
true	false	false	false	true
false	true	true	false	true
false	false	true	false	false

As with arithmetic operators, there is an order of precedence associated with the logical operators:

- .and. is carried out before
- .or. and .not.

In dealing with logicals, the operations are carried out within a given level, from left to right. Any expressions in brackets would be dealt with first. The logical operators are a lower order of precedence than the arithmetic operators, i.e., they are carried out later. Table 16.2 shows a more complete operator hierarchy.

Table 16.2 Fortran operator hierarchy

Expressions within brackets
Exponentiation
Multiplication and division
Addition and subtraction
Relational and logical
.and.
.or. and .not

Although you can build up complicated expressions with mixtures of operators, these are often difficult to comprehend, and it is generally more straightforward to break 'big' expressions down into smaller ones whose purpose is more readily appreciated.

Historically, logicals have not been in evidence extensively in Fortran programs, although clearly there are occasions on which they are of considerable use. Their use often aids significantly in making programs more modular and comprehensible. They can be used to make a complex section of code involving several choices much more transparent by the use of one logical function, with an appropriate name. Logicals may be used to control output; e.g.,

```
logical :: debug
...
debug=.true.
```

```
   . . .
if(debug)then
     . . .
   print *,'lots of printout'
     . . .
endif
```

ensures that, while debugging a program you have more output then, when the program is correct, run with debug=.false.

Note that Fortran does try to protect you while you use logical variables. You cannot do the following:

```
logical :: up, down
up=down+.false.
```

or

```
logical :: a2
real , dimension(10):: omega
  .
a2=omega(3)
```

The compiler will note that this is an error, and will not permit you to run the program. This is an example of strong typing, since only a limited number of predetermined operations are permitted. The real, integer and complex variable types are much more weakly typed (which helps lead to the confusion inherent in mixing variable types in arithmetic assignments).

16.2   I/O

Since logicals may take only the values .true. and .false., the possibilities in reading and writing logical values are clearly limited. The l edit descriptor or format allows logicals to be input and output. On input, if the first nonblank characters are either T or .T, the logical value .true. is stored in the corresponding list item; if the first nonblank characters are F or .F, then .false. is stored. (Note therefore that reading, say, ted and fahr in an l4 format would be acceptable.) if the first nonblank character is not F, T, .F or .T, then an error message will be generated. On output, the value T or F is written out, right justified, with blanks (if appropriate). Thus,

```
logical :: flag
flag=.true.
```

```
print 100, flag, .not.flag
100 format(2L3)
```

would produce

```
T    F
```

at the terminal.

Assigning a logical variable to anything other than a `.true.` or `.false.` value in your program will result in errors. The 'shorthand' forms of `.T`, `.F`, `F` and `T` are not acceptable in the program.

16.3 Summary

This chapter has introduced the `logical` data type. A logical variable may take one of two values, `.true.` or `.false.`.

- There are special operators for manipulating logicals:

  - `.not.`
  - `.and.`
  - `.or.`

- Logical operators have a lower order of precedence than any others.

16.4 Problems

16.1 Why are the full stops needed in a statement like `a = .true.`?

16.2 Generate a truth table like the one given in this chapter.

16.3 Write a program which will read in numerical data from the terminal, but will flag any data which is negative, and will also turn these negative values into positive ones.

Chapter 17
Introduction to Derived Types

> *Russell's theory of types leads to certain complexities in the foundations of mathematics…Its interesting features for our purposes are that types are used to prevent certain erroneous expressions from being used in logical and mathematical formulae; and that a check against violation of type constraints can be made purely by scanning the text, without any knowledge of the value which a particular symbol might happen to have*
> C.A.R. Hoare, Structured Programming

Aims

The aim of this chapter is to introduce the concepts and ideas involved in using the facilities offered in modern Fortran for the construction and use of derived or user defined types;

- defining our own types.
- declaring variables to be of a user defined type.
- manipulating variables of our own types.
- nesting types within types.

The examples are simple and are designed to highlight the syntax. More complex and realistic examples of the use of user defined data types are to be found in later chapters.

17.1 Introduction

In the coverage so far we have used the intrinsic types provided by Fortran. The only data structuring technique available has been to construct arrays of these intrinsic types. Whilst this enables us to solve a reasonable variety of problems, it is inadequate for many purposes. In this chapter we look at the facilities offered by Fortran for the construction of our own types and how we manipulate data of these new, user defined types.

© Springer International Publishing AG, part of Springer Nature 2018
I. Chivers and J. Sleightholme, *Introduction to Programming with Fortran*,
https://doi.org/10.1007/978-3-319-75502-1_17

With the ability to define our own types we can now construct aggregate data types that have components of a variety of base types. These are given a variety of names including

- Record in the Pascal family of languages and in many older books on computing and data structuring;
- Structs in C;
- Classes in C++, Java, C# and Eiffel;
- Cartesian product is often used in mathematics and this is the terminology adopted by Hoare;

Chapter 3 has details of some books for further reading:

- Dahl O.J., Dijkstra E.W., Hoare C.A.R., Structured Programming;
- Wirth N., Algorithms + Data Structures = Programs;
- Wirth N., Algorithms + Data Structures.

We will use the term user defined type and derived types interchangeably.

There are two stages in the process of creating and using our own data types: we must first define the type, and then create variables of this type.

17.2   Example 1: Dates

```
program ch1701

  implicit none

  type date

    integer :: day = 1
    integer :: month = 1
    integer :: year = 2000

  end type date

  type (date) :: d

  print *, d%day, d%month, d%year
  print *, ' type in the date, day, month, year'
  read *, d%day, d%month, d%year
  print *, d%day, d%month, d%year

end program ch1701
```

This complete program illustrates both the definition and use of the type. It also shows how you can define initial values within the type definition.

17.3   Type Definition

The type `date` is defined to have three component parts, comprising a day, a month and a year, all of integer type. The syntax of a type construction comprises:

```
type typename
    data type :: component_name
    etc
end type typename
```

Reference can then be made to this new type by the use of a single word, `date`, and we have a very powerful example of the use of abstraction.

17.4   Variable Definition

This is done by

```
type (typename) :: variablename
```

and we then define a variable d to be of this new type. The next thing we do is have a `read *` statement that prompts the user to type in three integer values, and the data are then echoed straight back to the user. We use the notation

```
variablename%component_name
```

to refer to each component of the new data type.

17.4.1   Example 2: Variant of Example 1 Using Modules

The following is a variant on the above and achieves the same result with a small amount of additional syntax.

```
module date_module

  type date

    integer :: day = 1
    integer :: month = 1
    integer :: year = 2000

  end type date

end module date_module

program ch1702

  use date_module

  implicit none
  type (date) :: d

  print *, d%day, d%month, d%year
  print *, ' type in the date, day, month, year'
  read *, d%day, d%month, d%year
  print *, d%day, d%month, d%year

end program ch1702
```

The key here is that we have embedded the type declaration inside a module, and then used the module in the main program. Modules are covered in more detail in a later chapter.

If you are only using the type within one program unit then the first form is satisfactory, but if you are going to use the type in several program units the second is the required form.

We will use the second form in the examples that follow.

17.5   Example 3: Address Lists

```
module address_module

  type address

    character (len=40) :: name
    character (len=60) :: street
    character (len=60) :: district
```

```fortran
      character (len=60) :: city
      character (len=8) :: post_code

   end type address

end module address_module

program ch1703

   use address_module

   implicit none

   integer :: n_of_address

   type (address), dimension (:), &
     allocatable :: addr

   integer :: i

   print *, 'input number of addresses'
   read *, n_of_address

   allocate (addr(1:n_of_address))

   open (unit=1, file='address.txt',status='old')

   do i = 1, n_of_address

      read (unit=1, fmt='(a40)') addr(i)%name
      read (unit=1, fmt='(a60)') addr(i)%street
      read (unit=1, fmt='(a60)') addr(i)%district
      read (unit=1, fmt='(a60)') addr(i)%city
      read (unit=1, fmt='(a8)') addr(i)%post_code

   end do

   do i = 1, n_of_address

      print *, addr(i)%name
      print *, addr(i)%street
      print *, addr(i)%district
      print *, addr(i)%city
      print *, addr(i)%post_code
```

```
   end do

end program ch1703
```

In this example we define a type `address` which has components that one would expect for a person's address. We then define an array `addr` of this type. Thus we are now creating arrays of our own user defined types. We index into the array in the way we would expect from our experience with integer, real and character arrays. The complete example is rather trivial in a sense in that the program merely reads from one file and prints the file out to the screen. However, it highlights many of the important ideas of the definition and use of user defined types.

17.6   Example 4: Nested User Defined Types

The following example builds on the two data types already introduced. Here we construct nested user defined data types based on them and construct a new data type containing them both plus additional information.

```
  module personal_module

    type address

      character (len=60) :: street
      character (len=60) :: district
      character (len=60) :: city
      character (len=8) :: post_code

    end type address

    type date_of_birth

      integer :: day
      integer :: month
      integer :: year

    end type date_of_birth

    type personal
      character (len=20) :: first_name
      character (len=20) :: other_names
      character (len=40) :: surname
      type (date_of_birth) :: dob
      character (len=1) :: gender
```

```fortran
    type (address) :: addr

  end type personal

end module personal_module

program ch1704

  use personal_module

  implicit none

  integer :: n_people
  integer :: i

  type (personal), dimension (:), &
    allocatable :: p

  print *, 'input number of people'
  read *, n_people

  allocate (p(1:n_people))

  open (unit=1, file='person.txt',status='old')

  do i = 1, n_people

    read (1, fmt=100) p(i)%first_name, &
      p(i)%other_names, p(i)%surname, &
      p(i)%dob%day, p(i)%dob%month, &
      p(i)%dob%year, p(i)%gender, p(i)%addr%street, &
      p(i)%addr%district, p(i)%addr%city, &
      p(i)%addr%post_code

  end do

  do i = 1, n_people

    write (*, fmt=110) p(i)%first_name, &
      p(i)%other_names, p(i)%surname, &
      p(i)%dob%day, p(i)%dob%month, &
      p(i)%dob%year, p(i)%gender, p(i)%addr%street, &
      p(i)%addr%district, p(i)%addr%city, &
      p(i)%addr%post_code
```

```
      end do

  100 format (a20, /, a20, /, a40, /, i2, 1x, i2, &
         1x, i4, /, a1, /, a60, /, a60, /, a60, /, &
         a8)

'  110 format (a20, a20, a40, /, i2, 1x, i2, 1x, &
         i4, /, a1, /, a60, /, a60, /, a60, /, a8)

  end program ch1704
```

Here we have a date of birth data type (date_of_birth) based on the date data type from the first example, plus a slightly modified address data type, incorporated into a new data type comprising personal details. Note the way in which we reference the component parts of this new, aggregate data type.

17.7   Problem

17.1 Modify the last example to include a more elegant printed name. The current example will pad with blanks the first_ name, other_names and surname and span 80 characters on one line, which looks rather ugly.

Add a new variable name which will comprise all three subcomponents and write out this new variable, instead of the three subcomponents.

Chapter 18
An Introduction to Pointers

Not to put too fine a point on it

Charles Dickens, Bleak House

Aim

The primary aim of the chapter is to introduce some of the key concepts of pointers in Fortran.

18.1   Introduction

All of the data types introduced so far, with the exception of the allocatable array, have been static. Even with the allocatable array a size has to be set at some stage during program execution. The facilities provided in Fortran by the concept of a pointer combined with those offered by a user defined type enable us to address a completely new problem area, previously extremely difficult to solve in Fortran. There are many problems where one genuinely does not know what requirements there are on the size of a data structure. Linked lists allow sparse matrix problems to be solved with minimal storage requirements, two-dimensional spatial problems can be addressed with quad-trees and three-dimensional spatial problems can be addressed with oct-trees. Many problems also have an irregular nature, and pointer arrays address this problem.

First we need to cover some of the technical aspects of pointers. A pointer is a variable that has the pointer attribute A pointer is associated with a target by allocation or pointer assignment. A pointer becomes associated as follows:

© Springer International Publishing AG, part of Springer Nature 2018
I. Chivers and J. Sleightholme, *Introduction to Programming with Fortran*,
https://doi.org/10.1007/978-3-319-75502-1_18

- The pointer is allocated as the result of the successful execution of an allocate statement referencing the pointer

  or

- The pointer is pointer-assigned to a target that is associated or is specified with the target attribute and, if allocatable, is currently allocated.

A pointer may have a pointer association status of associated, disassociated, or undefined. Its association status may change during execution of a program. Unless a pointer is initialised (explicitly or by default), it has an initial association status of undefined. A pointer may be initialised to have an association status of disassociated.

A pointer shall neither be referenced nor defined until it is associated. A pointer is disassociated following execution of a `deallocate` or `nullify` statement, following pointer association with a disassociated pointer, or initially through pointer initialisation.

Let us look at some examples to clarify these points.

18.2   Example 1: Illustrating Some Basic Pointer Concepts

With the introduction of pointers as a data type into Fortran we also have the introduction of a new assignment statement — the pointer assignment statement. Consider the following example:

```
program ch1801
  implicit none
  integer, pointer :: a => null(), b => null()
  integer, target :: c
  integer :: d

  c = 1
  a => c
  c = 2
  b => c
  d = a + b
  print *, a, b, c, d
end program ch1801
```

The following

```
integer , pointer :: a=>null(),b=>null()
```

is a declaration statement that defines a and b to be variables, with the `pointer` attribute. This means we can use a and b to refer or point to integer values. We also use the `null` intrinsic to set the status of the pointers a and b to disassociated. Using the `null` intrinsic means that we can test the status of a pointer variable and avoid making a number of common pointer programming errors. Note that in this case no space is set aside for the pointer variables a and b, i.e. a and b should not be referenced in this state.

The second declaration defines c to be an integer, with the `target` attribute, i.e., we can use pointers to refer or point to the value of the variable c.

The last declaration defines d to be an ordinary integer variable.

In the case of the last two declarations space is set aside to hold two integers.

Let us now look at the various executable statements in the program, one at a time:

```
c = 1
```

This is an example of the normal assignment statement with which we are already familiar. We use the variable name c in our program and whenever we use that name we get the value of the variable c.

```
a => c
```

This is an example of a pointer assignment statement. This means that both a and c now refer to the same value, in this case 1. a becomes associated with the target c. a can now be referenced.

```
c = 2
```

Conventional assignment statement, and c now has the value 2.

```
b => c
```

Second example of pointer assignment. b now points to the value that c has, in this case 2. b becomes associated with the target c. b can now be referenced.

```
d = a + b
```

Simple arithmetic assignment statement. The value that a points to is added to the value that b points to and the result is assigned to d.

The last statement prints out the values of a, b, c and d.

The output is

```
2 2 4
```

18.3   Example 2: The `associated` Intrinsic Function

The associated intrinsic returns the association status of a pointer variable. Consider the following example which is a simple variant on the first.

```
program ch1802
  implicit none
  integer, pointer :: a => null(), b => null()
  integer, target :: c
  integer :: d

  print *, associated(a)
  print *, associated(b)
  c = 1
  a => c
  c = 2
  b => c
  d = a + b
  print *, a, b, c, d
  print *, associated(a)
  print *, associated(b)
end program ch1802
```

The output from running this program is shown below

```
F
F
2 2 2 4
T
T
```

and as you can see we therefore have a mechanism to test pointers to see if they are in a valid state before use.

18.4   Example 3: Referencing Pointer Variables Before Allocation or Pointer Assignment

Consider the following example:

```
program ch1803
  implicit none
  integer, pointer :: a => null(), b => null()
```

```
  integer, target :: c
  integer :: d

  print *, a
  print *, b
  c = 1
  a => c
  c = 2
  b => c
  d = a + b
  print *, a, b, c, d
end program ch1803
```

Here we are actually referencing the pointers a and b, even though their status is disassociated. Most compilers generate a run time error with this example with the default compiler options, and the error message tends to be a little cryptic. It is recommended that you look at the diagnostic compilation switches for you compiler. We include some sample output below from gfortran, Intel and Nag. The error messages are now much more meaningful.

18.4.1   gfortran

Switches are

```
gfortran -W -Wall -fbounds-check -pedantic-errors
  -std=f2003 -Wunderflow
  -O -fbacktrace -ffpe-trap=zero,
  overflow,underflow -g
```

The program runs to completion with no error message. Here is the output.

```
ch1803.out
          0
          0
          2             2             2             4
```


18.4.2   Intel

Switches are

```
/check:all /traceback
```

Here is the output.

```
D:\document\fortran\newbook\examples\ch18>>
ch1803
forrtl: severe (408): fort: (7):
Attempt to use pointer A when it
is not associated with a target
Image           PC                  Routine Line
Source
ch1803.exe    000000013F0AC598   Unknown Unknown
Unknown
...
ntdll.dll     0000000077096611   Unknown Unknown
Unknown
```

18.4.3   Nag

Switches are

```
-C=all -C=undefined -info -g -gline
```

Here is the output.

```
Runtime Error: ch1803.f90, line 5:
Reference to disassociated POINTER A
Program terminated by fatal error
ch1803.f90, line 5: Error occurred in CH1803
```

18.5   Example 4: Pointer Allocation and Assignment

Consider the following example:

```
program ch1804
  implicit none
  integer, pointer :: a => null(), b => null()
  integer, target :: c
  integer :: d
```

```
   allocate (a)
   a = 1
   c = 2
   b => c
   d = a + b
   print *, a, b, c, d
   deallocate (a)
end program ch1804
```

In this example we allocate a and then can do conventional assignment. If we had not allocated a the assignment would be illegal. Try out problem 18.2 to see what will happen with your compiler.

Our simple recommendation when using pointers is to nullify them when declaring them and to explicitly allocate them before conventional assignment.

18.6   Memory Leak Examples

Dynamic memory brings greater versatility but requires greater responsibility.

18.6.1   Example 5: Simple Memory Leak

```
program ch1805
   implicit none
   integer, pointer :: a => null(), b => null()
   integer, target :: c
   integer :: d

   allocate (a)
   allocate (b)
   a = 100
   b = 200
   print *, a, b
   c = 1
   a => c
   c = 2
   b => c
   d = a + b
   print *, a, b, c, d
end program ch1805
```

What has happened to the memory allocated to a and b?

18.6.2   Example 6: More Memory Leaks

Now consider the following example.

```
program ch1806
  implicit none
  integer :: allocate_status = 0
  integer, parameter :: n1 = 10000000
  integer, parameter :: n2 = 5
  integer, dimension (:), pointer :: x
  integer, dimension (1:n2), target :: y
  integer :: i

  do
    allocate (x(1:n1), stat=allocate_status)
    if (allocate_status>0) then
      print *, ' allocate failed. program ends.'
      stop
    end if
    do i = 1, n1
      x(i) = i
    end do
    do i = 1, n2
      print *, x(i)
    end do
    do i = 1, n2
      y(i) = i*i
    end do
    do i = 1, n2
      print *, y(i)
    end do
    x => y               ! x now points to y
    do i = 1, n2
      print *, x(i)
    end do
!   what has happened to the memory that x
!   used to point to?
  end do
end program ch1806
```

Before running the above example we recommend starting up a memory monitoring program.

Under Microsoft Windows holding [CTRL] + [ALT] + [DEL] will bring up the Windows Task Manager. Choose the [Performance] tab to get a screen which will show CPU usage, PF Usage, CPU Usage History and Page File Usage History. You will also get details of Physical and Kernel memory usage.

Under Linux type

```
top
```

in a terminal window.

In these examples we also see the recommended form of the `allocate` statement when working with arrays. This enables us to test if the allocation has worked and take action accordingly. A positive value indicates an allocation error, zero indicates OK.

The second program can require a power off on a Windows operating system with a compiler that will remain anonymous!

18.7 Non-standard Pointer Example

Some Fortran compilers provide a non-standard `loc` intrinsic. This can be used to print out the address of the variable passed as an argument.

18.7.1 Example 7: Using the C *loc* Function

Some Fortran compilers provide non standard access to functions supported in the C language. This example uses the C `loc` function.

```
program ch1807
  implicit none
  integer, pointer :: a => null(), b => null()
  integer, target :: c
  integer :: d

  allocate (a)
  allocate (b)
  a = 100
  b = 200
  print *, a, b
  print *, loc(a)
  print *, loc(b)
  print *, loc(c)
  print *, loc(d)
  c = 1
```

```
    a => c
    c = 2
    b => c
    d = a + b
    print *, a, b, c, d
    print *, loc(a)
    print *, loc(b)
    print *, loc(c)
    print *, loc(d)
end program ch1807
```

Here is the output from a compiler with `loc` support.

```
       100              200
           13803552
           13803600
            2948080
            2948084
      2             2             2             4
            2948080
            2948080
            2948080
            2948084
```

This program clearly shows the memory leak.

18.8   Problems

18.1 Compile and run all of the example programs in this chapter with your compiler and examine the output.

18.2 Compile and run example 4 without the `allocate(a)` statement. See what happens with your compiler.
    Here is the output from the Nag compiler. The first run is with the default options.

```
nagfor ch1804p.f90
NAG Fortran Compiler:
[NAG Fortran Compiler normal termination]
a.exe
```

There is no meaningful output.
The following adds the -C=all compilation option.

```
nagfor ch1804p.f90 -C=all
NAG Fortran Compiler:
[NAG Fortran Compiler normal termination]
a.exe
Runtime Error: ch1804p.f90, line 5:
Reference to disassociated POINTER
A
Program terminated by fatal error
```

We now get a meaningful error message.

Chapter 19
Introduction to Subroutines

A man should keep his brain attic stacked with all the furniture he is likely to use, and the rest he can put away in the lumber room of his library, where he can get at it if he wants.
Sir Arthur Conan Doyle, Five Orange Pips

Aims

The aims of this chapter are:

- To consider some of the reasons for the inclusion of subroutines in a programming language.
- To introduce with a concrete example some of the concepts and ideas involved with the definition and use of subroutines.

  - Arguments or parameters.
  - The intent attribute for parameters.
  - The call statement.
  - Scope of variables.
  - Local variables and the save attribute.
  - The use of parameters to report on the status of the action carried out in the subroutine.

- Module procedures to provide interfaces.

19.1 Introduction

In the earlier chapter on functions we introduced two types of function

- Intrinsic functions - which are part of the language.
- User defined functions - by which we extend the language.

© Springer International Publishing AG, part of Springer Nature 2018
I. Chivers and J. Sleightholme, *Introduction to Programming with Fortran*,
https://doi.org/10.1007/978-3-319-75502-1_19

We now introduce subroutines which collectively with functions are given the name procedures. Procedures provide a very powerful extension to the language by:

- Providing us with the ability to break problems down into simpler more easily solvable subproblems.
- Allowing us to concentrate on one aspect of a problem at a time.
- Avoiding duplication of code.
- Hiding away messy code so that a main program is a sequence of calls to procedures.
- Providing us with the ability to put together collections of procedures that solve commonly occurring subproblems, often given the name libraries, and generally compiled.
- Allowing us to call procedures from libraries written, tested and documented by experts in a particular field. There is no point in reinventing the wheel!

There are a number of concepts required for the successful use of subroutines and we met some of them in Chap. 12 when we looked at user defined functions. We will extend the ideas introduced there of parameters and introduce the additional concept of an interface via the use of modules. The ideas are best explained with a concrete example.

Note that we use the terms parameters and arguments interchangeably.

19.2   Example 1: Roots of a Quadratic Equation

This example is one we met earlier that solves a quadratic equation, i.e., solves

$$ax^2 + bx + c = 0$$

The program to do this originally was just one program. In the example below we break that problem down into smaller parts and make each part a subroutine. The components are:

- Main program or driving routine.
- Interaction with user to get the coefficients of the equation.
- Solution of the quadratic.

Let us look now at how we do this with the use of subroutines:

```
module interact_module
contains
  subroutine interact(a, b, c, ok)
    implicit none
    real, intent (out) :: a
    real, intent (out) :: b
```

```fortran
      real, intent (out) :: c
      logical, intent (out) :: ok
      integer :: io_status = 0

      print *, &
        ' type in the coefficients a, b and c'
      read (unit=*, fmt=*, iostat=io_status) a, b, &
        c
      if (io_status==0) then
        ok = .true.
      else
        ok = .false.
      end if
    end subroutine interact
end module interact_module

module solve_module
contains
    subroutine solve(e, f, g, root1, root2, ifail)
      implicit none
      real, intent (in) :: e
      real, intent (in) :: f
      real, intent (in) :: g
      real, intent (out) :: root1
      real, intent (out) :: root2
      integer, intent (inout) :: ifail
!     local variables
      real :: term
      real :: a2

      term = f*f - 4.*e*g
      a2 = e*2.0
!     if term < 0, roots are complex
      if (term<0.0) then
        ifail = 1
      else
        term = sqrt(term)
        root1 = (-f+term)/a2
        root2 = (-f-term)/a2
      end if
    end subroutine solve
end module solve_module

program ch1901
  use interact_module
```

```
  use solve_module
  implicit none
! simple example of the use of a main program
! and two subroutines.
! one interacts with the user and the
! second solves a quadratic equation,
! based on the user input.
  real :: p, q, r, root1, root2
  integer :: ifail = 0
  logical :: ok = .true.

  call interact(p, q, r, ok)
  if (ok) then
    call solve(p, q, r, root1, root2, ifail)
    if (ifail==1) then
      print *, ' complex roots'
      print *, ' calculation abandoned'
    else
      print *, ' roots are ', root1, ' ', root2
    end if
  else
    print *, ' error in data input program ends'
  end if
end program ch1901
```

19.2.1   *Referencing a Subroutine*

To reference a subroutine you use the `call` statement:

```
call subroutine_name(optional actual argument list)
```

and from the earlier example the call to subroutine `interact` was of the form:

```
call interact(p,q,r,ok)
```

When a subroutine returns to the calling program unit control is passed to the statement following the call statement.

19.2.2   Dummy Arguments or Parameters and Actual Arguments

Procedures and their calling program units communicate through their arguments. We often use the terms parameter and arguments interchangeably through out this text. The `subroutine` statement normally contains a list of dummy arguments, separated by commas and enclosed in brackets. The dummy arguments have a type associated with them; for example, in subroutine `solve` x is of type `real`, but no space is put aside for this in memory. When the subroutine is referenced e.g., `call solve(p,q,r,root1,root2,ifail)`, then the dummy argument points to the actual argument p, which is a variable in the calling program unit. The dummy argument and the actual argument must be of the same type - in this case `real`.

19.2.3   The `intent` Attribute

It is recommended that dummy arguments have an `intent` attribute. In the earlier example subroutine `solve` has a dummy argument e with `intent(in)`, which means that when the subroutine is referenced or called it is expecting e to have a value, but its value cannot be changed inside the subroutine. This acts as an extra security measure besides making the program easier to understand. For each parameter it may have one of three attributes:

- `intent(in)`, where the parameter already has a value and cannot be altered in the called routine.
- `intent(out)`, where the parameter does not have a value, and is given one in the called routine.
- `intent(inout)`, where the parameter already has a value and this is changed in the called routine.

19.2.4   Local Variables

We saw with functions that variables could be essentially local to the function and unavailable elsewhere. The concept of local variables also applies to subroutines. In the example above `term` and `a2` are both local variables to the subroutine `solve`.

19.2.5   Local Variables and the `save` Attribute

Local variables are usually created when a procedure is called and their value lost when execution returns to the calling program unit. To make sure that a local variable retains its values between calls to a subprogram the `save` attribute can be used on a type statement: e.g.,

```
integer , save :: i
```

means that when this statement appears in a subprogram the value of the local variable `i` is saved between calls.

19.2.6   Scope of Variables

In most cases variables are only available within the program unit that defines them. The introduction of argument lists to procedures immediately opens up the possibility of data within one program unit becoming available in one or more other program units.

In the main program we declare the variables `p`, `q`, `r`, `root1`, `root2`, `ifail` and `ok`.

Subroutine `interact` has no variables locally declared. It works on the arguments `a`, `b`, `c` and `ok`; which map onto `p`, `q`, `r` and `ok` from the main program, i.e., it works with those variables.

Subroutine `solve` has two locally defined variables, `term` and `a2`. It works with the variables `e`, `f`, `g`, `root1`, `root2` and `ifail`, which map onto `p`, `q`, `r`, `root1`, `root2` and `ifail` from the main program.

19.2.7   Status of the Action Carried Out in the Subroutine

It is also useful to use parameters that carry information regarding the status of the action carried out by the subroutine. With the subroutine `interact` we use a logical variable `ok` to report on the status of the interaction with the user. In the subroutine `solve` we use the status of the integer variable `ifail` to report on the status of the solution of the equation.

19.2.8   Modules 'Containing' Procedures

At the same time as introducing procedures we have 'contained' them in a module and then the main program 'uses' the module in order to make the procedure available. Procedures 'contained' in modules are called module procedures.

With the `use` statement the interface to the procedure is available to the compiler so that the types and positions of the actual and dummy arguments can be checked. This was a major source of errors with Fortran 77.

The use statement must be the first statement in the main program or calling unit, also the modules must be compiled before the program or calling unit.

We will cover modules in more depth in later chapters.

There are times when an interface is mandatory in Fortran so it's good practice to use module procedures from the start. There are other ways of providing explicit interfaces and we will cover them later.

19.3   Why Bother with Subroutines?

Given the increase in the complexity of the overall program to solve a relatively straightforward problem, one must ask why bother. The answer lies in our ability to manage the solution of larger and larger problems. We need all the help we can get if we are to succeed in our task of developing large-scale reliable programs.

We need to be able to break our problems down into manageable subcomponents and solve each in turn. We are now in a very good position to be able to do this. Given a problem that requires a main program, one or more functions and one or more subroutines we can work on each subcomponent in relative isolation, and know that by using features like module procedures we will be able to glue all of the components together into a stable structure at the end. We can independently compile the main program and the modules containing the functions and subroutines and use the linker to generate the overall executable, and then test that. Providing we keep our interfaces the same we can alter the actual implementations of the functions and subroutines and just recompile the changed procedures.

19.4   Summary

We now have the following concepts for the use of subroutines:

- Module procedures providing interfaces.
- Intent attribute for parameters.
- Dummy parameters.
- The use of the call statement to invoke a subroutine.
- The concepts of variables that are local to the called routines and are unavailable elsewhere in the over all program.
- Communication between program units via the argument list.
- The concept of parameters on the call that enable us to report back on the status of the called routine.

19.5 Problems

19.1 Type the program and module procedures for Example 1 into one file. Compile, link and run providing data for complex roots to test this part of the code.

19.2 Split the main program and modules up into three separate files. Compile the modules and then compile the main program and link the object files to create one executable. Look at the file size of the executable and the individual object files. What do you notice?

The development of large programs is eased considerably by the ability to compile small program units and eradicate the compilation errors from one unit at a time. The linker obviously also has an important role to play in the development process.

19.3 Write a subroutine to calculate new coordinates (x', y') from (x, y) when the axes are rotated counter clockwise through an angle of a radians using:
$$x' = x cos a + y sin a$$
$$y' = -x sin a + y cos a$$

Hint:

The subroutine would look some thing like
```
subroutine ChangeCoordinate(x, y, a, xd, yd)
```
Write a main program to read in values of x, y and a and then call the subroutine and print out the new coordinates. Use a module procedure.

Chapter 20
Subroutines: 2

> *It is one thing to show a man he is in error, and another to put him in possession of the truth*

John Locke

Aims

The aims of this chapter are to extend the ideas in the earlier chapter on subroutines and look in more depth at parameter passing, in particular using a variety of ways of passing arrays.

20.1   More on Parameter Passing

So far we have seen scalar parameters of type real, integer and logical. We will now look at numeric array parameters and character parameters. We need to introduce some technical terminology first. Don't panic if you don't fully understand the terminology as the examples should clarify things.

20.1.1   Assumed-Shape Array

An assumed-shape array is a nonpointer dummy argument array that takes its shape from the associated actual argument array.

© Springer International Publishing AG, part of Springer Nature 2018
I. Chivers and J. Sleightholme, *Introduction to Programming with Fortran*,
https://doi.org/10.1007/978-3-319-75502-1_20

20.1.2   Deferred-Shape Array

A deferred-shape array is an allocatable array or an array pointer. An allocatable array is an array that has the allocatable attribute and a specified rank, but its bounds, and hence shape, are determined by allocation or argument association.

20.1.3   Automatic Arrays

An automatic array is an explicit-shape array that is a local variable. Automatic arrays are only allowed in function and subroutine subprograms, and are declared in the specification part of the subprogram. At least one bound of an automatic array must be a nonconstant specification expression. The bounds are determined when the subprogram is called.

20.1.4   Allocatable Dummy Arrays

Fortran provides the ability to declare an array in the main program and allocate in a subroutine.

20.1.5   Keyword and Optional Arguments

Fortran provides the ability to supply the actual arguments to a procedure by keyword, and hence in any order.

   To do this the name of the dummy argument is referred to as the keyword and is specified in the actual argument list in the form

```
dummy-argument = actual-argument
```

   A number of points need to be noted when using keyword and optional arguments:

- if all the actual arguments use keywords, they may appear in any order.
- When only some of the actual arguments use keywords, the first part of the list must be positional followed by keyword arguments in any order.
- When using a mixture of positional and keyword arguments, once a keyword argument is used all subsequent arguments must be specified by keyword.
- if an actual argument is omitted the corresponding optional dummy argument must not be redefined or referenced, except as an argument to the present intrinsic function.

- if an optional dummy argument is at the end of the argument list then it can just be omitted from the actual argument list.
- Keyword arguments are needed when an optional argument not at the end of an argument list is omitted, unless all the remaining arguments are omitted as well.
- Keyword and optional arguments require explicit procedure interfaces, i.e., the procedure must be internal, a module procedure or have an interface block available in the calling program unit.

A number of the intrinsic procedures have optional arguments. Consult Appendix D for details. We look at a complete example using optional arguments in a later chapter.

20.2   Example 1: Assumed Shape Parameter Passing

We are going to use an example based on a main program and a subroutine that calculates the mean and standard deviation of an array of numbers. The subroutine has the following parameters:

- x - the array containing the real numbers.
- n - the number of elements in the array.
- mean - the mean of the numbers.
- std_dev - the standard deviation of the numbers.

Consider the following program and subroutine.

```
module statistics_module
  implicit none

contains
  subroutine stats(x, n, mean, std_dev)
    implicit none
    integer, intent (in) :: n
    real, intent (in), dimension (:) :: x
    real, intent (out) :: mean
    real, intent (out) :: std_dev
    real :: variance
    real :: sumxi, sumxi2
    integer :: i

    variance = 0.0
    sumxi = 0.0
    sumxi2 = 0.0
    do i = 1, n
      sumxi = sumxi + x(i)
      sumxi2 = sumxi2 + x(i)*x(i)
```

```
      end do
      mean = sumxi/n
      variance = (sumxi2-sumxi*sumxi/n)/(n-1)
      std_dev = sqrt(variance)
    end subroutine stats
  end module statistics_module

  program ch2001
    use statistics_module
    implicit none
    integer, parameter :: n = 10
    real, dimension (1:n) :: x
    real, dimension (-4:5) :: y
    real, dimension (10) :: z
    real, allocatable, dimension (:) :: t
    real :: m, sd
    integer :: i

    do i = 1, n
      x(i) = real(i)
    end do
    call stats(x, n, m, sd)
    print *, ' x'
    print 100, m, sd
100 format (' Mean = ', f7.3, ' Std Dev = ', &
      f7.3)
    y = x
    call stats(y, n, m, sd)
    print *, ' y'
    print 100, m, sd
    z = x
    call stats(z, 10, m, sd)
    print *, ' z'
    print 100, m, sd
    allocate (t(n))
    t = x
    call stats(t, 10, m, sd)
    print *, ' t'
    print 100, m, sd
  end program ch2001
```

A fundamental rule in modern Fortran is that the shape of an actual array argument and its associated dummy arguments are the same, i.e., they both must have the same rank and the same extents in each dimension. The best way to apply this rule is to use assumed-shape dummy array arguments as shown in the example above.

In the subroutine we have

```
real , intent(in) , dimension(:) :: x
```

where x is an assumed-shape dummy array argument, and it will assume the shape of the actual argument when the subroutine is called.

In two of the calls we have passed a variable n as the size of the array and used a literal integer constant (10) in the other two cases. Both parameter passing mechanisms work.

20.2.1 Notes

There are several restrictions when using assumed-shape arrays:

- The rank is equal to the number of colons, in this case 1.
- The lower bounds of the assumed-shape array are the specified lower bounds, if present, and 1 otherwise. In the example above it is 1 because we haven't specified a lower bound.
- The upper bounds will be determined on entry to the procedure and will be whatever values are needed to make sure that the extents along each dimension of the dummy argument are the same as the actual argument. In this case the upper bound will be n.
- An assumed-shape array must not be defined with the pointer or allocatable attribute in Fortran.
- When using an assumed-shape array an interface is mandatory. In this example it is provided by the the stats subroutine being a contained subroutine in a module, and the use of the module in the main program.

20.3 Example 2: Character Arguments and Assumed-Length Dummy Arguments

The types of parameters considered so far have been real, integer and logical. Character variables are slightly different because they have a length associated with them. Consider the following program and subroutine which, given the name of a file, opens it and reads values into the real array x:

```
module read_module
  implicit none

contains
  subroutine readin(name, x, n)
```

```fortran
      implicit none
      integer, intent (in) :: n
      real, dimension (:), intent (out) :: x
      character (len=*), intent (in) :: name
      integer :: i

      open (unit=10, file=name, status='old')
      do i = 1, n
        read (10, *) x(i)
      end do
      close (unit=10)
    end subroutine readin
  end module read_module

program ch2002
  use read_module
  implicit none
  real, allocatable, dimension (:) :: a
  integer :: nos, i
  character (len=20) :: filename

  print *, ' Type in the name of the data file'
  read '(a)', filename
  print *, ' Input the number of items'
  read *, nos
  allocate (a(1:nos))
  call readin(filename, a, nos)
  print *, ' data read in was'
  do i = 1, nos
    print *, ' ', a(i)
  end do
end program ch2002
```

The main program reads the file name from the user and passes it to the subroutine that reads in the data. The dummy argument name is of type assumed-length, and picks up the length from the actual argument filename in the calling routine, which is in this case 20 characters. An interface must be provided with assumed-shape dummy arguments, and this is achieved in this case by the subroutine being in a module.

20.4   Example 3: Rank 2 and Higher Arrays as Parameters

The following example illustrates the modern way of passing rank 2 and higher arrays as parameters. We start with a simple rank 2 example.

```
module matrix_module
  implicit none

contains
  subroutine matrix_bits(a, b, c, a_t, n)
    implicit none
    integer, intent (in) :: n
    real, dimension (:, :), intent (in) :: a, b
    real, dimension (:, :), intent (out) :: c, &
      a_t
    integer :: i, j, k
    real :: temp
!   matrix multiplication c=ab
    do i = 1, n
      do j = 1, n
        temp = 0.0
        do k = 1, n
          temp = temp + a(i, k)*b(k, j)
        end do
        c(i, j) = temp
      end do
    end do
!   calculate a_t transpose of a
!   set a_t to be transpose matrix a
    do i = 1, n
      do j = 1, n
        a_t(i, j) = a(j, i)
      end do
    end do
  end subroutine matrix_bits
end module matrix_module

program ch2003
  use matrix_module
  implicit none
  real, allocatable, dimension (:, :) :: one, &
    two, three, one_t
  integer :: i, n
```

```
print *, 'input size of matrices'
read *, n
allocate (one(1:n,1:n))
allocate (two(1:n,1:n))
allocate (three(1:n,1:n))
allocate (one_t(1:n,1:n))
do i = 1, n
  print *, 'input row ', i, ' of one'
  read *, one(i, 1:n)
end do
do i = 1, n
  print *, 'input row ', i, ' of two'
  read *, two(i, 1:n)
end do
call matrix_bits(one, two, three, one_t, n)
print *, ' matrix three:'
do i = 1, n
  print *, three(i, 1:n)
end do
print *, ' matrix one_t:'
do i = 1, n
  print *, one_t(i, 1:n)
end do
end program ch2003
```

The subroutine is doing a matrix multiplication and transpose. There are intrinsic functions in Fortran called `matmul` and `transpose` that provide the same functionality as the subroutine. One of the problems at the end of the chapter is to replace the code in the subroutine with calls to the intrinsic functions.

20.4.1 Notes

The dummy array and actual array arguments look the same but there is a difference:

- The dummy array arguments a, b, c, a_t are all assumed-shape arrays and take the shape of the actual array arguments one, two, three and one_t, respectively.
- The actual array arguments one, two, three and one_t in the main program are allocatable arrays or deferred-shape arrays. An allocatable array is an array that has an allocatable attribute. Its bounds and shape are declared when the array is allocated, hence deferred-shape.

20.5   Example 4: Automatic Arrays and Median Calculation

This example looks at the calculation of the median of a set of numbers and also illustrates the use of an automatic array.

The median is the middle value of a list, i.e., the smallest number such that at least half the numbers in the list are no greater. If the list has an odd number of entries, the median is the middle entry in the list after sorting the list into ascending order. If the list has an even number of entries, the median is equal to the sum of the two middle (after sorting) numbers divided by two. One way to determine the median computationally is to sort the numbers and choose the item in the middle.

Wirth classifies sorting into simple and advanced, and his three simple methods are as follows:

- Insertion sorting — The items are considered one at a time and each new item is inserted into the appropriate position relative to the previously sorted item. If you have ever played bridge then you have probably used this method.
- Selection sorting — First the smallest (or largest) item is chosen and is set aside from the rest. Then the process is repeated for the next smallest item and set aside in the next position. This process is repeated until all items are sorted.
- Exchange sorting — if two items are found to be out of order they are interchanged. This process is repeated until no more exchanges take place.

Knuth also identifies the above three sorting methods. For more information on sorting the Knuth and Wirth books are good starting places. Knuth is a little old (1973) compared to Wirth (1986), but it is still a very good coverage. Knuth uses mix assembler to code the examples whilst the Wirth book uses Modula 2, and is therefore easier to translate into modern Fortran.

In the example below we use an exchange sort:

```
module statistics_module
  implicit none

contains
  subroutine stats(x, n, mean, std_dev, median)
    implicit none
    integer, intent (in) :: n
    real, intent (in), dimension (:) :: x
    real, intent (out) :: mean
    real, intent (out) :: std_dev
    real, intent (out) :: median
    real, dimension (1:n) :: y
    real :: variance
    real :: sumxi, sumxi2

    sumxi = 0.0
```

```
   sumxi2 = 0.0
   variance = 0.0
   sumxi = sum(x)
   sumxi2 = sum(x*x)
   mean = sumxi/n
   variance = (sumxi2-sumxi*sumxi/n)/(n-1)
   std_dev = sqrt(variance)
   y = x
   if (mod(n,2)==0) then
     median = (find(n/2)+find((n/2)+1))/2
   else
     median = find((n/2)+1)
   end if
contains
   real function find(k)
     implicit none
     integer, intent (in) :: k
     integer :: l, r, i, j
     real :: t1, t2

     l = 1
     r = n
     do while (l<r)
       t1 = y(k)
       i = l
       j = r
       do
         do while (y(i)<t1)
           i = i + 1
         end do
         do while (t1<y(j))
           j = j - 1
         end do
         if (i<=j) then
           t2 = y(i)
           y(i) = y(j)
           y(j) = t2
           i = i + 1
           j = j - 1
         end if
         if (i>j) exit
       end do
       if (j<k) then
         l = i
       end if
```

```
            if (k<i) then
              r = j
            end if
          end do
        find = y(k)
      end function find
    end subroutine stats
  end module statistics_module

  program ch2004
    use statistics_module
    implicit none
    integer :: n
    integer :: i
    real, allocatable, dimension (:) :: x
    real :: m, sd, median
    integer, dimension (8) :: timing

    n = 1000000
    do i = 1, 3
      print *, ' n = ', n
      allocate (x(1:n))
      call random_number(x)
      x = x*1000
      call date_and_time(values=timing)
      print *, ' initial '
      print *, timing(6), timing(7), timing(8)
      call stats(x, n, m, sd, median)
      print *, ' Mean = ', m
      print *, ' Standard deviation = ', sd
      print *, ' Median is = ', median
      call date_and_time(values=timing)
      print *, timing(6), timing(7), timing(8)
      n = n*10
      deallocate (x)
    end do
  end program ch2004
```

In the subroutine stats the array y is automatic. It will be allocated automatically when we call the subroutine. We use this array as a work array to hold the sorted data. We then use this sorted array to determine the median.

Note the use of the sum intrinsic in this example:

```
sumxi=sum(x)
sumxi2=sum(x*x)
```

These statements replace the do loop from the earlier example. A good optimising compiler would not make two passes over the data with these two statements.

20.5.1 Internal Subroutines and Scope

The `stats` subroutine contains the `find` subroutine. The `stats` subroutine has access to the following variables

- `x, n, mean, std_dev, median` — these are made available as they are passed in as parameters.
- `y, variance, sumxi, sumxi2` — are local to the subroutine `stats`.

The subroutine `find` has access to the above as it is contained within subroutine `stats`. It also has the following local variables that are only available within subroutine `selection`

- `i, j, k, minimum`

This program uses an algorithm developed by Hoare to determine the median. The number of computations required to find the median is approximately 2 * n.

The limiting factor with this algorithm is the amount of installed memory. The program will crash on systems with a failure to allocate the automatic array. This is a drawback of automatic arrays in that there is no mechanism to handle this failure gracefully. You would then need to use allocatable local work arrays. The drawback here is that the programmer is then responsible for the deallocation of these arrays. Memory leaks are then possible.

20.6 Example 5: Recursive Subroutines – Quicksort

In Chap. 12 we saw an example of recursive functions. This example illustrates the use of a recursive subroutine. In this example we use the additional form of the subroutine header that was required when recursive procedure support was introduced in Fortran 90. The Fortran 2018 standard makes this form optional. It uses a simple implementation of Hoare's Quicksort. References are given in the bibliography. We took the algorithm from Wirth's book for our example.

The program times the various components parts of the program

- dynamic allocation of the real array
- use the `random_number` subroutine to generate the numbers
- call the `sort_data` subroutine to sort the data
- print out the first 10 sorted elements
- deallocate the array

We also use the `date_and_time` intrinsic subroutine to provide the timing details.

```
module sort_data_module
  implicit none

contains
  subroutine sort_data(raw_data, how_many)
    implicit none
    integer, intent (in) :: how_many
    real, intent (inout), dimension (:) :: &
      raw_data

    call quicksort(1, how_many)
  contains
    recursive subroutine quicksort(l, r)
      implicit none
      integer, intent (in) :: l, r
!     local variables
      integer :: i, j
      real :: v, t

      i = l
      j = r
      v = raw_data(int((l+r)/2))
      do
        do while (raw_data(i)<v)
          i = i + 1
        end do
        do while (v<raw_data(j))
          j = j - 1
        end do
        if (i<=j) then
          t = raw_data(i)
          raw_data(i) = raw_data(j)
          raw_data(j) = t
          i = i + 1
          j = j - 1
        end if
        if (i>j) exit
      end do
      if (l<j) then
        call quicksort(l, j)
      end if
```

```
      if (i<r) then
        call quicksort(i, r)
      end if
    end subroutine quicksort
  end subroutine sort_data
end module sort_data_module

program ch2005
  use sort_data_module
  implicit none
  integer, parameter :: n = 10000000
  real, allocatable, dimension (:) :: x
  integer, dimension (8) :: timing
  real :: t1, t2
  character *30, dimension (4) :: heading = [ &
    ' Allocate =                    ', &
    ' Random number generation = ', &
    ' Sort =                       ', &
    ' Deallocate =                 ' ]

  call date_and_time(values=timing)
  print *, ' Program starts'
  write (unit=*, fmt=100) timing(1:3), &
    timing(5:7)
100 format (2x, i4, 2('/',i2), ' ', 2(i2,':'), &
    i2)
  t1 = td()
  allocate (x(n))
  t2 = td()
  write (unit=*, fmt=110) heading(1), (t2-t1)
110 format (a30, f8.3)
  t1 = t2
!
! Random number generation
  call random_number(x)
  t2 = td()
  write (unit=*, fmt=110) heading(2), (t2-t1)
  t1 = t2
!
! Sorting
  call sort_data(x, n)
  t2 = td()
  write (unit=*, fmt=110) heading(3), (t2-t1)
  print *, ' First 10 sorted numbers are'
  write (unit=*, fmt=120) x(1:10)
```

```
120 format (2x, e14.6)
   t1 = t2
!
! Deallocation
   deallocate (x)
   t2 = td()
   write (unit=*, fmt=110) heading(4), (t2-t1)
   call date_and_time(values=timing)
   print *, ' Program terminates'
   write (unit=*, fmt=100) timing(1:3), &
     timing(5:7)

contains

   function td()
     real :: td

     call date_and_time(values=timing)
     td = 60*timing(6) + timing(7) + &
       real(timing(8))/1000.0
   end function td
end program ch2005
```

20.6.1   Note — Recursive Subroutine

The actual sorting is done in the recursive subroutine QuickSort. The actual algorithm is taken from the Wirth book. See the bibliography for a reference.

Recursion provides us with a very clean and expressive way of solving many problems. There will be instances where it is worthwhile removing the overhead of recursion, but the first priority is the production of a program that is correct. It is pointless having a very efficient but incorrect solution.

We will look again at recursion and efficiency in a later chapter and see under what criteria we can replace recursion with iteration.

20.6.2   Note — Flexible Design

The QuickSort recursive routine can be replaced with another sorting algorithm and we can maintain the interface to sort_data. We can thus decouple the implementation of the actual sorting routine from the defined interface. We would only need to recompile the `sort_data` routine and we could relink using the already compiled main routine.

A later chapter looks at a non recursive implementation of quicksort where we look at some of the ways of rewriting the above program by replacing the recursive quicksort with the non recursive version.

We call the `date_and_time` intrinsic subroutine to get timing information. The first three values are the year, month and day, and 5, 6 and 7 provide the hour minute and second. The last element of the array is milliseconds.

20.7   Example 6: Allocatable Dummy Arrays

In the examples so far allocation of arrays has taken place in the main program and the arrays have been passed into subroutines and functions.

In this example the allocation takes place in the `read_data` subroutine.

```
module read_data_module
  implicit none

contains
  subroutine read_data(file_name, raw_data, &
    how_many)
    implicit none
    character (len=*), intent (in) :: file_name
    integer, intent (in) :: how_many
    real, intent (out), allocatable, &
      dimension (:) :: raw_data
!   local variables
    integer :: i

    allocate (raw_data(1:how_many))
    open (unit=1, file=file_name, status='old')
    do i = 1, how_many
      read (unit=1, fmt=*) raw_data(i)
    end do
  end subroutine read_data
end module read_data_module

module sort_data_module
  implicit none
```

```
contains
  subroutine sort_data(raw_data, how_many)
    implicit none
    integer, intent (in) :: how_many
    real, intent (inout), dimension (:) :: &
      raw_data

    call quicksort(1, how_many)
  contains
    recursive subroutine quicksort(l, r)
      implicit none
      integer, intent (in) :: l, r
!     local variables
      integer :: i, j
      real :: v, t


      i = l
      j = r
      v = raw_data(int((l+r)/2))
      do
        do while (raw_data(i)<v)
          i = i + 1
        end do
        do while (v<raw_data(j))
          j = j - 1
        end do
        if (i<=j) then
          t = raw_data(i)
          raw_data(i) = raw_data(j)
          raw_data(j) = t
          i = i + 1
          j = j - 1
        end if
        if (i>j) exit
      end do
      if (l<j) then
        call quicksort(l, j)
      end if
      if (i<r) then
        call quicksort(i, r)
      end if
    end subroutine quicksort
  end subroutine sort_data
end module sort_data_module
```

```
module print_data_module
  implicit none

contains
  subroutine print_data(raw_data, how_many)
    implicit none
    integer, intent (in) :: how_many
    real, intent (in), dimension (:) :: raw_data
!   local variables
    integer :: i

    open (file='sorted.txt', unit=2)
    do i = 1, how_many
      write (unit=2, fmt=*) raw_data(i)
    end do
    close (2)
  end subroutine print_data
end module print_data_module

program ch2006
  use read_data_module
  use sort_data_module
  use print_data_module
  implicit none
  integer :: how_many
  character (len=20) :: file_name
  real, allocatable, dimension (:) :: raw_data
  integer, dimension (8) :: timing

  print *, ' how many data items are there?'
  read *, how_many
  print *, ' what is the file name?'
  read '(a)', file_name
  call date_and_time(values=timing)
  print *, ' initial'
  print *, timing(6), timing(7), timing(8)
  call read_data(file_name, raw_data, how_many)
  call date_and_time(values=timing)
  print *, ' allocate and read'
  print *, timing(6), timing(7), timing(8)
  call sort_data(raw_data, how_many)
  call date_and_time(values=timing)
  print *, ' sort'
  print *, timing(6), timing(7), timing(8)
  call print_data(raw_data, how_many)
```

```
   call date_and_time(values=timing)
   print *, ' print'
   print *, timing(6), timing(7), timing(8)
   print *, ' '
   print *, ' data written to file sorted.txt'
end program ch2006
```

We now have a choice of where we do the allocation. This is more flexible than having to do the allocation in the main program, which is effectively a more Fortran 77 style of programming.

20.8   Example 7: Elemental Subroutines

We saw an example in Chap. 12 of elemental functions. Here is an example of an elemental subroutine.

```
module swap_module
   implicit none

contains
   elemental subroutine swap(x, y)
      integer, intent (inout) :: x, y
      integer :: temp

      temp = x
      x = y
      y = temp
   end subroutine swap
end module swap_module

program ch2007
   use swap_module
   implicit none
   integer, dimension (10) :: a, b
   integer :: i

   do i = 1, 10
     a(i) = i
     b(i) = i*i
   end do
   print *, a
   print *, b
   call swap(a, b)
```

```
   print *, a
   print *, b
end program ch2007
```

The subroutine is written as if the arguments are scalar, but works with arrays!
User defined elemental procedures came in with Fortran 95.

20.9   Summary

We now have a lot of the tools to start tackling problems in a structured and modular
way, breaking problems down into manageable chunks and designing subprograms
for each of the tasks.

20.10   Problems

20.1 Below is the random number program that was used to generate the data sets
for the Quicksort example:

```
program ch2008
   implicit none
   integer :: n
   integer :: i
   real, allocatable, dimension (:) :: x

   print *, ' how many values ?'
   read *, n
   allocate (x(1:n))
   call random_number(x)
   x = x*1000
   open (unit=10, file='random.txt')
   do i = 1, n
     write (10, 100) x(i)
   end do
100 format (f8.3)
end program ch2008
```

Run the Quick_Sort program in this chapter with the data file as input. Obtain
timing details.

What percentage of the time does the program spend in each subroutine? Is it
worth trying to make the sort much more efficient given these timings?

20.2 Try using the operating system SORT command to sort the file. What timing figures do you get now?

Was it worth writing a program?

20.3 Consider the following program:

```
program ch2009

! program to test array subscript checking
! when the array is passed as an argument.

  implicit none
  integer, parameter :: array_size = 10
  integer :: i
  integer, dimension (array_size) :: a

  do i = 1, array_size
    a(i) = i
  end do
  call sub01(a, array_size)
end program ch2009
subroutine sub01(a, array_size)
  implicit none
  integer, intent (in) :: array_size
  integer, intent (in), dimension (array_size) &
    :: a
  integer :: i
  integer :: atotal = 0
  integer :: rtotal = 0

  do i = 1, array_size
    rtotal = rtotal + a(i)
  end do
  do i = 1, array_size + 1
    atotal = atotal + a(i)
  end do
  print *, ' Apparent total is ', atotal
  print *, ' real total is ', rtotal
end subroutine sub01
```

The key thing to note is that we haven't used a module procedure (we haven't provided an interface for the subroutine) and we have an error in the subroutine where we go outside the array. Run this program. What answer do you get for the apparent total?

Are there any compiler flags or switches which will enable you to trap this error?

20.4 Use the intrinsic functions `matmul` and `transpose` to replace the current Fortran 77 style code in program ch2003.

20.11   Bibliography

Hoare C.A.R., Algorithm 63, Partition; Algorithm 64, Quicksort, p.321; Algorithm 65: FIND, Comm. of the ACM, 4 p.321–322, 1961.
Hoare C.A.R., Proof of a program: FIND, Comm A.C.M., 13, No 1 (1970) 39–45
Hoare C.A.R., Proof of a recursive program: Quicksort, Comp. J., 14, No 4 (1971) 391–95.
Knuth D.E., The Art of Computer programming, Volume 3 — Sorting and Searching, Addison-Wesley, 1973.
Wirth N., Algorithms and Data Structures, Prentice-Hall, 1986, ISBN 0-13-021999-1.

20.12   Commercial Numerical and Statistical Subroutine Libraries

There are two major suppliers of commercial numerical and statistical libraries:

- NAG: Numerical Algorithms Group

and

- Rogue Wave Software

  They can be found at:

  ```
  https://www.nag.co.uk/
  ```

and

  ```
  https://www.roguewave.com/
  ```

respectively. Their libraries are written by numerical analysts, and are fully tested and well documented. They are under constant development and available for a wide range of hardware platforms and compilers. Parallel versions are also available. In a later chapter we look at using a sorting routine from the Nag SMP & Multicore library.

Chapter 21
Modules

Common sense is the best distributed commodity in the world,
for every man is convinced that he is well supplied with it.

Descartes

Aims

The aims of this chapter are to look at the facilities found in Fortran provided by modules, in particular:

- The use of a module to aid in the consistent definition of precision throughout a program and subprograms.
- The use of modules for global data.
- The use of modules for derived data types.
- Modules containing procedures
- A module for timing programs
- Public, private and protected attributes
- The use statement and its extensions

21.1 Introduction

We have now covered the major executable building blocks in Fortran and they are

- The main program unit
- functions
- subroutines

© Springer International Publishing AG, part of Springer Nature 2018
I. Chivers and J. Sleightholme, *Introduction to Programming with Fortran*,
https://doi.org/10.1007/978-3-319-75502-1_21

and these provide us with the tools to solve many problems using just a main program, and one or more external and internal procedures. Both external and internal procedures communicate through their argument lists, whilst internal procedures have access to data in their host program units.

We have also introduced modules. The first set of examples was in the chapter on functions. The second set were in the chapter on derived types and the third set were in the subroutine chapters.

We will now look at examples of modules in more detail for

- Precision definition.
- Global data
- Modules containing procedures
- Derived type definition
- Simple timing information of a program

Modules provide the code organisational mechanism in Fortran and can be thought of as the equivalent of classes in C++, Java and C#. They are one of the most important features of modern Fortran.

21.2   Basic Module Syntax

The form of a module is

```
module module_name
  . .
  . .
  . .
end module module_name
```

and the specifications and definitions contained within it is made available in the program units that need to access it by

```
use module_name
```

The `use` statement must be the first statement after the program, function or subroutine statement.

21.3   Modules for Global Data

So far the only way that a program unit can communicate with a procedure is through the argument list. Sometimes this is very cumbersome, especially if a number of procedures want access to the same data, and it means long argument lists. The problem can be solved using modules; e.g., by defining the precision to which you wish to work and any constants defined to that precision which may be needed by a number of procedures.

21.4   Example 1: Modules for Precision Specification and Constant Definition

In the chapter on arithmetic we introduced the features in Fortran that enable us to specify the precision of real numbers.

For the real numeric kind types, we used

- sp - single precision
- dp - double precision
- qp - quad precision

and here is the Fortran code segment from the program example.

```
integer, parameter :: &
  sp = selected_real_kind( 6, 37)
integer, parameter :: &
  dp = selected_real_kind(15, 307)
integer, parameter :: &
  qp = selected_real_kind(30, 291)
```

In this example we are going to package the above in a module, and then use the module to enable us to choose a working precision for the program and associated functions and subroutines. This module will be referred to in many examples in the book.

We will also have a second module with a set of physical and mathematical constants.

```
module precision_module
  implicit none
  integer, parameter :: sp = selected_real_kind( &
    6, 37)
  integer, parameter :: dp = selected_real_kind( &
    15, 307)
  integer, parameter :: qp = selected_real_kind( &
    30, 291)
end module precision_module
```

```
module maths_module

  use precision_module, wp => dp

  implicit none

  real (wp), parameter :: c = 299792458.0_wp
! units m s-1

  real (wp), parameter :: e = &
     2.718281828459045235360287471352662497_wp

  real (wp), parameter :: g = 9.812420_wp
! 9.780 356 m s-2 at sea level on the equator
! 9.812 420 m s-2 at sea level in London
! 9.832 079 m s-2 at sea level at the poles

  real (wp), parameter :: pi = &
     3.141592653589793238462643383279502884_wp

end module maths_module

module sub1_module
  implicit none

contains

  subroutine sub1(radius, area, circumference)

    use precision_module, wp => dp
    use maths_module
    implicit none
    real (wp), intent (in) :: radius
    real (wp), intent (out) :: area, &
      circumference

    area = pi*radius*radius
    circumference = 2.0_wp*pi*radius

  end subroutine sub1

end module sub1_module
```

```
program ch2101

    use precision_module, wp => dp
    use sub1_module

    implicit none

    real (wp) :: r, a, c

    print *, 'radius?'
    read *, r
    call sub1(r, a, c)
    print *, ' for radius = ', r
    print *, ' area = ', a
    print *, ' circumference = ', c

end program ch2101
```

In our example we have

```
use precision_module , wp => dp
```

and the wp => dp is called a rename-list in Fortran terminology. We are using it in this example to make wp point to the dp precision in the module.

Thus we can chose the working precision of our program very easily.

The kind type parameter wp is then used with all the real type declaration e.g.,

```
real (wp):: r ,a,c
```

To make sure that all floating point calculations are performed to the working precision specified by wp any constants such as 2.0 in subroutine Sub1 are specified as const_wp e.g.,

```
2.0_wp
```

We set e and pi to over 33 digits as this is the number in a 128 bit real. This ensures that all calculations are carried out accurately to the maximum precision.

21.5 Example 2: Modules for Globally Sharing Data

The following example uses a module to define a parameter and two arrays. The module also contains three subroutines that have access to the data in the module. The main program has the statement

```
use data_module
```

which interfaces to the three subroutines.

Note that in this example the calls to the subroutines have no parameters. They
work with the data contained in the module.

```
module data_module
  implicit none
  integer, parameter :: n = 12
  real, dimension (1:n) :: rainfall
  real, dimension (1:n) :: sorted

contains
  subroutine readdata
    implicit none
    integer :: i
    character (len=40) :: filename

    print *, ' What is the filename ?'
    read *, filename
    open (unit=100, file=filename, status='old')
    do i = 1, n
      read (100, *) rainfall(i)
    end do
  end subroutine readdata

  subroutine sortdata
    implicit none

    sorted = rainfall
    call selection
  contains
    subroutine selection
      implicit none
      integer :: i, j, k
      real :: minimum

      do i = 1, n - 1
        k = i
        minimum = sorted(i)
        do j = i + 1, n
          if (sorted(j)<minimum) then
            k = j
            minimum = sorted(k)
          end if
```

```
              end do
            sorted(k) = sorted(i)
            sorted(i) = minimum
          end do
      end subroutine selection
    end subroutine sortdata

    subroutine printdata
      implicit none
      integer :: i

      print *, ' original data is '
      do i = 1, n
        print 100, rainfall(i)
      end do
      print *, ' Sorted data is '
      do i = 1, n
        print 100, sorted(i)
      end do
100   format (1x, f7.1)
      end subroutine printdata
    end module data_module

    program ch2102
      use data_module
      implicit none

      call readdata
      call sortdata
      call printdata
    end program ch2102
```

21.6 Modules for Derived Data Types

When using derived data types and passing them as arguments to procedures, both the actual arguments and dummy arguments must be of the same type, i.e., they must be declared with reference to the same type definition. The only way this can be achieved is by using modules. The user defined type is declared in a module and each program unit that requires that type uses the module.

21.7   Example 3: Person Data Type

In this example we have a user defined type person which we wish to use in the
main program and pass arguments of this type to the subroutines read_data and
stats. In order to have the type person available to two subroutines and the
main program we have defined person in a module personal_module and
then made the module available to each program unit with the statement

```
use personal_module
```

Note that we have put both subroutines in one module.

```
module personal_module
  implicit none
  type person
    real :: weight
    integer :: age
    character :: gender
  end type person
end module personal_module
module subs_module
  use personal_module
  implicit none
contains
  subroutine read_data(data, no)
    implicit none
    type (person), dimension (:), allocatable, &
      intent (out) :: data
    integer, intent (out) :: no
    integer :: i

    print *, 'input number of patients'
    read *, no
    allocate (data(1:no))

    do i = 1, no
      print *, 'for person ', i
      print *, 'weight ?'
      read *, data(i)%weight
      print *, 'age ?'
      read *, data(i)%age
      print *, 'gender ?'
      read *, data(i)%gender
    end do
  end subroutine read_data
```

```
    subroutine stats(data, no, m_a, f_a)
      implicit none
      type (person), dimension (:), &
        intent (in) :: data
      real, intent (out) :: m_a, f_a
      integer, intent (in) :: no
      integer :: i, no_f, no_m

      m_a = 0.0
      f_a = 0.0
      no_f = 0
      no_m = 0
      do i = 1, no
        if (data(i)%gender=='M' .or. &
                  data(i)%gender=='m' &
          ) then
          m_a = m_a + data(i)%weight
          no_m = no_m + 1
        else if (data(i)%gender=='F' .or. &
            data(i)%gender=='f') then
          f_a = f_a + data(i)%weight
          no_f = no_f + 1
        end if
      end do
      if (no_m>0) then
        m_a = m_a/no_m
      end if
      if (no_f>0) then
        f_a = f_a/no_f
      end if
    end subroutine stats
  end module subs_module
  program ch2103
    use personal_module
    use subs_module
    implicit none
    type (person), dimension (:), allocatable :: &
      patient
    integer :: no_of_patients
    real :: male_average, female_average

    call read_data(patient, no_of_patients)
    call stats(patient, no_of_patients, &
      male_average, female_average)
    print *, 'average male weight is ', &
```

```
      male_average
  print *, 'average female weight is ', &
      female_average
end program ch2103
```

21.8   Example 4: A Module for Simple Timing of a Program

It is a common requirement to need timing details on how long parts of a program take. In this module we have a `start_timing` and `end_timing` subroutines and a `time_difference` real function. We will be using this module in several examples in subsequent chapters.

```
module timing_module

  implicit none
  integer, dimension (8), private :: dt
  real, private :: h, m, s, ms, tt
  real, private :: last_tt

contains

  subroutine start_timing()
    implicit none

    call date_and_time(values=dt)
    print 100, dt(1:3), dt(5:8)
    h = real(dt(5))
    m = real(dt(6))
    s = real(dt(7))
    ms = real(dt(8))
    last_tt = 60*(60*h+m) + s + ms/1000.0
100 format (1x, i4, '/', i2, '/', i2, 1x, i2, &
        ':', i2, ':', i2, 1x, i3)
  end subroutine start_timing

  subroutine end_timing()
    implicit none

    call date_and_time(values=dt)
    print 100, dt(1:3), dt(5:8)
100 format (1x, i4, '/', i2, '/', i2, 1x, i2, &
```

```
      ':', i2, ':', i2, 1x, i3)
  end subroutine end_timing

  real function time_difference()
    implicit none

    tt = 0.0
    call date_and_time(values=dt)
    h = real(dt(5))
    m = real(dt(6))
    s = real(dt(7))
    ms = real(dt(8))
    tt = 60*(60*h+m) + s + ms/1000.0
    time_difference = tt - last_tt
    last_tt = tt
  end function time_difference

end module timing_module
```

21.9 private, public and protected Attributes

With the examples of modules so far every entity in a module has been accessible to each program unit that 'uses' the module. By default all entities in a module have the public attribute, but sometimes it is desirable to limit the access. If entities have the private attribute this limits the possibility of inadvertent changes to a variable by another program unit.

Example of using public and private attributes:

```
real, public    : : a, b, c
integer, private :: i, j, k
```

If a variable in a module is declared to be public, its access can be partially restricted by also giving it the protected attribute. This means that the variable can still be seen by program units that use the module but its value cannot be changed e.g.

```
integer, public, protected:: i
```

21.10   The use Statement

In its simplest form the use statement is

```
use module_name
```

which then makes all the module's public entities available to the program unit. There may be times when only certain entities should be available to a particular program unit. In Example 1 subroutine sub1 'uses' maths_module but only needs pi and not c, e and g. The use statement could therefore be

```
use maths_module, only: pi
```

There are also times when an entity in a module needs to have its name changed when used in a program unit. For example variable g in maths_module needs to be called gravity in subroutine sub1 so the use statement becomes

```
use maths_module, gravity=> g
```

We have also used this facility in example 1 where we renamed dp to wp.

21.11   Notes on Module Usage and Compilation

In the examples so far we have organised our code using one file. The file will comprise one or more of the following program units:

- main program
- subroutine
- function
- module

Another way of organising our code is to use several files and include statements.
   The next example shows a way of doing this.

21.12   Example 5: Modules and Include Statements

Here is the program source.

```
include 'precision_module.f90'
include 'maths_module.f90'
include 'sub1_module.f90'
```

```
program ch2105

  use precision_module, wp => dp
  use sub1_module

  implicit none

  real (wp) :: r, a, c

  print *, 'radius?'
  read *, r
  call sub1(r, a, c)
  print *, ' for radius = ', r
  print *, ' area = ', a
  print *, ' circumference = ', c

end program ch2105
```

and we will use both styles throughout the rest of the book.

21.13   Formal Syntax

The following is taken from the Fortran standard and describes more fully requirements in the interface area.

21.13.1 Interface

The interface of a procedure determines the forms of reference through which it may
be invoked. The procedures interface consists of its name, binding label, generic
identifiers, characteristics, and the names of its dummy arguments. The characteristics and binding label of a procedure are fixed, but the remainder of the interface
may differ in differing contexts, except that for a separate module procedure body
(15.6.2.5), the dummy argument names and whether it has the NON_RECURSIVE
attribute shall be the same as in its corresponding module procedure interface body
(15.4.3.2).

An abstract interface is a set of procedure characteristics with the dummy argument
names.

21.13.2   Implicit and Explicit Interfaces

Within the scope of a procedure identifier, the interface of the procedure is either explicit or implicit. The interface of an internal procedure, module procedure, or intrinsic procedure is always explicit in such a scope.

The interface of a subroutine or a function with a separate result name is explicit within the subprogram where the name is accessible.

21.13.3   Explicit Interface

A procedure other than a statement function shall have an explicit interface if it is referenced and

- a reference to the procedure appears

  - with an argument keyword, or
  - in a context that requires it to be pure,

- the procedure has a dummy argument that

  - has the `allocatable`, `optional`, `pointer`, `target`, or `value` attribute,
  - is an assumed-shape array,
  - is a coarray,
  - is polymorphic,

- the procedure has a result that

  - is an array,
  - is a pointer or is allocatable, or
  - has a nonassumed type parameter value that is not a constant expression,

- the procedure is elemental

21.14   Summary

We have now introduced the concept of a module, another type of program unit, probably one of the most important features of modern Fortran. We have seen in this chapter how they can be used:

- Define global data.
- Define derived data types.
- Contain explicit procedure interfaces.
- Package together procedures.

This is a very powerful addition to the language, especially when constructing large programs and procedure libraries.

21.15   Problems

21.1 Write two functions, one to calculate the volume of a cylinder $\pi r^2 l$ where the radius is r and the length is l, and the other to calculate the area of the base of the cylinder πr^2

Define π as a parameter in a module which is used by the two functions. Now write a main program which prompts the user for the values of r and l, calls the two functions and prints out the results.

21.2 Make all the real variables in the above problem have 15 significant digits and a range of 10^{-307} to 10^{+307}. Use a module.

Chapter 22
Data Structuring in Fortran

The good teacher is a guide who helps others to dispense with his services.

R. S. Peters, Ethics and Education

Aims

The aims of this chapter are to look at several complete examples illustrating data structuring in Fortran using the following

- Singly linked lists
- Ragged arrays
- A perfectly balanced tree
- A date data type

22.1 Introduction

This chapter looks at simple data structuring in Fortran using a range of examples. We use modules throughout to define the data structures that we will be working with. The chapter starts with a number of pointer examples.

22.2 Example 1: Singly Linked List: Reading an Unknown Amount of Text

Conceptually a singly linked list consists of a sequence of boxes with compartments. In the simplest case the first compartment holds a data item and the second contains directions to the next box.

© Springer International Publishing AG, part of Springer Nature 2018   359
I. Chivers and J. Sleightholme, *Introduction to Programming with Fortran*,
https://doi.org/10.1007/978-3-319-75502-1_22

In the diagram below we have a singly linked list that holds characters Jane. We assume that the address of the start of the list is 100. We assume 4 bytes per character (a 32 bit word) and 4 bytes per pointer.

- Element 1 is at address 100 and holds the character J and a pointer to the next element at address 108.
- Element 2 holds the character a and a pointer to the next element at address 116.
- Element 3 holds the character n and a pointer to the next element at address 124.
- Element 4 holds the character e and does not point to anything - we use the null pointer.

```
[J : 108] -> [a : 116] -> [n : 124] -> [e : null]
```

We can construct a data structure in Fortran to work with a singly linked list by defining a link data type with two components, a character variable and a pointer variable to a link data type. A complete program to do this is given below:

```
module link_module
  type link
    character (len=1) :: x
    type (link), pointer :: next => null()
  end type link
end module link_module

program ch2201
  use link_module
  implicit none
  character (len=80) :: fname
  integer :: io_stat_number = 0
  type (link), pointer :: root, current
  integer :: i = 0, n
  character (len=:), allocatable :: string

  print *, ' Type in the file name ? '
  read '(a)', fname
  open (unit=1, file=fname, status='old')

  allocate (root)

! read first data item

  read (unit=1, fmt='(a)', advance='no', &
    iostat=io_stat_number) root%x
  if (io_stat_number/=-1) then
    i = i + 1
    allocate (root%next)
```

```
      end if
      current => root

  ! read the rest

      do while (associated(current%next))
        current => current%next
        read (unit=1, fmt='(a)', advance='no', &
          iostat=io_stat_number) current%x
        if (io_stat_number/=-1) then
          i = i + 1
          allocate (current%next)
        end if
      end do

      print *, i, ' characters read'

      n = i
      allocate (character(len=n) :: string)
      i = 0
      current => root
      do while (associated(current%next))
        i = i + 1
        string(i:i) = current%x
        current => current%next
      end do
      print *, 'data read was:'
      print *, string
    end program ch2201
```

The first thing of interest is the type definition for the singly linked list. We have

```
    module link_module
      type link
        character (len=1) :: c
        type (link) , pointer   :: next => null()
      end type link
    end module link_module
```

and we call the new type `link`. It comprises two component parts: the first holds a character c, and the second holds a pointer called `next` to allow us to refer to another instance of type `link`.

We use the intrinsic `null()` to provide an initial value for the `next` pointer.

The next item of interest is the variable definition. Here we define two variables `root` and `current` to be pointers that point to items of type `link`. In Fortran when we define a variable to be a pointer we also have to define what it is allowed to point to. This is a very useful restriction on pointers, and helps make using them more secure. The first executable statement

```
allocate(root)
```

requests that the variable root be allocated memory. The next statement reads a character from the file. We are using a number of additional features of the read statement, including

```
iostat=io_stat_number
advance='no'
```

and the two options combine to provide the ability to read an arbitrary number of text from a file a character at a time. If there is data in the file we allocate root%next and increment the character count i. We then loop until we reach end of file. When end of file is reached the while loop will terminate as next is null(). The statement

```
current => root
```

means that both current and root point to the same physical memory location, and this holds a character data item and a pointer. We must do this as we have to know where the start of the list is. This is now our responsibility, not the compilers. Without this statement we are not able to do anything with the list except fill it up - hardly very useful.

When end of file is reached the while loop will terminate as next is null(). We then print out the number of characters read. We then allocate a character variable of the correct size. The next statement

```
current => root
```

means that we are back at the start of the list, and in a position to traverse the list and copy each character from the linked list to the word character variable.

There is thus the concept with the pointer variable current of it providing us with a window into memory where the complete linked list is held, and we look at one part of the list at a time. Both while loops use the intrinsic function associated to check the association status of a pointer.

It is recommended that this program be typed in, compiled and executed. It is surprisingly difficult to believe that it will actually read in a completely arbitrary amount of text from a file. Seeing is believing.

22.3 Example 2: Reading in an Arbitrary Number of Reals Using a Linked List and Copying to an Array

In this example we will look at using a singly linked list to read in an arbitrary amount of data and then allocating an array to copy it to for normal numeric calculations at run time. Here is the program.

```
module link_module
  type link
    real :: x
    type (link), pointer :: next => null()
  end type link
end module link_module

program ch2202
  use link_module
  implicit none
  character (len=80) :: fname
  integer :: io_stat_number = 0
  type (link), pointer :: root, current
  integer :: i = 0, n
  real, allocatable, dimension (:) :: y

  print *, ' Type in the file name ? '
  read '(a)', fname
  open (unit=1, file=fname, status='old')

  allocate (root)

! read first data item

  read (unit=1, fmt=*, &
    iostat=io_stat_number) root%x
  if (io_stat_number/=-1) then
    i = i + 1
    allocate (root%next)
  end if
  current => root

! read the rest

  do while (associated(current%next))
    current => current%next
    read (unit=1, fmt=*, &
```

```
      iostat=io_stat_number) current%x
    if (io_stat_number/=-1) then
      i = i + 1
      allocate (current%next)
    end if
  end do

  print *, i, ' numbers read'

  n = i
  allocate (y(1:n))
  i = 0
  current => root
  do while (associated(current%next))
    i = i + 1
    y(i) = current%x
    current => current%next
  end do
  print *, 'data read was:'
  do i = 1, n
    print *, y(i)
  end do

end program ch2202
```

A casual visual comparison of the two examples shows many similarities.

Diff is a line-oriented text file comparison utility. It tries to determine the smallest set of deletions and insertions to create one file from the other. The diff command displays the changes made in a standard format. Given one file and the changes, the other file can be created.

Here is the output from running this utility on these two examples.

```
3c3
<     character (len=1) :: x
---
>     real :: x
8c8
< program ch2201
---
> program ch2202
15c15
<     character (len=:), allocatable :: string
---
>     real, allocatable, dimension (:) :: y
25c25
```

```
<     read (unit=1, fmt='(a)', advance='no', &
---
>     read (unit=1, fmt=*, &
37c37
<       read (unit=1, fmt='(a)', advance='no', &
---
>       read (unit=1, fmt=*, &
45c45
<    print *, i, ' characters read'
---
>    print *, i, ' numbers read'
48c48
<    allocate (character(len=n) :: string)
---
>    allocate (y(1:n))
53c53
<       string(i:i) = current%x
---
>       y(i) = current%x
57,58c57,61
<    print *, string
< end program ch2201
---
>    do i = 1, n
>      print *, y(i)
>    end do
>
> end program ch2202
```

22.4 Example 3: Ragged Arrays

Arrays in Fortran are rectangular, even when allocatable. However if you wish to set up a lower triangular matrix that uses minimal memory Fortran provides a number of ways of doing this. The following example achieves it using allocatable components.

```
module ragged_module
  implicit none
  type ragged
    real, dimension (:), allocatable :: &
      ragged_row
  end type ragged
end module ragged_module
```

```
program ch2203
  use ragged_module
  implicit none
  integer :: i
  integer, parameter :: n = 3
  type (ragged), dimension (1:n) :: lower_diag

  do i = 1, n
    allocate (lower_diag(i)%ragged_row(1:i))
    print *, ' type in the values for row ', i
    read *, lower_diag(i)%ragged_row(1:i)
  end do
  do i = 1, n
    print *, lower_diag(i)%ragged_row(1:i)
  end do
end program ch2203
```

Within the first do loop we allocate a row at a time and each time we go around the loop the array allocated increases in size.

22.5   Example 4: Ragged Arrays and Variable Sized Data Sets

The previous example showed how to use allocatable components in a derived type to achieve ragged arrays.

In this example we are going to use data from the UK Met Office. Here is the current web address.

```
https://www.metoffice.gov.uk/public/weather/
climate-historic/#?tab=climateHistoric
```

In this example both the number of stations and the number of data items for each station is read in at run time and allocated accordingly. Notice that 0 is valid as the number of data items for a station.

```
module ragged_module
  type ragged
    real, allocatable, dimension (:) :: rainfall
  end type ragged
end module ragged_module
```

```
program ch2204
  use ragged_module
  implicit none
  integer :: i
  integer :: nr
  integer, allocatable, dimension (:) :: nc
  type (ragged), allocatable, dimension (:) :: &
    station

  print *, ' enter number of stations'
  read *, nr
  allocate (station(1:nr))
  allocate (nc(1:nr))
  do i = 1, nr
    print *, ' enter the number of data values ' &
      , 'for station ', i
    read *, nc(i)
    allocate (station(i)%rainfall(1:nc(i)))
    if (nc(i)==0) then
      cycle
    end if
    print *, ' Type in the values for station ', &
      i
    read *, station(i)%rainfall(1:nc(i))
  end do
  print *, ' Row    N    Data'
  do i = 1, nr
    print 100, i, nc(i), station(i)%rainfall(1: &
      nc(i))
100 format (3x, i3, 2x, i3, 2x, 12(1x,f6.2))
  end do
end program ch2204
```

Here is the input data file. It is the first 6 years rainfall data from the Met Office
Cwmystwyth site.

```
6
0
0
9
 144.8
 112.5
  77.2
 130.7
  66.3
```

```
     66.1
    141.1
    149.5
    134.8
8
    117.8
     72.8
     56.7
    236.2
    218.0
     69.7
     85.2
    204.4
10
    106.2
    159.7
    126.9
    121.6
     62.9
    154.3
    165.0
    139.0
    234.4
     19.7
12
     83.1
     38.5
     67.3
     76.4
     90.4
     83.5
    177.0
    180.5
     66.0
    171.9
    174.5
    334.8
```

Here is the output.

```
enter number of stations
enter the number of data values for station  1
enter the number of data values for station  2
enter the number of data values for station  3
Type in the values for station  3
```

```
enter the number of data values for station  4
Type in the values for station  4
enter the number of data values for station  5
Type in the values for station  5
enter the number of data values for station  6
Type in the values for station  6
 Row    N    Data
   1    0
   2    0
   3    9    144.80 112.50  77.20 130.70  66.30
             66.10 141.10 149.50 134.80
   4    8    117.80  72.80  56.70 236.20 218.00
             69.70  85.20 204.40
   5   10    106.20 159.70 126.90 121.60  62.90
            154.30 165.00 139.00 234.40  19.70
   6   12     83.10  38.50  67.30  76.40  90.40
             83.50 177.00 180.50  66.00 171.90
174.50 334.80
```

22.6   Example 5: Perfectly Balanced Tree

Let us now look at a more complex example that builds a perfectly balanced tree and
prints it out. A loose definition of a perfectly balanced tree is one that has minimum
depth for n nodes. More accurately a tree is perfectly balanced if for each node the
number of nodes in its left and right subtrees differ by at most 1:

```
module tree_node_module
  implicit none

  type tree_node
    integer :: number
    type (tree_node), pointer :: left => null(), &
      right => null()
  end type tree_node

end module tree_node_module

module tree_module
  implicit none

contains
```

```
recursive function tree(n) result (answer)
  use tree_node_module
  implicit none
  integer, intent (in) :: n
  type (tree_node), pointer :: answer
  type (tree_node), pointer :: new_node
  integer :: l, r, x

  if (n==0) then
    print *, ' terminate tree'
    nullify (answer)
  else
    l = n/2
    r = n - l - 1
    print *, l, r, n
    print *, ' next item'
    read *, x
    allocate (new_node)
    new_node%number = x
    print *, ' left branch'
    new_node%left => tree(l)
    print *, ' right branch'
    new_node%right => tree(r)
    answer => new_node
  end if
  print *, ' function tree ends'
end function tree

end module tree_module

module print_tree_module
  implicit none

contains

  recursive subroutine print_tree(t, h)
    use tree_node_module
    implicit none
    type (tree_node), pointer :: t
    integer :: i
    integer :: h

    if (associated(t)) then
      call print_tree(t%left, h+1)
      do i = 1, h
```

```
            write (unit=*, fmt=100, advance='no')
          end do
          print *, t%number
          call print_tree(t%right, h+1)
        end if
100 format (' ')

    end subroutine print_tree

  end module print_tree_module

  program ch2205
  ! construction of a perfectly balanced tree
    use tree_node_module
    use tree_module
    use print_tree_module
    implicit none
    type (tree_node), pointer :: root
    integer :: n_of_items

    print *, 'enter number of items'
    read *, n_of_items
    root => tree(n_of_items)
    call print_tree(root, 0)
  end program ch2205
```

There are a number of very important concepts contained in this example and they include:

- The use of a module to define a type. For user defined data types we must create a module to define the data type if we want it to be available in more than one program unit .
- The use of a function that returns a pointer as a result.
- As the function returns a pointer we must determine the allocation status before the function terminates. This means that in the above case we use the nullify(result) statement. The other option is to target the pointer.
- The use of associated to determine if the node of the tree is terminated or points to another node.

Type the program in and compile, link and run it. Note that the tree only has the minimal depth necessary to store all of the items. Experiment with the number of items and watch the tree change its depth to match the number of items.

22.7   Example 6: Date Class

The following is a complete manual rewrite of Skip Noble and Alan Millers date
module. Here are two urls for Alan Miller's Fortran 90 version of the code. The
original Skip Noble Fortran 77 version is in Chap. 38.

```
http://jblevins.org/mirror/amiller/
http://jblevins.org/mirror/amiller/datesub.f90
```

Here are some details about the function and subroutine naming conversion.

```
Skip Noble       Alan Miller
Fortran 77       Fortran 90       Current implementation

IDAY             iday             date_to_day_in_year
IZLR             izlr             date_to_weekday_number
CALEND           calend           year_and_day_to_date
CDATE            cdate            julian_to_date
NDAYS            ndays            ndays
DAYSUB           daysub           julian_to_date_and_week_and_day
JD               jd               calendar_to_julian
```

The original worked with the built-in Fortran intrinsic data types, i.e. year,
month and day were plain integer data types. It has been rewritten to work with a
derived date data type.

We have also added a function to print dates out in a variety of formats. This
is based on a subroutine called date_stamp from the original code. The first key
code segment is

```
type, public :: date
  private
  integer :: day
  integer :: month
  integer :: year
end type date
```

where the date data type is public but its components are private. This means that
access to the components must be done via subroutines and functions within the
date_module module. The next key segment is

```
character (9) :: day(0:6) = &
  (/ 'Sunday   ', 'Monday   ', 'Tuesday  ', &
     'Wednesday', 'Thursday ', 'Friday   ', &
          'Saturday ' /)
character (9) :: month(1:12) = &
```

```
(/ 'January   ', 'February ', 'March    ', &
   'April    ', 'May      ', 'June     ', &
   'July     ', 'August   ', 'September', &
   'October  ', 'November ', 'December ' /)
```

which declares the variable day to be an array of characters of length 9. They are initialised with the names of the days. The variable day is declared in the module and is available to all contained functions and subroutines.

The variable month is an array of characters of length 9 and is initialised to the names of the months. The variable month is declared in the module and is available to all contained functions and subroutines. The next key code segment is

```
public :: &
  calendar_to_julian, &
  date_, &
  date_to_day_in_year, &
  date_to_weekday_number, &
  get_day, &
  get_month, &
  get_year, &
  julian_to_date, &
  julian_to_date_and_week_and_day, &
  ndays, &
  print_date, &
  year_and_day_to_date
```

where we explicitly make the listed subroutines and functions public, as the code segment from the top of the module,

We have to provide a user defined constructor when the components of the derived type are private. This is given below:

```
function date_(dd,mm,yyyy) result (x)
  implicit none
  type (date) :: x
  integer, intent (in) :: dd, mm, yyyy
  x = date(dd,mm,yyyy)
end function date_
```

This in turn calls the built-in constructor date. As the date_ function is now an executable statement we cannot initialise in a declaration, i.e. the following is not allowed.

```
type (date) :: date1_(11,2,1952)
```

We also provide three additional procedures to access the components of the date class:

```
get_day
get_month
get_year
```

This is common programming practice in object oriented and object based programming.

The `print_date` function also has examples of internal write statements. These are

```
write(print_date(1:2),'(i2)')x%day
write(print_date(4:5),'(i2)')x%month
write(print_date(7:10) , '(i4)') x%year
write(print_date(pos:pos+1) ,'(i2)') x%day
write(print_date(pos:pos+3) , '(i4)') x%year
```

where we construct the elements of the character variable from the integer values of the `x%day`, `x%month` and `x%year` data.

```
module date_module
  implicit none

  private

  type, public :: date
    private
    integer :: day
    integer :: month
    integer :: year
  end type date

  character (9) :: day(0:6) = (/ 'Sunday   ', &
    'Monday   ', 'Tuesday  ', 'Wednesday', &
    'Thursday ', 'Friday   ', 'Saturday ' /)
  character (9) :: month(1:12) = (/ 'January  ', &
    'February ', 'March    ', 'April    ', &
    'May      ', 'June     ', 'July     ', &
    'August   ', 'September', 'October  ', &
    'November ', 'December ' /)

  public :: calendar_to_julian, date_, &
    date_to_day_in_year, date_to_weekday_number, &
```

```
        get_day, get_month, get_year, &
        julian_to_date, &
        julian_to_date_and_week_and_day, ndays, &
        print_date, year_and_day_to_date

contains

    function calendar_to_julian(x) result (ival)
      implicit none
      integer :: ival
      type (date), intent (in) :: x

      ival = x%day - 32075 + 1461*(x%year+4800+(x% &
        month-14)/12)/4 + 367*(x%month-2-((x%month &
        -14)/12)*12)/12 - 3*((x%year+4900+(x%month &
        -14)/12)/100)/4
    end function calendar_to_julian

    function date_(dd, mm, yyyy) result (x)
      implicit none
      type (date) :: x
      integer, intent (in) :: dd, mm, yyyy

      x = date(dd, mm, yyyy)
    end function date_

! functions
! "izlr"      date_to_day_in_year
! and
! "iday"      date_to_weekday_number
! are taken from remark on
! algorithm 398, by j. douglas robertson,
! cacm 15(10):918.

    function date_to_day_in_year(x)
      implicit none
      integer :: date_to_day_in_year
      type (date), intent (in) :: x
      intrinsic modulo

      date_to_day_in_year = 3055*(x%month+2)/100 - &
        (x%month+10)/13*2 - 91 + (1-(modulo(x%year &
        ,4)+3)/4+(modulo(x%year,100)+99)/100-( &
        modulo(x%year,400)+399)/400)*(x%month+10)/ &
        13 + x%day
```

```
    end function date_to_day_in_year

    function date_to_weekday_number(x)
      implicit none
      integer :: date_to_weekday_number
      type (date), intent (in) :: x
      intrinsic modulo

      date_to_weekday_number = modulo((13*( &
        x%month+10-(x%month+10)/13*12)-1)/5+x%day+ &
        77+5*(x%year+(x%month-14)/12-(x%year+ &
        (x%month-14)/12)/100*100)/4+(x%year+(x% &
        month-14)/12)/400-(x%year+(x%month- &
        14)/12)/100*2, 7)
    end function date_to_weekday_number


    function get_day(x)
      implicit none
      integer :: get_day
      type (date), intent (in) :: x

      get_day = x%day
    end function get_day

    function get_month(x)
      implicit none
      integer :: get_month
      type (date), intent (in) :: x

      get_month = x%month
    end function get_month

    function get_year(x)
      implicit none
      integer :: get_year
      type (date), intent (in) :: x

      get_year = x%year
    end function get_year

! cdate - julian_to_date
! see cacm 1968 11(10):657,
! letter to the editor by fliegel and van
! flandern.
```

```
function julian_to_date(julian) result (x)
  implicit none
  integer, intent (in) :: julian
  integer :: l, n
  type (date) :: x

  l = julian + 68569
  n = 4*l/146097
  l = l - (146097*n+3)/4
  x%year = 4000*(l+1)/1461001
  l = l - 1461*x%year/4 + 31
  x%month = 80*l/2447
  x%day = l - 2447*x%month/80
  l = x%month/11
  x%month = x%month + 2 - 12*l
  x%year = 100*(n-49) + x%year + 1
end function julian_to_date

subroutine julian_to_date_and_week_and_day(jd, &
  x, wd, ddd)
  implicit none
  integer, intent (out) :: ddd, wd
  integer, intent (in) :: jd
  type (date), intent (out) :: x

  x = julian_to_date(jd)
  wd = date_to_weekday_number(x)
  ddd = date_to_day_in_year(x)
end subroutine julian_to_date_and_week_and_day

function ndays(date1, date2)
  implicit none
  integer :: ndays
  type (date), intent (in) :: date1, date2

  ndays = calendar_to_julian(date1) - &
    calendar_to_julian(date2)
end function ndays

function print_date(x, day_names, &
  short_month_name, digits)
  implicit none
  type (date), intent (in) :: x
  logical, optional, intent (in) :: day_names, &
```

```fortran
     short_month_name, digits
character (40) :: print_date
integer :: pos
logical :: want_day, want_short_month_name, &
  want_digits
intrinsic len_trim, present, trim


want_day = .false.
want_short_month_name = .false.
want_digits = .false.
print_date = ' '
if (present(day_names)) then
  want_day = day_names
end if
if (present(short_month_name)) then
  want_short_month_name = short_month_name
end if
if (present(digits)) then
  want_digits = digits
end if
if (want_digits) then
  write (print_date(1:2), '(i2)') x%day
  print_date(3:3) = '/'
  write (print_date(4:5), '(i2)') x%month
  print_date(6:6) = '/'
  write (print_date(7:10), '(i4)') x%year
else
  if (want_day) then
    pos = date_to_weekday_number(x)
    print_date = trim(day(pos)) // ' '
    pos = len_trim(print_date) + 2
  else
    pos = 1
    print_date = ' '
  end if
  write (print_date(pos:pos+1), '(i2)') &
    x%day
  if (want_short_month_name) then
    print_date(pos+3:pos+5) = month(x%month) &
      (1:3)
    pos = pos + 7
  else
    print_date(pos+3:) = month(x%month)
    pos = len_trim(print_date) + 2
```

```
      end if
      write (print_date(pos:pos+3), '(i4)') &
        x%year
    end if

    return
  end function print_date

! calend - year_and_day_to_date
! see acm algorithm 398,
! tableless date conversion, by
! dick stone, cacm 13(10):621.

  function year_and_day_to_date(year, day) &
    result (x)
    implicit none
    type (date) :: x
    integer, intent (in) :: day, year
    integer :: t
    intrinsic modulo

    x%year = year
    t = 0
    if (modulo(year,4)==0) then
      t = 1
    end if
    if (modulo(year,400)/=0 .and. &
      modulo(year,100)==0) then
      t = 0
    end if
    x%day = day
    if (day>59+t) then
      x%day = x%day + 2 - t
    end if
    x%month = ((x%day+91)*100)/3055
    x%day = (x%day+91) - (x%month*3055)/100
    x%month = x%month - 2
    if (x%month>=1 .and. x%month<=12) then
      return
    end if
    write (unit=*, fmt='(a,i11,a)') '$$year_and_d&
      &ay_to_date: day of the year input &
      &=', day, ' is out of range.'
  end function year_and_day_to_date
```

```fortran
end module date_module


program ch2206
  use date_module, only: calendar_to_julian, &
    date, date_, date_to_day_in_year, &
    date_to_weekday_number, get_day, get_month, &
    get_year, julian_to_date_and_week_and_day, &
    ndays, print_date, year_and_day_to_date

  implicit none
  integer :: dd, ddd, i, mm, ndiff, wd, yyyy
  integer :: val(8)
  intrinsic date_and_time
  type (date) :: date1, date2, x

  call date_and_time(values=val)
  yyyy = val(1)
  mm = 10
  do i = 31, 26, -1
    x = date_(i, mm, yyyy)
    if (date_to_weekday_number(x)==0) then
      print *, 'Turn clocks  back to EST on: ', &
        i, ' October ', get_year(x)
      exit
    end if
  end do
  call date_and_time(values=val)
  yyyy = val(1)
  mm = 4
  do i = 1, 8
    x = date_(i, mm, yyyy)
    if (date_to_weekday_number(x)==0) then
      print *, 'Turn clocks ahead to DST on: ', &
        i, ' April   ', get_year(x)
      exit
    end if
  end do
  call date_and_time(values=val)
  yyyy = val(1)
  mm = 12
  dd = 31
  x = date_(dd, mm, yyyy)
  if (date_to_day_in_year(x)==366) then
    print *, get_year(x), ' is a leap year'
```

```
else
  print *, get_year(x), ' is not a leap year'
end if
x = date_(1, 1, 1970)
call julian_to_date_and_week_and_day &
  (calendar_to_julian(x), x, wd, ddd)
if (get_year(x)/=1970 .or. get_month(x)/=1 &
  .or. get_day(x)/=1 .or. wd/=4 .or. ddd/=1) &
  then
  print *, &
    'julian_to_date_and_week_and_day failed'
  print *, ' date, wd, ddd = ', get_year(x), &
    get_month(x), get_day(x), wd, ddd
  stop
end if
date1 = date_(22, 5, 1984)
date2 = date_(22, 5, 1983)
ndiff = ndays(date1, date2)
yyyy = 1970

x = year_and_day_to_date(yyyy, ddd)

if (ndiff/=366) then
  print *, 'ndays failed; ndiff = ', ndiff
else
  if (get_month(x)/=1 .and. get_day(x)/=1) &
    then
    print *, 'year_and_day_to_date failed'
    print *, ' mma, dda = ', get_month(x), &
      get_day(x)
  else
    print *, ' calendar_to_julian OK'
    print *, ' date_ OK'
    print *, ' date_to_day_in_year OK'
    print *, ' date_to_weekday_number OK'
    print *, ' get_day OK'
    print *, ' get_month OK'
    print *, ' get_year OK'
    print *, &
      ' julian_to_date_and_week_and_day OK'
    print *, ' ndays OK'
    print *, ' year_and_day_to_date OK'
  end if
end if
```

```
x = date_(11, 2, 1952)

print *, ' print_date test'
print *, ' Single parameter          ', &
  print_date(x)
print *, &
  ' day_names=false short_month_name=false ', &
  print_date(x, day_names=.false., &
  short_month_name=.false.)
print *, &
  ' day_names=true  short_month_name=false ', &
  print_date(x, day_names=.true., &
  short_month_name=.false.)
print *, &
  ' day_names=false short_month_name=true  ', &
  print_date(x, day_names=.false., &
  short_month_name=.true.)
print *, &
  ' day_names=true  short_month_name=true  ', &
  print_date(x, day_names=.true., &
  short_month_name=.true.)
print *, ' digits=true               ', &
  print_date(x, digits=.true.)

print *, ' Test out a month'

yyyy = 1970
do dd = 1, 31
  x = year_and_day_to_date(yyyy, dd)
  print *, print_date(x, day_names=.false., &
    short_month_name=.true.)
end do

end program ch2206
```

There are wrap problems with some of the lengthier arithmetic expressions. The version on the web site is obviously correct.

We also have an alternate form of array declaration in this program, which is given below. It is common in Fortran 77 style code:

```
integer :: val(8)
```

One improvement would be additional code to test the validity of dates. This would be called from within our constructor `date_`. This would mean that we could never have an invalid date when using the `date_module`. This is left as a programming exercise.

22.7.1   Notes: DST in the USA

The above program is no longer correct. Beginning in 2007, Daylight Saving Time was brought forward by 3 or 4 weeks in Spring and extended by one week in the Fall. Daylight Saving Time begins for most of the United States at 2 a.m. on the second Sunday of March. Time reverts to standard time at 2 a.m. on the first Sunday in November.

22.8   Example 7: Date Data Type with USA and ISO Support

The date derived type in this chapter handles conventional UK or world data types. To handle USA and ISO date formats we have added an extra component to this derived type. Here is the updated type.

```
type, public :: date
private
integer :: day
integer :: month
integer :: year
integer :: date_type = 1
end type date
```

When we use the default constructor we set the `date_type` to 1. An integer variable is often used in a problem like this. In the `date_iso` constructor we set `date_type` to 3 and in the `date_us` constructor set set `date_type` to 2.

The only other method we have to alter is the `print_date` method. In this method we have an `if then else` construct to choose how to print the date, based on the date type.

We have solved the problem of how to handle a variety of date formats in a simple, non object oriented fashion. First we have the date module.

```
module date_module
   implicit none

   private
```

```fortran
type, public :: date
  private
  integer :: day
  integer :: month
  integer :: year
  integer :: date_type = 1
end type date

character (9) :: day(0:6) = (/ 'Sunday   ', &
  'Monday   ', 'Tuesday  ', 'Wednesday', &
  'Thursday ', 'Friday   ', 'Saturday ' /)
character (9) :: month(1:12) = (/ 'January  ', &
  'February ', 'March    ', 'April    ', &
  'May      ', 'June     ', 'July     ', &
  'August   ', 'September', 'October  ', &
  'November ', 'December ' /)

public :: calendar_to_julian, date_, date_iso, &
  date_us, date_to_day_in_year, &
  date_to_weekday_number, get_day, get_month, &
  get_year, julian_to_date, &
  julian_to_date_and_week_and_day, ndays, &
  print_date, year_and_day_to_date

contains

  function date_(dd, mm, yyyy) result (x)
    implicit none
    type (date) :: x
    integer, intent (in) :: dd, mm, yyyy
    integer :: dt = 1

    x = date(dd, mm, yyyy, dt)
  end function date_

  function date_iso(yyyy, mm, dd) result (x)
    implicit none
    type (date) :: x
    integer, intent (in) :: dd, mm, yyyy
    integer :: dt = 3

    x = date(dd, mm, yyyy, dt)
  end function date_iso
```

```fortran
function date_us(mm, dd, yyyy) result (x)
  implicit none
  type (date) :: x
  integer, intent (in) :: dd, mm, yyyy
  integer :: dt = 2

  x = date(dd, mm, yyyy, dt)
end function date_us

include 'date_module_include_code.f90'

function print_date(x, day_names, &
  short_month_name, digits)
  implicit none
  type (date), intent (in) :: x
  logical, optional, intent (in) :: day_names, &
    short_month_name, digits
  character (30) :: print_date
  integer :: pos
  logical :: want_day, want_short_month_name, &
    want_digits
  integer :: l, t
  intrinsic len_trim, present, trim

  want_day = .false.
  want_short_month_name = .false.
  want_digits = .false.
  print_date = ' '
  if (present(day_names)) then
    want_day = day_names
  end if
  if (present(short_month_name)) then
    want_short_month_name = short_month_name
  end if
  if (present(digits)) then
    want_digits = digits
  end if
!     Start of code dependent on date_type
!     day month year
  if (x%date_type==1) then
    if (want_digits) then
      write (print_date(1:2), '(i2)') x%day
      print_date(3:3) = '/'
      write (print_date(4:5), '(i2)') x%month
      print_date(6:6) = '/'
```

```fortran
      write (print_date(7:10), '(i4)') x%year
    else
      if (want_day) then
        pos = date_to_weekday_number(x)
        print_date = trim(day(pos)) // ' '
        pos = len_trim(print_date) + 2
      else
        pos = 1
        print_date = ' '
      end if
      write (print_date(pos:pos+1), '(i2)') &
        x%day
      if (want_short_month_name) then
        print_date(pos+3:pos+5) &
          = month(x%month)(1:3)
        pos = pos + 7
      else
        print_date(pos+3:) = month(x%month)
        pos = len_trim(print_date) + 2
      end if
      write (print_date(pos:pos+3), '(i4)') &
        x%year
    end if

  else if (x%date_type==2) then
!     month day year
    if (want_digits) then
      write (print_date(1:2), '(i2)') x%month
      print_date(3:3) = '/'
      write (print_date(4:5), '(i2)') x%day
      print_date(6:6) = '/'
      write (print_date(7:10), '(i4)') x%year
    else
      pos = 1
      if (want_short_month_name) then
        print_date(pos:pos+2) = month(x%month) &
          (1:3)
        pos = pos + 4
      else
        print_date(pos:) = month(x%month)
        pos = len_trim(print_date) + 2
      end if
      if (want_day) then
        t = date_to_weekday_number(x)
        l = len_trim(day(t))
        print_date(pos:pos+l) = trim(day(t)) &
```

```
              // ' '
            pos = len_trim(print_date) + 2
          end if
          write (print_date(pos:pos+1), '(i2)') &
            x%day
          pos = pos + 3
          write (print_date(pos:pos+3), '(i4)') &
            x%year
        end if
      else if (x%date_type==3) then
!       year month day
        if (want_digits) then
          write (print_date(1:4), '(i4)') x%year
          print_date(5:5) = '/'
          write (print_date(6:7), '(i2)') x%month
          print_date(8:8) = '/'
          write (print_date(9:10), '(i2)') x%day
        else
          pos = 1
          write (print_date(pos:pos+3), '(i4)') &
            x%year
          pos = pos + 5
          if (want_short_month_name) then
            print_date(pos:pos+2) = month(x%month) &
              (1:3)
            pos = pos + 4
          else
            print_date(pos:) = month(x%month)
            pos = len_trim(print_date) + 2
          end if
          if (want_day) then
            t = date_to_weekday_number(x)
            l = len_trim(day(t))
            print_date(pos:pos+l) = trim(day(t))
            pos = pos + l + 1
          end if
          write (print_date(pos:pos+1), '(i2)') &
            x%day
        end if
      end if
      return
    end function print_date

end module date_module
```

Note that we have put the common executable code from the earlier date module into an include file.

```
include 'date_module_include_code.f90'
```

Next we have the program that uses the module.

```
include 'ch2207_date_module.f90'

program ch2207
  use date_module, only: calendar_to_julian, &
    date, date_, date_iso, date_us, &
    date_to_day_in_year, date_to_weekday_number, &
    get_day, get_month, get_year, &
    julian_to_date_and_week_and_day, ndays, &
    print_date, year_and_day_to_date

  implicit none
  integer :: i
  integer, parameter :: n = 3
  type (date), dimension (1:n) :: x

  x(1) = date_(11, 2, 1952)
  x(2) = date_us(2, 11, 1952)
  x(3) = date_iso(1952, 2, 11)

  do i = 1, 3
    print *, print_date(x(i))
  end do

end program ch2207
```

Note that we used the alternate syntax of using the

```
include 'ch2207_date_module.f90'
```

statement in this example.

22.9   Bibliography

Chapter 2 provided details of some books that address data structuring, but mainly from an historical viewpoint.

We provide a small number of references to books that look at data structuring more generally.

Schneider G.M., Bruell S.C., Advanced Programming and Problem Solving with Pascal, Wiley, 1981.

- The book is aimed at computer science students and follows the curriculum guidelines laid down in Communications of the ACM, August 1985, Course CS2. The book is very good for the complete beginner as the examples are very clearly laid out and well explained. There is a coverage of data structures, abstract data types and their implementation, algorithms for sorting and searching, the principles of software development as they relate to the specification, design, implementation and verification of programs in an orderly and disciplined fashion — their words.

Sedgewick, Robert (1993). Algorithms in Modula 3, Addison-Wesley. ISBN 0-201-53351-0.

- The Modula 3 algorithms are relatively easy to translate into Fortran.

22.10 Problems

22.1 Compile and run the examples in this chapter with your compiler.

22.2 Using ch2202.f90 as a starting point rewrite it to work with a file of integer data. You may find the diff output useful here.

22.3 Modify the ragged array example that processes a lower triangular matrix to work with an upper triangular matrix.

22.4 Using the balanced tree example as a basis and modify it to work with a character array rather than an integer. The routine that prints the tree will also have to be modified to reflect this.

22.5 Modify the Date program to account for the current DST in the USA.

22.6 Modify ch2204 to calculate and print the average rainfall for each station.

Chapter 23
An Introduction to Algorithms and the Big O Notation

> *Errors using inadequate data are much less than those using no data at all.*
>
> Charles Babbage

Aims

The aims of this chapter are to provide an introduction to algorithms and their behaviour. In Computer Science this is normally done using the so called big O notation.

We will cover briefly a small set of behaviour types including

- Order $O(1)$
- Order $O(n)$
- Order $O(\log n)$
- Order $O(n \log n)$

23.1 Introduction

A method for dealing with approximations was introduced by Bachman in 1892 in his work Analytische Zahlen Theorie. This is the big O notation.

The big O notation is used to classify algorithms by how they perform depending on the size of the input data set they are working on. This typically means looking at both their space and time behaviour.

A more detailed and mathematical coverage can be found in Knuth's Fundamental Algorithms.

Chapter one of this book looks at the basic concepts and mathematical preliminaries required for analysing algorithms, and is around 120 pages. Well worth a read.

© Springer International Publishing AG, part of Springer Nature 2018   391
I. Chivers and J. Sleightholme, *Introduction to Programming with Fortran*,
https://doi.org/10.1007/978-3-319-75502-1_23

23.2   Basic Background

Table 23.1 summarises some of the details regarding commonly occurring types of problem.

Table 23.1 Big O notation and complexity

Notation	Name
$O(1)$	Constant
$O(n)$	Linear
$O(\log n)$	Logarithmic
$O(n \log n) = O(\log n!)$	Linearithmic, loglinear, quasilinear
$O(\log \log n)$	Double logarithmic
$O(n \log^* n)$	n log-star n
$O(n^2)$	Quadratic
$O(n^c)\, 0 < c < 1$	Fractional power
$O(n^c)\, c > 1$	Polynomial or algebraic
$O(c^n)\, c > 1$	Exponential
$O(n!)$	Factorial

23.3   Brief Explanation

- $O(1)$ Determining if a number is even or odd; using a constant-size lookup table
- $O(\log \log n)$ Finding an item using interpolation search in a sorted array of uniformly distributed values.
- $O(\log n)$ Finding an item in a sorted array with a binary search or a balanced search tree as well as all operations in a Binomial heap.
- $O(n^c)\, 0 < c < 1$ Searching in a kd-tree
- $O(n)$ Finding an item in an unsorted list or a malformed tree (worst case) or in an unsorted array; Adding two n-bit integers by ripple carry.
- $O(n \log^* n)$ Performing triangulation of a simple polygon using Seidel's algorithm.
- $O(n \log n)$ Performing a Fast Fourier transform; heapsort, quicksort (best and average case), or merge sort.
- $O(n^2)$ Multiplying two n-digit numbers by a simple algorithm; bubble sort (worst case or naive implementation), Shell sort, quicksort (worst case), selection sort or insertion sort.
- $O(n^c)\, c > 1$ Tree-adjoining grammar parsing; maximum matching for bipartite graphs.

- $O(c^n)$ $c > 1$ Finding the (exact) solution to the travelling salesman problem using dynamic programming; determining if two logical statements are equivalent using brute-force search.
- $O(n!)$ Solving the traveling salesman problem via brute-force search; generating all unrestricted permutations of a poset; finding the determinant with expansion by minors.

23.4 Example 1: Order Calculations

This program calculates values for 4 of the above functions, for n from 1 to 10^9.

```
include 'precision_module.f90'

program ch2301

  use precision_module, wp => dp
  implicit none

  integer, parameter :: nn = 10
  integer :: n
  integer, dimension (nn) :: nvalues = [ 1, 10, &
    100, 1000, 10000, 100000, 1000000, 10000000, &
    100000000, 1000000000 ]
  integer :: i
  character *80 heading

  heading = ' i            n    O(1)        O(n)'
  heading = trim(heading) // &
    '        O(n*n) O(log n)   O(n log n)'
  print *, heading
  print *, ' '
  do i = 1, nn
    n = nvalues(i)
    print 100, i, n, order_1(), order_n(n), &
      order_n_squared(n), order_log_n(n), &
      order_n_log_n(n)
100 format (1x, i2, 2x, i10, 2x, i4, 2x, i10, &
      2x, e12.4, 2x, f7.2, 2x, e12.4)
  end do

contains

  integer function order_1()

    order_1 = 1
  end function order_1

  integer function order_n(n)
    integer, intent (in) :: n

    order_n = n
  end function order_n
```

```
function order_n_squared(n)
use precision_module, wp => dp
  integer, intent (in) :: n
  real (wp) :: order_n_squared

  order_n_squared = dble(n)*dble(n)
end function order_n_squared

real function order_log_n(n)
  integer, intent (in) :: n

  order_log_n = log(real(n))
end function order_log_n

real function order_n_log_n(n)
  integer, intent (in) :: n

  order_n_log_n = n*log(real(n))
end function order_n_log_n

end program ch2301
```

Here is the output from running the program.

i	n	O(1)	O(n)	O(n*n)	O(log n)	O(n log n)
1	1	1	1	0.1000E+01	0.00	0.0000E+00
2	10	1	10	0.1000E+03	2.30	0.2303E+02
3	100	1	100	0.1000E+05	4.61	0.4605E+03
4	1000	1	1000	0.1000E+07	6.91	0.6908E+04
5	10000	1	10000	0.1000E+09	9.21	0.9210E+05
6	100000	1	100000	0.1000E+11	11.51	0.1151E+07
7	1000000	1	1000000	0.1000E+13	13.82	0.1382E+08
8	10000000	1	10000000	0.1000E+15	16.12	0.1612E+09
9	100000000	1	100000000	0.1000E+17	18.42	0.1842E+10
10	1000000000	1	1000000000	0.1000E+19	20.72	0.2072E+11

23.5   Sorting

In the book we use two sorting algorithms

- Quicksort
- Insertion sort

Table 23.2 looks at their behaviour.

Table 23.2 Quicksort and insertion sort comparison

Algorithm	Data structure	Time complexity			Worst case auxiliary
					Space complexity
		Best	Average	Worst	Worst
Quicksort	Array	$O(n\,log(n))$	$O(n\,log(n))$	$O(n^2)$	$O(n)$
Insertion sort	Array	$O(n)$	$O(n^2)$	$O(n^2)$	$O(1)$

23.6 Basic Array and Linked List Performance

Table 23.3 summarises the array and linked list performance.

Table 23.3 Array and linked list performance

Data structure	Time complexity								Space complexity
	Average				Worst				Worst
	Index	Search	Insert	Delete	Index	Search	Insert	Delete	
Basic array	$O(1)$	$O(n)$	–	–	$O(1)$	$O(n)$	–	–	$O(n)$
Dynamic array	$O(1)$	$O(n)$	$O(n)$	$O(n)$	$O(1)$	$O(n)$	$O(n)$	$O(n)$	$O(n)$
Singly-linked list	$O(n)$	$O(n)$	$O(1)$	$O(1)$	$O(n)$	$O(n)$	$O(1)$	$O(1)$	$O(n)$

23.7 Bibliography

The earliest books that we have used in this area are those by Donald Knuth, and details are given below in chronological order.

Volume 1, Fundamental Algorithms, first edition, 1968, xxi+634pp, ISBN 0-201-03801-3.

Volume 2, Seminumerical Algorithms, first edition, 1969, xi+624pp, ISBN 0-201-03802-1.

Volume 3, Sorting and Searching, first edition, 1973, xi+723pp, ISBN 0-201-03803-X

Volume 1, second edition, 1973, xxi+634pp, ISBN 0-201-03809-9.

Volume 2, second edition, 1981, xiii+688pp, ISBN 0-201-03822-6.

- Knuth uses the Mix assembly language (an artificial language) and this limits the accessibility of the books.
- However within the Computer Science community they are generally regarded as the first and most comprehensive treatment of its subject.

For something more accessible, Sedgewick has written several programming language versions of a book on algorithms. He was a student of Knuth's.

The earliest used Pascal, and later editions have used C, C++ and Modula 2 and Modula 3.

Sedgewick, Robert (1992). Algorithms in C++, Addison-Wesley. ISBN 0-201-51059-6.

Sedgewick, Robert (1993). Algorithms in Modula 3, Addison-Wesley. ISBN 0-201-53351-0.

- The Modula 3 algorithms are relatively easy to translate into Fortran.

Chapter 24
Operator Overloading

All the persons in this book are real and none is fictitious even in part.

Flann O'Brien, The Hard Life

Aims

The aims of this chapter are to look at operator overloading in Fortran.

24.1 Introduction

In programming operator overloading can be regarded as a way of achieving polymorphism in that operators (e.g. $+$, $-$, $*$, $/$ or $=$) can have different implementations depending on the types of their arguments.

In some programming languages overloading is defined by the language. In Fortran for example, the addition $+$ operator invokes quite different code when used with integer, real or complex types.

Some languages allow the programmer to implement support for user defined types. Fortran introduced support for operator and assignment overloading in the 1990 standard.

24.2 Other Languages

Operator overloading is not new and several languages offer support for the feature including:

© Springer International Publishing AG, part of Springer Nature 2018

I. Chivers and J. Sleightholme, *Introduction to Programming with Fortran*,

https://doi.org/10.1007/978-3-319-75502-1_24

- Algol 68 - 1968
- Ada - Ada 83
- C++ - First standard, 1998
- Eiffel - 1986
- C# - 2001

Java, however does not.

24.3   Example 1: Overloading the Addition (+) Operator

The following example overloads the addition operator.

```
module t_position
  implicit none
  type position
    integer :: x
    integer :: y
    integer :: z
  end type position
  interface operator (+)
    module procedure new_position
  end interface operator (+)

contains
  function new_position(a, b)
    type (position), intent (in) :: a, b
    type (position) :: new_position

    new_position%x = a%x + b%x
    new_position%y = a%y + b%y
    new_position%z = a%z + b%z
  end function new_position
end module t_position

program ch2401
  use t_position
  implicit none
  type (position) :: a, b, c

  a%x = 10
  a%y = 10
  a%z = 10
  b%x = 20
```

```
    b%y = 20
    b%z = 20
    c = a + b
    print *, a
    print *, b
    print *, c
end program ch2401
```

We have extended the meaning of the addition operator so that we can write simple expressions in Fortran based on it and have our new position calculated using a user supplied function that actually implements the calculation of the new position.

24.4 Problem

24.1 Compile and run this example. Overload the subtraction operator as well.

Chapter 25
Generic Programming

General notions are generally wrong.
Letter to Mr. Wortley Montegu, 28th March 1710.

Aims

This chapter looks at some examples that implement generic programming in Fortran.

25.1 Introduction

Fortran 77 had several generic functions, e.g. the sine function could be called with arguments of type real, double precision or complex. Fortran 90 extended the idea so that a programmer could write their own generic functions or subroutines. For example we can now write a sort routine which works with arguments of a variety of types, e.g. integer, real etc.

25.2 Generic Programming and Other Languages

Generic programming has a wider meaning in computer science and effectively is a style of computer programming in which an algorithm is written once, but can be made to work with a variety of types.

This style of programming is provided in several programming languages and in a variety of ways.

Languages that support generics include

© Springer International Publishing AG, part of Springer Nature 2018
I. Chivers and J. Sleightholme, *Introduction to Programming with Fortran*,
https://doi.org/10.1007/978-3-319-75502-1_25

- Ada
- C#
- Eiffel
- Java
- C++

To quote the generic programming pioneer Alexander Stepanov;

> ... Generic programming is about abstracting and classifying algorithms and data structures. It gets its inspiration from Knuth and not from type theory. Its goal is the incremental construction of systematic catalogs of useful, efficient and abstract algorithms and data structures. Such an undertaking is still a dream.

and quoting Bjarne Stroustrup:

> ... lift algorithms and data structures from concrete examples to their most general and abstract form.

We'll look at a concrete example in Fortran next.

25.3   Example 1: Sorting Reals and Integers

In Chap. 20 Example 5 had a module called `sort_data_module` that contained a `sort_data` subroutine. The `sort_data` subroutine in turn contained an internal `quicksort` subroutine that did the actual sorting.

Here is the start of the `sort_data` subroutine.

```
subroutine sort_data(raw_data, how_many)
  implicit none
  integer, intent (in) :: how_many
  real, intent (inout), dimension (:) :: raw_data
```

and we called this subroutine as shown below from the main program.

```
call sort_data(x,n)
```

The subroutine worked with an array of default real type. We will use the module `sort_data_module` and subroutine `sort_data` as the basis of a module that will work with arrays of four integer types and three real types.

The first thing we need are modules that defines kind type parameters for the three real types and four integer types.

These two modules are shown below.

```
module precision_module
  implicit none
```

```
    integer, parameter :: sp = selected_real_kind( &
      6, 37)
    integer, parameter :: dp = selected_real_kind( &
      15, 307)
    integer, parameter :: qp = selected_real_kind( &
      30, 291)
  end module precision_module


module integer_kind_module
  implicit none
  integer, parameter :: i8 = selected_int_kind(2 &
    )
  integer, parameter :: i16 = selected_int_kind( &
    4)
  integer, parameter :: i32 = selected_int_kind( &
    9)
  integer, parameter :: i64 = selected_int_kind( &
    15)
end module integer_kind_module
```

We can now use these modules in the new module `sort_data_module` and main program.

We must use an interface to link the common calling name (`sort_data`) to the specific subroutines that handle each specific type.

Here is the interface block from the module `sort_data_module`.

```
    interface sort_data
      module procedure sort_real_sp
      module procedure sort_real_dp
      module procedure sort_real_qp
      module procedure sort_integer_8
      module procedure sort_integer_16
      module procedure sort_integer_32
      module procedure sort_integer_64
    end interface sort_data
```

In the original subroutine in Chap. 20 we had a call

```
call sort_date(raw_data,how_many)
```

and the subroutine `sort_data` had two arguments or parameters, a real array, and an integer for the size.

So the call is still the same, but now we can call the `sort_data` subroutine with an array of any of the four integer types or three real types.

The compiler will then look at the type, kind and ranks of the parameters in the call to the `sort_data` subroutine and call the appropriate module procedure.

Here is the new module `sort_data_module`.

```
module sort_data_module

  use precision_module
  use integer_kind_module

  interface sort_data
    module procedure sort_real_sp
    module procedure sort_real_dp
    module procedure sort_real_qp
    module procedure sort_integer_8
    module procedure sort_integer_16
    module procedure sort_integer_32
    module procedure sort_integer_64
  end interface sort_data

contains

  subroutine sort_real_sp(raw_data, how_many)
    use precision_module
    implicit none
    integer, intent (in) :: how_many
    real (sp), intent (inout), dimension (:) :: &
      raw_data

    call quicksort(1, how_many)

  contains

    recursive subroutine quicksort(l, r)
      implicit none
      integer, intent (in) :: l, r
      integer :: i, j
      real (sp) :: v, t

      include 'quicksort_include_code.f90'

    end subroutine quicksort

  end subroutine sort_real_sp
```

```fortran
subroutine sort_real_dp(raw_data, how_many)
  use precision_module
  implicit none
  integer, intent (in) :: how_many
  real (dp), intent (inout), dimension (:) :: &
    raw_data

  call quicksort(1, how_many)

contains
  recursive subroutine quicksort(l, r)
    implicit none
    integer, intent (in) :: l, r
    integer :: i, j
    real (dp) :: v, t

    include 'quicksort_include_code.f90'

  end subroutine quicksort
end subroutine sort_real_dp

subroutine sort_real_qp(raw_data, how_many)
  use precision_module
  implicit none
  integer, intent (in) :: how_many
  real (qp), intent (inout), dimension (:) :: &
    raw_data

  call quicksort(1, how_many)



contains
  recursive subroutine quicksort(l, r)
    implicit none
    integer, intent (in) :: l, r
    integer :: i, j
    real (qp) :: v, t

    include 'quicksort_include_code.f90'

  end subroutine quicksort
end subroutine sort_real_qp
```

```fortran
subroutine sort_integer_8(raw_data, how_many)
  use integer_kind_module
  implicit none
  integer, intent (in) :: how_many
  integer (i8), intent (inout), &
    dimension (:) :: raw_data

  call quicksort(1, how_many)

contains
  recursive subroutine quicksort(l, r)
    implicit none
    integer, intent (in) :: l, r
    integer :: i, j
    integer (i8) :: v, t

    include 'quicksort_include_code.f90'

  end subroutine quicksort
end subroutine sort_integer_8

subroutine sort_integer_16(raw_data, how_many)
  use integer_kind_module
  implicit none
  integer, intent (in) :: how_many
  integer (i16), intent (inout), &
    dimension (:) :: raw_data

  call quicksort(1, how_many)

contains
  recursive subroutine quicksort(l, r)
    implicit none
    integer, intent (in) :: l, r
    integer :: i, j
    integer (i16) :: v, t

    include 'quicksort_include_code.f90'

  end subroutine quicksort
end subroutine sort_integer_16



subroutine sort_integer_32(raw_data, how_many)
```

```fortran
      use integer_kind_module
      implicit none
      integer, intent (in) :: how_many
      integer (i32), intent (inout), &
        dimension (:) :: raw_data

      call quicksort(1, how_many)

contains
    recursive subroutine quicksort(l, r)
      implicit none
      integer, intent (in) :: l, r
      integer :: i, j
      integer (i32) :: v, t

      include 'quicksort_include_code.f90'

    end subroutine quicksort
  end subroutine sort_integer_32

  subroutine sort_integer_64(raw_data, how_many)
    use integer_kind_module
    implicit none
    integer, intent (in) :: how_many
    integer (i64), intent (inout), &
      dimension (:) :: raw_data

    call quicksort(1, how_many)

contains
    recursive subroutine quicksort(l, r)
      implicit none
      integer, intent (in) :: l, r
      integer :: i, j
      integer (i64) :: v, t

      include 'quicksort_include_code.f90'

    end subroutine quicksort

  end subroutine sort_integer_64

end module sort_data_module
```

In this module we have implementations for each of the module procedures listed in the interface block.

Here is the include file,

```
i = 1
j = r
v = raw_data(int((l+r)/2))
do
   do while (raw_data(i)<v)
     i = i + 1
   end do
   do while (v<raw_data(j))
     j = j - 1
   end do
   if (i<=j) then
     t = raw_data(i)
     raw_data(i) = raw_data(j)
     raw_data(j) = t
     i = i + 1
     j = j - 1
   end if
   if (i>j) exit
end do
if (l<j) then
   call quicksort(l, j)
end if
if (i<r) then
   call quicksort(i, r)
end if
```

which is used in each of the seven subroutines and is effectively a common algorithm between all seven subroutines.

Here is the main program to test the generic sort module.

```
include 'integer_kind_module.f90'
include 'precision_module.f90'
include 'sort_data_module.f90'

program ch2501

   use precision_module
   use integer_kind_module
   use sort_data_module
```

```
    implicit none
    integer, parameter :: n = 1000000
    real (sp), allocatable, dimension (:) :: x
    integer (i32), allocatable, dimension (:) :: y
    integer :: allocate_status

    allocate_status = 0

    print *, ' Program starts'
    allocate (x(1:n), stat=allocate_status)

    if (allocate_status/=0) then
      print *, ' Allocate failed.'
      print *, ' Program terminates'
      stop 10
    end if

    print *, ' Real allocate complete'
    call random_number(x)
    print *, ' Real array initialised'
    call sort_data(x, n)
    print *, ' Real sort ended'
    print *, ' First 10 reals'
    write (unit=*, fmt=100) x(1:10)
100 format (5(2x,e14.6))
    allocate (y(1:n), stat=allocate_status)
    if (allocate_status/=0) then
      print *, ' Allocate failed.'
      print *, ' Program terminates'
      stop 10
    end if
    y = int(x*1000000)
    deallocate (x)
    print *, ' Integer array initialised'
    call sort_data(y, n)
    print *, ' Sort ended'
    print *, ' First 10 integers'
    write (unit=*, fmt=110) y(1:10)
110 format (5(2x,i10))
    deallocate (y)
    print *, ' Deallocate'
    print *, ' Program terminates'

end program ch2501
```

This is obviously a very significant facility to have in a programming language.

Have a look at the following two examples which show the code for a generic quicksort in C++ and C#.

25.3.1   Generic Quicksort in C++

Here is the C++ program.

```
template <class Type>
void swap(Type array[],int i, int j)
{
  Type tmp=array[i];
  array[i]=array[j];
  array[j]=tmp;
}

template <class Type>
void quicksort( Type array[], int l, int r)
{
  int i=l;
  int j=r;
  Type v=array[int((l+r)/2)];
  for (;;)
  {
    while (array[i] < v) i=i+1;
    while (v < array[j]) j=j-1;
    if (i<=j)
      { swap(array,i,j); i=i+1 ; j=j-1; }
    if (i>j) goto ended ;
  }
  ended: ;
  if (l<j) quicksort(array,l,j);
  if (i<r) quicksort(array,i,r);
}

template <class Type>
void print(Type array[],int size)
{
  cout << " [ " ;
  for (int ix=0;ix<size; ++ix)
    cout << array[ix] << " ";
  cout << "] \n";
```

```
}

#include <iostream>
using namespace std;
int main()
{
  double da[] =
  {1.9,8.2,3.7,6.4,5.5,1.8,9.2,3.6,7.4,5.5};
  int ia[] = {1,10,2,9,3,8,4,7,6,5};
  int size=sizeof(da)/sizeof(double);
  cout << " Quicksort of double array is \n";
  quicksort(da,0,size-1);
  print(da,size);
  size=sizeof(ia)/sizeof(int);
  cout << " Quicksort of integer array is \n";
  quicksort(ia,0,size-1);
  print(ia,size);
  return(0);
}
```

25.3.2 Generic Quicksort in C#

Here is the C# version.

```
using System;
public static class generic
{

  public static void
swap< Type > (Type[] array,int i, int j)
  {
    Type tmp=array[i];
    array[i]=array[j];
    array[j]=tmp;
  }

  public static void
quicksort< Type > ( Type[] array, int l, int r)
    where Type : IComparable< Type >
  {
    int i=l;
    int j=r;
    Type v=array[(int)((l+r)/2)];
```

```
    for (;;)
    {
      while (array[i].CompareTo( v) < 0 ) i=i+1;
      while (v.CompareTo(array[j]) < 0) j=j-1;
      if (i<=j)
        { swap(array,i,j); i=i+1 ; j=j-1; }
      if (i>j) goto ended ;
    }
    ended: ;
    if (l<j) quicksort(array,l,j);
    if (i<r) quicksort(array,i,r);
  }

  public static void
print< Type > (Type[] array,int size)
  {
    int i;
    int l;
    l=array.Length;
    for (i=0;i<l;i++)
      Console.WriteLine(array[i]);
  }

  public static int Main()
  {
    double[] da =
    {1.9,8.2,3.7,6.4,5.5,1.8,9.2,3.6,7.4,5.5};
    int[]    ia = {1,10,2,9,3,8,4,7,6,5};
    int size;
    size=da.Length;
    Console.WriteLine("Original array");
    print(da,size);
    quicksort(da,0,size-1);
    Console.WriteLine("Sorted array");
    print(da,size);
    size=ia.Length;
    Console.WriteLine("Original array");
    print(ia,size);
    quicksort(ia,0,size-1);
    Console.WriteLine("Sorted array");
    print(ia,size);
    return(0);
  }

}
```

In C++ and C# we only have one version of the sort procedure and the compiler generates the code for us for each type of array we call the procedure with, which we have to actually write in Fortran.

25.4 Example 2: Generic Statistics Module

In this example we extend the statistics module from Chap. 20 (Example 4) to work with all three real kind types.

Here is the statistics module.

```
module statistics_module

  use precision_module

  interface calculate_statistics
    module procedure calculate_sp
    module procedure calculate_dp
    module procedure calculate_qp
  end interface calculate_statistics

contains


  subroutine calculate_sp(x, n, mean, std_dev, &
    median)
    implicit none
    integer, intent (in) :: n
    real (sp), intent (in), dimension (:) :: x
    real (sp), intent (out) :: mean
    real (sp), intent (out) :: std_dev
    real (sp), intent (out) :: median
    real (sp), dimension (1:n) :: y
    real (sp) :: variance
    real (sp) :: sumxi, sumxi2

    sumxi = 0.0
    sumxi2 = 0.0
    variance = 0.0
    sumxi = sum(x)
    sumxi2 = sum(x*x)
    mean = sumxi/n
    variance = (sumxi2-sumxi*sumxi/n)/(n-1)
    std_dev = sqrt(variance)
    y = x
```

```fortran
    if (mod(n,2)==0) then
      median = (find(n/2)+find((n/2)+1))/2
    else
      median = find((n/2)+1)
    end if
  contains

    function find(k)
      implicit none
      real (sp) :: find
      integer, intent (in) :: k
      integer :: l, r, i, j
      real (sp) :: t1, t2
include 'statistics_module_include_code.f90'
    end function find
  end subroutine calculate_sp

  subroutine calculate_dp(x, n, mean, std_dev, &
    median)
    implicit none
    integer, intent (in) :: n
    real (dp), intent (in), dimension (:) :: x
    real (dp), intent (out) :: mean
    real (dp), intent (out) :: std_dev
    real (dp), intent (out) :: median
    real (dp), dimension (1:n) :: y
    real (dp) :: variance
    real (dp) :: sumxi, sumxi2

    sumxi = 0.0
    sumxi2 = 0.0
    variance = 0.0
    sumxi = sum(x)
    sumxi2 = sum(x*x)
    mean = sumxi/n
    variance = (sumxi2-sumxi*sumxi/n)/(n-1)
    std_dev = sqrt(variance)
    y = x
    if (mod(n,2)==0) then
      median = (find(n/2)+find((n/2)+1))/2
    else
      median = find((n/2)+1)
    end if
```

```
    contains
      function find(k)
        implicit none
        real (dp) :: find
        integer, intent (in) :: k
        integer :: l, r, i, j
        real (dp) :: t1, t2
include 'statistics_module_include_code.f90'
      end function find
    end subroutine calculate_dp

  subroutine calculate_qp(x, n, mean, std_dev, &
    median)
    implicit none
    integer, intent (in) :: n
    real (qp), intent (in), dimension (:) :: x
    real (qp), intent (out) :: mean
    real (qp), intent (out) :: std_dev
    real (qp), intent (out) :: median
    real (qp), dimension (1:n) :: y
    real (qp) :: variance
    real (qp) :: sumxi, sumxi2

    sumxi = 0.0
    sumxi2 = 0.0
    variance = 0.0
    sumxi = sum(x)
    sumxi2 = sum(x*x)
    mean = sumxi/n
    variance = (sumxi2-sumxi*sumxi/n)/(n-1)
    std_dev = sqrt(variance)
    y = x
    if (mod(n,2)==0) then
      median = (find(n/2)+find((n/2)+1))/2
    else
      median = find((n/2)+1)
    end if
  contains
    function find(k)
      implicit none
      real (qp) :: find
      integer, intent (in) :: k
      integer :: l, r, i, j
      real (qp) :: t1, t2
include 'statistics_module_include_code.f90'
```

```
    end function find
  end subroutine calculate_qp

end module statistics_module
```

Here is the common include file.

```
l = 1
r = n
do while (l<r)
  t1 = y(k)
  i = l
  j = r
  do
    do while (y(i)<t1)
      i = i + 1
    end do
    do while (t1<y(j))
      j = j - 1
    end do
    if (i<=j) then
      t2 = y(i)
      y(i) = y(j)
      y(j) = t2
      i = i + 1
      j = j - 1
    end if
    if (i>j) exit
  end do
  if (j<k) then
    l = i
  end if
  if (k<i) then
    r = j
  end if
end do
find = y(k)
```

Here is the main program to test the statistics module.

```fortran
include 'precision_module.f90'
include 'statistics_module.f90'
include 'timing_module.f90'

program ch2502

  use precision_module
  use statistics_module
  use timing_module

  implicit none
  integer :: n
  real (sp), allocatable, dimension (:) :: x
  real (sp) :: x_m, x_sd, x_median
  real (dp), allocatable, dimension (:) :: y
  real (dp) :: y_m, y_sd, y_median
  real (qp), allocatable, dimension (:) :: z
  real (qp) :: z_m, z_sd, z_median
  character *20, dimension (3) :: heading = [ &
    ' Allocate    ', ' Random      ', &
    ' Statistics  ' ]

  call start_timing()
  n = 50000000
  print *, ' n = ', n

  print *, ' Single precision'

  allocate (x(1:n))
  print 100, heading(1), time_difference()
100 format (a20, 2x, f8.3)
  call random_number(x)
  print 100, heading(2), time_difference()
  call calculate_statistics(x, n, x_m, x_sd, &
    x_median)
  print 100, heading(3), time_difference()
  write (unit=*, fmt=110) x_m
110 format (' Mean              = ', f10.6)
  write (unit=*, fmt=120) x_sd
120 format (' Standard deviation = ', f10.6)
  write (unit=*, fmt=130) x_median
130 format (' Median            = ', f10.6)
```

```
deallocate (x)

print *, ' Double precision'

allocate (y(1:n))
print 100, heading(1), time_difference()
call random_number(y)
print 100, heading(2), time_difference()
call calculate_statistics(y, n, y_m, y_sd, &
  y_median)
print 100, heading(3), time_difference()
write (unit=*, fmt=110) y_m
write (unit=*, fmt=120) y_sd
write (unit=*, fmt=130) y_median
deallocate (y)

print *, ' Quad precision'

allocate (z(1:n))
print 100, heading(1), time_difference()
call random_number(z)
print 100, heading(2), time_difference()
call calculate_statistics(z, n, z_m, z_sd, &
  z_median)
print 100, heading(3), time_difference()
write (unit=*, fmt=110) z_m
write (unit=*, fmt=120) z_sd
write (unit=*, fmt=130) z_median
deallocate (z)

end program ch2502
```

Here are some results for the gfortran, Intel, Nag and Oracle compilers (Table 25.1).

Table 25.1 ch2502 results

Compiler	gfortran	Intel	Nag	Oracle	
n = 50,000,000					Average time
Single precision					
Allocate	0.000	0.000	0.000	0.000	0.000
Random	0.484	0.469	0.484	1.230	0.667
Statistics	1.312	0.766	1.031	0.773	0.971
Total time	1.796	1.235	1.515	2.003	1.637
Mean	0.335544	0.335544	0.335544	0.335544	
Standard deviation	0.465684	0.442725	0.442758	0.442686	
Median	0.500006	0.499965	0.500044	0.499957	
Double precision					
Allocate	0.020	0.016	0.016	0.000	0.013
Random	1.105	0.859	0.359	1.312	0.909
Statistics	1.520	0.953	1.172	1.055	1.175
Total time	2.645	1.828	1.547	2.367	2.097
Mean	0.500017	0.499931	0.499984	0.499984	
Standard deviation	0.288686	0.288691	0.288699	0.288695	
Median	0.500011	0.499889	0.499935	0.500012	
Quad precision					
Allocate	0.027	0.031	0.031	0.004	0.023
Random	6.363	2.500	0.734	2.395	2.998
Statistics	7.766	6.453	4.109	10.840	7.292
Total time	14.156	8.984	4.874	13.239	10.313
Mean	0.500019	0.499995	0.500030	0.500084	
Standard deviation	0.288659	0.288660	0.288662	0.288688	
Median	0.500041	0.499994	0.500065	0.500125	

25.5 Problems

25.1 Write a generic swap routine, that swaps two rank 1 integer arrays and two rank 1 real arrays.

25.2 Using Example 2 from Chap. 22 as a starting point convert it to a generic variant which handles files of integer data type and real data type.

25.6   Bibliography

25.6.1   Generic Programming References

This site is a collection of Alex Stepanov's papers, class notes, and source code, covering generic programming and other topics.

```
http://www.stepanovpapers.com/
```

25.6.2   Generic Programming and C++

C++ Templates: The Complete Guide, David Vandevoorde, Nicolai M Josuttis, 2003 Addison-Wesley. ISBN 0-201-73484-2

25.6.3   Generic Programming and C#

Visit the following site

```
http://msdn.microsoft.com/en-us/
library/512aeb7t(v=vs.80).aspx
```

for a very good coverage of generics and C#.

Chapter 26
Mathematical and Numerical Examples

You look at science (or at least talk of it) as some sort of demoralising invention of man, something apart from real life, and which must be cautiously guarded and kept separate from everyday existence. But science and everyday life cannot and should not be separated. Science, for me, gives a partial explanation for life. In so far as it goes, it is based on fact, experience and experiment.

Rosalind Franklin.

Aims

The aims of this chapter are to look at several mathematical and numeric examples in Fortran.

- Using linked lists for sparse matrix problems.
- The solution of a system of ordinary differential equations using the Runge–Kutta–Merson method, with the use of a procedure as a parameter, and the use of work arrays.
- The use of optional and keyword arguments
- Diagonal extraction of a matrix.
- The solution of a system of linear simultaneous equations using Gaussian Elimination
- An elemental e**x function
- Examples of the relative and absolute errors involved in subtraction with 32 and 64 bit precision

© Springer International Publishing AG, part of Springer Nature 2018   421
I. Chivers and J. Sleightholme, *Introduction to Programming with Fortran*,
https://doi.org/10.1007/978-3-319-75502-1_26

26.1 Introduction

This chapter looks at a small number of mathematical and numeric examples in Fortran.

26.2 Example 1: Using Linked Lists for Sparse Matrix Problems

A matrix is said to be sparse if many of its elements are zero. Mathematical models in areas such as management science, power systems analysis, circuit theory and structural analysis consist of very large sparse systems of linear equations. It is not possible to solve these systems with classical methods because the sparsity would be lost and the eventual system would become too large to solve. Many of these systems consist of tens of thousands, hundreds of thousands and millions of equations. As computer systems become ever more powerful with massive amounts of memory the solution of even larger problems becomes feasible.

Direct Methods for Sparse Matrices, by Duff I.S., Erismon A.M. and Reid J.K., looks at direct methods for solving sparse systems of linear equations.

Sparse matrix techniques lend themselves to the use of dynamic data structures in Fortran. Only the nonzero elements of a sparse matrix need be stored, together with their positions in the matrix. Other information also needs to be stored so that row or column manipulation can be performed without repeated scanning of a potentially very large data structure. Sparse methods may involve introducing some new nonzero elements, and a way is needed of inserting them into the data structure. This is where the Fortran pointer construct can be used. The sparse matrix can be implemented using a linked list to which entries can be easily added and from which they can be easily deleted.

As a simple introduction, consider the storage of sparse vectors. What we learn here can easily be applied to sparse matrices, which can be thought of as sets of sparse vectors.

26.2.1 Inner Product of Two Sparse Vectors

Assume that we have two sparse vectors x and y for example

$$
\underline{x} = \begin{bmatrix} 3 \\ 0 \\ 5 \\ 0 \\ 0 \\ 4 \end{bmatrix} \quad \underline{y} = \begin{bmatrix} 0 \\ 1 \\ 3 \\ 0 \\ 2 \\ 1 \end{bmatrix}
$$

and we wish to calculate the inner product

$$x^T y \equiv \sum_{i=1}^{n} x_i y_i$$

There are a number of approaches to doing this and the one we use in the program below stores them as two linked lists. Only the nonzero elements are stored (together with their indices):

```
x data file      y data file
   3   1              1   2
   5   3              3   3
   4   6              2   5
                      1   6
```

Here is the program.

```
module sparse_vector_module
  implicit none
  type sparse_vector
    integer :: index
    real :: value
    type (sparse_vector), pointer :: next => &
      null()
  end type sparse_vector
end module sparse_vector_module


module read_data_module

  implicit none

contains

  subroutine read_data(filename, root_z, ifail)

    use sparse_vector_module

    implicit none
    type (sparse_vector), pointer, &
      intent (inout) :: root_z
    character (len=*), intent (inout) :: &
      filename
    integer, intent (inout) :: ifail
```

```fortran
    integer :: io_status
    type (sparse_vector), pointer :: current_z

    ifail = 0

!   open file for reading data and read 1st
!   entry

    open (unit=1, file=filename, status='old', &
      iostat=io_status)
    if (io_status/=0) then
      ifail = 1
      return
    end if
    allocate (root_z)
    read (unit=1, fmt=*, iostat=io_status) &
      root_z%value, root_z%index
    if (io_status/=0) then
      ifail = 2
      return
    end if

!   read data from file until eof

    current_z => root_z
    allocate (current_z%next)
    do while (associated(current_z%next))
      current_z => current_z%next
      read (unit=1, fmt=*, iostat=io_status) &
        current_z%value, current_z%index
      if (io_status==0) then
        allocate (current_z%next)
        cycle
      else if (io_status>0) then
        ifail = 3
      end if
    end do
    close (unit=1)

    return
  end subroutine read_data

end module read_data_module
```

```fortran
program ch2601

! this program reads the non-zero elements of
! two sparse vectors x and y together with
! their indices, and stores them in two
! linked lists. using these linked lists it
! then calculates and prints out the inner
! product. it also prints the values.

  use sparse_vector_module
  use read_data_module

  implicit none
  character (len=30) :: filename

  type (sparse_vector), pointer :: root_x, &
    current_x, root_y, current_y
  real :: inner_prod = 0.0
  integer :: ifail = 0

! ask for name of file containing vector x
! non-zero values and indices

  print *, 'input file name for vector x'
  read '(a)', filename

! read vector x non-zero elements and indices
! into a linked list

  call read_data(filename, root_x, ifail)

  if (ifail==1) then
    print *, 'error opening file ', filename
    stop 10
  else if (ifail==2) then
    print *, &
      'error reading from beginning of file ', &
      filename
    stop 20
  else if (ifail==3) then
    print *, 'error reading from file ', &
      filename
    stop 30
  end if
```

```fortran
! ask for name of file containing vector y
! non-zero values and indices

  print *, 'input file name for vector y'
  read '(a)', filename

! read vector y non-zero elements and indices
! into a linked list

  call read_data(filename, root_y, ifail)
  if (ifail==1) then
    print *, 'error opening file ', filename
    stop 40
  else if (ifail==2) then
    print *, &
      'error reading from beginning of file ', &
      filename
    stop 50
  else if (ifail==3) then
    print *, 'error reading from file ', &
      filename
    stop 60
  end if

! data has now been read and stored in 2 linked
! lists. start at the beginning of x linked list
! and y linked list and compare indices
! in order to perform inner product

  current_x => root_x
  current_y => root_y
  do while (associated(current_x%next))
    do while (associated(current_y%next) .and. &
      current_y%index<current_x%index)

!     move through y list

      current_y => current_y%next
    end do

!   at this point
!   current_y%index >= current_x%index
!   or 2nd list is exhausted

    if (current_y%index==current_x%index) then
```

```
      inner_prod = inner_prod + current_x%value* &
        current_y%value
    end if
    current_x => current_x%next
  end do

! print non-zero values of vector x and indices

  print *, &
    'non-zero values of vector x and indices:'
  current_x => root_x
  do while (associated(current_x%next))
    print *, current_x%value, current_x%index
    current_x => current_x%next
  end do

! print non-zero values of vector y and indices

  print *, &
    'non-zero values of vector y and indices:'
  current_y => root_y
  do while (associated(current_y%next))
    print *, current_y%value, current_y%index
    current_y => current_y%next
  end do

! print out inner product

  print *, &
    'inner product of two sparse vectors is :', &
    inner_prod

end program ch2601
```

26.3   Example 2: Solving a System of First-Order Ordinary Differential Equations Using Runge–Kutta–Merson

Simulation and mathematical modelling of a wide range of physical processes often leads to a system of ordinary differential equations to be solved. Such equations also occur when approximate techniques are applied to more complex problems. We will restrict ourselves to a class of ordinary differential equations called initial value problems. These are systems for which all conditions are given at the same value of the independent variable. We will further restrict ourselves to first-order initial value problems of the form:

$$\frac{dy_1}{dt} = f_1(\underline{y}, t)$$

$$\frac{dy_2}{dt} = f_2(\underline{y}, t)$$

$$\dots$$

$$\frac{dy_n}{dt} = f_n(\underline{y}, t)$$

or

$$\underline{\dot{y}} = \underline{f}(\underline{y}, t) \tag{26.1}$$

with initial conditions

$$\underline{y}(t0) = \underline{y0}$$

where

$$\underline{y} = \begin{pmatrix} y_1 \\ \cdot \\ \cdot \\ \cdot \\ y_n \end{pmatrix} \quad \underline{f} = \begin{pmatrix} f_1 \\ \cdot \\ \cdot \\ \cdot \\ f_n \end{pmatrix} \quad \underline{y_0} = \begin{pmatrix} y_1(t_0) \\ \cdot \\ \cdot \\ \cdot \\ y_n t(_0) \end{pmatrix}$$

If we have a system of ordinary differential equations of higher order then they can be reformulated to a system of order one. See the NAG library documentation for solving ordinary differential equations.

One well-known class of methods for solving initial value ordinary differential equations is Runge-Kutta. In this example we have coded the Runge-Kutta-Merson algorithm, which is a fourth-order method and solves (26.1) from a point $t = a$ to a point $t = b$.

It starts with a step length $h = (b - a)/100$ and includes a local error control strategy such that the solution at $t + h$ is accepted if:

$$|error \; estimate| < user \; defined \; tolerance$$

If this isn't satisfied the step length h is halved and the solution attempt is repeated until the above is satisfied or the step length is too small and the problem is left unsolved. If the error criterion is satisfied the algorithm progresses with a suitable step length solving the equations at intermediate points until the end point b is reached. For a full discussion of the algorithm and the error control mechanism used see Numerical Methods in Practice by Tim Hopkins and Chris Phillips.

Here is a module containing the subroutine `runge_kutta_merson`.

```
module rkm_module
  use precision_module, wp => dp
  implicit none

contains
  subroutine runge_kutta_merson(y, fun, ifail, &
    n, a, b, tol)
!
!    runge-kutta-merson method for the solution
!    of a system of n 1st order initial value
!    ordinary differential equations.
!    the routine tries to integrate from
!    t=a to t=b with initial conditions in y,
!    subject to the condition that the
!    absolute error estimate <= tol. the step
!    length is adjusted automatically to meet
!    this condition.
!    if the routine is successful it returns with
!    ifail = 0, t=b and the solution in y.
!

    implicit none

!    define arguments

    real (wp), intent (inout), dimension (:) :: &
      y
    real (wp), intent (in) :: a, b, tol
    integer, intent (in) :: n
    integer, intent (out) :: ifail

    interface
      subroutine fun(t, y, f, n)
        use precision_module, wp => dp
        implicit none
        real (wp), intent (in), dimension (:) :: &
          y
        real (wp), intent (out), &
          dimension (:) :: f
        real (wp), intent (in) :: t
        integer, intent (in) :: n
      end subroutine fun
    end interface
```

```
!    local variables

     real (wp), dimension (1:size(y)) :: s1, s2, &
       s3, s4, s5, new_y_1, new_y_2, error
     real (wp) :: t, h, h2, h3, h6, h8, &
       factor = 1.e-2_wp
     real (wp) :: smallest_step = 1.e-6_wp, &
       max_error
     integer :: no_of_steps = 0

     ifail = 0

!    check input parameters

     if (n<=0 .or. a==b .or. tol<=0.0) then
       ifail = 1
       return
     end if

!    initialize t to be start of interval and
!    h to be 1/100 of interval

     t = a
     h = (b-a)/100.0_wp
     do

!        ##### beginning of
!        ##### repeat loop

         h2 = h/2.0_wp
         h3 = h/3.0_wp
         h6 = h/6.0_wp
         h8 = h/8.0_wp

!        calculate s1,s2,s3,s4,s5
!        s1=f(t,y)

         call fun(t, y, s1, n)
         new_y_1 = y + h3*s1

!        s2 = f(t+h/3,y+h/3*s1)

         call fun(t+h3, new_y_1, s2, n)
         new_y_1 = y + h6*s1 + h6*s2
```

```
!       s3=f(t+h/3,y+h/6*s1+h/6*s2)

        call fun(t+h3, new_y_1, s3, n)
        new_y_1 = y + h8*(s2+3.0_wp*s3)

!       s4=f(t+h/2,y+h/8*(s2+3*s3))

        call fun(t+h2, new_y_1, s4, n)
        new_y_1 = y + h2*(s1-3.0_wp*s3+4.0_wp*s4)

!       s5=f(t+h,y+h/2*(s1-3*s3+4*s4))

        call fun(t+h, new_y_1, s5, n)

!       calculate values at t+h

        new_y_1 = y + h6*(s1+4.0_wp*s4+s5)
        new_y_2 = y + h2*(s1-3.0_wp*s3+4.0_wp*s4)

!       calculate error estimate

        error = abs(0.2_wp*(new_y_1-new_y_2))
        max_error = maxval(error)
        if (max_error>tol) then

!         halve step length and try again

          if (abs(h2)<smallest_step) then
            ifail = 2
            return
          end if
          h = h2
        else

!         accepted approximation so overwrite
!         y with y_new_1, and t with t+h

          y = new_y_1
          t = t + h

!         can next step be doubled?

          if (max_error*factor<tol) then
            h = h*2.0_wp
          end if
```

```
!            does next step go beyond interval end b,
!            if so set h = b-t

             if (t+h>b) then
                h = b - t
             end if
             no_of_steps = no_of_steps + 1
          end if
          if (t>=b) exit

!         ##### end of
!         ##### repeat loop

       end do
     end subroutine runge_kutta_merson
   end module rkm_module
```

Consider trying to solve the following system of first-order ordinary differential equations:

$$\dot{y}_1 = \tan y_3$$

$$\dot{y}_2 = \frac{-0.032 \tan y_3}{y_2} - \frac{0.02 y_2}{\cos y_3}$$

$$\dot{y}_3 = -\frac{0.032}{y_2^2}$$

over an interval $t = 0.0$ to $t = 8.0$ with initial conditions

$$y1 = 0 \quad y2 = 0.5 \quad y3 = \pi/5$$

The user supplied subroutine, packaged as a module procedure, is:

```
module fun1_module
  implicit none
contains
  subroutine fun1(t, y, f, n)
    use precision_module, wp => dp
    implicit none
    real (wp), intent (in), dimension (:) :: y
    real (wp), intent (out), dimension (:) :: f
    real (wp), intent (in) :: t
    integer, intent (in) :: n
    f(1) = tan(y(3))
```

```
    f(2) = -0.032_wp*f(1)/y(2) - &
       0.02_wp*y(2)/cos(y(3))
    f(3) = -0.032_wp/(y(2)*y(2))
  end subroutine fun1
end module fun1_module
```

and the main program to solve this system of ordinary differential equations is

```
include 'precision_module.f90'
include 'ch2602_rkm_module.f90'
include 'ch2602_fun1_module.f90'

program ch2602
  use precision_module, wp => dp
  use rkm_module
  use fun1_module
  implicit none
  real (wp), dimension (:), allocatable :: y
  real (wp) :: a, b, tol
  integer :: n, ifail, all_stat

  print *, 'input no of equations'
  read *, n

! allocate space for y - checking to see that it
! allocates properly

  allocate (y(1:n), stat=all_stat)
  if (all_stat/=0) then
    print *, ' not enough memory'
    print *, ' array y is not allocated'
    stop
  end if
  print *, &
    ' input start and end of interval over'
  print *, ' which equations to be solved'
  read *, a, b
  print *, 'input initial conditions'
  read *, y(1:n)
  print *, 'input tolerance'
  read *, tol
  print 100, a
100 format ('at t= ', f5.2, &
    ' initial conditions are :')
  print 110, y(1:n)
```

```
110 format (4(f5.2,2x))
   call runge_kutta_merson(y, fun1, ifail, n, a, &
     b, tol)
   if (ifail/=0) then
     print *, 'integration stopped with ifail = ' &
       , ifail
   else
     print 120, b
120 format ('at t= ', f5.2, ' solution is:')
     print 110, y(1:n)
   end if
end program ch2602
```

The user is prompted for the number of equations, which is 3, the start and end of the interval over which the equations are to be solved (0.0, 8.0), the initial conditions (0.0, 0.5, $\pi/5$), and tolerance (1.0E-6).

26.3.1 Note: Alternative Form of the Allocate Statement

In   the main program ch2602 we have defined y to be a deferred-shape array, allocating it space after the variable n is read in. In order to make sure that enough memory is available to allocate space to array y the allocate statement is used as follows:

```
allocate(y(1:n),stat=all_stat)
```

If the allocation is successful variable all_stat returns zero; otherwise it is given a processor dependent positive value. We have included code to check for this and the program stops if all_stat is not zero.

26.3.2 Note: Automatic Arrays

The subroutine runge_kutta_merson needs a number of local rank 1 arrays s1, s2, s3, s4 and s5 for workspace, their shape and size being the same as the dummy argument y. Fortran supplies automatic arrays for this purpose and can be declared as

```
real(wp), dimension (1:size(y)) :: &
  s1, s2, s3, s4, s5
```

The size of automatic arrays can depend on the size of actual arrays: in our example they are the same shape and size as the dummy array y. Automatic arrays are created when the procedure is called and destroyed when control passes back to the calling program unit. They may have different shapes and sizes with different calls to the procedure, and because of this automatic arrays cannot be saved or initialised.

A word of warning should be given at this point. If there isn't enough memory available when an automatic array needs to be created problems will occur. Unlike allocatable arrays there is no way of testing to see if an automatic array has been created successfully. The general feeling is that even though they are nice, automatic arrays should be used with care and perhaps shouldn't be used in production code!

26.3.3   *Note: Subroutine as a Dummy Procedure Argument:*

In order to make the use of subroutine `runge_kutta_merson` as general as possible the user can choose the name of the subroutine in which the actual system of equations to be solved is defined. In this case we have chosen `fun1` as the name of the subroutine, which is then used as an actual argument when calling `runge_kutta_merson` from the main program e.g.

```
call runge_kutta_merson(y,fun1,ifail,n,a,b,tol)
```

An explicit interface for subroutine `fun1` is provided by it being contained in a module.

The equivalent dummy subroutine argument is `fun` and this needs an explicit interface in the subroutine `runge_kutta_merson`.

26.3.4   *Note: Compilation When Using Modules*

When compiling this program and the modules they must be done in the correct order:

- `precision_module`
- `rkm_module`
- `fun1_module`

  and then

- `main program`.

26.3.5   *Keyword and Optional Argument Variation*

In modern Fortran arguments to procedures can be optional, and can be supplied
by keyword. To illustrate this we will use the previous example. The definition of
subroutine `runge_kutta_merson` and its dummy arguments is:

```
subroutine runge_kutta_merson(y,fun,ifail,n,a,b,tol)
```

where a is the initial point, b is the end point at which the solution is required, `tol`
is the accuracy to which the solution is required and n is the number of equations.
The subroutine can be called as follows:

```
call runge_kutta_merson( y , fun1 , ifail , a=0.0 ,&
  b=8.0 , tol=1.0E-6 , n=3)
```

where the dummy arguments a, b, `tol` and n are now being used as keywords. The
use of keyword arguments makes the code easier to read and decreases the need to
remember their precise position in the argument list.

Also with Fortran comes the ability to specify that an argument is optional. This
is very useful when designing procedures for use by a range of programmers. Inside
a procedure defaults can be set for the optional arguments providing an easy-to-use
interface, while at the same time allowing sophisticated users a more comprehensive
one.

The `optional` attribute is needed to declare a dummy argument to be optional.
In the subroutine `runge_kutta_merson` the dummy argument `tol` could be
declared to be optional (although internally in the subroutine the code would have
to be changed to allow for this), e.g.,

```
subroutine runge_kutta_merson(y,fun,ifail,n,a,b,tol)
use precision_module  ,  wp => dp
real (wp) , intent(inout), optional :: tol
```

and because it is at the end of the dummy argument list, calling the subroutine
with a positional argument list, `tol` can be omitted, e.g.,

```
call runge_kutta_merson(y,fun1,ifail,n,a,b)
```

The code of the subroutine will need to be changed to check to see if the argument
`tol` is supplied, the intrinsic function `present` being available for this purpose.
Sample code is given below:

```
subroutine runge_kutta_merson(y,fun,ifail,n,a,b,tol)
use precision_module , wp => dp
! code left out
```

```
real (wp) , intent(in) , optional :: tol
real (wp) :: internal_tol = 1.0e-3_wp
  if(present(tol)) then
    internal_tol=tol
    print*,'tol = ', internal_tol,' is supplied'
  else
    print*,"tol isn't supplied, default tolerance = "
    print *,internal_tol,' is used'
  endif
! code left out but all references to tol
! would have to be changed to internal_tol
end subroutine runge_kutta_merson
```

26.4 Example 3: A Subroutine to Extract the Diagonal Elements of a Matrix

A common task mathematically is to extract the diagonal elements of a matrix. For example if

$$A = \begin{pmatrix} 21 & 6 & 7 \\ 9 & 3 & 2 \\ 4 & 1 & 8 \end{pmatrix}$$

the diagonal elements are $(21, 3, 8)$.

This can be thought of as extracting an array section, but the intrinsic function pack is needed. In its simplest form pack(array,vector) packs an array, array, into a rank 1 array, vector, according to array's array element order.

Below is a complete program to demonstrate this:

```
module md_module
  implicit none

contains
  subroutine matrix_diagonal(a, diag, n)
    implicit none
    real, intent (in), dimension (:, :) :: a
    real, intent (out), dimension (:) :: diag
    integer, intent (in) :: n
    real, dimension (1:size(a,1)*size(a,1)) :: &
      temp

!   subroutine to extract the diagonal
```

```
!    elements of an n * n matrix A

     temp = pack(a, .true.)
     diag = temp(1:n*n:n+1)
   end subroutine matrix_diagonal
end module md_module

program ch2603
! program reads the n * n matrix from a file
  use md_module
  implicit none
  integer :: i, n
  real, allocatable, dimension (:, :) :: a
  real, allocatable, dimension (:) :: adiag
  character (len=20) :: filename

  print *, 'input name of data file'
  read '(a)', filename
  open (unit=1, file=filename,status='old')
  read (1, *) n
  allocate (a(1:n,1:n), adiag(1:n))
  do i = 1, n
    read (1, *) a(i, 1:n)
  end do
  call matrix_diagonal(a, adiag, n)
  print *, ' diagonal elements of a are:'
  print *, adiag
end program ch2603
```

26.5   Example 4: The Solution of Linear Equations Using Gaussian Elimination

At   this stage we have introduced many of the concepts needed to write numerical code, and have included a popular algorithm, Gaussian Elimination, together with a main program which uses it and a module to bring together many of the features covered so far.

Finding the solution of a system of linear equations is very common in scientific and engineering problems, either as a direct physical problem or indirectly, for example, as the result of using finite difference methods to solve a partial differential equation. We will restrict ourselves to the case where the number of equations and the number of unknowns are the same. The problem can be defined as:

$$a_{11}x_1 + a_{12}x_2 + \ldots + a_{1n}x_n = b_1$$

$$a_{22}x_2 + a_{22}x_2 + \ldots + a_{2n}x_n = b_2$$

$$\ldots$$

$$a_{n1}x_1 + a_{n2}x_2 + \ldots + a_{nn}x_n = b_1$$

or

$$\begin{pmatrix} a_{11} & a_{12} & \ldots & a_{1n} \\ a_{21} & a_{22} & \ldots & a_{2n} \\ \ldots & \ldots & \ldots & \ldots \\ a_{n1} & a_{n2} & \ldots & a_{nn} \end{pmatrix} \begin{pmatrix} x_1 \\ x_2 \\ \ldots \\ x_n \end{pmatrix} = \begin{pmatrix} b_1 \\ b_2 \\ \ldots \\ b_n \end{pmatrix} \tag{26.2}$$

which can be written as:

$Ax = b$

where A is the n x n coefficient matrix, b is the right-hand-side vector and x is the vector of unknowns. We will also restrict ourselves to the case where A is a general real matrix.

Note that there is a unique solution to (26.2) if the inverse, A^{-1}, of the coefficient matrix A, exists. However, the system should never be solved by finding A^{-1} and then solving $A^{-1}b = x$ because of the problems of rounding error and the computational costs.

A well-known method for solving (26.2) is Gaussian Elimination, where multiples of equations are subtracted from others so that the coefficients below the diagonal become zero, producing a system of the form:

$$\begin{pmatrix} a_{11}^* & a_{12}^* & \ldots & a*_{1n} \\ 0 & a_{22}^* & \ldots & a_{2n}^* \\ \ldots & \ldots & \ldots & \ldots \\ 0 & 0 & 0 & a_{nn}^* \end{pmatrix} \begin{pmatrix} x_1 \\ x_2 \\ \ldots \\ x_n \end{pmatrix} = \begin{pmatrix} b_1^* \\ b_2^* \\ \ldots \\ b_n^* \end{pmatrix}$$

where A has been transformed into an upper triangular matrix. By a process of backward substitution the values of x drop out.

The subroutine `gaussian_elimination` implements the Gaussian Elimination algorithm with partial pivoting, which ensure that   the multipliers are less than 1 in magnitude, by interchanging rows if necessary. This is to try and prevent the buildup of errors.

This implementation is based on two LINPACK routines SGEFA and SGESL and a Fortran 77 subroutine written by Tim Hopkins and Chris Phillips and found in their book Numerical Methods in Practice.

When the subroutine `gaussian_elimination` is called on exit both a and b are overwritten. Mathematically Gaussian Elimination is described as working on rows, and using partial pivoting row interchanges may be necessary. Due to Fortran's row element ordering, to implement this algorithm efficiently it works on columns rather than rows by interchanging elements within a column if necessary.

```fortran
include 'precision_module.f90'

module ge_module
  use precision_module, wp => dp
  implicit none

contains
  subroutine gaussian_elimination(a, n, b, x, &
    singular)

!   routine to solve a system ax=b
!   using gaussian elimination
!   with partial pivoting
!   the code is based on the linpack routines
!   sgefa and sgesl
!   and operates on columns rather than rows!

    implicit none

!   matrix a and vector b are over-written
!   arguments

    integer, intent (in) :: n
    real (wp), intent (inout) :: a(:, :), b(:)
    real (wp), intent (out) :: x(:)
    logical, intent (out) :: singular

!   local variables

    integer :: i, j, k, pivot_row
    real (wp) :: pivot, sum, element
    real (wp), parameter :: eps = 1.e-13_wp

!   work through the matrix column by column

    do k = 1, n - 1

!     find largest element in column k for pivot
!
      pivot_row = maxval(maxloc(abs(a(k:n,k)))) &
        + k - 1

!     test to see if a is singular
!     if so return to main program
```

```
      if (abs(a(pivot_row,k))<=eps) then
        singular = .true.
        return
      else
        singular = .false.
      end if

!     exchange elements in column k if largest
!     is
!     not on the diagonal

      if (pivot_row/=k) then
        element = a(pivot_row, k)
        a(pivot_row, k) = a(k, k)
        a(k, k) = element
        element = b(pivot_row)
        b(pivot_row) = b(k)
        b(k) = element
      end if

!     compute multipliers
!     elements of column k below diagonal
!     are set to these multipliers for use
!     in elimination later on

      a(k+1:n, k) = a(k+1:n, k)/a(k, k)

!     row elimination performed by columns for
!     efficiency

      do j = k + 1, n
        pivot = a(pivot_row, j)
        if (pivot_row/=k) then

!         swap if pivot row is not k

          a(pivot_row, j) = a(k, j)
          a(k, j) = pivot
        end if
        a(k+1:n, j) = a(k+1:n, j) - &
          pivot*a(k+1:n, k)
      end do

!     apply same operations to b
```

```
    b(k+1:n) = b(k+1:n) - a(k+1:n, k)*b(k)
  end do

!   backward substitution

  do i = n, 1, -1
    sum = 0.0
    do j = i + 1, n
      sum = sum + a(i, j)*x(j)
    end do
    x(i) = (b(i)-sum)/a(i, i)
  end do
  end subroutine gaussian_elimination
end module ge_module

program ch2604
  use ge_module
  implicit none
  integer :: i, n
  real (wp), allocatable :: a(:, :), b(:), x(:)
  logical :: singular

  print *, 'number of equations?'
  read *, n
  allocate (a(1:n,1:n), b(1:n), x(1:n))
  do i = 1, n
    print *, 'input elements of row ', i, &
      ' of a'
    read *, a(i, 1:n)
    print *, 'input element ', i, ' of b'
    read *, b(i)
  end do
  call gaussian_elimination(a, n, b, x, &
    singular)
  if (singular) then
    print *, 'matrix is singular'
  else
    print *, 'solution x:'
    print *, x(1:n)
  end if
end program ch2604
```

26.5.1 Notes

26.5.1.1 Module for Precision Selection

We use the module precision_module from Chap. 21 and choose a working precision wp which maps to dp or double precision, to specify the floating point precision to which we wish to work. This module is then used by the main program and the subroutine, and wp is used with all the real type definitions and any constants, e.g.

```
real(wp), parameter :: eps=1.E-13_wp
```

26.5.1.2 Deferred-Shape Arrays

In the main program matrix a and vectors b and x are declared as deferred-shape arrays, by specifying their rank only and using the allocatable attribute . Their shape is determined at run time when the variable n is read in and then the statement

```
allocate(a(1:n,1:n), b(1:n), x(1:n))
```

is used.

26.5.1.3 Intrinsic Functions maxval and maxloc

In the context of subroutine gaussian_elimination we have used:

```
maxval ( maxloc (abs ( a ( k:n,k ) ) ) ) + k - 1
```

Breaking this down,

```
maxloc ( abs ( a (k:n,k) ) )
```

takes the rank 1 array

$$(|a(k, k)|, |a(k + 1, k)|, ...|a(n, k)|) \tag{26.3}$$

where $|a(k, k)| = abs(a(k, k))$ and of length $n - k + 1$. It returns the position of the largest element as a rank 1 array of size one, e.g. 1.

Applying maxval to this rank 1 array 1 returns 1 as a scalar, 1 being the position of the largest element of array (1).

What we actually want is the position of the largest element of (26.3), but in the kth column of matrix a. We therefore have to add $k-1$ to l to give the actual position in column k of a.

26.6   Example 5: Allocatable Function Results

A function may return an array, and in this example the array allocation takes place in the function.

```
module running_average_module
  implicit none

contains
  function running_average(r, how_many) &
    result (rarray)
    integer, intent (in) :: how_many
    real, intent (in), allocatable, &
      dimension (:) :: r
    real, allocatable, dimension (:) :: rarray
    integer :: i
    real :: sum = 0.0

    allocate (rarray(1:how_many))
    do i = 1, how_many
      sum = sum + r(i)
      rarray(i) = sum/i
    end do
  end function running_average
end module running_average_module
module read_data_module
  implicit none

contains
  subroutine read_data(file_name, raw_data, &
    how_many)
    implicit none
    character (len=*), intent (in) :: file_name
    integer, intent (in) :: how_many
    real, intent (out), allocatable, &
      dimension (:) :: raw_data
    integer :: i
```

```fortran
      allocate (raw_data(1:how_many))
      open (unit=1, file=file_name, status='old')
      do i = 1, how_many
        read (unit=1, fmt=*) raw_data(i)
      end do

    end subroutine read_data

  end module read_data_module

  program ch2605
    use running_average_module
    use read_data_module
    implicit none
    integer :: how_many
    character (len=20) :: file_name
    real, allocatable, dimension (:) :: raw_data
    real, allocatable, dimension (:) :: ra
    integer :: i

    print *, ' how many data items are there?'
    read *, how_many
    print *, ' what is the file name?'
    read '(a)', file_name
    call read_data(file_name, raw_data, how_many)
    allocate (ra(1:how_many))
    ra = running_average(raw_data, how_many)
    do i = 1, how_many
      print *, raw_data(i), ' ', ra(i)
    end do
  end program ch2605
```

This facility was introduced in Fortran 95.

26.7   Example 6: Elemental e**x Function

The following is an elemental version of the `etox` function covered in an earlier chapter.

```fortran
  module etox_module
    implicit none

  contains
```

```
  elemental real function etox(x)
    implicit none
    real, intent (in) :: x
    real :: term
    integer :: nterm
    real, parameter :: tol = 1.0e-6

    etox = 1.0
    term = 1.0
    nterm = 0
    do
      nterm = nterm + 1
      term = (x/nterm)*term
      etox = etox + term
      if (term<=tol) exit
    end do
  end function etox
end module etox_module
program ch2606
  use etox_module
  implicit none
  integer :: i
  real :: x
  real, dimension (10) :: y

  x = 1.0
  do i = 1, 10
    y(i) = i
  end do
  print *, y
  x = etox(x)
  print *, x
  y = etox(y)
  print *, y
end program ch2606
```

Elemental functions require the use of explicit interfaces, and we have therefore used modules to achieve this.

26.8 Example 7: Absolute and Relative Errors Involved in Subtraction Using 32 bit Reals

It should be apparent by now that floating point arithmetic is by its very nature inexact. Knuth and others identify the concept of significant digits or relative error as a useful measure. As a general rule the operations of multiplication and division do not magnify the relative error by very much, but floating point subtraction does.

In the next two examples we look at the the relative error involved with subtraction. In the first example we use 32 bit reals, our sp kind type from our precision module.

Here is the program source.

```
include 'precision_module.f90'

program ch2607

  use precision_module, wp => sp

  implicit none
  integer :: i
  integer, parameter :: n = 4
  real (wp), dimension (n) :: x1 = [ 1.1_wp, &
    1.01_wp, 1.001_wp, 1.0001_wp ]
  real (wp), dimension (n) :: x2 = [ 1.2_wp, &
    1.02_wp, 1.002_wp, 1.0002_wp ]
  real (wp), dimension (n) :: x3 = [ 0.1_wp, &
    0.01_wp, 0.001_wp, 0.0001_wp ]
  real (wp), dimension (n) :: rel_error = 0.0_wp
  real (wp), dimension (n) :: abs_error = 0.0_wp
  real (wp) :: z

  character (len=11), dimension (n) :: heading_1 &
    = [ '1 in 10    ', '1 in 100   ', &
    '1 in 1,000 ', '1 in 10,000' ]
  character (len=6), dimension (n) :: heading_2 &
    = [ '1.1   ', '1.01  ', '1.001 ', '1.0001' ]
  character (len=15), dimension (2) :: heading_3 &
    = [ 'Absolute error ', 'Relative error ' ]

  do i = 1, n
    z = x2(i) - x1(i)
    abs_error(i) = abs(z-x3(i))
    rel_error(i) = abs_error(i)/x3(i)
    print *, ' ', heading_1(i), '               ', &
      heading_2(i)
```

```
   print *, ' Calculated =              ', z, '    ', &
     heading_3(1), abs_error(i)
   print *, ' Expected    =            ', x3(i), &
      '   ', heading_3(2), rel_error(i)
 end do

end program ch2607
```

Here is sample output from the Nag compiler.

```
1 in 10                   1.1
Calculated =              0.1000000    Absolute error    2.2351742E-08
Expected    =             0.1000000    Relative error    2.2351742E-07
1 in 100                  1.01
Calculated =              9.9999905E-03   Absolute error   9.3132257E-09
Expected    =             9.9999998E-03   Relative error   9.3132257E-07
1 in 1,000                1.001
Calculated =              9.9992752E-04   Absolute error   7.2526745E-08
Expected    =             1.0000000E-03   Relative error   7.2526745E-05
1 in 10,000               1.0001
Calculated =              1.0001659E-04   Absolute error   1.6596459E-08
Expected    =             9.9999997E-05   Relative error   1.6596459E-04
```

26.9   Example 8: Absolute and Relative Errors Involved in Subtraction Using 64 bit Reals

Here is the program source.

```
include 'precision_module.f90'

program ch2608

  use precision_module, wp => dp

  implicit none
  integer :: i
  integer, parameter :: n = 5

  real (wp), dimension (n) :: x1 = [ &
    1.000000001_wp, 1.0000000001_wp, &
    1.00000000001_wp, 1.000000000001_wp, &
    1.0000000000001_wp ]

  real (wp), dimension (n) :: x2 = [ &
    1.000000002_wp, 1.0000000002_wp, &
    1.00000000002_wp, 1.000000000002_wp, &
    1.0000000000002_wp ]
```

```
real (wp), dimension (n) :: x3 = [ &
  0.000000001_wp, 0.0000000001_wp, &
  0.00000000001_wp, 0.000000000001_wp, &
  0.0000000000001_wp ]

real (wp), dimension (n) :: rel_error = 0.0_wp
real (wp), dimension (n) :: abs_error = 0.0_wp

real (wp) :: z

character (len=23), dimension (n) :: heading_1 &
  = [ '1 in        1,000,000,000', &
  '1 in       10,000,000,000', &
  '1 in      100,000,000,000', &
  '1 in    1,000,000,000,000', &
  '1 in 10,000,000,000,000' ]

character *15, dimension (n) :: heading_2 = [ &
  '1.000000001    ', '1.0000000001    ', &
  '1.00000000001  ', '1.000000000001 ', &
  '1.0000000000001' ]

character *15, dimension (2) :: heading_3 = [ &
  'Absolute error ', 'Relative error ' ]

do i = 1, n
  z = x2(i) - x1(i)
  abs_error(i) = abs(z-x3(i))
  rel_error(i) = abs_error(i)/x3(i)
  print *, heading_1(i), ' ', heading_2(i)
  print *, ' Calculated =          ', z, ' ', &
    heading_3(1), abs_error(i)
  print *, ' Expected   =          ', x3(i), &
    ' ', heading_3(2), rel_error(i)
end do

end program ch2608
```

Here is sample output from the Nag compiler.

```
1 in      1,000,000,000 1.000000001
Calculated =              9.9999986069576607E-10
                                  Absolute error   1.3930423398822253E-16
Expected   =              1.0000000000000001E-09
                                  Relative error   1.3930423398822253E-07
1 in     10,000,000,000 1.0000000001
Calculated =              1.0000000827403710E-10
                                  Absolute error   8.2740370962658176E-18
Expected   =              1.0000000000000000E-10
                                  Relative error   8.2740370962658176E-08
1 in    100,000,000,000 1.00000000001
Calculated =              1.0000000827403710E-11
```

```
                              Absolute error    8.2740371059593404E-19
      Expected   =           9.9999999999999994E-12
                              Relative error    8.2740371059593408E-08
1 in  1,000,000,000,000 1.000000000001
      Calculated =           9.9986685597741598E-13
                              Absolute error    1.3314402258399958E-16
      Expected   =           9.9999999999999998E-13
                              Relative error    1.3314402258399958E-04
1 in 10,000,000,000,000 1.0000000000001
      Calculated =           1.0014211682118912E-13
                              Absolute error    1.4211682118911691E-16
      Expected   =           1.0000000000000000E-13
                              Relative error    1.4211682118911691E-03
```

26.10   Problems

26.1 Compile and run the sparse matrix example with the data provided.

26.2 Compile and run the Runge Kutta Merson example with the data provided.

26.3 Compile and run the Gaussian Elimination example with the following data.

$$
A = \begin{pmatrix} 33 & 16 & 72 \\ -24 & -10 & -57 \\ -8 & -4 & -17 \end{pmatrix}
$$

$$
b = \begin{pmatrix} -359 \\ 281 \\ 85 \end{pmatrix}
$$

and the solution is

$$
x = \begin{pmatrix} 1 \\ -2 \\ -5 \end{pmatrix}
$$

26.4 Edit the Runge Kutta Merson subroutine so that `tol` is an optional argument. Compile and run the new code for the same set of ODE's but don't provide `tol` in the main program's call to the subroutine. Next provide `tol` with a value 1.0e-4. What results do you get?

26.11   Bibliography

Duff I.S., Erismon A.M., Reid J.K., Direct Methods for Sparse Matrices, Oxford Science Publications, 1986.

- Authoritative coverage of this area. Relatively old, but well regarded. Code segments and examples are a mixture of Fortran 77 and Algol 60 (which of course do not support pointers) and therefore the implementation of linked lists is done using the existing features of these languages. The onus is on the programmer to correctly implement linked lists using fixed size arrays rather than using the features provided by pointers in a language. It is remarkable how elegant these solutions are, given the lack of dynamic data structures in these two languages.

Hopkins T., Phillips C., Numerical Methods in Practice, Using the NAG Library. Addison-Wesley, 1988.

- Good adjunct to the NAG library documentation for the less numerate user.

Chapter 27
Parameterised Derived Types (PDTs) in Fortran

Aims

The aims of this chapter are to look at some additional data structuring examples in Fortran that use parameterised derived types - PDTs.

27.1 Introduction

Parameterised derived types were introduced in the Fortran 2003 standard. They allow the kind, length, or shape of a derived type's components to be chosen when the derived type is used.

This feature was only available in two compilers (Cray and IBM) at the time of the second edition. Support for this feature is now available in three additional compilers. At the time of writing they were available in the following compilers:

- Cray
- IBM
- Intel
- Nag (partial)
- PGI

Consult our *Compiler Support for the Fortran 2003 and 2008 Standards* document

```
https://www.fortranplus.co.uk/
fortran-information/
```

for up to date information.

A parameterised derived type can have the kind, length and shape of a derived type chosen at run time. All type parameters are of type `integer` and have a `kind`, `len` or `dim` attribute. A kind type parameter may be used in constant and specification expressions. A length type parameter may only be used in a specification expression, e.g. array declarations.

© Springer International Publishing AG, part of Springer Nature 2018 453
I. Chivers and J. Sleightholme, *Introduction to Programming with Fortran*,
https://doi.org/10.1007/978-3-319-75502-1_27

We have a small number of examples to illustrate their use.

27.2   Example 1: Linked List Parameterised by Real Kind

Here is the link module.

```
module link_module
  use precision_module
  type link(real_kind)
    integer, kind :: real_kind
    real (kind=real_kind) :: n
    type (link(real_kind)), pointer :: next
  end type link
end module link_module
```

Here is the complete program.

```
include 'precision_module.f90'
include 'ch2701_link_module.f90'

program ch2701
  use precision_module
  use link_module
  implicit none
  integer, parameter :: wp = dp
  type (link(real_kind=wp)), pointer :: root, &
    current
  integer :: i = 0
  integer :: error = 0
  integer :: io_stat_number = 0
  real (wp), allocatable, dimension (:) :: x

  allocate (root)
  print *, ' type in some numbers'
  read (unit=*, fmt=*, iostat=io_stat_number) &
    root%n
  if (io_stat_number>0) then
    error = error + 1
  else if (io_stat_number<0) then
    nullify (root%next)
  else
    i = i + 1
```

```
      allocate (root%next)
    end if
    current => root
    do while (associated(current%next))
      current => current%next
      read (unit=*, fmt=*, iostat=io_stat_number) &
        current%n
      if (io_stat_number>0) then
        error = error + 1
      else if (io_stat_number<0) then
        nullify (current%next)
      else
        i = i + 1
        allocate (current%next)
      end if
    end do
    print *, i, ' items read'
    print *, error, ' items in error'
    allocate (x(1:i))
    i = 1
    current => root
    do while (associated(current%next))
      x(i) = current%n
      i = i + 1
      print *, current%n
      current => current%next
    end do
    print *, x
end program ch2701
```

Let us look at the `link_module` in more depth.

```
    type link(real_kind)
      integer, kind :: real_kind
      real (kind=real_kind) :: n
      type (link(real_kind)), pointer :: next
    end type link
```

The key is in the type declaration for `link` where the `link` type takes a parameter `real_kind`.

We then can reference this parameter within the `link` kind type definition. Thus the declarations for `n` and `next` are parameterised by `real_kind`.

In the main program we have

```
integer, parameter :: wp = dp
type (link(real_kind=wp)), pointer :: root, &
  current
```

and the type declarations for `root` and `current` are parameterised by `wp`, where `wp = dp`.

This means that we write one type definition for the `link` type that will work with any supported real kind type.

Without parameterised derived type support we would have to write separate kind type definitions for each supported real kind.

27.3   Example 2: Ragged Array Parameterised by Real Kind Type

Here is the ragged module.

```
module ragged_module
  use precision_module
  implicit none
  type ragged(real_kind)
    integer, kind :: real_kind
    real (real_kind), dimension (:), &
      allocatable :: ragged_row
  end type ragged
end module ragged_module
```

Here is the complete program.

```
include 'precision_module.f90'
include 'ch2702_ragged_module.f90'

program ch2702

  use precision_module
  use ragged_module
  implicit none
  integer, parameter :: wp = sp
  integer :: i
  integer, parameter :: n = 3

  type (ragged(wp)), dimension (1:n) :: &
    lower_diag
```

```
    do i = 1, n
      allocate (lower_diag(i)%ragged_row(1:i))
      print *, ' type in the values for row ', i
      read *, lower_diag(i)%ragged_row(1:i)
    end do
    do i = 1, n
      print *, lower_diag(i)%ragged_row(1:i)
    end do

end program ch2702
```

Let us look at the `ragged_module` in more depth.

```
module ragged_module
  use precision_module
  implicit none
  type ragged(real_kind)
    integer, kind :: real_kind
    real (real_kind), dimension (:), &
      allocatable :: ragged_row
  end type ragged
end module ragged_module
```

The key is in the type declaration for the `ragged` type.
We have

```
type ragged(real_kind)
```

so the kind definition is parameterised by `real_kind`.
The `ragged_row` array declaration is parameterised by `real_kind`.
In the main program we have

```
type (ragged(wp)), dimension (1:n) :: &
  lower_diag
```

so that the `lower_diag` declaration is parameterised by wp, where wp = sp.
So we have one declaration for the `ragged` type and can use this type with any supported real kind type.

27.4   Example 3: Specifying `len` in a PDT

In this example we use both the `kind` attribute and the `len` attribute in the type specification.

Here is the matrix module.

```fortran
module pdt_matrix_module

  use precision_module
  implicit none

  type pdt_matrix(k, row, col)
    integer, kind :: k
    integer, len :: row, col
    real (kind=k), dimension (row, col) :: m
  end type pdt_matrix

  interface scale_matrix
    module procedure scale_matrix_sp
    module procedure scale_matrix_dp
  end interface scale_matrix

contains

  subroutine scale_matrix_sp(a, scale)
    type (pdt_matrix(sp,*,*)), intent (inout) :: &
      a
    real (sp) :: scale

    a%m = a%m + scale
  end subroutine scale_matrix_sp

  subroutine scale_matrix_dp(a, scale)
    type (pdt_matrix(dp,*,*)), intent (inout) :: &
      a
    real (dp) :: scale

    a%m = a%m + scale
  end subroutine scale_matrix_dp

end module pdt_matrix_module
```

Here is the complete program.

```fortran
include 'precision_module.f90'
include 'ch2703_matrix_module.f90'

program ch2703
```

```fortran
  use precision_module
  use pdt_matrix_module

  implicit none

  real (sp) :: scs
  real (dp) :: scd
  integer, parameter :: nr = 2, nc = 3
  integer :: i
  type (pdt_matrix(sp,nr,nc)) :: as
  type (pdt_matrix(dp,nr,nc)) :: ad
!
! single precision
!
  do i = 1, nr
    print *, 'input row ', i, ' of sp matrix'
    read *, as%m(i, 1:nc)
  end do
  print *, 'input sp scaling factor'
  read *, scs
  call scale_matrix(as, scs)
  print *, 'updated matrix:'
  do i = 1, nr
    print 100, as%m(i, 1:nc)
100 format (10(f6.2,2x))
  end do
!
! double precision
!
  do i = 1, nr
    print *, 'input row ', i, ' of dp matrix'
    read *, ad%m(i, 1:nc)
  end do
  print *, 'input dp scaling factor'
  read *, scd
  call scale_matrix(ad, scd)
  print *, 'updated matrix:'
  do i = 1, nr
    print 110, ad%m(i, 1:nc)
110 format (10(e12.5,2x))
  end do

end program ch2703
```

27.5   Problems

27.1 Modify example 1 to read the data from a file.

27.2 Rewrite the tree derived type in Chap. 22 as a parameterised derived type to work with an integer of any type. Test it out.

Chapter 28
Introduction to Object Oriented Programming

For Madmen only
Hermann Hesse, Steppenwolf

Aims

The aims of this chapter are to look at object oriented programming in Fortran.

28.1 Introduction

This chapter looks at object oriented programming in Fortran. The chapter on programming languages covers the topic in a broader context.

28.2 Brief Review of the History of Object Oriented Programming

Object oriented programming is not new. One of the first languages to offer support was Simula 67, a language designed for discrete event simulation by Ole Johan Dahl, Bjorn Myhrhaug and Kristen Nygaard whilst working at the Norwegian Computing Centre in Oslo in the 1960's.

One of the next major developments was in the 1970's at the Xerox Palo Alto Research Centre Learning Research Group who began working on a vision of the ways different people might effectively use computing power. One of the outcomes of their work was the Smalltalk 80 system. Objects are at the core of the Smalltalk 80 system.

© Springer International Publishing AG, part of Springer Nature 2018   461
I. Chivers and J. Sleightholme, *Introduction to Programming with Fortran*,
https://doi.org/10.1007/978-3-319-75502-1_28

The 1980's and 1990's saw a number of object oriented programming languages emerge. They include

- Eiffel. Bertrand Meyer, Eiffel Software.
- C++ from C with classes. Bjarne Stroustrup at Bell Labs.
- Oberon 2. Niklaus Wirth at ETH in Zurich.
- Java. James Gosling, originally Sun, now Oracle.
- C# is a recent Microsoft addition to the list.

Object-oriented programming is effectively a programming methodology or paradigm using objects (data structures made up of data and methods). We will use the concept of a shape class in our explanation and examples. The Simula Begin book starts with shapes, and it is often used in introductions to object oriented programming in other languages.

Some of the key concepts are

- encapsulation or information hiding - the implementation of the data is hidden inside an object and clients or users of the data only have access to an abstract view of it. Methods are used to access and manipulate the data. For example a shape class may have an x and y position, and methods exist to get and set the positions and draw and move the shape.
- data abstraction - if we have an abstract shape data type we can create multiple variables of that type.
- inheritance - an existing abstract data type can be extended. It will inherit the data and methods from the base type and add additional data and methods. A key to inheritance is that the extended type is compatible with the base type. Anything that works with objects or variables of the base type also works with objects of the extended type. A circle would have a radius in addition to an x and y position, a rectangle would have a width and height.
- dynamic binding - if we have a base shape class and derive circles and rectangles from it dynamic binding ensures that the correct method to calculate the area is called at run time.
- polymorphism - variables can therefore be polymorphic. Using the shape example we can therefore create an array of shapes, one may be a shape, one may be a circle and another may be a rectangle.

Extensible abstract data types with dynamically bound methods are often called classes. This is the terminology we will use in what follows.

28.3   Background Technical Material

We need to look more formally at a number of concepts so that we can actually do object oriented programming in Fortran. The following sections cover some of the introductory material we need, and are taken from the standard.

28.3.1 The Concept of Type

Fortran provides an abstract means whereby data can be categorized without relying on a particular physical representation. This abstract means is the concept of type. A type has a name, a set of valid values, a means to denote such values (constants), and a set of operations to manipulate the values.

28.3.2 Type Classification

A type is either an intrinsic type or a derived type. This document defines five intrinsic types: integer, real, complex, character, and logical. A derived type is one that is defined by a derived-type definition (7.5.2) or by an intrinsic module. It shall be used only where it is accessible (7.5.2.2). An intrinsic type is always accessible.

28.3.3 Set of Values

For each type, there is a set of valid values. The sets of valid values for integer, character, and real are processor dependent. The set of valid values for complex consists of the set of all the combinations of the values of the real and imaginary parts. The set of valid values for a derived type is as defined in 7.5.8.

28.3.4 Type

A `type` type specifier is used to declare entities that are assumed-type, or of an intrinsic or derived type.

An entity that is declared using the TYPE(*) type specifier is assumed-type and is an unlimited polymorphic entity. It is not declared to have a type, and is not considered to have the same declared type as any other entity, including another unlimited polymorphic entity. Its dynamic type and type parameters are assumed from its effective argument.

28.3.5 Class

The CLASS type specifier is used to declare polymorphic entities. A polymorphic entity is a data entity that is able to be of differing dynamic types during program execution.

The declared type of a polymorphic entity is the specified type if the CLASS type specifier contains a type name.

An entity declared with the CLASS(*) specifier is an unlimited polymorphic entity. It is not declared to have a type, and is not considered to have the same declared type as any other entity, including another unlimited polymorphic entity.

28.3.6   Attributes

The additional attributes that may appear in the attribute specification of a type declaration statement further specify the nature of the entities being declared or specify restrictions on their use in the program.

28.3.6.1   Accessibility Attribute

The accessibility attribute specifies the accessibility of an entity via a particular identifier. The following is taken from Sect. 8.5.2 of the Fortran 2018 standard.

- access-spec is `public` or `private`
- An access-spec shall appear only in the specification-part of a module.

Identifiers that are specified in a module or accessible in that module by use association have either the `public` or `private` attribute. Identifiers for which an access-spec is not explicitly specified in that module have the default accessibility attribute for that module. The default accessibility attribute for a module is `public` unless it has been changed by a `private` statement. Only identifiers that have the `public` attribute in that module are available to be accessed from that module by use association.

28.3.7   Passed Object Dummy Arguments

Section 3.107 of the Fortran 2018 standard introduces the concept of passed object dummy argument. Here is an extract from the standard:

- A passed-object dummy argument is a distinguished dummy argument of a procedure pointer component or type-bound procedure (7.5.5). It affects procedure overriding (7.5.7.3) and argument association (15.5.2.2).
- If NOPASS is specified, the procedure pointer component or type-bound procedure has no passed-object dummy argument.
- If neither PASS nor NOPASS is specified or PASS is specified without arg-name, the first dummy argument of a procedure pointer component or type-bound procedure is its passed-object dummy argument.

- If PASS (arg-name) is specified, the dummy argument named arg-name is the passed-object dummy argument of the procedure pointer component or named type-bound procedure.
- Constraint C761 The passed-object dummy argument shall be a scalar, nonpointer, nonallocatable dummy data object with the same declared type as the type being defined; all of its length type parameters shall be assumed; it shall be polymorphic (7.3.2.3) if and only if the type being defined is extensible (7.5.7). It shall not have the VALUE attribute.

The key here is that we are going to use the `pass` and `nopass` attributes with type bound procedures - a component of object oriented programming in Fortran.

28.3.8 Derived Types and Structure Constructors

A derived type is a type that is not defined by the language but requires a type definition to declare its components. A scalar object of such a derived type is called a structure. Assignment of structures is defined intrinsically, but there are no intrinsic operations for structures. For each derived type, a structure constructor is available to provide values.

A derived-type definition implicitly defines a corresponding structure constructor that allows construction of values of that derived type.

28.3.9 Structure Constructors and Generic Names

A generic name may be the same as a type name. This can be used to emulate user-defined structure constructors for that type, even if the type has private components. The following example is taken from the standard to illustrate this.

```
module mytype_module
type mytype
  private
    complex value
    logical exact
end type
interface mytype
  module procedure int_to_mytype
end interface
! Operator definitions etc.
...
contains
  type(mytype) function int_to_mytype(i)
    integer,intent(in) :: i
    int_to_mytype%value = i
```

```
        int_to_mytype%exact = .true.
   end function
 ! Procedures to support operators etc.
 ...
 end
```

28.3.10   Assignment

Execution of an assignment statement causes a variable to become defined or redefined. Simplistically

```
   variable = expression
```

28.3.11   Intrinsic Assignment Statement

An intrinsic assignment statement is an assignment statement that is not a defined assignment statement (10.2.1.4). In an intrinsic assignment statement,

- if the variable is polymorphic it shall be allocatable and not a coarray,
- if expr is an array then the variable shall also be an array,
- the variable and expr shall be conformable unless the variable is an allocatable array that has the same rank as expr and is not a coarray,
- if the variable is polymorphic it shall be type compatible with expr; otherwise the declared types of the variable and expr shall conform as specified in Table 10.8 of the standard,
- if the variable is of type character and of ISO 10646, ASCII, or default character kind, expr shall be of ISO 10646, ASCII, or default character kind,
- otherwise if the variable is of type character expr shall have the same kind type parameter,
- if the variable is of derived type each kind type parameter of the variable shall have the same value as the corresponding kind type parameter of expr, and
- if the variable is of derived type each length type parameter of the variable shall have the same value as the corresponding type parameter of expr unless the variable is allocatable, is not a coarray, and its corresponding type parameter is deferred.

28.3.12   Defined Assignment Statement

A defined assignment statement is an assignment statement that is defined by a subroutine and a generic interface that specifies ASSIGNMENT (=).

28.3.13   Polymorphic Variables

Here are some of the technical definitions regarding polymorphic taken from the standard.

- polymorphic - polymorphic data entity able to be of differing dynamic types during program execution (7.3.2.3)
- unlimited polymorphic - able to have any dynamic type during program execution (7.3.2.3)

A polymorphic variable must be a pointer or allocatable variable. We will use allocatable variables to achieve polymorphism in our examples.

28.3.14   Executable Constructs Containing Blocks

The following are executable constructs that contain blocks:

- associate construct
- case construct
- do construct
- if construct
- select type construct

We will look at the associate construct and select type construct next.

28.3.15   The *associate* Construct

The associate construct associates named entities with expressions or variables during the execution of its block. These named construct entities are associating entities. The names are associate names.

The following example illustrates an association with a derived-type variable.

```
associate ( xc => ax%b(i,i)%c )
xc%dv = xc%dv + product(xc%ev(1:n))
end associate
```

28.3.16   The *select type* Construct

The select type construct selects for execution at most one of its constituent blocks. The selection is based on the dynamic type of an expression. A name is associated with the expression, in the same way as for the associate construct.

Quite a lot to take in! Let's illustrate the use of the above in some actual examples.

28.4   Example 1: The Basic Shape Class

The code for the base shape class is given below.

- shape class data: integer variables x and y for the position.
- shape class methods: get and set for the x and y values, and moveto and draw.

We have used an include statement in the examples that follow to reduce code duplication. In this example we have used the default accessibility for the data and methods in the shape_module.

```
module shape_module

  type shape_type

    integer :: x_ = 0
    integer :: y_ = 0

  contains

    procedure, pass (this) :: get_x
    procedure, pass (this) :: get_y
    procedure, pass (this) :: set_x
    procedure, pass (this) :: set_y
    procedure, pass (this) :: moveto
    procedure, pass (this) :: draw

  end type shape_type

contains

  include 'shape_module_include_code.f90'

end module shape_module
```

Here is the code in the include file.

```
!start shape_module_common_code
integer function get_x(this)
  implicit none
  class (shape_type), intent (in) :: this

  get_x = this%x_
end function get_x
```

```fortran
integer function get_y(this)
  implicit none
  class (shape_type), intent (in) :: this

  get_y = this%y_
end function get_y

subroutine set_x(this, x)
  implicit none
  class (shape_type), intent (inout) :: this
  integer, intent (in) :: x

  this%x_ = x
end subroutine set_x

subroutine set_y(this, y)
  implicit none
  class (shape_type), intent (inout) :: this
  integer, intent (in) :: y

  this%y_ = y
end subroutine set_y

subroutine moveto(this, newx, newy)
  implicit none
  class (shape_type), intent (inout) :: this
  integer, intent (in) :: newx
  integer, intent (in) :: newy

  this%x_ = newx
  this%y_ = newy
end subroutine moveto

subroutine draw(this)
  implicit none
  class (shape_type), intent (in) :: this

  print *, ' x = ', this%x_
  print *, ' y = ', this%y_
end subroutine draw
!end shape_module_common_code
```

28.4.1 Key Points

Some of the key concepts are:

- We use a module as the organisational unit for the class.
- We use `type` and `end type` to contain the data and the procedures - called type bound procedures in Fortran terminology.
- The data in the base class is an x and y position.
- The type bound methods within the class are

  - `get_x` and `set_x`
  - `get_y` and `set_y`
  - `draw`
  - `moveto`

- We have used the default accessibility for the data and methods in the type.

  Let us look at the code in stages.

```
module shape_module
```

The module is called `shape_module`

```
    type shape_type
```

The type is called `shape_type`

```
        integer :: x_ = 0
        integer :: y_ = 0
```

The data associated with the shape type are integer variables that are the x and y coordinates of the shape. We initialise to zero.

```
    contains
```

The type also contains procedures or methods.

```
        procedure, pass(this) :: get_x
        procedure, pass(this) :: get_y
        procedure, pass(this) :: set_x
        procedure, pass(this) :: set_y
        procedure, pass(this) :: moveto
        procedure, pass(this) :: draw
```

These are called type bound procedures in Fortran terminology. It is common in object oriented programming to have get and set methods for each of the data components of the type or object. We also have a moveto and draw method.

Each of these methods has the pass attribute. When a type bound procedure is called or invoked the object through which is invoked is normally passed as a hidden parameter. We have used the pass attribute to explicitly confirm the default behaviour of passing the invoking object as the first parameter. We have also followed the convention in object oriented programming of using the word this to refer to the current object.

```
end type shape_type
```

This is the end of the type definition.

```
contains
```

The module then contains the actual implementation of the type bound procedures. We will look at a couple of these.

```
integer function get_x(this)
  implicit none
  class (shape_type), intent (in) :: this
    get_x = this%x_
end function get_x
```

As we stated earlier it is common in object oriented programming to have get and set methods for each data item in an object. This function implements the get_x method. The first argument is the current object, referred to as this. We then have the type declaration for this parameter. We declare the variable using class rather than type as we want the variable to be polymorphic. The rest of the function is self explanatory.

```
subroutine set_x(this,x)
  implicit none
  class (shape_type), intent (inout) :: this
  integer, intent (in) :: x
    this%x_ = x
end subroutine set_x
```

The set_x procedure is a subroutine. It takes two parameters, the current object and the new x value. Again we use the class declaration mechanism as we want the variable to be polymorphic.

Here is a program to test the above shape module out.

```
include 'ch2801_shape_module.f90'

program ch2801
  use shape_module
  implicit none
  type (shape_type) :: s1 = shape_type(10, 20)
  integer :: x1 = 100
  integer :: y1 = 200

  print *, ' get '
  print *, s1%get_x(), ' ', s1%get_y()
  print *, ' draw '
  call s1%draw()
  print *, ' moveto '
  call s1%moveto(x1, y1)
  print *, ' draw '
  call s1%draw()
  print *, ' set '
  call s1%set_x(99)
  call s1%set_y(99)
  print *, ' draw'
  call s1%draw()
end program ch2801
```

The first statement of interest is the use statement, where we make available the shape_module to the test program. The next statement of interest is

```
type (shape_type) :: s1 = shape_type(10,20)
```

We then have a type declaration for the variable s1. We also have the use of what Fortran calls a structure constructor shape_type to provide initial values to the x and y positions. The term constructor is used in other object oriented programming languages, e.g. C++, Java, C#. It has the same name as the type or class and is created automatically for us by the compiler in this example.

The

```
print *, s1%get_x(), ' ', s1%get_y()
```

statement prints out the x andy values for the object s1. We use the standard % notation that we used in derived types, to separate the components of the derived types. If one looks at the implementation of the get_x function and examines the first line, repeated below

```
integer function get_x(this)
```

how we refer to the current object, s1, through the syntax s1%get_x(). The
following call:

```
call s1%draw()
```

shows how to invoke the draw method for the s1 object, using the s1%draw()
syntax. The first line of the draw subroutine

```
subroutine draw(this)
```

shows how the current object is passed as the first argument.

28.4.2   *Notes*

In this example we have accepted the default Fortran accessibility behaviour. This
means that we can use the compiler provided structure constructor shape_type()

```
type (shape_type) :: s1 = shape_type(10,20)
```

in the type declaration to provide initial values, as they are public by default. Direct
access to the data is often not a good idea, as it is possible to makes changes to the
data anywhere in the program. The next example makes the data private.

28.5   Example 2: Base Class with Private Data

Here is the modified base class.

```
module shape_module

  type shape_type

    integer, private :: x_ = 0
    integer, private :: y_ = 0

  contains

    procedure, pass (this) :: get_x
    procedure, pass (this) :: get_y
    procedure, pass (this) :: set_x
    procedure, pass (this) :: set_y
    procedure, pass (this) :: moveto
```

```
    procedure, pass (this) :: draw

  end type shape_type

contains

  include 'shape_module_include_code.f90'

end module shape_module
```

Here is the diff output between the two shape modules.

```
5,6c5,6
<       integer :: x_ = 0
<       integer :: y_ = 0
---
>       integer, private :: x_ = 0
>       integer, private :: y_ = 0
```

This example will now not compile as the default compiler provided structure constructor does not have access to the private data.

The test program is the same as in the first example.

Here is the output from trying to compile this example.

```
Error: ch2802.f90, line 4:
Constructor for type SHAPE_TYPE has value
for PRIVATE component X_
Errors in declarations,
no further processing for CH2802
[NAG Fortran Compiler error termination, 1 error]
```

Not all compilers diagnose this problem. Test yours to see if you get an error message!

An earlier solution to this type of problem can be found in the date class in Chap. 22, where we provide our own structure constructor date_(). Most object oriented programming languages provide the ability to use the same name as a class as a constructor name even if the data is private. Modern Fortran provides another solution to this problem. In the example below we will provide our own structure constructor inside an interface.

28.6   Example 3: Using an Interface to Use the Class Name for the Structure Constructor

Here is the modified base class.

```
module shape_module

  type shape_type

    integer, private :: x_ = 0
    integer, private :: y_ = 0

  contains

    procedure, pass (this) :: get_x
    procedure, pass (this) :: get_y
    procedure, pass (this) :: set_x
    procedure, pass (this) :: set_y
    procedure, pass (this) :: moveto
    procedure, pass (this) :: draw

  end type shape_type

  interface shape_type
    module procedure shape_type_constructor
  end interface shape_type

contains

  type (shape_type) function &
    shape_type_constructor(x, y)
    implicit none
    integer, intent (in) :: x
    integer, intent (in) :: y

    shape_type_constructor%x_ = x
    shape_type_constructor%y_ = y
  end function shape_type_constructor

  include 'shape_module_include_code.f90'

end module shape_module
```

Here is the diff output between the second and third shape modules.

```
18a19,22
>    interface shape_type
>      module procedure shape_type_constructor
>    end interface shape_type
>
19a24,33
>
>    type (shape_type) function &
>      shape_type_constructor(x, y)
>      implicit none
>      integer, intent (in) :: x
>      integer, intent (in) :: y
>
>      shape_type_constructor%x_ = x
>      shape_type_constructor%y_ = y
>    end function shape_type_constructor
```

The key statements are

```
interface shape_type
  module procedure shape_type_constructor
end interface
```

which enables us to map a call or reference to shape_type (our structure constructor name) to our implementation of shape_type_constructor. Here is the implementation of this structure constructor.

```
type (shape_type) function &
  shape_type_constructor(x,y)
  implicit none
  integer, intent (in) :: x
  integer, intent (in) :: y
  shape_type_constructor%x_ = x
  shape_type_constructor%y_ = y
end function shape_type_constructor
```

The function is called shape_type_constructor hence we use this name to initialise the components of the type, and the function returns a value of type shape_type.

Here is the program to test the above out.

```
include 'ch2803_shape_module.f90'

program ch2803
```

```
  use shape_module
  implicit none
  type (shape_type) :: s1
  integer :: x1 = 100
  integer :: y1 = 200

  s1 = shape_type(10, 20)
  print *, ' get '
  print *, s1%get_x(), ' ', s1%get_y()
  print *, ' draw '
  call s1%draw()
  print *, ' moveto '
  call s1%moveto(x1, y1)
  print *, ' draw '
  call s1%draw()
  print *, ' set '
  call s1%set_x(99)
  call s1%set_y(99)
  print *, ' draw'
  call s1%draw()
end program ch2803
```

Note that in this example we cannot initialise s1 at definition time using our own (user defined) structure constructor. This must now be done within the execution part of the program. This is a Fortran restriction, and makes it consistent with the rest of the language.

These examples illustrate some of the basics of object oriented programming in Fortran. To summarise

- the data in our class is private;
- access to the data is via get and set methods;
- the data and methods are within the derived type definition - the methods are called type bound procedures in Fortran terminology;
- we can use interfaces to provide user defined structure constructors, which have the same name as the class - this is a common practice in object oriented programming;
- we have used class to declare the variables within the type bound methods. We need to use class when we want to use polymorphic variables in Fortran.

28.6.1 Public and Private Accessibility

We have only made the internal data in the class private in the above example. There will be cases where some of the methods are only used within the class, in which case they can be made private.

28.7   Example 4: Simple Inheritance

In this example we look at inheritance. We use the same base shape class and derive two classes from it - circle and rectangle.

A circle has a radius. This is the additional data component of the derived class. We also have get and set methods.

A rectangle has a width and height. These are the additional data components of the derived rectangle class. We also have get and set methods.

28.7.1   Base Shape Class

The base shape class is as in the previous example.

28.7.2   Circle - Derived Type 1

Here is the code.

```
module circle_module

  use shape_module

  type, extends (shape_type) :: circle_type

    integer, private :: radius_

  contains

    procedure, pass (this) :: get_radius
    procedure, pass (this) :: set_radius
    procedure, pass (this) :: draw => &
      draw_circle

  end type circle_type

  interface circle_type
    module procedure circle_type_constructor
  end interface circle_type

  contains
```

```
type (circle_type) function &
  circle_type_constructor(x, y, radius)
  implicit none
  integer, intent (in) :: x
  integer, intent (in) :: y
  integer, intent (in) :: radius

  call circle_type_constructor%set_x(x)
  call circle_type_constructor%set_y(y)
  circle_type_constructor%radius_ = radius
end function circle_type_constructor

integer function get_radius(this)
  implicit none
  class (circle_type), intent (in) :: this

  get_radius = this%radius_
end function get_radius

subroutine set_radius(this, radius)
  implicit none
  class (circle_type), intent (inout) :: this
  integer, intent (in) :: radius

  this%radius_ = radius
end subroutine set_radius

subroutine draw_circle(this)
  implicit none
  class (circle_type), intent (in) :: this

  print *, ' x = ', this%get_x()
  print *, ' y = ', this%get_y()
  print *, ' radius = ', this%radius_
end subroutine draw_circle

end module circle_module
```

Let us look more closely at the statements within this class. Firstly we have

```
module circle_module
```

which introduces our circle module. We then

```
use shape_module
```

within this module to make available the shape class. The next statement

```
type , extends(shape_type) :: circle_type
```

is the key statement in inheritance. What this statement says is base our new
`circle_type` on the base `shape_type`. It is an extension of the `shape_type`.
We then have the additional data in our `circle_type`

```
integer , private :: radius_
```

and the following additional type bound procedures.

```
procedure , pass(this) :: get_radius
procedure , pass(this) :: set_radius
procedure , pass(this) :: draw => draw_circle
```

and we have the simple get and set methods for the radius, and a type specific draw
method for our `circle_type`. It is this method that will be called when drawing
with a circle, rather than the `draw` method in the base `shape_type`.

We then have an interface to provide us with our own user defined structure
constructor for our `circle_type`.

```
interface circle_type
   module procedure circle_type_constructor
end interface
```

As has been stated earlier it is common practice in object oriented programming
to use the same name as the type for constructors.

We then have the implementation of the constructor.

```
type (circle_type) function &
   circle_type_constructor(x,y,radius)
   implicit none
   integer, intent (in) :: x
   integer, intent (in) :: y
   integer, intent (in) :: radius
   call circle_type_constructor%set_x(x)
   call circle_type_constructor%set_y(y)
   circle_type_constructor%radius_=radius
end function circle_type_constructor
```

Note that we use the `set_x` and `set_y` methods to provide initial values to the
x and y values. They are private in the base class so we need to use these methods.

We can directly initialise the radius as this is a data component of this class, and we have access to it.

We next have the get and set methods for the radius.

Finally we have the implementation for the draw circle method.

```
subroutine draw_circle(this)
implicit none
  class (circle_type), intent(in) :: this
  print *,' x = ' , this%get_x()
  print *,' y = ' , this%get_y()
  print *,' radius = ' , this%radius_
end subroutine draw_circle
```

Notice again that we use the get_x and get_y methods to access the x andy private data from the base shape class.

28.7.3   *Rectangle - Derived Type 2*

Here is the code for the second derived type.

```
module rectangle_module

  use shape_module

  type, extends (shape_type) :: rectangle_type

    integer, private :: width_
    integer, private :: height_

  contains

    procedure, pass (this) :: get_width
    procedure, pass (this) :: set_width
    procedure, pass (this) :: get_height
    procedure, pass (this) :: set_height
    procedure, pass (this) :: draw => &
      draw_rectangle

  end type rectangle_type

  interface rectangle_type
    module procedure rectangle_type_constructor
```

```fortran
    end interface rectangle_type

contains

  type (rectangle_type) function &
    rectangle_type_constructor(x, y, width, &
    height)
    implicit none
    integer, intent (in) :: x
    integer, intent (in) :: y
    integer, intent (in) :: width
    integer, intent (in) :: height

    call rectangle_type_constructor%set_x(x)
    call rectangle_type_constructor%set_y(y)
    rectangle_type_constructor%width_ = width
    rectangle_type_constructor%height_ = height
  end function rectangle_type_constructor

  integer function get_width(this)
    implicit none
    class (rectangle_type), intent (in) :: this

    get_width = this%width_
  end function get_width

  subroutine set_width(this, width)
    implicit none
    class (rectangle_type), intent (inout) :: &
      this
    integer, intent (in) :: width

    this%width_ = width
  end subroutine set_width

  integer function get_height(this)
    implicit none
    class (rectangle_type), intent (in) :: this

    get_height = this%height_
  end function get_height

  subroutine set_height(this, height)
    implicit none
    class (rectangle_type), intent (inout) :: &
```

```
      this
    integer, intent (in) :: height

    this%height_ = height
  end subroutine set_height

  subroutine draw_rectangle(this)
    implicit none
    class (rectangle_type), intent (in) :: this

    print *, ' x = ', this%get_x()
    print *, ' y = ', this%get_y()
    print *, ' width = ', this%width_
    print *, ' height = ', this%height_
  end subroutine draw_rectangle

end module rectangle_module
```

The code is obviously very similar to that of the first derived type.

28.7.4   Simple Inheritance Test Program

Here is a test program that illustrates the use of the shape type, circle type and
rectangle type.

```
include 'ch2803_shape_module.f90'
include 'ch2804_circle_module.f90'
include 'ch2804_rectangle_module.f90'

program ch2804

  use shape_module
  use circle_module
  use rectangle_module

  implicit none

  type (shape_type) :: vs
  type (circle_type) :: vc
  type (rectangle_type) :: vr

  vs = shape_type(10, 20)
  vc = circle_type(100, 200, 300)
```

```
     vr = rectangle_type(1000, 2000, 3000, 4000)
     print *, ' get '
     print *, ' shape      ', vs%get_x(), ' ', &
       vs%get_y()
     print *, ' circle     ', vc%get_x(), ' ', &
       vc%get_y(), 'radius = ', vc%get_radius()
     print *, ' rectangle ', vr%get_x(), ' ', &
       vr%get_y(), 'width = ', vr%get_width(), &
       'height ', vr%get_height()
     print *, ' draw '
     call vs%draw()
     call vc%draw()
     call vr%draw()
     print *, ' set '
     call vs%set_x(19)
     call vs%set_y(19)
     call vc%set_x(199)
     call vc%set_y(199)
     call vc%set_radius(199)
     call vr%set_x(1999)
     call vr%set_y(1999)
     call vr%set_width(1999)
     call vr%set_height(1999)
     print *, ' draw '
     call vs%draw()
     call vc%draw()
     call vr%draw()
end program ch2804
```

The first statements of note are

```
use shape_module
use circle_module
use rectangle_module
```

which make available the shape, circle and rectangle types within the program. The following statements

```
type (shape_type)     :: vs
type (circle_type)    :: vc
type (rectangle_type) :: vr
```

declare vs, vc and vr to be of type shape, circle and rectangle respectively. The following three statements

```
vs = shape_type(10,20)
vc = circle_type(100,200,300)
vr = rectangle_type(1000,2000,3000,4000)
```

call the three user defined structure constructor functions.

We then use the `get` functions to print out the values of the private data in each object.

```
print *,' shape      ', vs%get_x(),&
  ' ',vs%get_y()
print *,' circle     ', vc%get_x(),&
  ' ',vc%get_y(),' radius = ',vc%get_radius()
print *,' rectangle ', vr%get_x(),&
  ' ',vr%get_y(),' width  = ',vr%get_width(),'
height ',vr%get_height()
```

We then call the `draw` method for each type.

```
call vs%draw()
call vc%draw()
call vr%draw()
```

and the appropriate draw method is called for each type. We finally call the `set` functions for each variable and repeat the calls to the draw methods.

The draw methods in the derived types override the draw method in the base shape class.

28.8   Example 5: Polymorphism and Dynamic Binding

An inheritance hierarchy can provide considerable flexibility in our ability to manipulate objects, whilst still taking advantage of static or compile time type checking. If we combine inheritance with polymorphism and dynamic binding we have a very powerful programming tool. We will illustrate this with a concrete example.

28.8.1   Base Shape Class

This is our base class. A polymorphic variable is a variable whose data type may vary at run time. It must be a pointer or allocatable variable, and it must be declared using the `class` keyword. Our original base class declared variables using the `class` keyword from the beginning as we always intended to design a class that could be polymorphic.

We have had to make one change to the previous one. To make the polymorphism work we have had to provide our own assignment operator. So we have

```
interface assignment (=)
  module procedure generic_shape_assign
end interface
```

which means that our implementation of `generic_shape_assign` will replace the intrinsic assignment. Here is the actual implementation.

```
subroutine generic_shape_assign(lhs,rhs)
  implicit none
  class (shape_type), intent (out), &
    allocatable :: lhs
  class (shape_type), intent (in) :: rhs
  allocate (lhs,source=rhs)
end subroutine generic_shape_assign
```

In an assignment we obviously have

```
left_hand_side = right_hand_side
```

and in our code we have variables `lhs` and `rhs` to clarify what is happening. We also have an enhanced form of allocation statement:

```
allocate (lhs,source=rhs)
```

and the key is that the left hand side variable is allocated with the values and type of the right hand side variable. Here is the complete code.

```
module shape_module

  type shape_type

    integer, private :: x_ = 0
    integer, private :: y_ = 0

  contains

    procedure, pass (this) :: get_x
    procedure, pass (this) :: get_y
    procedure, pass (this) :: set_x
    procedure, pass (this) :: set_y
    procedure, pass (this) :: moveto
```

```
      procedure, pass (this) :: draw

   end type shape_type

   interface shape_type
     module procedure shape_type_constructor
   end interface shape_type

   interface assignment (=)
     module procedure generic_shape_assign
   end interface assignment (=)

contains

   type (shape_type) function &
     shape_type_constructor(x, y)
     implicit none
     integer, intent (in) :: x
     integer, intent (in) :: y

     shape_type_constructor%x_ = x
     shape_type_constructor%y_ = y
   end function shape_type_constructor

   include 'shape_module_include_code.f90'

   subroutine generic_shape_assign(lhs, rhs)
     implicit none
     class (shape_type), intent (out), &
       allocatable :: lhs
     class (shape_type), intent (in) :: rhs

     allocate (lhs, source=rhs)
   end subroutine generic_shape_assign

end module shape_module
```

28.8.2   Circle - Derived Type 1

The circle code is the same as before.

28.8.3   Rectangle - Derived Type 2

The rectangle code is as before.

28.8.4   Shape Wrapper Module

As was stated earlier a polymorphic variable must be a pointer or allocatable variable. We have chosen to go the allocatable route. The following is a wrapper routine to allow us to have a derived type whose types can be polymorphic.

```
module shape_wrapper_module
  use shape_module
  use circle_module
  use rectangle_module
  type shape_wrapper

    class (shape_type), allocatable :: x
  end type shape_wrapper
end module shape_wrapper_module
```

So now x can be of `shape_type` or of any type derived from `shape_type`. Don't panic if this isn't clear at the moment, the complete program should help out!

28.8.5   Display Subroutine

This is the key subroutine in this example. We can pass into this routine an array of type `shape_wrapper`. In the code so far we have variables of type

- `shape_type`
- `circle_type`
- `rectangle_type`

and we are passing in an array of elements and each element can be of any of these types, i.e. the `shape_array` is polymorphic.

The next statement of interest is

```
        call shape_array(i)%x%draw()
```

and at run time the correct `draw` method will be called. This is called dynamic binding. Here is the complete code.

```
module display_module

contains

  subroutine display(n_shapes, shape_array)
    use shape_wrapper_module
    implicit none
    integer, intent (in) :: n_shapes
    type (shape_wrapper), dimension (n_shapes) &
      :: shape_array
    integer :: i

    do i = 1, n_shapes
      call shape_array(i)%x%draw()
    end do
  end subroutine display

end module display_module
```

28.8.6   Test Program for Polymorphism and Dynamic Binding

We now have the complete program that illustrates polymorphism and dynamic binding in action.

```
include 'ch2805_shape_module.f90'
include 'ch2804_circle_module.f90'
include 'ch2804_rectangle_module.f90'
include 'ch2805_shape_wrapper_module.f90'
include 'ch2805_display_module.f90'

program ch2805
  use shape_module
  use circle_module
  use rectangle_module
  use shape_wrapper_module
  use display_module
  implicit none
  integer, parameter :: n = 6
  integer :: i
  type (shape_wrapper), dimension (n) :: s

  s(1)%x = shape_type(10, 20)
```

```fortran
s(2)%x = circle_type(100, 200, 300)
s(3)%x = rectangle_type(1000, 2000, 3000, &
  4000)
s(4)%x = s(1)%x
s(5)%x = s(2)%x
s(6)%x = s(3)%x
print *, ' calling display subroutine'
call display(n, s)
print *, ' select type with get methods'
do i = 1, n
  select type (t=>s(i)%x)
  class is (shape_type)
    print *, ' x = ', t%get_x(), ' y = ', &
      t%get_y()
  class is (circle_type)
    print *, ' x = ', t%get_x(), ' y = ', &
      t%get_y()
    print *, ' radius = ', t%get_radius()
  class is (rectangle_type)
    print *, ' x = ', t%get_x(), ' y = ', &
      t%get_y()
    print *, ' height = ', t%get_height()
    print *, ' width = ', t%get_width()
  class default
    print *, ' do nothing'
  end select
end do
print *, ' select type with set methods'
do i = 1, n
  select type (t=>s(i)%x)
  class is (shape_type)
    call t%set_x(19)
    call t%set_y(19)
  class is (circle_type)
    call t%set_x(199)
    call t%set_y(199)
    call t%set_radius(199)
  class is (rectangle_type)
    call t%set_x(1999)
    call t%set_y(1999)
    call t%set_height(1999)
    call t%set_width(1999)
  class default
    print *, ' do nothing'
  end select
```

```
   end do
   print *, ' calling display subroutine'
   call display(n, s)
end program ch2805
```

Let us look at the key statements in more detail.

```
type (shape_wrapper), dimension (n) :: s
```

This is the key declaration statement. s will be our polymorphic array. The following six assignment statements

```
s(1) %x = shape_type(10,20)
s(2) %x = circle_type(100,200,300)
s(3) %x = rectangle_type(1000,2000,3000,4000)
s(4) %x = s(1)%x
s(5) %x = s(2)%x
s(6) %x = s(3)%x
```

will call our own assignment subroutine to do the assignment. The allocation is hidden in the implementation. We then have

```
call display(n,s)
```

which calls the display subroutine. The compiler at run time works out which draw method to call depending of the type of the elements in the shape_wrapper array.

Imagine now adding another shape type, let us say a triangle. We need to do the following

- inherit from the base shape type
- add the additional data to define a triangle
- add the appropriate get and set methods
- add a draw triangle method
- add a use statement to the shape_wrapper_module
- add a use statement to the main program

and we now can work with the new triangle shape type. The display subroutine is unchanged! We can repeat the above steps for any additional shape type we want. Polymorphism and dynamic binding thus shorten our development and maintenance time, as it reduces the amount of code we need to write and test.

We then have an example of the use of the select type statement. The compiler determines the type of the elements in the array and then executes the matching block.

```
do i=1,n
  select type ( t=>s(i) %x )
    class is (shape_type)
      print *,' x =            ',    t%get_x(),' y = ',t%get_y()
    class is (circle_type)
      print *,' x =            ',    t%get_x(),' y = ',t%get_y()
      print *,' radius =   ',    t%get_radius()
    class is (rectangle_type)
      print *,' x =            ',    t%get_x(),' y = ',t%get_y()
      print *,' height =   ',    t%get_height()
      print *,' width =    ',    t%get_width()
    class default
      print *,' do nothing'
  end select
end do
```

Now imagine adding support for the new triangle type. Anywhere we have select type constructs we have to add support for our new triangle shape. There is obviously more work involved when we use the select type construct in our polymorphic code. However some problems will be amenable to polymorphism and dynamic binding, others will require the explicit use of select type statements. This example illustrates the use of both.

28.9   Fortran 2008 and Polymorphic Intrinsic Assignment

The previous example works with Fortran 2003 conformant compilers. This example illustrates a simple variant that will work if your compiler supports a feature from the 2008 standard - polymorphic intrinsic assignment. In this case we do not need to provide a user defined assignment subroutine.

Here is the modified shape module.

```
module shape_module

  type shape_type

    integer, private :: x_ = 0
    integer, private :: y_ = 0

  contains

    procedure, pass (this) :: get_x
    procedure, pass (this) :: get_y
    procedure, pass (this) :: set_x
```

```fortran
    procedure, pass (this) :: set_y
    procedure, pass (this) :: moveto
    procedure, pass (this) :: draw

  end type shape_type

  interface shape_type
    module procedure shape_type_constructor
  end interface shape_type

contains

  type (shape_type) function &
    shape_type_constructor(x, y)
    implicit none
    integer, intent (in) :: x
    integer, intent (in) :: y

    shape_type_constructor%x_ = x
    shape_type_constructor%y_ = y
  end function shape_type_constructor

  include 'shape_module_include_code.f90'

end module shape_module
```

The rest of the code is the same as in the previous example.

Compiling with gfortran 6.4 will generate the following error message.

Error: Assignment to an allocatable polymorphic variable at (1) is not yet supported

We maintain compiler standard conformance tables that document what features from the 2003, 2008 and 2018 standards are supported by current compilers.

Visit

```
https://www.fortranplus.co.uk/fortran-information/
```

to get up to date information. At the time of writing Table 28.1 was correct for compilers we have used in this edition.

Table 28.1 Polymorphic
intrinsic assignment support

Compiler	Version	Assignment support
Cray	7.4	Yes
gfortran	4.x	No
	5.x	No
	6.x	No
	7.1	Yes
Intel	17.x	No
	18.x	Yes
Nag	6.0	Yes
Oracle	12.6	No
Pathscale	6.0.1148	No
PGI	17.4.0	No

28.10   Summary

This chapter has introduced some of the essentials of object oriented programming. The first example looked at object oriented programming as an extension of basic data structuring. We used type bound procedures to implement our shape class. We used methods to access the internal data of the shape object.

The second example looked at simple inheritance. We saw in this example how we could reuse the methods from the base class and also add new data and methods specific to the new shapes - circles and rectangles.

The third example then looked at how to achieve polymorphism in Fortran. We could then create arrays of our base type and dynamically bind the appropriate methods at run rime. Dynamic binding is needed when multiple classes contain different implementations of the same method, i.e. to ensure in the following code

```
call shape_array(i) %x%draw()
```

that the correct draw method is invoked on the shape object.

28.11   Problems

28.1 Compile and run all of the examples in this chapter with your compiler.

28.2 Add a triangle type to the simple inheritance example.

28.3 Add a triangle type to the polymorphic example.

28.12   Further Reading

The following book

ISO/IEC DIS 1539-1 Information technology–Programming languages–Fortran–
Part 1: Base language

- Fortran 2018 draft standard.


```
https://www.iso.org/standard/72320.html
```

- Rouson D., Xia J., Xu X., Scientific Software Design: The Object Oriented Way,
  Cambridge University Press, 2011.

uses Fortran throughout and is a very good coverage of what is possible in modern
Fortran. Well worth a read.
   The second edition of the following book

- Meyer Bertrand, Object Oriented Software Construction, Prentice Hall, 1997.

provides a very good coverage and uses Eiffel throughout - he did design the language!

Chapter 29
Additional Object Oriented Examples

Smalltalk is a vision. Adele Goldberg and David Robson, Xerox Palo Alto Research Center

Aims

The aim of this chapter are to look at some additional object oriented programming examples in Fortran.

29.1   Introduction

The first set of examples are based on the date example (ch2206.f90) in the data structuring chapter. We are going to convert this example into an object oriented version.

- Example 1 - OO date example
  We use the following files.

  – ch2206_module.f90 - this is the module file for the example in Chap. 22
  – ch2206_program.f90 - the program to test out the date data structure
  – ch2901_day_and_month_name_module.f90 - a separate module containing the day and month names. Has the advantage that one can provide versions for different natural languages. We will be using Welsh.
  – ch2901_date_module.f90 - an object oriented implementation of the original date module.
  – ch2901.f90 - a program to test out the above module.

© Springer International Publishing AG, part of Springer Nature 2018   497
I. Chivers and J. Sleightholme, *Introduction to Programming with Fortran*,
https://doi.org/10.1007/978-3-319-75502-1_29

- Example 2 - OO date example with simple inheritance
  We use the following files.

  - ch2902_iso_date_module.f90 - simple inheritance module based on ISO date format (yyyymmdd)
  - ch2902.f90 - a program to test out the above module.

- Example 3 - OO date example with polymorphism
  We use the following files.

  - ch2903_date_wrapper_module.f90
  - ch2903.f90

- Example 4 - abstract shape base class and concrete derived class
  We use the following files.

  - ch2904_abstract_shape_module.f90
  - ch2904_square_module.f90
  - ch2904.f90

- Example 5 - date checking module
  We use the following file.

  - ch2905_valid_date_module.f90.

29.2   The Date Class

The first thing to do is split the complete example in Chap. 22 into a date module and a date test program.

We will convert the date module into an object oriented version.

We will then convert the date program into one that can be used to test our object oriented date module.

29.3   Example 1: The Base Date Class

Files used

- day and month name module
- oo date module
- oo date program.

The first thing we need to do is identify the functions and subroutines in the original program. Here is a list.

```
function calendar_to_julian(x) result (ival)
function date_(dd, mm, yyyy) result (x)
function date_to_day_in_year(x)
function date_to_weekday_number(x)
function get_day(x)
function get_month(x)
function get_year(x)
function julian_to_date(julian) result (x)
subroutine
  julian_to_date_and_week_and_day(jd,x, wd, ddd)
function ndays(date1, date2)
function
  print_date(x, day_names, short_month_name, digits)
function year_and_day_to_date(year, day) result (x)
```

The conversion means making the above type bound procedures.
We have also made the following changes

- add setter subroutines for the day, month and year
- add a date constructor
- add a separate module for the day and month names, so that we can access this
  data in any inherited versions
- change the calling syntax from a conventional Fortran function and subroutine
  syntax to an object oriented version

Here are the type bound procedures, with partial signatures.

```
procedure , pass(this) :: calendar_to_julian
procedure , pass(this) :: date_to_day_in_year
procedure , pass(this) :: date_to_weekday_number
procedure , pass(this) :: get_day
procedure , pass(this) :: get_month
procedure , pass(this) :: get_year
procedure , nopass     :: julian_to_date
procedure , nopass     ::
  julian_to_date_and_week_and_day
procedure , nopass     :: ndays
procedure , pass(this) :: print_date
procedure , pass(this) :: set_day
procedure , pass(this) :: set_month
procedure , pass(this) :: set_year
procedure , nopass     :: year_and_day_to_date
```

Here is the interface for the date constructor.

```
interface date
  module procedure date_constructor
end interface
```

Here is the complete source code.

29.3.1   Day and Month Name Module

```
module day_and_month_name_module

  implicit none

  character (9) :: day(0:6) = (/ 'Sunday   ', &
    'Monday   ', 'Tuesday  ', 'Wednesday', &
    'Thursday ', 'Friday   ', 'Saturday ' /)
  character (9) :: month(1:12) = (/ 'January  ', &
    'February ', 'March    ', 'April    ', &
    'May      ', 'June     ', 'July     ', &
    'August   ', 'September', 'October  ', &
    'November ', 'December ' /)

end module day_and_month_name_module
```

29.3.2   Date Module

```
module date_module

  use day_and_month_name_module

  implicit none

  private

  type, public :: date

    private
```

```
      integer :: day
      integer :: month
      integer :: year

  contains

    procedure, pass (this) :: calendar_to_julian
    procedure, pass (this) :: &
      date_to_day_in_year
    procedure, pass (this) :: &
      date_to_weekday_number
    procedure, pass (this) :: get_day
    procedure, pass (this) :: get_month
    procedure, pass (this) :: get_year
    procedure, nopass :: julian_to_date
    procedure, nopass :: &
      julian_to_date_and_week_and_day
    procedure, nopass :: ndays
    procedure, pass (this) :: print_date
    procedure, pass (this) :: set_day
    procedure, pass (this) :: set_month
    procedure, pass (this) :: set_year
    procedure, nopass :: year_and_day_to_date

  end type date

  interface date
    module procedure date_constructor
  end interface date

  public :: calendar_to_julian, &
    date_to_day_in_year, date_to_weekday_number, &
    get_day, get_month, get_year, &
    julian_to_date, &
    julian_to_date_and_week_and_day, ndays, &
    print_date, set_day, set_month, set_year, &
    year_and_day_to_date

contains

  function calendar_to_julian(this) &
    result (ival)
    implicit none
    integer :: ival
    class (date), intent (in) :: this
```

```
   ival = this%day - 32075 + 1461*(this%year+ &
     4800+(this%month-14)/12)/4 + &
     367*(this%month-2-((this%month- &
     14)/12)*12)/12 - 3*((this%year+4900+(this% &
     month-14)/12)/100)/4
end function calendar_to_julian

type (date) function date_constructor(dd, mm, &
  yyyy)

   implicit none
   integer, intent (in) :: dd, mm, yyyy

   date_constructor%day = dd
   date_constructor%month = mm
   date_constructor%year = yyyy

end function date_constructor

integer function date_to_day_in_year(this)
   implicit none
   class (date), intent (in) :: this
   intrinsic modulo

   date_to_day_in_year = 3055*(this%month+2)/ &
     100 - (this%month+10)/13*2 - 91 + &
     (1-(modulo(this%year,4)+3)/4+(modulo(this% &
     year,100)+99)/100--(modulo(this%year, &
     400)+399)/400)*(this%month+10)/13 + &
     this%day
end function date_to_day_in_year

integer function date_to_weekday_number(this)
   implicit none
   class (date), intent (in) :: this
   intrinsic modulo

   date_to_weekday_number = modulo((13*( &
     this%month+10-(this%month+10)/13*12)-1)/5+ &
     this%day+77+5*(this%year+(this%month- &
     14)/12-(this%year+(this%month-14)/12)/100* &
     100)/4+(this%year+(this%month- &
     14)/12)/400-(this%year+(this%month- &
     14)/12)/100*2, 7)
```

```fortran
  end function date_to_weekday_number

function get_day(this)
  implicit none
  integer :: get_day
  class (date), intent (in) :: this

  get_day = this%day
end function get_day

function get_month(this)
  implicit none
  integer :: get_month
  class (date), intent (in) :: this

  get_month = this%month
end function get_month

function get_year(this)
  implicit none
  integer :: get_year
  class (date), intent (in) :: this

  get_year = this%year
end function get_year

function julian_to_date(julian)
  implicit none
  type (date) :: julian_to_date
  integer, intent (in) :: julian

  integer :: l, n

  l = julian + 68569
  n = 4*l/146097
  l = l - (146097*n+3)/4
  julian_to_date%year = (4000*(l+1)/1461001)
  l = l - 1461*julian_to_date%year/4 + 31
  julian_to_date%month = (80*l/2447)
  julian_to_date%day = (l-2447*julian_to_date% &
    month/80)
  l = julian_to_date%month/11
  julian_to_date%month = (julian_to_date%month &
    +2-12*l)
```

```fortran
    julian_to_date%year = (100*(n-49)+ &
      julian_to_date%year+1)
end function julian_to_date

subroutine julian_to_date_and_week_and_day(jd, &
  d, wd, ddd)
  implicit none
  integer, intent (in) :: jd
  type (date), intent (out) :: d
  integer, intent (out) :: wd, ddd

  d = julian_to_date(jd)
  wd = date_to_weekday_number(d)
  ddd = date_to_day_in_year(d)
end subroutine julian_to_date_and_week_and_day

function ndays(date1, date2)
  implicit none
  integer :: ndays
  class (date), intent (in) :: date1, date2

  ndays = calendar_to_julian(date1) - &
    calendar_to_julian(date2)
end function ndays

function print_date(this, day_names, &
  short_month_name, digits)
  implicit none
  class (date), intent (in) :: this
  logical, optional, intent (in) :: day_names, &
    short_month_name, digits
  character (40) :: print_date
  integer :: pos
  logical :: want_day, want_short_month_name, &
    want_digits
  intrinsic len_trim, present, trim

  want_day = .false.
  want_short_month_name = .false.
  want_digits = .false.
  print_date = ' '
  if (present(day_names)) then
    want_day = day_names
  end if
```

```fortran
  if (present(short_month_name)) then
    want_short_month_name = short_month_name
  end if
  if (present(digits)) then
    want_digits = digits
  end if
  if (want_digits) then
    write (print_date(1:2), '(i2)') this%day
    print_date(3:3) = '/'
    write (print_date(4:5), '(i2)') this%month
    print_date(6:6) = '/'
    write (print_date(7:10), '(i4)') this%year
  else
    if (want_day) then
      pos = date_to_weekday_number(this)
      print_date = trim(day(pos)) // ' '
      pos = len_trim(print_date) + 2
    else
      pos = 1
      print_date = ' '
    end if
    write (print_date(pos:pos+1), '(i2)') &
      this%day
    if (want_short_month_name) then
      print_date(pos+3:pos+5) = month(this% &
        month)(1:3)
      pos = pos + 7
    else
      print_date(pos+3:) = month(this%month)
      pos = len_trim(print_date) + 2
    end if
    write (print_date(pos:pos+3), '(i4)') &
      this%year
  end if

  return
end function print_date

subroutine set_day(this, d)
  implicit none
  integer, intent (in) :: d
  class (date), intent (inout) :: this

  this%day = d
end subroutine set_day
```

```fortran
subroutine set_month(this, m)
  implicit none
  integer, intent (in) :: m
  class (date), intent (inout) :: this

  this%month = m
end subroutine set_month

subroutine set_year(this, y)
  implicit none
  integer, intent (in) :: y
  class (date), intent (inout) :: this

  this%year = y
end subroutine set_year

function year_and_day_to_date(year, &
  day_in_year)
  use day_and_month_name_module
  implicit none
  type (date) :: year_and_day_to_date
  integer, intent (in) :: day_in_year, year
  integer :: t
  intrinsic modulo

  year_and_day_to_date%year = year
  t = 0
  if (modulo(year,4)==0) then
    t = 1
  end if
  if (modulo(year,400)/=0 .and. &
    modulo(year,100)==0) then
    t = 0
  end if
  year_and_day_to_date%day = day_in_year
  if (day_in_year>59+t) then
    year_and_day_to_date%day = &
      year_and_day_to_date%day + 2 - t
  end if
  year_and_day_to_date%month = &
    ((year_and_day_to_date%day+91)*100)/3055
  year_and_day_to_date%day = ( &
    year_and_day_to_date%day+91) - &
```

```
      (year_and_day_to_date%month*3055)/100
    year_and_day_to_date%month = &
      year_and_day_to_date%month - 2
    if (year_and_day_to_date%month>=1 .and. &
      year_and_day_to_date%month<=12) then
      return
    end if
    write (unit=*, fmt='(a,i11,a)') '$$year_and_d&
      &ay_to_date: day of the year input &
      &=', day_in_year, ' is out of range.'
  end function year_and_day_to_date

end module date_module
```

29.3.3   Diff Output Between Original Module and New oo Module

Here is the diff output between the original module in example ch2206 and the new
oo module.

```
1c1,4
< module date_module
---
> module date_module_01
>
>   use day_and_month_name_module
>
6a10
>
7a12
>
10a16,36
>
>   contains
>
>     procedure, pass (this) :: calendar_to_julian
>     procedure, pass (this) :: &
>       date_to_day_in_year
>     procedure, pass (this) :: &
>       date_to_weekday_number
>     procedure, pass (this) :: get_day
>     procedure, pass (this) :: get_month
```

```
>        procedure, pass (this) :: get_year
>        procedure, nopass :: julian_to_date
>        procedure, nopass :: &
>          julian_to_date_and_week_and_day
>        procedure, nopass :: ndays
>        procedure, pass (this) :: print_date
>        procedure, pass (this) :: set_day
>        procedure, pass (this) :: set_month
>        procedure, pass (this) :: set_year
>        procedure, nopass :: year_and_day_to_date
>

13,20c39,41
<        character (9) :: day(0:6) = (/ 'Sunday    ', &
<        'Monday   ', 'Tuesday  ', 'Wednesday', &
<        'Thursday ', 'Friday ', 'Saturday ' /)
<      character (9) :: month(1:12) = (/ 'January  ', &
<        'February ', 'March    ', 'April    ', &
<        'May      ', 'June     ', 'July     ', &
<        'August   ', 'September', 'October ', &
<        'November ', 'December ' /)
---
>      interface date
>        module procedure date_constructor
>      end interface date
22c43
<    public :: calendar_to_julian, date_, &
---
>    public :: calendar_to_julian, &
27c48,49
<        print_date, year_and_day_to_date
---
>        print_date, set_day, set_month, set_year, &
>        year_and_day_to_date
31c53,54
<    function calendar_to_julian(x) result (ival)
---
>    function calendar_to_julian(this) &
>      result (ival)
34c57
<        type (date), intent (in) :: x
---
>        class (date), intent (in) :: this

36,39c59,63
<        ival = x%day - 32075 + 1461*(x%year+4800+(x% &
```

```
<          month-14)/12)/4 + 367*(x%month &
<          -14)/12)*12)/12 - 3*((x%year+4900+(x%month &
<          -14)/12)/100)/4
---
>      ival = this%day - 32075 + 1461*(this%year+ &
>          4800+(this%month-14)/12)/4 + &
>          367*(this%month-2-((this%month- &
>          14)/12)*12)/12 - 3*((this%year+4900+(this% &
>          month-14)/12)/100)/4
42c66,68
<    function date_(dd, mm, yyyy) result (x)
---
>    type (date) function date_constructor(dd, mm, &
>      yyyy)
>
44d69
<      type (date) :: x
47,48c72,74
<      x = date(dd, mm, yyyy)
<    end function date_
---
>      date_constructor%day = dd
>      date_constructor%month = mm
>      date_constructor%year = yyyy

50c76,78
<    function date_to_day_in_year(x)
---
>    end function date_constructor
>
>    integer function date_to_day_in_year(this)
52,53c80
<      integer :: date_to_day_in_year
<      type (date), intent (in) :: x
---
>      class (date), intent (in) :: this
56,60c83,88
<      date_to_day_in_year = 3055*(x%month+2)/100 - &
<          (x%month+10)/13*2 - 91 + (1-(modulo(x%year &
<          ,4)+3)/4+(modulo(x%year,100)+99)/100-( &
<          modulo(x%year,400)+399)/400)*(x%month+10)/ &
<          13 + x%day
---
>      date_to_day_in_year = 3055*(this%month+2)/ &
>          100 - (this%month+10)/13*2 - 91 + &
```

```
>            (1-(modulo(this%year,4)+3)/4+(modulo(this% &
>            year,100)+99)/100-(modulo(this%year, &
>            400)+399)/400)*(this%month+10)/13 + &
>            this%day
63c91
<    function date_to_weekday_number(x)
---
>    integer function date_to_weekday_number(this)

65,66c93
<       integer :: date_to_weekday_number
<       type (date), intent (in) :: x
---
>       class (date), intent (in) :: this
70,73c97,101
<          x%month+10-(x%month+10)/13*12)-1)/5+x%day+ &
<          77+5*(x%year+(x%month-14)/12-(x%year+ &
<          (x%month-14)/12)/100*100)/4+(x%year+(x% &
<          month-14)/12)/400-(x%year+(x%month- &
---
>          this%month+10-(this%month+10)/13*12)-1)/5+ &
>          this%day+77+5*(this%year+(this%month- &
>          14)/12-(this%year+(this%month-14)/12)/100* &
>          100)/4+(this%year+(this%month- &
>          14)/12)/400-(this%year+(this%month- &
77c105
<    function get_day(x)
---
>    function get_day(this)
80c108
<       type (date), intent (in) :: x
---
>       class (date), intent (in) :: this
82c110
<       get_day = x%day
---
>       get_day = this%day
85c113
<    function get_month(x)
---
>    function get_month(this)
88c116
<       type (date), intent (in) :: x
---
>       class (date), intent (in) :: this
```

```
90c118
<     get_month = x%month
---
>     get_month = this%month
93c121
<   function get_year(x)
---
>   function get_year(this)
96c124
<     type (date), intent (in) :: x
---
>     class (date), intent (in) :: this

98c126
<     get_year = x%year
---
>     get_year = this%year
101c129
<   function julian_to_date(julian) result (x)
---
>   function julian_to_date(julian)
102a131
>     type (date) :: julian_to_date
103a133
>
105d134
<     type (date) :: x 110,116c139,148
<     x%year = 4000*(l+1)/1461001
<     l = l - 1461*x%year/4 + 31
<     x%month = 80*l/2447
<     x%day = l - 2447*x%month/80
<     l = x%month/11
<     x%month = x%month + 2 - 12*l
<     x%year = 100*(n-49) + x%year + 1
---
>     julian_to_date%year = (4000*(l+1)/1461001)
>     l = l - 1461*julian_to_date%year/4 + 31
>     julian_to_date%month = (80*l/2447)
>     julian_to_date%day = (l-2447*julian_to_date% &
>       month/80)
>     l = julian_to_date%month/11
>     julian_to_date%month = (julian_to_date%month &
>       +2-12*l)
>     julian_to_date%year = (100*(n-49)+ &
>       julian_to_date%year+1)
```

```
120c152
<      x, wd, ddd)
---
>      d, wd, ddd)
122d153
<      integer, intent (out) :: ddd, wd
124c155,156
<      type (date), intent (out) :: x
---
>      type (date), intent (out) :: d
>      integer, intent (out) :: wd, ddd
126,128c158,160
<      x = julian_to_date(jd)
<      wd = date_to_weekday_number(x)
<      ddd = date_to_day_in_year(x)
---
>      d = julian_to_date(jd)
>      wd = date_to_weekday_number(d)
>      ddd = date_to_day_in_year(d)
134c166
<      type (date), intent (in) :: date1, date2
---
>      class (date), intent (in) :: date1, date2
140c172
<   function print_date(x, day_names, &
---
>   function print_date(this, day_names, &
143c175
<      type (date), intent (in) :: x
---
>      class (date), intent (in) :: this

166c198
<        write (print_date(1:2), '(i2)') x%day
---
>        write (print_date(1:2), '(i2)') this%day
168c200
<        write (print_date(4:5), '(i2)') x%month
---
>        write (print_date(4:5), '(i2)') this%month
170c202
<        write (print_date(7:10), '(i4)') x%year
---
>        write (print_date(7:10), '(i4)') this%year
173c205
```

```
<           pos = date_to_weekday_number(x)
---
>           pos = date_to_weekday_number(this)
181c213
<         x%day
---
>         this%day
183,184c215,216
<         print_date(pos+3:pos+5) = month(x%month) &
<           (1:3)
---
>         print_date(pos+3:pos+5) = month(this% &
>           month)(1:3)
187c219
<         print_date(pos+3:) = month(x%month)
---
>         print_date(pos+3:) = month(this%month)
191c223
<         x%year
---
>         this%year

197,198c229
<   function year_and_day_to_date(year, day) &
<   result (x)
---
>   subroutine set_day(this, d)
200,201c231,258
<     type (date) :: x
<     integer, intent (in) :: day, year
---
>     integer, intent (in) :: d
>     class (date), intent (inout) :: this
>
>     this%day = d
>   end subroutine set_day
>
>   subroutine set_month(this, m)
>     implicit none
>     integer, intent (in) :: m
>     class (date), intent (inout) :: this
>
>     this%month = m
>   end subroutine set_month
>
```

```
>    subroutine set_year(this, y)
>      implicit none
>      integer, intent (in) :: y
>      class (date), intent (inout) :: this
>
>      this%year = y
>    end subroutine set_year
>
>    function year_and_day_to_date(year, &
>      day_in_year)
>      use day_and_month_name_module
>      implicit none
>      type (date) :: year_and_day_to_date
>      integer, intent (in) :: day_in_year, year
205c262
<      x%year = year
---
>      year_and_day_to_date%year = year
214,221c271,284
<      x%day = day
<      if (day>59+t) then
<        x%day = x%day + 2 - t
<      end if
<      x%month = ((x%day+91)*100)/3055
<      x%day = (x%day+91) - (x%month*3055)/100
<      x%month = x%month - 2
<      if (x%month>=1 .and. x%month<=12) then
---
>      year_and_day_to_date%day = day_in_year
>      if (day_in_year>59+t) then
>        year_and_day_to_date%day = &
>          year_and_day_to_date%day + 2 - t
>      end if
>      year_and_day_to_date%month = &
>        ((year_and_day_to_date%day+91)*100)/3055
>      year_and_day_to_date%day = ( &
>        year_and_day_to_date%day+91) - &
>        (year_and_day_to_date%month*3055)/100
>      year_and_day_to_date%month = &
>        year_and_day_to_date%month - 2
>      if (year_and_day_to_date%month>=1 .and. &
>        year_and_day_to_date%month<=12) then
226c289
<        &=', day, ' is out of range.'
```

```
- - -
>            &=', day_in_year, ' is out of range.'
229c292
< end module date_module
- - -
> end module date_module_01
```

29.3.4 Main Program

This is the main test program. This is a conversion of the main program in example
ch2206.

```
include 'ch2901_day_and_month_name_module.f90'
include 'ch2901_date_module.f90'

program ch2901

  use date_module , only : calendar_to_julian, &
    date, date_to_day_in_year, &
    date_to_weekday_number, get_day, get_month, &
    get_year, julian_to_date, &
    julian_to_date_and_week_and_day, ndays, &
    print_date, year_and_day_to_date

  implicit none
  integer :: dd, ddd, i, mm, ndiff, wd, yyyy
  integer :: julian
  integer :: val(8)
  intrinsic date_and_time
  type (date) :: date1, date2, x, tx1, tx2

  call date_and_time(values=val)
  yyyy = val(1)
  mm = 10
  do i = 31, 26, -1
    x = date(i, mm, yyyy)
    if (x%date_to_weekday_number()==0) then
      print *, 'Turn clocks  back to EST on: ', &
        i, ' October ', x%get_year()
      exit
    end if
  end do
```

```
call date_and_time(values=val)
yyyy = val(1)
mm = 4
do i = 1, 8
  x = date(i, mm, yyyy)
  if (x%date_to_weekday_number()==0) then
    print *, 'Turn clocks ahead to DST on: ', &
        i, ' April    ', x%get_year()
    exit
  end if
end do
call date_and_time(values=val)
yyyy = val(1)
mm = 12
dd = 31
x = date(dd, mm, yyyy)
if (x%date_to_day_in_year()==366) then
  print *, x%get_year(), ' is a leap year'
else
  print *, x%get_year(), ' is not a leap year'
end if
x = date(1, 1, 1970)
call julian_to_date_and_week_and_day &
  (calendar_to_julian(x), x, wd, ddd)
if (x%get_year()/=1970 .or. x%get_month()/=1 &
  .or. x%get_day()/=1 .or. wd/=4 .or. ddd/=1) &
  then
  print *, &
    'julian_to_date_and_week_and_day failed'
  print *, ' date, wd, ddd = ', x%get_year(), &
    x%get_month(), x%get_day(), wd, ddd
  stop
end if
date1 = date(22, 5, 1984)
date2 = date(22, 5, 1983)
ndiff = ndays(date1, date2)
yyyy = 1970

x = year_and_day_to_date(yyyy, ddd)

if (ndiff/=366) then
  print *, 'ndays failed; ndiff = ', ndiff
else
  if (x%get_month()/=1 .and. x%get_day()/=1) &
```

```
    then
      print *, 'year_and_day_to_date failed'
      print *, ' mma, dda = ', x%get_month(), &
        x%get_day()
    else
      print *, ' calendar_to_julian OK'
      print *, ' date_ OK'
      print *, ' date_to_day_in_year OK'
      print *, ' date_to_weekday_number OK'
      print *, ' get_day OK'
      print *, ' get_month OK'
      print *, ' get_year OK'
      print *, &
        ' julian_to_date_and_week_and_day OK'
      print *, ' ndays OK'
      print *, ' year_and_day_to_date OK'
    end if
  end if

  tx1 = date(1, 1, 1970)
  julian = tx1%calendar_to_julian()
  tx2 = julian_to_date(julian)
  if (tx1%get_day()==tx2%get_day() .and. &
    tx1%get_month()==tx2%get_month() .and. &
    tx1%get_year()==tx2%get_year()) then
    print *, ' calendar_to_julian and '
    print *, ' julian_to_date worked'
  end if

  x = date(11, 2, 1952)


  print *, ' print_date test'
  print *, ' Single parameter       ', &
    x%print_date()
  print *, &
    ' day_names=false short_month_name=false ', &
    x%print_date(day_names=.false., &
    short_month_name=.false.)
  print *, &
    ' day_names=true  short_month_name=false ', &
    x%print_date(day_names=.true., &
    short_month_name=.false.)
  print *, &
```

```
       ' day_names=false short_month_name=true   ', &
       x%print_date(day_names=.false., &
       short_month_name=.true.)
   print *, &
       ' day_names=true   short_month_name=true   ', &
       x%print_date(day_names=.true., &
       short_month_name=.true.)
   print *, ' digits=true                ', &
       x%print_date(digits=.true.)

   print *, ' Test out a month'

   yyyy = 1970
   do dd = 1, 31
     x = year_and_day_to_date(yyyy, dd)
     print *, x%print_date(day_names=.false., &
       short_month_name=.true.)
   end do

end program ch2901
```

29.3.5   Diff Output Between Original Program and New oo Test Program

Here is the diff output between the original and the new oo one.

```
1,3c1,4
< program ch2206
<   use date_module, only: calendar_to_julian, &
<     date, date_, date_to_day_in_year, &
---
> program date_program_01
>
>   use date_module_01, only: calendar_to_julian, &
>     date, date_to_day_in_year, &
5,6c6,8
<     get_year, julian_to_date_and_week_and_day, &
<     ndays, print_date, year_and_day_to_date
---
>     get_year, julian_to_date, &
>     julian_to_date_and_week_and_day, ndays, &
>     print_date, year_and_day_to_date
```

```
9a12
>   integer :: julian
12c15
<   type (date) :: date1, date2, x
---
>   type (date) :: date1, date2, x, tx1, tx2
18,19c21,22
<     x = date_(i, mm, yyyy)
<     if (date_to_weekday_number(x)==0) then
---
>     x = date(i, mm, yyyy)
>     if (x%date_to_weekday_number()==0) then
21c24
<           i, ' October ', get_year(x)
---
>           i, ' October ', x%get_year()
29,30c32,33
<     x = date_(i, mm, yyyy)
<     if (date_to_weekday_number(x)==0) then
---
>     x = date(i, mm, yyyy)
>     if (x%date_to_weekday_number()==0) then
32c35
<           i, ' April   ', get_year(x)
---
>           i, ' April   ', x%get_year()
40,42c43,45
<   x = date_(dd, mm, yyyy)
<   if (date_to_day_in_year(x)==366) then
<     print *, get_year(x), ' is
a leap year'
---
>   x = date(dd, mm, yyyy)
>   if (x%date_to_day_in_year()==366) then
>     print *, x%get_year(), ' is a leap year'
44c47
<     print *, get_year(x), ' is not a leap year'
---
>     print *, x%get_year(), ' is not a leap year'
46c49
<   x = date_(1, 1, 1970)
---
>   x = date(1, 1, 1970)
49,50c52,53
```

```
<     if (get_year(x)/=1970 .or. get_month(x)/=1 &
<         .or. get_day(x)/=1 .or. wd/=4 .or. ddd/=1) &
---
>     if (x%get_year()/=1970 .or. x%get_month()/=1 &
>         .or. x%get_day()/=1 .or. wd/=4 .or. ddd/=1) &
54,55c57,58
<         print *, ' date, wd, ddd = ', get_year(x), &
<         get_month(x), get_day(x), wd, ddd
---
>         print *, ' date, wd, ddd = ', x%get_year(), &
>           x%get_month(), x%get_day(), wd, ddd
58,59c61,62
<    date1 = date_(22, 5, 1984)
<    date2 = date_(22, 5,
1983)
---
>    date1 = date(22, 5, 1984)
>    date2 = date(22, 5, 1983)
68c71
<     if (get_month(x)/=1 .and. get_day(x)/=1) &
---
>     if (x%get_month()/=1 .and. x%get_day()/=1) &
71,72c74,75
<        print *, ' mma, dda = ', get_month(x), &
<       get_day(x)
---
>         print *, ' mma, dda = ', x%get_month(), &
>           x%get_day()
88c91,101
<    x = date_(11, 2, 1952)
---
>    tx1 = date(1, 1, 1970)
>    julian = tx1%calendar_to_julian()
>    tx2 = julian_to_date(julian)
>    if (tx1%get_day()==tx2%get_day() .and. &
>      tx1%get_month()==tx2%get_month() .and. &
>      tx1%get_year()==tx2%get_year()) then
>      print *, ' calendar_to_julian and '
>      print *, ' julian_to_date worked'
>    end if
>
>    x = date(11, 2, 1952)
92c105
<       print_date(x)
```

```
---
>       x%print_date()
95c108
<       print_date(x, day_names=.false., &
---
>       x%print_date(day_names=.false., &
99c112
<       print_date(x, day_names=.true., &
---
>       x%print_date(day_names=.true., &
103c116
<       print_date(x, day_names=.false., &
---
>       x%print_date(day_names=.false., &
107c120
<       print_date(x, day_names=.true., &
---
>       x%print_date(day_names=.true., &
110c123
<       print_date(x, digits=.true.)
---
>       x%print_date(digits=.true.)
117c130
<       print *, print_date(x, day_names=.false., &
---
>       print *, x%print_date(day_names=.false., &
121c134
< end program ch2206
---
> end program date_program_01
```

Here is the build sequence

```
ch2901_day_and_month_name_module.f90
ch2901_date_module.f90
ch2901.f90
```

Here is the output from running the program.

```
Turn clocks ahead to DST on:  5  April     2015
2015  is not a leap year
calendar_to_julian OK
date_ OK
date_to_day_in_year OK
```

```
date_to_weekday_number OK
get_day OK
get_month OK
get_year OK
julian_to_date_and_week_and_day OK
ndays OK
year_and_day_to_date OK
calendar_to_julian and
julian_to_date worked
print_date test
Single parameter        11 February 1952
day_names=false short_month_name=false
11 February 1952
day_names=true   short_month_name=false
Monday 11 February 1952
day_names=false short_month_name=true
11 Feb 1952
day_names=true   short_month_name=true
Monday 11 Feb 1952
digits=true             11/ 2/1952

Test out a month
 1 Jan 1970
 2 Jan 1970
 3 Jan 1970
 4 Jan 1970
 5 Jan 1970
 6 Jan 1970
 7 Jan 1970
 8 Jan 1970
 9 Jan 1970
10 Jan 1970
11 Jan 1970
12 Jan 1970
13 Jan 1970
14 Jan 1970
15 Jan 1970
16 Jan 1970
17 Jan 1970
18 Jan 1970
19 Jan 1970
20 Jan 1970
21 Jan 1970
22 Jan 1970
23 Jan 1970
```

```
24 Jan 1970
25 Jan 1970
26 Jan 1970
27 Jan 1970
28 Jan 1970
29 Jan 1970
30 Jan 1970
31 Jan 1970
```

29.4 Example 2: Simple Inheritance Based on an ISO Date Format

Files used

- day and month name module
- oo date module
- iso date module
- iso date program.

29.4.1 ISO Date Module

Here is the source code for the ISO date module.

```
module iso_date_module

  use day_and_month_name_module

  use date_module

  implicit none

  public

  type, extends (date) :: iso_date

  contains

    procedure, pass (this) :: print_date => &
      print_iso_date
    procedure, nopass :: julian_to_iso_date
    procedure, nopass :: &
```

```
         julian_to_iso_date_and_week_and_day
      procedure, nopass :: &
        year_and_day_to_iso_date

   end type iso_date

   interface iso_date
     module procedure iso_date_constructor
   end interface iso_date

contains

   type (iso_date) function iso_date_constructor( &
     yyyy, mm, dd)

      implicit none
      integer, intent (in) :: dd, mm, yyyy

      call iso_date_constructor%set_day(dd)
      call iso_date_constructor%set_month(mm)
      call iso_date_constructor%set_year(yyyy)

   end function iso_date_constructor

   function julian_to_iso_date(julian)
      implicit none
      type (iso_date) :: julian_to_iso_date
      integer, intent (in) :: julian

      integer :: l, n

      l = julian + 68569
      n = 4*l/146097
      l = l - (146097*n+3)/4
      call julian_to_iso_date%set_year((4000*(1+ &
        l)/1461001))
      l = l - 1461*julian_to_iso_date%get_year()/4 &
        + 31
      call julian_to_iso_date%set_month((80*l/ &
        2447))
      call julian_to_iso_date%set_day((l- &
        2447*julian_to_iso_date%get_month()/80))
      l = julian_to_iso_date%get_month()/11
      call julian_to_iso_date%set_month &
```

```
      ((julian_to_iso_date%get_month()+2-12*l))
    call julian_to_iso_date%set_year((100*(n- &
      49)+julian_to_iso_date%get_year()+1))

end function julian_to_iso_date

subroutine julian_to_iso_date_and_week_and_day &
  (jd, d, wd, ddd)
  implicit none
  integer, intent (in) :: jd
  type (iso_date), intent (out) :: d
  integer, intent (out) :: wd, ddd

  d = julian_to_iso_date(jd)
  wd = date_to_weekday_number(d)
  ddd = date_to_day_in_year(d)
end subroutine &
  julian_to_iso_date_and_week_and_day

function print_iso_date(this, day_names, &
  short_month_name, digits)
  use day_and_month_name_module
  implicit none
  class (iso_date), intent (in) :: this
  logical, optional, intent (in) :: day_names, &
    short_month_name, digits
  character (40) :: print_iso_date
  integer :: pos
  logical :: want_day, want_short_month_name, &
    want_digits
  integer :: l, t
  intrinsic len_trim, present, trim

  want_day = .false.
  want_short_month_name = .false.
  want_digits = .false.
  print_iso_date = ' '
  if (present(day_names)) then
    want_day = day_names
  end if
  if (present(short_month_name)) then
    want_short_month_name = short_month_name
  end if
  if (present(digits)) then
```

```
        want_digits = digits
      end if
!   year month day
      if (want_digits) then
        write (print_iso_date(1:4), '(i4)') &
          this%get_year()
        print_iso_date(5:5) = '/'
        write (print_iso_date(6:7), '(i2)') &
          this%get_month()
        print_iso_date(8:8) = '/'
        write (print_iso_date(9:10), '(i2)') &
          this%get_day()
      else
        pos = 1
        write (print_iso_date(pos:pos+3), '(i4)') &
          this%get_year()
        pos = pos + 5
        if (want_short_month_name) then
          print_iso_date(pos:pos+2) &
            = month(this%get_month())(1:3)
          pos = pos + 4
        else
          print_iso_date(pos:) = month(this% &
            get_month())
          pos = len_trim(print_iso_date) + 2
        end if
        if (want_day) then
          t = date_to_weekday_number(this)
          l = len_trim(day(t))
          print_iso_date(pos:pos+l) = trim(day(t))
          pos = pos + l + 1
        end if
        write (print_iso_date(pos:pos+1), '(i2)') &
          this%get_day()
      end if

  end function print_iso_date

  function year_and_day_to_iso_date(year, &
    day_in_year)
    use day_and_month_name_module
    implicit none
    type (iso_date) :: year_and_day_to_iso_date
    integer, intent (in) :: day_in_year, year
    integer :: t
```

```
intrinsic modulo

call year_and_day_to_iso_date%set_year(year)
t = 0
if (modulo(year,4)==0) then
  t = 1
end if
if (modulo(year,400)/=0 .and. &
  modulo(year,100)==0) then
  t = 0
end if
call year_and_day_to_iso_date%set_day &
  (day_in_year)
if (day_in_year>59+t) then
  call year_and_day_to_iso_date%set_day &
    (year_and_day_to_iso_date%get_day()+2-t)
end if
call year_and_day_to_iso_date%set_month((( &
  year_and_day_to_iso_date%get_day()+ &
  91)*100)/3055)
call year_and_day_to_iso_date%set_day &
  ((year_and_day_to_iso_date%get_day( &
  )+91)-(year_and_day_to_iso_date%get_month( &
  )*3055)/100)
call year_and_day_to_iso_date%set_month &
  (year_and_day_to_iso_date%get_month()-2)
if (year_and_day_to_iso_date%get_month()>= &
  1 .and. year_and_day_to_iso_date%get_month &
  ()<=12) then
  return
end if
write (unit=*, fmt='(a,i11,a)') '$$year_and_d&
  &ay_to_date: day of the year input &
  &=', day_in_year, ' is out of range.'
end function year_and_day_to_iso_date

end module iso_date_module
```

29.4.2   ISO Test Program

Here is the source code for the ISO date test program.

```fortran
include 'ch2901_day_and_month_name_module.f90'
include 'ch2901_date_module.f90'
include 'ch2902_iso_date_module.f90'

program ch2902

  use date_module , only: calendar_to_julian, &
    date, date_to_day_in_year, &
    date_to_weekday_number, get_day, get_month, &
    get_year, julian_to_date, &
    julian_to_date_and_week_and_day, ndays, &
    print_date, year_and_day_to_date

  use iso_date_module

  implicit none
  integer :: dd, ddd, i, mm, ndiff, wd, yyyy
  integer :: julian
  integer :: val(8)
  intrinsic date_and_time
  type (iso_date) :: date1, date2, x, tx1, tx2

  call date_and_time(values=val)
  yyyy = val(1)
  mm = 10
  do i = 31, 26, -1
    x = iso_date(yyyy, mm, i)
    if (x%date_to_weekday_number()==0) then
      print *, 'Turn clocks  back to EST on: ', &
        i, ' October ', x%get_year()
      exit
    end if
  end do
  call date_and_time(values=val)
  yyyy = val(1)
  mm = 4
  do i = 1, 8
    x = iso_date(yyyy, mm, i)
    if (x%date_to_weekday_number()==0) then
      print *, 'Turn clocks ahead to DST on: ', &
        i, ' April   ', x%get_year()
      exit
    end if
  end do
```

```fortran
call date_and_time(values=val)
yyyy = val(1)
mm = 12
dd = 31
x = iso_date(yyyy, mm, dd)
if (x%date_to_day_in_year()==366) then
  print *, x%get_year(), ' is a leap year'
else
  print *, x%get_year(), ' is not a leap year'
end if
x = iso_date(1970, 1, 1)
call julian_to_iso_date_and_week_and_day &
  (calendar_to_julian(x), x, wd, ddd)
if (x%get_year()/=1970 .or. x%get_month()/=1 &
  .or. x%get_day()/=1 .or. wd/=4 .or. ddd/=1) &
  then
  print *, &
    'julian_to_date_and_week_and_day failed'
  print *, ' date, wd, ddd = ', x%get_year(), &
    x%get_month(), x%get_day(), wd, ddd
  stop
end if
date1 = iso_date(1984, 5, 22)
date2 = iso_date(1983, 5, 22)
ndiff = ndays(date1, date2)
yyyy = 1970

x = year_and_day_to_iso_date(yyyy, ddd)

if (ndiff/=366) then
  print *, 'ndays failed; ndiff = ', ndiff
else
  if (x%get_month()/=1 .and. x%get_day()/=1) &
    then
    print *, 'year_and_day_to_date failed'
    print *, ' mma, dda = ', x%get_month(), &
      x%get_day()
  else
    print *, ' calendar_to_julian OK'
    print *, ' date_ OK'
    print *, ' date_to_day_in_year OK'
    print *, ' date_to_weekday_number OK'
    print *, ' get_day OK'
    print *, ' get_month OK'
```

```
   print *, ' get_year OK'
   print *, &
      ' julian_to_date_and_week_and_day OK'
   print *, ' ndays OK'
   print *, ' year_and_day_to_date OK'
  end if
end if



tx1 = iso_date(1970, 1, 1)
julian = tx1%calendar_to_julian()
tx2 = julian_to_iso_date(julian)
if (tx1%get_day()==tx2%get_day() .and. &
  tx1%get_month()==tx2%get_month() .and. &
  tx1%get_year()==tx2%get_year()) then
  print *, ' calendar_to_julian and '
  print *, ' julian_to_iso_date worked'
end if

x = iso_date(1952, 2, 11)


print *, ' print iso date test'
print *, ' Single parameter         ', &
  x%print_date()
print *, &
  ' day_names=false short_month_name=false ', &
  x%print_date(day_names=.false., &
  short_month_name=.false.)
print *, &
  ' day_names=true  short_month_name=false ', &
  x%print_date(day_names=.true., &
  short_month_name=.false.)
print *, &
  ' day_names=false short_month_name=true  ', &
  x%print_date(day_names=.false., &
  short_month_name=.true.)
print *, &
  ' day_names=true  short_month_name=true  ', &
  x%print_date(day_names=.true., &
  short_month_name=.true.)
print *, &
  ' digits=true                            ', &
  x%print_date(digits=.true.)
```

```
print *, ' Test out a month'

yyyy = 1970
do dd = 1, 31
  x = year_and_day_to_iso_date(yyyy, dd)
  print *, x%print_date(day_names=.false., &
    short_month_name=.true.)
end do

end program ch2902
```

29.5   Example 3: Using the Two Date Formats and Showing Polymorphism and Dynamic Binding

Files used

- day and month name module
- date module
- date wrapper module
- iso date module
- test program.

29.5.1   Date Wrapper Module

Here is the source code for the date wrapper module.

```
module date_wrapper_module

  use date_module

  type date_wrapper
    class (date), allocatable :: date
  end type date_wrapper

end module date_wrapper_module
```

29.5.2   *Polymorphic and Dynamic Binding Test Program*

Here is the source code for the polymorphic date test program.

```
include 'ch2901_day_and_month_name_module.f90'
include 'ch2901_date_module.f90'
include 'ch2902_iso_date_module.f90'
include 'ch2903_date_wrapper_module.f90'

program ch2903

  use date_module
  use iso_date_module
  use date_wrapper_module
! use us_date_module_01

  implicit none
  integer :: i, ndiff
  integer, parameter :: n_dates = 2

  type (date_wrapper), dimension (1:n_dates) :: &
    x

  x(1)%date = date(1, 1, 1970)
  x(2)%date = iso_date(1980, 1, 1)
! x(3)%date = us_date(1, 1, 1990)

  do i = 1, n_dates
    if (x(i)%date%date_to_day_in_year()==366) &
      then
      print *, x(i)%date%get_year(), &
        ' is a leap year'
    else
      print *, x(i)%date%get_year(), &
        ' is not a leap year'
    end if
  end do

  ndiff = ndays(x(1)%date, x(2)%date)

  print *, ' Number of days = ', ndiff

  x(1)%date = date(1, 1, 1970)
  x(2)%date = iso_date(1980, 1, 1)
```

```
!  x(3)%date = us_date(1, 1, 1990)

  do i = 1, n_dates
    print *, ' print date test'
    print *, ' Single parameter        ', &
      x(i)%date%print_date()
    print *, &
      ' day_names=false short_month_name=false ' &
      , x(i)%date%print_date(day_names=.false., &
      short_month_name=.false.)
    print *, &
      ' day_names=true  short_month_name=false ' &
      , x(i)%date%print_date(day_names=.true., &
      short_month_name=.false.)
    print *, &
      ' day_names=false short_month_name=true  ' &
      , x(i)%date%print_date(day_names=.false., &
      short_month_name=.true.)
    print *, &
      ' day_names=true  short_month_name=true  ' &
      , x(i)%date%print_date(day_names=.true., &
      short_month_name=.true.)
    print *, &
      ' digits=true                           ' &
      , x(i)%date%print_date(digits=.true.)
  end do

end program ch2903
```

This example requires a compiler that supports polymorphic intrinsic assignment.

29.6 Dates, Date Validity and Calendars

In this section we look at dates, date validity and calendars.

29.6.1 Calendars

A calendar date is most commonly regarded as a reference to a particular day represented within a calendar system.

The most widely used calendar system is the Gregorian.

The Gregorian calendar, also called the Western calendar and the Christian calendar, is internationally the most widely used civil calendar. It is named for Pope Gregory XIII, who introduced it in October 1582.

The calendar was a refinement to the Julian calendar amounting to a 0.002% correction in the length of the year. The motivation for the reform was to stop the drift of the calendar with respect to the equinoxes and solstices particularly the vernal equinox, which set the date for Easter celebrations. Transition to the Gregorian calendar would restore the holiday to the time of the year in which it was celebrated when introduced by the early Church. The reform was adopted initially by the Catholic countries of Europe. Protestants and Eastern Orthodox countries continued to use the traditional Julian calendar and adopted the Gregorian reform after a time, for the sake of convenience in international trade. The last European country to adopt the reform was Greece, in 1923.

A particular day may be represented by a different date in another calendar as in the Gregorian calendar and the Julian calendar, which have been used simultaneously in different places.

The Julian calendar, introduced by Julius Caesar in 46 BC (708 AUC), was a reform of the Roman calendar. It took effect in 45 BC (AUC 709), shortly after the Roman conquest of Egypt. It was the predominant calendar in the Roman world, most of Europe, and in European settlements in the Americas and elsewhere, until it was refined and gradually replaced by the Gregorian calendar, promulgated in 1582 by Pope Gregory XIII. The Julian calendar gains against the mean tropical year at the rate of one day in 128 years. For the Gregorian the figure is one day in 3,226 years. The difference in the average length of the year between Julian (365.25 days) and Gregorian (365.2425 days) is 0.002%.

From a history point of view the course of the Sun and Moon have been the basis of timekeeping, and hence calendars.

29.6.2   Date Formats

There are a number of commonly used date formats. Here are some Gregorian variations, with figures for the countries that use these formats.

- DMY - Asia (Central, SE, West), Australia (24), New Zealand (5), parts of Europe (ca. 675), Latin America (570), North Africa; India (1240), Indonesia (250), Nigeria (170), Bangladesh (150), Russia (140) 3295
- YMD - China (1360), Koreas (75), Taiwan (23), Hungary (10), Iran (80), Japan (130), Lithuania. Known in other countries due to ISO 8601. 1660
- MDY - Federated States of Micronesia, United States (320) 320
- DMY, MDY Philippines (100), Saudi Arabia (30) 130
- DMY, YMD Albania (3), Austria (9), Croatia (4), Czech Republic (11), Denmark (6), [1] Germany (81), [2][not in citation given] Hong Kong (9), Kenya (45), Latvia (2), Macau (1), Nepal (50), South Africa (54), Slovenia (2), Sweden (10) [3] 290
- DMY, MDY, YMD Canada (40) 40

29.6.3 Other Calendar Systems

Quite a number of calendar systems exist, including

- Chinese
- Coptic
- Islamic
- Jewish
- Julian

29.6.4 Proleptic Gregorian Calendar

The proleptic Gregorian calendar is produced by extending the Gregorian calendar backward to dates preceding its official introduction in 1582. In countries that adopted the Gregorian calendar later, dates occurring in the interim (between 1582 and the local adoption) are sometimes "Gregorian-ized" as well. For example, George Washington was born on February 11, 1731 (Old Style), as Britain was using the Julian calendar. After the switch, that day became February 22, which is the date commonly given as Washington's birthday.

The proleptic Gregorian calendar is explicitly required for all dates before 1582 by ISO 8601:2004 (clause 4.3.2.1 The Gregorian calendar) if the partners to information exchange agree. It is also used by most Maya scholars, [2] especially when converting Long Count dates (1st century BC 10th century).

Extending the Gregorian calendar backwards to dates preceding its official introduction produces a proleptic calendar, which should be used with some caution. For ordinary purposes, the dates of events occurring prior to 15 October 1582 are generally shown as they appeared in the Julian calendar, with the year starting on 1 January, and no conversion to their Gregorian equivalents. For example, the Battle of Agincourt is universally considered to have been fought on 25 October 1415 which is Saint Crispin's Day.

29.6.5 References

Wikipedia is a good starting place.

```
https://en.wikipedia.org/wiki/Calendar
https://en.wikipedia.org/wiki/List_of_calendars
https://en.wikipedia.org/wiki/Date_format_by_country
```

29.7   An Abstract Base Class in Fortran

A type in Fortran can have the abstract attribute.

The DEFERRED attribute defers the implementation of a type-bound procedure to extensions of the type and it can appear only in an abstract type. The dynamic type of an object cannot be abstract; therefore, a deferred type-bound procedure cannot be invoked. An extension of an abstract type need not be abstract if it has no deferred type-bound procedures.

A short example of an abstract type taken from the standard is given below.

```fortran
TYPE, ABSTRACT :: FILE_HANDLE
CONTAINS
  PROCEDURE(OPEN_FILE), DEFERRED, &
    PASS(HANDLE) :: OPEN
  ...
END TYPE
```

Section C.2.4 of the standard has an additional example on abstract types. It illustrates how an abstract type can be used as the basis for a collection of related types, and how a non-abstract member of that collection can be created by type extension.

```fortran
TYPE, ABSTRACT :: DRAWABLE_OBJECT
  REAL, DIMENSION(3) :: &
      RGB_COLOR = (/1.0,1.0,1.0/) ! White
  REAL, DIMENSION(2) :: &
      POSITION = (/0.0,0.0/) ! Centroid
CONTAINS
  PROCEDURE(RENDER_X), &
      PASS(OBJECT), DEFERRED :: RENDER
END TYPE DRAWABLE_OBJECT

ABSTRACT INTERFACE
  SUBROUTINE RENDER_X(OBJECT, WINDOW)
    IMPORT DRAWABLE_OBJECT, X_WINDOW
    CLASS(DRAWABLE_OBJECT), INTENT(IN) :: OBJECT
    CLASS(X_WINDOW), INTENT(INOUT) :: WINDOW
  END SUBROUTINE RENDER_X
END INTERFACE

  ...

TYPE, EXTENDS(DRAWABLE_OBJECT) :: DRAWABLE_TRIANGLE
  ! Not ABSTRACT
```

```
    REAL, DIMENSION(2,3) :: VERTICES
    ! In relation to centroid
CONTAINS
  PROCEDURE, PASS(OBJECT) :: &
  RENDER=>RENDER_TRIANGLE_X
END TYPE DRAWABLE_TRIANGLE
```

The actual drawing procedure will draw a triangle in WINDOW with vertices at x and y coordinates at OBJECT%POSITION(1)+OBJECT%VERTICES(1,1:3) and OBJECT%POSITION(2)+OBJECT%VERTICES(2,1:3):

```
SUBROUTINE RENDER_TRIANGLE_X(OBJECT, WINDOW)
  CLASS(DRAWABLE_TRIANGLE), INTENT(IN) :: OBJECT
  CLASS(X_WINDOW), INTENT(INOUT) :: WINDOW
  ...
END SUBROUTINE RENDER_TRIANGLE_X
```

The following example is a variant of the shape class in the earlier chapter on object oriented programming.

```
module shape_module

  type, abstract :: shape_type

    integer, private :: x_ = 0
    integer, private :: y_ = 0

  contains

    procedure, pass (this) :: get_x
    procedure, pass (this) :: get_y
    procedure, pass (this) :: set_x
    procedure, pass (this) :: set_y

    procedure (calculate_area), pass (this), &
      deferred :: area

  end type shape_type

  abstract interface
    integer function calculate_area(this)
      import :: shape_type
      class (shape_type), intent (in) :: this
    end function calculate_area
```

```
      end interface

  contains

    integer function get_x(this)
      implicit none

      class (shape_type), intent (in) :: this

      get_x = this%x_
    end function get_x

    integer function get_y(this)
      implicit none

      class (shape_type), intent (in) :: this

      get_y = this%y_
    end function get_y

    subroutine set_x(this, x)
      implicit none

      class (shape_type), intent (inout) :: this
      integer, intent (in) :: x

      this%x_ = x
    end subroutine set_x

    subroutine set_y(this, y)
      implicit none

      class (shape_type), intent (inout) :: this
      integer, intent (in) :: y

      this%y_ = y
    end subroutine set_y

  end module shape_module
```

Let us look at this example in more depth.
Here is the derived class.

```
module square_module
```

```fortran
    use shape_module

    type, extends (shape_type) :: square_type

      integer, private :: side_ = 0

    contains

      procedure, pass (this) :: area => &
        square_area

    end type square_type

    interface square_type
      module procedure square_type_constructor
    end interface square_type

  contains

    type (square_type) function &
      square_type_constructor(x, y, side)
      implicit none
      integer, intent (in) :: x
      integer, intent (in) :: y
      integer, intent (in) :: side

      call square_type_constructor%set_x(x)
      call square_type_constructor%set_y(y)
      square_type_constructor%side_ = side

    end function square_type_constructor

    integer function square_area(this)
      implicit none
      class (square_type), intent (in) :: this

      square_area = this%side_*this%side_
    end function square_area

  end module square_module
```

here is the test program that demonstrates the use of an abstract base class and simple concrete derived class.

```
include 'ch2904_abstract_shape_module.f90'
include 'ch2904_square_module.f90'

program ch2904

  use square_module

  type (square_type) :: x

  x = square_type(1, 2, 3)

  print *, ' Square area = ', x%area()

end program ch2904
```

29.8   Problems

29.1 Compile and run the examples in this chapter.

29.2 Add a US date module and test program for simple inheritance.

29.3 Add the US date data type to the polymorphic example.

29.4 The names of the days of the week and months in the year are English. Here are their Welsh equivalents.

```
Llun       Monday
Mawrth     Tuesday
Mercher    Wednesday
Iau        Thursday
Gwener     Friday
Sadwrn     Saturday
Sul        Sunday
```

```
January    Ionawr     July       Gorffennaf
February   Chwefror   August     Awst
March      Mawrth     September   Medi
April      Ebrill     October    Hydref
May        Mai        November   Tachwedd
June       Mehefin    December   Rhagfyr
```

Choose a language of you own, and write another language version of the date class. Test it out.

29.5 The following module contains code that tests the validity of a date using a date expressed in terms of days, months and years.

```
module valid_date_module

  implicit none

contains

  logical function leap_year(year)
    implicit none
    integer, intent (in) :: year

    if ((year/4)*4==year) then
      leap_year = .true.
      if ((year/400)*400==year) then
        leap_year = .true.
      else if ((year/100)*100==year) then
        leap_year = .false.
      end if
    else
      leap_year = .false.
    end if
  end function leap_year

  subroutine check_date(day, month, year, ifail)
    implicit none

    integer, intent (in) :: day
    integer, intent (in) :: month
    integer, intent (in) :: year
    integer, intent (inout) :: ifail

    integer, parameter :: n_months = 12
    integer, dimension (1:n_months) :: &
      days_in_month = [ 31, 28, 31, 30, 31, 30, &
      31, 31, 30, 31, 30, 31 ]

!   Initialise ifail to 0

    ifail = 0

!   Simple test for Gregorian start date
!   This is a warning. See the book for more
!   details
```

```
!    about dates and calendars.

     if (year<1582) then
       ifail = 1
     end if

     if ((month<1) .or. (month>12)) then
       ifail = ifail + 2
       return
     end if



!    Now have a valid month

!    reset in case of leap year in previous call

     days_in_month(2) = 28

     if (leap_year(year)) then
       days_in_month(2) = 29
     end if

     if ((day<1) .or. (day>days_in_month(month))) &
       then
       ifail = ifail + 4
       return
     end if

     return

   end subroutine check_date

 end module valid_date_module
```

How easy would it be to add date checking to the base class?

29.9   Bibliography

ISO/IEC DIS 1539-1 Information technology – Programming languages – Fortran – Part 1: Base language

- Fortran 2018 draft standard.

```
https://www.iso.org/standard/72320.html
```

Chapter 30
Introduction to Submodules

> *The competent programmer is fully aware of the limited size of his own skull. He therefore approaches his task with full humility, and avoids clever tricks like the plague*
>
> Edsger Dijkstra

Aims

The aims of this chapter is to provide a short introduction to submodules.

30.1 Introduction

Modules were introduced into Fortran in the 1990 standard. Over the next ten or so years a number of issues arose that lead to the TR on Enhanced Module Facilities, N1602, which was the starting point for the submodule facility in Fortran. A copy can be found at the WG5 site. Visit

```
https://wg5-fortran.org/
```

to obtain a copy.

The actual published technical report (TR 19767) can be found at the ISO site.

```
https://www.iso.org/standard/37995.html
```

The document discussed the fact that the module system of Fortran was adequate for a wide range of problems, but had shortcomings when one ended up with large modules.

Four areas of concern were identified in this document:

© Springer International Publishing AG, part of Springer Nature 2018
I. Chivers and J. Sleightholme, *Introduction to Programming with Fortran*,
https://doi.org/10.1007/978-3-319-75502-1_30

- Decomposing large and interconnected facilities. If an intellectual concept is large and internally interconnected, it requires a large module to implement it. Decomposing such a concept into components of tractable size using modules may require one to convert private data to public data. One problem occurs during maintenance, when one must then answer the question where is this entity used?
- Avoiding recompilation cascades. Once the design of a program is stable, few changes to a module occur in its interface, that is, in its public data, public types, the interfaces of its public procedures, and private entities that affect their definitions. We refer to the rest of a module, that is, private entities that do not affect the definitions of public entities, and the bodies of its public procedures, as its implementation. Changes in the implementation have no effect on the translation of other program units that access the module. The existing module facility, however, draws no structural distinction between the interface and the implementation. Therefore, if one changes any part of a module, most language translation systems have no alternative but to conclude that a change might have occurred that could affect the translation of other modules that access the changed module. This effect cascades into modules that access modules that access the changed module, and so on. This can cause a substantial expense to re-translate and re-certify a large program. Re-certification can be several orders of magnitude more costly than retranslation.
- Packaging proprietary software. If a module is used to package proprietary software, the source text of the module cannot be published as authoritative documentation of the interface of the module, without either exposing trade secrets, or requiring the expense of separating the implementation from the interface every time a revision is published.
- Easier library creation. Most Fortran translator systems produce a single file of computer instructions and data, frequently called an object file, for each module. This is easier than producing an object file for the specification part and one for each module procedure. It is also convenient, and conserves space and time, when a program uses all or most of the procedures in each module. It is inconvenient, and results in a larger program, when only a few of the procedures in a general purpose module are needed in a particular program.

We provide a brief technical background below and then look at an example based on the date class from the second object oriented chapter.

30.2   Brief Technical Background

The following is taken from Sect. 14.2.3 of the Fortran 2018 standard.

A submodule is a program unit that extends a module or another submodule. The program unit that it extends is its host, and is specified by the parent-identifier in the submodule-stmt.

A module or submodule is an ancestor program unit of all of its descendants, which are its submodules and their descendants. The submodule identifier is the ordered pair whose first element is the ancestor module name and whose second element is the submodule name; the submodule name by itself is not a local or global identifier.

A module and its submodules stand in a tree-like relationship one to another, with the module at the root. Therefore, a submodule has exactly one ancestor module and can have one or more ancestor submodules.

A submodule may provide implementations for separate module procedures (15.6.2.5), each of which is declared within that submodule or one of its ancestors, and declarations and definitions of other entities that are accessible by host association in its descendants.

Here is an example taken from N1602.

The example module POINTS below declares a type POINT and a module procedure interface body for a module function POINT_DIST. Because the interface body includes the MODULE prefix, it accesses the scoping unit of the module by host association, without needing an IMPORT statement; indeed, an IMPORT statement is prohibited.

```
MODULE POINTS

  TYPE :: POINT
    REAL :: X, Y
  END TYPE POINT

  INTERFACE
    REAL MODULE FUNCTION POINT_DIST ( A, B ) &
  RESULT ( DISTANCE )
    TYPE(POINT), INTENT(IN) :: A, B
! POINT is accessed by host association
      REAL :: DISTANCE
    END FUNCTION POINT_DIST
  END INTERFACE

END MODULE POINTS
```

The example submodule POINTS A below is a submodule of the POINTS module. The type POINT and the interface POINT_DIST are accessible in the submodule by host association. The characteristics of the function POINT_DIST are redeclared in the module function body, and the dummy arguments have the same names. The function POINT_DIST is accessible by use association because its module procedure interface body is in the ancestor module and has the PUBLIC attribute.

```
SUBMODULE ( POINTS ) POINTS_A
```

```
CONTAINS
  REAL MODULE FUNCTION POINT_DIST ( A, B ) &
RESULT ( DISTANCE )
    TYPE(POINT), INTENT(IN) :: A, B
    DISTANCE = SQRT( (A%X-B%X)**2 + (A%Y-B%Y)**2 )
  END FUNCTION POINT_DIST
END SUBMODULE POINTS_A
```

A complete example is given below.

30.3 Example 1: Rewrite of the Date Class Using Submodules

In this example we rewrite the base date module to have type declarations and interfaces for each of the contained module procedures.

The submodule will be based on the base date module and will have the implementations of the contained methods.

We have thus effectively decoupled the interface from the implementation.

The stages we followed are

- Duplicate the original module, creating an interface module and a implementation submodule
- Add interfaces for each function and subroutine to the interface module
- Add the new syntax to the interfaces in the module, i.e. add the MODULE keyword to each function and subroutine
- Remove all executable code from the interface module, in this example all code after the contains statement
- Remove all code before the contains statement in the implementation module
- Add the new submodule syntax
- Add the new syntax to each contained procedure, i.e. add the MODULE keyword to each function and subroutine
- Copy the module test program
- Change the test program to use the new module names

We can distribute the module interface, and effectively keep the implementation functions and subroutines hidden.

Here is the first source file. This is the base date class, but now rewritten just to have the interfaces, and no executable or implementation code.

```
module date_module_interface

  use day_and_month_name_module
```

```
implicit none

private

type, public :: date

  private

  integer :: day
  integer :: month
  integer :: year

contains

  procedure, pass (this) :: calendar_to_julian
  procedure, pass (this) :: date_to_day_in_year
  procedure, pass (this) :: &
date_to_weekday_number
  procedure, pass (this) :: get_day
  procedure, pass (this) :: get_month
  procedure, pass (this) :: get_year
  procedure, nopass :: julian_to_date
  procedure, nopass :: &
julian_to_date_and_week_and_day.
  procedure, nopass :: ndays
  procedure, pass (this) :: print_date
  procedure, pass (this) :: set_day
  procedure, pass (this) :: set_month
  procedure, pass (this) :: set_year
  procedure, nopass :: year_and_day_to_date

end type date

interface date
  module procedure date_constructor
end interface date

interface
  module function calendar_to_julian(this) &
result (ival)
    implicit none
    integer :: ival
    class (date), intent (in) :: this
  end function calendar_to_julian
end interface
```

```fortran
interface
  type (date) module function &
date_constructor(dd, mm, yyyy)

    implicit none
    integer, intent (in) :: dd, mm, yyyy
  end function date_constructor
end interface

interface
  integer module function &
date_to_day_in_year(this)
    implicit none
    class (date), intent (in) :: this
    intrinsic modulo
  end function date_to_day_in_year
end interface

interface
  integer module function &
date_to_weekday_number(this)
    implicit none
    class (date), intent (in) :: this
    intrinsic modulo
  end function date_to_weekday_number
end interface

interface
  module function get_day(this)
    implicit none
    integer :: get_day
    class (date), intent (in) :: this
  end function get_day
end interface

interface
  module function get_month(this)
    implicit none
    integer :: get_month
    class (date), intent (in) :: this
  end function get_month
end interface
```

```
interface
  module function get_year(this)
    implicit none
    integer :: get_year
    class (date), intent (in) :: this
  end function get_year
end interface

interface
  module function julian_to_date(julian)
    implicit none
    type (date) :: julian_to_date
    integer, intent (in) :: julian
  end function julian_to_date
end interface

interface
  module subroutine &
julian_to_date_and_week_and_day &
(jd, d, wd, ddd)
    implicit none
    integer, intent (in) :: jd
    type (date), intent (out) :: d
    integer, intent (out) :: wd, ddd
  end subroutine &
julian_to_date_and_week_and_day
end interface

interface
  module function ndays(date1, date2)
    implicit none
    integer :: ndays
    class (date), intent (in) :: date1, date2
  end function ndays
end interface

interface
  module function &
print_date(this, day_names, &
short_month_name, digits)
    implicit none
    class (date), intent (in) :: this
    logical, optional, intent (in) :: &
day_names, short_month_name, digits
    character (len=40) :: print_date
```

```
      end function print_date
    end interface

    interface
      module subroutine set_day(this, d)
        implicit none
        integer, intent (in) :: d
        class (date), intent (inout) :: this
      end subroutine set_day
    end interface

    interface
      module subroutine set_month(this, m)
        implicit none
        integer, intent (in) :: m
        class (date), intent (inout) :: this
      end subroutine set_month
    end interface

    interface
      module subroutine set_year(this, y)
        implicit none
        integer, intent (in) :: y
        class (date), intent (inout) :: this
      end subroutine set_year
    end interface

    interface
      module function &
    year_and_day_to_date(year, day_in_year)
        use day_and_month_name_module
        implicit none
        type (date) :: year_and_day_to_date
        integer, intent (in) :: day_in_year, year
      end function year_and_day_to_date
    end interface

    public :: calendar_to_julian, &
     date_to_day_in_year, &
       date_to_weekday_number, get_day, &
    get_month, &
    get_year, julian_to_date, &
       julian_to_date_and_week_and_day, &
    ndays, print_date, &
       set_day, set_month, set_year, &
```

```
 year_and_day_to_date

end module date_module_interface
```

Here is the submodule that actually has the implementation.

```
submodule (date_module_interface) &
  date_module_implementation


contains

  module function &
    calendar_to_julian(this) &
    result (ival)
    implicit none
    integer :: ival
    class (date), intent (in) :: this

    ival = this%day - 32075 + 1461*&
      (this%year+ &
      4800+(this%month-14)/12)/4 + &
      367*(this%month-2-((this%month- &
      14)/12)*12)/12 - 3*&
      ((this%year+4900+(this% &
      month-14)/12)/100)/4
  end function calendar_to_julian

  type (date) module function &
    date_constructor(dd, mm, &
    yyyy)

    implicit none
    integer, intent (in) :: dd, mm, yyyy

    date_constructor%day = dd
    date_constructor%month = mm
    date_constructor%year = yyyy

  end function date_constructor

  integer module function &
    date_to_day_in_year(this)
    implicit none
    class (date), intent (in) :: this
```

```
    intrinsic modulo

    date_to_day_in_year = 3055*&
        (this%month+2)/ &
      100 - (this%month+10)/13*2 - &
        91 + &
      (1-(modulo(this%year,4)+3)/4+&
        (modulo(this% &
      year,100)+99)/100-(modulo(this%year, &
      400)+399)/400*(this%month+10)/13 + &
      this%day
  end function date_to_day_in_year

  integer module function &
    date_to_weekday_number(this)
    implicit none
    class (date), intent (in) :: this
    intrinsic modulo

    date_to_weekday_number = modulo((13*( &
      this%month+10-&
        (this%month+10)/13*12)-1)/5+ &
      this%day+77+5*(this%year+(this%month- &
      14)/12-(this%year+&
        (this%month-14)/12)/100* &
      100)/4+(this%year+(this%month- &
      14)/12)/400-(this%year+(this%month- &
      14)/12)/100*2, 7)
  end function date_to_weekday_number

  module function get_day(this)
    implicit none
    integer :: get_day
    class (date), intent (in) :: this

    get_day = this%day
  end function get_day

  module function get_month(this)
    implicit none
    integer :: get_month
    class (date), intent (in) :: this

    get_month = this%month
  end function get_month
```

```
module function get_year(this)
  implicit none
  integer :: get_year
  class (date), intent (in) :: this

  get_year = this%year
end function get_year

module function julian_to_date(julian)
  implicit none
  type (date) :: julian_to_date
  integer, intent (in) :: julian

  integer :: l, n

  l = julian + 68569
  n = 4*l/146097
  l = l - (146097*n+3)/4
  julian_to_date%year = (4000*(l+1)/1461001)
  l = l - 1461*julian_to_date%year/4 + 31
  julian_to_date%month = (80*l/2447)
  julian_to_date%day = &
    (l-2447*julian_to_date% &
    month/80)
  l = julian_to_date%month/11
  julian_to_date%month = &
     (julian_to_date%month &
    +2-12*l)
  julian_to_date%year = (100*(n-49)+ &
    julian_to_date%year+1)
end function julian_to_date

module subroutine &
  julian_to_date_and_week_and_day(jd, &
  d, wd, ddd)
  implicit none
  integer, intent (in) :: jd
  type (date), intent (out) :: d
  integer, intent (out) :: wd, ddd

  d = julian_to_date(jd)
  wd = date_to_weekday_number(d)
  ddd = date_to_day_in_year(d)
end subroutine &
```

```fortran
    julian_to_date_and_week_and_day

module function ndays(date1, date2)
  implicit none
  integer :: ndays
  class (date), intent (in) :: date1, date2

  ndays = calendar_to_julian(date1) - &
    calendar_to_julian(date2)
end function ndays

module function &
  print_date(this, day_names, &
  short_month_name, digits)
  implicit none
  class (date), intent (in) :: this
  logical, optional, intent (in) :: &
    day_names, &
    short_month_name, digits
  character (40) :: print_date
  integer :: pos
  logical :: want_day, &
    want_short_month_name, &
    want_digits
  intrinsic len_trim, present, trim

  want_day = .false.
  want_short_month_name = .false.
  want_digits = .false.
  print_date = ' '
  if (present(day_names)) then
    want_day = day_names
  end if
  if (present(short_month_name)) then
    want_short_month_name = short_month_name
  end if
  if (present(digits)) then
    want_digits = digits
  end if
  if (want_digits) then
    write (print_date(1:2), '(i2)') this%day
    print_date(3:3) = '/'
    write (print_date(4:5), '(i2)') &
      this%month
    print_date(6:6) = '/'
```

```
      write (print_date(7:10), '(i4)') this%year
    else
      if (want_day) then
        pos = date_to_weekday_number(this)
        print_date = trim(day(pos)) // ' '
        pos = len_trim(print_date) + 2
      else
        pos = 1
        print_date = ' '
      end if
      write (print_date(pos:pos+1), '(i2)') &
        this%day
      if (want_short_month_name) then
        print_date(pos+3:pos+5) = month(this% &
          month)(1:3)
        pos = pos + 7
      else
        print_date(pos+3:) = month(this%month)
        pos = len_trim(print_date) + 2
      end if
      write (print_date(pos:pos+3), '(i4)') &
        this%year
    end if

    return
  end function print_date

  module subroutine set_day(this, d)
    implicit none
    integer, intent (in) :: d
    class (date), intent (inout) :: this

    this%day = d
  end subroutine set_day

  module subroutine set_month(this, m)
    implicit none
    integer, intent (in) :: m
    class (date), intent (inout) :: this

    this%month = m
  end subroutine set_month

  module subroutine set_year(this, y)
    implicit none
```

```
      integer, intent (in) :: y
      class (date), intent (inout) :: this

      this%year = y
   end subroutine set_year

   module function year_and_day_to_date(year, &
      day_in_year)
      use day_and_month_name_module
      implicit none
      type (date) :: year_and_day_to_date
      integer, intent (in) :: day_in_year, year
      integer :: t
      intrinsic modulo

      year_and_day_to_date%year = year
      t = 0
      if (modulo(year,4)==0) then
        t = 1
      end if
      if (modulo(year,400)/=0 .and. &
        modulo(year,100)==0) then
        t = 0
      end if
      year_and_day_to_date%day = day_in_year
      if (day_in_year>59+t) then
        year_and_day_to_date%day = &
          year_and_day_to_date%day + 2 - t
      end if
      year_and_day_to_date%month = &
        ((year_and_day_to_date%day+91)*100)/3055
      year_and_day_to_date%day = ( &
        year_and_day_to_date%day+91) - &
        (year_and_day_to_date%month*3055)/100
      year_and_day_to_date%month = &
        year_and_day_to_date%month - 2
      if (year_and_day_to_date%month>=1 .and. &
        year_and_day_to_date%month<=12) then
        return
      end if
      write (unit=*, fmt='(a,i11,a)') &
        '$$year_and_d&
        &ay_to_date: day of the year input &
        &=', day_in_year, ' is out of range.'
   end function year_and_day_to_date
```

```
      end submodule date_module_implementation
```

Here is the Fortran driving program to test the submodule out.

```
include 'day_and_month_name_module.f90'
include 'date_module_interface.f90'
include 'date_module_implementation.f90'

program ch3001

  use date_module_interface , only : &
  calendar_to_julian, &
    date, date_to_day_in_year, &
    date_to_weekday_number, get_day, get_month, &
    get_year, julian_to_date, &
    julian_to_date_and_week_and_day, ndays, &
    print_date, year_and_day_to_date

  implicit none
  integer :: dd, ddd, i, mm, ndiff, wd, yyyy
  integer :: julian
  integer :: val(8)
  intrinsic date_and_time
  type (date) :: date1, date2, x, tx1, tx2

  call date_and_time(values=val)
  yyyy = val(1)
  mm = 10
  do i = 31, 26, -1
    x = date(i, mm, yyyy)
    if (x%date_to_weekday_number()==0) then
      print *, 'Turn clocks  back to EST on: ', &
        i, ' October ', x%get_year()
      exit
    end if
  end do
  call date_and_time(values=val)
  yyyy = val(1)
  mm = 4
  do i = 1, 8
    x = date(i, mm, yyyy)
    if (x%date_to_weekday_number()==0) then
      print *, 'Turn clocks ahead to DST on: ', &
        i, ' April    ', x%get_year()
      exit
```

```
    end if
  end do
  call date_and_time(values=val)
  yyyy = val(1)
  mm = 12
  dd = 31
  x = date(dd, mm, yyyy)
  if (x%date_to_day_in_year()==366) then
    print *, x%get_year(), ' is a leap year'
  else
    print *, x%get_year(), ' is not a leap year'
  end if
  x = date(1, 1, 1970)
  call julian_to_date_and_week_and_day &
    (calendar_to_julian(x), x, wd, ddd)
  if (x%get_year()/=1970 .or. x%get_month()/=1 &
    .or. x%get_day()/=1 .or. wd/=4 .or. ddd/=1) &
    then
    print *, &
      'julian_to_date_and_week_and_day failed'
    print *, ' date, wd, ddd = ', x%get_year(), &
      x%get_month(), x%get_day(), wd, ddd
    stop
  end if
  date1 = date(22, 5, 1984)
  date2 = date(22, 5, 1983)
  ndiff = ndays(date1, date2)
  yyyy = 1970

  x = year_and_day_to_date(yyyy, ddd)

  if (ndiff/=366) then
    print *, 'ndays failed; ndiff = ', ndiff
  else
    if (x%get_month()/=1 .and. x%get_day()/=1) &
      then
      print *, 'year_and_day_to_date failed'
      print *, ' mma, dda = ', x%get_month(), &
        x%get_day()
    else
      print *, ' calendar_to_julian OK'
      print *, ' date_ OK'
      print *, ' date_to_day_in_year OK'
      print *, ' date_to_weekday_number OK'
      print *, ' get_day OK'
```

```
      print *, ' get_month OK'
      print *, ' get_year OK'
      print *, &
        ' julian_to_date_and_week_and_day OK'
      print *, ' ndays OK'
      print *, ' year_and_day_to_date OK'
    end if
  end if

  tx1 = date(1, 1, 1970)
  julian = tx1%calendar_to_julian()
  tx2 = julian_to_date(julian)
  if (tx1%get_day()==tx2%get_day() .and. &
    tx1%get_month()==tx2%get_month() .and. &
    tx1%get_year()==tx2%get_year()) then
    print *, ' calendar_to_julian and '
    print *, ' julian_to_date worked'
  end if

  x = date(11, 2, 1952)

  print *, ' print_date test'
  print *, ' Single parameter         ', &
    x%print_date()
  print *, &
    ' day_names=false short_month_name=false ', &
    x%print_date(day_names=.false., &
    short_month_name=.false.)
  print *, &
    ' day_names=true  short_month_name=false ', &
    x%print_date(day_names=.true., &
    short_month_name=.false.)
  print *, &
    ' day_names=false short_month_name=true  ', &
    x%print_date(day_names=.false., &
    short_month_name=.true.)
  print *, &
    ' day_names=true  short_month_name=true  ', &
    x%print_date(day_names=.true., &
    short_month_name=.true.)
  print *, ' digits=true              ', &
    x%print_date(digits=.true.)

  print *, ' Test out a month'
```

```
yyyy = 1970
do dd = 1, 31
  x = year_and_day_to_date(yyyy, dd)
  print *, x%print_date(day_names=.false., &
    short_month_name=.true.)
end do

end program ch3001
```

As can be seen the test or driving program is identical to the earlier, non submodule version.

30.4   Example 2: Rewrite of the First Order RKM ODE Solver Using Modules

The module rkm_module from Chap. 26 contained the runge_kutta_merson subroutine which was an implementation of the Runge Kutta Merson (RKM) algorithm.

We have now introduced a submodule called rkm_module_implementation which contains the runge_kutta_merson subroutine. By moving the body of the procedure into a submodule any subsequent changes to the body will typically only require recompilation of the submodule. Here is the new RKM module code.

```
module rkm_module

interface

  module subroutine &
    runge_kutta_merson(y, fun, ifail, n, a, b, tol)

  use precision_module, wp=> dp

    implicit none

    real (wp), intent (inout), dimension (:) :: y
    real (wp), intent (in) :: a, b, tol
    integer, intent (in) :: n
    integer, intent (out) :: ifail

    interface

      subroutine fun(t, y, f, n)
```

```
            use precision_module, wp => dp
            implicit none
            real (wp), intent (in), dimension (:) :: y
            real (wp), intent (out), dimension (:) :: f
            real (wp), intent (in) :: t
            integer, intent (in) :: n
         end subroutine fun

     end interface

   end subroutine runge_kutta_merson

 end interface

 end module rkm_module
```

Here is the RKM submodule.

```
submodule (rkm_module) rkm_module_implementation

 contains

  module subroutine &
  runge_kutta_merson(y, fun, ifail, n, a, b, tol)
  use precision_module, wp => dp

!    runge-kutta-merson method for the solution
!    of a system of n 1st order initial value
!    ordinary differential equations.
!    the routine tries to integrate from
!    t=a to t=b with initial conditions in y,
!    subject to the condition that the
!    absolute error estimate <= tol. the step
!    length is adjusted automatically to meet
!    this condition.
!    if the routine is successful it returns with
!    ifail = 0, t=b and the solution in y.

    implicit none

!    define arguments

    real (wp), intent (inout), &
  dimension (:) :: y
    real (wp), intent (in) :: a, b, tol
```

```
      integer, intent (in) :: n
      integer, intent (out) :: ifail

      interface
        subroutine fun(t, y, f, n)
          use precision_module, wp => dp
          implicit none
          real (wp), intent (in), &
    dimension (:) :: y
          real (wp), intent (out), &
    dimension (:) :: f
          real (wp), intent (in) :: t
          integer, intent (in) :: n
        end subroutine fun
      end interface

!   local variables

      real (wp), dimension (1:size(y)) :: &
    s1, s2, s3, s4, s5, new_y_1, new_y_2, error
      real (wp) :: &
    t, h, h2, h3, h6, h8, factor = 1.e-2_wp
      real (wp) :: &
    smallest_step = 1.e-6_wp, max_error
      integer :: no_of_steps = 0

      ifail = 0

!   check input parameters

      if (n<=0 .or. a==b .or. tol<=0.0) then
        ifail = 1
        return
      end if

!   initialize t to be start of interval and
!   h to be 1/100 of interval

      t = a
      h = (b-a)/100.0_wp
      do

!       ##### beginning of
!       ##### repeat loop
```

```
      h2 = h/2.0_wp
      h3 = h/3.0_wp
      h6 = h/6.0_wp
      h8 = h/8.0_wp

!     calculate s1,s2,s3,s4,s5 !
      s1=f(t,y)

      call fun(t, y, s1, n)
      new_y_1 = y + h3*s1

!     s2 = f(t+h/3,y+h/3*s1)

      call fun(t+h3, new_y_1, s2, n)
      new_y_1 = y + h6*s1 + h6*s2

!     s3=f(t+h/3,y+h/6*s1+h/6*s2)

      call fun(t+h3, new_y_1, s3, n)
      new_y_1 = y + h8*(s2+3.0_wp*s3)

!     s4=f(t+h/2,y+h/8*(s2+3*s3))

      call fun(t+h2, new_y_1, s4, n)
      new_y_1 = y + h2*(s1-3.0_wp*s3+4.0_wp*s4)

!     s5=f(t+h,y+h/2*(s1-3*s3+4*s4))

      call fun(t+h, new_y_1, s5, n)

!     calculate values at t+h

      new_y_1 = y + h6*(s1+4.0_wp*s4+s5)
      new_y_2 = y + h2*(s1-3.0_wp*s3+4.0_wp*s4)

!     calculate error estimate

      error = abs(0.2_wp*(new_y_1-new_y_2))
      max_error = maxval(error)
      if (max_error>tol) then

!       halve step length and try again

        if (abs(h2)<smallest_step) then
          ifail = 2
```

```
              return
           end if
           h = h2
        else

!         accepted approximation so overwrite
!         y with y_new_1, and t with t+h

          y = new_y_1
          t = t + h

!         can next step be doubled?

          if (max_error*factor<tol) then
            h = h*2.0_wp
          end if

!         does next step go beyond interval end b,
!         if so set h = b-t

          if (t+h>b) then
            h = b - t
          end if
          no_of_steps = no_of_steps + 1
        end if
        if (t>=b) exit

!       ##### end of
!       ##### repeat loop

    end do
  end subroutine runge_kutta_merson

end submodule rkm_module_implementation
```

Here is the fun1_module, which is the same code as in Chap. 26.

```
module fun1_module

  implicit none

contains

  subroutine fun1(t, y, f, n)
    use precision_module, wp => dp
```

```
      implicit none
      real (wp), intent (in), dimension (:) :: y
      real (wp), intent (out), dimension (:) :: f
      real (wp), intent (in) :: t
      integer, intent (in) :: n
      f(1) = tan(y(3))
      f(2) = -0.032_wp*f(1)/y(2) - &
                  0.02_wp*y(2)/cos(y(3))
      f(3) = -0.032_wp/(y(2)*y(2))
    end subroutine fun1

end module fun1_module
```

Here is the main program, which is the same code as in Chap. 26.

```
include 'precision_module.f90'
include 'ch3002_fun1_module.f90'
include 'ch3002_rkm_interface_module.f90'
include 'ch3002_rkm_implementation_module.f90'

program ch3002

  use precision_module, wp => dp
  use rkm_module
  use fun1_module

  implicit none

  real (wp), dimension (:), allocatable :: y
  real (wp) :: a, b, tol
  integer :: n, ifail, all_stat

  print *, 'input no of equations'
  read *, n

! allocate space for y - checking to see that it
! allocates properly

  allocate (y(1:n), stat=all_stat)
  if (all_stat/=0) then
    print *, ' not enough memory'
    print *, ' array y is not allocated'
    stop
  end if
  print *, ' input start and end of interval over'
```

```
      print *, ' which equations to be solved'
      read *, a, b
      print *, 'input initial conditions'
      read *, y(1:n)
      print *, 'input tolerance'
      read *, tol
      print 100, a
 100 format &
      ('at t= ', f5.2, ' initial conditions are :')
      print 110, y(1:n)
 110 format (4(f5.2,2x))
      call &
      runge_kutta_merson(y, fun1, ifail, n, a, b, tol)
      if (ifail/=0) then
        print *, &
   'integration stopped with ifail = ', ifail
      else
        print 120, b
 120 format ('at t= ', f5.2, ' solution is:')
        print 110, y(1:n)
      end if

 end program ch3002
```

30.5   Problems

30.1 Compile and run the above example. Compare the output to the previous version.

30.2 Convert an earlier module example to use submodules, with an interface module and an implementation submodule.

30.6   Bibliography

ISO/IEC DIS 1539-1 Information technology – Programming languages – Fortran – Part 1: Base language

- Fortran 2018 draft standard.

```
   https://www.iso.org/standard/72320.html
```

Chapter 31
Introduction to Parallel Programming

> *'Can you do addition?'* the White Queen asked. *'What's one and one and one and one and one and one and one and one and one and one?'*
> *'I don't know'* said Alice. *'I lost count.'*
> *'She can't do addition,'* the Red Queen interrupted.
>   Lewis Carroll, Through the Looking Glass and What Alice Found There

Aims

The aims of this chapter is to provide a short introduction to parallel programming.

31.1 Introduction

Parallel programming involves breaking a program down into parts that can be executed concurrently. Here is a simple diagram to illustrate the idea.

```
Sequential  Parallel    Step
Execution   Execution
    |           |         1
              /   \       #
    |         |   |       2
    |         |   |       3
              \   /       @
    |           |         4
```

© Springer International Publishing AG, part of Springer Nature 2018
I. Chivers and J. Sleightholme, *Introduction to Programming with Fortran*,
https://doi.org/10.1007/978-3-319-75502-1_31

On the left hand side we have a sequential program and this steps through linearly from beginning to end. The right hand side has the same program that has been partially parallelised. There are two parallel regions and the work here is now shared between two processes or threads. At each parallel part of the program we have the following

	Parallel Region 1	Parallel Region 2
Set up cost	Step #	Step ##
Parallel section	Steps 2,3	Steps 6,7
Synchronisation cost	Step @	Step @@

The theory is that the overall run time of the program will have been reduced or we will have been able to solve a larger problem by parallelising our code. In the above example we have divided the work between two processes or threads. Here are some details of a range of processors which support multiple cores. Visit the AMD and Intel sites for up to date information.

Processor	Cores	Hyper Threading
AMD Phenom II X6	6	
Intel Core i7 920	4	* 2
Intel Core i7 2600K	4	* 2
AMD Opteron Shanghai	4	
Istanbul	6	
Magny Cours	8	
Magny Cours	12	
Intel E5-2697	12	* 2

Intel introduced hyperthreading technology in 2002. For each physical processor core the Intel chip has the operating system can see or address two virtual or logical cores, and can share the workload between them when possible. See the Wikipedia entry for more information.

```
http://en.wikipedia.org/wiki/Hyper-threading
```

There are several ways of doing parallel programming, and this chapter will look at three ways of doing this in Fortran. There are a common set of concepts and terminology that are useful to know about, whichever method we use, and we will cover these first.

31.2 Parallel Computing Classification

Parallel computing is often classified by the way the hardware supports parallelism. Two of the most common are:

- multi-processor and multi-core computers having multiple processing elements within a single system
- clusters or grids with multiple computers connected to work together.

Modern large systems are increasingly hybrids of the two above.

31.3 Amdahl's Law

Amdahl's law is a simple equation for the speedup of a program when parallelised. It assumes that the problem size remains the same when parallelised. In the equation below

- P is the proportion of the program that can be parallelised
- (1-P) is the serial proportion
- N is the number of processors
- speedup = 1 / ((1-P) + P/N).

We have included a couple of graphs to illustrate the above. We have written programs that use the dislin graphics library to do the plots. More information on these programs can be found in Chap. 35, where we have a look at third party numeric and graphics libraries.

31.3.1   Amdahl's Law Graph 1–8 Processors or Cores

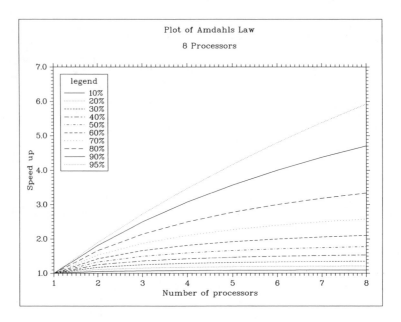

31.3.2   Amdahl's Law Graph 2–64 Processors or Cores

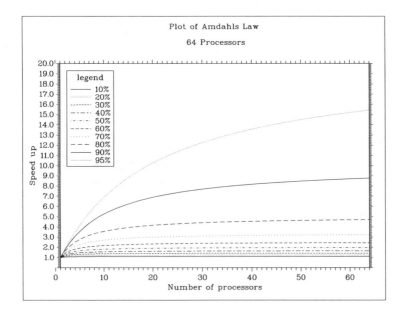

31.4 Gustafson's Law

Gustafson's Law is often seen as a contradiction of Amdahl's Law. Simplistically it states that programmers solve larger problems when parallelising programs.

The equation for Gustafson's Law is given below.

- N is the number of processors
- Serial is the proportion that remains serial
- Speedup(N) = N - Serial * (N - 1).

We have again included a graph to illustrate the above.

31.4.1 Gustafson's Law Graph 1–64 Processors or Cores

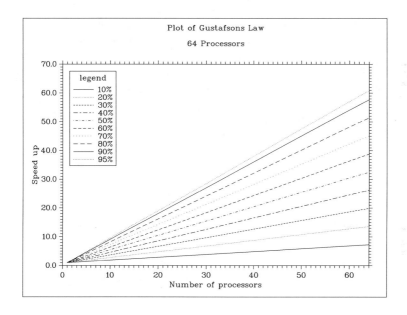

31.5 Memory Access

Memory access times fall into two main categories that are of interest in parallel computing

- uma - uniform memory access. Each element of main memory can be accessed with the same latency and bandwidth. Multi-processor and multi-core computers typically have this behaviour.

- numa - non uniform memory access. Distributed memory systems have non-uniform memory access. Clusters or grids with multiple computers connected to work together have this behaviour.

31.6   Cache

Modern processors have a memory hierarchy. They typically have two or more levels:

- main memory
- cpu memory

and there is a speed and cost link. Main memory is cheap and relatively slow in comparison to the cpu memory.

The cpu memory or cache is used to reduce the effective access time to memory. If the information that the program requires is in the cpu cache then the average latency of memory accesses will be closer to the cache latency than to the latency of main memory. Getting high performance from a computer normally means writing cache friendly programs. This means that the data and instructions that the program needs are already in the cache and don't need to be accessed from the much slower main memory.

In a multi-core and multi-cpu system each core and cpu will have their own memory or cache. This introduces the problem of cache coherency - i.e. the consistency of data stored in local caches compared to the data in the common shared memory. This problem must obviously be addressed when doing parallel programming.

31.7   Bandwidth and Latency

Bandwidth is the rate at which data can be transferred. Latency is the start up time for a data transfer. We normally want a high bandwidth and low latency. Table 31.1 looks at some figures for several interconnects.

Table 31.1 Bandwidth and latency

	MPI bandwidth or theoretical maximum GB/s	latency μs
Gigabit ethernet	0.125	≈ 100
Infiniband	1.3	4.0
Myrinet 10-G	1.2	2.1
Quadrics QsNet II	0.9	2.7
Cray SeStar2	2.1	4.5

31.8 Flynn's Taxonomy

Flynn's taxonomy is an old, but still widely used, classification scheme for computer architecture.

- Single Instruction, Single Data stream (SISD) A sequential computer which exploits no parallelism in either the instruction or data streams. Term rarely used.
- Single Instruction, Multiple Data streams (SIMD) A computer which exploits multiple data streams against a single instruction stream to perform operations which may be naturally parallelised. For example, an array processor or GPU.
- Multiple Instruction, Single Data stream (MISD) Multiple instructions operate on a single data stream. Term rarely used.
- Multiple Instruction, Multiple Data streams (MIMD) Multiple autonomous processors simultaneously executing different instructions on different data. Distributed systems are generally recognized to be MIMD architectures; either exploiting a single shared memory space or a distributed memory space. Essentially separate computers working together to solve a problem.

We also have the term

- Single Program Multiple Data - An identical program executes on a MIMD computer system. Conditional statements in the code mean that different parts of the program execute on each system.

31.9 Consistency Models

Parallel programming languages and parallel computers must have a consistency model (also known as a memory model). The consistency model defines rules for how operations on computer memory occur and how results are produced.

31.10 Threads and Threading

In computing a thread of execution is often regarded as the smallest unit of processing that can be scheduled by an operating system. The implementation of threads and processes generally varies with operating system.

31.11   Threads and Processes

From a strict computer science point of view threads and processes are different. However when looking simply at parallel programming the term can often be used interchangeably. In the following we use the term thread.

31.12   Data Dependencies

A data dependency is when one statement in a program depends on a calculation from a previous statement. This will obviously hinder parallelism.

31.13   Race Conditions

Race conditions can occur in programs when separate threads depend on a shared state or variable.

31.14   Mutual Exclusion - Mutex

A mutex is a programming construct that is used to allow multiple threads to share a resource. The sharing is not simultaneous. One thread will acquire the mutex and then lock the other threads from accessing it until it has completed.

31.15   Monitors

In concurrent programming, a monitor is an object or module intended to be used safely by more than one thread. The defining characteristic of a monitor is that its methods are executed with mutual exclusion. That is, at each point in time, at most one thread may be executing any of its methods. This mutual exclusion greatly simplifies reasoning about the implementation of monitors compared with code that may be executed in parallel.

31.16   Locks

In computing a lock is a synchronization mechanism for enforcing limits on access to a resource in an environment where there are many threads of execution. Locks are one way of enforcing concurrency control policies.

31.17 Synchronization

The concept of synchronisation is often split into process and data synchronisation.

In process synchronisation several processes or threads come together at a certain part of a program.

Data synchronisation is concerned with keeping data consistent.

31.18 Granularity and Types of Parallelism

Granularity is a useful concept in parallel programming. A common classification is

- Fine-grained - a lot of small components, larger amounts of communication and synchronisation
- Coarse-grained - a small number of larger components, hence smaller amounts of communication and less synchronisation

  The terms are of course relative.
  We also have the concept of

- Embarrassingly parallel - very little effort is required to partition the task and there is little or no communication and synchronisation.

  A simple example of this would be a graphics processor processing individual pixels.

31.19 Partitioned Global Address Space - PGAS

PGAS is a parallel programming model. It assumes a global memory address space that is logically partitioned and a portion of it is local to each processor. The PGAS model is the basis of Unified Parallel C, Coarray Fortran, Titanium, Fortress, Chapel and X10.

31.20 Fortran and Parallel Programming

Most Fortran compilers now offer support for parallel programming. We next provide a brief coverage of three methods

- MPI - Message Passing Interface
- OpenMP - Open Multi-Processing
- CoArray Fortran.

  Subsequent chapters look at simple examples using each method.

31.21   MPI

MPI started with a meeting that was held at the Supercomputing 92 conference. The attendants agreed to develop and implement a common standard for message passing. The first MPI standard, called MPI-1 was completed in May 1994. The second MPI standard, MPI-2, was completed in 1998.

MPI is effectively a library of C and Fortran callable routines. It has become widely used and is available on a number of platforms. Some useful web addresses are given below. The first is hosted at Argonne National Laboratory.

```
http://www.mcs.anl.gov/research/projects/mpi/
```

MPI was designed by a broad group of parallel computer users, vendors, and software writers. These included

- Vendors - IBM, Intel, TMC, Meiko, Cray, Convex, Ncube
- Library writers - PVM, p4, Zipcode, TCGMSG, Chameleon, Express, Linda
- Companies - ARCO, Convex, Cray Research, IBM, Intel, KAI, Meiko, NAG, nCUBE, Parasoft, Shell, TMC
- Laboratories - ANL, GMD, LANL, LLNL, NOAA, NSF, ORNL, PNL, Sandia, SDSC, SRC
- Universities - UC Santa Barbara, Syracuse University, Michigan State University, Oregon Grad Inst, University of New Mexico, Mississippi State University, University of Southampton, University of Colorado, Yale University, University of Tennessee, University of Maryland, Western Michigan University, University of Edinburgh, Cornell University, Rice University, University of San Francisco.

So whilst MPI is not a formal standard like Fortran, C or C++, its development has involved quite a wide range of people. The following site has details of MPI meetings.

```
http://meetings.mpi-forum.org/
```

The steering committee (March 2015) and affiliations are given below

- Jack Dongarra - Computer Science Department, University of Tennessee
- Al Geist - Group Leader, Computer Science Research Group, Oak Ridge National Laboratory
- Richard Graham
- Bill Gropp - Computer Science Department, University of Illinois Urbana-Champaign
- Andrew Lumsdaine - Computer Science Department, Indianna University
- Ewing Lusk - Mathematics and Computer Science Division, Argonne National Laboratory
- Rolf Rabenseifner - High Performance Computing Center, Germany.

Another useful site is the Open MPI site.

```
http://www.open-mpi.org/
```

The following is taken from their site.

The Open MPI Project is an open source MPI implementation that is developed and maintained by a consortium of academic, research, and industry partners. Open MPI is therefore able to combine the expertise, technologies, and resources from all across the High Performance Computing community in order to build the best MPI library available. Open MPI offers advantages for system and software vendors, application developers and computer science researchers.

Both sites provide free down loadable implementations. Commercial implementations are available from

- Cray
- IBM
- Intel
- Microsoft

amongst others.

MPI is, at the time of writing, the dominant parallel programming method used in Fortran. MPI and Fortran currently account for over 80% of the code running on the Archer Service in Edinburgh. Archer is the UK's national supercomputing resource, funded by the UK Research Councils. Visit

```
http://www.archer.ac.uk
```

for more information.

31.22 OpenMP

OpenMP (Open Multi-Processing) is an application programming interface that supports shared memory multiprocessing programming in three main languages (C, C++, and Fortran) on a range of hardware platforms and operating systems. It consists of a set of compiler directives, library routines, and environment variables that determine the run time behaviour of a program.

The OpenMP Architecture Review Board (ARB) has published several versions

- October 1997 - OpenMP for Fortran 1.0. October the following year they released the C/C++ standard.
- 2000 - Fortran version
- 2005 - Fortran 2.5
- 2008 - OpenMP 3.0. Included in the new features in 3.0 is the concept of tasks and the task construct.

- 2011 - OpenMP 3.1
- 2013 - OpenMP 4.0 was released in July 2013.

A number of compilers from various vendors or open source communities implement the OpenMP API, including

- Absoft
- Cray
- gnu
- Hewlett Packard
- IBM
- Intel
- Lahey/Fujitsu
- Nag
- Oracle/Sun
- PGI

The main OpenMP web site is:

```
http://www.openmp.org/
```

31.23   Coarray Fortran

Coarrays became part of Fortran in the 2008 standard. The original ideas came from work by Robert Numrich and John Reid in the 1990s. They are based on a single program multiple data model. A coarray Fortran program is interpreted as if it were duplicated several times and all copies execute asynchronously. Each copy has its own set of data objects and is termed an image. The array syntax of Fortran is extended with additional trailing subscripts in square brackets to provide a concise representation of references to data that is spread across images.

The syntax is architecture independent and may be implemented on:

- Distributed memory machines.
- Shared memory machines.
- Clustered machines.

Work has now been completed on additional Coarray functionality and is in the Fortran 2018 standard.

31.24   Other Parallel Options

There are a number of additional parallel methods. They are covered for completeness.

31.24.1 PVM

Parallel Virtual Machine consists of a library and a run-time environment which allow the distribution of a program over a network of (even heterogeneous) computers. Visit

- http://www.netlib.org/pvm3/

for more details.

31.24.2 HPF

To quote their home page

http://hpff.rice.edu/index.htm

'The High Performance Fortran Forum (HPFF), a coalition of industry, academic and laboratory representatives, works to define a set of extensions to Fortran 90 known collectively as High Performance Fortran (HPF). HPF extensions provide access to high-performance architecture features while maintaining portability across platforms.'

They also provide details of:

- Surveys of HPF compilers and tools.
- Currently available commercial HPF compilers.
- public domain HPF compilation systems.
- Research prototypes of HPF and HPF-related compilation systems.
- Mailing list.

31.25 Top 500 Supercomputers

Have a look at

https://www.top500.org/

for a lot of links to supercomputing centres and information on parallel computing in general. To see what can be done with all this processing power visit:

http://www.metoffice.gov.uk/

31.26 Summary

Fortran has long been one of the main languages used in parallel programming. This chapter has provided a brief coverage of some of the background to parallel programming in general, and Fortran in particular.

In the next three chapters we will look at a small number of programs that introduce some of the basic syntax of parallel programming with MPI, OpenMP and Coarray Fortran. We will also look at solving one problem serially and then solve it using the parallel features provided by MPI, OpenMP and Coarray Fortran. We provide timing details so that we can see the benefits that parallel solutions offer.

Bibliography

The ideas involved in parallel computing are not new and we've included a couple of references about computer hardware and operating systems, which provide information for the more inquisitive reader. Wikipedia is an on-line source of information in this area.

Up to date hardware information can be found at most hardware vendor sites. Here are the web sites for AMD, IBM and Intel.

```
AMD
http://developer.amd.com/pages/default.aspx
IBM
http://www.ibm.com/products
Intel
http://www.intel.com/en_UK/
products/processor/index.htm
```

Baer J.L., Computer Systems Architecture, Computer Science Press, 1980.

The chapters on the memory hierarchy and memory management are old, but well written.

Deitel H.M., Operating Systems, Addison Wesley, 1990.

Part two of the book (process management) has chapters on process concepts, asynchronous concurrent processes, concurrent programming and deadlock and indefinite postponement. The bibliographies at the end of each chapter are quite extensive.

The following four books provide a good coverage of the essentials of MPI and OpenMP.

Chandra R., Dagum L., Kohr D., Maydan D., McDonald J., Menon R., Parallel Programming in OpenMP, Morgan Kaufmann.

Chapman B., Jost G., Van Der Pas R., Using OpenMP, MIT Press.

Gropp W., Lusk E., Skjellum A., Using MPI: Portable Parallel Programming with the Message Passing Interface, MIT Press.

Pacheco P., Parallel Programming with MPI, Morgan Kaufmann.

Chapter 32
MPI - Message Passing Interface

> *In almost every computation a great variety of arrangements for
> the succession of the processes is possible, and various
> considerations must influence the selections amongst them for
> the purposes of a calculating engine. One essential object is to
> choose that arrangement which shall tend to reduce to a
> minimum the time necessary for completing the calculation.*
>
> Ada Lovelace

Aim

The aims of this chapter is to provide a short introduction to MPI programming in
Fortran.

32.1 Introduction

Documents for the MPI standard are available from the MPI Forum. Their web
address is

```
http://www.mpi-forum.org
```

If you are going to do MPI programming we recommend getting hold of the
document that refers to your implementation.

32.2 MPI Programming

MPI programming typically requires two components, a compiler and an MPI implementation. Two common ways of doing MPI programming are

- a cluster or multiple systems running MPI

© Springer International Publishing AG, part of Springer Nature 2018   581
I. Chivers and J. Sleightholme, *Introduction to Programming with Fortran*,
https://doi.org/10.1007/978-3-319-75502-1_32

• a single system running MPI

In both cases an MPI installation will normally provide an MPI daemon or service that can then be called from an MPI program.

32.3   Compiler and Implementation Combination

A number of commercial companies provide a combined bundle including

• Cray
• IBM
• Intel
• PGI

The Cray and IBM offerings will most likely be for a cluster. Intel and PGI provide products for both clusters and single systems. You should check their sites for up to date information.

32.4   Individual Implementation

A low cost option is to get hold of an MPI implementation that works with your existing compiler, and install it yourself on your own system.

The Intel MPI product is available as a free download for evaluation purposes.

There are a number of free MPI implementations, and details are given below for two of them.

32.4.1   MPICH2

They are based at Argonne National Laboratory

```
http://www.mpich.org/
```

MPICH2 is distributed as source (with an open-source, freely available license). It has been tested on several platforms, including Linux (on IA32 and x86-64), Mac OS/X (PowerPC and Intel), Solaris (32- and 64-bit), and Windows.

32.4.2   Open MPI

They can be found at

```
http://www.open-mpi.org/
```

They develop Open MPI on Linux, OS X, Solaris (both 32 and 64 on all platforms) and Windows (Windows XP, Windows HPC Server 2003/2008 and also Windows 7 RC).

32.5   Compiler and MPI Combinations Used in the Book

We have used a variety of compilers and MPI combinations, including

- Intel compiler + mpich2, Windows
- Intel compiler + Intel MPI, Windows
- gfortran + openmpi, openSuSe Linux
- Cray compiler, Hector Service
- Cray compiler, Archer Service
- PGI compiler, Hector Service
- IBM compiler, Met Office Slovakia

We haven't tried out all of the examples with all of the compiler and MPI implementations.

32.5.1   Cray Archer System

The Archer hardware consists of the Cray XC30 MPP supercomputer, external login nodes and postprocessing nodes, and the associated filesystems. There are 4920 compute nodes in Archer phase 2 and each compute node has two 12-core Intel Ivy Bridge Xeon series processors (2.7 GHz Intel E5-2697) giving a total of 118,080 processing cores. Each node has a total of 64 GB of memory with a subset of large memory nodes having 128 GB. A high-performance Lustre storage system is available to all compute nodes. There is no local disk on the compute nodes as they are housed in 4-node blades (the image below shows an XC30 blade with 4 compute nodes).

32.6   The MPI Memory Model

MPI is characterised generally by distributed memory and

- All threads/processes have access to their own private memory only
- Data transfer and most synchronization has to be programmed explicitly
- All data is private
- Data is shared explicitly by exchanging buffers in MPI terminology

but in this chapter we will also show the use of MPI on one system.

32.7   Example 1: Hello World

The first example is the classic hello world program.

```
program ch3201
  use mpi
  implicit none
  integer :: error_number
  integer :: this_process_number
  integer :: number_of_processes

  call mpi_init(error_number)
  call mpi_comm_size(mpi_comm_world, &
    number_of_processes, error_number)
  call mpi_comm_rank(mpi_comm_world, &
    this_process_number, error_number)
  print *, ' Hello from process ', &
    this_process_number, ' of ', &
    number_of_processes, 'processes!'
  call mpi_finalize(error_number)
end program ch3201
```

Let us look at each statement in turn.

```
use mpi
```

With most modern MPI implementations we can make available the MPI setup
with a use statement. Older implementations required an include file option.

```
    call mpi_init( error_number )
```

This must be the first MPI routine called. The Fortran binding only takes one argument, an integer variable that is used to return an `error number`. It sets up the MPI environment.

```
call mpi_comm_size( mpi_comm_world, &
number_of_processes , error_number )
```

is typically the second MPI routine called. All MPI communication is associated with a so called communicator that describes the communication context and an associated set of processes. In this simple example we use the default communicator, called `mpi_comm_world`. The number of processes available is returned via the second argument. This means that the above program is duplicated on each process, i.e. `number_of_processes` determines how many copies are running.

```
call mpi_comm_rank( mpi_comm_world, &
  this_process_number , error_number )
```

The call above returns the process number for this process or copy of the program.

```
print *, " Hello from process " , &
  this_process_number , " of ", &
  number_of_processes , " processes!"
```

Each copy of the program will print out this message.

```
call mpi_finalize(error_number)
```

The call to `mpi_finalize` is the last call to the MPI system we need to make. Here is the output from the Intel compiler and Intel MPI option under a Windows system.

```
mpiexec -n 8 ch3201
   Hello from process     0  of     8  processes!
   Hello from process     4  of     8  processes!
   Hello from process     1  of     8  processes!
   Hello from process     5  of     8  processes!
   Hello from process     7  of     8  processes!
   Hello from process     6  of     8  processes!
   Hello from process     3  of     8  processes!
   Hello from process     2  of     8  processes!
```

Notice that process numbering starts at 0. Note also that there is no particular order to the process numbers.

Here is the output from gfortran and openmpi on a openSuSe system. This is the same system as the above, as it is dual boot.

```
mpiexec -n 8 ch3201.out
   Hello from process    0   of    8   processes!
   Hello from process    1   of    8   processes!
   Hello from process    2   of    8   processes!
   Hello from process    3   of    8   processes!
   Hello from process    4   of    8   processes!
   Hello from process    5   of    8   processes!
   Hello from process    6   of    8   processes!
   Hello from process    7   of    8   processes!
```

Now the ordering is sequential.

Here is the output from the Cray Archer service. This uses 48 processes. The job is submitted as a batch job, via a queueing mechanism. This is a common mechanism on larger multi user systems.

```
   Hello world from image  16
   Hello world from image  6
   Hello world from image  13
   Hello world from image  25
   Hello world from image  34

lines deleted

   Hello world from image  38
   Hello world from image  44
   Hello world from image  35
   Hello world from image  28
   Hello world from image  33
   Hello world from image  32
   Hello world from image  30
   Hello world from image  29
```

The order appears to be pretty random!

32.8   Example 2: Hello World Using Send and Receive

The following is a variation of the above. In the first example we had no communication between processes. Sending and receiving of messages by processes is the basic MPI communication mechanism. The basic point-to-point communication

operations are send and receive. Their use is shown in the example below. These
are blocking send and receive operations. A blocking send does not return until the
message data and envelope have been safely stored away so that the sender is free
to modify the send buffer. The message might be copied directly into the matching
receive buffer, or it might be copied into a temporary system buffer.

In this example process 0 is the master process and this communicates with every
other process or program.

```
program ch3202
  use mpi
  implicit none
  integer :: error_number
  integer :: this_process_number
  integer :: number_of_processes
  integer :: i
  integer, dimension (mpi_status_size) :: status

  call mpi_init(error_number)
  call mpi_comm_size(mpi_comm_world, &
    number_of_processes, error_number)
  call mpi_comm_rank(mpi_comm_world, &
    this_process_number, error_number)
  if (this_process_number==0) then
    print *, ' Hello from process ', &
      this_process_number, ' of ', &
      number_of_processes, 'processes.'
    do i = 1, number_of_processes - 1
      call mpi_recv(this_process_number, 1, &
        mpi_integer, i, 1, mpi_comm_world, &
        status, error_number)
      print *, ' Hello from process ', &
        this_process_number, ' of ', &
        number_of_processes, 'processes.'
    end do
  else
    call mpi_send(this_process_number, 1, &
      mpi_integer, 0, 1, mpi_comm_world, &
      error_number)
  end if
  call mpi_finalize(error_number)
end program ch3202
```

The calls to

- mpi_init

- `mpi_comm_size`
- `mpi_comm_rank`
- `mpi_finalize`

are the same as in the first example. We have the additional code

- A test to see if we are process 0. If we are we then print out a message saying that we are process 0. We next loop from 1 to `number_of_processes` -1 and call `mpi_recv`.
- If we are not process 0 we make a call to `mpi_send` - remember that the program executes on all processes.

Let us look at the calls to `mpi_recv` and `mpi_send` in more depth. Here is an extract from the MPI 2.2 specification describing `mpi_recv`

```
<> buf(*)
  initial address of receive buffer
integer count
  number of elements in the receive buffer
datatype
  data type of each receive buffer element
source -   rank of source
tag -   message tag
comm -   communicator
status(mpi_status_size),
ierror
```

The following shows the mapping between MPI data types and Fortran data types.

```
mpi datatype              fortran datatype

mpi_integer               integer
mpi_real                  real
mpi_double_precision      double precision
mpi_complex               complex
mpi_logical               logical
mpi_character             character(1)
```

our arguments to `mpi_recv` are

- `this_process_number` - process 0 is doing the receiving
- 1 item
- `mpi_integer` - an `mpi_integer` variable
- i - receive from this process
- 1 - tag
- `mpi_comm_world` - the communicator

- `status` - an integer array of size `mpi_status_size`
- `error_number`

Here is an extract from the 2.2 specification regarding `mpi_send`

```
<> buf(*) - initial address of send buffer
integer count - number of elements in send buffer
datatype - data type of each send buffer element
dest - rank of destination
tag - message tag
comm - communicator
ierror - error number\index{Error number}
```

the arguments to our `mpi_send` are

- `this_process_number` - send from this process
- 1
- `mpi_integer`
- 0 - send to this process number
- 1
- `mpi_comm_world` - the communicator
- `error_number`

and as you can see the sends and receives are in matching pairs.
   Here is an Intel sample run.

```
Hello from process   0   of    8 processes.
Hello from process   1   of    8 processes.
Hello from process   2   of    8 processes.
Hello from process   3   of    8 processes.
Hello from process   4   of    8 processes.
Hello from process   5   of    8 processes.
Hello from process   6   of    8 processes.
Hello from process   7   of    8 processes.
```

Here is a Cray Archer sample run.

```
Hello from process   0   of   48 processes.
Hello from process   1   of   48 processes.
Hello from process   2   of   48 processes.
Hello from process   3   of   48 processes.
Hello from process   4   of   48 processes.

lines deleted
```

```
Hello from process   43   of   48 processes.
Hello from process   44   of   48 processes.
Hello from process   45   of   48 processes.
Hello from process   46   of   48 processes.
Hello from process   47   of   48 processes.
```

32.9   Example 3: Serial Solution for pi Calculation

We choose numerical integration in this example. The following integral

$$\int_0^1 \frac{4}{1+x^2}\, dx$$

is one way of calculating an approximation to π, and is a problem that is easy to parallelise. The integral can be approximated by

$$1/n \sum_1^n \frac{4}{1+\left(\frac{i-0.5}{n}\right)^2}$$

According to Wikipedia π to 50 digits is
3.14159265358979323846264338327950288419716939937510
Another way of calculating π is using the formula $4\,tan^{-1}(1)$ and in Fortran this is $4.0*atan(1.0)$.
Consider the following plot of the above equation.

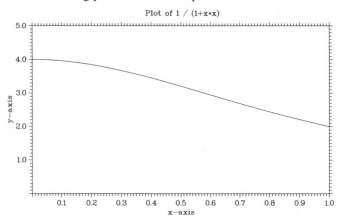

To do the evaluation numerically we divide the interval between 0 and 1 into n sub intervals. The higher the value of n the more accurate our value of π will be, or should be.
Here is a serial program to do this calculation. The program is in three main parts. These are

- The module `precision_module` - to set the precision throughout the whole code.
- The module `timing_module` - a timing module to enable us to time parts of the program. We will be using this module throughout the parallel examples to provide information about the performance of the algorithms.
- the program - that actually does the integration.

The first two modules are straightforward and we will only cover the integration solution in depth. We will be using this integration example in this chapter on MPI and the subsequent two on OpenMP and coarray Fortran.

```fortran
include 'precision_module.f90'

include 'timing_module.f90'

program ch3203
  use precision_module
  use timing_module
  implicit none
  integer :: i, j
  integer :: n_intervals
  real (dp) :: interval_width, x, total, pi
  real (dp) :: fortran_internal_pi

  call start_timing()
  n_intervals = 1000000
  fortran_internal_pi = 4.0_dp*atan(1.0_dp)
  print *, ' fortran_internal_pi = ', &
    fortran_internal_pi
  print *, ' '
  do j = 1, 4
    interval_width = 1.0_dp/n_intervals
    total = 0.0_dp
    do i = 1, n_intervals
      x = interval_width*(real(i,dp)-0.5_dp)
      total = total + f(x)
    end do
    pi = interval_width*total
    print 100, n_intervals, time_difference()
    print 110, pi, abs(pi-fortran_internal_pi)
    n_intervals = n_intervals*10
  end do
100 format (' N intervals = ', i12, ' time = ', &
    f8.3)
110 format (' pi = ', f20.16, /, &
```

```
      ' difference = ', f20.16)
    call end_timing()
    stop

contains

    real (dp) function f(x)
      implicit none
      real (dp), intent (in) :: x

      f = 4.0_dp/(1.0_dp+x*x)
    end function f

end program ch3203
```

The first part of the code has the declarations for the variables we will be using. These are

```
integer :: n_intervals
real (dp) :: interval_width, x, total, pi
real (dp) :: fortran_internal_pi
```

We have an integer variable for the number of intervals we will be using. We have made this of default integer type, which will be 32 bit on most platforms, and will be up to 2, 147, 483, 647.

We then have the following variables

- `interval_width`
- z - the variable we will be calculating numerically
- `total` - our total for the integration
- `pi` - our calculated value of π
- `fortran_internal_pi` - we use a common way of defining this using the internal `atan` function.

We then call the `start_timing` routine to print out details of the start time.

We next set the number of intervals. We choose 10 as an initial value. We will be doing the calculation for a number of interval sizes.

We calculate π using the `atan` intrinsic and print out its value. We will be using this value to determine the accuracy of our calculations.

We then have the loop that does the calculations for 9 values of the interval size from 10 to 1,000,000,000.

We calculate the interval width at the start of each loop and reset the total to zero at the start of each loop.

The following

```
do i = 1, n_intervals
  x = interval_width*(real(i,dp)-0.5_dp)
  total = total + f(x)
end do
```

is the code that actually does the integration. We calculate x each time round the loop and then use this calculated value in our call to our function, summing up as we go along. We need to subtract a as we need the mid point of the interval for our value of x.

The loop finishes and we then calculate the value of π and print out details of the number of intervals, the calculated value of pi and the difference between the internal value of π and the calculated value.

We also print out timing information about this calculation. We then increment the number of intervals and repeat the above.

We need to know how long the serial version takes and how accurate our calculated value for π is.

Here is output from this program on a couple of systems and compilers.

Compiler 1 - Intel compiler, Windows

```
2015/ 3/12 13:16:55 739
  fortran_internal_pi =     3.14159265358979

N intervals =       1000000 time =     0.000
pi =    3.1415926535899033
difference =    0.0000000000001101
N intervals =      10000000 time =     0.031
pi =    3.1415926535896861
difference =    0.0000000000001070
N intervals =     100000000 time =     0.281
pi =    3.1415926535902168
difference =    0.0000000000004237
N intervals =    1000000000 time =     2.871
pi =    3.1415926535897682
difference =    0.0000000000000249
2015/ 3/12 13:16:58 922
```

Compiler 2 - gfortran, Windows

```
2015/ 3/12 15:14:42 110
  fortran_internal_pi =     3.1415926535897931

N intervals =       1000000 time =     0.016
pi =    3.1415926535899601
difference =    0.0000000000001670
```

```
N intervals =       10000000 time =      0.016
pi =    3.1415926535897216
difference =    0.0000000000000715
N intervals =      100000000 time =      0.281
pi =    3.1415926535900236
difference =    0.0000000000002305
N intervals =     1000000000 time =      2.793
pi =    3.1415926535896523
difference =    0.0000000000001408
2015/ 3/12 15:14:45 214
```

Compiler 3 - Cray, Archer Service. Hardware details of this system are given earlier.

```
sttp1553@eslogin008:~> ./ch3003.x
 2015/ 3/22 11:42: 5   50
   fortran_internal_pi =   3.1415926535897931

 N intervals =        1000000 time =      0.000
 pi =    3.1415926535899033
 difference =    0.0000000000001101
 N intervals =       10000000 time =      0.023
 pi =    3.1415926535896861
 difference =    0.0000000000001070
 N intervals =      100000000 time =      0.207
 pi =    3.1415926535902168
 difference =    0.0000000000004237
 N intervals =     1000000000 time =      2.074
 pi =    3.1415926535897682
 difference =    0.0000000000000249
 2015/ 3/22 11:42: 7 356
 STOP
```

The three sample serial runs provide us with information that we can use as a basis for an analysis of our parallel solution. We have information about the accuracy of the solution and timing details.

32.10 Example 4: Parallel Solution for pi Calculation

This example is a parallel solution to the above problem using MPI. We only show the parallel program. The precision and timing modules are the same as in the previous example.

```fortran
include 'precision_module.f90'

include 'timing_module.f90'

program ch3204
  use precision_module
  use timing_module
  use mpi
  implicit none
  real (dp) :: fortran_internal_pi
  real (dp) :: partial_pi
  real (dp) :: total_pi
  real (dp) :: width
  real (dp) :: partial_sum
  real (dp) :: x
  integer :: n
  integer :: this_process
  integer :: n_processes
  integer :: i
  integer :: j
  integer :: error_number

  call mpi_init(error_number)
  call mpi_comm_size(mpi_comm_world, &
    n_processes, error_number)
  call mpi_comm_rank(mpi_comm_world, &
    this_process, error_number)
  n = 100000
  fortran_internal_pi = 4.0_dp*atan(1.0_dp)
  if (this_process==0) then
    call start_timing()
    print *, ' fortran_internal_pi = ', &
      fortran_internal_pi
  end if
  do j = 1, 5
    width = 1.0_dp/n
    partial_sum = 0.0_dp
    do i = this_process + 1, n, n_processes
      x = width*(real(i,dp)-0.5_dp)
      partial_sum = partial_sum + f(x)
    end do
    partial_pi = width*partial_sum
    call mpi_reduce(partial_pi, total_pi, 1, &
      mpi_double_precision, mpi_sum, 0, &
      mpi_comm_world, error_number)
```

```fortran
    if (this_process==0) then
      print 100, n, time_difference()
      print 110, total_pi, abs(total_pi- &
        fortran_internal_pi)
    end if
    n = n*10
  end do
  call mpi_finalize(error_number)
100 format (' N intervals = ', i12, ' time = ', &
    f8.3)
110 format (' pi = ', f20.16, /, &
    ' difference = ', f20.16)

contains

  real (dp) function f(x)
    implicit none
    real (dp), intent (in) :: x

    f = 4.0_dp/(1.0_dp+x*x)
  end function f

end program ch3204
```

The first difference is the

```fortran
use mpi
```

statement. This makes available the MPI functionality. We next have several variable declarations.

```fortran
real (dp) :: fortran_internal_pi
real (dp) :: partial_pi
real (dp) :: total_pi
real (dp) :: width
real (dp) :: partial_sum
real (dp) :: x
integer :: n
integer :: this_process
integer :: n_processes
integer :: i
integer :: j
integer :: error_number
```

The variables `partial_pi`, `total_pi` and `partial_sum` are required by our parallel algorithm. The variable n is the number of intervals and we start this at 100,000 rather than 10 as we have seen from the serial solution that there are quite large differences between the internal value of pi and the calculated value below 100,000.

The variables `this_process`, `n_processes` and `error_number` are required for the MPI solution.

The real work is done in the following do loop.

```
do i = this_process + 1, n, n_processes
  x = width*(real(i,dp)-0.5_dp)
  partial_sum = partial_sum + f(x)
end do
```

The key is to split up the work of the calculation between the processes we have available. The following shows how the work will be split up for n = 10 and with the number of processes ranging from 1 to 8.

```
n_processes=1 do i=1,n,1  1,2,3,4,5,6,7,8,9,10
n_processes=2 do i=1,n,2  1,3,5,7,9
              do i=2,n,2  2,4,6,8,10
n_processes=4 do i=1,n,4  1,5,9
              do i=2,n,4  2,6,10
              do i=3,n,5  3,7
              do i=4,n,4  4,8
n_processes=8 do i=1,n,8  1,9
              do i=2,n,8  2,10
              do i=3,n,8  3
              do i=4,n,8  4
              do i=5,n,8  5
              do i=6,n,8  6
              do i=7,n,8  7
              do i=8,n,8  8
```

The above also shows how the algorithm balances the load of the computation across the processes.

Each process has its own `partial_sum` and `partial_pi`. We then use the call to the MPI subroutine `mpi_reduce` to calculate the total value of pi from the partial values of pi. Here is the MPI description of the `mpi_reduce` routine

```
MPI_REDUCE( sendbuf, recvbuf, count,
            datatype, op, root, comm)
IN   sendbuf address of send buffer (choice)
OUT recvbuf address of receive buffer
```

```
    (choice, significant only at root)
IN  count number of elements in send buffer
    (non-negative integer)
IN  datatype data type of elements of send buffer
    (handle)
IN  op reduce operation (handle)
IN  root rank of root process (integer)
IN  comm communicator (handle)
```

and

```
partial_pi is our send buffer
total_pi is our receive buffer
1 - the number of elements
mpi_double_precision - the type of the elements
mpi_sum - the reduction operation
0 - the root process
mpi_comm_world  - the communicator
error_number - the error number
```

We then control the printing from process 0.
Here is sample output from the Intel compiler on a 6 core AMD system.

```
mpiexec -n 6 ch3004.exe
 2015/ 3/12 13:16:39 671
  fortran_internal_pi =    3.14159265358979
 N intervals =       100000 time =    0.000
 pi =   3.1415926535981256
 difference =   0.0000000000083324
 N intervals =      1000000 time =    0.000
 pi =   3.1415926535898762
 difference =   0.0000000000000830
 N intervals =     10000000 time =    0.000
 pi =   3.1415926535897674
 difference =   0.0000000000000258
 N intervals =    100000000 time =    0.062
 pi =   3.1415926535897389
 difference =   0.0000000000000542
 N intervals =   1000000000 time =    0.637
 pi =   3.1415926535898402
 difference =   0.0000000000000471
```

We get a nearly linear speed up over the serial version, which shows how good
the parallel solution is. Note that the time value is not the total time taken by all

processes, but rather the effective running time of the program. If we are sat in front of the pc the program would complete in about a quarter of the time of the serial version. The numerical results are similar to the serial solution.

Table 32.1 summarises the output from the Intel compiler on an Intel I7 system. The table has the execution time details when running the program on 1 to 8 cores. The timing for cores 1–4 are for the program runs on real physical cores. The timing for cores 5–8 are when running on hyperthreaded cores. The execution time is worse when running on 5–7 cores. You should time your programs on hyperthreaded systems to see if running on the extra cores brings any benefit.

Table 32.1 Intel I7 with hyperthreading

	Cores							
Intervals	1	2	3	4	5	6	7	8
100,000	0.000	0.000	0.000	0.000	0.000	0.000	0.000	0.000
1,000,000	0.000	0.000	0.000	0.000	0.000	0.000	0.000	0.000
10,000,000	0.016	0.016	0.012	0.000	0.016	0.000	0.000	0.016
100,000,000	0.234	0.109	0.078	0.062	0.094	0.094	0.078	0.062
1,000,000,000	2.203	1.141	0.816	0.609	0.984	0.812	0.703	0.594

As can be seen the performance for 5–8 cores is similar to that for 4 cores. Cores 5–8 represent the hyperthreaded cores.

Here is the output from the Cray at the Archer service. This is for 48 processes running on 2 nodes.

```
2015/ 3/21  1:11:47 841
  fortran_internal_pi =  3.1415926535897931
N intervals =        1000000 time =     0.004
pi =    3.1415926535898757
difference =    0.0000000000000826
N intervals =       10000000 time =     0.000
pi =    3.1415926535897958
difference =    0.0000000000000027
N intervals =      100000000 time =     0.006
pi =    3.1415926535897909
difference =    0.0000000000000022
N intervals =     1000000000 time =     0.054
pi =    3.1415926535897949
difference =    0.0000000000000018
```

32.11   Example 5: Work Sharing Between Processes

This example looks at one way of splitting work up between processes. We use the
process number of determine which process does which work.

```fortran
program ch3205
  use mpi
  implicit none
  integer :: error_number
  integer :: this_process_number
  integer :: number_of_processes
  integer, dimension (mpi_status_size) :: status
  integer, allocatable, dimension (:) :: x
  integer :: n
  integer, parameter :: factor = 5
  integer :: i, j, k
  integer :: start
  integer :: end
  integer :: recv_start

  call mpi_init(error_number)
  call mpi_comm_size(mpi_comm_world, &
    number_of_processes, error_number)
  call mpi_comm_rank(mpi_comm_world, &
    this_process_number, error_number)
  n = number_of_processes*factor
  allocate (x(1:n))
  x = 0
  start = (factor*this_process_number) + 1
  end = factor*(this_process_number+1)
  print 100, this_process_number, start, end
  do i = start, end
    x(i) = i*factor
  end do
  do i = 1, n
    print 110, this_process_number, i, x(i)
  end do
  if (this_process_number==0) then
    do i = 1, number_of_processes - 1
      recv_start = (factor*i) + 1
      call mpi_recv(x(recv_start), factor, &
        mpi_integer, i, 1, mpi_comm_world, &
        status, error_number)
    end do
```

```
    else
      call mpi_send(x(start), factor, mpi_integer, &
        0, 1, mpi_comm_world, error_number)
    end if
    if (this_process_number==0) then
      do i = 1, n
        print 120, i, factor, x(i)
      end do
    end if
    call mpi_finalize(error_number)
100 format (' Process number = ', i3, ' start ', &
      i3, ' end ', i3)
110 format (1x, i4, ' i ', i4, ' x(i) ', i4)
120 format (1x, i4, ' * ', i2, ' = ', i5)
end program ch3205
```

What we are going to do is allocate an array based on the number of processes and then split the (simple) work on the array up between the processes. We will calculate array indices from the process numbers.

```
n = number_of_processes*factor
```

This statement calculates the array size based on the number of processes and a constant factor.

```
allocate (x(1:n))
```

This statement allocates the array.

```
x = 0
```

This statement initialises the whole array to zero. The following statements define the start and end points for the array processing for each process.

```
start = (factor*this_process_number) + 1
end = factor*(this_process_number+1)
```

and partition the work up between the processes. Each process will have its own start and end values. The following do loop does the work:

```
do i = start, end
  x(i) = i*factor
end do
```

and all we are doing as this is filling sections of the array up with data based in process numbers.

The following

```
if (this_process_number==0) then
  do i = 1, number_of_processes - 1
    recv_start = (factor*I) + 1
    call mpi_recv(x(recv_start), &
      factor,mpi_integer,i,1,mpi_comm_world,&
      status ,error_number)
  end do
else
  call mpi_send(x(start),factor, &
    mpi_integer,0,1,mpi_comm_world,error_number)
end if
```

uses sends and receives to transfer the updated array sections back to process zero. We are using `recv_start` to specify the starting point for the array transfer, and `x(start)` is the starting point for the transfer from the x array to process zero.

Here is sample output from the program when the number of processes is three.

```
mpiexec -n 3 ch3205
 Process number =    2 start  11 end   15
 Process number =    1 start   6 end   10
       1 I     1 x(i)     0
       1 I     2 x(i)     0
       1 I     3 x(i)     0
       1 I     4 x(i)     0
       1 I     5 x(i)     0
       1 I     6 x(i)    30
       1 I     7 x(i)    35
       1 I     8 x(i)    40
       1 I     9 x(i)    45
       1 I    10 x(i)    50
       1 I    11 x(i)     0
       1 I    12 x(i)     0
 Process number =    0 start   1 end    5
       0 I     1 x(i)     5
       0 I     2 x(i)    10
       0 I     3 x(i)    15
       0 I     4 x(i)    20
       0 I     5 x(i)    25
       0 I     6 x(i)     0
       0 I     7 x(i)     0
```

```
 0  I      8  x(i)      0
 0  I      9  x(i)      0
 0  I     10  x(i)      0
 0  I     11  x(i)      0
 0  I     12  x(i)      0
 0  I     13  x(i)      0
 0  I     14  x(i)      0
 0  I     15  x(i)      0
 1  *   5  =        5
 2  *   5  =       10
 3  *   5  =       15
 4  *   5  =       20
 5  *   5  =       25
 6  *   5  =       30
 7  *   5  =       35
 2  I      1  x(i)      0
 2  I      2  x(i)      0
 2  I      3  x(i)      0
 2  I      4  x(i)      0
 2  I      5  x(i)      0
 2  I      6  x(i)      0
 2  I      7  x(i)      0
 2  I      8  x(i)      0
 2  I      9  x(i)      0
 2  I     10  x(i)      0
 2  I     11  x(i)     55
 2  I     12  x(i)     60
 2  I     13  x(i)     65
 2  I     14  x(i)     70
 2  I     15  x(i)     75
 1  I     13  x(i)      0
 1  I     14  x(i)      0
 1  I     15  x(i)      0
 8  *   5  =       40
 9  *   5  =       45
10  *   5  =       50
11  *   5  =       55
12  *   5  =       60
13  *   5  =       65
14  *   5  =       70
15  *   5  =       75
```

So with three processes we have an array of size 15, and the work that each process does is

```
Process number =    0 start   1 end    5
Process number =    1 start   6 end   10
Process number =    2 start  11 end   15
```

and each process works on its own section of the array. At the end we use the sends and receives to make sure that the x array on process zero now has all of the updated values.

This code achieves load balancing across the processes.

32.12 Summary

The programs in this chapter provide an introduction to the use of MPI to achieve parallel programs in Fortran. We have also seen some of the timing benefits of parallel programming with MPI.

32.13 Problem

32.1 Compile and run the programs with your compiler and implementation of MPI. You should get similar results.

Chapter 33
OpenMP

The best way to have a good idea is to have a lot of ideas.

Linus Pauling

Aim

The aims of this chapter is to provide a short introduction to OpenMP programming in Fortran.

33.1 Introduction

The main OpenMP site is

```
http://www.openmp.org/
```

and this has details about the various specifications

```
http://www.openmp.org/specifications/
```

We recommend downloading the documentation if you are going to do OpenMP programming. You should visit

```
http://www.openmp.org/resources/openmp-compilers/
```

to see an up to date list of what compilers support the OpenMP specification, and at what level.

© Springer International Publishing AG, part of Springer Nature 2018
I. Chivers and J. Sleightholme, *Introduction to Programming with Fortran*,
https://doi.org/10.1007/978-3-319-75502-1_33

The OpenMP site has a range of resources available, check out

```
http://www.openmp.org/resources/
```

for more information.

We've run the examples in this chapter with one or more of the following compilers

- Cray
- gfortran
- Intel
- Nag

33.2   OpenMP Memory Model

OpenMP is a shared memory programming model. It has several features including

- All threads have access to the same shared memory
- Data can be shared or private
- Data transfer is transparent to the programmer
- Synchronization takes place and is generally implicit

We will look at a small number of examples to highlight some of the key features. We provide a brief coverage of some of the OpenMP glossary to provide a basic background to OpenMP.

- Threading Concepts

  - Thread - An execution entity with a stack and associated static memory, called thread private memory.
  - OpenMP thread - A thread that is managed by the OpenMP run time system.
  - Thread-safe routine - A routine that performs the intended function even when executed concurrently (by more than one thread).

- OpenMP language terminology

  - Structured block - For Fortran, a block of executable statements with a single entry at the top and a single exit at the bottom.
  - Loop directive - An OpenMP executable directive whose associated user code must be a loop that is a structured block. For Fortran, only the do directive and the optional end do directive are loop directives.
  - Master thread - The thread that encounters a parallel construct, creates a team, generates a set of tasks, then executes one of those tasks as thread number 0.
  - Work sharing construct - A construct that defines units of work, each of which is executed exactly once by one of the threads in the team executing the construct. For Fortran, work sharing constructs are do, sections, single and work share.

- Barrier - A point in the execution of a program encountered by a team of threads, beyond which no thread in the team may execute until all threads in the team have reached the barrier and all explicit tasks generated by the team have executed to completion.

- Data Terminology

  - Variable - A named data object, whose value can be defined and redefined during the execution of a program. Only an object that is not part of another object is considered a variable. For example, array elements, structure components, array sections and substrings are not considered variables.
  - Private variable - With respect to a given set of task regions that bind to the same parallel region, a variable whose name provides access to a different block of storage for each task region.
  - Shared variable - With respect to a given set of task regions that bind to the same parallel region, a variable whose name provides access to the same block of storage for each task region.

- Execution Model

  - The OpenMP API uses the fork-join model of parallel execution. Multiple threads of execution perform tasks defined implicitly or explicitly by OpenMP directives. OpenMP is intended to support programs that will execute correctly both as parallel programs (multiple threads of execution and a full OpenMP support library) and as sequential programs (directives ignored and a simple OpenMP stubs library).

The above coverage should be enough to get started with OpenMP and understand the examples that follow.

33.3 Example 1: Hello World

This is the classic hello world program.

```
program ch3301
  use omp_lib
  implicit none
  integer :: nthreads
  integer :: thread_number
  integer :: i

  nthreads = omp_get_max_threads()
  print *, ' Number of threads = ', nthreads
! $omp parallel do
```

```
  do i = 1, nthreads
    print *, ' Hello from thread ', &
      omp_get_thread_num()
  end do
! $omp end parallel do
end program ch3301
```

Let us go through the program one statement at a time.

```
use omp_lib
```

This use statement makes available the OpenMP environment. OpenMP statements are treated as comments without this statement.

```
nthreads = omp_get_max_threads()
print *, ' Number of threads = ', nthreads
```

The first statement sets the variable nthread to the value returned by the OpenMP function omp_get_max_threads(). We then print out this value.

```
!$omp parallel do
```

OpenMP directives in Fortran start with the comment character (!), followed by a $ symbol and the characters omp. We use this form as it is works with both free format and fixed format Fortran source code.

The parallel do words indicate that the code that follows is a parallel region construct. In this case a do loop. Here is a small table listing some of the OpenMP directives.

```
                    Parallel region construct

!$omp parallel [clause]
structured block
!$omp end parallel

                    Work sharing constructs

!$omp do [clause] ...
do loop
!$omp end parallel
!$omp sections [clause] ...
[!$omp section
    structured block ] ...
```

```
!$omp end sections [nowait]
!$omp single [clause]
structured block
!$omp end single [nowait]
```

```
                    Combined parallel work
                    sharing constructs
```

```
!$omp parallel do [clause]
structured block
!$omp end parallel do
!$omp parallel sections [clause] ...
[!$omp section
structured block ] ...
!$omp end parallel sections
```

```
              Synchronisation constructs
```

```
!$omp master
structured block
!$omp end master
!$omp critical [(name)]
structured block
!$omp end critical [(name)]
!$omp barrier
$omp atomic
expression list
!$omp flush
!$omp ordered
structured block
!$omp end ordered
```

```
                    Data environment
```

```
!$omp threadprivate (/c1/,/c2/)
```

We next have the parallel do.

```
  do i = 1, nthreads
    print *, ' Hello from thread ', &
      omp_get_thread_num()
  end do
```

This loop prints out a message from each thread showing the thread number.

```
!$omp end parallel do
```

This marks the end of the OpenMP parallel loop.

So at the start of the loop the OpenMP run time system does a fork and creates multiple threads. At the end of the loop we have a join operation and we are back to one thread of execution.

Here is the output from the Intel compiler on an Intel i7 system.

```
Number of threads =              8
Hello from thread        0
Hello from thread        4
Hello from thread        2
Hello from thread        3
Hello from thread        1
Hello from thread        7
Hello from thread        6
Hello from thread        5
```

These Intel systems have four real cores and each core supports hyper threading in Intel terminology. So the OpenMP system sees eight threads.

Here is the output from the gfortran compiler on the same system.

```
Number of threads =              8
Hello from thread        1
Hello from thread        3
Hello from thread        2
Hello from thread        4
Hello from thread        5
Hello from thread        6
Hello from thread        0
Hello from thread        7
```

The output is very similar, as one would expect.

33.4   Example 2: Hello World Using Default Variable Data Scoping

This is a simple variation on the first example. At first sight it appears to be identical in effect to example one.

```
program ch3302
  use omp_lib
```

```
      implicit none
      integer :: nthreads
      integer :: thread_number
      integer :: i

      nthreads = omp_get_max_threads()
      print *, ' Number of threads = ', nthreads
!$omp parallel do
      do i = 1, nthreads
        thread_number = omp_get_thread_num()
        print *, ' Hello from thread ', &
          thread_number
      end do
!$omp end parallel do end program ch3302
```

However we have introduced a variable thread_number and are using the OpenMP default data scoping rules, i.e. we have said nothing. Here is the output from the Intel compiler.

```
Number of threads =              8
Hello from thread     4
Hello from thread     5
Hello from thread     0
Hello from thread     1
Hello from thread     2
Hello from thread     3
Hello from thread     7
Hello from thread     6
```

We appear to have a working program. Here is the output from the gfortran compiler.

```
$ ./a.exe
Number of threads =              8
Hello from thread     6
Hello from thread     7
Hello from thread     7
Hello from thread     7
Hello from thread     7
Hello from thread     7
Hello from thread     7
Hello from thread     7
```

Now something appears to be not quite right! The default variable scoping rules mean that the variable thread_number is available to all threads - in OpenMP

terminology it is shared. The opposite of shared is private and each thread has their
own copy. Example 3 corrects this problem.

33.5   Example 3: Hello World with Private
`thread_number` variable

```
program ch3303
  use omp_lib
  implicit none
  integer :: nthreads
  integer :: thread_number
  integer :: i

  nthreads = omp_get_max_threads()
  print *, ' Number of threads = ', nthreads
!$omp parallel do private(thread_number)
  do i = 1, nthreads
    thread_number = omp_get_thread_num()
    print *, ' Hello from thread ', &
      thread_number
  end do
!$omp end parallel do
  end program ch3303
```

Here is the output from the gfortran compiler.

```
$ ./a.exe
  Number of threads =             8
  Hello from thread        2
  Hello from thread        1
  Hello from thread        4
  Hello from thread        3
  Hello from thread        0
  Hello from thread        6
  Hello from thread        5
  Hello from thread        7
```

Care must be taken with variables in OpenMP to ensure they have the correct data
scoping state.

33.6 Example 4: Parallel Solution for pi Calculation

This is an OpenMP parallel implementation of the integration problem (Example 3) from the previous chapter. You should compare it with the MPI solution - Example 4 in the last chapter.

```fortran
include 'precision_module.f90'

include 'timing_module.f90'

program ch3304
  use precision_module
  use timing_module
  use omp_lib
  implicit none
  real (dp) :: fortran_internal_pi
  real (dp) :: partial_pi
  real (dp) :: openmp_pi
  real (dp) :: width
  real (dp) :: x
  integer :: nthreads
  integer :: i
  integer :: j
  integer :: k
  integer :: n

  nthreads = omp_get_max_threads()
  fortran_internal_pi = 4.0_dp*atan(1.0_dp)
  print *, ' Maximum number of threads is ', &
    nthreads
  do k = 1, nthreads
    call start_timing()
    n = 100000
    call omp_set_num_threads(k)
    print *, ' Number of threads = ', k
    do j = 1, 5
      width = 1.0_dp/n
      partial_pi = 0.0_dp
!$omp parallel do private(x) &
!$omp shared(width) reduction(+:partial_pi)
      do i = 1, n
        x = width*(real(i,dp)-0.5_dp)
        partial_pi = partial_pi + f(x)
      end do
```

```
!$omp end parallel do
      openmp_pi = width*partial_pi
      print 100, n, time_difference()
      print 110, openmp_pi, abs(openmp_pi- &
        fortran_internal_pi)
      n = n*10
    end do
  end do
100 format (' N intervals = ', i12, ' time =', &
    f8.3)
110 format (' openmp_pi = ', f20.16, /, &
    'difference = ', f20.16)
  call end_timing()
  stop

contains

  real (dp) function f(x)
    implicit none
    real (dp), intent (in) :: x

    f = 4.0_dp/(1.0_dp+x*x)
  end function f

end program ch3304
```

Here is the output from the Intel compiler.

```
 Maximum number of threads is                8
 ..
  Number of threads =                1
 N intervals =         100000 time =    0.004
 openmp_pi =    3.1415926535981167
difference =    0.0000000000083236
 N intervals =        1000000 time =    0.012
 openmp_pi =    3.1415926535899033
difference =    0.0000000000001101
 N intervals =       10000000 time =    0.051
 openmp_pi =    3.1415926535896861
difference =    0.0000000000001070
 N intervals =      100000000 time =    0.449
 openmp_pi =    3.1415926535902168
difference =    0.0000000000004237
 N intervals =     1000000000 time =    4.398
 openmp_pi =    3.1415926535897682
```

```
difference =   0.0000000000000249
..
  Number of threads =             2
 N intervals =          100000 time =   0.000
 openmp_pi =   3.1415926535981260
difference =   0.0000000000083329
 N intervals =         1000000 time =   0.000
 openmp_pi =   3.1415926535898624
difference =   0.0000000000000693
 N intervals =        10000000 time =   0.020
 openmp_pi =   3.1415926535897829
difference =   0.0000000000000102
 N intervals =       100000000 time =   0.219
 openmp_pi =   3.1415926535898926
difference =   0.0000000000000995
 N intervals =      1000000000 time =   2.195
 openmp_pi =   3.1415926535897380
difference =   0.0000000000000551
..
  Number of threads =             4
 N intervals =          100000 time =   0.004
 openmp_pi =   3.1415926535981287
difference =   0.0000000000083356
 N intervals =         1000000 time =   0.004
 openmp_pi =   3.1415926535898726
difference =   0.0000000000000795
 N intervals =        10000000 time =   0.027
 openmp_pi =   3.1415926535898153
difference =   0.0000000000000222
 N intervals =       100000000 time =   0.137
 openmp_pi =   3.1415926535898038
difference =   0.0000000000000107
 N intervals =      1000000000 time =   1.781
 openmp_pi =   3.1415926535898544
difference =   0.0000000000000613
..
  Number of threads =             8
 N intervals =          100000 time =   0.000
 openmp_pi =   3.1415926535981278
difference =   0.0000000000083347
 N intervals =         1000000 time =   0.004
 openmp_pi =   3.1415926535898784
difference =   0.0000000000000853
 N intervals =        10000000 time =   0.016
 openmp_pi =   3.1415926535897962
```

```
difference =    0.0000000000000031
 N intervals =     100000000 time =     0.113
 openmp_pi =    3.1415926535898162
difference =    0.0000000000000231
 N intervals =    1000000000 time =     1.137
 openmp_pi =    3.1415926535898824
difference =    0.0000000000000893
```

We have similar timing improvements to the MPI solutions.

33.7   Example 5: Comparing the Timing of Whole Array Syntax, Simple Do Loops, Do Concurrent and an OpenMP Solution

The chapter on data structuring introduced the do concurrent statement. In the example we solve a summation problem using the following four methods:

- whole array syntax
- simple do loop
- do concurrent loop
- OpenMP parallel loop

Here is the program.

```
include 'timing_module.f90'
include 'precision_module.f90'

program ch3305

use timing_module
use precision_module
use omp_lib

implicit none

integer , parameter :: n=10000000
integer , parameter ::loop_count=10
integer , parameter :: n_types=4
integer :: i
integer :: j
integer :: nthreads

real (dp) , allocatable , dimension(:) :: x
```

```
real (dp) , allocatable, dimension(:)  :: y
real (dp) , allocatable , dimension(:) :: z

 real , dimension(n_types,loop_count) :: &
  timing_details = 0.0
real , dimension(n_types) :: t_sum  = 0.0
real , dimension(n_types) :: t_average = 0.0
real :: reset = 0.0

character (15)  , dimension(n_types) :: &
  heading_1 = &
    [ ' Whole array   ' , &
       ' Do loop       ' , &
       ' Do concurrent ' , &
       ' openmp        ' ]

  call start_timing()
  print *,' '

  nthreads = omp_get_max_threads()
  open(unit=20,file='ch3305.dat')
  print 10,nthreads
  10 format(' Nthreads = ',i3)
  allocate (x(n))
  allocate (y(n))
  allocate (z(n))

  call random_number(x)
  call random_number(y)
  z=0.0_dp
  print 20,time_difference()
  20 format(' Initialise time = ',f6.3)
  write(20,30) x(1),y(1),z(1)
  30 format(3(2x,f6.3))
  print  *, ' '

  do j=1,loop_count

    print 40,j
    40 format(' Iteration = ',i3)
!
!  Whole array syntax
!
    z=x+y
    timing_details(1,j) = time_difference()
```

```fortran
      write(20,30) x(1),y(1),z(1)
      z = 0.0_dp
      reset = time_difference()
!
! Simple traditional do loop
!
      do i=1,n
        z(i)=x(i)+y(i)
      end do
      timing_details(2,j) = time_difference()
      z = 0.0_dp
      reset = time_difference()
!
! do concurrent loop
!
      do concurrent (i=1:n)
        z(i)=x(i)+y(i)
      end do
      timing_details(3,j) = time_difference()
      write(20,30) x(1),y(1),z(1)
      z = 0.0_dp
      reset = time_difference()
!
! OpenMP parallel loop
!
    !$omp parallel do
      do i=1,n
        z(i)=x(i)+y(i)
      end do
    !$omp end parallel do
      timing_details(4,j) = time_difference()
      write(20,30) x(1),y(1),z(1)
      z = 0.0_dp
      reset = time_difference()

    end do
    close(20)
    print 50
50  format(15x,70x,'    Sum       Average')

    do i=1,n_types
      t_sum(i) = &
        sum(timing_details(i,1:loop_count))
      t_average(i) = t_sum(i)/loop_count
      print 60,heading_1(i) , &
```

```
      timing_details(i,1:loop_count),&
      t_sum(i),t_average(i)
   60 format(a,10(1x,f6.3),2(3x,f6.3))
   end do

   print *,' '
   call end_timing()
 end program ch3305
```

Here are some timing details for three compilers on one system under both Linux and Windows.

	gfortran		Intel		Nag	
	Linux	Windows	Linux	Windows	Linux	Windows
Whole array	0.019	0.018	0.013	0.015	0.034	0.053
Do loop	0.019	0.019	0.018	0.019	0.020	0.019
Do concurrent	0.019	0.018	0.018	0.020	0.019	0.020
openmp	0.016	0.016	0.012	0.012	0.016	0.016

33.8 Summary

This chapter briefly introduced the essentials of OpenMP programming. We have also seen the timing benefits that OpenMP programming can offer in the solution of the same problem as in the MPI chapter. We finished off by doing a comparison of summation in Fortran using four methods.

33.9 Problem

33.1 Compile and run the examples in this chapter with your compiler and compare the results.

Chapter 34
Coarray Fortran

Science is a wonderful thing if one does not have to earn one's living at it.

Einstein

Aim

The aims of this chapter is to provide a short introduction to coarray programming in Fortran.

34.1 Introduction

Coarrays were the major component of the Fortran 2008 standard. As stated earlier they are based on a single program multiple data model. Coarrays are a simple parallel programming extension to Fortran. They are effectively variables that can be shared across multiple instances of the same program or images in Fortran terminology.

Coarray variables look like conventional Fortran arrays, except that they use [] brackets instead of () brackets. In the simple declaration below

```
character(len=20)  ::  name[*]='*****'
```

We declare name to be a `coarray` and the * in the [] brackets means that the bounds of the coarray are calculated at run time, rather than compile time.

```
read  *, name
```

is a reference to the coarray on the current image.

We can then use the following statement

```
name[i] = name
```

© Springer International Publishing AG, part of Springer Nature 2018
I. Chivers and J. Sleightholme, *Introduction to Programming with Fortran*,
https://doi.org/10.1007/978-3-319-75502-1_34

to broadcast the value read in to each of the other images.

Note the Fortran coarray syntax here. We use the [] brackets to reference the coarray variable on other images and the omission of the [] brackets is a reference to the coarray variable on the current image.

34.2   Some Basic Coarray Terminology

The following is taken from the Fortran 2018 standard and covers some of the basic coarray terminology.

- `codimension` attribute - The `codimension` attribute species that an entity is a coarray. The coarray-spec specifies its corank or corank and cobounds.
- Allocatable coarray - A coarray with the allocatable attribute has a specified corank, but its cobounds are determined by allocation or argument association.
- Explicit-coshape coarray - An explicit-coshape coarray is a named coarray that has its corank and cobounds declared by an explicit-coshape-spec.
- Coindexed named objects - A coindexed-named-object is a named scalar coarray variable followed by an image selector.
- Image selectors - An image selector determines the image index for a coindexed object.
- Image execution control and image control statements - The execution sequence on each image is specified in 5.3.5 of the standard.
- Execution of an image control statement divides the execution sequence on an image into segments. Each of the following is an image control statement:

  - `sync all` statement;
  - `sync images` statement;
  - `sync memory` statement;
  - `allocate` or `deallocate` statement that has a coarray allocate-object;
  - `critical` or `end critical`;
  - `lock` or `unlock` statement;
  - Any statement that completes execution of a block or procedure and which results in the implicit deallocation of a coarray;
  - `stop` statement;
  - `end` statement of a main program.

- Coarray - A coarray is a data entity that has nonzero corank; it can be directly referenced or defined by any image. It may be a scalar or an array.
- Coarray dummy variables - If the dummy argument is a coarray, the corresponding actual argument shall be a coarray and shall have the `volatile` attribute if and only if the dummy argument has the `volatile` attribute.
- Some coarray intrinsics

  - `image_index` - convert a cosubscript to an image index

- lcobound - cobounds of a coarray
- num_images - the number of images
- this_image - image index or cosubscripts
- ucobound - cobounds of a coarray

Let us look now at some simple examples.

34.3 Example 1: Hello World

The first is the classic Hello world.

```
program ch3401

  implicit none

  print *, ' Hello world from image ', &
    this_image()

end program ch3401
```

Here is the output from the Intel compiler.

```
Hello world from image              5
Hello world from image              3
Hello world from image              4
Hello world from image              8
Hello world from image              1
Hello world from image              6
Hello world from image              2
Hello world from image              7
```

Here is sample output from the Cray Archer service.

```
Hello world from image   16
Hello world from image   6
Hello world from image   13
Hello world from image   25
Hello world from image   34

lines deleted

Hello world from image   38
Hello world from image   44
```

```
Hello world from image  35
Hello world from image  28
Hello world from image  33
Hello world from image  32
Hello world from image  30
Hello world from image  29
```

The output is obviously very similar to the corresponding MPI and OpenMP versions.

34.4   Example 2: Broadcasting Data

Here is a simple program that broadcasts data from one image to the rest. This is a common requirement in parallel programming.

```
program ch3402

  implicit none

  integer :: i
  character (len=20) :: name [ * ] = '*****'

  print 100, name, this_image()

  if (this_image()==1) then
    print *, ' Type in your name'
    read *, name
    do i = 2, num_images()
      name [ i ] = name
    end do
  end if

  sync all

  print 100, name, this_image()
100 format (1x, ' Hello ', a20, ' from image ', &
    i3)

end program ch3402
```

Here is the output from the Intel compiler.

```
Hello *****                    from image   1
```

```
Hello *****                        from image    3
Hello *****                        from image    5
Hello *****                        from image    7
Hello *****                        from image    2
Hello *****                        from image    4
Hello *****                        from image    8
Type in your name
Hello *****                        from image    6
Jane
Hello Jane                         from image    4
Hello Jane                         from image    8
Hello Jane                         from image    2
Hello Jane                         from image    6
Hello Jane                         from image    7
Hello Jane                         from image    3
Hello Jane                         from image    5
Hello Jane                         from image    1
```

Again no particular ordering of the image numbers.

34.5   Example 3: Parallel Solution for pi Calculation

```
include 'precision_module.f90'

include 'timing_module.f90'

program ch3403

  use precision_module
  use timing_module

  implicit none

  real (dp) :: fortran_internal_pi
  real (dp) :: partial_pi
  real (dp) :: coarray_pi
  real (dp) :: width
  real (dp) :: total_sum
  real (dp) :: x
  real (dp), codimension [ * ] :: partial_sum

  integer :: n_intervals
```

```fortran
   integer :: i
   integer :: j
   integer :: current_image
   integer :: n_images

   fortran_internal_pi = 4.0_dp*atan(1.0_dp)
   n_images = num_images()
   current_image = this_image()

   if (current_image==1) then
     print *, ' Number of images = ', n_images
   end if

   n_intervals = 100000

   do j = 1, 5
     if (current_image==1) then
       call start_timing()
     end if
     width = 1.0_dp/real(n_intervals, dp)
     total_sum = 0.0_dp
     partial_sum = 0.0_dp
     do i = current_image, n_intervals, n_images
       x = (real(i,dp)-0.5_dp)*width
       partial_sum = partial_sum + f(x)
     end do
     partial_sum = partial_sum*width
     sync all
     if (current_image==1) then
       do i = 1, n_images
         total_sum = total_sum + partial_sum [ i &
           ]
       end do
       coarray_pi = total_sum
       print 100, n_intervals, time_difference()
       print 110, coarray_pi, abs(coarray_pi- &
         fortran_internal_pi)
     end if
     n_intervals = n_intervals*10
     sync all
   end do

100 format (' n intervals = ', i12, ' time =', &
     f8.3)
110 format (' pi = ', f20.16, /, &
```

```
      ' difference = ', f20.16)

contains

  real (dp) function f(x)
    implicit none
    real (dp), intent (in) :: x

    f = 4.0_dp/(1.0_dp+x*x)

  end function f

end program ch3403
```

Here is the   output from the Intel compiler.

```
Number of images =            8
2011/ 6/10 13:40:48 479
n intervals =        100000 time =   0.004
pi =    3.1415926535981260
difference =    0.0000000000083329
2011/ 6/10 13:40:48 486
n intervals =       1000000 time =   0.004
pi =    3.1415926535898802
difference =    0.0000000000000870
2011/ 6/10 13:40:48 490
n intervals =      10000000 time =   0.012
pi =    3.1415926535897936
difference =    0.0000000000000004
2011/ 6/10 13:40:48 500
n intervals =     100000000 time =   0.105
pi =    3.1415926535897749
difference =    0.0000000000000182
2011/ 6/10 13:40:48 605
n intervals =    1000000000 time =   0.992
pi =    3.1415926535898455
difference =    0.0000000000000524
```

Here is the output from the Cray compiler.

```
 Number of images =  48
2015/ 3/21  1:11:50 130
n intervals =        100000 time =   0.005
pi =    3.1415926535981265
```

```
difference =    0.0000000000083333
2015/ 3/21  1:11:50 135
n intervals =        1000000 time =    0.000
pi =   3.1415926535898762
difference =    0.0000000000000830
2015/ 3/21  1:11:50 135
n intervals =       10000000 time =    0.001
pi =   3.1415926535897953
difference =    0.0000000000000022
2015/ 3/21  1:11:50 136
n intervals =      100000000 time =    0.006
pi =   3.1415926535897905
difference =    0.0000000000000027
2015/ 3/21  1:11:50 142
n intervals =     1000000000 time =    0.054
pi =   3.1415926535897949
difference =    0.0000000000000018
```

We get the time improvement we have seen with both the MPI and OpenMP solutions.

34.6   Example 4: Work Sharing

This example looks at one way of splitting work up between images. We use the image number to determine which image does which work. It is a coarray version of the MPI work sharing example.

```
program ch3404
  implicit none
  integer :: n, i, j
  integer :: me, nim, start, end
  integer, parameter :: factor = 5
  integer, dimension (1:factor), &
    codimension [ * ] :: x

  nim = num_images()
  me = this_image()
  n = nim*factor
  x = 0
  start = factor*(me-1) + 1
  end = factor*me
  j = 1
  do i = start, end
```

```
      x(j) = i*factor
      print *, 'on image ', me, 'j = ', j, &
        ' x(j) = ', x(j)
      j = j + 1
   end do
   sync all
   if (me==1) then
     print *, 'coarray x on image ', me, ' is: ', &
       x
     do i = 2, nim
       print *, 'coarray x on image ', i, &
         ' is: ', x(:) [ i ]
     end do
   end if
end program ch3404
```

The following statements define the start and end points for the array processing for each image:

```
   start = factor*(me-1) + 1
   end   = factor*me
```

and partitions the work between the images. Each image will have its own start and end values. The following do loop does the work:

```
   do i=start,end
      x(j) = i*factor
      print*,'on image ',me, 'j = ',j,' x(j) = ',x(j)
      j    = j + 1
   end do
```

We need the

```
   sync all
```

to ensure that each image has completed before further processing, and we then print out the data from each image on image 1.

Here is a subset of the output from the Intel compiler. This example runs on 8 images.

```
on image     2 j =     1  x(j) =      30
on image     7 j =     1  x(j) =     155
on image     8 j =     1  x(j) =     180
on image     8 j =     2  x(j) =     185
on image     8 j =     3  x(j) =     190
```

```
on image      8 j =      4  x(j) =     195
on image      8 j =      5  x(j) =     200
on image      6 j =      1  x(j) =     130
on image      6 j =      2  x(j) =     135
on image      6 j =      3  x(j) =     140
...
...
...
coarray x on image            1  is:
         5              10
15
         20             25
on image      4 j =      1  x(j) =      80
on image      4 j =      2  x(j) =      85
on image      4 j =      3  x(j) =      90
on image      4 j =      4  x(j) =      95
on image      4 j =      5  x(j) =     100
coarray x on image            2  is:
         30             35
40
         45             50
coarray x on image            3  is:
         55             60
65
         70             75
coarray x on image            4  is:
         80             85
90
         95            100
coarray x on image            5  is:
         105            110
115dir
         120            125
coarray x on image            6  is:
         130            135
140
         145            150
coarray x on image            7  is:
         155            160
165
         170            175
coarray x on image            8  is:
         180            185
190
         195            200
```

Here is a sample of the output from the Cray compiler on the Archer service. This
example runs on 48 images.

```
on image  1 j =  1  x(j) =   5
on image  1 j =  2  x(j) =  10
on image  3 j =  1  x(j) =  55
on image  3 j =  2  x(j) =  60

stuff deleted

on image  22 j =  5  x(j) =  550
coarray x on image  1  is:  5,  10,  15,  20,  25
on image  21 j =  1  x(j) =  505

stuff deleted

on image  20 j =  3  x(j) =  490
on image  6 j =  3  x(j) =  140
on image  13 j =  2  x(j) =  310
on image  6 j =  4  x(j) =  145

stuff deleted

on image  7 j =  1  x(j) =  155
on image  10 j =  2  x(j) =  235

stuff deleted

on image  27 j =  2  x(j) =  660
on image  41 j =  4  x(j) =  1020
on image  28 j =  2  x(j) =  685

stuff deleted

on image  33 j =  5  x(j) =  825
on image  36 j =  5  x(j) =  900
on image  40 j =  1  x(j) =  980

stuff deleted

on image  40 j =  2  x(j) =  985
on image  40 j =  3  x(j) =  990
on image  40 j =  4  x(j) =  995
on image  40 j =  5  x(j) =  1000
```

```
  on image   45 j =   4  x(j) =   1120
  on image   46 j =   5  x(j) =   1150
  on image   45 j =   5  x(j) =   1125
Application 13271719 resources: utime ~7s,
stime ~52s, Rss ~4288,
inblocks ~22292, outblocks ~39436
```

34.7   Summary

This chapter has looked briefly at some of the simple syntax of coarrays using a small set of examples. We have also seen the timing benefits that coarray programming can offer in the solution of the same problem.

34.8   Problem

34.1 Compile and run the examples in this chapter with your compiler.

Chapter 35
C Interop

> *We can't solve problems by using the same kind of thinking we used when we created them.*
>
> Einstein

Aim

This chapter looks briefly at C interoperability.

35.1 Introduction

C is a widely used programming language and there is a considerable amount of software written in C or with a C calling interface. Fortran 2003 introduced a standardised mechanism for interoperating with C.

There were limitations to this interoperability and ISO TS 29113 significantly extended the scope of the interoperation facilities. The TS was published in 2012.

In this chapter we provide a brief coverage of some of the technical details required for interoperability and then have a look at a couple of examples.

35.2 The `iso_c_binding` Module

There is an intrinsic module called `iso_c_binding` that contains named constants, derived types and module procedures to support interoperability.

© Springer International Publishing AG, part of Springer Nature 2018
I. Chivers and J. Sleightholme, *Introduction to Programming with Fortran*,
https://doi.org/10.1007/978-3-319-75502-1_35

35.3   Named Constants and Derived Types in the Module

In Table 35.1 the entities listed in the second column are named constants of type
default integer.

Table 35.1 `iso_c_binding` module - named constants

Fortran type	Named constant from the iso_c_binding module (kind type parameter is positive if supported)	C type
integer	c_int	int
	c_short	short int
	c_long	long int
	c_long_long	long long int
	c_signed_char	signed char
		unsigned char
	c_size_t	size_t
	c_int8_t	int8_t
	c_int16_t	int16_t
	c_int32_t	int32_t
	c_int64_t	int64_t
	c_int_least8_t	int_least8_t
	c_int_least16_t	int_least16_t
	c_int_least32_t	int_least32_t
	c_int_least64_t	int_least64_t
	c_int_fast8_t	int_fast8_t
	c_int_fast16_t	int_fast16_t
	c_int_fast32_t	int_fast32_t
	c_int_fast64_t	int_fast64_t
	c_intmax_t	intmax_t
	c_intptr_t	intptr_t
real	c_float	float
	c_double	double
	c_long_double	long double
complex	c_float_complex	float complex
	c_double_complex	double complex
	c_long_double_complex	long double complex
logical	c_bool	bool
character	c_char	char

35.4   Character Interoperability

Table 35.2 shows the mapping between Fortran and C character types. The semantics of these values are explained in 5.2.1 and 5.2.2 of the C International Standard.

Table 35.2   C Interop character interoperability

Name	C definition	c_char = −1	c_char /= −1
c_null_char	Null character	char(0)	`'\0'`
c_alert	Alert	achar(7)	`'\a'`
c_backspace	Backspace	achar(8)	`'\b'`
c_form_feed	Form feed	achar(12)	`'\f'`
c_new_line	New line	achar(10)	`'\n'`
c_carriage_return	Carriage return	achar(13)	`'\r'`
c_horizontal_tab	Horizontal tab	achar(9)	`'\t'`
c_vertical_tab	Vertical tab	achar(11)	`'\v'`

35.5   Procedures in the Module

There are several procedures in this module. In the descriptions below, procedure names are generic and not specific.

A C procedure argument is often defined in terms of a C address. The c_loc and c_funloc functions are provided so that Fortran applications can determine the appropriate value to use with C facilities.

The c_associated function is provided so that Fortran programs can compare C addresses.

The c_f_pointer and c_f_procpointer subroutines provide a means of associating a Fortran pointer with the target of a C pointer.

More information can be found in Chap. 18 of the Fortran 2018 standard.

35.6   Interoperability of Intrinsic Types

Table 35.1 shows the interoperability between Fortran intrinsic types and C types. A Fortran intrinsic type with particular type parameter values is interoperable with a C type if the type and kind type parameter value are listed in the table on the same row as that C type; if the type is character, interoperability also requires that the length type parameter be omitted or be specified by an initialization expression whose value is one. A combination of Fortran type and type parameters that is interoperable with a C type listed in the table is also interoperable with any unqualified C type that is compatible with the listed C type.

The second column of the table refers to the named constants made accessible by the `iso_c_binding` intrinsic module.

A combination of intrinsic type and type parameters is interoperable if it is interoperable with a C type.

The above mentioned C types are defined in the C International Standard, clauses 6.2.5, 7.17, and 7.18.1.

35.7   Other Aspects of Interoperability

There are considerable restrictions on other aspects of interoperability. The following provides some brief details of other areas:

35.7.1   Interoperability with C Pointer Types

`c_ptr` and `c_funptr` shall be derived types with private components. `c_ptr` is interoperable with any C object pointer type. `c_funptr` is interoperable with any C function pointer type.

35.7.2   Interoperability of Scalar Variables

A scalar Fortran variable is interoperable if its type and type parameters are interoperable and it has neither the pointer nor the allocatable attribute.

An interoperable scalar Fortran variable is interoperable with a scalar C entity if their types and type parameters are interoperable.

35.7.3   Interoperability of Array Variables

An array Fortran variable is interoperable if its type and type parameters are interoperable and it is of explicit shape or assumed size.

35.7.4   Interoperability of Procedures and Procedure Interfaces

A Fortran procedure is interoperable if it has the `bind` attribute, that is, if its interface is specified with a proc-language-binding-spec.

35.7.5   Interoperation with C Global Variables

A C variable with external linkage may interoperate with a common block or with a variable declared in the scope of a module. The common block or variable shall be specified to have the `bind` attribute.

35.7.6 Binding Labels for Common Blocks and Variables

The binding label of a variable or common block is a value of type default character that specifies the name by which the variable or common block is known to the companion processor.

35.7.7 Interoperation with C Functions

A procedure that is interoperable may be defined either by means other than Fortran or by means of a Fortran subprogram, but not both.

Another useful source can be found in the December 2009 edition of Fortran Forum. Details are given at the end of the chapter.

35.8 Compilers Used in the Examples

Not all Fortran compilers work with all C and C++ compilers and vice versa.

Table 35.3 has some details of the compilers we have used in the examples that follow.

Table 35.3 Compilers used

Main program	Subprogram	Operating system
gfortran	gcc	cygwin, Windows
gfortran	gcc	MinGW-W64, Windows
gfortran	gcc	openSuSe Linux
Intel Fortran	Microsoft Visual C++	Windows
Intel Fortran	Intel C++	Windows
Nag Fortran	Nag integrated gcc	Windows
Nag Fortran	gcc	MinGW-W64, Windows
Oracle Fortran	Oracle cc	openSuSe Linux
gcc	gfortran	cygwin, Windows
gcc	gfortran	openSuSe Linux
Intel C	Intel Fortran	openSuSe Linux
Nag C	Nag Fortran	Windows
Oracle C	Oracle Fortran	openSuSe Linux
g++	gfortran	cygwin, Windows
g++	gfortran	openSuSe Linux
Intel C++	Intel Fortran	openSuSe Linux
Intel C++	Intel Fortran	Windows
Microsoft Visual C++	Intel Fortran	Windows
Nag C++	Nag Fortran	Windows
Oracle C++	Oracle Fortran	openSuSe Linux

35.9   Example 1: Kind Type Support

This example uses Table 35.1 as its basis. It prints out the kind types for each of the kind types in the table. If the value of one of the named constants is positive it will be a valid kind value for the intrinsic type, i.e. the corresponding C type is interoperable with the Fortran intrinsic type of that kind. If the value of one of the named constants is negative then there is no interoperable Fortran kind for that C type.

```
program ch3501
  use iso_c_binding
  implicit none

  print *, 'integer support'
  print *, '  c_int = ', c_int
  print *, '  c_short = ', c_short
  print *, '  c_long = ', c_long
  print *, '  c_long_long = ', c_long_long
  print *, '  c_signed_char = ', c_signed_char
  print *, '  c_size_t = ', c_size_t
  print *, '  c_int8_t = ', c_int8_t
  print *, '  c_int16_t = ', c_int16_t
  print *, '  c_int32_t = ', c_int32_t
  print *, '  c_int64_t = ', c_int64_t
  print *, '  c_int_least8_t = ', c_int_least8_t
  print *, '  c_int_least16_t = ', &
    c_int_least16_t
  print *, '  c_int_least32_t = ', &
    c_int_least32_t
  print *, '  c_int_least64_t = ', &
    c_int_least64_t
  print *, '  c_int_fast8_t = ', c_int_fast8_t
  print *, '  c_int_fast16_t = ', c_int_fast16_t
  print *, '  c_int_fast32_t = ', c_int_fast32_t
  print *, '  c_int_fast64_t = ', c_int_fast64_t
  print *, '  c_intmax_t = ', c_intmax_t
  print *, '  c_intptr_t = ', c_intptr_t
  print *, 'real support'
  print *, '  c_float = ', c_float
  print *, '  c_double = ', c_double
  print *, '  c_long_double = ', c_long_double
  print *, 'complex support'
  print *, '  c_float_complex = ', &
    c_float_complex
  print *, '  c_double_complex = ', &
```

```
      c_double_complex
  print *, '  c_long_double_complex = ', &
    c_long_double_complex
  print *, 'logical support'
  print *, '  c_bool = ', c_bool
  print *, 'character support'
  print *, '  c_char = ', c_char
end program ch3501
```

Table 35.4 summarises support for several compilers.
A negative number means not supported.

Table 35.4 Basic C Interop table

Compiler vendors	gfortran	Intel	Nag	Sun
C interop type				
C_INT	4	4	4	4
C_SHORT	2	2	2	2
C_LONG	8	4	4	8
C_LONG_LONG	8	8	8	8
C_SIGNED_CHAR	1	1	1	1
C_SIZE_T	8	8	8	8
C_INT8_T	1	1	1	1
C_INT16_T	2	2	2	2
C_INT32_T	4	4	4	4
C_INT64_T	8	8	8	8
C_INT_LEAST8_T	1	1	1	1
C_INT_LEAST16_T	2	2	2	2
C_INT_LEAST32_T	4	4	4	4
C_INT_LEAST64_T	8	8	8	8
C_INT_FAST8_T	1	1	1	1
C_INT_FAST16_T	8	2	2	2
C_INT_FAST32_T	8	4	4	4
C_INT_FAST64_T	8	8	8	8
C_INTMAX_T	8	8	8	8
C_INTPTR_T	8	8	8	8
C_FLOAT	4	4	4	4
C_DOUBLE	8	8	8	8
C_LONG_DOUBLE	10	8	-4	-3
C_FLOAT_COMPLEX	4	4	4	4
C_DOUBLE_COMPLEX	8	8	8	8
C_LONG_DOUBLE_COMPLEX	10	8	-4	-3
C_BOOL	1	1	1	1
C_CHAR	1	1	1	1

35.10   Example 2: Fortran Calling a C Function

Here is the Fortran source.

```
program ch3502
  use iso_c_binding
  interface
    real (c_float) function reciprocal(x) &
      bind (c, name='reciprocal')
      use iso_c_binding
      real (c_float), value :: x
    end function reciprocal
  end interface
  real :: x

  x = 10.0
  print *, ' Fortran calling C function'
  print *, x, ' reciprocal = ', reciprocal(x)
end program ch3502
```

Here is the C source.

```
float reciprocal(float x)
{
  return(1.0f/x);
}
```

The first key statement is

```
use iso_c_binding
```

which makes available named constants, derived types and module procedures to support interoperability.

The next part of the program

```
interface
  real (c_float) function reciprocal(x) &
    bind(c,name='reciprocal')
  use iso_c_binding
  real (c_float) , value :: x
  end function reciprocal
end interface
```

provides the compiler with details of the C function that is being called. It is called
reciprocal, takes an argument of type `real` in Fortran or `float` in C terminology, and returns a value of type `real` in Fortran or `float` in C terminology.

35.11   Example 3: C Calling a Fortran Function

Here is the Fortran source.

```
function reciprocal(x) bind (c, name= &
  'reciprocal')
  use iso_c_binding
  implicit none
  real (c_float), intent (in) :: x
  real (c_float) :: reciprocal

  reciprocal = 1.0/x
end function reciprocal
```

Here is the C source.

```
#include <stdio.h>
float reciprocal(float *x);

int main()
{
  float x;
  x=10.0f;
  printf(" C calling a Fortran function\n");
  printf(" (1 / %f ) = %f \n" ,x,reciprocal(&x));
  return(0);
}
```

Let us look at the Fortran code first.

```
function reciprocal(x) bind(c,name=reciprocal)
```

This line tells the compiler that the reciprocal function has to have a name
and calling convention that is interoperable with C.

```
real (c_float), intent(in) :: x
```

says that the argument x is intent(in) and is of type `real` in Fortran and type
`float` in C.

```
real (c_float) :: reciprocal
```

says that the function will return a value of type `real` in Fortran or `float` in C terminology.

The function prototype

```
float reciprocal(float *x);
```

is required in the C source code to tell the compiler about the `reciprocal` function.

35.12   Example 4: C++ Calling a Fortran Function

Here is the Fortran source.

```
function reciprocal(x) bind (c, name= &
  'reciprocal')
  use iso_c_binding
  implicit none
  real (c_float), intent (in) :: x
  real (c_float) :: reciprocal

  reciprocal = 1.0/x
end function reciprocal
```

Here is the C++ source.

```
#include <iostream> using namespace std;
extern "C" { float reciprocal(float *); }
int main()
{
  float x;
  x=10.0f;
  cout << " C++ calling a Fortan function" << endl;
  cout << " x = " << x << " reciprocal = ";
  cout << reciprocal(&x) << endl;
  return(0);
}
```

The Fortran code and explanation is as for the previous example.
The

```
extern "C" { float reciprocal(float *); }
```

code is required in the C++ code to tell the compiler about the Fortran function
`reciprocal`.

In C++ we have to tell the compiler that the function has C calling semantics.

35.13   Example 5: Passing an Array from Fortran to C

Here is the Fortran source.

```fortran
program ch3505
  use iso_c_binding
  interface
    function summation(x, n) bind (c, &
      name='summation')
      use iso_c_binding
      integer (c_int), value :: n
      real (c_float), dimension (1:n), &
        intent (in) :: x
      real (c_float) :: summation
    end function summation
  end interface
  integer, parameter :: n = 10
  real, dimension (1:n) :: x = 1.0

  print *, ' Fortran calling c function'
  print *, ' 1 d array as parameter'
  print *, summation(x, n)
end program ch3505
```

Here is the C source.

```c
float summation(float *x,int n)
{
  int i;
  float t;
    t=0.0f;
    for (i=0;i<n;i++)
    {
      t+=x[i];
    }
    return(t);
}
```

The following code

```
interface
  function summation(x,n) bind(c,name=summation)
    use iso_c_binding
    integer (c_int) , value :: n
    real (c_float), dimension(1:n) , intent(in) :: x
    real (c_float) :: summation
  end function summation
end interface
```

is required to tell the Fortran compiler the details of the C function.

Arrays in C are passed as pointers or by address so we have the following signature

```
float summation(float *x,int n)
```

in the C code.

35.14   Example 6: Passing an Array from C to Fortran

Here is the Fortran source.

```
function summation(x, n) bind (c, &
  name='summation')
  use iso_c_binding
  implicit none
  integer (c_int), value :: n
  real (c_float), dimension (1:n), &
    intent (in) :: x
  real (c_float) :: summation
  integer :: i

  summation = sum(x(1:n))
end function summation
```

Here is the C source.

```
#include <stdio.h>
float summation(float *x,int n);

int main()
{
  const int n=10;
```

```
      float x[n];
      int i;
      for (i=0;i<n;i++)
        x[i]=1.0;
      printf(" C calling Fortran\n");
      printf(" 1 d array as parameter\n");
      printf(" Sum is = %f \n " ,summation(x,n));
      return(0);
  }
```

The `bind(c)` attribute is required to tell the Fortran compiler that the function will be called from C.

The other declarations provide details of the parameters passed into the function from the C calling routine.

The following function prototype

```
float summation(float *x,int n);
```

is required to tell the C compiler the details of the Fortran function.

35.15   Example 7: Passing an Array from C++ to Fortran

Here is the Fortran source.

```
function summation(x, n) bind (c, &
  name='summation')
  use iso_c_binding
  implicit none
  integer (c_int), value :: n
  real (c_float), dimension (1:n), &
    intent (in) :: x
  real (c_float) :: summation
  integer :: i

  summation = sum(x(1:n))
end function summation
```

Here is the C++ source.

```
#include <iostream>
using namespace std;
extern "C" float summation(float *,int );
int main()
{
```

```
  const int n=10;
  float *x;
  int i;
  x = new  float[n];
  for (i=0;i<n;i++)
    x[i]=1.0f;
  cout << " C++ calling Fortran" << endl;
  cout << " 1 d array as parameter" << endl;
  cout << " Sum is " << summation(x,n) << endl;
  return(0);
}
```

The explanation of the Fortran source is the same as for the previous example.
The following function prototype

```
float summation(float *x,int n);
```

is required to tell the C++ compiler about the Fortran function.

35.16   Example 8: Passing a Rank 2 Array from Fortran to C

Here is the Fortran source.

```
program ch3508
  use iso_c_binding
  interface
    subroutine reciprocal(nr, nc, x, y) bind (c, &
      name='reciprocal')
      use iso_c_binding
      integer (c_int), value :: nr
      integer (c_int), value :: nc
      real (c_float), dimension (nr, nc) :: x
      real (c_float), dimension (nr, nc) :: y
    end subroutine reciprocal
  end interface
  integer, parameter :: nr = 2
  integer, parameter :: nc = 6
  integer :: i
  real, dimension (nr, nc) :: x
  real, dimension (nr, nc) :: y
  real, dimension (nr*nc) :: t = [ (i,i=1,nr*nc) &
    ]
```

```
  integer :: r
  integer :: c

  x = reshape(t, (/nr,nc/), order=(/2,1/) )
  print *, ' Fortran calling C'
  print *, ' two d array as parameter'
  print *, ' using C 99 VLA'
  do r = 1, nr
    print 100, x(r, 1:nc)
100 format (10(f5.1))
  end do
  call reciprocal(nr, nc, x, y)
  do r = 1, nr
    print 110, y(r, 1:nc)
110 format (10(f6.3))
  end do
end program ch3508
```

Here is the C source.

```
void reciprocal(int nrow,int ncol,
  float matrix1[nrow][ncol],
  float matrix2[nrow][ncol])
{
  int i;
  int j;
  for (i=0;i<nrow;i++)
    for (j=0;j<ncol;j++)
      matrix2[i][j]=1.0f/matrix1[i][j];
}
```

In this example we are using the variable length array syntax that was introduced in the C 99 standard.

This feature is not supported in all C compilers.

This enables us to use the following syntax in C.

```
void reciprocal(int nrow,int ncol,
float matrix1[nrow][ncol],
float matrix2[nrow][ncol])
```

35.17   Example 9: Passing a Rank 2 Array from C to Fortran

Here is the Fortran source.

```
subroutine reciprocal(nr, nc, x, y) bind (c, &
  name='reciprocal')
  use iso_c_binding
  implicit none
  integer (c_int), value :: nr
  integer (c_int), value :: nc
  real (c_float), dimension (1:nr, 1:nc), &
    intent (in) :: x
  real (c_float), dimension (1:nr, 1:nc), &
    intent (out) :: y

  y = 1.0/x
end subroutine reciprocal
```

Here is the C source.

```c
#include <stdio.h>
void reciprocal(int nr,int nc,
                float x[nr][nc],
                float y[nr][nc]);
int main()
{
  const int nr=2;
  const int nc=5;
  float x[nr][nc];
  float y[nr][nc];
  int r;
  int c;
  int i=1;
  for (r=0;r<nr;r++)
    for (c=0;c<nc;c++)
    {
      x[r][c]=(float)(i);
      i++;
    }
  printf(" C calling Fortran\n");
  printf(" 2 d array as parameter\n");
  printf(" C99 vla\n");
  for (r=0;r<nr;r++)
  {
    for (c=0;c<nc;c++)
    {
      printf(" %5.2f " , x[r][c]);
    }
    printf("\n");
```

```
  }
  reciprocal(nr,nc,x,y);
  for (r=0;r<nr;r++)
  {
    for (c=0;c<nc;c++)
    {
      printf(" 1 / %5.2f = %6.3f \n"
, x[r][c],y[r][c]);
    }
    printf("\n");
  }
  return(0);
}
```

We use C99 VLAs in this example too.

35.18   Example 10: Passing a Rank 2 Array from C++ to Fortran

Here is the Fortran source.

```
subroutine reciprocal(nr, nc, x, y) bind (c, &
  name='reciprocal')
  use iso_c_binding
  implicit none
  integer (c_int), value :: nr
  integer (c_int), value :: nc
  real (c_float), dimension (1:nr, 1:nc), &
    intent (in) :: x
  real (c_float), dimension (1:nr, 1:nc), &
    intent (out) :: y

  y = 1.0/x
end subroutine reciprocal
```

Here is the C++ source.

```
#include <iostream>
using namespace std;
extern "C" void reciprocal(int nr,int nc,
                           float *x,float *y);
int main()
```

```
{
  const int nr=2;
  const int nc=5;
  float x[nr][nc];
  float y[nr][nc];
  int r;
  int c;
  int i=1;
  for (r=0;r<nr;r++)
    for (c=0;c<nc;c++)
    {
      x[r][c]=(float)(i);
      i++;
    }
  cout << " C++ calling Fortran" << endl;
  cout << " 2 d array as parameter\n";
  for (r=0;r<nr;r++)
  {
    for (c=0;c<nc;c++)
    {
      cout << " " << x[r][c] << " ";
    }
    cout << endl;
  }
  reciprocal(nr,nc,(float*)x,(float*)y);
  for (r=0;r<nr;r++)
  {
    for (c=0;c<nc;c++)
      cout << " 1 / " << x[r][c] << " = "
                << y[r][c] << endl;
  }
  return(0);
}
```

The key syntax in this example is

```
extern "C" void reciprocal(int nr,int nc,
float *x,float *y);
```

where we have to pass pointers to the two d arrays.

35.19 Example 11: Passing a Rank 2 Array from C++ to Fortran and Taking Care of Array Storage

Two dimensional arrays are stored by column in Fortran and by row in C++. In this example we take care of the array element ordering changes between C++ and Fortran. We handle the change in the Fortran subroutine.

Here is the C++ calling program.

```
#include <iostream>
#include <iomanip>
using namespace std;
extern "C" void sums(int nr,int nc,
  int *x,int *rsum, int *csum);
int main()
{
  const int nr=2;
  const int nc=6;
  int x[nr][nc];
  int rsum[nr];
  int csum[nc];
  int r;
  int c;
  int i=1;
  for (r=0;r<nr;r++)
    for (c=0;c<nc;c++)
    {
      x[r][c]=i;
      i++;
    }
  for (r=0;r<nr;r++)
    rsum[r]=0;
  for (c=0;c<nc;c++)
    csum[c]=0;
  cout << " C++ calling Fortran" << endl;
  cout << " 2 d array as parameter\n";
  cout << " Original 2 d array" << endl;
  cout << endl;
  for (r=0;r<nr;r++)
  {
    for (c=0;c<nc;c++)
    {
      cout << setw(3) << x[r][c] << " ";
    }
    cout << endl;
```

```
    }
    cout << endl;
    sums(nr,nc,(int*)x,rsum,csum);
    for (r=0;r<nr;r++)
    {
       for (c=0;c<nc;c++)
       {
          cout << setw(3) << x[r][c] << " ";
       }
       cout << " = " << rsum[r] << endl;
    }
    cout << endl;
    for (c=0;c<nc;c++)
       cout << setw(3) << csum[c] << " " ;
    cout << endl;
    return(0);
}
```

Here is the Fortran subroutine.

```
subroutine sums(nr, nc, x, rsum, csum) bind (c, &
   name='sums')
! g++ needs -lgfortran to link
   use iso_c_binding
   implicit none
   integer (c_int), value :: nr
   integer (c_int), value :: nc
   integer (c_int), dimension (1:nr, 1:nc), &
      intent (in) :: x
   integer (c_int), dimension (1:nr), &
      intent (out) :: rsum
   integer (c_int), dimension (1:nc), &
      intent (out) :: csum
   integer (c_int), dimension (1:nc, 1:nr) :: t

   t = reshape(x, (/nc,nr/) )
   rsum = sum(t, dim=1)
   csum = sum(t, dim=2)
end subroutine sums
```

The key syntax in the C++ code is shown below.

```
extern "C" void sums(int nr,int nc,
int *x,int *rsum, int *csum);
```

where all arrays are passed by address.

The key statements in the Fortran are

```
t=reshape(x,(/nc,nr/))
```

where we use the `reshape` intrinsic to transform from row storage to column storage.

The `reshape` intrinsic and the following statements

```
rsum=sum(t,dim=1)
csum=sum(t,dim=2)
```

show the power and expressiveness of array handling in Fortran compared to the C family of languages (C, C++, C# and Java).

Here is some sample output.

```
C++ calling Fortran
2 d array as parameter
Original 2 d array

 1   2   3   4    5    6
 7   8   9  10   11   12

 1   2   3   4    5    6  = 21
 7   8   9  10   11   12  = 57

 8  10  12  14   16   18
```

35.19.1 Compiler Switches

We now have to ensure that we include the necessary components of the Fortran run time system.

Here are details of how to make this work with the following compiler combinations.

```
gfortran and g++, openSuSe Linux and Windows

gfortran -c ch3511.f90 -o ch3511_f.o
g++          ch3511.cxx     ch3511_f.o -lgfortran


ifort and icc, openSuSe Linux
```

```
ifort  -c ch3511.f90 -o ch3511_f.o
icc       ch3511.cxx    ch3511_f.o


nagfor, openSuSe linux

nagfor -c ch3511.f90 -o ch3511_nag.o
nagfor    ch3511.cxx    ch3511_nag.o


sunf90 and sunCC, openSuSe Linux

sunf90 -c ch3511.f90 -o ch3511_f.o
sunCC     ch3512.cxx    ch3511_c.o -xlang=f90
```

35.20   Example 12: Passing a Rank 2 Array from C to Fortran and Taking Care of Array Storage

Two dimensional arrays are stored by column in Fortran and by row in C. In this example we take care of the array element ordering changes between C and Fortran. We handle the change in the Fortran subroutine.

Here is the C calling program.

```
#include <stdio.h>
void sums(int nr,int nc,int x[nr][nc],
  int * rsum, int * csum);
int main()
{
  const int nr=2;
  const int nc=6;
  int x[nr][nc];
  int rsum[nr];
  int csum[nc];
  int r;
  int c;
  int i=1;
  for (r=0;r<nr;r++)
    rsum[r]=0;
  for (c=0;c<nc;c++)
    csum[c]=0;
  for (r=0;r<nr;r++)
    for (c=0;c<nc;c++)
    {
      x[r][c]=i;
```

```
      i++;
    }
  printf(" C calling Fortran\n");
  printf(" 2 d array as parameter\n");
  printf(" c99 vla\n");
  for (r=0;r<nr;r++)
  {
    for (c=0;c<nc;c++)
    {
      printf(" %3d " , x[r][c]);
    }
    printf("\n");
  }
  printf("\n");
  sums(nr,nc,x,rsum,csum);
  for (r=0;r<nr;r++)
  {
    for (c=0;c<nc;c++)
    {
      printf(" %3d " , x[r][c]);
    }
    printf(" %3d ",rsum[r]);
    printf("\n");
  }
  printf("\n");
  for (c=0;c<nc;c++)
    printf(" %3d ",csum[c]);
  printf("\n");
  return(0);
}
```

Here is the Fortran subroutine.

```
subroutine sums(nr, nc, x, rsum, csum) bind (c, &
  name='sums')
! gcc requires -lgfortran
  use iso_c_binding
  implicit none
  integer (c_int), value :: nr
  integer (c_int), value :: nc
  integer (c_int), dimension (1:nr, 1:nc), &
    intent (in) :: x
  integer (c_int), dimension (1:nr), &
    intent (out) :: rsum
  integer (c_int), dimension (1:nc), &
```

```
   intent (out) :: csum
   integer (c_int), dimension (1:nc, 1:nr) :: t

   t = reshape(x, (/nc,nr/) )
   rsum = sum(t, dim=1)
   csum = sum(t, dim=2)
end subroutine sums
```

Here is some sample output.

```
C calling Fortran
2 d array as parameter
c99 vla
    1    2    3    4    5    6
    7    8    9   10   11   12

    1    2    3    4    5    6   21
    7    8    9   10   11   12   57

    8   10   12   14   16   18
```

35.20.1 Compiler Switches

In this example we are calling a Fortran subroutine from C++ and the subroutine calls the reshape intrinsic function.

We now have to ensure that we include the necessary components of the Fortran run time system.

Here are details of how to make this work with the following compiler combinations.

```
gfortran and gcc, openSuSe Linux and Windows

gfortran -c ch3512.f90 -o ch3512_f.o
gcc         ch3512.c       ch3512_f.o -lgfortran

ifort and icc, openSuSe Linux

ifort -c ch3512.f90 -o ch3512_f.o
icc        ch3512.c       ch3512_f.o

nagfor, openSuSe linux and Windows

nagfor -c ch3512.f90 -o ch3512_nag.o
```

```
nagfor     ch3512.c        ch3512_nag.o

sunf90 and sunc99, openSuSe Linux

sunf90 -c ch3512.f90 -o ch3512_f.o
sunc99 -c ch3512.c   -o ch3512_c.o
sunf90    ch3512_f.o    ch3512_c.o
```

35.21   Example 13: Passing a Fortran Character Variable to C

A Fortran character variable normally has a length type parameter. In this example we will pass a Fortran character variable to three C routines.

We use a module to provide functions that help convert from Fortran style character variables to C style character variables.

Here is the C source.

```c
#include <stdio.h>
#include <string.h>

void print_string(char * string)
{
  printf("                         %s\n",string);
}

void replace_string(char * string)
{
  strcpy(string,"Hello Hello");
}

void concatenate_string(char * string)
{
  strcat(string," Hello Hello");
}
```

Here is the Fortran source. The font size has been reduced to fit the page width.

```fortran
include 'c_interop_module.f90'

program ch3513

  use iso_c_binding

  use c_interop_module
```

```
implicit none

interface

   subroutine print_string(x)            bind (c, name='print_string')
     use iso_c_binding
     character (c_char) :: x(*)
   end subroutine print_string

   subroutine replace_string(x)          bind (c, name='replace_string')
     use iso_c_binding
     character (c_char)  :: x(*)
   end subroutine replace_string

   subroutine concatenate_string(x) bind (c, name='concatenate_string')
     use iso_c_binding
     character (c_char)  :: x(*)
   end subroutine concatenate_string

end interface

integer , parameter :: line_length=80

character ( len=line_length )                 ::   fortran_string
character ( len=line_length , kind=c_char ) :: c_string

fortran_string = 'Hello'
c_string       = f_to_c(fortran_string)

print *, ' print_string '
call print_string( c_string )

fortran_string = 'Hello'
c_string       = f_to_c(fortran_string)

print *, ' replace_string '
call replace_string( c_string )
fortran_string = c_to_f( c_string )
print *, ' After                 ' , fortran_string

fortran_string = 'Hello'
c_string       = f_to_c(fortran_string)

print *, ' concatenate_string '
call concatenate_string( c_string )
fortran_string = c_to_f( c_string )
print *, ' After                 ' , fortran_string

end program ch3513
```

Here is the module that has the functions that help converting from Fortran style string variables to C style string variables.

```
module c_interop_module

use iso_c_binding
```

```
implicit none

integer , parameter :: n=80

contains

  function f_to_c(fortran_string)
    implicit none
    character (len=n,kind=c_char) :: f_to_c
    character (len=n)             :: fortran_string
    integer :: f_length
    f_length = len_trim(fortran_string)
    if (f_length >= n) then
      f_length = 79
    end if
    f_to_c = fortran_string(1:f_length) // c_null_char
  end function f_to_c

  function c_to_f(c_string)
    implicit none
    character (len=n)             :: c_to_f
    character (len=n,kind=c_char) :: c_string
    integer :: c_length
    integer :: i
    c_length = 1
    c_to_f = ' '
    do i=1,n
      if ( c_string(i:i) == c_null_char ) exit
      c_length = c_length +1
    end do
    c_length = c_length -1
    c_to_f = c_string(1:c_length)
  end function c_to_f

end module c_interop_module
```

Here is the sample output.

```
print_string
                Hello
replace_string
After           Hello Hello
concatenate_string
After           Hello Hello Hello
```

35.22 Example 14: Passing a Fortran Character Variable to C++

This is a C++ version of the previous one.

Here is the Fortran source. The font size has been reduced to fit the page width.

```fortran
include 'c_interop_module.f90'

program ch3514

  use iso_c_binding

  use c_interop_module

  implicit none

  interface

    subroutine print_string(x)        bind (c, name='print_string')
      use iso_c_binding
      character (c_char) :: x(*)
    end subroutine print_string

    subroutine replace_string(x)      bind (c, name='replace_string')
      use iso_c_binding
      character (c_char)  :: x(*)
    end subroutine replace_string

    subroutine concatenate_string(x) bind (c, name='concatenate_string')
      use iso_c_binding
      character (c_char)  :: x(*)
    end subroutine concatenate_string

  end interface

  integer , parameter :: line_length=80

  character ( len=line_length )                :: fortran_string
  character ( len=line_length , kind=c_char ) :: c_string

  fortran_string = 'Hello'
  c_string       = f_to_c(fortran_string)

  print *, ' print_string '
  call print_string( c_string )

  fortran_string = 'Hello'
  c_string       = f_to_c(fortran_string)

  print *, ' replace_string '
  call replace_string( c_string )
  fortran_string = c_to_f( c_string )
  print *, ' After             ' , fortran_string
```

```
  fortran_string = 'Hello'
  c_string       = f_to_c(fortran_string)

  print *, ' concatenate_string '
  call concatenate_string( c_string )
  fortran_string = c_to_f( c_string )
  print *, ' After                 ' , fortran_string

end program ch3514
```

Here is the C++ source.

```
#include <cstring>
#include <cstdio>

using namespace std;

extern "C"
{
void print_string(char *);
}

extern "C"
{
void replace_string(char *);
}

extern "C"
{
void concatenate_string(char *);
}

void print_string(char * string)
{
  printf("                          %s\n",string);
}

void replace_string(char * string)
{
  strcpy(string,"Hello Hello");
}

void concatenate_string(char * string)
{
  strcat(string," Hello Hello");
}
```

We use the same module.
Here is the sample output.

```
print_string
                        Hello
replace_string
After               Hello Hello
concatenate_string
After               Hello Hello Hello
```

35.23   **c_loc Examples on Our Web Site**

We have examples of using the c_loc function on our web site for both 32 bit and 64 bit operating systems.

```
https://www.fortranplus.co.uk/
```

Here is some background technical information on c_loc from the Fortran 2008 standard.

35.23.1   *c_loc(x) Description*

Description: Returns the C address of the argument.
   Class: Inquiry function.
   Argument: x shall either

- (1) have interoperable type and type parameters and be

  - (a) a variable that has the target attribute and is interoperable,
  - (b) an allocated allocatable variable that has the target attribute and is not an array of zero size, or
  - (c) an associated scalar pointer, or

- (2) be a nonpolymorphic scalar, have no length type parameters, and be

  - (a) a nonallocatable, nonpointer variable that has the target attribute,
  - (b) an allocated allocatable variable that has the target attribute, or
  - (c) an associated pointer.

   Result Characteristics: Scalar of type c_ptr.
   Result Value: The result value will be described using the result name cptr.

- (1) If x is a scalar data entity, the result is determined as if c_ptr were a derived type containing a scalar pointer component px of the type and type parameters of x and the pointer assignment

```
cptr%px => x
```

were executed.
- (2) If x is an array data entity, the result is determined as if c_ptr were a derived type containing a scalar pointer component px of the type and type parameters of x and the pointer assignment of cptr%px to the first element of x were executed.

If x is a data entity that is interoperable or has interoperable type and type parameters, the result is the value that the C processor returns as the result of applying the unary & operator (as defined in the C International Standard, 6.5.3.2) to the target of cptr

The result is a value that can be used as an actual cptr argument in a call to c_f_pointer where fptr has attributes that would allow the pointer assignment

```
fptr => x
```

Such a call to c_f_pointer shall have the effect of the pointer assignment

```
fptr => x
```

NOTE 15.6 - Where the actual argument is of noninteroperable type or type parameters, the result of c_loc provides an opaque "handle" for it. In an actual implementation, this handle may be the C address of the argument; however, portable C functions should treat it as a void (generic) C pointer that cannot be dereferenced (6.5.3.2 in the C International Standard).

The key issues are that we must take care with the argument to the function, the return value is of type c_ptr, and that this is an opaque type. Let us now look at some examples using this function.

Bibliography

Standardized Mixed Language Programming for Fortran and C, Bo Einarsson, Richard J. Hanson and Tim Hopkins. Fortran Forum, Volume 28, Number 3, December 2009.
The C VLA information was taken from the standard.
ISO/IEC 9899:2011, Programming languages C. The official standard.

```
http://www.iso.org/iso/iso_catalogue/
catalogue_tc/catalogue_detail.htm?csnumber=57853
```

Harbison S.P., Steele G.L., A C Reference Manual, Prentice-Hall, 2002.

Kernighan B.W., Ritchie D.M., The C programming Language, Prentice-Hall; first edition 1978; second edition 1988.

Both of the following texts cover C++11.

Josuttis N.M., The C++ Standard Library, second edition, Addison Wesley, 2012.

Stroustrup B., The C++ Programming Language, 4th edition, Addison Wesley, 2013.

ISO/IEC 14882:2011, Programming Languages - C++.

```
http://www.iso.org/iso/home/store/catalogue_ics/
   catalogue_detail_ics.htm?csnumber=50372
```

35.24   Problem

35.1 Compile and run the example programs in this chapter with your compiler and examine the output.

Acknowledgements Thanks to Steve Clamage of Oracle and Themos Tsikas of Nag for technical advice with some of C interop examples.

Chapter 36
IEEE Arithmetic

*Any effectively generated theory capable of expressing
elementary arithmetic cannot be both consistent and complete.
In particular, for any consistent, effectively generated formal
theory that proves certain basic arithmetic truths, there is an
arithmetical statement that is true, but not provable in the theory.*
Godel, First incompleteness theorem

Aims

The aims of this chapter are to look in more depth at arithmetic and in particular at
the support that Fortran provides for the IEEE 754 and later standards. There is a
coverage of:

- hardware support for arithmetic.
- integer formats.
- floating point formats: single and double.
- special values: denormal, infinity and not a number — nan.
- exceptions and flags: divide by zero, inexact, invalid, overflow, underflow.

36.1 Introduction

The literature contains details of the IEEE arithmetic standards. The bibliography
contains details of a number of printed and on-line sources.

36.2 History

When we use programming languages to do arithmetic two major concerns are the
ability to develop reliable and portable numerical software. Arithmetic is done in
hardware and there are a number of things to consider:

© Springer International Publishing AG, part of Springer Nature 2018   665
I. Chivers and J. Sleightholme, *Introduction to Programming with Fortran*,
https://doi.org/10.1007/978-3-319-75502-1_36

- the range of hardware available both now and in the past.
- the evolution of hardware.

There has been a very considerable change in arithmetic units since the first computers. Table 36.1 is a list of hardware and computing systems that the authors have used or have heard of. It is not exhaustive or definitive, but rather reflects the authors' age and experience.

Table 36.1 Computer hardware and manufacturers

CDC	Cray	IBM	ICL
Fujitsu	DEC	Compaq	Gateway
Sun	Silicon graphics	Hewlett Packard	Data general
Harris	Honeywell	Elliot	Mostek
National semiconductors	Intel	Zilog	Motorola
Signetics	Amdahl	Texas instruments	Cyrix
AMD	NEC		

Table 36.2 lists some of the operating systems.

Table 36.2 Operating systems

NOS	NOS/BE	Kronos	UNIX
VMS	Dos	Windows 3.x	Windows 95
Windows 98	Windows NT	Windows 2000	Windows XP
Windows vista	Windows 7.x	Windows 8.x	MVS
VM	VM/CMS	CP/M	Macintosh
OS/2	Linux (too many)		

Again the list is not exhaustive or definitive. The intention is simply to provide some idea of the wide range of hardware, computer manufacturers and operating systems that have been around in the past 50 years.

To cope with the anarchy in this area Doctor Robert Stewart (acting on behalf of the IEEE) convened a meeting which led to the birth of IEEE 754.

The first draft, which was prepared by William Kahan, Jerome Coonen and Harold Stone, was called the KCS draft and eventually adopted as IEEE 754. A fascinating account of the development of this standard can be found in An Interview with the Old Man of Floating Point, and the bibliography provides a web address for this interview. Kahan went on to get the ACM Turing Award in 1989 for his work in this area.

This has become a de facto standard amongst arithmetic units in modern hardware. Note that it is not possible to describe precisely the answers a program will give, and the authors of the standard knew this. This goal is virtually impossible to achieve when one considers floating point arithmetic. Reasons for this include:

- the conversions of numbers between decimal and binary formats.
- the use of elementary library functions.
- results of calculations may be in hardware inaccessible to the programmer.
- intermediate results in subexpressions or arguments to procedures.

The bibliography contains details of a paper that addresses this issue in much greater depth — Differences Among IEEE 754 Implementations.

Fortran is one of a small number of languages that provides access to IEEE arithmetic, and it achieves this via TR1880 which is an integral part of Fortran 2003. The C standard (C9X) addresses this issue and Java offers limited IEEE arithmetic support. More information can be found in the references at the end of the chapter.

36.3 IEEE Specifications

There have been several IEEE arithmetic standards. The following information is taken from the ISO site.

The url is

```
https://www.iso.org/standard/57469.html
```

ISO/IEC/IEEE 60559:2011(E) specifies formats and methods for floating-point arithmetic in computer systems - standard and extended functions with single, double, extended, and extendable precision and recommends formats for data interchange. Exception conditions are defined and standard handling of these conditions is specified. It provides a method for computation with floating-point numbers that will yield the same result whether the processing is done in hardware, software, or a combination of the two. The results of the computation will be identical, independent of implementation, given the same input data. Errors, and error conditions, in the mathematical processing will be reported in a consistent manner regardless of implementation. This first edition, published as ISO/IEC/IEEE 60559, replaces the second edition of IEC 60559.

Here is the standard history.

- ISO/IEC/IEEE 60559:2011(E)
- IEC 559:1989
- IEC 559:1982

The standard provides coverage of the following areas, which is taken from the table of contents.

- Floating-point formats

  - Overview
  - Specification levels

  - Sets of floating-point data
  - Binary interchange format encodings
  - Decimal interchange format encodings
  - Interchange format parameters
  - Extended and extendable precisions

- Attributes and rounding

  - Attribute specification
  - Dynamic modes for attributes
  - Rounding-direction attributes

- Operations

  - Overview
  - Decimal exponent calculation
  - Homogeneous general-computational operations
  - Format of general-computational operations
  - Quiet-computational operations
  - Signaling-computational operations
  - Non-computational operations
  - Details of conversions from floating-point to integer formats
  - Details of operations to round a floating-point datum to integral value
  - Details of totalorder predicate
  - Details of comparison predicates
  - Details of conversion between floating-point data and external character sequences

- Infinity, NaNs, and sign bit

  - Infinity arithmetic
  - Operations with NaNs
  - The sign bit

- Default exception handling

  - Overview: exceptions and flags
  - Invalid operation
  - Division by zero
  - Overflow
  - Underflow
  - Inexact

- Alternate exception handling attributes

  - Overview
  - Resuming alternate exception handling attributes
  - Immediate and delayed alternate exception handling attributes

- Recommended operations

  - Conforming language- and implementation-defined functions
  - Recommended correctly rounded functions
  - Operations on dynamic modes for attributes
  - Reduction operations

- Expression evaluation

  - Expression evaluation rules
  - Assignments, parameters, and function values
  - preferred width attributes for expression evaluation
  - Literal meaning and value-changing optimizations

- Reproducible floating-point results

36.4 Floating Point Formats

Table 36.3 summarises the formats specified in the IEEE 754-2008 standard.

Table 36.3 IEEE formats

Name	Common name	Base	Digits	Decimal digits	Exponent bits	Decimal E max	Exponent bias[1]	E min E min	
Binary16	Half precision	2	11	3.31	5	4.51	2**4−1 = 15	−14 +15	[2]
Binary32	Single precision	2	24	7.22	8	38.23	2**7−1 = 127	−126 +127	
Binary64	Double precision	2	53	15.95	11	307.95	2**10−1 = 1023	−1022 +1023	
Binary128	Quadruple precision	2	113	34.02	15	4931.77	2**14−1 = 16383	−16382 +16383	
Binary256	Octuple precision	2	237	71.34	19	78913.2	2**18−1 = 262143	−262142 +262143	[2]
Decimal32		10	7	7	7.58	96	101	−95 +96	[2]
Decimal64		10	16	16	9.58	384	398	−383 +384	
Decimal128		10	34	34	13.58	6144	6176	−6143 +6144	

36.5 Procedure Summary

Tables 36.4 and 36.5 summarise the procedures.

Table 36.4   IEEE Arithmetic module procedure summary

Procedure arguments	Class	Description
IEEE_CLASS(X)	E	Classify number
IEEE_COPY_SIGN(X,Y)	E	Copy sign
IEEE_FMA(A,B,C)	E	Fused multiply-add operation
IEEE_GET_ROUNDING_MODE	S	Get rounding mode
(ROUND_VALUE[,RADIX])	S	Get rounding mode
IEEE_GET_UNDERFLOW_MODE	S	Get underflow mode
(GRADUAL)	S	Get underflow mode
IEEE_INT(A,ROUND[, KIND])	E	Conversion to integer type
IEEE_IS_FINITE(X)	E	Whether a value is finite
IEEE_IS_NAN(X)	E	Whether a value is an IEEE NaN
IEEE_IS_NEGATIVE(X)	E	Whether a value is negative
IEEE_IS_NORMAL(X)	E	Whether a value is a normal number
IEEE_LOGB(X)	E	Exponent
IEEE_MAX_NUM(X,Y)	E	Maximum numeric value
IEEE_MAX_NUM_MAG(X,Y)	E	Maximum magnitude numeric value
IEEE_MIN_NUM(X,Y)	E	Minimum numeric value
IEEE_MIN_NUM_MAG(X,Y)	E	Minimum magnitude numeric value
IEEE_NEXT_AFTER(X,Y)	E	Adjacent machine number
IEEE_NEXT_DOWN(X)	E	Adjacent lower machine number
IEEE_NEXT_UP(X)	E	Adjacent higher machine number
IEEE_QUIET_EQ(A,B)	E	Quiet compares equal
IEEE_QUIET_GE(A,B)	E	Quiet compares greater than or equal
IEEE_QUIET_GT(A,B)	E	Quiet compares greater than
IEEE_QUIET_LE(A,B)	E	Quiet compares less than or equal
IEEE_QUIET_LT(A,B)	E	Quiet compares less than
IEEE_QUIET_NE(A,B)	E	Quiet compares not equal
IEEE_REAL(A[,KIND])	E	Conversion to real type
IEEE_REM(X,Y)	E	Exact remainder
IEEE_RINT(X)	E	Round to integer
IEEE_SCALB(X,I)	E	X 2I
IEEE_SELECTED_REAL_KIND	T	IEEE kind type parameter value
([P,R,RADIX])	S	IEEE kind type parameter value
IEEE_SET_ROUNDING_MODE	S	Set
(ROUND_VALUE[,RADIX])	S	Set
IEEE_SET_UNDERFLOW_MODE	S	Set underflow mode
(GRADUAL)	S	Set underflow mode
IEEE_SIGNALING_EQ(A,B)	E	Signaling compares equal
IEEE_SIGNALING_GE(A,B)	E	Signaling compares greater than or equal
IEEE_SIGNALING_GT(A,B)	E	Signaling compares greater than
IEEE_SIGNALING_LE(A,B)	E	Signaling compares less than or equal
IEEE_SIGNALING_LT(A,B)	E	Signaling compares less than
IEEE_SIGNALING_NE(A,B)	E	Signaling compares not equal
IEEE_SIGNBIT(X)	E	Test sign bit
IEEE_SUPPORT_DATATYPE([X])	I	Query IEEE arithmetic support
IEEE_SUPPORT_DENORMAL([X])	I	Query subnormal number support
IEEE_SUPPORT_DIVIDE([X])	I	Query IEEE division support
IEEE_SUPPORT_INF([X])	I	Query IEEE infinity support
IEEE_SUPPORT_IO([X])	I	Query IEEE formatting support
IEEE_SUPPORT_NAN([X])	I	Query IEEE NaN support
IEEE_SUPPORT_ROUNDING	T	Query IEEE rounding support
(ROUND_VALUE[,X])	T	Query IEEE rounding support

Table 36.4 (continued)

Procedure Arguments	Class	Description
IEEE_SUPPORT_SQRT([X])	I	Query IEEE square root support
IEEE_SUPPORT_SUBNORMAL([X])	I	Query subnormal number support
IEEE_SUPPORT_STANDARD([X])	I	Query IEEE standard support
IEEE_SUPPORT_UNDERFLOW	I	Query underflow control support
_CONTROL([X])	I	Query underflow control support
IEEE_UNORDERED(X,Y)	E	Whether two values are unordered
IEEE_VALUE(X,CLASS)	E	Return number in a class

Table 36.5 IEEE Exceptions module procedure summary

Procedure	Arguments	Class	Description
IEEE_GET_FLAG	(FLAG,FLAG_VALUE)	ES	Get an exception flag
IEEE_GET_HALTING_MODE	(FLAG,HALTING)	ES	Get a halting mode
IEEE_GET_MODES	(MODES)	S	Get floating-point modes
IEEE_GET_STATUS	(STATUS_VALUE)	S	Get floating-point status
IEEE_SET_FLAG	(FLAG,FLAG_VALUE)	PS	Set an exception flag
IEEE_SET_HALTING_MODE	(FLAG,HALTING)	PS	Set a halting mode
IEEE_SET_MODES	(MODES)	S	Set floating-point modes
IEEE_SET_STATUS	(STATUS_VALUE)	S	Restore floating-point status
IEEE_SUPPORT_FLAG	(FLAG [,X])	T	Query exception support
IEEE_SUPPORT_HALTING	(FLAG)	T	Query halting mode support

36.6   General Comments About the Standard

The special bit patterns provide the following:

- +0
- −0
- subnormal numbers in the range 1.17549421E-38 to 1.40129846E-45
- +∞
- −∞
- quiet NaN (Not a Number)
- signalling NaN

One of the first systems that the authors worked with that had special bit patterns set aside was the CDC 6000 range of computers that had negative indefinite and infinity. Thus the ideas are not new, as this was in the late 1970s.

The support of positive and negative zero means that certain problems can be handled correctly including:

- The evaluation of the log function which has a discontinuity at zero.
- The equation $\sqrt{1/z} = 1/z$ can be solved when $z = -1$

See also the Kahan paper *Branch Cuts for complex Elementary functions, or Much Ado About Nothing's Sign Bit* for more details.

Subnormals, which permit gradual underflow, fill the gap between 0 and the smallest normal number.

Simply stated underflow occurs when the result of an arithmetic operation is so small that it is subject to a larger than normal rounding error when stored. The existence of subnormals means that greater precision is available with these small numbers than with normal numbers. The key features of gradual underflow are:

- When underflow does occur there should never be a loss of accuracy any greater than that from ordinary roundoff.
- The operations of addition, subtraction, comparison and remainder are always exact.
- Algorithms written to take advantage of subnormal numbers have smaller error bounds than other systems.
- if x and y are within a factor of 2 then x-y is error free, which is used in a number of algorithms that increase the precision at critical regions.

The combination of positive and negative zero and subnormal numbers means that when x and y are small and x-y has been flushed to zero the evaluation of $1/(x - y)$ can be flagged and located.

Certain arithmetic operations cause problems including:

- $0 * \infty$
- $0/0$
- $\sqrt{x}$ when $x < 0$

and the support for NaN handles these cases.

The support for positive and negative infinity allows the handling of $x/0$ when x is nonzero and of either sign, and the outcome of this means that we write our programs to take the appropriate action. In some cases this would mean recalculating using another approach.

For more information see the references in the bibliography.

36.7   Resume

The above has provided a quick tour of the IEEE standard. We'll now look at what Fortran has to offer to support it.

36.8 Fortran Support for IEEE Arithmetic

Fortran first introduced support for IEEE arithmetic in ISO TR 15580. The Fortran 2003 standard integrated support into the main standard. Fortran 2018 offers more support, and for more details one should consult Chap. 17 of that document.

The intrinsic modules

- `ieee_features`
- `ieee_exceptions`
- `ieee_arithmetic`

provide support for exceptions and IEEE arithmetic. Whether the modules are provided is processor dependent. If the module `ieee_features` is provided, which of the named constants defined in this standard are included is processor dependent. The module `ieee_arithmetic` behaves as if it contained a `use` statement for `ieee_exceptions`; everything that is public in `ieee_exceptions` is public in `ieee_arithmetic`.

The first thing to consider is the degree of conformance to the IEEE standard. It is possible that not all of the features are supported. Thus the first thing to do is to run one or more test programs to determine the degree of support for a particular system.

36.9 Derived Types and Constants Defined in the Modules

The modules

- `ieee_exceptions`
- `ieee_arithmetic`
- `ieee_features`

define five derived types, whose components are all private.

36.9.1 *ieee_exceptions*

This module defines `ieee_flag_type`, for identifying a particular exception flag.
Possible values are

```
ieee_invalid
ieee_overflow
ieee_divide_by_zero
ieee_underflow
ieee_inexact
```

The module also defines the array named constants

```
ieee_usual = (/ ieee_overflow,
   ieee_divide_by_zero, ieee_invalid /)
```

```
ieee_all = (/ ieee_usual, ieee_underflow,
                ieee_inexact /)
```

```
ieee_status_type
```

The last is for saving the current floating point status.

36.9.2 *ieee_arithmetic*

This module defines `ieee_class_type`, for identifying a class of floating-point values.
   Possible values are:

```
ieee_signalling_nan
ieee_quiet_nan
ieee_negative_inf
ieee_negative_normal
ieee_negative_denormal
ieee_negative_zero
ieee_positive_zero
ieee_positive_denormal
ieee_positive_normal
ieee_positive_inf
ieee_other_value
```

The module defines `ieee_round_type`, for identifying a particular rounding mode. Its only possible values are those of named constants defined in the module: `ieee_nearest`, `ieee_to_zero`, `ieee_up`, and `ieee_down` for the `ieee_modes`; and `ieee_other` for any other mode.
   The elemental operator `==` for two values of one of these types to return true if the values are the same and false otherwise.
   The elemental operator `/=` for two values of one of these types to return true if the values differ and false otherwise.

36.9.3   `ieee_features`

This module defines `ieee_features_type`, for expressing the need for particular `ieee_features`. Its only possible values are those of named constants defined in the module:

- `ieee_datatype`
- `ieee_denormal`
- `ieee_divide`
- `ieee_halting`
- `ieee_inexact_flag`
- `ieee_inf`
- `ieee_invalid_flag`
- `ieee_nan`
- `ieee_rounding`
- `ieee_sqrt`
- `ieee_underflow_flag`

36.9.4   *Further Information*

There are a number of additional sources of information.

- the Fortran standard.
- documentation that comes with your compiler.

  The latter has the benefit of describing what is supported in that compiler.

36.10   Example 1: Testing IEEE Support

The first examples test basic IEEE arithmetic support.
  Here is a program to illustrate the above.

```
include 'precision_module.f90'

program ch3601

  use precision_module
  use ieee_arithmetic

  implicit none

  real (sp) :: x = 1.0
```

```
real (dp) :: y = 1.0_dp
real (qp) :: z = 1.0_qp

if (ieee_support_datatype(x)) then
  print *, '  32 bit IEEE support'
end if
if (ieee_support_datatype(y)) then
  print *, '  64 bit IEEE support'
end if
if (ieee_support_datatype(z)) then
  print *, ' 128 bit IEEE support'
end if

end program ch3601
```

Table 36.6 summarises the support for a number of compilers.

Table 36.6 Compiler IEEE support for various precisions

Precision	gfortran	intel	nag	sun
32 bit IEEE support	Yes	Yes	Yes	Yes
64 bit IEEE support	Yes	Yes	Yes	Yes
128 bit IEEE support	No	Yes	No	Yes

36.11   Example 2: Testing What Flags Are Supported

Here is a program to illustrate the above.

```
include 'precision_module.f90'

program ch3602

  use precision_module
  use ieee_arithmetic

  implicit none

  real (sp) :: x = 1.0
```

```
   real (dp) :: y = 1.0_dp
   real (qp) :: z = 1.0_qp

   integer :: i

   character *20, dimension (5) :: flags = (/ &
     'IEEE_DIVIDE_BY_ZERO ', &
     'IEEE_INEXACT        ', &
     'IEEE_INVALID        ', &
     'IEEE_OVERFLOW       ', &
     'IEEE_UNDERFLOW      ' /)

   do i = 1, 5
     if (ieee_support_flag(ieee_all(i),x)) then
       write (unit=*, fmt=100) flags(i)
100    format (a20, ' 32 bit support')
     end if
     if (ieee_support_flag(ieee_all(i),y)) then
       write (unit=*, fmt=110) flags(i)
110    format (a20, ' 64 bit support')

     end if
     if (ieee_support_flag(ieee_all(i),z)) then
       write (unit=*, fmt=120) flags(i)
120    format (a20, '128 bit support')
     end if
   end do

end program ch3602
```

Here is the output from the Intel compiler.

```
IEEE_DIVIDE_BY_ZERO  32 bit support
IEEE_DIVIDE_BY_ZERO  64 bit support
IEEE_DIVIDE_BY_ZERO 128 bit support
IEEE_INEXACT         32 bit support
IEEE_INEXACT         64 bit support
IEEE_INEXACT        128 bit support
IEEE_INVALID         32 bit support
IEEE_INVALID         64 bit support
IEEE_INVALID        128 bit support
IEEE_OVERFLOW        32 bit support
IEEE_OVERFLOW        64 bit support
IEEE_OVERFLOW       128 bit support
IEEE_UNDERFLOW       32 bit support
```

```
IEEE_UNDERFLOW              64 bit support
IEEE_UNDERFLOW             128 bit support
```

36.12   Example 3: Overflow

Here is a program to illustrate the above.

```
program ch3603

  use ieee_arithmetic

  implicit none
  integer :: i
  real :: x = 1.0
  logical :: overflow_happened = .false.

  if (ieee_support_datatype(x)) then
    print *, &
      ' IEEE support for default precision'
  end if

  do i = 1, 50
    if (overflow_happened) then
      print *, ' overflow occurred '
      print *, ' program terminates'
      stop 20
    else
      print 100, i, x
100   format (' ', i3, ' ', e12.4)
    end if
    x = x*10.0
    call ieee_get_flag(ieee_overflow, &
      overflow_happened)
  end do
end program ch3603
```

36.13   Example 4: Underflow

Here is a program to illustrate the above.

```
program ch3604

  use ieee_arithmetic

  implicit none
  integer :: i
  real :: x = 1.0
  logical :: underflow_happened = .false.

  if (ieee_support_datatype(x)) then
    print *, ' IEEE arithmetic '
    print *, &
      ' is supported for default precision'
  end if

  do i = 1, 50
    if (underflow_happened) then
      print *, ' underflow occurred '
      print *, ' program terminates'
      stop 20
    else
      print 100, i, x
100   format (' ', i3, ' ', e12.4)
    end if
    x = x/10.0
    call ieee_get_flag(ieee_underflow, &
      underflow_happened)
  end do
end program ch3604
```

36.14   Example 5: Inexact Summation

Here is a program to illustrate the above.

```
program ch3605

  use ieee_arithmetic
  implicit none

  integer :: i
  real :: computed_sum
  real :: real_sum
```

```fortran
      integer :: array_size

      logical :: inexact_happened = .false.
      integer :: allocate_status

      character *13, dimension (3) :: heading = (/ &
         '   10,000,000', '  100,000,000', &
         '1,000,000,000' /)

      real, allocatable, dimension (:) :: x

      if (ieee_support_datatype(x)) then
        print *, &
          ' IEEE support for default precision'
      end if

!                10,000,000

      array_size = 10000000

      do i = 1, 3
        write (unit=*, fmt=100) array_size, &
          heading(i)
100   format (' Array size = ', i15, 2x, a13)
        allocate (x(1:array_size), stat= &
          allocate_status)
        if (allocate_status/=0) then
          print *, ' Allocate fails, program ends'
          stop
        end if
        x = 1.0
        computed_sum = sum(x)
        call ieee_get_flag(ieee_inexact, &
          inexact_happened)
        real_sum = array_size*1.0
        write (unit=*, fmt=110) computed_sum
110   format (' Computed sum = ', e12.4)
        write (unit=*, fmt=120) real_sum
120   format (' Real sum     = ', e12.4)
        if (inexact_happened) then
          print *, ' inexact arithmetic'
          print *, ' in the summation'
          print *, ' program terminates'
          stop 20
        end if
```

```
   deallocate (x)
   array_size = array_size*10
 end do

end program ch3605
```

Here is the output from several compilers.

```
gfortran
```

```
 IEEE support for default precision
 Array size =          10000000      10,000,000
 Computed sum =   0.1000E+08
 Real sum     =   0.1000E+08
 Array size =         100000000     100,000,000
 Computed sum =   0.1000E+09
 Real sum     =   0.1000E+09
  inexact arithmetic
  in the summation
  program terminates
```

```
Intel
```

```
 IEEE support for default precision
 Array size =          10000000      10,000,000
 Computed sum =   0.1000E+08
 Real sum     =   0.1000E+08
 Array size =         100000000     100,000,000
 Computed sum =   0.1000E+09
 Real sum     =   0.1000E+09
  inexact arithmetic
  in the summation
  program terminates
```

```
nag
```

```
 IEEE support for default precision
 Array size =          10000000      10,000,000
 Computed sum =   0.1000E+08
 Real sum     =   0.1000E+08
 Array size =         100000000     100,000,000
 Computed sum =   0.1678E+08
 Real sum     =   0.1000E+09
  inexact arithmetic
```

```
  in the summation
  program terminates


sun/oracle

  IEEE support for default precision
  Array size =            10000000      10,000,000
  Computed sum =     0.1000E+08
  Real sum      =     0.1000E+08
  Array size =           100000000     100,000,000
  Computed sum =     0.1678E+08
  Real sum      =     0.1000E+09
   inexact arithmetic
   in the summation
   program terminates
```

What do you notice about the value of the computed sum?

36.15   Example 6: NAN and Other Specials

Here is a program to illustrate some additional IEEE functionality.

```
program ch3606

  use precision_module
  use ieee_arithmetic
  implicit none

  real (sp) :: x0 = 0.0
  real (dp) :: y0 = 0.0_dp
  real (qp) :: z0 = 0.0_qp

  real (sp) :: x1 = 1.0
  real (dp) :: y1 = 1.0_dp
  real (qp) :: z1 = 1.0_qp

  real (sp) :: xnan = 1.0
  real (dp) :: ynan = 1.0_dp
  real (qp) :: znan = 1.0_qp

  real (sp) :: xinfinite = 1.0
  real (dp) :: yinfinite = 1.0_dp
```

```
      real (qp) :: zinfinite = 1.0_qp

      xinfinite = x1/x0
      yinfinite = y1/y0
      zinfinite = z1/z0
      xnan = x0/x0
      ynan = y0/y0
      znan = z0/z0

      if (ieee_support_datatype(x1)) then
        print *, '  32 bit IEEE support'
        print *, '     inf ', ieee_support_inf(x1)
        print *, '     nan ', ieee_support_nan(x1)
        print *, ' 1/0 finite', ieee_is_finite( &
          xinfinite)
        print *, ' 0/0 nan', ieee_is_nan(xnan)
      end if

      if (ieee_support_datatype(y1)) then
        print *, '  64 bit IEEE support'
        print *, '     inf ', ieee_support_inf(y1)
        print *, '     nan ', ieee_support_nan(y1)
        print *, ' 1/0 finite', ieee_is_finite( &
          yinfinite)
        print *, ' 0/0 nan', ieee_is_nan(ynan)
      end if
      if (ieee_support_datatype(z1)) then
        print *, ' 128 bit IEEE support'
        print *, '     inf ', ieee_support_inf(z1)
        print *, '     nan ', ieee_support_nan(z1)
        print *, ' 1/0 finite', ieee_is_finite( &
          zinfinite)
        print *, ' 0/0 nan', ieee_is_nan(znan)
      end if

  end program ch3606
```

36.16 Summary

Compiler support in this area is now quite widespread as the above examples have
shown.

36.17   Bibliography

Hauser J.R., Handling Floating Point Exceptions in Numeric programs, ACM Trans-action on programming Languages and Systems, Vol. 18, No. 2, March 1996, pp. 139–174.

- The paper looks at a number of techniques for handling floating point exceptions in numeric code. One of the conclusions is for better structured support for floating point exception handling in new programming languages, or of course better standards for existing languages.

  IEEE, IEEE Standard for Binary Floating-Point Arithmetic, ANSI/IEEE Std 754-2008, Institute of Electrical and Electronic Engineers Inc.

- The formal definition of IEEE 754. This is available for purchase as both a pdf and printed version - see the address below.

```
http://www.techstreet.com/standards/
IEEE/754_2008?product_id=1745167
```

This standard specifies formats and methods for floating-point arithmetic in computer systems: standard and extended functions with single, double, extended, and extendable precision, and recommends formats for data interchange. Exception conditions are defined and standard handling of these conditions is specified. Keywords: 754-2008, arithmetic, binary, computer, decimal, exponent, floating-point, format, interchange, NaN,number, rounding, significand, subnormal. Product Code(s): STDPD95802,STD95802

Knuth D., Seminumerical Algorithms, Addison-Wesley, 1969.

- There is a coverage of floating point arithmetic, multiple precision arithmetic, radix conversion and rational arithmetic.

  Sun, Numerical Computation Guide, SunPro.

- Very good coverage of the numeric formats for IEEE Standard 754 for Binary Floating-Point Arithmetic. All SunPro compiler products support the features of the IEEE 754 standard.

36.17.1   Web-Based Sources

- Differences Among IEEE 754 Implementations. The material in this paper will eventually be included in the Sun Numerical Computation Guide as an addendum to Appendix C, David Goldberg's What Every Computer Scientist Should Know about Floating Point Arithmetic.

```
http://docs.oracle.com/cd/
E19422-01/819-3693/819-3693.pdf
https://docs.oracle.com/en/
```

- The Numerical Computation Guide can be browsed on-line or downloaded as a pdf file. The last time we checked it was 294 pages. Good source of information if you have Sun equipment.

```
http://www-users.math.umn.edu/
~arnold/disasters/ariane.html
```

- The Explosion of the Ariane 5: A 64-bit floating point number relating to the horizontal velocity of the rocket with respect to the platform was converted to a 16-bit signed integer. The number was larger than 32,768, the largest integer storeable in a 16-bit signed integer, and thus the conversion failed.

36.17.2 Hardware Sources

Amd - Visit

```
https://developer.amd.com/resources/
```

for details of the AMD manuals. The following five manuals are available for download as pdf's from the above site.

- AMD64 Architecture Programmer's Manual Volume 1: Application Programming
- AMD64 Architecture Programmer's Manual Volume 2: System Programming
- AMD64 Architecture Programmer's Manual Volume 3: General Purpose and System Instructions
- AMD64 Architecture Programmer's Manual Volume 4: 128-bit and 256 bit media instructions
- AMD64 Architecture Programmer's Manual Volume 5: 64-Bit Media and x87 Floating-Point Instructions

  Intel - Visit

```
https://software.intel.com/en-us/articles/intel-sdm
```

for a list of manuals. The following three manuals are available for download as pdf's from the above site.

- Intel 64 and IA-32 Architectures Software Developer's Manual. Volume 1: Basic Architecture
- Intel 64 and IA-32 Architectures Software Developer's Manual. Combined Volumes 2A and 2B: Instruction Set Reference, A-Z.
- Intel 64 and IA-32 Architectures Software Developer's Manual. Combined Volumes 3A and 3B: System Programming Guide, Parts 1 and 2

   Osbourne A., Kane G., 4-bit and 8-bit Microprocessor Handbook, Osbourne and McGraw Hill, 1981.

- Good source of information on 4-bit and 8-bit microprocessors.

   Osbourne A., Kane G., 16-Bit Microprocessor Handbook, Osbourne and McGraw Hill, 1981.

- Ditto 16-bit microprocessors.

   Bhandarkar D.P., Alpha Implementations and Architecture: Complete Reference and Guide, Digital Press, 1996.

- Looks at some of the trade-offs and design philosophy behind the alpha chip. The author worked with VAX, MicroVAX and VAX vectors as well as the Prism. Also looks at the GEM compiler technology that DEC/Compaq use.

   Various companies home pages.

```
http://www.ibm.com/
IBM home page.
http://www.sgi.com/
Silicon Graphics home page.
```

36.17.3   Operating Systems

Deitel H.M., An Introduction to Operating Systems, Addison-Wesley, 1990.

- The revised first edition includes case studies of UNIX, VMS, CP/M, MVS and VM. The second edition adds OS/2 and the Macintosh operating systems. There is a coverage of hardware, software, firmware, process management, process concepts, asynchronous concurrent processes, concurrent programming, deadlock and indefinite postponement, storage management, real storage, virtual storage, processor management, distributed computing, disk performance optimisation, file and database systems, performance, coprocessors, risc, data flow, analytic modelling, networks, security and it concludes with case studies of the these operating systems. The book is well written and an easy read.

36.18   Problem

36.1 Compile and run each of the examples in this chapter with your compiler(s). If you have access to more than one compiler do the compilers behave in the same way?

Chapter 37
Derived Type I/O

37.1   Introduction

In this chapter we look at a facility introduced in the Fortran 2003 standard - derived type I/O. The Fortran 2018 standard calls it defined type input/output, and is now widely available in current compilers.

When a derived type is encountered in an I/O list, we can arrange to call a Fortran subroutine. For a particular derived type and a particular set of kind type parameter values, there are four possible sets of characteristics for defined input/output procedures; one each for

- formatted input
- formatted output
- unformatted input
- unformatted output

A program need not supply all four procedures.

We will look at formatted I/O and the use of the DT edit descriptor in the examples that follow.

The following information is taken from Sect. 12.6.4.8.2 of the 2018 standard. The characteristics for a formatted read are the same as those specified by the following interface:

```
SUBROUTINE my_read_routine_formatted (dtv, &
                                       unit, &
                          iotype, v_list, &
                                iostat, iomsg)
   ! the derived-type variable
   dtv-type-spec , INTENT(INOUT) :: dtv
   INTEGER, INTENT(IN) :: unit ! unit number
   ! the edit descriptor string
   CHARACTER (LEN=*), INTENT(IN) :: iotype
```

© Springer International Publishing AG, part of Springer Nature 2018
I. Chivers and J. Sleightholme, *Introduction to Programming with Fortran*,
https://doi.org/10.1007/978-3-319-75502-1_37

```
   INTEGER, INTENT(IN) :: v_list(:)
   INTEGER, INTENT(OUT) :: iostat
   CHARACTER (LEN=*), INTENT(INOUT) :: iomsg
END
```

The characteristics for a formatted write are the same as those specified by the following interface:

```
SUBROUTINE my_write_routine_formatted (dtv, &
                                        unit, &
                             iotype, v_list, &
                                 iostat, iomsg)
   ! the derived-type value/variable
   dtv-type-spec , INTENT(IN) :: dtv
   INTEGER, INTENT(IN) :: unit
   ! the edit descriptor string
   CHARACTER (LEN=*), INTENT(IN) :: iotype
   INTEGER, INTENT(IN) :: v_list(:)
   INTEGER, INTENT(OUT) :: iostat
   CHARACTER (LEN=*), INTENT(INOUT) :: iomsg
END
```

Let us look at each parameter in turn.

```
dtv-type-spec , INTENT(IN) :: dtv
```

This is the derived type we are interested in printing out.

```
INTEGER, INTENT(IN) :: unit
```

The unit number for the I/O. It is a scalar of default integer type. It is negative if on an internal file.

```
CHARACTER (LEN=*), INTENT(IN) :: iotype
```

For formatted data transfer, the processor shall pass an iotype argument that has the value:

- LISTDIRECTED if the parent data transfer statement specified list directed formatting,
- NAMELIST if the parent data transfer statement specified namelist formatting, or
- DT concatenated with the char-literal-constant, if any, of the DT edit descriptor in the format specification of the parent data transfer statement.

```
INTEGER, INTENT(IN) :: v_list(:)
```

The v_list array. It is a rank one array of intent in and type default integer.

```
INTEGER, INTENT(OUT) :: iostat
```

The iostat value.

```
CHARACTER (LEN=*), INTENT(INOUT) :: iomsg
```

The iomsg value.

For the edit descriptor DT'Link List'(10, 4, 2), iotype is "DTLink List" and v_list is [10, 4, 2].

If the v-list of the edit descriptor appears in the parent data transfer statement, the processor shall provide the values from it in the v_list dummy argument, with the same number of elements in the same order as v-list. If there is no v-list in the edit descriptor or if the data transfer statement specifies list-directed or namelist formatting, the processor shall provide v_list as a zero-sized array.

The elements of the v_list array can be used for anything in the subroutine. In our examples below we will use them to control the fields widths.

It can also choose an arbitrary interpretation (or none) for iotype.

37.2   User-Defined Derived-Type Editing

We have examples illustrating some of the basics of defined type I/O.

37.3   Example 1: Basic Syntax, No Parameters in Call

Here is the derived type.

```
module ch3701_person_module

  implicit none

  type :: person

    character (len=30) :: name
    integer            :: age
    real               :: height
    real               :: weight
```

```fortran
contains

    procedure :: print_person
    generic   :: write(formatted) => print_person
    procedure :: read_person
    generic   :: read(formatted)  => read_person

  end type person

contains

subroutine print_person(p,unit_number,&
  iotype,vlist,iostat,iomsg)

    implicit none

    class (person)           , intent(in)    :: p
    integer                  , &
      intent(in)    :: unit_number
    character (len=*)        , intent(in)    :: iotype
    integer , dimension(:)   , intent(in)    :: vlist
    integer                  , intent(out)   :: iostat
    character (len=*)        , intent(inout) :: iomsg

    character (len=40) :: person_format

    person_format="(a,2x,i3,2x,f4.2,2x,f3.0)"

    write (unit_number,fmt=person_format) &
      p%name,p%age,p%height,p%weight

    iostat=0

  end subroutine print_person

 subroutine read_person(p,unit_number,&
    iotype,vlist,iostat,iomsg)

    implicit none

    class (person)             , intent(inout) :: p
    integer                    , &
      intent(in)    :: unit_number
    character (len=*)        , intent(in)    :: iotype
```

```
      integer , dimension(:) , intent(in)     :: vlist
      integer                 , intent(out)   :: iostat
      character (len=*)       , intent(inout) :: iomsg

      character (len=40) :: person_format

      person_format='(a,2x,i3,2x,f4.2,2x,f3.0)'

      read (unit_number,fmt=person_format) &
        p%name,p%age,p%height,p%weight

      iostat=0

    end subroutine read_person

end module ch3701_person_module
```

Here is the driving program.

```
include 'ch3701_person_module.f90'

program ch3701

  use ch3701_person_module

  integer , parameter :: n=4
  type (person) , dimension(n) :: p
  integer :: i

  open(unit=99,file='ch3701_input_file.txt')

  do i=1,n
    read( 99 , 10 ) p(i)
    10 format( DT )
    write( * , 20 ) p(i)
    20 format( DT )
  end do

end program ch3701
```

Here is the data input file.

```
Zahpod Beeblebrox              42  1.85  75
Ford Prefect                   25  1.75  65
```

```
Arthur Dent                          30   1.72   68
Trillian                             30   1.65   45
12345678901234567890123456789012345678901234 5
          1         2         3         4
```

Extra lines have been added at the end to indicate the column positions in the read statement. Here is the output.

```
Zahpod Beeblebrox                    42   1.85   75.
Ford Prefect                         25   1.75   65.
Arthur Dent                          30   1.72   68.
Trillian                             30   1.65   45.
```

37.4   Example 2: Extended Syntax, Passing Parameters

Here is the derived type.

```
module ch3702_person_module

  implicit none

  type :: person

    character (len=30) :: name
    integer            :: age
    real               :: height
    real               :: weight

    contains

      procedure :: print_person
      generic   :: write(formatted) &
                => print_person
      procedure :: read_person
      generic   :: read(formatted)  &
                => read_person

  end type person

  contains

  subroutine print_person(p,unit_number,&
```

```
        iotype,vlist,iostat,iomsg)

    implicit none

    class (person)          , intent(in)      :: p
    integer                 , &
      intent(in)      :: unit_number
    character (len=*)       , intent(in)    :: iotype
    integer , dimension(:) , intent(in)    :: vlist
    integer                 , intent(out)   :: iostat
    character (len=*)       , intent(inout) :: iomsg

    character (len=40) :: person_format

    write(person_format,10)'(a',vlist(1),&
                           ',',            ,&
                           'i',vlist(2),&
                           ',2x,'          ,&
                           'f',vlist(3),&
                           '.',vlist(4),&
                           ',2x,'          ,&
                           'f',vlist(5),&
                           '.0)'
10  format(a,i2,&
           a,   &
           a,i1,&
           a,   &
           a,i1,&
           a,i1,&
           a,   &
           a,i1,&
           a)

  write (unit_number,fmt=person_format) &
    p%name,p%age,p%height,p%weight

  iostat=0

end subroutine print_person

subroutine read_person(p,unit_number,&
  iotype,vlist,iostat,iomsg)

  implicit none
```

```fortran
      class (person)            , intent(inout) :: p
      integer                   , &
        intent(in)      :: unit_number
      character (len=*)         , intent(in)    :: iotype
      integer , dimension(:)  , intent(in)    :: vlist
      integer                   , intent(out)   :: iostat
      character (len=*)         , intent(inout) :: iomsg

      character (len=40) :: person_format

      write(person_format,10)'(a',vlist(1),&
                             ',2x,'              ,&
                             'i',vlist(2),&
                             ',2x,'              ,&
                             'f',vlist(3),&
                             '.',vlist(4),&
                             ',2x,'              ,&
                             'f',vlist(5),&
                             '.0)'
   10 format(a,i2,&
             a,    &
             a,i1,&
             a,    &
             a,i1,&
             a,i1,&
             a,    &
             a,i1,&
             a)

      read (unit_number,fmt=person_format) &
        p%name,p%age,p%height,p%weight

      iostat=0

  end subroutine read_person

end module ch3702_person_module
```

Here is the driving program.

```fortran
include 'ch3702_person_module.f90'

program ch3702

  use ch3702_person_module
```

```
      integer , parameter :: n=4
      type (person) , dimension(n) :: p
      integer :: i
      integer :: file_stat = 0

      open(unit=99 , file='ch3701_input_file.txt' , &
        status='old' , iostat = file_stat)

      if (file_stat /=0) then
        print *,' File not found'
        print *,' Program terminates'
        stop
      end if

      do i=1,n
        read( 99 , 10 ) p(i)
        10 format( DT(30,3,4,2,3) )
        write( * , 20 ) p(i)
        20 format( DT(20,5,4,2,3) )
      end do

end program ch3702
```

Here is the diff output between the two main programs.

```
1c1
< include 'ch3701_person_module.f90'
---
> include 'ch3702_person_module.f90'
3,5c3
< program ch3701
<
<     use ch3701_person_module
---
> program ch3702
6a5
>     use ch3702_person_module
23c22
<     10 format( DT )
---
>     10 format( DT(30,3,4,2,3) )
25c24
<     20 format( DT )
---
>     20 format( DT(20,5,4,2,3) )
```

```
28c27
< end program ch3701
---
> end program ch3702
```

Here is the diff output between the two person modules.

```
1c1
< module ch3701_person_module
---
> module ch3702_person_module
14,17c14,19
<      procedure :: print_person
<      generic   :: write(formatted) => print_person
<      procedure :: read_person
<      generic   :: read(formatted)  => read_person
---
>      procedure :: print_person
>      generic   :: write(formatted) &
>                          => print_person
>      procedure :: read_person
>      generic   :: read(formatted)  &
>                          => read_person
38c40,57
<     person_format="(a,2x,i3,2x,f4.2,2x,f3.0)"
---
>     write(person_format,10)'(a',vlist(1),&
>                             ',',            ,&
>                             'i',vlist(2),&
>                             ',2x,',          ,&
>                             'f',vlist(3),&
>                             '.',vlist(4),&
>                             ',2x,',          ,&
>                             'f',vlist(5),&
>                             '.0)'
>    10 format(a,i2,&
>                a,   &
>                a,i1,&
>                a,   &
>                a,i1,&
>                a,i1,&
>                a,   &
>                a,i1,&
>                a)
62c81,98
```

```
<         person_format='(a,2x,i3,2x,f4.2,2x,f3.0)'
---
>         write(person_format,10)'(a',vlist(1),&
>                                 ',2x,'          ,&
>                                 'i',vlist(2),&
>                                 ',2x,'          ,&
>                                 'f',vlist(3),&
>                                 '.',vlist(4),&
>                                 ',2x,'          ,&
>                                 'f',vlist(5),&
>                                 '.0)'
>      10 format(a,i2,&
>                  a,   &
>                  a,i1,&
>                  a,   &
>                  a,i1,&
>                  a,i1,&
>                  a,   &
>                  a,i1,&
>                  a)
71,72c107
< end module ch3701_person_module
<
---
> end module ch3702_person_module
```

The data input file is the same as in the last example.
Here is the output.

```
Zahpod Beeblebrox       42   1.85   75.
Ford Prefect            25   1.75   65.
Arthur Dent             30   1.72   68.
Trillian                30   1.65   45.
```

37.5   Example 3: Basic Syntax with Timing

This example is a variation on the first example. We are now interested in timing the
I/O.
Here is the driving program.

```
include 'timing_module.f90'
include 'ch3701_person_module.f90'

program ch3703
```

```
use ch3701_person_module
use timing_module

implicit none

integer :: i
integer , parameter :: n=1000000

type (person) :: p1 = &
  person('Zaphod Beeblebrox',42,1.85,70)

open(unit=10,file='ch3703.txt')

call start_timing()

do i=1,n
  write(10,100)  p1%name,p1%age,p1%height,p1%weight
  100 format(a39,2x,i2,2x,f4.2,2x,f3.0)
end do

print 200,time_difference()
200 format(2x,f8.3)

do i=1,n
  write( 10 , 10 ) p1
  10 format( DT )
end do

print 200,time_difference()

close(10)

call end_timing()

end program ch3703
```

Here is the output from one compiler.

```
2017/11/24 13: 7:44 790
   15.613
   17.266
2017/11/24 13: 8:17 685
```

37.6   Example 4: Extended Syntax with Timing

This example is a variation on the second example. We are now interested in timing the I/O.

Here is the driving program.

```
include 'timing_module.f90'
include 'ch3702_person_module.f90'

program ch3704

  use ch3702_person_module
  use timing_module

  implicit none

  integer :: i
  integer , parameter :: n=1000000

  type (person) :: p1 = &
    person('Zaphod Beeblebrox',42,1.85,70)

  open(unit=10,file='ch3704.txt')

  call start_timing()

  do i=1,n
    write(10,100)  p1%name,p1%age,p1%height,p1%weight
    100 format(a30,2x,i2,2x,f4.2,2x,f3.0)
  end do

  print 200,time_difference()
  200 format(2x,f8.3)

  do i=1,n
    write( 10 , 10 ) p1
    10 format( DT(20,5,4,2,3) )
  end do

  print 200,time_difference()

  close(10)

  call end_timing()
```

```
end program ch3704
```

Here is the output from one compiler.

```
2017/11/24 13:12:32 523
    15.547
    19.941
2017/11/24 13:13: 8   12
```

37.7   Summary

This chapter has illustrated simple usage of derived type I/O.

37.8   Problem

37.1 Compile and run the examples in this chapter. What timing figures do you get with your compiler for the last two examples?

Chapter 38
Sorting and Searching

The Analytical Engine weaves algebraic patterns, just as the Jacquard loom weaves flowers and leaves.

Ada Lovelace

Aims

We look at a number of sorting and searching examples:

- three numeric sorting examples, using a recursive algorithm, a non recursive algorithm and a parallelised subroutine from the Nag library

  - timing details for our generic serial Quicksort algorithm for five of the numeric kind types
  - timing details of the Netlib serial non recursive Quicksort for 32 bit integers, 32 bit reals and 64 bit reals
  - a comparison of the timing of the above two sorting algorithms
  - the Nag SMP sorting routine m01caf for 64 bit reals
  - timing details of the parallel Nag sorting subroutine

- Sorting an array of a derived type
- A searching example

38.1 Example 1: Generic Recursive Quicksort Example with Timing Details

This example has several components

- a module called `precision_module` from Chap. 21
- a module called `integer_kind_module` from Chap. 25

© Springer International Publishing AG, part of Springer Nature 2018
I. Chivers and J. Sleightholme, *Introduction to Programming with Fortran*,
https://doi.org/10.1007/978-3-319-75502-1_38

- a timing module
- the generic Quicksort module from Chap. 25
- a main program to provide the timing information

Here is the source code for the main program. The source code for the other modules is the same as in earlier chapters.

```
include 'integer_kind_module.f90'
include 'precision_module.f90'
include 'sort_data_module.f90'
include 'timing_module.f90'

program ch3801

  use sort_data_module
  use timing_module

  implicit none
  integer, parameter :: n = 100000000
  character *12 :: nn = '100,000,000'
  character *80 :: report_file_name = &
    'ch3601.report'

  real (sp), allocatable, dimension (:) :: x_sp
  real (dp), allocatable, dimension (:) :: x_dp
  real (qp), allocatable, dimension (:) :: x_qp
  integer (i32), allocatable, dimension (:) :: &
    y_i32
  integer (i64), allocatable, dimension (:) :: &
    y_i64

  integer :: allocate_status = 0

  character *20, dimension (5) :: heading1 = [ &
    '  32 bit real', '  32 bit int ', &
    '  64 bit real', '  64 bit int ', &
    ' 128 bit real' ]

  character *20, dimension (3) :: heading2 = [ &
    '      Allocate ', '      Random   ', &
    '      Sort     ' ]

  print *, 'Program starts'
  print *, 'N = ', nn
  call start_timing()
```

```
  open (unit=100, file=report_file_name)

  print *, heading1(1)

  allocate (x_sp(1:n), stat=allocate_status)
  if (allocate_status/=0) then
    print *, &
      ' Allocate failed. Program terminates'
    stop 10
  end if

  print 100, heading2(1), time_difference()
100 format (a20, 2x, f8.3)
  call random_number(x_sp)
  print 100, heading2(2), time_difference()
  call sort_data(x_sp, n)
  print 100, heading2(3), time_difference()
  write (unit=100, fmt='(a)') &
    ' First 10 32 bit reals'
  write (unit=100, fmt=110) x_sp(1:10)
110 format (5(2x,e14.6))

  print *, heading1(2)

  allocate (y_i32(1:n), stat=allocate_status)
  if (allocate_status/=0) then
    print *, &
      'Allocate failed. Program terminates'
    stop 20
  end if
  print 100, heading2(1), time_difference()
  y_i32 = int(x_sp*1000000000, i32)
  deallocate (x_sp)
  print 100, heading2(2), time_difference()
  call sort_data(y_i32, n)
  print 100, heading2(3), time_difference()
  write (unit=100, fmt='(a)') &
    'First 10 32 bit integers'
  write (unit=100, fmt=120) y_i32(1:10)
120 format (5(2x,i10))
  deallocate (y_i32)

  print *, heading1(3)
```

```fortran
allocate (x_dp(1:n), stat=allocate_status)
if (allocate_status/=0) then
  print *, &
    'Allocate failed. Program terminates'
  stop 30
end if


print 100, heading2(1), time_difference()
call random_number(x_dp)
print 100, heading2(2), time_difference()
call sort_data(x_dp, n)
print 100, heading2(3), time_difference()
write (unit=100, fmt='(a)') &
  'First 10 64 bit reals'
write (unit=100, fmt=110) x_dp(1:10)

print *, heading1(4)

allocate (y_i64(1:n), stat=allocate_status)
if (allocate_status/=0) then
  print *, &
    'Allocate failed. Program terminates'
  stop 40
end if

print 100, heading2(1), time_difference()
y_i64 = int(x_dp*1000000000000000_i64, i64)
deallocate (x_dp)
print 100, heading2(2), time_difference()
call sort_data(y_i64, n)
print 100, heading2(3), time_difference()
write (unit=100, fmt='(a)') &
  'First 10 64 bit integers'
write (unit=100, fmt=120) y_i64(1:10)
deallocate (y_i64)

print *, heading1(5)

allocate (x_qp(1:n), stat=allocate_status)
if (allocate_status/=0) then
  print *, &
    'Allocate failed. Program terminates'
  stop 50
end if
```

```
  print 100, heading2(1), time_difference()
  call random_number(x_qp)
  print 100, heading2(2), time_difference()
  call sort_data(x_qp, n)
  print 100, heading2(3), time_difference()
  write (unit=100, fmt='(a)') &
    'First 10 128 bitreals'
  write (unit=100, fmt=110) x_qp(1:10)

  close (200)
  print *, 'Program terminates'
  call end_timing()

end program ch3801
```

Table 38.1 has timing information for four compilers.

Table 38.1 Generic recursive quicksort timing

		gfortran	Intel	Nag	Oracle	Mean	StdDev
Allocate	32 bit real	0.008	0.000	0.000	0.000	0.002	0.004
Allocate	32 bit int	0.000	0.000	0.000	0.008	0.002	0.004
Allocate	64 bit real	0.094	0.031	0.031	0.000	0.039	0.039
Allocate	64 bit int	0.016	0.000	0.016	0.000	0.008	0.009
Allocate	128 bit real	0.156	0.047	0.047	0.000	0.063	0.066
Allocate	Total	0.274	0.078	0.094	0.008	0.114	0.113
Random	32 bit real	0.562	0.422	0.609	2.125	0.930	0.801
Random	32 bit int	0.219	0.172	0.328	0.062	0.195	0.110
Random	64 bit real	1.492	0.594	0.531	2.219	1.209	0.804
Random	64 bit int	0.414	0.328	0.609	0.133	0.371	0.197
Random	128 bit real	11.203	3.797	1.070	3.625	4.924	4.368
Random	Total	13.890	5.313	3.147	8.164	7.629	4.653
Sort	32 bit real	13.742	12.328	15.063	11.586	13.180	1.541
Sort	32 bit int	3.492	2.891	4.781	2.203	3.342	1.095
Sort	64 bit real	14.945	13.266	16.078	12.664	14.238	1.561
Sort	64 bit int	2.742	2.312	2.906	1.633	2.398	0.568
Sort	128 bit real	45.703	33.141	18.750	36.633	33.557	11.201
Sort	Total	80.624	63.938	57.578	64.719	66.715	9.809
Overall	Total	94.788	69.329	60.819	72.891	74.457	14.469

Here are some simple observations about the timing information in this table:

- allocation is a negligible component of the overall time

- random number generation takes between 5 and 15% of total timing
- integer sorting is much faster than real sorting
- sorting of 32 and 64 bit reals is similar
- overall processing of the Nag format 128 bit real is faster than the other 128 bit formats

38.2 Example 2: Non Recursive Quicksort Example with Timing Details

The subroutines in this example are taken from the Netlib site. They are 3 non recursive Fortran 77 implementation of Quicksort.

Visit the Netlib site for more details.

```
http://www.netlib.org/
```

The following is taken directly from their FAQ.

- What is Netlib? The Netlib repository contains freely available software, documents, and databases of interest to the numerical, scientific computing, and other communities. The repository is maintained by AT&T Bell Laboratories, the University of Tennessee and Oak Ridge National Laboratory, and by colleagues worldwide. The collection is replicated at several sites around the world, automatically synchronized, to provide reliable and network efficient service to the global community.

The routines we are interested in are in the following directory.

```
http://www.netlib.org/slatec/src/
```

Three versions are provided.

```
http://www.netlib.org/slatec/src/isort.f
http://www.netlib.org/slatec/src/ssort.f
http://www.netlib.org/slatec/src/dsort.f
```

They are fixed form Fortran 77. A small set of changes need to be made to enable them to be compiled and used in this example.

We will cover the changes we have made for the double precision sort routine dsort.f.

Here is the subroutine header for the double precision subroutine.

```
SUBROUTINE DSORT (DX, DY, N, KFLAG)
```

The routine takes 4 parameters and we look at the implementation of the dsort routine to find out more details about each parameter. This line

```
C***TYPE DOUBLE PRECISION (SSORT-S, DSORT-D, ISORT-I)
```

provides the first clue as to the nature of the parameters.
The following provide some more.

```
C    Description of Parameters
C        DX - array of values to be sorted   (usually abscissas)
C        DY - array to be (optionally) carried along
C        N  - number of values in array DX to be sorted
C        KFLAG - control parameter
C             =  2  means sort DX in increasing order and carry DY
along.
C             =  1  means sort DX in increasing order (ignoring DY)
C             = -1  means sort DX in decreasing order (ignoring DY)
C             = -2  means sort DX in decreasing order and carry DY
along.
```

The following lines then complete the information.

```
C        .. Scalar Arguments ..
         INTEGER KFLAG, N
C        .. Array Arguments ..
         DOUBLE PRECISION DX(*), DY(*)
```

If we set the fourth parameter to 1, we can use the same array for the first and
second arguments.

We have made source code changes to the three subroutines.

The changes are summarised below, and we have included details of the line
numbers in each sort subroutine. The changes involve commenting out 4 sets of
lines.

	Line number(s) in subroutines		
	dsort.f	ssort.f	isort.f
*DECK	1	1	1
EXTERNAL XERMSG	61	60	60
1st Call to XERMSG	66-70	65-69	65-69
2nd call to XERMSG	73-78	72-77	72-77

Here are the lines that need to be commented out.

```
*DECK DSORT
..
..

      EXTERNAL XERMSG
..
..

      IF (NN .LT. 1) THEN
         CALL XERMSG ('SLATEC', 'DSORT',
     +      'The number of values to be sorted is not positive.',
1, 1)
         RETURN
      ENDIF
..
..

      IF (KK.NE.1 .AND. KK.NE.2) THEN
         CALL XERMSG ('SLATEC', 'DSORT',
     +      'The sort control parameter, K, is not 2, 1, -1, or -2.',
2,
     +         1)
         RETURN
      ENDIF
..
..
```

The following lines

```
C***REFERENCES  R. C. Singleton, Algorithm 347, An efficient algorithm
C                  for sorting with minimal storage, Communications
of
C                  the ACM, 12, 3 (1969), pp. 185-187.
C***ROUTINES CALLED  XERMSG
C***REVISION HISTORY  (YYMMDD)
C   761101  DATE WRITTEN
C   761118  Modified to use the Singleton quicksort algorithm.  (JAW)
C   890531  Changed all specific intrinsics to generic.  (WRB)
C   890831  Modified array declarations.  (WRB)
C   891009  Removed unreferenced statement labels.  (WRB)
C   891024  Changed category.  (WRB)
C   891024  REVISION DATE from Version 3.2
C   891214  Prologue converted to Version 4.0 format.  (BAB)
C   900315  CALLs to XERROR changed to CALLs to XERMSG.  (THJ)
C   901012  Declared all variables; changed X,Y to DX,DY; changed
C           code to parallel SSORT. (M. McClain)
C   920501  Reformatted the REFERENCES section.  (DWL, WRB)
C   920519  Clarified error messages.  (DWL)
C   920801  Declarations section rebuilt and code restructured to use
C           IF-THEN-ELSE-ENDIF.  (RWC, WRB)
```

provide details about the algorithm and its revision history. This information is extremely useful when working with the subroutine.

We are now going to look at one solution to the problem of how to integrate the original program and the three sorting subroutines.

The simplest solution is to independently compile the three routines as Fortran 77 source. Here is the Nag compiler command to achieve this

```
nagfor -c -O4 dsort.f ssort.f isort.f
```

On the Windows platform this will generate the following files

```
dsort.o
ssort.o
isort.o
```

The following command will then compile the modern Fortran code and link the Fortran 77 compiled code into the executable.

```
nagfor -O4 ch3802.f90 dsort.o ssort.o isort.o
```

Here is the command line for the Intel compiler to compile the Fortran 77 netlib routines.

```
ifort /c /fast /Qparallel dsort.f ssort.f isort.f
```

Here is the command line for gfortran to compile the Fortran 77 Netlib routines.

```
gfortran -c -O3 -ffast-math -funroll-loops
  dsort.f ssort.f isort.f
```

Here is the main program.

```
include 'precision_module.f90'
include 'integer_kind_module.f90'
include 'timing_module.f90'

program ch3802
  use precision_module
  use integer_kind_module
  use timing_module
  implicit none
  integer, parameter :: n = 100000000
  character *12 :: nn = '100,000,000'
  character *80 :: report_file_name = 'ch3502.report'
  real (sp), allocatable, dimension (:) :: x_sp
  real (dp), allocatable, dimension (:) :: x_dp
  integer (i32), allocatable, dimension (:) :: y_i32

  integer :: allocate_status
  character *20, dimension (5) :: heading1 = &
```

```fortran
   [ '   32 bit real   ', &
   '  32 bit int    ', &
 '   64 bit real   ', &
 '   64 bit int    ', &
     ' 128 bit real  ' ]

   character *20, dimension (3) :: heading2 = &
   [ '        Allocate ', &
   '        Random     ', &
 '       Sort         ' ]

   allocate_status = 0

   print *, 'Program starts'
   print *, 'N = ', nn
   call start_timing()

   open (unit=100, file=report_file_name)

   print *, heading1(1)

   allocate (x_sp(1:n), stat=allocate_status)
   if (allocate_status/=0) then
     print *, ' Allocate failed. Program terminates'
     stop 10
   end if
   print 100, heading2(1), time_difference()
100 format (a20, 2x, f8.3)
   call random_number(x_sp)
   print 100, heading2(2), time_difference()
   call ssort(x_sp, x_sp, n, 1)
   print 100, heading2(3), time_difference()
   write (unit=100, fmt='(a)') &
   ' First 10 32 bit reals'
   write (unit=100, fmt=110) x_sp(1:10)
110 format (5(2x,e14.6))

   print *, heading1(2)

   allocate (y_i32(1:n), stat=allocate_status)
   if (allocate_status/=0) then
     print *, ' Allocate failed. Program terminates'
     stop 20
   end if
   print 100, heading2(1), time_difference()
```

```
   y_i32 = int(x_sp*1000000000, i32)
   deallocate (x_sp)
   print 100, heading2(2), time_difference()
   call isort(y_i32, y_i32, n, 1)
   print 100, heading2(3), time_difference()
   write (unit=100, fmt='(a)') &
   'First 10 32 bit integers'
   write (unit=100, fmt=120) y_i32(1:10)
120 format (5(2x,i10))
   deallocate (y_i32)


   print *, heading1(3)

   allocate (x_dp(1:n), stat=allocate_status)
   if (allocate_status/=0) then
     print *, ' Allocate failed. Program terminates'
     stop 30
   end if
   print 100, heading2(1), time_difference()
   call random_number(x_dp)
   print 100, heading2(2), time_difference()
   call dsort(x_dp, x_dp, n, 1)
   print 100, heading2(3), time_difference()
   write (unit=100, fmt='(a)') &
   'First 10 64 bit reals'
   write (unit=100, fmt=110) x_dp(1:10)

   print *, ' Program terminates'
   call end_timing()

end program ch3802
```

It is then possible to link to the already compiled subroutines when compiling the main program.

The following command will then compile the modern Fortran code and link the Fortran 77 compiled code into the executable using the Nag compiler.

```
nagfor -O4 ch3802.f90 dsort.o ssort.o isort.o
```

Table 38.2 summarises the timing information for the above four compilers.

Table 38.2 Non recursive quicksort timing

		gfortran	Intel	Nag	Oracle	Mean	StdDev
Allocate	32 bit real	0.000	0.016	0.008	0.000	0.006	0.008
Allocate	32 bit int	0.000	0.000	0.000	0.000	0.000	0.000
Allocate	64 bit real	0.094	0.023	0.031	0.004	0.038	0.039
Allocate	Sum	0.094	0.039	0.039	0.004	0.044	0.037
Random	32 bit real	0.562	0.609	0.625	2.062	0.965	0.732
Random	32 bit int	0.203	0.375	0.297	0.066	0.235	0.133
Random	64 bit real	1.484	0.523	0.516	2.090	1.153	0.772
Random	Sum	2.249	1.507	1.438	4.218	2.353	1.296
Sort	32 bit real	11.508	11.563	11.852	12.207	11.783	0.321
Sort	32 bit int	2.945	2.961	3.000	2.242	2.787	0.364
Sort	64 bit real	12.625	12.406	12.320	12.953	12.576	0.282
Sort	Sum	27.078	26.930	27.172	27.402	27.146	0.198
Overall	Sum	29.421	28.476	28.649	31.624	29.543	1.447

Here are some simple observations about the timing information in this table:

- allocation is again a negligible component of the overall time
- random number generation takes between 5% and 15% of total timing
- integer sorting is much faster than real sorting
- sorting of 32 and 64 bit reals is similar
- the sums for the sorting are very similar, as the standard deviation shows

38.2.1   Notes - Version Control Systems

The original program had the following statement

```
*DECK DSORT
```

and this statement was one used in version control or revision control software of the time. Two version control programs that were available on CDC systems from the 1970s and 1980s were called update and modify that used the above. In computer programming, revision control is any practice that tracks and provides control over changes to source code. Software developers also use revision control software to maintain documentation and configuration files as well as source code.

The use of this kind of software is common for medium to large scale program development.

Wikipedia provides a comparison of what is currently available. See

```
http://en.wikipedia.org/wiki/
Comparison_of_revision_control_software
```

for more information.

38.3   Subroutine and Function Libraries

A software library is a set of precompiled program units (functions and subroutines) that has been written to solve common problems.

In a university environment many departments (e.g. Mechanical Engineering, Electrical Engineering, Mathematics, Physics etc) have libraries that solve common problems in each discipline.

38.4   The Nag Library for SMP and Multicore

The major commercial cross platform numerical library is the Nag library. Nag provide an SMP and multicore version of their library.

More information can be found at:-

```
https://www.nag.co.uk/numeric/numerical_libraries.asp
https://www.nag.co.uk/numeric/FL/FSdescription.asp
```

The library is available on a range of platforms.

- Windows
- Linux (including 64-bit)
- Solaris
- Mac OS X
- AIX

A subset of the library is thread safe.

Many of the algorithms, or routines, in the library are specifically tuned to run significantly faster on multi-socket and multicore systems. We will look at timing information for one of the sorting routines and compare the times to those of our serial sorting routines.

38.5   Example 3: Calling the Nag m01caf Sorting Routine

Here is the program source.

```fortran
include 'precision_module.f90'
include 'timing_module.f90'

program ch3803

  use precision_module
  use timing_module

  implicit none
  integer, parameter :: n = 100000000
  character *12 :: nn = '100,000,000'
  character *80 :: report_file_name = 'ch3505.report'

  real (dp), allocatable, dimension (:) :: x_dp

  integer :: allocate_status = 0
  integer :: ifail = 0

  character *20, dimension (5) :: heading1 = &
    [ '   32 bit real', &
      '   32 bit int ', &
      '   64 bit real', &
      '   64 bit int ', &
      ' 128 bit real' ]

  character *20, dimension (3) :: heading2 = &
    [ '      Allocate ', &
      '      Random   ', &
      '        Sort    ' ]

  print *, 'Program starts'
  print *, 'N = ', nn
  call start_timing()

  open (unit=100, file=report_file_name)

100 format (a20, 2x, f8.3)
110 format (5(2x,e14.6))
120 format (5(2x,i10))

  print *, heading1(3)

  allocate (x_dp(1:n), stat=allocate_status)
  if (allocate_status/=0) then
    print *, 'Allocate failed. Program terminates'
```

```
      stop 30
   end if

   print 100, heading2(1), time_difference()
   call random_number(x_dp)
   print 100, heading2(2), time_difference()
   call m01caf(x_dp, 1, n, 'A', ifail)
   if (ifail/=0) then
     print *, 'sort failed. Program terminates'
     stop 100
   end if

   print 100, heading2(3), time_difference()
   write (unit=100, fmt='(a)') 'First 10 64 bit reals'
   write (unit=100, fmt=110) x_dp(1:10)

   close (200)
   print *, 'Program terminates'
   call end_timing()

end program ch3803
```

Table 38.3 has details of timing information for the serial sorting algorithms.

Table 38.3 Sixty four bit real sort timings

		gfortran	Intel	Nag	Oracle	Mean	StdDev
Recursive sort	64 bit real	14.945	13.266	16.078	12.664	14.238	1.561
Non-recursive Sort	64 bit real	12.625	12.406	12.320	12.953	12.576	0.282

The non recursive solution is faster for three out of four compilers.

Table 38.4 has the timing information for the Nag SMP routine, for 1–8 cores.

Table 38.4 Nag sort m01caf timing

N threads	Time
1	11.938
2	6.773
3	5.047
4	4.211
5	4.094
6	3.703
7	3.586
8	3.391

As can be seen the Nag `m01caf` timing is faster for one core and shows a very impressive speed up as the number of cores goes up. The system is an Intel I7 system, which has 4 physical cores and is also hyper-threaded giving 8 cores overall.

This link

```
https://www.nag.co.uk/numeric/fl/
performance_examples.asp
```

has some examples of how the NAG SMP library performance scales on multiple cores. At the time of writing they were drawn from the following library chapters

- Sorting
- Correlation and Regression Analysis
- Wavelet Transforms
- Interpolation
- Random number generators
- Special Functions

This link

```
https://www.nag.co.uk/numeric/fl/
nagdoc_f124/html/GENINT/smptuned.html
```

has details of the tuned routines in the SMP library.

Here are some details that were correct at the time of writing.

- There are 77 tuned LAPACK routines
- There are 149 Tuned NAG-specific routines within the Library

The Nag library may well offer you a very cost effective way to improve the speed of your programs. Nag have effectively done the work of parallelising many common problems and sub problems and thus the use of their library routines may save you significant development time and help you produce programs that run faster.

As you are probably aware by now parallelising your own code can be hard work!

38.6   Example 4: Sorting an Array of a Derived Type

In this section we look at rewriting the quicksort algorithm to work with an array of a user defined type, or Fortran derived type. We will use the date data type from an earlier chapter to illustrate the key points.

38.6.1   Compare Function

For each derived type the user needs needs to implement a logical function that compares two variables of that type. This comparison function will replace the < and > comparison tests in the quicksort sorting routine.

38.6.2   Fortran Sources

There are three source files:

- The date module with comparison function
- the new sort routine
- the Fortran test program

They are listed below.

38.6.3   Date Module

```
module date_module

    implicit none

    private

    type, public :: date
      private
      integer :: day
      integer :: month
      integer :: year
    end type date

    character (9) :: day(0:6) = (/ 'Sunday   ', &
       'Monday   ', 'Tuesday  ', 'Wednesday', &
       'Thursday ', 'Friday   ', 'Saturday ' /)
    character (9) :: month(1:12) = (/ 'January  ', &
       'February ', 'March    ', 'April    ', &
       'May      ', 'June     ', 'July     ', &
       'August   ', 'September', 'October  ', &
       'November ', 'December ' /)


    public :: calendar_to_julian, date_, &
       date_to_day_in_year, date_to_weekday_number, &
```

```
        get_day, get_month, get_year, &
        julian_to_date, &
        julian_to_date_and_week_and_day, ndays, &
        print_date, year_and_day_to_date, less_than


   contains

     function calendar_to_julian(x) result (ival)
       implicit none
       integer :: ival
       type (date), intent (in) :: x

       ival = x%day - 32075 + 1461*(x%year+4800+(x% &
         month-14)/12)/4 + 367*(x%month-2-((x%month &
         -14)/12)*12)/12 - 3*((x%year+4900+(x%month &
         -14)/12)/100)/4
     end function calendar_to_julian

     function date_(dd, mm, yyyy) result (x)
       implicit none
       type (date) :: x
       integer, intent (in) :: dd, mm, yyyy

       x = date(dd, mm, yyyy)
     end function date_

     function date_to_day_in_year(x)
       implicit none
       integer :: date_to_day_in_year
       type (date), intent (in) :: x
       intrinsic modulo

       date_to_day_in_year = 3055*(x%month+2)/100 - &
         (x%month+10)/13*2 - 91 + (1-(modulo(x%year &
         ,4)+3)/4+(modulo(x%year,100)+99)/100-( &
         modulo(x%year,400)+399)/400)*(x%month+10)/ &
         13 + x%day
     end function date_to_day_in_year

     function date_to_weekday_number(x)
       implicit none
       integer :: date_to_weekday_number
       type (date), intent (in) :: x
       intrinsic modulo
```

```
    date_to_weekday_number = modulo((13*( &
      x%month+10-(x%month+10)/13*12)-1)/5+x%day+ &
      77+5*(x%year+(x%month-14)/12-(x%year+ &
      (x%month-14)/12)/100*100)/4+(x%year+(x% &
      month-14)/12)/400-(x%year+(x%month- &
      14)/12)/100*2, 7)
  end function date_to_weekday_number


function get_day(x)
  implicit none
  integer :: get_day
  type (date), intent (in) :: x

  get_day = x%day
end function get_day

function get_month(x)
  implicit none
  integer :: get_month
  type (date), intent (in) :: x

  get_month = x%month
end function get_month

function get_year(x)
  implicit none
  integer :: get_year
  type (date), intent (in) :: x

  get_year = x%year
end function get_year

function julian_to_date(julian) result (x)
  implicit none
  integer, intent (in) :: julian
  integer :: l, n
  type (date) :: x

  l = julian + 68569
  n = 4*l/146097
  l = l - (146097*n+3)/4
  x%year = 4000*(l+1)/1461001
  l = l - 1461*x%year/4 + 31
```

```fortran
    x%month = 80*l/2447
    x%day = l - 2447*x%month/80
    l = x%month/11
    x%month = x%month + 2 - 12*l
    x%year = 100*(n-49) + x%year + 1
  end function julian_to_date


  subroutine julian_to_date_and_week_and_day(jd, &
    x, wd, ddd)
    implicit none
    integer, intent (out) :: ddd, wd
    integer, intent (in) :: jd
    type (date), intent (out) :: x

    x = julian_to_date(jd)
    wd = date_to_weekday_number(x)
    ddd = date_to_day_in_year(x)
  end subroutine julian_to_date_and_week_and_day

  logical function less_than(x1, x2)
    implicit none
    type (date), intent (in) :: x1
    type (date), intent (in) :: x2

    if (calendar_to_julian(x1)< &
      calendar_to_julian(x2)) then
      less_than = .true.
    else
      less_than = .false.
    end if
  end function less_than

  function ndays(date1, date2)
    implicit none
    integer :: ndays
    type (date), intent (in) :: date1, date2

    ndays = calendar_to_julian(date1) - &
      calendar_to_julian(date2)
  end function ndays


  function print_date(x, day_names, &
    short_month_name, digits)
```

```fortran
    implicit none
    type (date), intent (in) :: x
    logical, optional, intent (in) :: day_names, &
      short_month_name, digits
    character (40) :: print_date
    integer :: pos
    logical :: want_day, want_short_month_name, &
      want_digits
    intrinsic len_trim, present, trim

    want_day = .false.
    want_short_month_name = .false.
    want_digits = .false.
    print_date = ' '
    if (present(day_names)) then
      want_day = day_names
    end if
    if (present(short_month_name)) then
      want_short_month_name = short_month_name
    end if
    if (present(digits)) then
      want_digits = digits
    end if
    if (want_digits) then
      write (print_date(1:2), '(i2)') x%day
      print_date(3:3) = '/'
      write (print_date(4:5), '(i2)') x%month
      print_date(6:6) = '/'
      write (print_date(7:10), '(i4)') x%year
    else
      if (want_day) then
        pos = date_to_weekday_number(x)
        print_date = trim(day(pos)) // ' '
        pos = len_trim(print_date) + 2
      else
        pos = 1
        print_date = ' '
      end if
      write (print_date(pos:pos+1), '(i2)') &
        x%day
      if (want_short_month_name) then
        print_date(pos+3:pos+5) = month(x%month) &
          (1:3)
        pos = pos + 7
      else
```

```
        print_date(pos+3:) = month(x%month)
        pos = len_trim(print_date) + 2
      end if
      write (print_date(pos:pos+3), '(i4)') &
        x%year
    end if


    return
  end function print_date

  function year_and_day_to_date(year, day) &
    result (x)
    implicit none
    type (date) :: x
    integer, intent (in) :: day, year
    integer :: t
    intrinsic modulo

    x%year = year
    t = 0
    if (modulo(year,4)==0) then
      t = 1
    end if
    if (modulo(year,400)/=0 .and. &
      modulo(year,100)==0) then
      t = 0
    end if
    x%day = day
    if (day>59+t) then
      x%day = x%day + 2 - t
    end if
    x%month = ((x%day+91)*100)/3055
    x%day = (x%day+91) - (x%month*3055)/100
    x%month = x%month - 2
    if (x%month>=1 .and. x%month<=12) then
      return
    end if
    write (unit=*, fmt='(a,i11,a)') '$$year_and_d&
      &ay_to_date: day of the year input &
      &=', day, ' is out of range.'
  end function year_and_day_to_date

end module date_module
```

38.6.4 Sort Module

```
module generic_sort_module

! use user_module , internal_type => user_type
! less_than is a logical function in the module

  use date_module, internal_type => date

  implicit none

contains

  subroutine sort(x, n)
    integer, intent (in) :: n
    type (internal_type), intent (inout), &
      dimension (n) :: x

    call quicksort(1, n)

  contains

    recursive subroutine quicksort(l, r)
      implicit none
      integer, intent (in) :: l, r
!     local variables
      integer :: i, j
      type (internal_type) :: v, t

      i = l
      j = r
      v = x(int((l+r)/2))
      do
        do while (less_than(x(i),v))
          i = i + 1
        end do
        do while (less_than(v,x(j)))
          j = j - 1
        end do
        if (i<=j) then
          t = x(i)
          x(i) = x(j)
          x(j) = t
          i = i + 1
```

```
        j = j - 1
      end if
      if (i>j) exit
    end do
    if (l<j) then
      call quicksort(l, j)
    end if
    if (i<r) then
      call quicksort(i, r)
    end if
  end subroutine quicksort

  end subroutine sort

end module generic_sort_module
```

38.6.5   Main Program

```
include 'ch3804_date_module.f90'
include 'ch3804_generic_sort_module.f90'
include 'timing_module.f90'

program ch3804

  use date_module
  use generic_sort_module
  use timing_module

  implicit none
  integer :: i
  integer, parameter :: n = 1000000
  integer, dimension (1:n) :: julian_dates
  type (date), dimension (n) :: x
  character *20 :: heading

  call start_timing()
  print *, ' '

  open (unit=100, file='julian_dates.dat', &
    form='unformatted')

  heading = 'open'
```

```
   print 100, heading, time_difference()
100 format (a20, f7.3)

   read (100) julian_dates
   heading = 'read'
   print 100, heading, time_difference()

   do i = 1, n
     x(i) = julian_to_date(julian_dates(i))
   end do

   heading = 'copy'
   print 100, heading, time_difference()

   call sort(x, n)

   heading = 'sort'
   print 100, heading, time_difference()
   print *, ' '


   do i = 1, n, 100000
     print *, print_date(x(i))
   end do

   print *, ' '
   call end_timing()

end program ch3804
```

Here is some sample output.

```
 2016/12/ 5 16:56:24 112
```

```
open                    0.023
read                    0.004
copy                    0.031
sort                    0.344

  1 January 1859
 31 January 1887
  6 June 1914
  1 November 1941
 28 March 1969
 22 June 1996
```

```
21 November 2023
15 March 2051
20 August 2078
28 February 2106

2016/12/ 5 16:56:24 540
```

38.7   Example 5: Binary Search Example

Searching is a common problem in programming. Wirth's book has a short chapter on searching, with coverage of

- linear search
- binary search
- table search
- straight string search
- the Knuth-Morris-Pratt string search
- the Boyer-Moore string search

A linear search of a collection can obviously be quite an expensive operation. The worst case is that the object of interest is the last member of the collection.

In this example we make the assumption that the data is sorted and can then use a very efficient algorithm - a binary search. Here is the program.

```fortran
include 'timing_module.f90'

module character_binary_search_module

contains

  function binary_search(x, n, key) &
    result (position)
    implicit none

!   Algorithm taken from Algorithms +
!   Data Structures - N. Wirth
!   ISBN 0-13-021999-1
!   Pages 57:59
    integer, intent (in) :: n
    character *32, dimension (1:n), &
      intent (in) :: x
    character *32, intent (in) :: key
```

```
      integer :: position
      integer :: l, r, m

      l = 1
      r = n

      do while (l<r)
        m = (l+r)/2
        if (x(m)<key) then
          l = m + 1
        else
          r = m
        end if
      end do

      if (x(r)==key) then
        position = r
      else
        position = 0
      end if

   end function binary_search

end module character_binary_search_module


program ch3805
  use character_binary_search_module
  use timing_module
  implicit none

  integer, parameter :: nwords = 173528
  character *32, dimension (1:nwords) :: &
    dictionary
  character *32 :: word
  character *1 :: answer
  integer :: position

  call start_timing()

  call read_words()

  write (*, 100) time_difference()
100 format (2x, f7.3)
```

```fortran
  do

    print *, &
      'Type in the word you are looking for'
    read *, word

    write (*, 100) time_difference()

    position = binary_search(dictionary, nwords, &
      word)

    write (*, 100) time_difference()

    if (position==0) then
      print *, ' Word not found'
    else
      write (*, 110) trim(word), position
110   format (a, ' found at position ', i6)
    end if

    print *, ' Try again (y/n) ?'
    read *, answer

    if ((answer=='y') .or. (answer=='Y')) then
      cycle
    else
      exit
    end if

  end do

  call end_timing()

contains

  subroutine read_words()
    implicit none
    integer :: i
    character *80 :: file_name = 'words.txt'

    open (unit=10, file=file_name, status='old')
    do i = 1, nwords
      read (10, 100) dictionary(i)
100   format (a)
    end do
```

```
      close (10)

    end subroutine read_words

  end program ch3805
```

The program reads in a dictionary. Historically on Unix systems there was a spelling checker, and there would be a *words* file, often in

```
/etc
```

This is an example of one of these files. Many language versions were available. We then search the dictionary to see if the word entered is in the dictionary. The program provides timing information.

Here is the output from a sample run. The data was read from a file.

```
 2015/ 3/10 14:56: 8 430
     0.070
 Type in the word you are looking for
     0.000
     0.000
 qwerty found at position 122712
   Try again (y/n) ?
 Type in the word you are looking for
     0.000
     0.000
   Word not found
   Try again (y/n) ?
 Type in the word you are looking for
     0.000
     0.000
 albumin found at position    3309
   Try again (y/n) ?
 Type in the word you are looking for
     0.000
     0.000
 transubstantiation found at position 158170
   Try again (y/n) ?
 2015/ 3/10 14:56: 8 500
```

As can be seen the timing reading in the file takes less than one tenth of a second, and the search takes less than a microsecond - the resolution made available via the date_time subroutine.

The dictionary has over 170,000 words. Handy for Scrabble!

The dictionary word file is called

`words.txt`

in the program.

38.8   Problems

38.1 Try out the examples on your system. What timing details do you get?

38.2 Using the non recursive 32 bit integer sort subroutine as a starting point produce a 64 bit integer version. How long did it take to get a working version?

38.3 If you have successfully solved the above problem now produce subroutines for 8 bit and 16 bit integers.

38.4 Using the non recursive 64 bit real subroutine as a starting point produce a 128 bit version. How long did this take?

Chapter 39
Handling Missing Data in Statistics Calculations

Jupiter and beyond the infinite
Stanley Kubrick - 2001: A Space Odyssey

39.1 Introduction

In this chapter we look at a case study of processing the Met Office historic data files and generating statistics accommodating missing data values.

Several steps are involved

- a program to download and save the data files locally
- a sed script to convert the missing values.
- a modified statistics module that will process and report on missing values.
- a module that encapsulates the Met Office station data information.
- a program that actually does the calculations and generates the summary information.
- a site description module that encapsulates the site information.
- a program to generate the site information summary data.

39.2 Example 1: Program to Download and Save the Data Files Locally

This is a C# program. We have programs in Python and Java on our web site that have the same functionality.

Here is the Met Office web address.

```
http://www.metoffice.gov.uk/public/weather/
climate-historic/#?tab=climateHistoric
```

© Springer International Publishing AG, part of Springer Nature 2018
I. Chivers and J. Sleightholme, *Introduction to Programming with Fortran*,
https://doi.org/10.1007/978-3-319-75502-1_39

Here is the program.

```
using System;
using System.Net;
using System.Net.Sockets;
using System.IO;
using System.Text;

class ch3901 {

  static int Main()
  {

    const int n_sites=37;

    string base_address =
    @"http://www.metoffice.gov.uk/pub/"
    +"data/weather/uk/climate/stationdata/";

    string [] station_name =
    {
    "aberporth",        "armagh",
    "ballypatrick",     "bradford",
    "braemar",          "camborne",
    "cambridge",        "cardiff",
    "chivenor",         "cwmystwyth",
    "dunstaffnage",     "durham",
    "eastbourne",       "eskdalemuir",
    "heathrow",         "hurn",
    "lerwick",          "leuchars",
    "lowestoft",        "manston",
    "nairn",            "newtonrigg",
    "oxford",           "paisley",
    "ringway",          "rossonwye",
    "shawbury",         "sheffield",
    "southampton",      "stornoway",
    "suttonbonington",  "tiree",
    "valley",           "waddington",
    "whitby",           "wickairport",
    "yeovilton",
    };

    string [] web_address = new string[n_sites];

    string last_part="data.txt";

    string input_string;

    int i;

    // create the web address of each file

    for (i=0;i<n_sites;i++)
    {
      web_address[i]=
      base_address+station_name[i]+last_part;
      System.Console.WriteLine(web_address[i]);
    }

    string[] local_data_file =
```

```
    {
        "aberporthdata.txt",         "armaghdata.txt",
        "ballypatrickdata.txt",      "bradforddata.txt",
        "braemardata.txt",           "cambornedata.txt",
        "cambridgedata.txt",         "cardiffdata.txt",
        "chivenordata.txt",          "cwmystwythdata.txt",
        "dunstaffnagedata.txt",      "durhamdata.txt",
        "eastbournedata.txt",        "eskdalemuirdata.txt",
        "heathrowdata.txt",          "hurndata.txt",
        "lerwickdata.txt",           "leucharsdata.txt",
        "lowestoftdata.txt",         "manstondata.txt",
        "nairndata.txt",             "newtonriggdata.txt",
        "oxforddata.txt",            "paisleydata.txt",
        "ringwaydata.txt",           "rossonwyedata.txt",
        "shawburydata.txt",          "sheffielddata.txt",
        "southamptondata.txt",       "stornowaydata.txt",
        "suttonboningtondata.txt",   "tireedata.txt",
        "valleydata.txt",            "waddingtondata.txt",
        "whitbydata.txt",            "wickairportdata.txt",
        "yeoviltondata.txt"
    };

    StreamWriter output_file;

    for (i=0;i<n_sites;i++)
    {
      // create the web addresses

      HttpWebRequest  httpwreq   = (HttpWebRequest)
      WebRequest.Create(web_address[i]);

      // set up connection

      HttpWebResponse httpwresp  = (HttpWebResponse)
      httpwreq.GetResponse();

      // set up input stream

      StreamReader input_stream = new
        StreamReader
        (httpwresp.GetResponseStream(),Encoding.ASCII);

      // read the whole file

      input_string=input_stream.ReadToEnd();

      // create the output file

      output_file =
      File.CreateText("before_"+local_data_file[i]);

      output_file.WriteLine(input_string);

      input_stream.Close();
      output_file.Close();
    }
    return(0);
}}
```

39.3   Example 2: The Sed Script and Command File That Converts the Missing Values

Here is an extract from one of the Met Office station files.

yyyy	mm	tmax degC	tmin degC	af days	rain mm	sun hours
1959	1	4.5	-1.9	20	---	57.2
1959	2	7.3	0.9	15	---	87.2
1959	3	8.4	3.1	3	---	81.6
1959	4	10.8	3.7	1	---	107.4
1959	5	15.8	5.8	1	---	213.5
1959	6	16.9	8.2	0	---	209.4
1959	7	18.5	9.5	0	---	167.8
1959	8	19.0	10.5	0	---	164.8
1959	9	18.3	5.9	0	---	196.5
1959	10	14.8	7.9	1	---	101.1
1959	11	8.8	3.9	3	---	38.9
1959	12	7.2	2.5	3	---	19.2
1960	1	6.3	0.6	15	---	30.7
1960	2	5.3	-0.3	17	---	50.2
1960	3	8.2	2.4	4	---	73.9
1960	4	11.2	2.6	7	---	146.8
1960	5	15.4	6.5	2	---	153.9
1960	6	18.5	8.2	0	---	225.6
1960	7	16.0	9.3	0	---	111.3
1960	8	16.5	9.4	0	---	119.2
1960	9	15.0	7.9	0	---	120.3
1960	10	12.0	5.3	5	---	---
1960	11	8.8	2.9	5	---	37.3
1960	12	5.9	0.4	13	---	33.9
1961	1	5.4	0.2	11	144.8	31.0
1961	2	8.7	2.9	2	112.5	45.2
1961	3	10.2	2.1	10	77.2	102.6
1961	4	11.9	5.0	1	130.7	83.9
1961	5	---	---	---	66.3	173.7
1961	6	---	7.4	---	66.1	190.6
1961	7	16.7	8.2	0	141.1	149.2
1961	8	16.8	10.1	0	149.5	106.6
1961	9	17.4	9.3	0	134.8	79.7

The Met Office uses

---

to indicate a missing value. One way of processing the missing values is to convert the

---

into a number that cannot occur in the data.

We convert

```
--- to
-999
```

in this case study. We use the Unix sed command.

sed (stream editor) is a Unix utility that parses and transforms text, using a simple programming language syntax. sed was developed from 1973 to 1974 by Lee E. McMahon of Bell Labs, and is available today for most operating systems. sed was based on the scripting features of the interactive editor ed. ed and vi are sometimes the only editors one has access to on a Unix system. ed is the command driven component of vi. sed was one of the earliest tools to support regular expressions.

The bibliography has some references to sed material.

We can then read the whole file in and adjust the statistics routines to ignore the −999 data values.

Here is the sed command to do the conversion.

```
s/ ---/-999/g
```

Here is an example of the sed command to convert one of the Met Office data files.

```
sed -f convert.sed before_aberporthdata.txt
                    > aberporthdata.txt
```

The -f means read the sed command from a file. sed will read from the file before_aberporthdata.txt and write the converted output to the file aberporth-data.txt

39.4   Example 3: The Program to Do the Statistics Calculations

The complete solution is made up of three source files.

Here is the source code for the statistics module.

```
module statistics_module

  implicit none

contains

  subroutine calculate_month_averages(x, n, &
    n_months, sum_x, average_x, index_by_month, &
    month_names)

    implicit none

    real, dimension (:), intent (in) :: x
```

```
   integer, intent (in) :: n
   integer, intent (in) :: n_months

   real, dimension (1:n_months), &
     intent (inout) :: sum_x
   real, dimension (1:n_months), &
     intent (inout) :: average_x

   integer, dimension (1:n), intent (in) :: &
     index_by_month
   character *9, dimension (1:n_months), &
     intent (in) :: month_names

   integer, dimension (1:n_months) :: n_missing
   integer, dimension (1:n_months) :: n_actual

   integer :: m

   sum_x = 0.0
   average_x = 0.0
   n_missing = 0
   n_actual = 0

   do m = 1, n
     if (x(m)>-98.9) then
       sum_x(index_by_month(m)) &
         = sum_x(index_by_month(m)) + x(m)
       n_actual(index_by_month(m)) &
         = n_actual(index_by_month(m)) + 1
     else
       n_missing(index_by_month(m)) &
         = n_missing(index_by_month(m)) + 1
     end if
   end do

   do m = 1, n_months
     average_x(m) = sum_x(m)/(n_actual(m))
   end do

   print *, ' Summary of actual    missing'
   print *, '                 values    values'
   do m = 1, n_months
     print 100, month_names(m), n_actual(m), &
       n_missing(m)
100  format (2x, a9, 2x, i6, 2x, i6)
   end do
 end subroutine calculate_month_averages
end module statistics_module
```

The following Fortran segment

```
   do m = 1, n
     if (x(m)>-98.9) then
       sum_x(index_by_month(m)) &
         = sum_x(index_by_month(m)) + x(m)
       n_actual(index_by_month(m)) &
         = n_actual(index_by_month(m)) + 1
     else
       n_missing(index_by_month(m)) &
```

```
                        = n_missing(index_by_month(m)) + 1
            end if
        end do
```

is the code to skip processing of the missing data.

Here is the source code for the Met Office station module.

```
module met_office_station_module

    implicit none

    type station_type

        integer :: year
        integer :: month
        real :: tmax
        real :: tmin
        integer :: af_days
        real :: rainfall
        real :: sunshine

    end type station_type

! Number of stations

    integer, parameter :: n_stations = 37

! Number of lines per station, read in later

    integer, dimension (n_stations) :: nl = 0

! Site names

    character *15, dimension (n_stations) :: &
        site_name = (/ 'aberporth       ', &
        'armagh         ', 'ballypatrick   ', &
        'bradford       ', 'braemar        ', &
        'camborne       ', 'cambridge      ', &
        'cardiff        ', 'chivenor       ', &
        'cwmystwyth     ', 'dunstaffnage   ', &
        'durham         ', 'eastbourne     ', &
        'eskdalemuir    ', 'heathrow       ', &
        'hurn           ', 'lerwick        ', &
        'leuchars       ', 'lowestoft      ', &
        'manston        ', 'nairn          ', &
        'newtonrigg     ', 'oxford         ', &
        'paisley        ', 'ringway        ', &
        'rossonwye      ', 'shawbury       ', &
        'sheffield      ', 'southampton    ', &
        'stornoway      ', 'suttonbonington', &
        'tiree          ', 'valley         ', &
        'waddington     ', 'whitby         ', &
        'wickairport    ', 'yeovilton      ' /)


! Station data file names

    character *23, dimension (n_stations) :: &
        station_data_file_name = (/ &
```

```fortran
          'aberporthdata.txt         ', &
          'armaghdata.txt            ', &
          'ballypatrickdata.txt      ', &
          'bradforddata.txt          ', &
          'braemardata.txt           ', &
          'cambornedata.txt          ', &
          'cambridgedata.txt         ', &
          'cardiffdata.txt           ', &
          'chivenordata.txt          ', &
          'cwmystwythdata.txt        ', &
          'dunstaffnagedata.txt      ', &
          'durhamdata.txt            ', &
          'eastbournedata.txt        ', &
          'eskdalemuirdata.txt       ', &
          'heathrowdata.txt          ', &
          'hurndata.txt              ', &
          'lerwickdata.txt           ', &
          'leucharsdata.txt          ', &
          'lowestoftdata.txt         ', &
          'manstondata.txt           ', &
          'nairndata.txt             ', &
          'newtonriggdata.txt        ', &
          'oxforddata.txt            ', &
          'paisleydata.txt           ', &
          'ringwaydata.txt           ', &
          'rossonwyedata.txt         ', &
          'shawburydata.txt          ', &
          'sheffielddata.txt         ', &
          'southamptondata.txt       ', &
          'stornowaydata.txt         ', &
          'suttonboningtondata.txt', &
          'tireedata.txt             ', &
          'valleydata.txt            ', &
          'waddingtondata.txt        ', &
          'whitbydata.txt            ', &
          'wickairportdata.txt       ', &
          'yeoviltondata.txt         ' /)

! cwmystwyth   1959 - 2011
! ringway      1946 - 2004
! southampton  1855 - 2000

! default header line count

  integer, dimension (1:n_stations) :: hl = 7

  integer, parameter :: n_months = 12

  character *9, dimension (1:n_months) :: &
    month_names = (/ 'January  ', 'February ', &
    'March    ', 'April    ', 'May      ', &
    'June     ', 'July     ', 'August   ', &
    'September', 'October  ', 'November ', &
    'December ' /)

contains

  subroutine initialise_station_data()
    implicit none
```

```
      integer :: i

!     Braemar, Lowestoft, Nairn, Southampton,
!     Whitby
!     have 8 header lines, as the position of
!     the station moved.

      hl(5) = 8
      hl(19) = 8
      hl(21) = 8
      hl(29) = 8
      hl(35) = 8

!     Next read in the current number of
!     lines per station
!     This changes as the data is collected,
!     and when you
!     run the C# program that gets the files.
!
!     I generate this information using wc on the
!     data files.

      open (unit=100, file='line_count.txt',&
              status='old')

      do i = 1, n_stations
        read (100, 100) nl(i)
100     format (i7)
        nl(i) = nl(i) - hl(i)
        print 110, station_data_file_name(i), &
          nl(i)
110     format (' Station ', a30, ' = ', i6, &
          ' records')
      end do

      close (100)

   end subroutine initialise_station_data

   subroutine skip_header_lines(j)

      implicit none
      integer, intent (in) :: j
      integer :: i

!     Skip header lines

      do i = 1, hl(j)
        read (unit=100, fmt='(a)')
      end do

   end subroutine skip_header_lines

end module met_office_station_module
```

Here is the source code for the driving program.

```
include 'ch3903_statistics_module.f90'
include 'ch3903_met_office_station_module.f90'
```

```
program ch3903

  use met_office_station_module
  use statistics_module

  implicit none

! met office data user defined type

  type (station_type), dimension (:), &
    allocatable :: station_data

! Temporary variables used on the read

  integer :: year
  integer :: month
  real :: tmax
  real :: tmin
  integer :: af_days
  real :: rainfall
  real :: sunshine

! Currently we only calculate the
! rainfall sum and averages.

! real, dimension (1:n_months) :: sum_tmax
! real, dimension (1:n_months) :: sum_tmin
! real, dimension (1:n_months) :: sum_af_days
  real, dimension (1:n_months) :: sum_rainfall
! real, dimension (1:n_months) :: sum_sunshine

! real, dimension (1:n_months) :: average_tmax
! real, dimension (1:n_months) :: average_tmin
! real, dimension (1:n_months) ::
! average_af_days
  real, dimension (1:n_months) :: &
    average_rainfall
! real, dimension (1:n_months) ::
! average_sunshine

! Table to hold the monthly rainfall averages
! for all stations.

  real, dimension (1:n_months, 1:n_stations) :: &
    rainfall_table = 0

  integer :: n_years

  integer :: i, j

  call initialise_station_data()

! Process each station

  do j = 1, n_stations

    print *, ' '
    print *, ' Processing ', &
```

```
        station_data_file_name(j)
        print *, ' '

        open (unit=100,&
              file=station_data_file_name(j),&
              status='old')

!    skip the header lines before starting to
!    read the data

        call skip_header_lines(j)

!    the number of observations at each station
!    is stored in the nl array.

        allocate (station_data(1:nl(j)))

!    Read in the data for each station

        do i = 1, nl(j)
          read (unit=100, fmt=100) year, month, &
            tmax, tmin, af_days, rainfall, sunshine
100       format (3x, i4, 2x, i2, 2x, f5.1, 3x, &
            f5.1, 3x, i5, 2x, f6.1, 1x, f6.1)
          station_data(i) = station_type(year, &
            month, tmax, tmin, af_days, rainfall, &
            sunshine)
        end do

        close (100)

!    Do the monthly average calculations
!    for each station

        call calculate_month_averages(station_data% &
          rainfall, nl(j), n_months, sum_rainfall, &
          average_rainfall, station_data%month, &
          month_names)

        n_years = station_data(nl(j))%year - &
          station_data(1)%year + 1

        print *, ' '
        print *, ' Start date ', station_data(1)% &
          year, ' ', station_data(1)%month
        print *, ' '
        print *, ' Rainfall monthly averages over'
        print 110, n_years
110     format (' ~ ', i5, &
          ' years            mm     ins')
        do i = 1, n_months
          print 120, month_names(i), &
            average_rainfall(i), (average_rainfall(i &
            )/25.4)
120       format (2x, a9, 8x, f7.2, 2x, f5.2)
        end do
        print 130, sum(average_rainfall), &
          (sum(average_rainfall)/25.4)
130     format ('  Annual rainfall', /, &
```

```
          '   average               ', f8.2, 2x, f5.2)
      print *, ' '
      print *, ' End date  ', station_data(nl(j))% &
        year, ' ', station_data(nl(j))%month

      rainfall_table(1:n_months, j) &
        = average_rainfall

!   Deallocate the arrays

    deallocate (station_data)

!   move on to next station

  end do

  print *, ' '
  print 140, site_name(1:n_stations)
140 format (37(2x,a7))
  print *, ' '

  do i = 1, n_months
    print 150, rainfall_table(i, 1:n_stations)/ &
      25.4
150 format (37(2x,f7.2))
  end do

end program ch3903
```

Here are the required files.

```
line_count.txt
```

Here is some sample output from running the program. It is a subset of the complete output, which can be found on our web site.

```
    Station        aberporthdata.txt      =      906 records
    Station        armaghdata.txt         =     1962 records
    Station        ballypatrickdata.txt   =      660 records
    Station        bradforddata.txt       =     1302 records

... lines deleted

  Processing aberporthdata.txt

  Summary of actual    missing
            values     values
  January      76        0
  February     76        0
  March        76        0
  April        76        0
  May          76        0
  June         76        0
  July         75        0
  August       75        0
  September    75        0
  October      75        0
  November     75        0
```

```
December          75          0

Start date   1941    1

Rainfall monthly averages over
~     76 years              mm     ins
January                  90.71   3.57
February                 62.75   2.47
March                    59.25   2.33
April                    53.98   2.13
May                      57.99   2.28
June                     57.23   2.25
July                     61.94   2.44
August                   73.03   2.88
September                79.43   3.13
October                 104.40   4.11
November                107.61   4.24
December                102.01   4.02
Annual rainfall
average                 910.35  35.84

End date    2016    6
```

... lines deleted

```
Processing ballypatrickdata.txt

Summary of actual      missing
              values     values
January          28         27
February         28         27
March            28         27
April            28         27
May              28         27
June             28         27
July             27         28
August           27         28
September        27         28
October          26         29
November         28         27
December         27         28

Start date   1961    7

Rainfall monthly averages over
~     56 years              mm     ins
January                 133.76   5.27
February                108.66   4.28
March                    95.51   3.76
April                    87.12   3.43
May                      81.26   3.20
June                     87.10   3.43
July                     90.06   3.55
August                  104.44   4.11
September                98.58   3.88
October                 148.92   5.86
November                146.29   5.76
December                146.13   5.75
Annual rainfall
```

```
average              1327.85   52.28

End date    2016    6

... lines deleted

... following lines truncated
... to fit page

aberpor   armagh    ballypa   bradfor

   3.57      3.00      5.27      3.60
   2.47      2.25      4.28      2.78
   2.33      2.27      3.76      2.45
   2.13      2.18      3.43      2.28
   2.28      2.35      3.20      2.34
   2.25      2.45      3.43      2.40
   2.44      2.82      3.55      2.61
   2.88      3.23      4.11      3.01
   3.13      2.71      3.88      2.66
   4.11      3.20      5.86      3.16
   4.24      2.90      5.76      3.48
   4.02      3.19      5.75      3.68
```

39.5   Example 4: Met Office Utility Program

The complete solution is made up of two source files.
    Here is the source for the site description module.

```fortran
module site_description_module

  type site_description
    character *15 :: site_name = ' '
    character *7 :: easting_1 = ' '
    character *7 :: northing_1 = ' '
    real :: lat_1 = 0.0
    real :: long_1 = 0.0
    integer :: height_1 = 0
    character *7 :: easting_2 = ' '
    character *7 :: northing_2 = ' '
    real :: lat_2 = 0.0
    real :: long_2 = 0.0
    integer :: height_2 = 0
    integer :: start_date_month_1 = 0
    integer :: start_date_year_1 = 0
    integer :: end_date_month_1 = 0
    integer :: end_date_year_1 = 0
    integer :: start_date_month_2 = 0
    integer :: start_date_year_2 = 0
    integer :: end_date_month_2 = 0
    integer :: end_date_year_2 = 0
  end type site_description

end module site_description_module
```

Here is the source for the driving program.

```
include 'ch3904_site_description_module.f90'

program ch3904

  use site_description_module

  implicit none

  integer, parameter :: n_stations = 37

! site names

  character *15, dimension (n_stations) :: &
    site_name = (/ 'aberporth       ', &
    'armagh         ', 'ballypatrick   ', &
    'bradford       ', 'braemar        ', &
    'camborne       ', 'cambridge      ', &
    'cardiff        ', 'chivenor       ', &
    'cwmystwyth     ', 'dunstaffnage   ', &
    'durham         ', 'eastbourne     ', &
    'eskdalemuir    ', 'heathrow       ', &
    'hurn           ', 'lerwick        ', &
    'leuchars       ', 'lowestoft      ', &
    'manston        ', 'nairn          ', &
    'newtonrigg     ', 'oxford         ', &
    'paisley        ', 'ringway        ', &
    'rossonwye      ', 'shawbury       ', &
    'sheffield      ', 'southampton    ', &
    'stornoway      ', 'suttonbonington', &
    'tiree          ', 'valley         ', &
    'waddington     ', 'whitby         ', &
    'wickairport    ', 'yeovilton      ' /)

! Braemar, Lowestoft, Nairn,
! Southampton, Whitby
! have 8 header lines, as the position
! of the station moved.

  type (site_description), dimension (1: &
    n_stations) :: site_details

  integer :: i

  open (unit=10, &
        file='location_line.txt',&
        status='old')

  do i = 1, n_stations

    site_details(i)%site_name = site_name(i)
    read (unit=10, fmt=100) site_details(i) &
      %easting_1, site_details(i)%northing_1, &
      site_details(i)%lat_1, site_details(i)% &
      long_1, site_details(i)%height_1
100 format (10x, a6, 2x, a7, 7x, f6.3, 5x, f6.3, &
      2x, i3)
  end do
```

```
  close (10)

  open (unit=20,&
        file='third_line.txt',&
        status='old')

! Update Braemar

! print *,' Braemar'

  read (unit=20, fmt=110) site_details(5) &
    %easting_2, site_details(5)%northing_2, &
    site_details(5)%lat_2, site_details(5)% &
    long_2, site_details(5)%height_2

110 format (2x, a6, 2x, a6, 7x, f6.3, 5x, f6.3, &
    2x, i3)

  site_details(5)%end_date_month_1 = 4
  site_details(5)%end_date_year_1 = 2005
  site_details(5)%start_date_month_2 = 8
  site_details(5)%start_date_year_2 = 2005

! Update Lowestoft

! print *,' Lowestoft'

  read (unit=20, fmt=110) site_details(19) &
    %easting_2, site_details(19)%northing_2, &
    site_details(19)%lat_2, site_details(19)% &
    long_2, site_details(19)%height_2

  site_details(19)%end_date_month_1 = 8
  site_details(19)%end_date_year_1 = 2007
  site_details(19)%start_date_month_2 = 9
  site_details(19)%start_date_year_2 = 2007

! Update Nairn

! print *,' Nairn'

  read (unit=20, fmt=110) site_details(21) &
    %easting_2, site_details(21)%northing_2, &
    site_details(21)%lat_2, site_details(21)% &
    long_2, site_details(21)%height_2

  site_details(21)%end_date_month_1 = 12
  site_details(21)%end_date_year_1 = 1997
  site_details(21)%start_date_month_2 = 1
  site_details(21)%start_date_year_2 = 1998

! Update Southampton

! print *,' Southampton'

  read (unit=20, fmt=110) site_details(29) &
    %easting_2, site_details(29)%northing_2, &
    site_details(29)%lat_2, site_details(29)% &
```

```
       long_2, site_details(29)%height_2

    site_details(29)%end_date_month_1 = 12
    site_details(29)%end_date_year_1 = 1969
    site_details(29)%start_date_month_2 = 1
    site_details(29)%start_date_year_2 = 1970


  ! Update Whitby

  ! print *,' Whitby'

    read (unit=20, fmt=110) site_details(35) &
      %easting_2, site_details(35)%northing_2, &
      site_details(35)%lat_2, site_details(35)% &
      long_2, site_details(35)%height_2

    site_details(35)%end_date_month_1 = 12
    site_details(35)%end_date_year_1 = 1999
    site_details(35)%start_date_month_2 = 1
    site_details(35)%start_date_year_2 = 2000

    close (20)

  ! Start dates

    open (unit=30, &
          file='first_data_line.txt',&
          status='old')

    do i = 1, n_stations
      read (30, fmt=120) site_details(i) &
        %start_date_year_1, site_details(i)% &
        start_date_month_1
120 format (3x, i4, 2x, i2)
    end do

    close (30)

  ! End dates

    open (unit=40, &
          file='end_data_line.txt',&
          status='old')

    do i = 1, n_stations
      select case (i)
      case (5, 19, 21, 29, 35)
        read (40, fmt=130) site_details(i) &
          %end_date_year_2, site_details(i)% &
          end_date_month_2
      case default
        read (40, fmt=130) site_details(i) &
          %end_date_year_1, site_details(i)% &
          end_date_month_1
130     format (3x, i4, 2x, i2)
      end select
    end do
```

```
   close (40)

   do i = 1, n_stations
     print 140, site_details(i)
140 format (a15, 2x, a7, 2x, a7, 2x, f6.3, 2x, &
       f6.3, 2x, i3, 2x, a7, 2x, a7, f6.3, 2x, &
       f6.3, 2x, i3, 4(2x,i2,2x,i4))
   end do

end program ch3904
```

Here are the required files.

```
location_line.txt
third_line.txt
first_data_line.txt
end_data_line.txt
```

Here is sample output. It has been reformatted to fit the printed page.

```
aberporth         224100    252100  52.139  -4.570  133
         0.000    0.000     0   1  1941   6  2016   0      0    0     0
armagh            287800    345800  54.352  -6.649   62
         0.000    0.000     0   1  1853   6  2016   0      0    0     0
ballypatrick      317600    438600  55.181  -6.153  156
         0.000    0.000     0   7  1961   6  2016   0      0    0     0
bradford          414900    435200  53.813  -1.772  134
         0.000    0.000     0   1  1908   6  2016   0      0    0     0
braemar           315200    791400   0.000   0.000  339
    315200   791900 57.006  -3.396  327   1
1959    4   2005   8  2005   6  2016
camborne          162700     40700  50.218  -5.327   87
         0.000    0.000     0   9  1978   6  2016   0      0    0     0
cambridge         543500    260600  52.245   0.102   26
         0.000    0.000     0   1  1959   6  2016   0      0    0     0
cardiff           317600    177300  51.488  -3.187    9
         0.000    0.000     0   9  1977   6  2016   0      0    0     0
chivenor          249600    134400  51.089  -4.147    6
         0.000    0.000     0   1  1951   6  2016   0      0    0     0
cwmystwyth        277300    274900  52.358  -3.802  301
         0.000    0.000     0   1  1959   3  2011   0      0    0     0
dunstaffnage      188100    734000  56.451  -5.439    3
         0.000    0.000     0   6  1971   6  2016   0      0    0     0
durham            426700    541500  54.768  -1.585  102
         0.000    0.000     0   1  1880   6  2016   0      0    0     0
eastbourne        561100     98300  50.762   0.285    7
         0.000    0.000     0   1  1959   6  2016   0      0    0     0
eskdalemuir       323400    602600  55.311  -3.206  242
         0.000    0.000     0   1  1911   6  2016   0      0    0     0
heathrow          507800    176700  51.479  -0.449   25
         0.000    0.000     0   1  1948   6  2016   0      0    0     0
hurn              411700     97800  50.779  -1.835   10
         0.000    0.000     0   1  1957   6  2016   0      0    0     0
lerwick           445300   1139700  60.139  -1.183   82
         0.000    0.000     0  12  1930   6  2016   0      0    0     0
leuchars          346800    720900  56.377  -2.861   10
         0.000    0.000     0   1  1957   6  2016   0      0    0     0
lowestoft         654300    294600   0.000   0.000   25
```

```
   653000    293800 52.483    1.727    18    1
1914   8   2007   9   2007   6   2016
manston            632300    166100  51.346    1.337    49
         0.000    0.000    0    7  1934   6  2016   0      0   0      0
nairn              286900    856800   0.000    0.000     8
   291200    857300 57.593  -3.821    23    1
1931  12  1997   1  1998   6  2016
newtonrigg         349300    530800  54.670  -2.786   169
         0.000    0.000    0    1  1959   6  2016   0      0   0      0
oxford             450900    207200  51.761  -1.262    63
         0.000    0.000    0    1  1853   6  2016   0      0   0      0
paisley            247800    664200  55.846  -4.430    32
         0.000    0.000    0    1  1959   6  2016   0      0   0      0
ringway            381400    384400  53.356  -2.279    69
         0.000    0.000    0    1  1946  10  2004   0      0   0      0
rossonwye          359800    223800  51.911  -2.584    67
         0.000    0.000    0   12  1930   6  2016   0      0   0      0
shawbury           355200    322100  52.794  -2.663    72
         0.000    0.000    0    1  1946   6  2016   0      0   0      0
sheffield          433900    387200  53.381  -1.490   131
         0.000    0.000    0    1  1883   6  2016   0      0   0      0
southampton        442000    112500   0.000    0.000    20
   441600    111200 50.898  -1.408     3    1
1855  12  1969   1  1970   3  2000
stornoway          146400    933200  58.214  -6.318    15
         0.000    0.000    0    7  1873   6  2016   0      0   0      0
suttonbonington    450700    325900  52.833  -1.250    48
         0.000    0.000    0    1  1959   6  2016   0      0   0      0
tiree               99800    744800  56.500  -6.880    12
         0.000    0.000    0    1  1928   6  2016   0      0   0      0
valley             230800    375800  53.252  -4.535    10
         0.000    0.000    0   12  1930   6  2016   0      0   0      0
waddington         498800    365300  53.175  -0.522    68
         0.000    0.000    0    1  1947   6  2016   0      0   0      0
whitby             490400    511400   0.000    0.000    60
   489100    510400 54.481  -0.624    41    9
1961  12  1999   1  2000   6  2016
wickairport        336500    952200  58.454  -3.088    36
         0.000    0.000    0    1  1914   6  2016   0      0   0      0
yeovilton          355100    123200  51.006  -2.641    20
         0.000    0.000    0    9  1964   6  2016   0      0   0      0
```

39.6   Bibliography

Dougherty D., Robbins A., sed and awk, O'Reilly

- One of the classic O'Reilly texts.

Unix in a Nutshell, O'Reilly.

- The classic Nutshell text on Unix. Essential reading for Unix and Linux users. The wikipedia entry is a good starting place.

  https://en.wikipedia.org/wiki/Sed

39.7   Problem

39.1 Compile and run the examples in this chapter.

Chapter 40
Converting from Fortran 77

Twas brillig, and the slithy toves did gyre and gimble in the wabe; All mimsy were the borogoves, And the mome raths outgrabe.

Lewis Carroll

Aim

This chapter looks at some of the options available when working with older Fortran code.

40.1 Introduction

This chapter looks at converting Fortran 77 code to a modern Fortran style.

The aim is to provide the Fortran 77 programmer (and in particular the person with legacy code) with some simple guidelines for conversion.

The first thing that one must have is a thorough understanding of the newer, better language features of Fortran. It is essential that the material in the earlier chapters of this book are covered, and some of the problems attempted. This will provide a feel for modern Fortran.

The second thing one must have is a thorough understanding of the language constructs used in your legacy code. Use should be made of the compiler documentation for whatever Fortran 77 compiler you are using, as this will provide the detailed (often system specific) information required. The recommendations below are therefore brief.

It is possible to move gradually from Fortran 77 to modern Fortran. In many cases existing code can be quite simply recompiled by a suitable choice of compiler options. This enables us to mix and match old and new in one program. This process is likely to highlight nonstandard language features in your old code. There will inevitably be some problems here.

© Springer International Publishing AG, part of Springer Nature 2018   753
I. Chivers and J. Sleightholme, *Introduction to Programming with Fortran*,
https://doi.org/10.1007/978-3-319-75502-1_40

The standard identifies two kinds of decremented features; deleted and obsolescent. In the long-term these features are candidates for removal from future standards. These deleted and obsolescent features may well be supported by compilers even though they have been removed from the standard.

The following information is taken from the Fortran 2018 standard.

40.2   Deleted Features from Fortran 90

These deleted features are those features of Fortran 90 that were redundant and considered largely unused. The following Fortran 90 features are not required.

- (1) Real and double precision DO variables.
  In Fortran 77 and Fortran 90, a DO variable was allowed to be of type real or double precision in addition to type integer; this has been deleted. A similar result can be achieved by using a DO construct with no loop control and the appropriate exit test.
- (2) Branching to an END IF statement from outside its block.
  In Fortran 77 and Fortran 90, it was possible to branch to an END IF statement from outside the IF construct; this has been deleted. A similar result can be achieved by branching to a CONTINUE statement that is immediately after the END IF statement.
- (3) PAUSE statement.
  The PAUSE statement, provided in Fortran 66, Fortran 77, and Fortran 90, has been deleted. A similar result can be achieved by writing a message to the appropriate unit, followed by reading from the appropriate unit.
- (4) ASSIGN and assigned GO TO statements, and assigned format specifiers.
  The ASSIGN statement and the related assigned GO TO statement, provided in Fortran 66, Fortran 77, and Fortran 90, have been deleted. Further, the ability to use an assigned integer as a format, provided in Fortran 77 and Fortran 90, has been deleted. A similar result can be achieved by using other control constructs instead of the assigned GO TO statement and by using a default character variable to hold a format specification instead of using an assigned integer.
- (5) H edit descriptor.
  In Fortran 77 and Fortran 90, there was an alternative form of character string edit descriptor, which had been the only such form in Fortran 66; this has been deleted. A similar result can be achieved by using a character string edit descriptor.
- (6) Vertical format control.
  In Fortran 66, Fortran 77, Fortran 90, and Fortran 95 formatted output to certain units resulted in the first character of each record being interpreted as controlling vertical spacing. There was no standard way to detect whether output to a unit resulted in this vertical format control, and no way to specify that it should be applied; this has been deleted. The effect can be achieved by post-processing a

formatted file. See ISO/IEC 1539:1991 for detailed rules of how these deleted features worked.

40.3   Deleted Features from Fortran 2008

These deleted features are those features of Fortran 2008 that were redundant and considered largely unused. The following Fortran 2008 features are not required.

- (1) Arithmetic IF statement.
  The arithmetic IF statement is incompatible with ISO/IEC/IEEE 60559:2011 and necessarily involves the use of statement labels; statement labels can hinder optimization, and make code hard to read and maintain. Similar logic can be more clearly encoded using other conditional statements.
- (2) Nonblock DO construct
  The nonblock forms of the DO loop were confusing and hard to maintain. Shared termination and dual use of labeled action statements as do termination and branch targets were especially error11 prone.

40.4   Obsolescent Features

The obsolescent features are those features of Fortran 90 that were redundant and for which better methods were available in Fortran 90. Subclause 4.4.3 describes the nature of the obsolescent features. The obsolescent features in this document are the following.

- (1) Alternate return
- (2) Computed GO TO
- (3) Statement functions
- (4) DATA statements amongst executable statements
- (5) Assumed length character functions
- (6) Fixed form source
- (7) CHARACTER* form of CHARACTER declaration
- (8) ENTRY statements
- (9) Label form of DO statement
- (10) COMMON and EQUIVALENCE statements, and the block data program unit
- (11) Specific names for intrinsic functions
- (12) FORALL construct and statement

40.4.1   Alternate Return

An alternate return introduces labels into an argument list to allow the called procedure to direct the execution of the caller upon return. The same effect can be achieved
with a return code that is used in a SELECT CASE construct on return. This avoids
an irregularity in the syntax and semantics of argument association. For example,

```
CALL SUBR_NAME (X, Y, Z, *100, *200, *300)
```

can be replaced by

```
CALL SUBR_NAME (X, Y, Z, RETURN_CODE)
SELECT CASE (RETURN_CODE)
CASE (1)
...
CASE (2)
...
CASE (3)
...
CASE DEFAULT
...
END SELECT
```

40.4.2   Computed GO TO Statement

The computed GO TO statement has been superseded by the SELECT CASE construct, which is a generalized, easier to use, and clearer means of expressing the same
computation.

40.4.3   Statement Functions

Statement functions are subject to a number of nonintuitive restrictions and are a
potential source of error because their syntax is easily confused with that of an
assignment statement. The internal function is a more generalized form of the statement function and completely supersedes it.

40.4.4   DATA Statements Among Executables

The statement ordering rules allow DATA statements to appear anywhere in a program unit after the specification statements. The ability to position DATA statements amongst executable statements is very rarely used, unnecessary, and a potential
source of error.

40.4.5 Assumed Character Length Functions

Assumed character length for functions is an irregularity in the language in that elsewhere in Fortran the philosophy is that the attributes of a function result depend only on the actual arguments of the invocation and on any data accessible by the function through host or use association. Some uses of this facility can be replaced with an automatic character length function, where the length of the function result is declared in a specification expression. Other uses can be replaced by the use of a subroutine whose arguments correspond to the function result and the function arguments. Note that dummy arguments of a function can have assumed character length.

40.4.6 Fixed Form Source

Fixed form source was designed when the principal machine-readable input medium for new programs was punched cards. Now that new and amended programs are generally entered via keyboards with screen displays, it is an unnecessary overhead, and is potentially error-prone, to have to locate positions 6, 7, or 72 on a line. Free form source was designed expressly for this more modern technology. It is a simple matter for a software tool to convert from fixed to free form source.

40.4.7 CHARACTER* Form of CHARACTER Declaration

In addition to the CHARACTER*char-length form introduced in Fortran 77, Fortran 90 provided the CHAR3 ACTER([LEN =] type-param-value) form. The older form (CHARACTER*char-length) is redundant.

40.4.8 ENTRY Statements

ENTRY statements allow more than one entry point to a subprogram, facilitating sharing of data items and executable statements local to that subprogram. This can be replaced by a module containing the (private) data items, with a module procedure for each entry point and the shared code in a private module procedure.

40.4.9   Label DO Statement

The label in the DO statement is redundant with the construct name. Furthermore, the label allows unrestricted branches and, for its main purpose (the target of a conditional branch to skip the rest of the current iteration), is redundant with the CYCLE statement, which is clearer.

40.4.10   COMMON and EQUIVALENCE Statements and the Block Data Program Unit

Common blocks are error-prone and have largely been superseded by modules. EQUIVALENCE similarly is error-prone. Whilst use of these statements was invaluable prior to Fortran 90 they are now redundant and can inhibit performance. The block data program unit exists only to serve common blocks and hence is also redundant.

40.4.11   Specific Names for Intrinsic Functions

The specific names of the intrinsic functions are often obscure and hinder portability. They have been redundant since Fortran 90. Use generic names for references to intrinsic procedures.

40.4.12   FORALL Construct and Statement

The FORALL construct and statement were added to the language in the expectation that they would enable highly efficient execution, especially on parallel processors. However, experience indicates that they are too complex and have too many restrictions for compilers to take advantage of them. They are redundant with the DO CONCURRENT construct, and many of the manipulations for which they might be used can be done more effectively using pointers, especially using pointer rank remapping.

40.5   Better Alternatives

Below we are looking at the new features of the Fortran standard, and how we can replace our current coding practices with the better facilities that now exist.

- double precision — use the module `precision_module` which was introduced in Chap. 21 and used subsequently throughout the book.
- fixed format — use free format
- implicit typing — use implicit none
- block data — use modules
- common statement — use modules
- equivalence — Invariably the use of this feature requires considerable system specific knowledge. There will be cases where there have been extremely good reasons why this feature has been used, normally efficiency related. However with the rapid changes taking place in the power and speed of hardware these reasons are diminishing.
- assumed-size/explicit-shape dummy array arguments — if a dummy argument is assumed-size or explicit-shape (the only ones available in Fortran 77) then the ranks of the actual argument and the associated argument don't have to be the same. With modern Fortran arrays are now objects instead of a linear sequence of elements, as was the case with Fortran 77, and now for array arguments the fundamental rule is that actual and dummy arguments have the same rank and same extents in each dimension, i.e., the same shape, and this is done using assumed-shape dummy array arguments. An explicit interface is mandatory for assumed-shape arrays.
- entry statement — use module plus use statement.
- statement functions — use internal function, see Chap. 12, and examples later this chapter.
- computed goto — use case statement, see Chap. 13.
- alternate return — use error flags on calling routine.
- external statement for dummy procedure arguments - use modules and interface blocks. See the Runge-Kutta-Merson example in Chap. 26.

Use explicit interfaces everywhere, i.e. use module procedures.
This also provides argument checking and other benefits.

40.6 Free and Commercial Conversion Tools

At the time of writing there are several options. Have a look at our Fortran resource file:

```
https://www.fortranplus.co.uk/
```

for up to date information.

Here are brief details of the tools currently available.

40.6.1   Convert

Fortran 77 to Fortran 90 converter by Mike Metcalf.

```
http://rhymneyconsulting.co.uk/fortran/convert.f90
```

Here are some of the comments from the program.

```
!    A program to convert FORTRAN 77 source form to Fortran 90 source  *
!  form. It also formats the code by indenting the bodies of DO-loops   *
!  and IF-blocks by ISHIFT columns. Statement keywords are              *
!  followed if necessary by a blank, and blanks within tokens are       *
!  are suppressed; this handling of blanks is optional.                 *
!    If a CONTINUE statement terminates a single DO loop, it is         *
!  replaced by END DO.                                                  *
!    Procedure END statements have the procedure name added, if         *
!  blanks are handled.                                                  *
!    Statements like INTEGER*2 are converted to INTEGER(2), if blanks   *
!  are handled. Depending on the target processor, a further global     *
!  edit might be required (e.g. where 2 bytes correspond to KIND=1).    *
!  Typed functions and assumed-length character specifications are      *
!  treated similarly. The length specification *4 is removed for all    *
!  data types except CHARACTER, as is *8 for COMPLEX. This              *
!  treatment of non-standard type declarations includes any            *
!  non-standard IMPLICIT statements.                                    *
!    Optionally, interface blocks only may be produced; this requires   *
!  blanks processing to be requested. The interface blocks are         *
!  compatible with both the old and new source forms.                   *
```

40.6.2   Forcheck

A Fortran analyser and programming aid.

```
http://www.forcheck.nl/
```

40.6.3   Nag Compiler Polish Tool

Here is the home page for the Nag compiler.

```
https://www.nag.co.uk/nag-compiler
```

Here is a brief description of the tools.

In addition the Compiler provides software tools to: convert fixed-format code to free-format; pretty print ("polish") code; list dependency information of modules and include files; produce callgraphs; and generate explicit procedure interfaces as module or INCLUDE files.

40.6.4   Plusfort

Fortran 77 to Fortran 90 converter.

```
https://www.polyhedron.com/
```

40.7   Example 1: Using the plusFORT Tool Suite from Polyhedron Software

Below is an example from their site that looks at the same subroutine in Fortran 66, 77 and 90 styles.

40.7.1   Original Fortran 66

This subroutine picks off digits from an integer and branches depending on their value.

```
      SUBROUTINE OBACT(TODO)
      INTEGER TODO,DONE,IP,BASE
      COMMON /EG1/N,L,DONE
      PARAMETER (BASE=10)
   13 if(TODO.EQ.0) GO TO 12
      I=MOD(TODO,BASE)
      TODO=TODO/BASE
      GO TO(62,42,43,62,404,45,62,62,62),I
      GO TO 13
   42 CALL COPY
      GO TO 127
   43 CALL MOVE
      GO TO 144
  404 N=-N
   44 CALL DELETE
      GO TO 127
   45 CALL print
      GO TO 144
   62 CALL BADACT(i)
      GO TO 12
  127 L=L+N
  144 DONE=DONE+1
      CALL RESYNC
      GO TO 13
   12 RETURN
      END
```

40.7.2   Fortran 77 Version

In addition to restructuring, SPAG has renamed some variables, removed the unused variable IP, inserted declarations, and used upper and lower case to distinguish different types of variable:

```
          SUBROUTINE OBACT(TODO)
          IMPLICIT NONE
C*** START OF DECLARATIONS INSERTED BY SPAG
          INTEGER ACT , LENGTH , NCHAR
C*** END OF DECLARATIONS INSERTED BY SPAG
          INTEGER TODO , DONE , BASE
          COMMON /EG1   / NCHAR , LENGTH , DONE
          PARAMETER (BASE=10)
  100 IF ( TODO.NE.0 ) THEN
            ACT = MOD(TODO,BASE)
            TODO = TODO/BASE
            IF ( ACT.EQ.1 .OR. ACT.EQ.4 .OR.
     &          ACT.EQ.7 .OR. ACT.EQ.8 .OR.
     &          ACT.EQ.9 ) THEN
              CALL BADACT(ACT)
              GOTO 200
            ELSEIF ( ACT.EQ.2 ) THEN
              CALL COPY
              LENGTH = LENGTH + NCHAR
            ELSEIF ( ACT.EQ.3 ) THEN
              CALL MOVE
            ELSEIF ( ACT.EQ.5 ) THEN
              NCHAR = -NCHAR
              CALL DELETE
              LENGTH = LENGTH + NCHAR
            ELSEIF ( ACT.EQ.6 ) THEN
              CALL PRINT
            ELSE
              GOTO 100
            ENDIF
            DONE = DONE + 1
            CALL RESYNC
            GOTO 100
          ENDIF
  200 RETURN
          END
```

40.7.3   Fortran 90 Version

SPAG has used do while, select case, exit and cycle. No GOTOs or labels remain.

```
          subroutine obact(todo)
          implicit none
!*** start of declarations inserted by spag
          integer act , length , nchar
!*** end of declarations inserted by spag
```

```
integer todo , done , base
common /eg1    / nchar , length , done
parameter (base=10)
do while ( todo.ne.0 )
   act = mod(todo,base)
   todo = todo/base
   select case (act)
   case (1,4,7,8,9)
      call badact(act)
      exit
   case (2)
      call copy
      length = length + nchar
   case (3)
      call move
   case (5)
      nchar = -nchar
      call delete
      length = length + nchar
   case (6)
      call print
   case default
      cycle
   end select
   done = done + 1
   call resync
enddo
return
end
```

This tool suite can also be used in the maintenance of code during development.

40.8   Example 2: Leaving as Fortran 77

The simplest option if the function or subroutine works and does not need updating
is to leave it as Fortran 66 or 77 fixed source form. The Netlib routines in Chap. 36
are a good example of this. They are

```
dsort.f
ssort.f
isort.f
```

We had to make some changes to get them to compile, and the changes are
documented in the earlier chapter.

40.9   Example 3: Simple Conversion to Fortran 90

The Metcalf convert program can be used to simply convert from Fortran 77 to
Fortran 90.

Using this utility on the Netlib dsort.f Fortran 77 code will produce a Fortran 90
equivalent. Here is the converted code.

```
      SUBROUTINE DSORT (DX, DY, N, KFLAG)
!***BEGIN PROLOGUE  DSORT
!***PURPOSE  Sort an array and optionally make the same interchanges in
!            an auxiliary array.  The array may be sorted in increasing
!            or decreasing order. A slightly modified QUICKSORT
!            algorithm is used.
!***LIBRARY   SLATEC
!***CATEGORY  N6A2B
!***TYPE      DOUBLE PRECISION (SSORT-S, DSORT-D, ISORT-I)
!***KEYWORDS  SINGLETON QUICKSORT, SORT, SORTING
!***AUTHOR  Jones, R. E., (SNLA)
!           Wisniewski, J. A., (SNLA)
!***DESCRIPTION
!
!    DSORT sorts array DX and optionally makes the same interchanges in
!    array DY.  The array DX may be sorted in increasing order or
!    decreasing order. A slightly modified quicksort algorithm is used.
!
!    Description of Parameters
!       DX - array of values to be sorted   (usually abscissas)
!       DY - array to be (optionally) carried along
!       N  - number of values in array DX to be sorted
!       KFLAG - control parameter
!             =  2  means sort DX in increasing order and carry DY along.
!             =  1  means sort DX in increasing order (ignoring DY)
!             = -1  means sort DX in decreasing order (ignoring DY)
!             = -2  means sort DX in decreasing order and carry DY along.
!
!***REFERENCES  R. C. Singleton, Algorithm 347, An efficient algorithm
!                 for sorting with minimal storage, Communications of
!                 the ACM, 12, 3 (1969), pp. 185-187.
!***ROUTINES CALLED  XERMSG
!***REVISION HISTORY  (YYMMDD)
!     761101  DATE WRITTEN
!     761118  Modified to use the Singleton quicksort algorithm.  (JAW)
!     890531  Changed all specific intrinsics to generic.  (WRB)
!     890831  Modified array declarations.  (WRB)
!     891009  Removed unreferenced statement labels.  (WRB)
!     891024  Changed category.  (WRB)
!     891024  REVISION DATE from Version 3.2
!     891214  Prologue converted to Version 4.0 format.  (BAB)
!     900315  CALLs to XERROR changed to CALLs to XERMSG.  (THJ)
!     901012  Declared all variables; changed X,Y to DX,DY; changed
!               code to  parallel SSORT. (M. McClain)
!     920501  Reformatted the REFERENCES section.  (DWL, WRB)
!     920519  Clarified error messages.  (DWL)
!     920801  Declarations section rebuilt and code restructured to use
!               IF-THEN-ELSE-ENDIF.  (RWC, WRB)
!***END PROLOGUE  DSORT
!     .. Scalar Arguments ..
```

```
          INTEGER KFLAG, N
!         .. Array Arguments ..
          DOUBLE PRECISION DX(*), DY(*)
!         .. Local Scalars ..
          DOUBLE PRECISION R, T, TT, TTY, TY
          INTEGER I, IJ, J, K, KK, L, M, NN
!         .. Local Arrays ..
          INTEGER IL(21), IU(21)
!         .. External Subroutines ..
!         EXTERNAL XERMSG
!         .. Intrinsic Functions ..
          INTRINSIC ABS, INT
!***FIRST EXECUTABLE STATEMENT  DSORT
          NN = N
!          IF (NN .LT. 1) THEN
!             CALL XERMSG ('SLATEC', 'DSORT',
!        +       'The number of values to be sorted is not positive.', 1, 1)
!             RETURN
!          ENDIF
!
          KK = ABS(KFLAG)
!          IF (KK.NE.1 .AND. KK.NE.2) THEN
!             CALL XERMSG ('SLATEC', 'DSORT',
!        +       'The sort control parameter, K, is not 2, 1, -1, or -2.', 2
!        +        1)
!             RETURN
!          ENDIF
!
!         Alter array DX to get decreasing order if needed
!
          IF (KFLAG .LE. -1) THEN
             DO 10 I=1,NN
                DX(I) = -DX(I)
   10        CONTINUE
          ENDIF
!
          IF (KK .EQ. 2) GO TO 100
!
!         Sort DX only
!
          M = 1
          I = 1
          J = NN
          R = 0.375D0
!
   20 IF (I .EQ. J) GO TO 60
          IF (R .LE. 0.5898437D0) THEN
             R = R+3.90625D-2
          ELSE
             R = R-0.21875D0
          ENDIF
!
   30 K = I
!
!         Select a central element of the array and save it in location T
!
          IJ = I + INT((J-I)*R)
          T = DX(IJ)
!
```

```
!      If first element of array is greater than T, interchange with T
!
       IF (DX(I) .GT. T) THEN
          DX(IJ) = DX(I)
          DX(I) = T
          T = DX(IJ)
       ENDIF
       L = J
!
!      If last element of array is less than than T, interchange with T
!
       IF (DX(J) .LT. T) THEN
          DX(IJ) = DX(J)
          DX(J) = T
          T = DX(IJ)
!
!         If first element of array is greater than T, interchange with T
!
          IF (DX(I) .GT. T) THEN
             DX(IJ) = DX(I)
             DX(I) = T
             T = DX(IJ)
          ENDIF
       ENDIF
!
!      Find an element in the second half of the array which is smaller
!      than T
!
   40 L = L-1
        IF (DX(L) .GT. T) GO TO 40
!
!      Find an element in the first half of the array which is greater
!      than T
!
   50 K = K+1
       IF (DX(K) .LT. T) GO TO 50
!
!      Interchange these elements
!
       IF (K .LE. L) THEN
          TT = DX(L)
          DX(L) = DX(K)
          DX(K) = TT
          GO TO 40
       ENDIF
!
!      Save upper and lower subscripts of the array yet to be sorted
!
       IF (L-I .GT. J-K) THEN
          IL(M) = I
          IU(M) = L
          I = K
          M = M+1
       ELSE
          IL(M) = K
          IU(M) = J
          J = L
          M = M+1
       ENDIF
```

```
      GO TO 70
!
!     Begin again on another portion of the unsorted array
!
   60 M = M-1
      IF (M .EQ. 0) GO TO 190
      I = IL(M)
      J = IU(M)
!
   70 IF (J-I .GE. 1) GO TO 30
      IF (I .EQ. 1) GO TO 20
      I = I-1
!
   80 I = I+1
      IF (I .EQ. J) GO TO 60
      T = DX(I+1)
      IF (DX(I) .LE. T) GO TO 80
      K = I
!
   90 DX(K+1) = DX(K)
      K = K-1
      IF (T .LT. DX(K)) GO TO 90
      DX(K+1) = T
      GO TO 80
!
!     Sort DX and carry DY along
!
  100 M = 1
      I = 1
      J = NN
      R = 0.375D0
!
  110 IF (I .EQ. J) GO TO 150
      IF (R .LE. 0.5898437D0) THEN
         R = R+3.90625D-2
      ELSE
         R = R-0.21875D0
      ENDIF
!
  120 K = I
!
!     Select a central element of the array and save it in location T
!
      IJ = I + INT((J-I)*R)
      T = DX(IJ)
      TY = DY(IJ)
!
!     If first element of array is greater than T, interchange with T
!
      IF (DX(I) .GT. T) THEN
         DX(IJ) = DX(I)
         DX(I) = T
         T = DX(IJ)
         DY(IJ) = DY(I)
         DY(I) = TY
         TY = DY(IJ)
      ENDIF
      L = J
!
```

```
!     If last element of array is less than T, interchange with T
!
      IF (DX(J) .LT. T) THEN
         DX(IJ) = DX(J)
         DX(J) = T
         T = DX(IJ)
         DY(IJ) = DY(J)
         DY(J) = TY
         TY = DY(IJ)
!
!        If first element of array is greater than T, interchange with T
!
         IF (DX(I) .GT. T) THEN
            DX(IJ) = DX(I)
            DX(I) = T
            T = DX(IJ)
            DY(IJ) = DY(I)
            DY(I) = TY
            TY = DY(IJ)
         ENDIF
      ENDIF
!
!     Find an element in the second half of the array which is smaller
!     than T
!
  130 L = L-1
      IF (DX(L) .GT. T) GO TO 130
!
!     Find an element in the first half of the array which is greater
!     than T
!
  140 K = K+1
      IF (DX(K) .LT. T) GO TO 140
!
!     Interchange these elements
!
      IF (K .LE. L) THEN
         TT = DX(L)
         DX(L) = DX(K)
         DX(K) = TT
         TTY = DY(L)
         DY(L) = DY(K)
         DY(K) = TTY
         GO TO 130
      ENDIF
!
!     Save upper and lower subscripts of the array yet to be sorted
!
      IF (L-I .GT. J-K) THEN
         IL(M) = I
         IU(M) = L
         I = K
         M = M+1
      ELSE
         IL(M) = K
         IU(M) = J
         J = L
         M = M+1
      ENDIF
```

```
         GO TO 160
!
!        Begin again on another portion of the unsorted array
!
   150 M = M-1
         IF (M .EQ. 0) GO TO 190
         I = IL(M)
         J = IU(M)
!
   160 IF (J-I .GE. 1) GO TO 120
         IF (I .EQ. 1) GO TO 110
         I = I-1
!
   170 I = I+1
         IF (I .EQ. J) GO TO 150
         T = DX(I+1)
         TY = DY(I+1)
         IF (DX(I) .LE. T) GO TO 170
         K = I
!
   180 DX(K+1) = DX(K)
         DY(K+1) = DY(K)
         K = K-1
         IF (T .LT. DX(K)) GO TO 180
         DX(K+1) = T
         DY(K+1) = TY
         GO TO 170
!
!        Clean up
!
   190 IF (KFLAG .LE. -1) THEN
            DO 200 I=1,NN
               DX(I) = -DX(I)
   200      CONTINUE
         ENDIF
         RETURN
         END
```

The Unix diff command will document the changes between the original Fortran 77 and the new Fortran 90 version.

As can be seen, converting the comment symbol from a C in column 1 to the ! character makes it valid free form Fortran 90.

40.10   Example 4: Simple Syntax Conversion to Modern Fortran

The Nag compiler offers a Polish option that will automatically convert Fortran 77 to Fortran 90.

Here is the converted version of the Netlib dsort.f subroutine.

```
subroutine dsort(dx, dy, n, kflag)
!***BEGIN PROLOGUE  DSORT
!***PURPOSE  Sort an array and optionally make the same interchanges in
!            an auxiliary array.  The array may be sorted in increasing
!            or decreasing order.  A slightly modified QUICKSORT
!            algorithm is used.
!***LIBRARY   SLATEC
!***CATEGORY  N6A2B
!***TYPE      DOUBLE PRECISION (SSORT-S, DSORT-D, ISORT-I)
!***KEYWORDS  SINGLETON QUICKSORT, SORT, SORTING
!***AUTHOR  Jones, R. E., (SNLA)
!           Wisniewski, J. A., (SNLA)
!***DESCRIPTION
!
!   DSORT sorts array DX and optionally makes the same interchanges in
!   array DY.  The array DX may be sorted in increasing order or
!   decreasing order.  A slightly modified quicksort algorithm is used.
!
!   Description of Parameters
!      DX - array of values to be sorted   (usually abscissas)
!      DY - array to be (optionally) carried along
!      N  - number of values in array DX to be sorted
!      KFLAG - control parameter
!            =  2  means sort DX in increasing order and carry DY along.
!            =  1  means sort DX in increasing order (ignoring DY)
!            = -1  means sort DX in decreasing order (ignoring DY)
!            = -2  means sort DX in decreasing order and carry DY along.
!
!***REFERENCES  R. C. Singleton, Algorithm 347, An efficient algorithm
!                 for sorting with minimal storage, Communications of
!                 the ACM, 12, 3 (1969), pp. 185-187.
!***ROUTINES CALLED  XERMSG
!***REVISION HISTORY  (YYMMDD)
!   761101  DATE WRITTEN
!   761118 Modified to use the Singleton quicksort algorithm.  (JAW)
!   890531 Changed all specific intrinsics to generic.  (WRB)
!   890831 Modified array declarations.  (WRB)
!   891009  Removed unreferenced statement labels.  (WRB)
!   891024  Changed category.  (WRB)
!   891024  REVISION DATE from Version 3.2
!   891214  Prologue converted to Version 4.0 format.  (BAB)
!   900315  CALLs to XERROR changed to CALLs to XERMSG.  (THJ)
!   901012  Declared all variables; changed X,Y to DX,DY; changed
!              code to parallel SSORT. (M. McClain)
!   920501  Reformatted the REFERENCES section.  (DWL, WRB)
!   920519  Clarified error messages.  (DWL)
!   920801  Declarations section rebuilt and code restructured to use
!              IF-THEN-ELSE-ENDIF.  (RWC, WRB)
!***END PROLOGUE  DSORT
!     .. Scalar Arguments ..
  integer kflag, n
!     .. Array Arguments ..
  double precision dx(*), dy(*)
!     .. Local Scalars ..
  double precision r, t, tt, tty, ty
  integer i, ij, j, k, kk, l, m, nn
!     .. Local Arrays ..
```

```
      integer il(21), iu(21)
!        .. External Subroutines ..
!        EXTERNAL XERMSG
!        ..  Intrinsic Functions ..
      intrinsic abs, int
!***FIRST EXECUTABLE STATEMENT  DSORT
      nn = n
!        IF (NN .LT. 1) THEN
!           CALL XERMSG ('SLATEC', 'DSORT',
!     +         'The number of values to be sorted is not positive.', 1, 1)
!           RETURN
!        ENDIF
!
      kk = abs(kflag)
!        IF (KK.NE.1 .AND. KK.NE.2) THEN
!           CALL XERMSG ('SLATEC', 'DSORT',
!     +         'The sort control parameter, K, is not 2, 1, -1, or -2.', 2,
!     +         1)
!          RETURN
!      ENDIF
!
!      Alter array DX to get decreasing order if needed
!
      if (kflag<=-1) then
        do i = 1, nn
          dx(i) = -dx(i)
        end do
      end if
!
      if (kk==2) go to 180
!
!      Sort DX only
!
      m = 1
      i = 1
      j = nn
      r = 0.375d0
!
100   if (i==j) go to 140
      if (r<=0.5898437d0) then
        r = r + 3.90625d-2
      else
        r = r - 0.21875d0
      end if
!
110   k = i
!
!      Select a central element of the array and save it in location T
!
      ij = i + int((j-i)*r)
      t = dx(ij)
!
!      If first element of array is greater than T, interchange with T
!
      if (dx(i)>t) then
        dx(ij) = dx(i)
        dx(i) = t
        t = dx(ij)
      end if
      l = j
```

```
!
!      If last element of array is less than than T, interchange with T
!
  if (dx(j)<t) then
    dx(ij) = dx(j)
    dx(j) = t
    t = dx(ij)
!
!          If first element of array is greater than T, interchange with T
!
    if (dx(i)>t) then
      dx(ij) = dx(i)
      dx(i) = t
      t = dx(ij)
    end if
  end if
!
!      Find an element in the second half of the array which is smaller
!      than T
!
120 l = l - 1
    if (dx(l)>t) go to 120
!
!      Find an element in the first half of the array which is greater
!      than T
! 130 k = k + 1
    if (dx(k)<t) go to 130
!
!      Interchange these elements
!
  if (k<=l) then
    tt = dx(l)
    dx(l) = dx(k)
    dx(k) = tt
    go to 120
  end if
!
!      Save upper and lower subscripts of the array yet to be sorted
!
  if (l-i>j-k) then
    il(m) = i
    iu(m) = l
    i = k
    m = m + 1
  else
    il(m) = k
    iu(m) = j
    j = l
    m = m + 1
  end if
  go to 150
!
!      Begin again on another portion of the unsorted array
!
140 m = m - 1
    if (m==0) go to 270

        i = il(m)
```

```
      j = iu(m)
!
150 if (j-i>=1) go to 110
    if (i==1) go to 100
    i = i - 1
!
160 i = i + 1
    if (i==j) go to 140
    t = dx(i+1)
    if (dx(i)<=t) go to 160
    k = i
!
170 dx(k+1) = dx(k)
    k = k - 1
    if (t<dx(k)) go to 170
    dx(k+1) = t
    go to 160
!
!        Sort DX and carry DY along
!
180 m = 1
    i = 1
    j = nn
    r = 0.375d0
!
190 if (i==j) go to 230
    if (r<=0.5898437d0) then
       r = r + 3.90625d-2
  else
       r = r - 0.21875d0
  end if
!
200 k = i
!
!     Select a central element of the array and save it in location T
!
   ij = i + int((j-i)*r)
   t = dx(ij)
   ty = dy(ij)
!
!     If first element of array is greater than T, interchange with T
!
  if (dx(i)>t) then
    dx(ij) = dx(i)
    dx(i) = t
    t = dx(ij)
    dy(ij) = dy(i)
    dy(i) = ty
    ty = dy(ij)
  end if
  l = j
!
!     If last element of array is less than T, interchange with T
!
  if (dx(j)<t) then
    dx(ij) = dx(j)
    dx(j) = t
    t = dx(ij)
    dy(ij) = dy(j)
```

```
      dy(j) = ty
      ty = dy(ij)
!
!         If first element of array is greater than T, interchange with T
!
      if (dx(i)>t) then
        dx(ij) = dx(i)
        dx(i) = t
        t = dx(ij)
        dy(ij) = dy(i)
        dy(i) = ty
        ty = dy(ij)
      end if
    end if
!
!     Find an element in the second half of the array which is smaller
!     than T
!
210 l = l - 1
  if (dx(l)>t) go to 210
!
!     Find an element in the first half of the array which is greater
!     than T
!
220 k = k + 1
  if (dx(k)<t) go to 220
!
!     Interchange these elements
!
  if (k<=l) then
    tt = dx(l)
    dx(l) = dx(k)
    dx(k) = tt
    tty = dy(l)
    dy(l) = dy(k)
    dy(k) = tty
    go to 210
  end if
!
!     Save upper and lower subscripts of the array yet to be sorted
!
  if (l-i>j-k) then
    il(m) = i
    iu(m) = l
    i = k
    m = m + 1
  else
    il(m) = k
    iu(m) = j
    j = l
    m = m + 1
  end if
  go to 240
!
!     Begin again on another portion of the unsorted array
!
230 m = m - 1
  if (m==0) go to 270
  i = il(m)
  j = iu(m)
```

```
!
240 if (j-i>=1) go to 200
   if (i==1) go to 190
   i = i - 1
!
250 i = i + 1
   if (i==j) go to 230
   t = dx(i+1)
   ty = dy(i+1)
   if (dx(i)<=t) go to 250
   k = i
!
260 dx(k+1) = dx(k)
   dy(k+1) = dy(k)
   k = k - 1
   if (t<dx(k)) go to 260
   dx(k+1) = t
   dy(k+1) = ty
   go to 250
!
!     Clean up
!
270 if (kflag<=-1) then
     do i = 1, nn
       dx(i) = -dx(i)
     end do
   end if
   return
end subroutine
```

As can be seen we have a much more Fortran 90 style after conversion. We use the Nag compiler polish option on all of our old Fortran 77 style code.

40.11   Example 5: Date Case Study

In this example we look at a variety of conversions. We start with a set of Fortran 77 functions and subroutines for date manipulation put together by Skip Noble.

We next look at a modern Fortran 90 version written by Alan Miller.

Both of these versions manipulate dates using independent integer variables to represent days, months, and years.

We next refer to the version in Chap. 22, where we introduce a date derived type throughout.

We will start by looking at the Fortran 77 version.

```
C======DATESUB.FOR with Sample Drivers.
C      COLLECTED AND PUT TOGETHER JANUARY 1972, H. D. KNOBLE .
C      ORIGINAL REFERENCES ARE CITED IN EACH ROUTINE.
C
```

```
      INTEGER YYYY,MM,DD,JD,WD,DDD,MMA,DDA,NDIFF,I
      INTEGER*2 YYYY2,MM2,DD2
C
C------IDAY IS A COMPANION TO CALEND; GIVEN A CALENDAR DATE, YYYY, MM,
C        DD, IDAY IS RETURNED AS THE DAY OF THE YEAR.
C          EXAMPLE: IDAY(1984,4,22)=113
      IDAY(YYYY,MM,DD)=3055*(MM+2)/100-(MM+10)/13*2-91
     ,            +(1-(MOD(YYYY,4)+3)/4+(MOD(YYYY,100)+99)/100
     ,            -(MOD(YYYY,400)+399)/400)*(MM+10)/13+DD
C
C------IZLR(YYYY,MM,DD) GIVES THE WEEKDAY NUMBER 0=SUNDAY, 1=MONDAY,
C      ... 6=SATURDAY.  EXAMPLE: IZLR(1970,1,1)=4=THURSDAY
      IZLR(YYYY,MM,DD)=MOD((13*(MM+10-(MM+10)/13*12)-1)/5+DD+77
     ,            +5*(YYYY+(MM-14)/12-(YYYY+(MM-14)/12)/100*100)/4
     ,            + (YYYY+(MM-14)/12)/400-(YYYY+(MM-14)/12)/100*2,7)
C
C Compute date this year for changing clocks back to EST.
C I.e., compute date for the last Sunday in October for this year.
      CALL GETDAT(YYYY2,MM2,DD2)
      YYYY=YYYY2
      DO I=31,26,-1
       IF (IZLR(YYYY,10,I).EQ.0) THEN
         WRITE(*,*) 'Turn Clocks back to EST on: ',I,' October ',YYYY
         EXIT
       ENDIF
      END DO
C Compute date this year for turning clocks ahead to DST
C I.e., compute date for the first Sunday in April for this year.
      CALL GETDAT(YYYY2,MM2,DD2)
      YYYY=YYYY2
      DO I=1,8
       IF (IZLR(YYYY,4,I).EQ.0) THEN
         WRITE(*,*) 'Turn Clocks ahead to DST on: ',I,' April ',YYYY
         EXIT
       ENDIF
      END DO
C
C Is this a leap year? I.e. is 12/31/yyyy the 366th day of the year?
      CALL GETDAT(YYYY2,MM2,DD2)
C---GETDAT is builtin using most Compilers.
      YYYY=YYYY2
      IF(IDAY(YYYY,12,31).EQ.366) THEN
         WRITE(*,*) YYYY,' is a Leap Year'
      ELSE
         WRITE(*,*) YYYY,' is not a Leap Year'
      ENDIF


C
C DAYSUB SHOULD RETURN: 1970, 1, 1, 4, 1
         CALL DAYSUB(JD(1970,1,1),YYYY,MM,DD,WD,DDD)
         IF(YYYY.NE.1970.OR.MM.NE.1.OR.DD.NE.1.OR.WD.NE.4.OR.DDD.NE.1)
     *   THEN
         WRITE(*,*)'DAYSUB Failed; YYYY,MM,DD,WD,DDD=',YYYY,MM,DD,WD,DDD
         STOP 1
      ENDIF
C DIFFERENCE BETWEEN TWO SAME MONTHS AND DAYS OVER 1 LEAP YEAR IS 366.
      NDIFF=NDAYS(5,22,1984,5,22,1983)
      IF(NDIFF.NE.366) THEN
         WRITE(*,*) 'NDAYS FAILED; NDIFF=',NDIFF
```

```
            ELSE
C  RECOVER MONTH AND DAY FROM YEAR AND DAY NUMBER.
            CALL CALEND(YYYY,DDD,MMA,DDA)
            IF(MMA.NE.1.AND.DDA.NE.1) THEN
               WRITE(*,*) 'CALEND FAILED; MMA,DDA=',MMA,DDA
                               ELSE
               WRITE(*,*) '** DATE MANIPULATION SUBROUTINES SIMPLE TEST OK.'
            END IF
         END IF
         STOP
         END


         SUBROUTINE CALEND(YYYY,DDD,MM,DD)
C=============CALEND WHEN GIVEN A VALID YEAR, YYYY, AND DAY OF THE
C             YEAR, DDD, RETURNS THE MONTH, MM, AND DAY OF THE
C             MONTH, DD.
C              SEE ACM ALGORITHM 398, TABLELESS DATE CONVERSION, BY
C              DICK STONE, CACM 13(10):621.
         INTEGER YYYY,DDD,MM,DD,T
         T=0
         IF(MOD(YYYY,4).EQ.0) T=1
C-----------THE FOLLOWING STATEMENT IS NECESSARY IF YYYY IS LESS TNAN
C             1900 OR GREATER THAN 2100.
         IF(MOD(YYYY,400).NE.0.AND.MOD(YYYY,100).EQ.0) T=0
         DD=DDD
         IF(DDD.GT.59+T) DD=DD+2-T
         MM=((DD+91)*100)/3055
         DD=(DD+91)-(MM*3055)/100
         MM=MM-2
C----------MM WILL BE CORRECT IFF DDD IS CORRECT FOR YYYY.
         IF(MM.GE.1 .AND. MM.LE.12) RETURN
         WRITE(*,1) DDD
1        FORMAT('0$$$CALEND: DAY OF THE YEAR INPUT =',I11,
       ,        ' IS OUT OF RANGE.')
         STOP 8
         END


         SUBROUTINE CDATE(JD,YYYY,MM,DD)
C=======GIVEN A JULIAN DAY NUMBER, NNNNNNNN, YYYY,MM,DD ARE RETURNED AS
C               AS THE CALENDAR DATE. JD=NNNNNNNN IS THE JULIAN DATE
C               FROM AN EPOCK IN THE VERY DISTANT PAST.  SEE CACM
C               1968 11(10):657, LETTER TO THE EDITOR BY FLIEGEL AND
C               VAN FLANDERN.
C    EXAMPLE CALL CDATE(2440588,YYYY,MM,DD) RETURNS 1970 1 1 .
C
         INTEGER JD,YYYY,MM,DD,L,N
         L=JD+68569
         N=4*L/146097
         L=L-(146097*N + 3)/4
         YYYY=4000*(L+1)/1461001
         L=L-1461*YYYY/4+31
         MM=80*L/2447
         DD=L-2447*MM/80
         L=MM/11
         MM=MM + 2 - 12*L
         YYYY=100*(N-49) + YYYY + L
         RETURN
         END
```

```
       SUBROUTINE DAYSUB(JD,YYYY,MM,DD,WD,DDD)
C=======GIVEN JD, A JULIAN DAY # (SEE ASF JD), THIS ROUTINE
C       CALCULATES DD, THE DAY NUMBER OF THE MONTH; MM, THE MONTH
C       NUMBER; YYYY THE YEAR; WD THE WEEKDAY NUMBER, AND DDD
C       THE DAY NUMBER OF THE YEAR.
C       ARITHMETIC STATEMENT FUNCTIONS 'IZLR' AND 'IDAY' ARE TAKEN
C       FROM REMARK ON ALGORITHM 398, BY J. DOUGLAS ROBERTSON,
C       CACM 15(10):918.
C
C  EXAMPLE:  CALL DAYSUB(2440588,YYYY,MM,DD,WD,DDD) YIELDS 1970 1 1 4 1.
C
       INTEGER JD,YYYY,MM,DD,WD,DDD
C
C------IZLR(YYYY,MM,DD) GIVES THE WEEKDAY NUMBER 0=SUNDAY, 1=MONDAY,
C      ... 6=SATURDAY.  EXAMPLE: IZLR(1970,1,1)=4=THURSDAY
C
       IZLR(YYYY,MM,DD)=MOD((13*(MM+10-(MM+10)/13*12)-1)/5+DD+77
     ,             +5*(YYYY+(MM-14)/12-(YYYY+(MM-14)/12)/100*100)/4
     ,             + (YYYY+(MM-14)/12)/400-(YYYY+(MM-14)/12)/100*2,7)
C
C------IDAY IS A COMPANION TO CALEND; GIVEN A CALENDAR DATE, YYYY, MM,
C       DD, IDAY IS RETURNED AS THE DAY OF THE YEAR.
C       EXAMPLE: IDAY(1984,4,22)=113
C
       IDAY(YYYY,MM,DD)=3055*(MM+2)/100-(MM+10)/13*2-91
     ,                 +(1-(MOD(YYYY,4)+3)/4+(MOD(YYYY,100)+99)/100
     ,                 -(MOD(YYYY,400)+399)/400)*(MM+10)/13+DD
C
       CALL CDATE(JD,YYYY,MM,DD)
       WD=IZLR(YYYY,MM,DD)
       DDD=IDAY(YYYY,MM,DD)
       RETURN
       END


       FUNCTION JD(YYYY,MM,DD)
       INTEGER YYYY,MM,DD
C               DATE ROUTINE JD(YYYY,MM,DD) CONVERTS CALENDER DATE TO
C               JULIAN DATE.  SEE CACM 1968 11(10):657, LETTER TO THE
C               EDITOR BY HENRY F. FLIEGEL AND THOMAS C. VAN FLANDERN.
C  EXAMPLE JD(1970,1,1)=2440588
       JD=DD-32075+1461*(YYYY+4800+(MM-14)/12)/4
     ,             +367*(MM-2-((MM-14)/12)*12)/12-3*
     ,             ((YYYY+4900+(MM-14)/12)/100)/4
       RETURN
       END


       FUNCTION NDAYS(MM1,DD1,YYYY1, MM2,DD2,YYYY2)
       INTEGER YYYY1,MM1,DD1,YYYY2,MM2,DD2
C==============NDAYS IS RETURNED AS THE NUMBER OF DAYS BETWEEN TWO
C              DATES; THAT IS  MM1/DD1/YYYY1 MINUS MM2/DD2/YYYY2,
C              WHERE DATEI AND DATEJ HAVE ELEMENTS MM, DD, YYYY.
C-------NDAYS WILL BE POSITIVE IFF DATE1 IS MORE RECENT THAN DATE2.
       NDAYS=JD(YYYY1,MM1,DD1)-JD(YYYY2,MM2,DD2)
       RETURN
       END
```

Here some comments about the code.

- it is fixed format
- the Fortran code is upper case only
- variables names are a maximum of 6 characters
- There is no program statement at the start of the program
- default typing is in effect, with variables that begin with I-N as integer
- the following is a statement function

```
C
C------IDAY IS A COMPANION TO CALEND; GIVEN A CALENDAR DATE, YYYY, MM,
C           DD, IDAY IS RETURNED AS THE DAY OF THE YEAR.
C           EXAMPLE: IDAY(1984,4,22)=113
      IDAY(YYYY,MM,DD)=3055*(MM+2)/100-(MM+10)/13*2-91
     ,                +(1-(MOD(YYYY,4)+3)/4+(MOD(YYYY,100)+99)/100
     ,                -(MOD(YYYY,400)+399)/400)*(MM+10)/13+DD
```

- the following is a statement function

```
C
C------IZLR(YYYY,MM,DD) GIVES THE WEEKDAY NUMBER 0=SUNDAY, 1=MONDAY,
C       ... 6=SATURDAY.  EXAMPLE: IZLR(1970,1,1)=4=THURSDAY
      IZLR(YYYY,MM,DD)=MOD((13*(MM+10-(MM+10)/13*12)-1)/5+DD+77
     ,                +5*(YYYY+(MM-14)/12-(YYYY+(MM-14)/12)/100*100)/4
     ,                + (YYYY+(MM-14)/12)/400-(YYYY+(MM-14)/12)/100*2,7)
```

- The program has calls to a non-standard routine GETDAT

Here is the modern Fortran 90 version using independent integer variables for the days, months and years.

```
module date_sub

! COLLECTED AND PUT TOGETHER JANUARY 1972, H. D.
! KNOBLE .

! ORIGINAL REFERENCES ARE CITED IN EACH ROUTINE.

! Code converted using TO_F90 by Alan Miller
! Date: 1999-12-22 Time: 10:23:47
! Compatible with Imagine1 F compiler:
! 2002-07-19

  implicit none

  public :: iday, izlr, calend, cdate, ndays, &
    daysub, jd

contains

! ARITHMETIC FUNCTIONS "IZLR" AND "IDAY" ARE
! TAKEN FROM REMARK ON
! ALGORITHM 398, BY J. DOUGLAS ROBERTSON, CACM
! 15(10):918.
```

```
  function iday(yyyy, mm, dd) result (ival)
! IDAY IS A COMPANION TO CALEND; GIVEN A
! CALENDAR DATE, YYYY, MM,
! DD, IDAY IS RETURNED AS THE DAY OF THE YEAR.
! EXAMPLE: IDAY(1984, 4, 22) = 113

    integer, intent (in) :: yyyy, mm, dd
    integer :: ival

    ival = 3055*(mm+2)/100 - (mm+10)/13*2 - 91 + &
      (1-(modulo(yyyy,4)+3)/4+(modulo(yyyy, &
      100)+99)/100-(modulo(yyyy, &
      400)+399)/400*(mm+10)/13 + dd

    return
  end function iday


  function izlr(yyyy, mm, dd) result (ival)
! IZLR(YYYY, MM, DD) GIVES THE WEEKDAY NUMBER
! 0 = SUNDAY, 1 = MONDAY,
! ... 6 = SATURDAY.  EXAMPLE: IZLR(1970, 1, 1)
! = 4 = THURSDAY

    integer, intent (in) :: yyyy, mm, dd
    integer :: ival

    ival = modulo((13*(mm+10-(mm+10)/13*12)-1)/5 &
      +dd+77+5*(yyyy+(mm-14)/12-(yyyy+ &
      (mm-14)/12)/100*100)/4+(yyyy+(mm- &
      14)/12)/400-(yyyy+(mm-14)/12)/100*2, 7)

    return
  end function izlr

  subroutine calend(yyyy, ddd, mm, dd)
! CALEND WHEN GIVEN A VALID YEAR, YYYY, AND
! DAY OF THE YEAR, DDD,
! RETURNS THE MONTH, MM, AND DAY OF THE MONTH,
! DD.
! SEE ACM ALGORITHM 398, TABLELESS DATE
! CONVERSION, BY
! DICK STONE, CACM 13(10):621.

    integer, intent (in) :: yyyy
    integer, intent (in) :: ddd
    integer, intent (out) :: mm
    integer, intent (out) :: dd

    integer :: t

    t = 0
    if (modulo(yyyy,4)==0) t = 1

! ------THE FOLLOWING STATEMENT IS NECESSARY
! IF YYYY IS < 1900 OR > 2100.
    if (modulo(yyyy,400)/=0 .and. &
      modulo(yyyy,100)==0) t = 0

    dd = ddd
```

```
      if (ddd>59+t) dd = dd + 2 - t
      mm = ((dd+91)*100)/3055
      dd = (dd+91) - (mm*3055)/100
      mm = mm - 2
!     ----------MM WILL BE CORRECT IFF DDD IS
!     CORRECT FOR YYYY.
      if (mm>=1 .and. mm<=12) return
      write (unit=*, fmt='(a,i11,a)') &
        '$$CALEND: DAY OF THE YEAR INPUT =', ddd, &
        ' IS OUT OF RANGE.'
      stop
    end subroutine calend

  subroutine cdate(jd, yyyy, mm, dd)
!   GIVEN A JULIAN DAY NUMBER, NNNNNNNN,
!   YYYY,MM,DD ARE RETURNED AS THE
!   CALENDAR DATE. JD = NNNNNNNN IS THE JULIAN
!   DATE FROM AN EPOCH
!   IN THE VERY DISTANT PAST.  SEE CACM 1968
!   11(10):657,
!   LETTER TO THE EDITOR BY FLIEGEL AND VAN
!   FLANDERN.
!   EXAMPLE CALL CDATE(2440588, YYYY, MM, DD)
!   RETURNS 1970 1 1 .

      integer, intent (in) :: jd
      integer, intent (out) :: yyyy
      integer, intent (out) :: mm
      integer, intent (out) :: dd

      integer :: l, n

      l = jd + 68569
      n = 4*l/146097
      l = l - (146097*n+3)/4
      yyyy = 4000*(l+1)/1461001
      l = l - 1461*yyyy/4 + 31
      mm = 80*l/2447
      dd = l - 2447*mm/80
      l = mm/11
      mm = mm + 2 - 12*l
      yyyy = 100*(n-49) + yyyy + l
      return
    end subroutine cdate


  subroutine daysub(jd, yyyy, mm, dd, wd, ddd)
!   GIVEN JD, A JULIAN DAY # (SEE ASF JD), THIS
!   ROUTINE CALCULATES DD,
!   THE DAY NUMBER OF THE MONTH; MM, THE MONTH
!   NUMBER; YYYY THE YEAR;
!   WD THE WEEKDAY NUMBER, AND DDD THE DAY
!   NUMBER OF THE YEAR.

!   EXAMPLE:
!   CALL DAYSUB(2440588, YYYY, MM, DD, WD, DDD)
!   YIELDS 1970 1 1 4 1.

      integer, intent (in) :: jd
      integer, intent (out) :: yyyy
```

```
   integer, intent (out) :: mm
   integer, intent (out) :: dd
   integer, intent (out) :: wd
   integer, intent (out) :: ddd

   call cdate(jd, yyyy, mm, dd)
   wd = izlr(yyyy, mm, dd)
   ddd = iday(yyyy, mm, dd)

   return
  end subroutine daysub


  function jd(yyyy, mm, dd) result (ival)

   integer, intent (in) :: yyyy
   integer, intent (in) :: mm
   integer, intent (in) :: dd
   integer :: ival

!    DATE ROUTINE JD(YYYY, MM, DD) CONVERTS
!    CALENDER DATE TO
!    JULIAN DATE.  SEE CACM 1968 11(10):657,
!    LETTER TO THE
!    EDITOR BY HENRY F. FLIEGEL AND THOMAS C. VAN
!    FLANDERN.
!    EXAMPLE JD(1970, 1, 1) = 2440588

   ival = dd - 32075 + 1461*(yyyy+4800+(mm-14)/ &
     12)/4 + 367*(mm-2-((mm-14)/12)*12)/12 - &
     3*((yyyy+4900+(mm-14)/12)/100)/4

   return
  end function jd

  function ndays(mm1, dd1, yyyy1, mm2, dd2, &
    yyyy2) result (ival)

   integer, intent (in) :: mm1
   integer, intent (in) :: dd1
   integer, intent (in) :: yyyy1
   integer, intent (in) :: mm2
   integer, intent (in) :: dd2
   integer, intent (in) :: yyyy2
   integer :: ival

!    NDAYS IS RETURNED AS THE NUMBER OF DAYS
!    BETWEEN TWO
!    DATES; THAT IS  MM1/DD1/YYYY1 MINUS
!    MM2/DD2/YYYY2,
!    WHERE DATEI AND DATEJ HAVE ELEMENTS MM, DD,
!    YYYY.
!    NDAYS WILL BE POSITIVE IFF DATE1 IS MORE
!    RECENT THAN DATE2.

   ival = jd(yyyy1, mm1, dd1) - &
     jd(yyyy2, mm2, dd2)

   return
```

```
    end function ndays

  end module date_sub


  program test_datesub

  ! ======DATESUB.FOR with Sample Drivers.

    use date_sub
    implicit none
    integer :: yyyy, mm, dd, wd, ddd, mma, dda, &
      ndiff, i
    integer, dimension (8) :: val

  ! Compute date this year for changing clocks
  ! back to EST.
  ! I.e.compute date for the last Sunday in
  ! October for this year.
    call date_and_time(values=val)
    yyyy = val(1)
    do i = 31, 26, -1
      if (izlr(yyyy,10,i)==0) then
        print *, 'Turn Clocks back to EST on: ', &
          i, ' October ', yyyy
        exit
      end if
    end do
  ! Compute date this year for turning clocks
  ! ahead to DST
  ! I.e., compute date for the first Sunday in
  ! April for this year.
    call date_and_time(values=val)
    yyyy = val(1)
    do i = 1, 8
      if (izlr(yyyy,4,i)==0) then
        print *, 'Turn Clocks ahead to DST on: ', &
          i, ' April ', yyyy
        exit
      end if
    end do


    call date_and_time(values=val)
    yyyy = val(1)

  ! Is this a leap year? I.e. is 12/31/yyyy the
  ! 366th day of the year?
    if (iday(yyyy,12,31)==366) then
      print *, yyyy, ' is a Leap Year'
    else
      print *, yyyy, ' is not a Leap Year'
    end if

  ! DAYSUB SHOULD RETURN: 1970, 1, 1, 4, 1
    call daysub(jd(1970,1,1), yyyy, mm, dd, wd, &
      ddd)
    if (yyyy/=1970 .or. mm/=1 .or. dd/=1 .or. &
      wd/=4 .or. ddd/=1) then
      print *, &
```

```
          'DAYSUB Failed; YYYY, MM, DD, WD, DDD = ', &
          yyyy, mm, dd, wd, ddd
      stop
    end if

! DIFFERENCE BETWEEN TO SAME MONTHS AND DAYS
! OVER 1 LEAP YEAR IS 366.
    ndiff = ndays(5, 22, 1984, 5, 22, 1983)
    if (ndiff/=366) then
      print *, 'NDAYS FAILED; NDIFF = ', ndiff
    else
!     RECOVER MONTH AND DAY FROM YEAR AND DAY
!     NUMBER.
      call calend(yyyy, ddd, mma, dda)
      if (mma/=1 .and. dda/=1) then
        print *, 'CALEND FAILED; MMA, DDA = ', &
          mma, dda
      else
        print *, '** DATE MANIPULATION SUBROUTINES &
          &SIMPLE TEST OK.'
      end if
    end if

    stop
  end program test_datesub
```

The next version using derived types and a modern Fortran 90 syntax can be found in Chap. 22.

This version required manual conversion. As can be seen by comparing the versions there is quite a difference.

The final version using an object oriented style can be found in Chap. 29. Again this required manual conversion.

40.12   Example 6: Creating 64 Bit Integer and 128 Bit Real Sorting Subroutines from the Netlib Sorting Routines

Netlib provides three non recursive sorting routines and they are

- dsort.f - Fortran 77 double precision, 64 bit normally
- ssort.f - Fortran default real type, 32 bit normally
- isort.f - Fortran default integer type, 32 bit normally

The aim is to provide a 64 bit integer sorting subroutine and a 128 bit real sorting subroutine, to accompany the above routines.

The first step is to rewrite the double precision version to use our precision module, and use that to create the 128 bit real subroutine.

The second step is to rewrite the 32 bit integer subroutine to use our integer kind module. We can then create our 64 bit integer sorting routine from that one.

Here are some of the major differences between the original Netlib version which uses double precision and the latest real versions which use kind types.

```
> subroutine dsort_dp(dx, dy, n, kflag)
> use precision_module , wp => dp
> implicit none
54c7
<    double precision dx(*), dy(*)
---
>    real (wp) ::  dx(*), dy(*)
56c9
<    double precision r, t, tt, tty, ty
---
>    real (wp) ::  r, t, tt, tty, ty

95c34
<    r = 0.375d0
---
>    r = 0.375_wp
97,99c36,38
< 100 if (i==j) go to 140
<    if (r<=0.5898437d0) then
<       r = r + 3.90625d-2
---
>    20 if (i==j) go to 60
>    if (r<=0.5898437_wp) then
>       r = r + 3.90625_wp/100.0_wp
101c40    ·
<       r = r - 0.21875d0
---
>       r = r - 0.21875_wp

200c139
<    r = 0.375d0
---
>    r = 0.375_wp
202,204c141,143
< 190 if (i==j) go to 230
<    if (r<=0.5898437d0) then
<       r = r + 3.90625d-2
---
>    110 if (i==j) go to 150
>    if (r<=0.5898437_wp) then
>       r = r + 3.90625_wp/100.0_wp
206c145
<       r = r - 0.21875d0
---
>       r = r - 0.21875_wp
```

Here is the 128 bit real sort subroutine.

```
subroutine dsort_qp(dx, dy, n, kflag)
  use precision_module, wp => qp
  implicit none
```

```
! .. Scalar Arguments ..
  integer kflag, n
! .. Array Arguments ..
  real (wp) :: dx(*), dy(*)
! .. Local Scalars ..
  real (wp) :: r, t, tt, tty, ty
  integer i, ij, j, k, kk, l, m, nn
! .. Local Arrays ..
  integer il(21), iu(21)
! .. Intrinsic Functions ..
  intrinsic abs, int
! ***FIRST EXECUTABLE STATEMENT  DSORT
  nn = n
  kk = abs(kflag)
!
! Alter array DX to get decreasing order if
! needed
!
  if (kflag<=-1) then
    do i = 1, nn
      dx(i) = -dx(i)
    end do
  end if
!
  if (kk==2) go to 180
!
! Sort DX only
!
  m = 1
  i = 1
  j = nn
  r = 0.375_wp
!
100 if (i==j) go to 140
  if (r<=0.5898437_wp) then
    r = r + 3.90625_wp/100.0_wp
  else
    r = r - 0.21875_wp
  end if
!
110 k = i
!
! Select a central element of the array and save
! it in location T
!
  ij = i + int((j-i)*r)
  t = dx(ij)
!
! If first element of array is greater than T,
! interchange with T
!
  if (dx(i)>t) then
    dx(ij) = dx(i)
    dx(i) = t
    t = dx(ij)
  end if
  l = j
!
! If last element of array is less than than T,
```

```
! interchange with T
!
  if (dx(j)<t) then
    dx(ij) = dx(j)
    dx(j) = t
    t = dx(ij)
!
!   If first element of array is greater than T,
!   interchange with T
!
    if (dx(i)>t) then
      dx(ij) = dx(i)
      dx(i) = t
      t = dx(ij)
    end if
  end if
!
! Find an element in the second half of the
! array which is smaller
! than T
!
120 l = l - 1
  if (dx(l)>t) go to 120
!
! Find an element in the first half of the array
! which is greater
! than T
!
130 k = k + 1
  if (dx(k)<t) go to 130
!
! Interchange these elements
!
  if (k<=l) then
    tt = dx(l)
    dx(l) = dx(k)
    dx(k) = tt
    go to 120
  end if
!
! Save upper and lower subscripts of the array
! yet to be sorted
!
  if (l-i>j-k) then
    il(m) = i
    iu(m) = l
    i = k
    m = m + 1
  else
    il(m) = k
    iu(m) = j
    j = l
    m = m + 1
  end if
  go to 150
```

```
!
! Begin again on another portion of the unsorted
! array
!
140 m = m - 1
  if (m==0) go to 270
  i = il(m)
  j = iu(m)
!
150 if (j-i>=1) go to 110
  if (i==1) go to 100
  i = i - 1
!
160 i = i + 1
  if (i==j) go to 140
  t = dx(i+1)
  if (dx(i)<=t) go to 160
  k = i
!
170 dx(k+1) = dx(k)
  k = k - 1
  if (t<dx(k)) go to 170
  dx(k+1) = t
  go to 160
!
! Sort DX and carry DY along
!
180 m = 1
  i = 1
  j = nn
  r = 0.375_wp
!
190 if (i==j) go to 230
  if (r<=0.5898437_wp) then
    r = r + 3.90625_wp/100.0_wp
  else
    r = r - 0.21875_wp
  end if

!
200 k = i
!
! Select a central element of the array and save
! it in location T
!
  ij = i + int((j-i)*r)
  t = dx(ij)
  ty = dy(ij)
!
! If first element of array is greater than T,
! interchange with T
!
  if (dx(i)>t) then
    dx(ij) = dx(i)
    dx(i) = t
    t = dx(ij)
    dy(ij) = dy(i)
    dy(i) = ty
    ty = dy(ij)
  end if
```

```
  l = j
!
! If last element of array is less than T,
! interchange with T
!
  if (dx(j)<t) then
    dx(ij) = dx(j)
    dx(j) = t
    t = dx(ij)
    dy(ij) = dy(j)
    dy(j) = ty
    ty = dy(ij)
!
!   If first element of array is greater than T,
!   interchange with T
!
    if (dx(i)>t) then
      dx(ij) = dx(i)
      dx(i) = t
      t = dx(ij)
      dy(ij) = dy(i)
      dy(i) = ty
      ty = dy(ij)
    end if
  end if
!
! Find an element in the second half of the
! array which is smaller
! than T
!
210 l = l - 1
  if (dx(l)>t) go to 210
!
! Find an element in the first half of the array
! which is greater
! than T
!
220 k = k + 1
  if (dx(k)<t) go to 220
!
! Interchange these elements
!
  if (k<=l) then
    tt = dx(l)
    dx(l) = dx(k)
    dx(k) = tt
    tty = dy(l)
    dy(l) = dy(k)
    dy(k) = tty
    go to 210
  end if
!
! Save upper and lower subscripts of the array
! yet to be sorted
!
  if (l-i>j-k) then
    il(m) = i
    iu(m) = l
    i = k
    m = m + 1
```

```
      else
        il(m) = k
        iu(m) = j
        j = l
        m = m + 1
      end if
      go to 240
!
! Begin again on another portion of the unsorted
! array
!
230 m = m - 1
    if (m==0) go to 270
    i = il(m)
    j = iu(m)
!
240 if (j-i>=1) go to 200
    if (i==1) go to 190
    i = i - 1
!
250 i = i + 1
    if (i==j) go to 230
    t = dx(i+1)
    ty = dy(i+1)
    if (dx(i)<=t) go to 250
    k = i
!
260 dx(k+1) = dx(k)
    dy(k+1) = dy(k)
    k = k - 1
    if (t<dx(k)) go to 260
    dx(k+1) = t
    dy(k+1) = ty
    go to 250
!
! Clean up
!
270 if (kflag<=-1) then
      do i = 1, nn
        dx(i) = -dx(i)
      end do
    end if
    return
end subroutine dsort_qp
```

Here is the 64 bit integer sort subroutine.

```
subroutine isort_64(ix, iy, n, kflag)
  use integer_kind_module, wp => i64
  implicit none
! .. Scalar Arguments ..
  integer (wp) :: kflag, n
! .. Array Arguments ..
  integer (wp) :: ix(*), iy(*)
! .. Local Scalars ..
  real r
  integer (wp) :: i, ij, j, k, kk, l, m, nn, t, &
    tt, tty, ty
```

```fortran
! .. Local Arrays ..
  integer (wp) :: il(21), iu(21)
! .. Intrinsic Functions ..
  intrinsic abs, int
! ***FIRST EXECUTABLE STATEMENT  ISORT
  nn = n
!
  kk = abs(kflag)
!
! Alter array IX to get decreasing order if
! needed
!
  if (kflag<=-1) then
    do i = 1, nn
      ix(i) = -ix(i)
    end do
  end if
!
  if (kk==2) go to 180
!
! Sort IX only
!
  m = 1
  i = 1
  j = nn
  r = 0.375e0
!
100 if (i==j) go to 140
  if (r<=0.5898437e0) then
    r = r + 3.90625e-2
  else
    r = r - 0.21875e0
  end if
!
110 k = i
!
! Select a central element of the array and save
! it in location T
!
  ij = i + int(((j-i)*r), wp)
  t = ix(ij)
!
! If first element of array is greater than T,
! interchange with T
!
  if (ix(i)>t) then
    ix(ij) = ix(i)
    ix(i) = t
    t = ix(ij)
  end if
  l = j
!
! If last element of array is less than than T,
! interchange with T
!
  if (ix(j)<t) then
    ix(ij) = ix(j)
    ix(j) = t
    t = ix(ij)
!
```

```
!   If first element of array is greater than T,
!   interchange with T
!

   if (ix(i)>t) then
     ix(ij) = ix(i)
     ix(i) = t
     t = ix(ij)
   end if
 end if
!
! Find an element in the second half of the
! array which is smaller
! than T
!
120 l = l - 1
  if (ix(l)>t) go to 120
!
! Find an element in the first half of the array
! which is greater
! than T
!
130 k = k + 1
  if (ix(k)<t) go to 130
!
! Interchange these elements
!
  if (k<=l) then
    tt = ix(l)
    ix(l) = ix(k)
    ix(k) = tt
    go to 120
  end if
!
! Save upper and lower subscripts of the array
! yet to be sorted
!
  if (l-i>j-k) then
    il(m) = i
    iu(m) = l
    i = k
    m = m + 1
  else
    il(m) = k
    iu(m) = j
    j = l
    m = m + 1
  end if
  go to 150
!
! Begin again on another portion of the unsorted
! array
!
140 m = m - 1
  if (m==0) go to 270
  i = il(m)
  j = iu(m)
!
150 if (j-i>=1) go to 110
  if (i==1) go to 100
  i = i - 1
```

```
!
160 i = i + 1
  if (i==j) go to 140
  t = ix(i+1)
  if (ix(i)<=t) go to 160
  k = i
!
170 ix(k+1) = ix(k)
  k = k - 1
  if (t<ix(k)) go to 170
  ix(k+1) = t
  go to 160
!
! Sort IX and carry IY along
!
180 m = 1
  i = 1
  j = nn
  r = 0.375e0
! 190 if (i==j) go to 230
  if (r<=0.5898437e0) then
    r = r + 3.90625e-2
  else
    r = r - 0.21875e0
  end if
!
200 k = i
!
! Select a central element of the array and save
! it in location T
!
  ij = i + int(((j-i)*r), wp)
  t = ix(ij)
  ty = iy(ij)
!
! If first element of array is greater than T,
! interchange with T
!
  if (ix(i)>t) then
    ix(ij) = ix(i)
    ix(i) = t
    t = ix(ij)
    iy(ij) = iy(i)
    iy(i) = ty
    ty = iy(ij)
  end if
  l = j
!
! If last element of array is less than T,
! interchange with T
!
  if (ix(j)<t) then
    ix(ij) = ix(j)
    ix(j) = t
    t = ix(ij)
    iy(ij) = iy(j)
    iy(j) = ty
    ty = iy(ij)
!
!    If first element of array is greater than T,
```

```
!    interchange with T
!
     if (ix(i)>t) then
       ix(ij) = ix(i)
       ix(i) = t
       t = ix(ij)
       iy(ij) = iy(i)
       iy(i) = ty
       ty = iy(ij)
     end if
   end if
!
! Find an element in the second half of the
! array which is smaller
! than T
!
210 l = l - 1
   if (ix(l)>t) go to 210
!
! Find an element in the first half of the array
! which is greater
! than T
!
220 k = k + 1
   if (ix(k)<t) go to 220
!
! Interchange these elements
!
   if (k<=l) then
     tt = ix(l)
     ix(l) = ix(k)
     ix(k) = tt
     tty = iy(l)
     iy(l) = iy(k)
     iy(k) = tty
     go to 210
   end if
!
! Save upper and lower subscripts of the array
! yet to be sorted
!
   if (l-i>j-k) then
     il(m) = i
     iu(m) = l
     i = k
     m = m + 1
   else
     il(m) = k
     iu(m) = j
     j = l
     m = m + 1
   end if
   go to 240
```

```
!
! Begin again on another portion of the unsorted
! array
!
230 m = m - 1
  if (m==0) go to 270
  i = il(m)
  j = iu(m)
!
240 if (j-i>=1) go to 200
  if (i==1) go to 190
  i = i - 1
!
250 i = i + 1
  if (i==j) go to 230
  t = ix(i+1)
  ty = iy(i+1)
  if (ix(i)<=t) go to 250
  k = i
!
260 ix(k+1) = ix(k)
  iy(k+1) = iy(k)
  k = k - 1
  if (t<ix(k)) go to 260
  ix(k+1) = t
  iy(k+1) = ty
  go to 250
!
! Clean up
!
270 if (kflag<=-1) then
    do i = 1, nn
      ix(i) = -ix(i)
    end do
  end if
  return
end subroutine isort_64
```

All five subroutines are available on our web site.

```
isort_32.f90
isort_64.f90
dsort_sp.f90
dsort_dp.f90
dsort_qp.f90
```

We have also taken the generic recursive sort module from an earlier chapter and converted it to work with the Netlib routines. A copy of this module can also be found on our web site.

40.13   Summary

This chapter has shown some of the options open to you when working with legacy code. The emphasis has been on relatively straightforward code restructuring. The use of software tools to aid in this is highly recommended as converting manually using an editor is obviously going to involve much more work.

40.14   Problems

40.1 Compile and run the examples in this chapter.

40.2 Create a 16 bit integer sorting routine using the 32 bit integer sort subroutine in Example 5.

40.3 Create a generic sorting module from the subroutines in Example 5.

Chapter 41
Graphics Libraries - Simple Dislin Usage

*Modern data graphics can do much more than simply substitute
for small statistical tables. At their best, graphics are
instruments for reasoning about quantitative information. Often
the most effective way to describe, explore and summarise a set
of numbers — even a large set — is to look at pictures of those
numbers.*

Edward R Tufte, The Visual Display of Quantitative
Information.

A picture paints a thousand words.

Reportedly first used by Frederick R. Barnard in Printer's Ink
(December, 1921), while commenting that graphics can tell a
story as effectively as a large amount of descriptive text.

41.1 Introduction

In science and engineering graphics are essential part of the presentation of information.

A graphics library is generally a set of routines that can be called from one or
more programming languages to help in the display of graphical output to a screen
or monitor with the option normally of targetting a hard copy device.

Our resource file

```
https://www.fortranplus.co.uk/
fortran-information/
```

provides details of some of the graphics libraries available.

We will be using the Dislin library in our examples.

41.2 The Dislin Graphics Library

This is the dislin home page.

© Springer International Publishing AG, part of Springer Nature 2018
I. Chivers and J. Sleightholme, *Introduction to Programming with Fortran*,
https://doi.org/10.1007/978-3-319-75502-1_41

```
http://www.mps.mpg.de/dislin/
```

Here is a description of the software from the above page.

- Dislin is a high-level and easy to use plotting library for displaying data as curves, bar graphs, pie charts, 3D-colour plots, surfaces, contours, and maps. The library contains about 500 plotting and parameter setting routines. The approach used is to have only a few graphics routines with short parameter lists. A large variety of parameter setting routines can then be used to create customized graphics. Several output formats are supported such as X11, VGA, PostScript, PDF, SVG, CGM, HPGL, TIFF, GIF, PNG and BMP. Dislin is available for the programming languages C, Fortran 77, Fortran 90, Perl, Python and Java.

41.3   Example 1: Using Dislin to Plot Amdahl's Law Graph 1 – 8 Processors or Cores

Here is the source code for this program.

```
program ch41_dislin_01
  use dislin
  implicit none
  integer :: i, j
! Total number of processors and hence data ! points
  integer, parameter :: nprocs = 8
! Number of percentage values from
! 10% -> 90% 9
! 95% 1
! Total 10
  integer, parameter :: nn = 10
  real, dimension (nn) :: pp = (/ 0.1, 0.2, 0.3, &
    0.4, 0.5, 0.6, 0.7, 0.8, 0.9, 0.95 /)
  real, dimension (nprocs) :: x
  real, dimension (nprocs) :: y
  real, dimension (nprocs, nn) :: ydata
  integer :: nx
  integer :: ny
  character *30 cbuf

  do i = 1, nprocs
    x(i) = real(i)
  end do
! Amdahl calculations. Store in 2 d array and
! then
```

```
! assign to 1 d array for plotting.
  do i = 1, nprocs
    do j = 1, nn
      ydata(i, j) = 1/((1-pp(j))+pp(j)/i)
    end do
  end do
! Write the data to a file for verification
! purposes
  open (unit=10, file='amdahl_table_08.txt')
  do i = 1, nprocs
    write (unit=10, fmt=100) x(i), &
      ydata(i, 1:nn)
100 format (11(f7.2,2x))
  end do
  close (10)
  call disini
  call complx
  call axspos(450, 1800)
  call axslen(2200, 1400)
  call name('Number of processors', 'x')
  call name('Speed up', 'y')
  call titlin('Plot of Amdahls Law', 1)
  call titlin('8 Processors', 3)
  call labdig(-1, 'x')
  call ticks(10, 'xy')
  call graf(1.0, 8.0, 1.0, 1.0, 1.0, 7.0, 1.0, &
    1.0)
  call title
  call xaxgit
  call chncrv('line')
! Plot the curves. Copy from 2 d array to 1 d
! array
! before the call to curve.
  do i = 1, nn
    y = ydata(1:nprocs, i)
    call curve(x, y, nprocs)
  end do
  call legini(cbuf, 10, 3)
! Coordinates of the start of the legend
! for the curves.
  nx = 500
  ny = 450
  call legpos(nx, ny)
  call leglin(cbuf, '10%', 1)
  call leglin(cbuf, '20%', 2)
```

```
       call leglin(cbuf, '30%', 3)
       call leglin(cbuf, '40%', 4)
       call leglin(cbuf, '50%', 5)
       call leglin(cbuf, '60%', 6)
       call leglin(cbuf, '70%', 7)
       call leglin(cbuf, '80%', 8)
       call leglin(cbuf, '90%', 9)
       call leglin(cbuf, '95%', 10)
       call legtit('legend')
       call legend(cbuf, 3)
       call disfin
     end program ch41_dislin_01
```

41.4   Example 2: Using Dislin to Plot Amdahl's Law Graph 2 – 64 Processors or Cores

Here is the source code for this program.

```
program ch41_dislin_02
  use dislin
  implicit none
  integer :: i, j
! Total number of processors and hence data
! points
  integer, parameter :: nprocs = 64
! Number of percentage values from
! 10% -> 90% 9
! 95% 1
! Total 10
  integer, parameter :: nn = 10
  real, dimension (nn) :: pp = (/ 0.1, 0.2, 0.3, &
    0.4, 0.5, 0.6, 0.7, 0.8, 0.9, 0.95 /)
  real, dimension (nprocs) :: x
  real, dimension (nprocs) :: y
  real, dimension (nprocs, nn) :: ydata
  integer :: nx
  integer :: ny
  character *30 cbuf

  do i = 1, nprocs
    x(i) = real(i)
  end do
! Amdahl calculations. Store in 2 d array and
```

```fortran
! then
! assign to 1 d array for plotting.
  do i = 1, nprocs
    do j = 1, nn
      ydata(i, j) = 1/((1-pp(j))+pp(j)/i)
    end do
  end do
! Write the data to a file for verification
! purposes
  open (unit=10, file='amdahl_table_08.txt')
  do i = 1, nprocs
    write (unit=10, fmt=100) x(i), &
      ydata(i, 1:nn)
100 format (11(f7.2,2x))
  end do
  close (10)
  call disini
  call complx
  call axspos(450, 1800)
  call axslen(2200, 1400)
  call name('Number of processors', 'x')
  call name('Speed up', 'y')
  call titlin('Plot of Amdahls Law', 1)
  call titlin('8 Processors', 3)
  call labdig(-1, 'x')
  call ticks(10, 'xy')
  call graf(1.0, 8.0, 1.0, 1.0, 1.0, 7.0, 1.0, &
    1.0)
  call title
  call xaxgit
  call chncrv('line')
! Plot the curves. Copy from 2 d array to 1 d
! array
! before the call to curve.
  do i = 1, nn
    y = ydata(1:nprocs, i)
    call curve(x, y, nprocs)
  end do
  call legini(cbuf, 10, 3)
! Coordinates of the start of the legend
! for the curves.
  nx = 500
  ny = 450
  call legpos(nx, ny)
  call leglin(cbuf, '10%', 1)
```

```
   call leglin(cbuf, '20%', 2)
   call leglin(cbuf, '30%', 3)
   call leglin(cbuf, '40%', 4)
   call leglin(cbuf, '50%', 5)
   call leglin(cbuf, '60%', 6)
   call leglin(cbuf, '70%', 7)
   call leglin(cbuf, '80%', 8)
   call leglin(cbuf, '90%', 9)
   call leglin(cbuf, '95%', 10)
   call legtit('legend')
   call legend(cbuf, 3)
   call disfin
end program ch41_dislin_02
```

It is similar to the previous example.

41.5   Example 3: Using Dislin to Plot Gustafson's Law Graph 1 – 64 Processors or Cores

Here is the source code for this program.

```
program ch41_dislin_03
  use dislin
  implicit none
  integer :: i, j
! Total number of processors and hence data
! points
  integer, parameter :: nprocs = 64
! Number of percentage values from
! 10% -> 90% 9
! 95% 1
! Total 10
  integer, parameter :: nn = 10
  real, dimension (nn) :: pp = (/ 0.1, 0.2, 0.3, &
    0.4, 0.5, 0.6, 0.7, 0.8, 0.9, 0.95 /)
  real, dimension (nprocs) :: x
  real, dimension (nprocs) :: y
  real, dimension (nprocs, nn) :: ydata
  integer :: nx
  integer :: ny
  character *30 cbuf

  do i = 1, nprocs
```

```
    x(i) = real(i)
  end do
! gustafson calculations. Store in 2 d array and
! then
! assign to 1 d array for plotting.
  do i = 1, nprocs
    do j = 1, nn
      ydata(i, j) = i - (1-pp(j))*(i-1)
    end do
  end do
! Write the data to a file for verification
! purposes
  open (unit=10, file='gustafson_table.txt')
  do i = 1, nprocs
    write (unit=10, fmt=100) x(i), &
      ydata(i, 1:nn)
100 format (11(f7.2,2x))
  end do
  close (10)
  call disini
  call complx
  call axspos(450, 1800)
  call axslen(2200, 1400)
  call name('Number of processors', 'x')
  call name('Speed up', 'y')
  call titlin('Plot of Gustafsons Law', 1)
  call titlin('64 Processors', 3)
  call labdig(-1, 'x')
  call ticks(10, 'xy')
  call graf(0.0, 64.0, 0.0, 10.0, 0.0, 70.0, &
    0.0, 10.0)
  call title
  call xaxgit
  call chncrv('line')
! Plot the curves. Copy from 2 d array to 1 d
! array
! before the call to curve.
  do i = 1, nn
    y = ydata(1:nprocs, i)
    call curve(x, y, nprocs)
  end do
  call legini(cbuf, 10, 3)
! Coordinates of the start of the legend
! for the curves.
  nx = 500
```

```
   ny = 450
   call legpos(nx, ny)
   call leglin(cbuf, '10%', 1)
   call leglin(cbuf, '20%', 2)
   call leglin(cbuf, '30%', 3)
   call leglin(cbuf, '40%', 4)
   call leglin(cbuf, '50%', 5)
   call leglin(cbuf, '60%', 6)
   call leglin(cbuf, '70%', 7)
   call leglin(cbuf, '80%', 8)
   call leglin(cbuf, '90%', 9)
   call leglin(cbuf, '95%', 10)
   call legtit('legend')
   call legend(cbuf, 3)
   call disfin
end program ch41_dislin_03
```

It is similar to the first example.

41.6   Example 4: Using Dislin to Plot Tsunami Events

Here is the source code for this program.

```
program ch41_dislin_04
  use dislin
  logical :: trial, screen
  real :: long, lat

  screen = .false.
  trial = .false.

! read in the tsunami data

  call datain(trial)

! I now have all the tsunami data latitude and
! longitude values read in to the arrays in the
! tsunam common block.

  iproj = 1
  lat = 0.0
  long = 180.0
```

```
    nreg = 0

! dislin initialisation routines and setting of
! some basic components
! of the plot. these are based on two sample
! dislin programs.

! initialise dislin

    call disini

! choose font

    call psfont('times-roman')

! determines the position of an axis system.
! the lower left corner of the axis system

    call axspos(400, 1850)

! the size of the axis system
! are the length and height of an axis system in
! plot coordinates. the default
! values are set to 2/3 of the page length and ! height.

    call axslen(2400, 1400)

! define axis title

    call name('longitude', 'x')

! define axis title

    call name('latitude', 'y')

! this routine plots a title over an axis
! system.

    call titlin('plot of 3034 tsunami events ', 3)

! determines which label types will be plotted
! on an axis.
! map defines geographical labels which are
! plotted as non negative floating-point
! numbers with the following characters 'w', ! 'e', 'n'
```

```
  and 's'.

    call labels('map', 'xy')

! plots a geographical axis system.

    call grafmp(-180., 180., -180., 90., -90., &
      90., -90., 30.)

! the statement call gridmp (i, j) overlays an
! axis system with a longitude
! and latitude grid where i and j are the number
! of grid lines between  labels in
! the x- and y-direction.

    call gridmp(1, 1)

! the routine world plots coastlines and lakes.

    call world

! the angle and height of the characters can be
! changed with the routines
! angle and height.

    call height(50)

! this routine plots a title over an axis
! system.
! the title may contain up to four lines of text
! designated
! with titlin.

    call title

! this is a call to the routine that actually
! plots each event.

    call plotem(trial, nreg)

! disfin terminates dislin and prints a message
! on the screen.
! the level is set back to 0.

    call disfin
```

```
end program ch41_dislin_04

subroutine datain(trial)
  common /tsunam/reg0la(378), reg0lo(378), &
    reg1la(206), reg1lo(206), reg2la(41), &
    reg2lo(41), reg3la(54), reg3lo(54), &
    reg4la(60), reg4lo(60), reg5la(1540), &
    reg5lo(1540), reg6la(80), reg6lo(80), &
    reg7la(144), reg7lo(144), reg8la(245), &
    reg8lo(245), reg9la(285), reg9lo(285)

  logical :: trial
  character (80) :: filnam

  if (trial) then
    print *, ' entering data input phase'
  end if
  filnam = 'tsunami.txt'
  open (unit=50, file=filnam, err=100, &
    status='old')
  go to 110
100 print *, ' error opening data file'
  print *, ' program terminates'
  stop
110 do i = 1, 378
    read (unit=50, fmt=120) reg0la(i), reg0lo(i)
  end do
100 format (1x, f7.2, 2x, f7.2)
  do i = 1, 206
    read (unit=50, fmt=120) reg1la(i), reg1lo(i)
  end do
  do i = 1, 41
    read (unit=50, fmt=120) reg2la(i), reg2lo(i)
  end do
  do i = 1, 54
    read (unit=50, fmt=120) reg3la(i), reg3lo(i)
  end do
  do i = 1, 60
    read (unit=50, fmt=120) reg4la(i), reg4lo(i)
  end do
  do i = 1, 1540
    read (unit=50, fmt=120) reg5la(i), reg5lo(i)
  end do
  do i = 1, 80
```

```
      read (unit=50, fmt=120) reg6la(i), reg6lo(i)
    end do
    do i = 1, 144
      read (unit=50, fmt=120) reg7la(i), reg7lo(i)
    end do
    do i = 1, 245
      read (unit=50, fmt=120) reg8la(i), reg8lo(i)
    end do
    do i = 1, 285
      read (unit=50, fmt=120) reg9la(i), reg9lo(i)
    end do
    if (trial) then
      do i = 1, 10
        print *, reg0la(i), '    ', reg0lo(i)
      end do
      print *, ' exiting data input phase'
      read *, dummy
    end if
  end subroutine datain

  subroutine plotem(trial, nreg)
    use dislin
    common /tsunam/reg0la(378), reg0lo(378), &
      reg1la(206), reg1lo(206), reg2la(41), &
      reg2lo(41), reg3la(54), reg3lo(54), &
      reg4la(60), reg4lo(60), reg5la(1540), &
      reg5lo(1540), reg6la(80), reg6lo(80), &
      reg7la(144), reg7lo(144), reg8la(245), &
      reg8lo(245), reg9la(285), reg9lo(285)

! this subroutine plots all of the tsunamis onto
! the map as coloured
! points, with a different colour per region. i
! have chosen
! a dot size of 1 mm, and step through the
! colour pallette.
! the default may not be appropriate.

    logical :: trial
    integer :: nreg
    integer :: kolour = 10
    data dwidth/1.0/

    if (trial) then
      dwidth = 5.0
```

```
  print *, ' entering plot points'
end if
call incmrk(-1)
if (nreg==0) then
  call setclr(kolour)
  call curvmp(reg0lo, reg0la, 378)
  kolour = kolour + 30
  call setclr(kolour)
  call curvmp(reg1lo, reg1la, 206)
  kolour = kolour + 30
  call setclr(kolour)
  call curvmp(reg2lo, reg2la, 41)
  kolour = kolour + 30
  call setclr(kolour)
  call curvmp(reg3lo, reg3la, 54)
  kolour = kolour + 30
  call setclr(kolour)
  call curvmp(reg4lo, reg4la, 60)
  kolour = kolour + 30
  call setclr(kolour)
  call curvmp(reg5lo, reg5la, 1540)
  kolour = kolour + 30
  call setclr(kolour)
  call curvmp(reg6lo, reg6la, 80)
  kolour = kolour + 30
  call setclr(kolour)
  call curvmp(reg7lo, reg7la, 144)
  kolour = kolour + 30
  call setclr(kolour)
  call curvmp(reg8lo, reg8la, 245)
  kolour = kolour + 30
  call setclr(kolour)
  call curvmp(reg9lo, reg9la, 285)
else if (nreg==1) then
  kolour = 10
  call setclr(kolour)
  call curvmp(reg0lo, reg0la, 378)
else if (nreg==2) then
  kolour = 20
  call setclr(kolour)
  call curvmp(reg1lo, reg1la, 206)
else if (nreg==3) then
  kolour = 30
  call setclr(kolour)
  call curvmp(reg2lo, reg2la, 41)
```

```
  else if (nreg==4) then
    kolour = 40
    call setclr(kolour)
    call curvmp(reg3lo, reg3la, 54)
  else if (nreg==5) then
    kolour = 50
    call setclr(kolour)
    call curvmp(reg4lo, reg4la, 60)
  else if (nreg==6) then
    kolour = 60
    call setclr(kolour)
    call curvmp(reg5lo, reg5la, 1540)
  else if (nreg==7) then
    kolour = 70
    call setclr(kolour)
    call curvmp(reg6lo, reg6la, 80)
  else if (nreg==8) then
    kolour = 80
    call setclr(kolour)
    call curvmp(reg7lo, reg7la, 144)
  else if (nreg==9) then
    kolour = 90
    call setclr(kolour)
    call curvmp(reg8lo, reg8la, 245)
  else if (nreg==10) then
    kolour = 100
    call setclr(kolour)
    call curvmp(reg9lo, reg9la, 285)
  end if
  if (trial) then
    print *, ' exiting plot points'
  end if


end subroutine plotem
```

The original program on which this is based was written by Ian whilst he was on secondment to the United Nations Environment Programme. Section 9 of their Environmental Data Reports cover natural disasters and these include

- Earthquakes
- Volcanoes
- Tsunamis
- Floods
- Landslides
- Natural dams

- Droughts
- Wildfires

See the bibliography for more details of these publications. The tsunami data sets are from this chapter.

The tsunami data file and graphics program can be found at:

```
https://www.fortranplus.co.uk/
```

Here is the plot produced by this program.

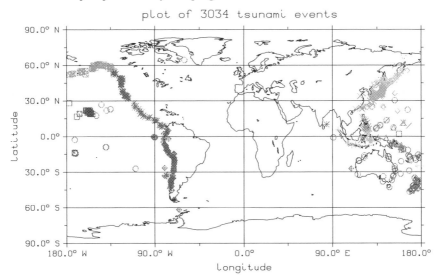

As you can see there are a lot of tsunami events in the Pacific rim area. A colour A4 pdf of the plot can be found at the Fortranplus website.

41.7   Example 5: Using Dislin to Plot the Met Office Data

Here is the source code for this program.

```fortran
program ch41_dislin_05

  use dislin

  parameter (n=906)
  dimension x(n), y(n)

  open (unit=100, file='aberporth_rainfall.csv',&
        status='old')

  do i = 1, n
    read (100, 100) x(i), y(i)
100 format (f3.0, 6x, f4.2)
  end do

! Must call initialisation routine

  call disini

! Plot a border round a page

  call pagera

! Bounding box
!
! 0 ,    0         2969 ,    0
! 0 , 2099         2969, 2099

! Position of axis systems

  call axspos(450, 1800)

! axis length

  call axslen(2400, 1400)

! Change symbol rectangle by default

  call symbol(4, 0, 0)

! X axis

  call name('Months', 'X')

! Y axis
```

```
  call name('Rainfall inches', 'Y')

  call labdig(1, 'X')
  call ticks(1, 'XY')

  call titlin('Demonstration of scatterplot', 1)
  call titlin('of rainfall by month', 3)

! call mylab('Jan',1,'X')
! call mylab('Feb',2,'X')
! call mylab('Mar',3,'X')
! call mylab('Apr',4,'X')
! call mylab('May',5,'X')
! call mylab('Jun',6,'X')
! call mylab('Jul',7,'X')
! call mylab('Aug',8,'X')
! call mylab('Sep',9,'X')
! call mylab('Oct',10,'X')
! call mylab('Nov',11,'X')
! call mylab('Dec',12,'X')

! Plot a 2 d axis system

  call graf(0.0, 13.0, 1.0, 1.0, 0.0, 11.0, 0.0, &
    1.0)

! Scatter plot

  call qplsca(x, y, n)

! Must call terminating routine

  call disfin

end program ch41_dislin_05
```

Here is dislin output.

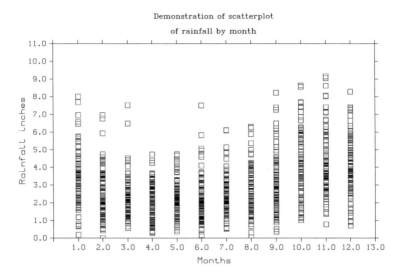

These examples have shown some of the capability of the dislin library. Most graphics libraries will offer similar functionality.

41.8   Graphics Production Notes

Most graphics libraries will enable you to view the image on the screen. They will also have the option to generate the image in one or more file formats.

We used Postscript and encapsulated postscript in the production of the graphics included in the book.

There is a brief coverage of the postscript programming language in Chap. 3.

Encapsulated PostScript (EPS) is a postscript document with additional restrictions which is intended to be usable as a graphics file format. EPS files can be thought of as more-or-less self-contained postscript documents that describe an image or drawing and can be placed within another postscript document.

When generating the book we use the $\LaTeX$ $->$ ps $->$ pdf print option.

41.9   Bibliography

United Nations Environment Programme, Environmental Data Report: 1989–1990, Second Edition, Blackwell Reference, 1989.

United Nations Environment Programme, Environmental Data Report: 1991–1992, Third Edition, Blackwell Reference, 1991.

- Part 9 of these two publications are dedicated to natural disasters

Andries Van Dam; James D. Foley, The Fundamentals of Interactive Computer Graphics Addison-Wesley.

- The classic graphics textbook. Dated, but very good.

Edward R Tufte, Visual Explanations, Images and quantities, evidence and narrative, Graphics Press, Chesire, Connecticut.
Edward R Tufte, The Visual Display of Quantitative Information, Graphics Press, Chesire, Connecticut.

- Two very good books on how to present information visually

41.10 Problems

41.1 Try out the examples in this chapter.

41.2 Have a look at our resource file to find out more about what libraries are available.

Chapter 42
Abstract Interfaces and Procedure Pointers

No amount of experimentation can ever prove me right; a single experiment can prove me wrong.

Albert Einstein

42.1 Introduction

We look at an example that illustrates the use of abstract interfaces and procedure pointers.

42.2 Example 1: Abstract Interfaces and Procedure Pointers

Abstract interfaces and procedure pointers were introduced into Fortran in the 2003 standard. One of the things their addition did was simplify the way we could program where several procedures shared a common interface.

Their addition also made it possible to solve problems involving procedure pointer components and abstract type bound procedures.

Here is some background technical material taken from the standard.

A procedure pointer is a procedure that has the EXTERNAL and POINTER attributes; it may be pointer associated with an external procedure, an internal procedure, an intrinsic procedure, a module procedure, or a dummy procedure that is not a procedure pointer.

An interface body in a generic or specific interface block specifies the EXTERNAL attribute and an explicit specific interface for an external procedure, dummy procedure, or procedure pointer.

A procedure declaration statement declares procedure pointers, dummy procedures, and external procedures. It specifies the EXTERNAL attribute for all entities in the proc-decl-list.

© Springer International Publishing AG, part of Springer Nature 2018   817
I. Chivers and J. Sleightholme, *Introduction to Programming with Fortran*,
https://doi.org/10.1007/978-3-319-75502-1_42

Here is the syntax for a procedure declaration statement.

```
PROCEDURE ( [ proc-interface ] )
  [ [ , proc-attr-spec ] ... :: ] proc-decl-list
```

We use abstract interfaces and procedure pointers in the example below.

```
module abstract_function_interface_module

  abstract interface
    real function f(i)
      implicit none
      integer , intent(in) :: i
    end function f
  end interface

end module abstract_function_interface_module

module fun01

  implicit none

contains

  real function f1(i)

    implicit none
    integer, intent (in) :: i

    f1 = 1.0/i

  end function f1

  real function f2(i)

    implicit none
    integer, intent (in) :: i

    f2 = 1.0/(i*i)

  end function f2

end module fun01

module fun02
```

```
use abstract_function_interface_module

contains

  real function f3(fun, i)

    implicit none
    integer, intent (in) :: i

    procedure (f) :: fun

    f3 = fun(i)

  end function f3

  real function f4(fun, i)

    implicit none
    integer, intent (in) :: i

    procedure (f) :: fun

    integer :: n
    real :: t

    t = 0.0

    do n = 1, 5
      t = t + fun(i)
    end do

    f4 = t

  end function f4

end module fun02

program ch4201

  use abstract_function_interface_module

  use fun01

  use fun02
```

```
implicit none

procedure (f) , pointer :: p1

p1 => f1

print *, ' p1 => f1, calling f3'
print *, f3(p1, 2)

p1 => f2

print *, ' p1 => f2, calling f3'
print *, f3(p1, 2)

p1 => f1

print *, ' p1 => f1, calling f4'
print *, f4(p1, 2)

p1 => f2

print *, ' p1 => f2, calling f4'
print *, f4(p1, 2)

end program ch4201
```

Here is sample output.

```
p1 => f1, calling f3
  0.5000000
p1 => f2, calling f3
  0.2500000
p1 => f1, calling f4
  2.5000000
p1 => f2, calling f4
  1.2500000
```

42.3   Problem

42.1 Try out the example in this chapter.

Appendix A
Glossary

This appendix is based on the terms and definitions chapter in the standard. References are to the standard.

Actual argument entity (R1524) that appears in a procedure reference

Allocatable having the ALLOCATABLE attribute (8.5.3)

Array set of scalar data, all of the same type and type parameters, whose individual elements are arranged in a rectangular pattern (8.5.8, 9.5)

> **Array element**   scalar individual element of an array
>
> **Array pointer**   array with the POINTER attribute (8.5.14)
>
> **Array section**   array subobject designated by array-section, and which is itself an array (9.5.3.3)
>
> **Assumed-shape array**   nonallocatable nonpointer dummy argument array that takes its shape from its effective argument (8.5.8.3)
>
> **Assumed-size array**   dummy argument array whose size is assumed from that of its effective argument (8.5.8.5)
>
> **Deferred-shape array**   allocatable array or array pointer, declared with a deferred-shape-spec-list (8.5.8.4)
>
> **Explicit-shape array**   array declared with an explicit-shape-spec-list, which specifies explicit values for the bounds in each dimension of the array (8.5.8.2)

ASCII character character whose representation method corresponds to ISO/IEC 646:1991 (International Reference Version)

Associate name name of construct entity associated with a selector of an ASSOCIATE, CHANGE TEAM, SELECT RANK, or SELECT TYPE construct (11.1.3, 11.1.5, 11.1.10, 11.1.11)

Associating entity 'in a dynamically-established association' the entity that did not exist prior to the establishment of the association (19.5.5)

Association inheritance association, name association, pointer association, or storage association.

> **Argument association**   association between an effective argument and a dummy argument

© Springer International Publishing AG, part of Springer Nature 2018
I. Chivers and J. Sleightholme, *Introduction to Programming with Fortran*,
https://doi.org/10.1007/978-3-319-75502-1

Construct association association between a selector and an associate name in an ASSOCIATE, CHANGE TEAM, SELECT RANK, or SELECT TYPE construct (11.1.3, 11.1.5, 11.1.10, 11.1.11, 19.5.1.6)

Host association name association, other than argument association, between entities in a submodule or contained scoping unit and entities in its host (19.5.1.4)

Inheritance association association between the inherited components of an extended type and the components of its parent component (19.5.4)

Linkage association association between a variable or common block with the BIND attribute and a C global variable (18.9, 19.5.1.5)

Name association argument association, construct association, host association, linkage association, or use association (19.5.1)

Pointer association association between a pointer and an entity with the TARGET attribute (19.5.2)

Storage association association between storage sequences (19.5.3)

Use association association between entities in a module and entities in a scoping unit or construct that references that module, as specified by a USE statement (14.2.2)

Assumed-rank dummy data object dummy data object that assumes the rank, shape, and size of its effective argument (8.5.8.7)

Assumed-type declared with a TYPE(*) type specifier (7.3.2)

Attribute property of an entity that determines its uses (8.1)

Automatic data object nondummy data object with a type parameter or array bound that depends on the value of a specification-expr that is not a constant expression (8.3)

Base object 'data-ref' object designated by the leftmost part-name (9.4.2)

Binding type-bound procedure or final subroutine (7.5.5)

Binding name name given to a specific or generic type-bound procedure in the type definition (7.5.5)

Binding label default character value specifying the name by which a global entity with the BIND attribute is known to the companion processor (18.10.2, 18.9.2)

Block sequence of executable constructs formed by the syntactic class block and which is treated as a unit by the executable constructs described in 11.1

Bound array bound limit of a dimension of an array (8.5.8)

Branch target statement action-stmt, associate-stmt, end-associate-stmt, if-then-stmt, end-if-stmt, select-case-stmt, end-select-stmt, selectrank-stmt, end-select-rank-stmt, select-type-stmt, end-select-type-stmt, do-stmt, end-do-stmt, block-stmt, endblock-stmt, critical-stmt, end-critical-stmt, forall-construct-stmt, where-construct-stmt, end-function-stmt, end-mp-subprogram-stmt, end-program-stmt, or end-subroutine-stmt.

C address value identifying the location of a data object or procedure either defined by the companion processor or which might be accessible to the companion processor NOTE 3.1 This is the concept that ISO/IEC 9899:2011 calls the address.

C descriptor C structure of type CFI_cdesc_t defined in the source file ISO_Fortran_binding.h (18.4, 18.5)

Character context within a character literal constant (7.4.4) or within a character string edit descriptor (13.3.2)

Characteristics 'dummy argument' being a dummy data object, dummy procedure, or an asterisk (alternate return indicator)

Characteristics 'dummy data object' properties listed in 15.3.2.2

Characteristics 'dummy procedure or dummy procedure pointer' properties listed in 15.3.2.3

Characteristics 'function result' properties listed in 15.3.3

Characteristics 'procedure' properties listed in 15.3.1

Coarray data entity that has nonzero corank (5.4.7)

> **Established coarray** coarray that is accessible using an image-selector (5.4.8)

Cobound bound (limit) of a codimension (8.5.6)

Codimension dimension of the pattern formed by a set of corresponding coarrays (8.5.6)

Coindexed object data object whose designator includes an image-selector (R924, 9.6)

Collating sequence one-to-one mapping from a character set into the nonnegative integers (7.4.4.4)

Common block block of physical storage specified by a COMMON statement (8.10.2)

> **Blank common** unnamed common block

Companion processor processor-dependent mechanism by which global data and procedures may be referenced or defined (5.5.7)

Component part of a derived type, or of an object of derived type, defined by a component-def-stmt (7.5.4)

> **Direct component** one of the components, or one of the direct components of a nonpointer nonallocatable component (7.5.1)
>
> **Parent component** component of an extended type whose type is that of the parent type and whose components are inheritance associated with the inherited components of the parent type (7.5.7.2)
>
> **Potential subobject component** nonpointer component, or potential subobject component of a nonpointer component (7.5.1)
>
> **Subcomponent** 'structure' direct component that is a subobject of the structure (9.4.2)
>
> **Ultimate component** component that is of intrinsic type, a pointer, or allocatable; or an ultimate component of a nonpointer nonallocatable component of derived type

Component order ordering of the nonparent components of a derived type that is used for intrinsic formatted input/output and structure constructors (where component keywords are not used) (7.5.4.7)

Conformable 'of two data entities' having the same shape, or one being an array and the other being scalar

Connected relationship between a unit and a file: each is connected if and only if the unit refers to the file (12.5.4)

Constant data object that has a value and which cannot be defined, redefined, or become undefined during execution of a program (6.2.3, 9.3)

> **Literal constant**   constant that does not have a name (R605, 7.4)
> **Named constant**   named data object with the PARAMETER attribute (8.5.13)

Construct entity entity whose identifier has the scope of a construct (19.1, 19.4)

Constant expression expression satisfying the requirements specified in 10.1.12, thus ensuring that its value is constant

Contiguous 'array' having array elements in order that are not separated by other data objects, as specified in 8.5.7

Contiguous 'multi-part data object' that the parts in order are not separated by other data objects

Corank number of codimensions of a coarray (zero for objects that are not coarrays) (8.5.6)

Cosubscript (R925) scalar integer expression in an image-selector (R924)

Data entity data object, result of the evaluation of an expression, or the result of the execution of a function reference

Data object object constant, variable, or subobject of a constant

Decimal symbol character that separates the whole and fractional parts in the decimal representation of a real number in a file (13.6)

Declaration specification of attributes for various program entities NOTE 3.2 Often this involves specifying the type of a named data object or specifying the shape of a named array object.

Default initialization mechanism for automatically initializing pointer components to have a defined pointer association status, and nonpointer components to have a particular value (7.5.4.6)

Default-initialized 'subcomponent' subject to a default initialization specified in the type definition for that component (7.5.4.6)

Definable capable of definition and permitted to become defined

Defined 'data object' has a valid value

Defined 'pointer' has a pointer association status of associated or disassociated (19.5.2.2)

Defined assignment assignment defined by a procedure (10.2.1.4, 15.4.3.4.3)

Defined input/output input/output defined by a procedure and accessed via a defined-io-generic-spec (R1509, 12.6.4.8)

Defined operation operation defined by a procedure (10.1.6.1, 15.4.3.4.2)

Definition 'data object' process by which the data object becomes defined (19.6.5)

Definition 'derived type (7.5.2), enumeration (7.6), or procedure (15.6)' specification of the type, enumeration, or procedure

Descendant 'module or submodule' submodule that extends that module or submodule or that extends another descendant thereof (14.2.3)

Designator name followed by zero or more component selectors, complex part selectors, array section selectors, array element selectors, image selectors, and substring selectors (9.1)

> **Complex part designator**   designator that designates the real or imaginary part of a complex data object, independently of the other part (9.4.4)
> **Object designator**   data object designator designator for a data object NOTE 3.3 An object name is a special case of an object designator.
> **Procedure designator**   designator for a procedure

Disassociated 'pointer association' pointer association status of not being associated with any target and not being undefined (19.5.2.2)
Disassociated 'pointer' has a pointer association status of disassociated
Dummy argument entity whose identifier appears in a dummy argument list in a FUNCTION, SUBROUTINE, ENTRY, or statement function statement, or whose name can be used as an argument keyword in a reference to an intrinsic procedure or a procedure in an intrinsic module

> **Dummy data object**   dummy argument that is a data object
> **Dummy function**   dummy procedure that is a function

Effective argument entity that is argument-associated with a dummy argument (15.5.2.3)
Effective item scalar object resulting from the application of the rules in 12.6.3 to an input/output list
Elemental independent scalar application of an action or operation to elements of an array or corresponding elements of a set of conformable arrays and scalars, or possessing the capability of elemental operation NOTE 3.4 Combination of scalar and array operands or arguments combine the scalar operand(s) with each element of the array operand(s).

> **Elemental assignment**   assignment that operates elementally
> **Elemental operation**   operation that operates elementally
> **Elemental operator**   operator in an elemental operation
> **Elemental procedure**   elemental intrinsic procedure or procedure defined by an elemental subprogram (15.8)
> **Elemental reference**   reference to an elemental procedure with at least one array actual argument
> **Elemental subprogram**   subprogram with the ELEMENTAL prefix (15.8.1)

END statement end-block-data-stmt, end-function-stmt, end-module-stmt, end-mp-subprogram-stmt, end-program-stmt, end-submodule-stmt, or end-subroutine-stmt
Explicit initialization initialization of a data object by a specification statement (8.4, 8.6.7)
Extent number of elements in a single dimension of an array
External file file that exists in a medium external to the program (12.3)
External unit external input/output unit entity that can be connected to an external file (12.5.3, 12.5.4)

File storage unit unit of storage in a stream file or an unformatted record file (12.3.5)
Final subroutine subroutine whose name appears in a FINAL statement (7.5.6) in a type definition, and which can be automatically invoked by the processor when an object of that type is finalized (7.5.6.2)
Finalizable 'type' has a final subroutine or a nonpointer nonallocatable component of finalizable type
Finalizable 'nonpointer data entity' of finalizable type
Finalization process of calling final subroutines when one of the events listed in 7.5.6.3 occurs
Function procedure that is invoked by an expression
Function result entity that returns the value of a function (15.6.2.2)
Generic identifier lexical token that identifies a generic set of procedures, intrinsic operations, and/or intrinsic assignments (15.4.3.4.1)
Host instance 'internal procedure, or dummy procedure or procedure pointer associated with an internal procedure' instance of the host procedure that supplies the host environment of the internal procedure (15.6.2.4)
Host scoping unit host scoping unit immediately surrounding another scoping unit, or the scoping unit extended by a submodule
IEEE infinity ISO/IEC/IEEE 60559:2011 conformant infinite floating-point value
IEEE NaN ISO/IEC/IEEE 60559:2011 conformant floating-point datum that does not represent a number
Image instance of a Fortran program (5.3.4)

> **Active image**   image that has not failed or stopped (5.3.6)
> **Failed image**   image that has not initiated termination but which has ceased to participate in program execution (5.3.6)
> **Stopped image**   image that has initiated normal termination (5.3.6)

Image index integer value identifying an image within a team
Image control statement statement that affects the execution ordering between images (11.6)
Inclusive scope nonblock scoping unit plus every block scoping unit whose host is that scoping unit or that is nested within such a block scoping unit NOTE 3.5 That is, inclusive scope is the scope as if BLOCK constructs were not scoping units.
Inherit 'extended type' acquire entities (components, type-bound procedures, and type parameters) through type extension from the parent type (7.5.7.2)
Inquiry function intrinsic function, or function in an intrinsic module, whose result depends on the properties of one or more of its arguments instead of their values
Interface 'procedure' name, procedure characteristics, dummy argument names, binding label, and generic identifiers (15.4.1)

> **Abstract interface**   set of procedure characteristics with dummy argument names (15.4.1)
> **Explicit interface**   interface of a procedure that includes all the characteristics of the procedure and names for its dummy arguments except for asterisk dummy arguments (15.4.2)

Generic interface set of procedure interfaces identified by a generic identifier

Implicit interface interface of a procedure that is not an explicit interface (15.4.2, 15.4.3.8)

Specific interface interface identified by a nongeneric name

Interface block abstract interface block, generic interface block, or specific interface block (15.4.3.2)

Abstract interface block interface block with the ABSTRACT keyword; collection of interface bodies that specify named abstract interfaces

Generic interface block interface block with a generic-spec; collection of interface bodies and procedure statements that are to be given that generic identifier

Specific interface block interface block with no generic-spec or ABSTRACT keyword; collection of interface bodies that specify the interfaces of procedures

Interoperable 'Fortran entity' equivalent to an entity defined by or definable by the companion processor (18.3)

Intrinsic type, procedure, module, assignment, operator, or input/output operation defined in this document and accessible without further definition or specification, or a procedure or module provided by a processor but not defined in this document

Standard intrinsic 'procedure or module' defined in this document (16)

Nonstandard intrinsic 'procedure or module' provided by a processor but not defined in this document

Internal file character variable that is connected to an internal unit (12.4)

Internal unit input/output unit that is connected to an internal file (12.5.4)

ISO 10646 character character whose representation method corresponds to UCS-4 in ISO/IEC 10646

Keyword statement keyword, argument keyword, type parameter keyword, or component keyword

Argument keyword word that identifies the corresponding dummy argument in an actual argument list (15.5.2.1)

Component keyword word that identifies a component in a structure constructor (7.5.10)

Statement keyword word that is part of the syntax of a statement (5.5.2)

Type parameter keyword word that identifies a type parameter in a type parameter list

Lexical token keyword, name, literal constant other than a complex literal constant, operator, label, delimiter, comma, =, =>, :, ::, ;, or % (6.2)

Line sequence of zero or more characters

Main program program unit that is not a subprogram, module, submodule, or block data program unit (14.1)

Masked array assignment assignment statement in a WHERE statement or WHERE construct

Module program unit containing (or accessing from other modules) definitions that are to be made accessible to other program units (14.2)

Name identifier of a program constituent, formed according to the rules given in 6.2.2

NaN Not a Number, a symbolic floating-point datum (ISO/IEC/IEEE 60559:2011)

Operand data value that is the subject of an operator

Operator intrinsic-operator, defined-unary-op, or defined-binary-op (R608, R1003, R1023)

Passed-object dummy argument dummy argument of a type-bound procedure or procedure pointer component that becomes associated with the object through which the procedure is invoked (7.5.4.5)

Pointer data pointer or procedure pointer

> **Data pointer**   data entity with the POINTER attribute (8.5.14)
>
> **Procedure pointer**   procedure with the EXTERNAL and POINTER attributes (8.5.9, 8.5.14)
>
> **Local procedure pointer**   procedure pointer that is part of a local variable, or a named procedure pointer that is not a dummy argument or accessed by use or host association

Pointer assignment association of a pointer with a target, by execution of a pointer assignment statement (10.2.2) or an intrinsic assignment statement (10.2.1.2) for a derived-type object that has the pointer as a subobject

Polymorphic 'data entity' able to be of differing dynamic types during program execution (7.3.2.3)

Preconnected 'file or unit' connected at the beginning of execution of the program (12.5.5)

Procedure entity encapsulating an arbitrary sequence of actions that can be invoked directly during program execution

> **Dummy procedure**   procedure that is a dummy argument (15.2.2.3)
>
> **External procedure**   procedure defined by an external subprogram (R503) or by means other than Fortran (15.6.3)
>
> **Internal procedure**   procedure defined by an internal subprogram (R512)
>
> **Module procedure**   procedure defined by a module subprogram, or a procedure provided by an intrinsic module (R1408)
>
> **Pure procedure**   procedure declared or defined to be pure (15.7)
>
> **Type-bound procedure**   procedure that is bound to a derived type and referenced via an object of that type (7.5.5)

Processor combination of a computing system and mechanism by which programs are transformed for use on that computing system

Processor dependent not completely specified in this document, having methods and semantics determined by the processor

Program set of Fortran program units and entities defined by means other than Fortran that includes exactly one main program

Program unit main program, external subprogram, module, submodule, or block data program unit (5.2.1)

Rank number of array dimensions of a data entity (zero for a scalar entity)

Record sequence of values or characters in a file (12.2)

Record file file composed of a sequence of records (12.1)

Reference data object reference, procedure reference, or module reference

> **Data object reference**   appearance of a data object designator (9.1) in a context requiring its value at that point during execution
>
> **Function reference**   appearance of the procedure designator for a function, or operator symbol for a defined operation, in a context requiring execution of the function during expression evaluation (15.5.3)
>
> **Module reference**   appearance of a module name in a USE statement (14.2.2)
>
> **Procedure reference**   appearance of a procedure designator, operator symbol, or assignment symbol in a context requiring execution of the procedure at that point during execution; or occurrence of defined input/output (13.7.6) or derived-type finalization (7.5.6.2)

Saved having the SAVE attribute (8.5.16)

Scalar data entity that can be represented by a single value of the type and that is not an array (9.5)

Scoping unit BLOCK construct, derived-type definition, interface body, program unit, or subprogram, excluding all nested scoping units in it

> **Block scoping unit**   scoping unit of a BLOCK construct

Sequence set of elements ordered by a one-to-one correspondence with the numbers 1, 2, to n

Sequence structure scalar data object of a sequence type (7.5.2.3)

Sequence type derived type with the SEQUENCE attribute (7.5.2.3)

> **Character sequence type**   sequence type with no allocatable or pointer components, and whose components are all default character or of another character sequence type
>
> **Numeric sequence type**   sequence type with no allocatable or pointer components, and whose components are all default complex, default integer, default logical, default real, double precision real, or of another numeric sequence type

Shape array dimensionality of a data entity, represented as a rank-one array whose size is the rank of the data entity and whose elements are the extents of the data entity NOTE 3.6 Thus the shape of a scalar data entity is an array with rank one and size zero.

Simply contiguous 'array designator or variable' satisfying the conditions specified in 9.5.4 NOTE 3.7 These conditions are simple ones which make it clear that the designator or variable designates a contiguous array.

Size 'array' total number of elements in the array

Specification expression expression satisfying the requirements specified in 10.1.11, thus being suitable for use in specifications

Specific name name that is not a generic name

Standard-conforming program program that uses only those forms and relationships described in, and has an interpretation according to, this document

Statement sequence of one or more complete or partial lines satisfying a syntax rule that ends in -stmt (6.3)

> **Executable statement** end-function-stmt, end-mp-subprogram-stmt, end-program-stmt, end-subroutine-stmt, or statement that is a member of the syntactic class executable-construct, excluding those in the block-specification-part of a BLOCK construct
>
> **Nonexecutable statement** statement that is not an executable statement

"aStatement entity entity whose identifier has the scope of a statement or part of a statement (19.1, 19.4)

Statement label label unsigned positive number of up to five digits that refers to an individual statement (6.2.5)

Storage sequence contiguous sequence of storage units (19.5.3.2)

Storage unit character storage unit, numeric storage unit, file storage unit, or unspecified storage unit (19.5.3.2)

> **Character storage unit** unit of storage that holds a default character value (19.5.3.2)
>
> **Numeric storage unit** unit of storage that holds a default real, default integer, or default logical value (19.5.3.2)
>
> **Unspecified storage unit** unit of storage that holds a value that is not default character, default real, double precision real, default logical, or default complex (19.5.3.2)

Stream file file composed of a sequence of file storage units (12.1)

Structure scalar data object of derived type (7.5)

> **Structure component** component of a structure
>
> **Structure constructor** syntax (structure-constructor, 7.5.10) that specifies a structure value or creates such a value

Submodule program unit that extends a module or another submodule (14.2.3)

Subobject portion of data object that can be referenced, and if it is a variable defined, independently of any other portion

Subprogram function-subprogram (R1529) or subroutine-subprogram (R1534)

> **External subprogram** subprogram that is not contained in a main program, module, submodule, or another subprogram
>
> **Internal subprogram** subprogram that is contained in a main program or another subprogram
>
> **Module subprogram** subprogram that is contained in a module or submodule but is not an internal subprogram

Subroutine procedure invoked by a CALL statement, by defined assignment, or by some operations on derived-type entities

Atomic subroutine   intrinsic subroutine that performs an action on its ATOM argument atomically

Collective subroutine   intrinsic subroutine that performs a calculation on a team of images without requiring synchronization

Target entity that is pointer associated with a pointer (19.5.2.2), entity on the right-hand-side of a pointer assignment statement (R1033), or entity with the TARGET attribute (8.5.17)

Team ordered set of images created by execution of a FORM TEAM statement, or the initial ordered set of all images

Current team   team specified by the most recently executed CHANGE TEAM statement of a CHANGE TEAM construct that has not completed execution (11.1.5), or initial team if no CHANGE TEAM construct is being executed

Initial team   team existing at the beginning of program execution, consisting of all images

Parent team   'team except for initial team' current team at time of execution of the FORM TEAM statement that created the team (11.6.9)

Team number   -1 which identifies the initial team, or positive integer that identifies a team within its parent team

Transformational function intrinsic function, or function in an intrinsic module, that is neither elemental nor an inquiry function

Type data type named category of data characterized by a set of values, a syntax for denoting these values, and a set of operations that interpret and manipulate the values (7.1)

Abstract type   type with the ABSTRACT attribute (7.5.7.1)

Declared type   type that a data entity is declared to have, either explicitly or implicitly (7.3.2, 10.1.9)

Derived type   type defined by a type definition (7.5) or by an intrinsic module

Dynamic type   type of a data entity at a particular point during execution of a program (7.3.2.3, 10.1.9)

Extended type   type with the EXTENDS attribute (7.5.7.1)

Extensible type   type that may be extended using the EXTENDS clause (7.5.7.1)

Extension type   'of one type with respect to another' is the same type or is an extended type whose parent type is an extension type of the other type

Intrinsic type   type defined by this document that is always accessible (7.4)

Numeric type   one of the types integer, real, and complex

Parent type   'extended type' type named in the EXTENDS clause

Type compatible   compatibility of the type of one entity with respect to another for purposes such as argument association, pointer association, and allocation (7.3.2)

Type parameter value used to parameterize a type (7.2)

Assumed type parameter length type parameter that assumes the type parameter value from another entity NOTE 3.8 The other entity is the selector for an associate name, the constant-expr for a named constant of type character, or NOTE 3.8 (cont.) the effective argument for a dummy argument.

Deferred type parameter length type parameter whose value can change during execution of a program and whose type-param-value is a colon

Kind type parameter type parameter whose value is required to be defaulted or given by a constant expression

Length type parameter type parameter whose value is permitted to be assumed, deferred, or given by a specification expression

Type parameter inquiry syntax (type-param-inquiry) that is used to inquire the value of a type parameter of a data object (9.4.5)

Type parameter order ordering of the type parameters of a type (7.5.3.2) used for derived-type specifiers (derived-type-spec, 7.5.9)

Ultimate argument nondummy entity with which a dummy argument is associated via a chain of argument associations (15.5.2.3)

Undefined 'data object' does not have a valid value

Undefined 'pointer' does not have a pointer association status of associated or disassociated (19.5.2.2)

Unit input/output unit means, specified by an io-unit, for referring to a file (12.5.1)

Unlimited polymorphic able to have any dynamic type during program execution (7.3.2.3)

Unsaved not having the SAVE attribute (8.5.16)

Variable data entity that can be defined and redefined during execution of a program

Event variable scalar variable of type EVENT_TYPE (16.10.2.10) from the intrinsic module ISO_FORTRAN_ENV

Local variable variable in a scoping unit that is not a dummy argument or part thereof, is not a global entity or part thereof, and is not an entity or part of an entity that is accessible outside that scoping unit

Lock variable scalar variable of type LOCK_TYPE (16.10.2.19) from the intrinsic module ISO_FORTRAN_ENV

Team variable scalar variable of type TEAM_TYPE (16.10.2.32) from the intrinsic module ISO_FORTRAN_ENV

Vector subscript section-subscript that is an array (9.5.3.3.2)

Whole array array component or array name without further qualification (9.5.2)

Appendix B
Attribute Declarations and Specifications

This appendix is based on Chap. 8 in the standard. References are to the standard.

Attributes of Procedures and Data Objects

Every data object has a type and rank and may have type parameters and other properties that determine the uses of the object. Collectively, these properties are the attributes of the object. The declared type of a named data object is either specified explicitly in a type declaration statement or determined implicitly by the first letter of its name (8.7). All of its attributes may be specified in a type declaration statement or individually in separate specification statements.

A function has a type and rank and may have type parameters and other attributes that determine the uses of the function. The type, rank, and type parameters are the same as those of the function result.

A subroutine does not have a type, rank, or type parameters, but may have other attributes that determine the uses of the subroutine.

Type Declaration Statement

A type declaration statement specifies the declared type of the entities in the entity declaration list.

Attribute Specification

An attribute specifier can be one or more of

- ALLOCATABLE
- ASYNCHRONOUS
- BIND C
- CODIMENSION
- CONTIGUOUS
- DIMENSION
- EXTERNAL
- INTENT
- INTRINSIC

© Springer International Publishing AG, part of Springer Nature 2018
I. Chivers and J. Sleightholme, *Introduction to Programming with Fortran*,
https://doi.org/10.1007/978-3-319-75502-1

- OPTIONAL
- PARAMETER
- POINTER
- PRIVATE
- PROTECTED
- PUBLIC
- SAVE
- TARGET
- VALUE
- VOLATILE

Attribute Specification Statements

These include

- ALLOCATABLE
- ASYNCHRONOUS
- BIND C
- CODIMENSION
- CONTIGUOUS
- DATA
- DIMENSION
- INTENT
- OPTIONAL
- PARAMETER
- POINTER
- PROTECTED
- SAVE
- TARGET
- VALUE
- VOLATILE

Appendix C
Compatibility

Previous Fortran Standards

Table C.1 lists the previous editions of the Fortran International Standard, along with their informal names.

Table C.1 Previous editions of the Fortran standard

Official name	Informal name
ISO R 1539-1972	Fortran 66
ISO 1539-1980	Fortran 77
ISO/IEC 1539:1991	Fortran 90
ISO/IEC 1539-1:1997	Fortran 95
ISO/IEC 1539-1:2004	Fortran 2003
ISO/IEC 1539-1:2010	Fortran 2008

New Intrinsic Procedures

Each Fortran International Standard since ISO 1539:1980 (Fortran 77), defines more intrinsic procedures than the previous one. Therefore, a Fortran program conforming to an older standard might have a different interpretation under a newer standard if it invokes an external procedure having the same name as one of the new standard intrinsic procedures, unless that procedure is specified to have the EXTERNAL attribute.

Fortran 2008 Compatibility

Except as identified in this subclause, and except for the deleted features noted in Annex B.2, the Fortran 2018 standard is an upward compatible extension to the preceding Fortran International Standard, ISO/IEC 1539-1:2010 (Fortran). Any standard-conforming Fortran 2008 program that does not use any deleted features,

© Springer International Publishing AG, part of Springer Nature 2018
I. Chivers and J. Sleightholme, *Introduction to Programming with Fortran*,
https://doi.org/10.1007/978-3-319-75502-1

and does not use any feature identified in this subclause as being no longer permitted, remains standard-conforming in the Fortran 2018 standard.

Fortran 2008 specifies that the IOSTAT = variable shall be set to a processor-dependent negative value if the flush operation is not supported for the unit specified. the Fortran 2018 standard specifies that the processor-dependent negative integer value shall be different from the named constants IOSTAT_EOR or IOSTAT_END from the intrinsic module ISO_FORTRAN_ENV.

Fortran 2008 permitted a noncontiguous array that was supplied as an actual argument corresponding to a contiguous INTENT (INOUT) dummy argument in one iteration of a DO CONCURRENT construct, without being previously defined in that iteration, to be defined in another iteration;

Fortran 2008 permitted a pure statement function to reference a volatile variable, and permitted a local variable of a pure subprogram or of a BLOCK construct within a pure subprogram to be volatile (provided it was not used); the Fortran 2018 standard does not permit this.

Fortran 2008 permitted a pure function to have a result that has a polymorphic allocatable ultimate component; the Fortran 2018 standard does not permit this.

Fortran 2008 permitted a PROTECTED TARGET variable accessed by use association to be used as an initial7 data-target; the Fortran 2018 standard does not permit this.

Fortran 2008 permitted a named constant to have declared type LOCK_TYPE, or have a noncoarray potential subobject component with declared type LOCK_TYPE; the Fortran 2018 standard does not permit this.

Fortran 2008 permitted a polymorphic object to be finalized within a DO CON-CURRENT construct; the Fortran 2018 standard does not permit this.

Fortran 2003 Compatibility

Except as identified in this subclause, the Fortran 2018 standard is an upward compatible extension to ISO/IEC 1539-1:2004 (Fortran 2003). Except as identified in this subclause, any standard-conforming Fortran 2003 program remains standard-conforming in the Fortran 2018 standard.

Fortran 2003 permitted a sequence type to have type parameters; that is not permitted by the Fortran 2018 standard.

Fortran 2003 specified that array constructors and structure constructors of finalizable type are finalized. The Fortran 2018 standard specifies that these constructors are not finalized.

The form produced by the G edit descriptor for some values and some input/output rounding modes differs from that specified by Fortran 2003.

Fortran 2003 required an explicit interface only for a procedure that was actually referenced in the scope, not merely passed as an actual argument. the Fortran 2018 standard requires an explicit interface for a procedure under the conditions listed in 15.4.2.2, regardless of whether the procedure is referenced in the scope.

Fortran 2003 permitted the function result of a pure function to be a polymorphic allocatable variable, to have a polymorphic allocatable ultimate component, or to be finalizable by an impure final subroutine. These are not permitted by the Fortran 2018 standard.

Fortran 2003 permitted an INTENT (OUT) argument of a pure subroutine to be polymorphic; that is not permitted by the Fortran 2018 standard.

Fortran 2003 interpreted assignment to an allocatable variable from a nonconformable array as intrinsic assignment, even when an elemental defined assignment was in scope; the Fortran 2018 standard does not permit assignment from a nonconformable array in this context.

Fortran 2003 permitted a statement function to be of parameterized derived type; the Fortran 2018 standard does not permit this.

Fortran 2003 permitted a pure statement function to reference a volatile variable, and permitted a local variable of a pure subprogram to be volatile (provided it was not used); the Fortran 2018 standard does not permit this

Fortran 95 Compatibility

Except as identified in this subclause, the Fortran 2018 standard is an upward compatible extension to ISO/IEC 1539-1:1997 (Fortran 95). Except as identified in this subclause, any standard-conforming Fortran 95 program remains standard-conforming in the Fortran 2018 standard.

Fortran 95 permitted defined assignment between character strings of the same rank and different kinds. This document does not permit that if both of the different kinds are ASCII, ISO 10646, or default kind.

The following Fortran 95 features might have different interpretations in the Fortran 2018 standard.

Earlier Fortran standards had the concept of printing, meaning that column one of formatted output had special meaning for a processor-dependent (possibly empty) set of external files. This could be neither detected nor specified by a standard-specified means. The interpretation of the first column is not specified by the Fortran 2018 standard.

The Fortran 2018 standard specifies a different output format for real zero values in list-directed and namelist output.

If the processor distinguishes between positive and negative real zero, the Fortran 2018 standard requires different returned values for ATAN2(Y,X) when $X < 0$ and Y is negative real zero and for LOG(X) and SQRT(X) when X is complex with $X\%RE < 0$ and $X\%IM$ is negative real zero.

The Fortran 2018 standard has fewer restrictions on constant expressions than Fortran 95; this might affect whether a variable is considered to be an automatic data object.

The form produced by the G edit descriptor with d equal to zero differs from that specified by Fortran 95 for some values.

Fortran 90 Compatibility

Except for the deleted features noted in Annex B.1, and except as identified in this subclause, the Fortran 2018 standard is an upward compatible extension to ISO/IEC 1539:1991 (Fortran 90). Any standard-conforming Fortran 90 program that does not use one of the deleted features remains standard-conforming in the Fortran 2018 standard.

The PAD = specifier in the INQUIRE statement in the Fortran 2018 standard returns the value UNDEFINED if there is no connection or the connection is for unformatted input/output. Fortran 90 specified YES.

Fortran 90 specified that if the second argument to MOD or MODULO was zero, the result was processor dependent. The Fortran 2018 standard specifies that the second argument shall not be zero.

Fortran 90 permitted defined assignment between character strings of the same rank and different kinds. This document does not permit that if both of the different kinds are ASCII, ISO 10646, or default kind.

The following Fortran 90 features have different interpretations in the Fortran 2018 standard:

if the processor distinguishes between positive and negative real zero, the result value of the intrinsic function SIGN when the second argument is a negative real zero;

formatted output of negative real values (when the output value is zero);

whether an expression is a constant expression (thus whether a variable is considered to be an automatic data object);

the G edit descriptor with d equal to zero for some values.

FORTRAN 77 Compatibility

Except for the deleted features noted in Annex B.1, and except as identified in this subclause, the Fortran 2018 standard is an upward compatible extension to ISO 1539:1980 (Fortran 77). Any standard-conforming Fortran 77 program that does not use one of the deleted features noted in Annex B.1 and that does not depend on the differences specified here remains standard-conforming in the Fortran 2018 standard. the Fortran 2018 standard restricts the behaviour for some features that were processor dependent in Fortran 77. Therefore, a standard-conforming Fortran 77 program that uses one of these processor-dependent features might have a different interpretation in the Fortran 2018 standard, yet remain a standard-conforming program. The following Fortran 77 features might have different interpretations in the Fortran 2018 standard.

Fortran 77 permitted a processor to supply more precision derived from a default real constant than can be represented in a default real datum when the constant is used to initialize a double precision real data object in a DATA statement. the Fortran 2018 standard does not permit a processor this option.

If a named variable that was not in a common block was initialized in a DATA statement and did not have the SAVE attribute specified, Fortran 77 left its SAVE attribute processor dependent. the Fortran 2018 standard specifies (8.6.7) that this named variable has the SAVE attribute.

Fortran 77 specified that the number 1 of characters required by the input list was to be less than or equal to the number of characters in the record during formatted input. the Fortran 2018 standard specifies (12.6.4.5.3) that the input record is logically padded with blanks if there are not enough characters in the record, unless the PAD= specifier with the value 'NO' is specified in an appropriate OPEN or READ statement.

A value of 0 for a list item in a formatted output statement will be formatted in a different form for some G edit descriptors. In addition, the Fortran 2018 standard specifies how rounding of values will affect the output field form, but Fortran 77 did not address this issue. Therefore, the form produced for certain combinations of values and G edit descriptors might differ from that produced by some Fortran 77 processors.

Fortran 77 did not permit a processor to distinguish between positive and negative real zero; if the processor does so distinguish, the result will differ for the intrinsic function SIGN when the second argument is negative real zero, and formatted output of negative real zero will be different.

Appendix D
Intrinsic Functions and Procedures

This appendix has a brief coverage of some of the more commonly used intrinsic functions and procedures. Chapter 16 of the standard should be consulted for an exhaustive coverage.

The following abbreviations and typographic conventions are used in this appendix.

D.1 Argument Type and Return Type

These are documented in Table D.1.

Table D.1 Argument and return type abbreviations

Abbreviation	Meaning
a	Any
i	Integer
r	Real
c	Complex
n	Numeric (any of integer, real, complex)
l	Logical
p	Pointer
p*	Polymorphic
t	Target
dp	Double precision
char	Character, length = 1
s	Character
boz	Boz-literal-constant
co	Coarray or coindexed object
te	Team type

© Springer International Publishing AG, part of Springer Nature 2018
I. Chivers and J. Sleightholme, *Introduction to Programming with Fortran*,
https://doi.org/10.1007/978-3-319-75502-1

D.2 Classes of Function

There are several classes of function in Fortran and they are documented below (Table D.2).

Table D.2 Classes of function

Class	Description
a	Indicates that the procedure is an atomic subroutine
e	Indicates that the procedure is an elemental function
es	Indicates that the procedure is an elemental subroutine
i	Indicates that the procedure is an inquiry function
ps	Indicates that the procedure is a pure subroutine
s	Indicates that the procedure is an impure subroutine
t	Indicates that the procedure in a transformational function

D.3 Optional Arguments

Arguments in italics or [] brackets are optional arguments.
     In the example ALL(mask, *dim*) dim may be omitted.

D.4 Common Optional Arguments

These are documented in Table D.3.

Table D.3 Common optional arguments

Argument	Description
Back	Controls the direction of string scan, forward or backward
Dim	A selected dimension of an array argument
Kind	Describes the kind type parameter of the result If the kind argument is absent the result is the same type as the first argument.
Mask size	A mask may be applied to the arguments f an array, the total number of elements

D.5   Double Precision

Before Fortran 90 if you required real variables to have greater precision than the default real then the only option available was to declare them as double precision. With the introduction of kind types with Fortran 90 the use of double precision declarations is not recommended, and instead real entities with a kind type offering more than the default precision should be used.

D.6   Result Type

When the result type is the same as the argument type then the result is not just the same type as the argument but also the same kind.

D.7   Miscellaneous Rules

All intrinsic procedures may be invoked with either positional arguments or argument keywords.

Many of the intrinsic functions have optional arguments.

Unless otherwise specified the intrinsc inquiry functions accept array arguments for which the shape need not be defined. The shape of array arguments to transformational and elemental intrinsic functions shall be defined.

Some array intrinsic functions are reduction functions - they reduce the rank of an array by collapsing one dimension (or all dimensions, usually producing a scalar result).

When the argument is `back` it is of logical type.

When the argument is `count_rate`, `count_max`, `dim`, `kind`, `len`, `order`, `n_copies`, `shape`, `shift`, `values` it is of integer type.

When the argument is `mask` it is of logical type.

When the argument is `target` it is of `pointer` or `target` type.

Fortran 2008 introduced several changes to Fortran 2003 that affected intrinsic procedures.

- The following functions can now have arguments of type complex: `acos`, `asin`, `atan`, `cosh`, `sinh`, `tan` and `tanh`.
- The intrinsic function `atan2` can be referenced by the name `atan`.
- The intrinsic functions `lge`, `lgt`, `lle` and `llt` can have arguments of ASCII kind.
- The intrinsic functions `maxloc` and `minloc` have an additional `back` argument.
- The intrinsic function `selected_real_kind` has an additional `radix` argument.

Fortran 2018 introduced the following intrinsic functions and procedures

- ATOMIC_ADD (ATOM, VALUE [, STAT])
- ATOMIC_AND (ATOM, VALUE [, STAT])
- ATOMIC_CAS (ATOM, OLD, COMPARE, NEW [, STAT])
- ATOMIC_DEFINE (ATOM, VALUE [, STAT])
- ATOMIC_FETCH_ADD (ATOM, VALUE, OLD [, STAT])
- ATOMIC_FETCH_AND (ATOM, VALUE, OLD [, STAT])
- ATOMIC_FETCH_OR (ATOM, VALUE, OLD [, STAT])
- ATOMIC_FETCH_XOR (ATOM, VALUE, OLD [, STAT])
- ATOMIC_OR (ATOM, VALUE [, STAT])
- ATOMIC_REF (VALUE, ATOM [, STAT])
- ATOMIC_XOR (ATOM, VALUE [, STAT])
- CO_BROADCAST(A, SOURCE_IMAGE [, STAT, ERRMSG])
- CO_MAX(A [, RESULT_IMAGE, STAT, ERRMSG])
- CO_MIN(A [, RESULT_IMAGE, STAT, ERRMSG])
- CO_REDUCE(A, OPERATION [, RESULT_IMAGE, STAT, ERRMSG])
- CO_SUM(A [, RESULT_IMAGE, STAT, ERRMSG])
- COSHAPE (COARRAY [, KIND])
- FAILED_IMAGES([TEAM, KIND])
- FINDLOC (ARRAY, VALUE, DIM [, MASK, KIND, BACK])
- FINDLOC (ARRAY, VALUE [, MASK, KIND, BACK])
- GET_TEAM([LEVEL])
- IMAGE_STATUS (IMAGE [, TEAM])
- LCOBOUND (COARRAY [, DIM, KIND])
- OUT_OF_RANGE (X, MOLD [, ROUND])
- RANDOM_INIT (REPEATABLE, IMAGE_DISTINCT)
- RANK (A)
- REDUCE (ARRAY, OPERATION [, MASK, IDENTITY, ORDERED])
- REDUCE (ARRAY, OPERATION, DIM [, MASK, IDENTITY,ORDERED])
- STOPPED_IMAGES([TEAM, KIND])
- TEAM_NUMBER([TEAM])
- THIS_IMAGE ([TEAM]) or THIS_IMAGE (COARRAY [, TEAM])
- THIS_IMAGE (COARRAY, DIM [, TEAM])
- UCOBOUND (COARRAY [, DIM, KIND])

D.8   Intrinsic functions list

These are documented in Table D.4, where some of the procedure names are split over multiple lines.

Table D.4 Standard generic intrinsic procedure summary

Procedure	Class	Description
ABS	E	Absolute value
ACHAR	E	Character from ASCII code value
ACOS	E	function
ACOSH	E	Inverse hyperbolic cosine function
ADJUSTL	E	Left-justified string value
ADJUSTR	E	Right-justified string value
AIMAG	E	Imaginary part of a complex number
AINT	E	Truncation toward 0 to a whole number
ALL	T	Array reduced by AND operator
ALLOCATED	I	Allocation status of allocatable variable
ANINT	E	Nearest whole number
ANY	T	Array reduced by OR operator
ASIN	E	function
ASINH	E	Inverse hyperbolic sine function
ASSOCIATED	I	Pointer association status inquiry
ATAN	E	function
ATAN2	E	function
ATANH	E	Inverse hyperbolic tangent function
ATOMIC_ADD	A	Atomic addition
ATOMIC_AND	A	Atomic bitwise AND
ATOMIC_CAS	A	Atomic compare and swap
ATOMIC_DEFINE	A	Define a variable atomically
ATOMIC_FETCH_ADD	A	Atomic fetch and add
ATOMIC_FETCH_AND	A	Atomic fetch and bitwise AND
ATOMIC_FETCH_OR	A	Atomic fetch and bitwise OR
ATOMIC_FETCH_XOR	A	Atomic fetch and bitwise exclusive OR
ATOMIC_OR	A	Atomic bitwise OR
ATOMIC_REF	A	Reference a variable atomically
ATOMIC_XOR	A	Atomic bitwise exclusive OR
BESSEL_J0	E	Bessel function of the 1st kind, order 0
BESSEL_J1	E	Bessel function of the 1st kind, order 1
BESSEL_JN	E	Bessel function of the 1st kind, order N
BESSEL_JN	T	Bessel functions of the 1st kind
BESSEL_Y0	E	Bessel function of the 2nd kind, order 0
BESSEL_Y1	E	Bessel function of the 2nd kind, order 1
BESSEL_YN	E	Bessel function of the 2nd kind, order N
BESSEL_YN	T	Bessel functions of the 2nd kind
BGE	E	Bitwise greater than or equal to
BGT	E	Bitwise greater than
BIT_SIZE	I	Number of bits in integer model

Table D.4 (continued)

BLE	E	Bitwise less than or equal to
BLT	E	Bitwise less than
BTEST	E	Test single bit in an integer
CEILING	E	Least integer greater than or equal to A
CHAR	E	Character from code value
CMPLX	E	Conversion to complex type
CO_BROADCAST	C	Broadcast value to images
CO_MAX	C	Compute maximum value across images
CO_MIN	C	Compute minimum value across images
CO_REDUCE	C	Generalized reduction across images
CO_SUM	C	Compute sum across images
COMMAND_ARGUMENT_COUNT	T	Number of command arguments
CONJG	E	Conjugate of a complex number
COS	E	Cosine function
COSH	E	Hyperbolic cosine function
COSHAPE	I	Sizes of codimensions of a coarray
COUNT	T	Logical array reduced by counting true values
CPU_TIME	S	Processor time used
CSHIFT	T	Circular shift of an array
DATE_AND_TIME	S	Date and time
DBLE	E	Conversion to double precision real
DIGITS	I	Significant digits in numeric model
DIM	E	Maximum of X - Y and zero
DOT_PRODUCT	T	Dot product of two vectors
DPROD	E	Double precision real product
DSHIFTL	E	Combined left shift
DSHIFTR	E	Combined right shift
EOSHIFT	T	End-off shift of the elements of an array
EPSILON	I	Model number that is small compared to 1
ERF	E	Error function
ERFC	E	Complementary error function
ERFC_SCALED	E	Scaled complementary error function
EVENT_QUERY	S	Query event count
EXECUTE_COMMAND_LINE	S	Execute a command line
EXP	E	Exponential function
EXPONENT	E	Exponent of floating-point number
EXTENDS_TYPE_OF	I	Dynamic type extension inquiry
FAILED_IMAGES	T	Indices of failed images
FINDLOC	T	Location(s) of a specified value
FLOOR	E	Greatest integer less than or equal to A

Table D.4 (continued)

FRACTION	E	Fractional part of number
GAMMA	E	Gamma function
GET_COMMAND	S	Get program invocation command
GET_COMMAND_ ARGUMENT	S	Get program invocation argument
GET_ENVIRONMENT_VARIABLE	S	Get environment variable
GET_TEAM	T	Team
HUGE	I	Largest model number
HYPOT	E	Euclidean distance function
IACHAR	E	ASCII code value for character
IALL	T	Array reduced by IAND function
IAND	E	Bitwise AND
IANY	T	Array reduced by IOR function
IBCLR	E	I with bit POS replaced by zero
IBITS	E	Specified sequence of bits
IBSET	E	I with bit POS replaced by one
ICHAR	E	Code value for character
IEOR	E	Bitwise exclusive OR
IMAGE_INDEX	I	Image index from cosubscripts
IMAGE_STATUS	T	Image execution state
INDEX	E	Character string search
INT	E	Conversion to integer type
IOR	E	Bitwise inclusive OR
IPARITY	T	Array reduced by IEOR function
ISHFT	E	Logical shift
ISHFTC	E	Circular shift of the rightmost bits
IS_CONTIGUOUS	I	Array contiguity test
IS_IOSTAT_END	E	IOSTAT value test for end of file
IS_IOSTAT_EOR	E	IOSTAT value test for end of record
KIND	I	Value of the kind type parameter of X
LBOUND	I	Lower bound(s)
LCOBOUND	I	Lower cobound(s) of a coarray
LEADZ	E	Number of leading zero bits
LEN	I	Length of a character entity
LEN_TRIM	E	Length without trailing blanks
LGE	E	ASCII greater than or equal
LGT	E	ASCII greater than
LLE	E	ASCII less than or equal
LLT	E	ASCII less than
LOG	E	Natural logarithm
LOG_GAMMA	E	Logarithm of the absolute value of the gamma function

Table D.4 (continued)

LOG10	E	Common logarithm
LOGICAL	E	Conversion between kinds of logical
MASKL	E	Left justified mask
MASKR	E	Right justified mask
MATMUL	T	Matrix multiplication
MAX	E	Maximum value
MAXEXPONENT	I	Maximum exponent of a real model
MAXLOC	T	Location(s) of maximum value
MAXVAL	T	Maximum value(s) of array
MERGE	E	Expression value selection
MERGE_BITS	E	Merge of bits under mask
MIN	E	Minimum value
MINEXPONENT	I	Minimum exponent of a real model
MINLOC	T	Location(s) of minimum value
MINVAL	T	Minimum value(s) of array
MOD	E	Remainder function
MODULO	E	Modulo function
MOVE_ALLOC	PS	Move an allocation
MVBITS	ES	Copy a sequence of bits
NEAREST	E	Adjacent machine number
NEW_LINE	I	Newline character
NINT	E	Nearest integer
NORM2	T	L2 norm of an array
NOT	E	Bitwise complement
NULL	T	Disassociated pointer or unallocated allocatable entity
NUM_IMAGES	T	Number of images
OUT_OF_RANGE	E	Whether a value cannot be converted safely
PACK	T	Array packed into a vector
PARITY	T	Array reduced by NEQV operator
POPCNT	E	Number of one bits
POPPAR	E	Parity expressed as 0 or 1
PRECISION	I	Decimal precision of a real model
PRESENT	I	Presence of optional argument
PRODUCT	T	Array reduced by multiplication
RADIX	I	Base of a numeric model
RANDOM_INIT	S	Initialise the pseudorandom number generator
RANDOM_NUMBER	S	Generate pseudorandom number(s)
RANDOM_SEED	S	Restart or query the pseudorandom number generator
RANGE	I	Decimal exponent range of a numeric model

Table D.4 (continued)

RANK	I	Rank of a data object
REAL	E	Conversion to real type
REDUCE	T	General reduction of array
REPEAT	T	Repetitive string concatenation
RESHAPE	T	Arbitrary shape array construction
RRSPACING	E	Reciprocal of relative spacing of model numbers
SAME_TYPE_AS	I	Dynamic type equality test
SCALE	E	Real number scaled by radix power
SCAN	E	Character set membership search
SELECTED_CHAR_KIND	T	Character kind selection
SELECTED_INT_KIND	T	Integer kind selection
SELECTED_REAL_KIND	T	Real kind selection
SET_EXPONENT	E	Real value with specified exponent
SHAPE	I	Shape of an array or a scalar
SHIFTA	E	Right shift with fill
SHIFTL	E	Left shift
SHIFTR	E	Right shift
SIGN	E	Magnitude of A with the sign of B
SIN	E	Sine function
SINH	E	Hyperbolic sine function
SIZE	I	Size of an array or one extent
SPACING	E	Spacing of model numbers
SPREAD	T	Value replicated in a new dimension
SQRT	E	Square root
STOPPED_IMAGES	T	Indices of stopped images
STORAGE_SIZE	I	Storage size in bits
SUM	T	Array reduced by addition
SYSTEM_CLOCK	S	Query system clock
TAN	E	Tangent function
TANH	E	Hyperbolic tangent function
TEAM_NUMBER	T	Team number
THIS_IMAGE	T	Index of the invoking image
THIS_IMAGE	T	Cosubscript(s) of this image
TINY	I	Smallest positive model number
TRAILZ	E	Number of trailing zero bits
TRANSFER	T	Transfer physical representation
TRANSPOSE	T	Transpose of an array of rank two
TRIM	T	String without trailing blanks
UBOUND	I	Upper bound(s)
UCOBOUND	I	Upper cobound(s) of a coarray
UNPACK	T	Vector unpacked into an array
VERIFY	E	Character manipulation

D.9 Intrinsic Function Examples

In this section we provide coverage of a large subset of the intrinsic functions and procedures.

ABS(a) : Absolute value.

argument: a	**type**: n
result: as argument	**class**: e

Note(s):

If a is complex(x,y) then the functions returns $\sqrt{x^2 + y^2}$

Example(s): r1=abs(a)

ACHAR(i, *kind*) : Returns character in the ASCII character set.

argument: i	**type**: i
result: char	**class**: e

Note(s):

Inverse of the iachar function.

Example(s): c=achar(i)

ACOS(x) : Arccosine, inverse cosine.

argument: x	**type**: r,c
result: as argument	**class**: e

Note(s):

$|x| <= 1$

Example(s): y=acos(x)

ACOSH(x) : Inverse hyperbolic cosine function.

argument: x	**type**: r,c
result: as argument	**class**: e

Example(s): y = acosh(x)

ADJUSTL(string) : Adjust string left, removing leading blanks and inserting trailing blanks.

argument: string   **type**: s
result: as argument   **class**: e

Example(s): `s=adjustl(s)`

ADJUSTR(string) : Adjust `string` right, removing trailing blanks and inserting leading blanks.

argument: string   **type**: s
result: as argument   **class**: e

Example(s): `s=adjustr(s)`

AIMAG(z) : Imaginary part of complex argument.

argument: z   **type**: c
result: as argument   **class**: e

Example(s): `y=aimag(z)`

AINT(a, _kind_) : Truncation toward zero to a whole number.

argument: a   **type**: r
result: as a   **class**: e

Example(s): `y=aint(z)`

```
   z        y
  0.3       0
  2.73      2.0
 -2.73     -2.0
```

ALL(mask, _dim_) : Determines whether all values are true in `mask`.

argument: mask   **type**: l
result: l   **class**: t

Note(s):

    `dim` is optional and must be a scalar in the range $1 <= dim <= n$ where n is the rank of mask. The result is scalar if `dim` is absent or mask has rank 1. Otherwise it works on the dimension `dim` of mask and the result is an array of rank $n - 1$

Example(s): `t=all(m)`

ALLOCATED(variable) : Returns true if and only if the allocatable variable is allocated.

argument: variable	**type**: any
result: l	**class**: i

Note(s):

    `variable` must be declared with the allocatable attribute and can be an array or a scalar.

Example(s): `if (allocated(array) ) then ...`

ANINT(a, *kind*) : Nearest whole number.

argument: a	**type**: r
result: as a	**class**: e

Example(s): `z=anint(a)`

```
   a       z
  5.63     6
 -5.7    -6.0
```

ANY(mask, *dim*) : Determines whether any value is true in `mask` along dimension `dim`.

argument: mask	**type**: l
result: l	**class**: t

Note(s):

    `mask` must be an array. The result is a scalar if `dim` is absent or if `mask` is of rank 1. Otherwise it works on the dimension `dim` of `mask` and the result is an array of rank $n - 1$

Example(s): `t=any(a)`

ASIN(x) : Arcsine.

argument: x	**type**: r,c
result: as argument	**class**: e

Example(s): z=asin(x)

ASINH(x) : Inverse hyperbolic sine function.

argument: x	**type**: r,c
result: as argument	**class**: e

Example(s): y = asinh(x)

ASSOCIATED(pointer, *target*) : Returns the association status of the pointer.

argument: pointer	**type**: p
result: l	**class**: i

Note(s):
1. If target is absent then the result is true if pointer is associated with a target, otherwise false.
2. If target is present and is a target, the result is true if pointer is currently associated with target and false if it is not.
3. If target is present and is a pointer, the result is true if both pointer and target are currently associated with the same target, and is false otherwise. If either pointer or target is disassociated the result is false.
Example(s): t=associated(p)

ATAN(x) or
ATAN(y,x) : Arctangent.

argument: x	**type**: r,c
argument: y	**type**: r
result: as argument	**class**: e

Note(s):
 If y appears, x shall be of type real with the same kind type parameter as y.
 If y has the value zero, x shall not have the value zero.
 If y does not appear, x shall be of type real or complex.
Example(s): z=atan(x)

ATAN2(y,x) : Arctangent of y / x.

argument: y	**type**: r
result: as arguments	**class**: e

Example(s): z=atan2(y,x)

ATANH(x) : Inverse hyperbolic tangent function.

argument: x	**type**: r,c
result: as argument	**class**: e

Example(s): y = atanh(x)

BESSEL_J0(x) : Bessel function of the first kind, order 0.

argument: x	**type**: r
result: as argument	**class**: e

Example(s): y = bessel_j0(1.0) has the value 0.765 (approximately)

BESSEL_J1(x) : Bessel function of the first kind, order 1.

argument: x	**type**: r
result: as argument	**class**: e

Example(s): y = bessel_j1(1.0) has the value 0.440 (approximately).

BESSEL_JN(n, x) : Bessel functions of the first kind. Elemental
BESSEL_JN(n1,n2,x) : Bessel function of the first kind. Transformational.

arguments: n	**type**: i
arguments: n1	**type**: i
arguments: n2	**type**: i
arguments: x	**type**: r
result: as x	**class**: e or t

Note(s):

n shall be nonnegative.

n1 shall be nonnegative.

n2 shall be nonnegative.

x if the function is transformational, x shall be scalar.

Additional Note(s):

The result of bessel_jn(n, x) is processor dependent approximation to the Bessel function of the first kind and order n of x.

Element i of the result value of `bessel_jn(n1,n2,x)` is a processor dependent approximation to the bessel function of the first kind and order $n1 + i - 1$ of
x.

Example(s): `y = bessel_jn(2, 1.0)` has the value 0.115 (approximately).

BESSEL_Y0(x) : Bessel function of the second kind, order 0.

argument: x	**type**: r
result: as argument	**class**: e

Example(s): `y = bessel_y0(1.0)` has the value 0.088 (approximately).

BESSEL_Y1(x) : Bessel function of the second kind, order 1.

argument: x	**type**: r
result: as argument	**class**: e

Example(s): `y = bessel_y1(1.0)` has the value -0.781 (approximately).

BESSEL_YN(n1,n2,x) Bessel functions of the second kind. Transformational.
BESSEL_YN(n, x) : Bessel functions of the second kind. Elemental.

arguments: n	**type**: i
arguments: n1	**type**: i
arguments: n2	**type**: i
arguments: x	**type**: r
result: as x	**class**: e or t

Note(s):

n nonnegative.

n1 nonnegative.

n2 nonnegative.

x if the function is transformational, x shall be scalar. Its value shall be greater
than zero.

Example(s): `y = bessel_yn(2, 1.0)` has the value -1.651 (approximately).

BGE(i, j) : True if i is bitwise greater than or equal to j.

arguments: i,j	**type**: i or boz
result: l	**class**: e

Example(s): If `bit_size(j)` has the value 8, `bge(z'ff', j)` has the value true for any value of j. `bge(0, -1)` has the value false.

BGT(i, j) : True if `i` is bitwise greater than `j`

arguments: i,j	type: i or boz
result: l	class: e

The result is true if the sequence of bits represented by `i` is greater than the sequence of bits represented by `j`, according to the method of bit sequence comparison in 16.3.2 of the standard; otherwise the result is false.
Example(s): `bgt(z'ff', z'fc')` has the value true. `bgt(0, -1)` has the value false.

BLE(i, j) : True if `i` is bitwise less than or equal to `j`.

arguments: i,j	type: i or boz
result: l	class: e

The result is true if the sequence of bits represented by `i` is less than or equal to the sequence of bits represented by `j`, according to the method of bit sequence comparison in 16.3.2 of the standard; otherwise the result is false.
Example(s): `ble(0, j)` has the value true for any value of j. `ble(-1, 0)` has the value false.

BLT(i, j) : Bitwise less than.

arguments: i,j	type: i or boz
result: l	class: e

The result is true if the sequence of bits represented by `i` is less than the sequence of bits represented by `j`, according to the method of bit sequence comparison in 16.3.2 of the standard; otherwise the result is false.
Example(s): `blt(0, -1)` has the value true. `blt(z'ff', z'fc')` has the value false.

BIT_SIZE(i) : Returns the number of bits, as defined by the bit model of Sect. 16.3 of the standard.

argument: i	type: i
result: as argument	class: i

Example(s): `n_bits=bit_size(i)`

BTEST(i, pos) : True if and only if a specified bit of an integer value is one.

argument: i	**type**: i
result: l	**class**: e

Example(s): `t=btest(i,pos)`

CEILING(a, *kind*) : Least integer greater than or equal to a.

argument: a	**type**: r
result: i	**class**: e

Note(s):
If `kind` is present the result has the kind type parameter `kind`. otherwise the result is of type default integer.

Example(s): `i=ceiling(a)` If $a = 12.21$ then $i = 13$, if $a = -3.16$ then $i = -3$.

CHAR(i, *kind*) : Returns the character in a given position in the processor collating sequence associated with the specified `kind` type parameter. It is the inverse of the `ICHAR` function.

argument: i	**type**: i
result: char	**class**: e

Note(s):
ASCII is the default character set.

Example(s): `c=char(65)` and for the ASCII character set c='a'.

CMPLX(x,*kind*) or
CMPLX(x, y, *kind*) : Converts to complex type.
First form.

argument: x	**type**: c
result: c	**class**: e

Second form.

argument: x   **type**: i, r, boz
argument: y   **type**: i, r boz
result: c   **class**: e

Note(s):

1. The result is of type complex. If `kind` is present, the kind type parameter is that specified by the value of `kind`; otherwise, the kind type parameter is that of default real kind

2. If Y is absent and X is not complex, it is as if Y were present with the value zero. If `kind` is absent, it is as if `kind` were present with the value `kind` (0.0). If X is complex, the result is the same as that of `cmplx (real (x), aimag (x), kind)`. The result of `cmplx (x, y, kind)` has the complex value whose real part is `real (x, kind)` and whose imaginary part is `real (y, kind)`.

Example(s): `z=cmplx(x,y)`

COMMAND_ARGUMENT_COUNT( ) : Number of command arguments.

arguments: none   **result**: i
class: t

The result value is equal to the number of command arguments available. If there are no command arguments available or if the processor does not support command arguments, then the result has the value zero. if the processor has a concept of a command name, the command name does not count as one of the command arguments.

Example(s): `i = command_argument_count ( )`

CONJG(z) : Conjugate of a complex argument.

argument: z   **type**: c
result: as z   **class**: e

Example(s): `z1=conjg(z)`

COS(x) : Cosine.

argument: x   **type**: r, c
result: as argument   **class**: e

Note(s):

The arguments of all trigonometric functions should be in radians, not degrees.

Example(s): `a=cos(x)`

COSH(x) : Hyperbolic cosine.

argument: x	type: r,c
result: as argument	class: e

Example(s): z=cosh(x)

COUNT(mask, *dim, kind*) : Returns the number of true elements in mask along dimension dim.

argument: mask	type: l
result: i	class: t

Note(s):

dim must be a scalar in the range $1 <= dim <= n$, where n is the rank of mask. The result is scalar if dim is absent or mask has rank 1. Otherwise it works on the dimension dim of mask and the result is an array of rank $n - 1$

Example(s): n=count(a)

CPU_TIME(time) : Returns the processor time.

argument: time	type: r
result: n/a	class: s

Example(s): call cpu_time(time)

CSHIFT(array, shift, *dim)* : Circular shift on a rank 1 array or rank 1 sections of higher-rank arrays.

argument: array	type: any
result: as array	class: t

Note(s):

array must be an array

shift must be a scalar if array has rank 1, otherwise it is an array of rank $n - 1$, where n is the rank of array.

dim must be a scalar with a value in the range $1 < dim <= n$.

Example(s): array=cshift(array,10)

DATE_AND_TIME(*date, time, zone, values)* : Returns the current date and time (compatible with ISO 8601:1988).

Note(s):

1. Date is optional and must be scalar and 8 characters long in order to return the complete value of the form ccyymmdd, where cc is the century, yy is the year, mm is the month and dd is the day. It is intent(out).

2. Time is optional and must be scalar and 10 characters long in order to return the complete value of the form hhmmss.sss where hh is the hour, mm is the minutes and ss.sss is the seconds and milliseconds. It is intent(out).

3. Zone is optional and must be scalar and must be 5 characters long in order to return the complete value of the form hhmm where hh and mm are the time differences with respect to coordinated universal time in hours and minutes. It is intent(out).

4. Values is optional and a rank 1 array of size 8. It is intent(out). The values returned are as shown below.

```
values(1)    year
values(2)    month
values(3)    day
values(4)    time with respect to coordinated
             universal time in minutes.
values(5)    hour (24 hour clock)
values(6)    minutes
values(7)    seconds
values(8)    milliseconds in the range 0 - 999.
```

Example(s): call date_time(d,t,z,v)

DBLE(a) : Converts to double precision from integer, real, and complex

argument: a	**type**: n
result: dp	**class**: e

Example(s): d=dble(a)

DIGITS(x) : Returns the number of significant digits of the argument as defined in the numeric models for integer and reals in Chap. 5.

argument: x	**type**: i,r
result: i	**class**: i

Example(s): i=digits(x)

DIM(x,y) : Difference of two values if positive or zero otherwise.

argument: x	**type**: i
result: as arguments	**class**: e

Example(s): z=dim(x,y)

DOT_PRODUCT(vector_1,vector_2) : Performs the mathematical dot product of two rank 1 arrays.

argument: vector_ 1	**type**: n
argument: vector_ 2	**type**: n
result: as arguments	**class**: t

vector_2 is as vector_1.
Note(s):
   1. For integer and real vector_1 result has the value sum(vector_1*vector_2).
   2. For complex vector_1 result has the value sum(conjg(vector_1)*vector_2).
   3. For logical vector_1 result has the value any(vector_1 .and. vector_2).
Example(s): a=dot_product(x,y)

DPROD(x,y) : Double precision product of two reals.

argument: x	**type**: r
result: dp	**class**: e

Example(s): d=dprod(x,y)

DSHIFTL(i, j, shift) : Combined left shift.

arguments: i,j	**type**: i or boz
argument: shift	**type**: i
result: See note below.	**class**: e

Note(s):
   Result type: Same as i if i is of type integer; otherwise, same as j. If either i or j is a boz-literal-constant, it is first converted as if by the intrinsic function int to type integer with the kind type parameter of the other. The rightmost shift bits of the result value are the same as the leftmost bits of j, and the remaining bits of the result value are the same as the rightmost bits of i. This is equal to ior(shiftl(i, shift), shiftr(j, bit size(j)-shift)). The model for the interpretation of an integer value as a sequence of bits is in Sect. 16.3 of the standard.

Example(s): dshiftl(1, 2**30, 2) has the value 5 if default integer has 32 bits. dshiftl(i, i, shift) has the same result value as ishftc(i, shift).

DSHIFTR(i, j, shift) : Combined right shift.

arguments: i,j	**type**: i or boz
argument: shift	**type**: i
result: See note below.	**class**: e

Note(s):

Result: Same as i if i is of type integer; otherwise, same as j. If either i or j is a boz-literal-constant, it is first converted as if by the intrinsic function int to type integer with the kind type parameter of the other. The leftmost shift bits of the result value are the same as the rightmost bits of i, and the remaining bits of the result value are the same as the leftmost bits of j. This is equal to ior(shiftl(i, bit size(i)-shift), shiftr(j, shift)). The model for the interpretation of an integer value as a sequence of bits is in 16.3 of the standard.

Example(s): dshiftr(1, 16, 3) has the value 229 +2 if default integer has 32 bits. dshiftr(i, i, shift) has the same result value as ishftc(i,-shift).

EOSHIFT(array, shift, *boundary, dim*) : End of shift of a rank 1 array or rank 1 section of a higher-rank array.

argument: array	**type**: any
argument: shift	**type**: n
argument: boundary	**type**: n
result: as array	**class**: t

Note(s):

1. boundary is as array.

2. array must be an array, shift must be a scalar if array has rank 1, otherwise it is an array of rank $n - 1$, where n is the rank of array.

3. boundary shall be of the same type and type parameters as array. It must be scalar if array has rank 1, otherwise it must be either scalar or of rank $n - 1$. See section 16.9.67 of the standard for additional information.

4. dim must be a scalar with a value in the range $1 <= dim <= n$.

Example(s): a=eoshift(a,shift)

EPSILON(x) : Smallest difference between two reals of that kind. See Chap. 5 and real numeric model.

argument: x	**type**: r
result: as argument	**class**: i

Example(s): `tiny=epsilon(x)`

ERF(x) : Error function.

argument: x	**type**: r
result: as x	**class**: e

Example(s): `y = erf(1.0)` has the value 0.843 (approximately).

ERFC(x) : Complementary error function.

argument: x	**type**: r
result: as x	**class**: e

Example(s): `y = erfc(1.0)` has the value 0.157 (approximately).

ERFC_SCALED(x) : Scaled complementary error function.

argument: x	**type**: r
result: as x	**class**: e

Example(s): `y = erfc_scaled(20.0)` has the value 0.0282 (approximately).

EXECUTE_COMMAND_LINE(command, *wait, exitstat,cmdstat, cmdmsg* **)** : Execute a command line.

Note(s):

command shall be a default character scalar. It is an `intent(in)` argument. Its value is the command line to be executed. the interpretation is processor dependent.

wait shall be a default logical scalar. It is an `intent(in)` argument. If wait is present with the value false, and the processor supports asynchronous execution of the command, the command is executed asynchronously; otherwise it is executed synchronously.

exitstat shall be a default integer scalar. It is an intent(inout) argument. If the command is executed synchronously, it is assigned the value of the processor-dependent exit status. Otherwise, the value of exitstat is unchanged.

cmdstat shall be a default integer scalar. It is an `intent(out)` argument. It is assigned the value -1 if the processor does not support command line execution, a processor-dependent positive value if an error condition occurs, or the value -2 if no error condition occurs but wait is present with the value false and the processor does not support asynchronous execution. otherwise it is assigned the value 0.

cmdmsg shall be a default character scalar. It is an `intent(inout)` argument. If an error condition occurs, it is assigned a processor-dependent explanatory message. otherwise, it is unchanged.

Example(s): `call execute_command_line('pwd')` will print the full path-name of the current directory under unix and an error message from windows.

EXP(x) : Exponential. e^x

argument: x	**type**: r, c
result: as argument	**class**: e

Example(s): `y=exp(x)`

EXPONENT(x) : Returns the exponent component of the argument. See Chap. 5 and the real numeric model.

argument: x	**type**: r
result: i	**class**: e

Example(s): `i=exponent(x)`

EXTENDS_TYPE_OF(a, mold) : Query dynamic type for extension.

arguments: a, mold	**type**: p*
result: l	**class**: i

Note(s):

a shall be an object of extensible declared type or unlimited polymorphic. If it is a polymorphic pointer, it shall not have an undefined association status.

mold shall be an object of extensible declared type or unlimited polymorphic. If it is a polymorphic pointer, it shall not have an undefined association status.

If mold is unlimited polymorphic and is either a disassociated pointer or unallocated allocatable variable, the result is true; otherwise if a is unlimited polymorphic and is either a disassociated pointer or unallocated allocatable variable, the result is false; otherwise if the dynamic type of a or mold is extensible, the result is true if and only if the dynamic type of a is an extension type of the dynamic type of mold; otherwise the result is processor dependent.

Example(s):

```
if(extends_type_of(a, mold)) then
   print *,'dynamic type of a is an'
   print *,'extension of dynamic type of mold'
end if
```

FINDLOC(array, value, dim, *mask, kind, back*) or
FINDLOC(array, value, *mask, kind, back*) : Location(s) of a specified value.

argument: array	**type**: intrinsic type
argument: value	**type**: as array
argument: dim	**type**: i
argument: mask	**type**: l
argument: kind	**type**: i
argument: back	**type**: l
result: i	**class**: t

Note(s):

1. dim shall be an integer scalar with a value in the range $1 <= dim <= n$, where n is the rank of array.

2. mask shall be conformable with array.

3. **result characteristics**: If kind is present, the kind type parameter is that specified by the value of kind; otherwise the kind type parameter is that of default integer type. If dim does not appear, the result is an array of rank one and of size equal to the rank of array; otherwise, the result is of rank $n - 1$ and shape $[d_1, d_2, ..., d_{DIM-1}, d_{DIM+1}, ..., d_n]$, where $[d_1, d_2, ..., d_n]$ is the shape of array.

Example(s):

```
1. The value of
findloc ([1, 3, 5, 3, 1], value=3)
is [2]
The value of
findloc ([1, 3, 5, 3, 1], value=3, back=.true.)
is [4]
The value of
findloc ([1, 3, 5, 3, 1], value=3, dim=1)
is [2]
```

2. If B has the value

$$\begin{bmatrix} 1 & 2 & -9 \\ 2 & 2 & 6 \end{bmatrix}$$

findloc (b, value=2, dim=1) has the value [2, 1, 0] and
findloc (b, value=2, dim=2) has the value [2, 1]. This is independent of the declared lower bounds for b.

FLOOR(a, *kind*) : Returns the greatest integer less than or equal to the argument

argument: a	**type**: r
result: i	**class**: e

Note(s):

If kind is present the result has the kind type parameter kind, otherwise the result is of type default integer.

Example(s): i=floor(a) when a = 5.2 i has the value 5, when a = − 9.7 i has the value −10.

FRACTION(x) : Returns the fractional part of the real numeric model of the argument. See Chap. 5 and the real numeric model.

argument: x	**type**: r
result: as x	**class**: e

Example(s): f=fraction(x)

GAMMA(x) : Gamma function.

argument: x	**type**: r
result: as x	**class**: e

Example(s): y = gamma(1.0) has the value 1.000 (approximately).

GET_COMMAND(*command, length, status*) : Query program invocation command.

GET_COMMAND_ARGUMENT(number, *value, length, status*) : Query arguments from program invocation.

GET_ENVIRONMENT_VARIABLE(name, *value, length, status, trim name*) : Query environment variable.

HUGE(x) : Returns the largest number for the kind type of the argument. See Chap. 5 and the real and integer numeric models.

argument: x	**type**: i,r
result: as argument	**class**: i

Example(s): h=huge(x)

HYPOT(x, y) : Euclidean distance function.

arguments: x,y	**type**: r
result: r	**class**: e

Example(s): h = hypot(3.0, 4.0) has the value 5.0 (approximately).

IACHAR(c) : Returns the position of the character argument in the ASCII collating sequence.

argument: c	**type**: char
result: i	**class**: e

Example(s): i=iachar('a') returns the value 65.

IALL(array, dim, *mask*) or
IALL(array, *mask*) : Reduce array with bitwise and operation.
IAND(i,j) : Performs a logical and on the arguments.

argument: i	**type**: i
result: as arguments	**class**: e

Example(s): k=iand(i,j)

IANY(array, dim, *mask*) or
IANY(array, *mask*) : Reduce array with bitwise or operation.
IBCLR(i,pos) : Clears one bit of the argument to zero.

argument: i	**type**: i
result: as i	**class**: e

Example(s): i=ibclr(i,pos)

IBITS(i,pos,len) : Returns a sequence of bits.

argument: i	**type**: i
result: as i	**class**: e

Example(s): slice=ibits(i,pos,len)

IBSET(i,pos) : Sets one bit of the argument to one.

argument: i	**type**: i
result: as i	**class**: e

Note(s):

$0 <= pos <= bit\_size(i)$

Example(s): i=ibset(i,pos)

ICHAR(c) : Returns the position of a character in the processor collating sequence associated with the kind type parameter of the argument. Normally the position in the ASCII collating sequence.

argument: c	**type**: char
result: i	**class**: e

Example(s): i=ichar('a') would return the value 65 for the ASCII character set.

IEOR(i, j) : Performs an exclusive or on the arguments.

argument: i	**type**: i
result: Same as i if i is of type integer; otherwise, same as j.	**class**: e

Example(s): i=ieor(i,j)

IMAGE_INDEX(coarray, sub) or
IMAGE_INDEX(coarray, sub, team) or
IMAGE_INDEX(coarray, sub, team_number) : Convert cosubscripts to image index.

argument: coarray	**type**: co
argument: sub	**type**: rank-one integer array
argument: team	**type**: te
argument: team_ number	**type**: i
result: i	**class**: i

Note(s):

1. coarray is of any type.
2. team is scalar.
3. team_number is scalar.

Example(s):

```
integer, codimension[0:*]:: x
integer, dimension(10,15), &
    codimension[3,0:1,-1:*]:: z
  print*, image_index(x,(/0/));
  print*, image_index(z,(/2,0,-1/))
```

would print 1 and 2 respectively.

INDEX(string, substring, *back, kind*) : Locates one substring in another, i.e., returns position of substring in character expression string.

argument: string	**type**: s
argument: substring	**type**: s
argument: back	**type**: l
result: i	**class**: e

Note(s):

If $len(string) < len(substring)$ the result is zero.

Otherwise, if there is an integer i in the range

$1 <= i <= (len(string) - len(substring) + 1)$

such that `string(i : i + len(substring) - 1)` is equal to `substring`, the result has the value of the smallest such i if `back` is absent or present with the value false, and the greatest such i if `back` is present with the value true.

If the substring is not found the result is zero.

Example(s):

```
where=index(' hello world hello','hello')
```
the result 2 is returned.
```
where=index(' hello world hello','hello',.true.)
```
the result 14 is returned.

INT(a, *kind*) : Converts to integer from integer, real, and complex.

argument: a	**type**: n
result: i	**class**: e

Example(s): `i=int(f)`

IOR(i, j) : Performs an inclusive or on the arguments.

argument: i	**type**: i
result: as i	**class**: e

Example(s): i=ior(i,j)

IPARITY(array, dim, *mask*) or
IPARITY(array, *mask*) : Array reduced by ieor function. Transformational.

argument: array	**type**: i
argument: dim	**type**: i
argument: mask	**type**: l
result: as i	**class**: e

Note(s):

dim integer scalar with a value in the range $1 <= dim <= n$, where n is the rank of array.

mask shall be of type logical and shall be conformable with array.

Example(s):

iparity ([14, 13, 8]) has the value 11.
iparity ([14, 13, 8], mask=[.true., .false., .true])
has the value 6.

ISHFT(i, shift) : Performs a logical shift. The bits of i are shifted by shift positions.

argument: i	**type**: i
result: as i	**class**: e

Note(s):

$|shift| <= bit\_size(i)$

If shift is positive, the shift is to the left.

If shift is negative, the shift is to the right.

If shift is zero, no shift is performed.

Bits shifted out from the left or from the right, as appropriate, are lost. Zeros are shifted in from the opposite end.

Example(s): i=ishft(i,shift).

ISHFTC(i, shift, *size*) : Performs a circular shift of the rightmost bits. The size rightmost bits of i are circularly shifted by shift positions.

argument: i	**type**: i
result: i	**class**: e

Note(s):

$|shift| <= size$

The result has the value obtained by shifting the `size` rightmost bits of `i` circularly by `shift` positions.

If `shift` is positive, the shift is to the left.

If `shift` is negative, the shift is to the right.

If `shift` is zero, no shift is performed.

No bits are lost. The unshifted bits are unaltered.

Example(s): i=ishftc(i,shift,size)

IS_CONTIGUOUS(array) : Test contiguity of an array.

argument: array	**type**: any
result: l	**class**: i

Example(s):

```
integer,target, dimension(10)::a
integer,pointer,dimension(:) :: p
   p= a(1:10:2); print*,is_contiguous(p)
```

would print 'f'.

IS_IOSTAT_END(i) : Test iostat value for end-of-file.

argument: i	**type**: i
result: l	**class**: e

Example(s): is_iostat_end(i) returns value true if i is an i/o status value that corresponds to an end-of-file condition, and false otherwise.

```
read(unit=1,fmt=*, iostat=ist)y(i)
if (is_iostat_end(ist)) then
  print*,'end of file!'
endif
```

IS_IOSTAT_EOR(i) : Test iostat value for end-of-record.

argument: i	**type**: i
result: l	**class**: e

Example(s): is_iostat_eor(i) returns the value true if i is an i/o status value that corresponds to an end-of-record condition, and false otherwise.

KIND(x) : Returns the kind type parameter of the argument.

argument: x	**type**: any
result: i	**class**: i

Example(s): `i=kind(x)`

LBOUND(array, *dim, kind*) : Lower bound(s) of an array.

argument: array	**type**: any
result: i	**class**: i

Note(s):

1. `dim` optional. $1 <= dim <= n$ where n is the rank of array. The result is scalar if `dim` is present otherwise the result is an array of rank 1 and size n. The result is scalar if `dim` is present, otherwise a rank 1 array and size n.

2. If `array` is a whole array and either array is an assumed-size array of rank `dim` or dimension `dim` of array has nonzero extent, `lbound (array, dim)` has a value equal to the lower bound for subscript `dim` of `array`. Otherwise the result value is 1.

Example(s): `i=lbound(array)`

LCOBOUND(coarray, *dim, kind*]) : Lower cobound(s) of a coarray.

argument: coarray	**type**: co
argument: dim (optional)	**type**: i
argument: kind(optional)	**type**: i
result: i	**class**: i

Example(s):

```
integer, codimension[:,:], allocatable::a
allocate(a[2:3,7:*])
```

`lcbound(a)` is [2,7] and `lcobound(a,dim=2)` is 7

LEADZ(i) : Number of leading zero bits.

argument: i	**type**: i
result: i	**class**: e

Example(s): `leadz (1)` has the value 31 if bit size(1) has the value 32.

LEN(string) : Length of a character entity.

> **argument**: string   **type**: s
> **result**: i   **class**: i

Example(s): i=len(string)

LEN_TRIM(string) : Length of character argument less the number of trailing blanks.

> **argument**: string   **type**: s
> **result**: i   **class**: e

Example(s): i=len_trim(string)

LGE(string_1, string_2) :
   Lexically greater than or equal to and this is default character or ASCII.

> **argument**: string_1   **type**: s,ASCII
> **result**: l   **class**: e

   string_2 is of type s.
Example(s): l=lge(s1,s2)

LGT(string_1, string_2) : Lexically greater than and this is based on the ASCII collating sequence.

> **argument**: string_1   **type**: s

Example(s): l=lgt(s1,s2)

LLE(string_1, string_2) : Lexically less than or equal to and this is based on the ASCII collating sequence.

> **argument**: string_1   **type**: s
> **result**: l   **class**: e

   string_2 is of type s.
Example(s): l=lle(s1,s2)

LLT(string_1, string_2) : Lexically less than and this is based on the ASCII collating sequence.

argument: string_ l	**type**: s
result: l	**class**: e

Example(s): `l=llt(s1,s2)`

LOG(x) : Natural logarithm.

argument: x	**type**: r, c
result: as argument	**class**: e

Example(s): `y=log(x)`

LOG_GAMMA(x) : Logarithm of the absolute value of the gamma function.

argument: x	**type**: r
result: r	**class**: e

Example(s): `log_gamma(3.0)` has the value 0.693 (approximately).

LOG10(x) : Common logarithm, log10

argument: x	**type**: r
result: as argument	**class**: e

Example(s): `y=log10(x)`

LOGICAL(l, *kind*) : Converts between different logical kind types, i.e., performs a type cast.

argument: l	**type**: l
result: l	**class**: e

Example(s): `l=logical(k,kind)`

MASKL(i, *kind*) : Left justified mask.

argument : i	**type** : i
result: i	**class**: e

Example(s): `maskl(4)` has the value `shiftl(15, bit_size(0) - 4)`

MASKR(i, *kind*) : Right justified mask.

argument: i	type: i
result: i	class: e

Example(s): `maskr(4)` has the value 15.

MATMUL(matrix_1, matrix_2) : Performs mathematical matrix multiplication of the array arguments.

argument: matrix_1	type: n,l
argument: matrix_2	type: n,l
result: as arguments	class: t

matrix_2 is as matrix_1.

Note(s):

    `matrix_a` shall be a rank-one or rank-two array of numeric type or logical type.

    `matrix_b` shall be of numeric type if `matrix_a` is of numeric type and of logical type if `matrix_a` is of logical type. It shall be an array of rank one or two.

    `matrix_a` and `matrix_b` shall not both have rank one.

    The size of the first (or only) dimension of `matrix_b` shall equal the size of the last (or only) dimension of `matrix_a`.

    The shape of the result depends on the shapes of the arguments as follows:

If `matrix_a` has shape [n,m] and `matrix_b` has shape [m, k], the result has shape [n, k].

If `matrix_a` has shape [m] and `matrix_b` has shape [m, k], the result has shape [k].

If `matrix_a` has shape [n,m] and `matrix_b` has shape [m], the result has shape [n].

Example(s): `r=matmul(m_1,m_2)`

MAX(a1, a2, *a3*,...) : Returns the largest value.

argument: a1	type: i,r,s
result: as arguments	class: e

a2, a3,.. are as a1.

Example(s): `a=max(a1,a2,a3,a4)`

MAXEXPONENT(x) : Returns the maximum exponent. See Chap. 5 and numeric models.

argument: x   **type**: r
result: i   **class**: i

Example(s): `i=maxexponent(x)`

MAXLOC(array, *mask, kind, back*) or
MAXLOC(array, dim, *mask, kind, back*) : Location(s) of maximum value.

argument: array   **type**: i,r,s
argument: dim   **type**: i
argument: mask   **type**: l
argument: kind   **type**: i
argument: back   **type**: l
result: i   **class**: t

Note(s):

1. `dim` shall be an integer scalar with a value in the range $1 <= dim <= n$, where n is the rank of `array`. The corresponding actual argument shall not be an optional dummy argument.

2. `mask` shall be of type logical and shall be conformable with `array`.

3. `kind` shall be a scalar integer constant expression.

4. `back` shall be scalar and of type logical.

Example(s):

```
a=(/5,6,7,8/)
i=maxloc(a)
```

is (4), which is the subscript of the location of the first occurrence of the maximum value in the rank 1 array.

If

$$A = \begin{pmatrix} 1 & 8 & 5 \\ 9 & 3 & 6 \\ 4 & 2 & 7 \end{pmatrix}$$

```
i = maxloc(a, dim=1)
```
is (2,1,3) returning the position of the largest in each column.
```
i = maxloc(a, dim=2)
```
is (2,1,3) returning the position of the largest in each row.

MAXVAL(array, *mask*) or
MAXVAL(array, dim, *mask*) : Maximum value(s) of `array`.

argument: array	**type**: i,r,s
argument: mask	**type**: l
argument: dim	**type**: i
result: as argument	**class**: t

Note(s):

1. dim shall be an integer scalar with a value in the range $1 <= dim <= n$, where n is the rank of `array`.

2. mask (optional) shall be of type logical and shall be conformable with `array`.

Example(s): `maxval((/1,2,3/))` returns the value 3.

```
maxval( c , mask = c < 0.0)
```

returns the maximum of the negative elements of c.

For

$$B = \begin{pmatrix} 1 & 3 & 5 \\ 2 & 4 & 6 \end{pmatrix}$$

```
maxval(b, dim=1) returns(2,4,6)
maxval(b, dim=2) returns(5,6)
```

MERGE(true, false, mask) : Chooses alternative values according to the value of a mask.

argument: true	**type**: any
result: as true	**class**: e

Example(s): For

$$true = \begin{pmatrix} 2 & 6 & 10 \\ 4 & 8 & 12 \end{pmatrix}, false = \begin{pmatrix} 1 & 5 & 9 \\ 3 & 7 & 11 \end{pmatrix}, and \ mask = \begin{pmatrix} T & F & T \\ F & T & F \end{pmatrix}$$

$$result = \begin{pmatrix} 2 & 5 & 10 \\ 3 & 8 & 11 \end{pmatrix}$$

MERGE_BITS(i, j, mask) : Merge of bits under mask.

argument: i	**type**: i or boz
argument: j i or boz	
argument: mask i or boz	
result: same as i if integer, otherwise same as j.	
class: e	

Example(s): `merge_bits(14,18,22)` has the value 6.

MIN(a1, a2, a3,...) : Chooses the smallest value.

argument: a1	**type**: i, r, s
result: as arguments	**class**: e

Example(s): `y=min(x1,x2,x3,x4,x5)`

MINEXPONENT(x) : Returns the minimum exponent. See Chap. 5 and numeric models.

argument: x	**type**: r
result: i	**class**: i

Example(s): `i=minexponent(x)`

MINLOC(array,*mask,kind,back*) or
MINLOC(array,dim,*mask,kind,back*) : Location of minimum value.

argument: array	**type**: i,r,s
argument: dim	**type**: i
argument: mask	**type**: l
argument: kind	**type**: i
argument: back	**type**: l
result: i	**class**: t

Note(s):

1. `dim` shall be an integer scalar with a value in the range $1 <= dim <= n$, where n is the rank of `array`. The corresponding actual argument shall not be an optional dummy argument.

2. `mask` shall be of type logical and shall be conformable with `array`.

3. `kind` shall be a scalar integer constant expression.

4. `back` shall be scalar and of type logical.

Example(s): `i=minloc(array)`

In the above example if array is a rank 2 array of shape(5,10) and the smallest value is in position(2,1) then the result is the rank 1 array i with shape(2) and i(1) = 2 and i(2) = 1.

MINVAL(array, *mask* or
MINVAL(array, dim, mask) : Minimum value(s) of `array`.

argument: array	**type**: i,r,s
argument: mask	**type**: l
argument: dim	**type**: i
result: as array	**class**: t

Note(s):

1. dim shall be an integer scalar with a value in the range $1 <= dim <= n$, where n is the rank of array. The corresponding actual argument shall not be an optional dummy argument.

2. mask shall be of type logical and shall be conformable with array.

Example(s):

minval((/1,2,3/)) returns the value 1.

minval(c,mask=c>0.0) returns the minimum of the positive elements of c.

For

$$B = \begin{pmatrix} 1 & 3 & 5 \\ 2 & 4 & 6 \end{pmatrix}$$

minval(b,dim=1) returns(1,3,5).

minval(b,dim=2) returns(1,2).

MOD(a, b) : Returns the remainder when first argument divided by second.

argument: a	**type**: i, r
argument: b	**type**: as a
result: as arguments	**class**: e

Note(s):

b shall not be zero.

The result is $a - int(a/b) * b$.

Example(s): r=mod(a,b)

a	b	r
8	5	3
-8	5	-3
8	-5	3
-8	-5	-3

MODULO(a, b) : Returns the modulo of the arguments.

argument: a	**type**: i,r
argument: b	**type**: as a
result: as a	**class**: e

Note(s):

b shall not be zero.

If a is of typr integer, modulo (a, b) has the value r such that $a = qb + r$, where q is an integer, the inequalities $0 <= r < b$ hold if $b > 0$, and $b < r <= 0$ hold if $b < 0$.

If a is a type real modulo (a,b) has the result $a - floor(a/b) * b$.

Example(s): r=modulo(a,b)

a	b	r
8	5	3
-8	5	2
8	-5	-2
-8	-5	-3

MOVE_ALLOC (from, to [, stat, errmsg]) : Move an allocation.

Note(s):

1. Subroutine, pure if and only if from is not a coarray.

2. from may be of any type, rank, and corank. It shall be allocatable and shall not be a coindexed object. It is an intent (inout) argument.

3. to shall be type compatible with from and have the same rank and corank. It shall be allocatable and shall not be a coindexed object. It shall be polymorphic if from is polymorphic. It is an intent (out) argument.

4. stat shall be a noncoindexed integer scalar with a decimal exponent range of at least four. It is an intent (out) argument.

5. errmsg shall be a noncoindexed default character scalar. It is an intent (inout) argument.

6. It is expected that the implementation of allocatable objects will typically involve descriptors to locate the allocated storage; move_alloc could then be implemented by transferring the the contents of the descriptor for from to the descriptor for to and clearing the descriptor for from.

Example(s):

```
real,allocatable :: grid(:),tempgrid(:)
. . .
allocate(grid(-n:n))
! initial allocation of grid
. . .
allocate(tempgrid(-2*n:2*n))
! allocate bigger grid
tempgrid(::2)=grid
! distribute values to new locations
call move_alloc(to=grid,from=tempgrid)
```

The old grid is deallocated because to is intent (out), and grid then takes over the new grid allocation.

MVBITS(from, frompos, len, to, topos) : Copies a sequence of bits from one data object to another.

argument: from	**type**: i
argument: frompos	**type**: i
argument: len	**type**: i
argument: to	**type**: i
argument: topos	**type**: i
result: n/a	**class**: s

All arguments are of integer type.

Note(s):

from It is an intent(in) argument.

frompos shall be nonnegative. It is an intent(in) argument. $frompos + len <= bit\_size(from)$.

len shall be nonnegative. It is an intent(in) argument.

to shall be a variable of the same type and kind type parameter value as from and may be associated with from. It is an intent(inout) argument.

to is defined by copying the sequence of bits of length len, starting at position frompos of from to position topos of to. No other bits of to are altered. On return, the len bits of to starting at topos are equal to the value that the len bits of from starting at frompos had on entry.

topos shall be nonnegative. It is an intent(in) argument. $topos + len <= bit\_size(to)$.

Example(s): If to has the initial value 6, the value of to after the statement call mvbits (7, 2, 2, to, 0) is 5.

Example(s): call mvbits(f,fp,l,t,tp)

NEAREST(x,next) : Returns the nearest different number. See Chap. 5 and the real numeric model.

argument: x	**type**: r
argument: next	**type**: r
result: as x	**class**: e

Note(s):

next Not equal to zero.

The result has a value equal to the machine-representable number distinct from x and nearest to it in the direction of infinity with the same sign as next.

Unlike other floating point manipulation functions, nearest operates on machine representable numbers rather than model numbers. On many systems there are machine representable numbers that lie between adjacent model numbers.

Example(s): n=nearest(x,next)

NEW_LINE(a) : Returns newline character used for formatted stream output.

argument: a	**type**: char
result: char	**class**: i

Note(s):

If a is default character and the character in position 10 of the ASCII collating sequence is representable in the default character set, then the result is achar (10).

If a is ASCII character or ISO 10646 character, then the result is char (10, kind (a)).

Otherwise, the result is a processor-dependent character that represents a newline in output to files connected for formatted stream output if there is such a character.

Otherwise, the result is the blank character.

Example(s):

```
open(2,file='nline.txt', access='stream', form='formatted')
write(2,'(a)')'hola'//new_line('a')//'mundo'
```

This will write 2 lines to the file nline.txt.

NINT(a, *kind*) : Yields nearest integer.

argument: a	**type**: r
result: i	**class**: e

Note(s):

1. $a > 0$, the result is int(a+0.5).
2. $a <= 0$, the result is int(a-0.5).

Example(s): i=nint(x)

NORM2(x) or
NORM2(x, *dim*) : Norm of an array.

argument: x	**type**:*r*
argument: dim	**type**: i
result: r	**class**: t

Note(s):

1. dim shall be an integer scalar with a value in the range $1 <= dim <= n$, where n is the rank of x. The corresponding actual argument shall not be an optional dummy argument.

2. The result of `norm2(x)` has a value equal to a processor-dependent approximation to the generalized l2 norm of `x`, which is the square root of the sum of the squares of the elements of `x`.

3. If `dim` is present the array is reduced as for `sum(x,dim)` except that `norm2` is applied to the reduced vectors.

Example(s): See below.

```
norm2([3.0, 4.0]) is 5.0.
If x has the value
   1.0 2.0
   3.0 4.0
norm2(x,dim=1) is [3.162, 4.472]
norm2(x,dim=2) is [2.236,5.0]
approximately.
```

NOT(i) : Returns the logical complement of the argument.

argument: i	**type**: i
result: as i	**class**: e

Example(s): `i=not(i)`

NULL(*mold*) : Returns a disassociated pointer.

argument: mold	**type**: p
result: as argument	**class**: t

Note(s):

If the argument mold is present the result is the same as mold. Otherwise it is determined by context.

Example(s): `real, pointer :: p=>null()`

NUM_IMAGES( ) or
NUM_IMAGES(team) or
NUM_IMAGES(team_number) : Number of images.

argument: none	
argument: team	**type**: te
argument: team_ number	**type**: i
result: i	**class**: t

Notes(s):

team shall be a scalar of type team_type from the intrinsic module iso_fortran_env, with a value that identifies the current or an ancestor team.

team_number shall be an integer scalar. It shall identify the initial team or a team whose parent is the same as that of the current team.

The result is the number of images in the specified team, or in the current team if no team is specified.

Example(s): print*,' number of images = ',num_images( )

The following code uses image 1 to read data and broadcast it to other images.

```
REAL :: P[*]
  IF (THIS_IMAGE()==1) THEN
    READ (6,*) P
    DO I = 2, NUM_IMAGES()
      P[I] = P
    END DO
  END IF
SYNC ALL
```

OUT_OF_RANGE (x, mold [, round]) Whether a value cannot be converted safely.

argument: x	**type**: i,r
argument: mold	**type**: i,r scalar
argument: round	**type**: l scalar
result: l	**class**: e

Note(s):

1. mold If it is a variable, it need not be defined.

2. round shall be present only if x is of type real and mold is of type integer.

Example(s): If INT8 is the kind value for an 8-bit binary integer type, OUT_OF_RANGE (-128.5, 0_INT8) will have the value false and OUT_OF_RANGE (-128.5, 0_INT8, .TRUE.) will have the value true.

PACK(array, mask, *vector*) : Packs an array into an array of rank 1, under the control of a mask.

argument: array	**type**: any
argument: mask	**type**: l
argument: vector	**type**: same type as array
result: as array	**class**: t

Note(s):

1. array must be an array.

2. mask be conformable with array.

3. vector must have rank 1 and have at least as many elements as there are true elements in mask.

4. If mask is scalar with the value true vector must have at least as many elements as there are in array.

5. The result is an array of rank 1.

6. If vector is present the result size is that of vector.

7. If vector is not present the result size is t, the number of true elements in mask, unless mask is scalar with a value true in which case the result size is the size of array.

Example(s): r=pack(a,m)

The nonzero elements of an array m with the value

```
0 0 0
9 0 0
0 0 7
```

can be *gathered* by the function pack. The result of
pack (m, mask = m/= 0) is [9, 7] and the result of
pack (m, m /= 0, vector = [2, 4, 6, 8, 10, 12])
is [9, 7, 6, 8, 10, 12].

PARITY(mask, *dim*) : Reduce array with .neqv. operation.

argument:mask	**type**: l array
argument:dim shall be an integer scalar in the range $1 <= dim <= n$ where n is rank of mask.	

Example(s): If t has the value true and f has the value false
parity([t,t,t,f]) is true.

POPCNT(i) : Number of one bits in the sequence of bits of i.

argument: i	**type**: i
result: i	**class**: e

Example(s): popcnt([1, 2, 3, 4, 5, 6, 7])
has the value [1, 1, 2, 1, 2, 2, 3].

POPPAR(i) : Returns the parity of the bit count of an integer expressed as 0 or 1.

argument: i   **type**: i
result: i   **type**: e

Example(s): `poppar([1, 2, 3, 4, 5, 6, 7])`
has the value [1, 1, 0, 1, 0, 0, 1]

PRECISION(x) : Returns the decimal precision of the argument. See Chap. 5 and numeric models.

argument: x   **type**: r, c
result: i   **class**: i

Example(s): `i=precision(x)`

PRESENT(a) : Returns whether an optional argument is present.

argument: a   **type**: any
result: l   **class**: i

Note(s):
a must be an optional argument of the procedure in which the `present` function reference appears.
Example(s): `if(present(a)) then`

PRODUCT(array, *mask*) or
PRODUCT(array, dim, *mask*)
The product of all of the elements of `array` along the dimension `dim` corresponding to the true elements of `mask`.

argument: array   **type**: n
argument: dim   **type**: i
argument: mask   **type**: l
result: as array   **class**: t

Note(s):
1. `array` must be an array.
2. $1 <= dim <= n$ where n is the rank of array.
3. `mask` must be conformable with array.
Example(s):
`product((/1,2,3/))` the result is 6.
`product( c , mask = c > 0.0)` forms the product of the positive elements of c.

If

$$B = \begin{pmatrix} 1\ 3\ 5 \\ 2\ 4\ 6 \end{pmatrix}$$

```
product(b,dim=1)
```
is (2,12,30)
```
product(b,dim=2)
```
is (15,48)

RADIX(x) : Returns the base of the numeric argument. See Chap. 5 and numeric models.

argument: x	**type**: i,r
result: i	**class**: i

Example(s): `base=radix(x)`

RANDOM_INIT (repeatable, image_distinct) Initialize the pseudorandom number generator.

argument: repeatable	**type**: l
argument: image_ distinct	**type**: l
result: n/a	**class**: e

Note(s):

1. `repeatable` shall be a logical scalar. It is an `intent (in)` argument. If it has the value `true`, the seed accessed by the pseudorandom number generator is set to a processor-dependent value that is the same each time `random_init` is called from the same image. If it has the value `false`, the seed is set to a processor-dependent, unpredictably different value on each call.

2. `image_distinct` shall be a logical scalar. It is an `intent (in)` argument. If it has the value `true`, the seed accessed by the pseudorandom number generator is set to a processor-dependent value that is distinct from the value that would be set by a call to `random_init` by another image. If it has the value `false`, the value to which the seed is set does not depend on which image calls `random_init`.

Example(s):

```
call random_init (repeatable=.false.,
   image_distinct=.false.)
```

Initializes the pseudorandom number generator so that the seed is different on each call and that the sequence generated will differ from that of another image:

RANDOM_NUMBER(harvest) : Returns one pseudorandom number or an array of pseudorandom numbers from the uniform distribution over the range $0 <= x < 1$

argument: harvest	**type**: r
result: n/a	**class**: s

Note(s):

harvest is intent(out).

Example(s): call random_number(harvest=x)
call random_number(y)
x and y contain uniformly distributed random numbers.

RANDOM_SEED(*size,put,get*) : Restarts(seeds) or queries the pseudorandom generator used by random_number.

argument: size	**type**: i
result: n/a	**class**: s

All arguments are of integer type.

Note(s):

1. size is intent(out). It is set to the number n of integers that the processor uses to hold the value of the seed.

2. put is intent(in). It is an array of rank 1 and $size >= n$ It is used by the processor to set the seed value.

3. get is intent(out). It is an array of rank 1 and $size >= n$ It is set by the processor to the current value of the seed.

Example(s): call random_seed

RANGE(x) : Returns the decimal exponent range of the real argument. See Chap. 5 and the numeric model representing the argument.

argument: x	**type**: n
result: i	**class**: i

Example(s): i=range(n)

RANK (a) : Rank of a data object.

argument: a	**type**: n
result: i	**class**: e

Note(s):
  1. a shall be a data object of any type.
  2. Result Characteristics. Default integer scalar.
Example(s): If X is an assumed-rank dummy argument and its associated effective argument is an array of rank 3, RANK(X) has the value 3.

REAL(a,*kind*) : Converts to real from integer, real or complex.

argument: a	**type**: n
result: r	**class**: e

Example(s): x=real(a)

REDUCE (array, operation [, mask, identity, ordered]) or
REDUCE (array, operation , dim [, mask, identity, ordered]) : General reduction of array.

argument: array	**type**: ANY
argument: operation	**type**: See notes
argument: mask	**type**: l
argument: identity	**type**: n
argument: ordered	**type**: n
argument: dim	**type**: n
result: ?	**class**: t

Notes(s):
  operation shall be a pure function with exactly two arguments; each argument shall be a scalar, nonallocatable, nonpointer, nonpolymorphic, nonoptional dummy data object with the same type and type parameters as array. If one argument has the asynchronous, target, value attribute, the other shall have that attribute. Its result shall be a nonpolymorphic scalar and have the same type and type parameters as array. operation should implement a mathematically associative operation. It need not be commutative.
  dim shall be an integer scalar with a value in the range $1 <= dim <= n$, where n is the rank of ARRAY.
  mask shall be of type logical and shall be conformable with array.
  identity shall be scalar with the same type and type parameters as array.
  ordered shall be a logical scalar.
  If operation is not computationally associative, reduce without ordered=.true. with the same argument values might not always produce the same result, as the processor can apply the associative law to the evaluation.
Example(s):

The following examples all use the function `my_mult`, which returns the product of its two integer arguments.

The value of

```
reduce ([1, 2, 3], my_mult)
```

is 6.

```
reduce (c, my_mult, mask= c > 0, identity=1)
```

forms the product of the positive elements of `c`.

If B is the array

```
1 3 5
2 4 6
```

```
reduce (b, my_mult, dim = 1)
```

is [2, 12, 30] and

```
reduce (b,my_mult, dim = 2)
```

is [15, 48].

REPEAT(string, n_copies) : Concatenate several copies of a string.

argument: string	**type**: s
result: s	**class**: t

Example(s): `new_s=repeat(s,10)`

RESHAPE(source,shape,pad,order) : Constructs an array of a specified shape from the elements of a given array.

argument: source	**type**: any
result: as source	**class**: t

Note(s):

1. `source` must be an array. If `pad` is absent or of size zero the size of `source` must be `product(shape)`.

2. `shape` must be a rank 1 array and $0 <= size < 16$

3. `pad` must be an array.

4. order must have the same shape as shape and its value must be a permutation of (1,2,... ,n) where n is the size of shape. If absent it is as if it were present with the value (1,2,...,n).

5. the result is an array of shape shape

Example(s):

    reshape((/1,2,3,4,5,6/),(/2,3/))

has the value

$$\begin{pmatrix} 1\ 3\ 5 \\ 2\ 4\ 6 \end{pmatrix}$$

    reshape((/1,2,3,4,5,6/) ,(/2,4/) ,(/0,0/) ,(/2,1/))

has the value

$$\begin{pmatrix} 1\ 2\ 3\ 4 \\ 5\ 6\ 0\ 0 \end{pmatrix}$$

RRSPACING(x) : Returns the reciprocal of the relative spacing of model numbers near the argument value. See Chap. 5 and the real numeric model.

argument: x	type: r
result: as x	class: e

Example(s): z=rrspacing(x)

SAME_TYPE_AS(a, b) : Query dynamic types for equality. If the dynamic type of a or b is extensible, the result is true if and only if the dynamic type of a is the same as the dynamic type of b. If neither a nor b has extensible dynamic type, the result is processor dependent.

Note(s):

a an object of extensible declared type or unlimited polymorphic. If it is a pointer, it shall not have an undefined association status.

b an object of extensible declared type or unlimited polymorphic. If it is a pointer, it shall not have an undefined association status.

The dynamic type of a disassociated pointer or unallocated allocatable variable is its declared type. An unlimited polymorphic entity has no declared type.

result: l

type: i

SCALE(x, i) : Returns xb^i where b is the base in the model representation of x. See Chap. 5 and the real numeric model.

> **argument**: x   **type**: r
> **argument**: i   **type**: i
> **result**: as x   **class**: e

Example(s): z=scale(x,i)

SCAN(string, set, *back*) : Scans a string for any one of the characters in a set of characters.

> **argument**: string   **type**: s
> **result**: i   **class**: e

Note(s):

1. The default is to scan from the left, and will only be from the right when back is present and has the value true.

2. Zero is returned if the scan fails.

Example(s): w=scan(string,set)

SELECTED_CHAR_KIND(name) : Returns the kind value for the character set whose name is given by the character string name or -1 if not supported.

> **argument**: name   **type**: char
> **result**: i   **class**: t

Note(s):

If name has the value default, then the result has a value equal to that of the kind type parameter of default character.

If name has the value ASCII, then the result has a value equal to that of the kind type parameter of ASCII character if the processor supports such a kind; otherwise the result has the value 1.

If name has the value ISO_10646, then the result has a value equal to that of the kind type parameter of the ISO 10646 character kind (corresponding to UCS-4 as specified in ISO/IEC 10646) if the processor supports such a kind; otherwise the result has the value 1.

If name is a processor-defined name of some other character kind supported by the processor, then the result has a value equal to that kind type parameter value.

If name is not the name of a supported character type, then the result has the value 1. The name is interpreted without respect to case or trailing blanks.

SELECTED_INT_KIND(r) : Returns a value of the kind type parameter of an integer data type that represents all integer values n with $-10^r < n < 10^r$

argument: r   **type**: i
result: i   **class**: t

Note(s):

r must be scalar.

If a kind type parameter is not available then the value -1 is returned.

Example(s): i=selected_int_kind(2)

SELECTED_REAL_KIND(*p,r,radix*) : Returns a value of the kind type parameter of a real data type with decimal precision of at least p digits and a decimal exponent range of at least r.

argument: p and r   **type**: i
result: i   **class**: t

Note(s):

0. at least one argument must be present.

1. p, r and radix must be integer scalars.

2. The result is -1 if the processor supports a real type with radix radix and exponent range of at least r but not with precision of at least p; -2 if the processor supports a real type with radix radix and precision of at least p but not with exponent range of at least r; -3 if the processor supports a real type with radix radix but with neither precision of at least p nor exponent range of at least r; -4 if the processor supports a real type with radix radix and either precision of at least p or exponent range of at least r but not both together; -5 if the processor supports no real type with radix radix.

Example(s): i=selected_real_kind(p,r)

SET_EXPONENT(x,i) : Returns the model number whose fractional part is the fractional part of the model representation of x and whose exponent part is i.

argument: x   **type**: r
argument: i   **type**: i
result: as x   **class**: e

Example(s): exp_part=set_exponent(x,i)

SHAPE(source, *kind*) : Returns the shape of the array argument or scalar.

argument: source   **type**: any
result: i   **class**: i

Note(s):

1. `source` may be array valued or scalar. It must not be a pointer that is disassociated or an allocatable array that is not allocated. It must not be an assumed-size array.

2. the result is an array of rank 1 whose size is equal to the rank of `source`.

Example(s): s=shape(a(2:5,-1:1)) yields s=(4,3)

SHIFTA(i, shift) : Right shift with fill.

argument: i	**type**: i
argument: shift	**type**: i
result: same as i	**class**: e

Note(s):

1. `shift` shall be nonnegative and less than or equal to `bit_size(i)`

2. If `shift` is zero the result is i. Bits shifted out from the right are lost. The model for the interpretation of an integer value as a sequence of bits is in 16.3 of the standard.

Example(s): shifta (ibset (0, bit_size (0)), 2)
is equal to shiftl (7, bit_size (0) 3).

SHIFTL(i, shift) : Shift left.

argument: i	**type**: i
argument: shift	**type**: i
result: same as i	**class**: e

Note(s):

1. shift shall be nonnegative and less than or equal to `bit_size(i)`

Example(s): shiftl(4, 1) is 8

SHIFTR(i, shift) : Shift right.

argument: i	**type**: i
argument: shift	**type**: i
result: same as i	**class**: e
class: e	

Note(s):

1. shift shall be nonnegative and less than or equal to `bit_size(i)`

Example(s): shiftr(4, 1) is 2.

SIGN(a, b) : Absolute value of a times the sign of b.

argument: a	**type**: i, r
result: as a	**class**: e

Note(s):

1. If $b > 0$, the value of the result is $|a|$.

2. If $b < 0$, the value of the result is $-|a|$.

3. If b is of type integer and $b = 0$, the value of the result is $|a|$.

4. If b is of type real and is zero, then:

if the processor cannot distinguish between positive and negative real zero, or if b is positive real zero, the value of the result is $|a|$;

if b is negative real zero, the value of the result is $-|a|$.

Example(s): a=sign(a,b)

SIN(x) : Sine.

argument: x	**type**: r, c
result: as argument	**class**: e

Note(s):

The argument is in radians.

Example(s): z=sin(x)

SINH(x) : Hyperbolic sine.

argument: x	**type**: r,c
result: as argument	**class**: e

Example(s): z=sinh(x)

SIZE(array, *dim, kind*) : Extent of an array along a specified dimension or the total number of elements in the array.

argument: array	**type**: any
result: i	**class**: i

Note(s):

1. array shall be a scalar or array of any type. It shall not be an unallocated allocatable variable or a pointer that is not associated. If array is an assumed-size array, dim shall be present with a value less than the rank of array.

2. dim (optional) shall be an integer scalar with a value in the range $1 <= dim <= n$, where n is the rank of array.

3. kind shall be a scalar integer constant expression.

4. result is equal to the extent of dimension dim of array, or if dim is absent, the total number of elements of array.

Example(s): a=size(array)

SPACING(x) : Returns the absolute spacing of model numbers near the argument value. See Chap. 5 and the real numeric model.

argument: x	**type**: r
result: as x	**class**: e

Example(s): s=spacing(x)

SPREAD(source, dim, n_copies) : Creates an array with an additional dimension, replicating the values in the original array.

argument: source	**type**: any
result: as source	**class**: t

Note(s):

1. source may be array valued or scalar, with rank less than 15.

2. dim must be scalar and in the range $1 <= dim <= n + 1$ where n is the rank of source.

3. n_copies must be scalar.

4. the result is an array of rank $n + 1$.

Example(s):

If a is the array(2,3,4) then spread(a,dim=1,ncopies=3) then the result is the array

$$\begin{pmatrix} 2\ 3\ 4 \\ 2\ 3\ 4 \\ 2\ 3\ 4 \end{pmatrix}$$

SQRT(x) : Square root.

argument: x	**type**: r, c
result: as argument	**class**: e

Example(s): a=sqrt(b)

STORAGE_SIZE(a, *kind*) : Storage size in bits.

argument: a	**type**: any type.
argument: kind(optional)	**result**: i
class: i	

Note(s):

If a is polymorphic it shall not be an undefined pointer. If it is unlimited polymorphic or has any deferred type parameters, it shall not be an unallocated allocatable variable or a disassociated or undefined pointer.

If kind is present, the kind type parameter is that specified by the value of kind; otherwise, the kind type parameter is that of default integer type.

The result value is the size expressed in bits for an element of an array that has the dynamic type and type parameters of a. If the type and type parameters are such that storage association applies, the result is consistent with the named constants defined in the intrinsic module ISO_FORTRAN_ENV.

An array element might take more bits to store than an isolated scalar, since any hardware-imposed alignment requirements for array elements might not apply to a simple scalar variable.

This is intended to be the size in memory that an object takes when it is stored; this might differ from the size it takes during expression handling (which might be the native register size) or when stored in a file. If an object is never stored in memory but only in a register, this function nonetheless returns the size it would take if it were stored in memory.

Example(s): storage_size(1.0) has the same value as the named constant numeric_storage_size in the intrinsic module iso_fortran_env.

SUM(array, *dim, mask*) or
SUM(array, *mask*) : Returns the sum of all elements of array along the dimension dim corresponding to the true elements of mask.

argument: array	**type**: n
argument: dim	**type**: i
argument: mask	**type**: l
result: as array	**class**: t

Note(s):

1. array must be an array.

2. $1 <= dim <= n$ where n is the rank of array.

3. mask must be conformable with array.

4. result is scalar if dim is absent, or array has rank 1, otherwise the result is an array of rank $n - 1$.

Example(s):

sum((/1,2,3/))

the result is 6.
```
sum(c,mask=c> 0.0)
```
forms the arithmetic sum of the positive elements of c.
If

$$B = \begin{pmatrix} 1 & 3 & 5 \\ 2 & 4 & 6 \end{pmatrix}$$

```
sum(b,dim=1)
```
is (3,7,11)
```
sum(b,dim=2)
```
is (9,12)

SYSTEM_CLOCK(*count,count_rate,count_max*) : Returns integer data from a real time clock.

argument: count	**type**: i
result: n/a	**class**: s

Note(s):

1. `count` is `intent(out)` and is set to a processor dependent value based on the current value of the processor clock or to `-huge(0)` if there is no clock. It lies in the range 0 to `count_max` if there is a clock.

2. `count_rate` is `intent(out)` and it is set to the number of processor clock counts per second, or zero if there is no clock.

3. `count_max` is `intent(out)` and is set to the maximum value that count can have or to zero if there is no clock.
```
call system_clock(c,r,m)
```

TAN(x) : Tangent.

argument: x	**type**: r,c
result: as argument	**class**: e

Note(s):

x must be in radians.

Example(s): `y=tan(x)`

TANH(x) : Hyperbolic tangent.

argument: x	**type**: r,c
result: as argument	**class**: e

```
y=tanh(x)
```

THIS_IMAGE(team) or
THIS_IMAGE(coarray [,team]) or
THIS_IMAGE(coarray, dim [,team]) : Index of the invoking image, a single cosubscript, or a list of cosubscripts.

argument: team	**type**: te
argument: coarray	**type**: a
argument: dim	**type**: i
result: as argument	**class**: e

Note(s):

1. coarray shall be a coarray of any type. If it is allocatable it shall be allocated. If its designator has more than one part-ref, the rightmost part-ref shall have nonzero corank. If it is of type team_type from the intrinsic module ISO_FORTRAN_ENV, the team argument shall appear.

2. dim shall be an integer scalar. Its value shall be in the range $1 <= dim <= n$, where n is the corank of coarray.

3. team shall be a scalar of type team_type from the intrinsic module ISO_FORTRAN_ENV, whose value identifies the current or an ancestor team. If coarray appears, it shall be established in that team.

Example(s):

```
integer, dimension(10,20), &
        codimension[10,0:9,0:*] :: a
```

then on image 5, this_image() has the value 5 and this_image(a) has the value [3,1,2].

TINY(x) : Returns the smallest positive number in the model representing numbers of the same type and kind type parameter as the argument.

argument: x	**type**: r
result: as x	**class**: i

Example(s): t=tiny(x)

TRAILZ(i) : Number of trailing zero bits. If all of the bits of i are zero, the result value is bit_size(i). Otherwise, the result value is the position of the rightmost 1 bit in i.

argument: i	**type**: i
result: i	**class**: e

Example(s):

```
trailz(4)
has the value 2.
```

TRANSFER(source, mold, *size*) : Returns a result with a physical representation identical to that of `source`, but interpreted with the type and type parameters of `mold`.

argument: source	**type**: any
result: as mold	**class**: t

Warning: A thorough understanding of the implementation specific internal representation of the data types involved is necessary for successful use of this function. Consult the documentation that accompanies the compiler that you work with before using this function.

TRANSPOSE(matrix) : Transposes an array of rank 2.

argument: matrix	**type**: any
result: as argument	**class**: t

Note(s):

`matrix` must be of rank 2. If its shape is (n, m) then the resultant matrix has shape (m, n)

Example(s):

```
transpose(a)
```

$$a = \begin{pmatrix} 1\ 2\ 3 \\ 4\ 5\ 6 \\ 7\ 8\ 9 \end{pmatrix} \; yields \; \begin{pmatrix} 1\ 4\ 7 \\ 2\ 5\ 8 \\ 3\ 6\ 9 \end{pmatrix}$$

TRIM(string) : Returns the argument with trailing blanks removed.

argument: string	**type**: s
result: as string	**class**: t

Note(s):

`string` must be a scalar.

Example(s): `t_s=trim(s)`

UBOUND(array, *dim, kind*) : Upper bound(s).

argument: array	**type**: any
result: i	**class**: i

Note(s):

1. `dim` optional. Shall be an integer scalar with a value in the range $1 <= dim <= n$, where n is the rank of array. The corresponding actual argument shall not be an optional dummy argument.

2. For an array section or for an array expression, other than a whole array, `ubound(array, dim)` has a value equal to the number of elements in the given dimension; otherwise, it has a value equal to the upper bound for subscript `dim` of `array` if dimension `dim` of `array` does not have size zero and has the value zero if dimension `dim` has size zero.

Example(s): `z=ubound(a)`

UCOBOUND(coarray, *dim, kind*) : Upper cobound(s) of a coarray.

argument: coarray	**type**: co
argument: dim (optional)	**type**: i
argument: kind(optional)	**type**: i
result: i	**class**: i

UNPACK(vector, mask, field) : Unpacks an array of rank 1 into an array under the control of a mask.

argument: vector	**type**: any
result: as vector	**class**: t

Note(s):

1. `vector` must have rank 1. Its size must be at least t, where t is the number of true elements in mask.

2. `mask` must be array valued.

3. `field` must be conformable with `mask`. Result is an array with the same shape as `mask`.

Example(s):

With `vector=(1,2,3)`

$$and\ mask = \begin{pmatrix} f & t & f \\ t & f & f \\ f & f & t \end{pmatrix}\ and\ field \begin{pmatrix} 1 & 0 & 0 \\ 0 & 1 & 0 \\ 0 & 0 & 1 \end{pmatrix}\ the\ result\ is \begin{pmatrix} 1 & 2 & 0 \\ 1 & 1 & 0 \\ 0 & 0 & 3 \end{pmatrix}$$

VERIFY(string,set,*back,kind*) : Verify that a set of characters contains all the characters in a string by identifying the position of the first character in a string of characters that does not appear in a given set of characters.

argument: string	**type**: s
argument: set	**type**: s
argument: back	**type**: l
result: kind	**class**: i
result: i	**class**: e

Note(s):

1. The default is to scan from the left, and will only be from the right when back is present and has the value true.

2. The value of the result is zero if each character in `string` is in set, or if `string` has zero length.

Example(s) `i=verify(string,set)`

D.10   Fortran Intrinsics by Standard

We use a + character in the table to indicate that the name of the intrinsic continues on the next line. The intrinsics by standard year are in Table D.5.

Table D.5 Intrinsic functions by standard - Fortran 90 to Fortran 2018

Fortran 90	Fortran 95	Fortran 2003	Fortran 2008	Fortran 2018
ABS	ABS	ABS	ABS	ABS
ACHAR	ACHAR	ACHAR	ACHAR	ACHAR
ACOS	ACOS	ACOS	ACOS	ACOS
			ACOSH	ACOSH
ADJUSTL	ADJUSTL	ADJUSTL	ADJUSTL	ADJUSTL
ADJUSTR	ADJUSTR	ADJUSTR	ADJUSTR	ADJUSTR
AIMAG	AIMAG	AIMAG	AIMAG	AIMAG
AINT	AINT	AINT	AINT	AINT
ALL	ALL	ALL	ALL	ALL
ALLOCATED	ALLOCATED	ALLOCATED	ALLOCATED	ALLOCATED
ANINT	ANINT	ANINT	ANINT	ANINT
ANY	ANY	ANY	ANY	ANY
ASIN	ASIN	ASIN	ASIN	ASIN
			ASINH	ASINH
ASSOCIATED	ASSOCIATED	ASSOCIATED	ASSOCIATED	ASSOCIATED
ATAN	ATAN	ATAN	ATAN	ATAN
ATAN2	ATAN2	ATAN2	ATAN2	ATAN2
			ATANH	ATANH
				ATOMIC_ADD
				ATOMIC_AND
				ATOMIC_CAS
				ATOMIC_DEFINE
				ATOMIC_FETCH+_ADD
				ATOMIC_FETCH+_AND
				ATOMIC_FETCH+_OR
				ATOMIC_FETCH+_XOR
				ATOMIC_OR
				ATOMIC_REF
				ATOMIC_XOR
			BESSEL_J0	BESSEL_J0
			BESSEL_J1	BESSEL_J1
			BESSEL_JN	BESSEL_JN
			BESSEL_Y0	BESSEL_Y0
			BESSEL_Y1	BESSEL_Y1
			BESSEL_YN	BESSEL_YN
			BGE	BGE
			BGT	BGT
BIT_SIZE	BIT_SIZE	BIT_SIZE	BIT_SIZE	BIT_SIZE
			BLE	BLE
			BLT	BLT
BTEST	BTEST	BTEST	BTEST	BTEST
CEILING	CEILING	CEILING	CEILING	CEILING
CHAR	CHAR	CHAR	CHAR	CHAR

Table D.5 (continued)

Fortran 90	Fortran 95	Fortran 2003	Fortran 2008	Fortran 2018
CMPLX	CMPLX	CMPLX	CMPLX	CMPLX
				CO_BROADCAST
			CO_LBOUND	CO_LBOUND
				CO_MAX
				CO_MIN
				CO_REDUCE
				CO_SUM
			CO_UBOUND	CO_UBOUND
		COMMAND+	COMMAND+	COMMAND+
		_ARGUMENT+	_ARGUMENT+	_ARGUMENT+
		_COUNT	_COUNT	_COUNT
CONJG	CONJG	CONJG	CONJG	CONJG
COS	COS	COS	COS	COS
COSH	COSH	COSH	COSH	COSH
				COSHAPE
COUNT	COUNT	COUNT	COUNT	COUNT
	CPU_TIME	CPU_TIME	CPU_TIME	CPU_TIME
CSHIFT	CSHIFT	CSHIFT	CSHIFT	CSHIFT
DATE_AND_TIME	DATE_AND_TIME	DATE_AND_TIME	DATE_AND_TIME	DATE_AND_TIME
DBLE	DBLE	DBLE	DBLE	DBLE
DIGITS	DIGITS	DIGITS	DIGITS	DIGITS
DIM	DIM	DIM	DIM	DIM
DOT_PRODUCT	DOT_PRODUCT	DOT_PRODUCT	DOT_PRODUCT	DOT_PRODUCT
DPROD	DPROD	DPROD	DPROD	DPROD
			DSHIFTL	DSHIFTL
			DSHIFTR	DSHIFTR
EOSHIFT	EOSHIFT	EOSHIFT	EOSHIFT	EOSHIFT
EPSILON	EPSILON	EPSILON	EPSILON	EPSILON
			ERF	ERF
			ERFC	ERFC
			ERFC_SCALED	ERFC_SCALED
				EVENT_QUERY
			EXECUTE+	EXECUTE+
			_COMMAND+	_COMMAND+
			_LINE	_LINE
EXP	EXP	EXP	EXP	EXP
EXPONENT	EXPONENT	EXPONENT	EXPONENT	EXPONENT
		EXTENDS+	EXTENDS+	EXTENDS+
		_TYPE_OF	_TYPE_OF	_TYPE_OF
				FAILED_IMAGES
				FINDLOC
FLOOR	FLOOR	FLOOR	FLOOR	FLOOR
FRACTION	FRACTION	FRACTION	FRACTION	FRACTION
			GAMMA	GAMMA
		GET_COMMAND	GET_COMMAND	GET_COMMAND
		GET_COMMAND+	GET_COMMAND+	GET_COMMAND+
		_ARGUMENT	_ARGUMENT	_ARGUMENT
		GET+	GET+	GET+
		_ENVIRONMENT+	_ENVIRONMENT+	_ENVIRONMENT+
		_VARIABLE	_VARIABLE	_VARIABLE
				GET_TEAM

Table D.5 (continued)

Fortran 90	Fortran 95	Fortran 2003	Fortran 2008	Fortran 2018
HUGE	HUGE	HUGE	HUGE	HUGE
			HYPOT	HYPOT
IACHAR	IACHAR	IACHAR	IACHAR	IACHAR
IAND	IAND	IAND	IAND	IALL
IBCLR	IBCLR	IBCLR	IBCLR	IAND
IBITS	IBITS	IBITS	IBITS	IANY
IBSET	IBSET	IBSET	IBSET	IBCLR
				IBITS
				IBSET
ICHAR	ICHAR	ICHAR	ICHAR	ICHAR
IEOR	IEOR	IEOR	IEOR	IEOR
		IMAGE_INDEX	IMAGE_INDEX	
				IMAGE_STATUS
INDEX	INDEX	INDEX	INDEX	INDEX
INT	INT	INT	INT	INT
IOR	IOR	IOR	IOR	IOR
				IPARITY
		IS_CONTIGUOUS	IS_CONTIGUOUS	IS_CONTIGUOUS
		IS_IOSTAT_END	IS_IOSTAT_END	IS_IOSTAT_END
		IS_IOSTAT_EOR	IS_IOSTAT_EOR	IS_IOSTAT_EOR
ISHFT	ISHFT	ISHFT	ISHFT	ISHFT
ISHFTC	ISHFTC	ISHFTC	ISHFTC	ISHFTC
KIND	KIND	KIND	KIND	KIND
LBOUND	LBOUND	LBOUND	LBOUND	LBOUND
				LCOBOUND
			LEADZ	LEADZ
LEN	LEN	LEN	LEN	LEN
LEN_TRIM	LEN_TRIM	LEN_TRIM	LEN_TRIM	LEN_TRIM
LGE	LGE	LGE	LGE	LGE
LGT	LGT	LGT	LGT	LGT
LLE	LLE	LLE	LLE	LLE
LLT	LLT	LLT	LLT	LLT
LOG	LOG	LOG	LOG	LOG
			LOG_GAMMA	LOG_GAMMA
LOG10	LOG10	LOG10	LOG10	LOG10
LOGICAL	LOGICAL	LOGICAL	LOGICAL	LOGICAL
			MASKL	MASKL
			MASKR	MASKR
MATMUL	MATMUL	MATMUL	MATMUL	MATMUL
MAX	MAX	MAX	MAX	MAX
MAXEXPONENT	MAXEXPONENT	MAXEXPONENT	MAXEXPONENT	MAXEXPONENT
MAXLOC	MAXLOC	MAXLOC	MAXLOC	MAXLOC
MAXVAL	MAXVAL	MAXVAL	MAXVAL	MAXVAL
MERGE	MERGE	MERGE	MERGE	MERGE
			MERGE_BITS	MERGE_BITS
MIN	MIN	MIN	MIN	MIN
MINEXPONENT	MINEXPONENT	MINEXPONENT	MINEXPONENT	MINEXPONENT
MINLOC	MINLOC	MINLOC	MINLOC	MINLOC
MINVAL	MINVAL	MINVAL	MINVAL	MINVAL
MOD	MOD	MOD	MOD	MOD
MODULO	MODULO	MODULO	MODULO	MODULO
	MOVE_ALLOC	MOVE_ALLOC	MOVE_ALLOC	MOVE_ALLOC

Table D.5 (continued)

Fortran 90	Fortran 95	Fortran 2003	Fortran 2008	Fortran 2018
MVBITS	MVBITS	MVBITS	MVBITS	MVBITS
NEAREST	NEAREST	NEAREST	NEAREST	NEAREST
		NEW_LINE	NEW_LINE	NEW_LINE
NINT	NINT	NINT	NINT	NINT
			NORM2	NORM2
NOT	NOT	NOT	NOT	NOT
	NULL	NULL	NULL	NULL
			NUM_IMAGES	NUM_IMAGES
				OUT_OF_RANGE
PACK	PACK	PACK	PACK	PACK
			PARITY	PARITY
			POPCNT	POPCNT
			POPPAR	POPPAR
PRECISION	PRECISION	PRECISION	PRECISION	PRECISION
PRESENT	PRESENT	PRESENT	PRESENT	PRESENT
PRODUCT	PRODUCT	PRODUCT	PRODUCT	PRODUCT
RADIX	RADIX	RADIX	RADIX	RADIX
				RANDOM_INIT
RANDOM+ _NUMBER	RANDOM+ _NUMBER	RANDOM+ _NUMBER	RANDOM+ _NUMBER	RANDOM+ _NUMBER
RANDOM_SEED	RANDOM_SEED	RANDOM_SEED	RANDOM_SEED	RANDOM_SEED
RANGE	RANGE	RANGE	RANGE	RANGE
				RANK
REAL	REAL	REAL	REAL	REAL
				REDUCE
REPEAT	REPEAT	REPEAT	REPEAT	REPEAT
RESHAPE	RESHAPE	RESHAPE	RESHAPE	RESHAPE
RRSPACING	RRSPACING	RRSPACING	RRSPACING	RRSPACING
		SAME_TYPE_AS	SAME_TYPE_AS	SAME_TYPE_AS
SCALE	SCALE	SCALE	SCALE	SCALE
SCAN	SCAN	SCAN	SCAN	SCAN
		SELECTED+ _CHAR+ _KIND	SELECTED+ _CHAR+ _KIND	SELECTED+ _CHAR+ _KIND
SELECTED_INT+ _KIND	SELECTED_INT+ _KIND	SELECTED_INT+ _KIND	SELECTED_INT+ _KIND	SELECTED_INT+ _KIND
SELECTED+ _REAL+ _KIND	SELECTED+ _REAL+ _KIND	SELECTED+ _REAL+ _KIND	SELECTED+ _REAL+ _KIND	SELECTED+ _REAL+ _KIND
SET_EXPONENT	SET_EXPONENT	SET_EXPONENT	SET_EXPONENT	SET_EXPONENT
SHAPE	SHAPE	SHAPE	SHAPE	SHAPE
			SHIFTA	SHIFTA
			SHIFTL	SHIFTL
			SHIFTR	SHIFTR
SIGN	SIGN	SIGN	SIGN	SIGN
SIN	SIN	SIN	SIN	SIN
SINH	SINH	SINH	SINH	SINH
SIZE	SIZE	SIZE	SIZE	SIZE
SPACING	SPACING	SPACING	SPACING	SPACING
SPREAD	SPREAD	SPREAD	SPREAD	SPREAD
SQRT	SQRT	SQRT	SQRT	SQRT
				STOPPED_IMAGES
			STORAGE_SIZE	STORAGE_SIZE

Table D.5 (continued)

Fortran 90	Fortran 95	Fortran 2003	Fortran 2008	Fortran 2018
SUM	SUM	SUM	SUM	SUM
SYSTEM_CLOCK	SYSTEM_CLOCK	SYSTEM_CLOCK	SYSTEM_CLOCK	SYSTEM_CLOCK
TAN	TAN	TAN	TAN	TAN
TANH	TANH	TANH	TANH	TANH
				TEAM_NUMBER
				THIS_IMAGE
TINY	TINY	TINY	TINY	TINY
			TRAILZ	TRAILZ
TRANSFER	TRANSFER	TRANSFER	TRANSFER	TRANSFER
TRANSPOSE	TRANSPOSE	TRANSPOSE	TRANSPOSE	TRANSPOSE
TRIM	TRIM	TRIM	TRIM	TRIM
UBOUND	UBOUND	UBOUND	UBOUND	UBOUND
				UCOBOUND
UNPACK	UNPACK	UNPACK	UNPACK	UNPACK
VERIFY	VERIFY	VERIFY	VERIFY	VERIFY
N = 113	N = 115	N = 126	N = 166	N = 200

D.11   Standard Intrinsic Modules

The standard defines five standard intrinsic modules:

- a Fortran environment module
- a set of three modules to support floating-point exceptions and IEEE arithmetic
- a module to support interoperability with the C programming language

   The intrinsic modules

- IEEE_EXCEPTIONS
- IEEE_ARITHMETIC
- IEEE_FEATURES are described in Clause 17 of the standard.

   The intrinsic module ISO_C_BINDING is described in Clause 18 of the standard.
   The intrinsic module ISO_FORTRAN_ENV provides public entities relating to the Fortran environment.
   The processor shall provide the named constants, derived types, and procedures described in subclause 16.10.2. of the standard.
   Here is a complete list of the public entities in this module.

- ATOMIC_INT_KIND
- ATOMIC_LOGICAL_KIND
- CHARACTER_KINDS
- CHARACTER_STORAGE_SIZE
- COMPILER_OPTIONS ( )
- COMPILER_VERSION ( )
- CURRENT_TEAM
- ERROR_UNIT
- EVENT_TYPE
- FILE_STORAGE_SIZE
- INITIAL_TEAM
- INPUT_UNIT
- INT8, INT16, INT32, and INT64
- INTEGER_KINDS
- IOSTAT_END
- IOSTAT_EOR
- IOSTAT_INQUIRE_INTERNAL_UNIT
- LOCK_TYPE
- LOGICAL_KINDS
- NUMERIC_STORAGE_SIZE
- OUTPUT_UNIT
- PARENT_TEAM
- REAL_KINDS
- REAL32, REAL64, and REAL128
- STAT_FAILED_IMAGE

- STAT_LOCKED
- STAT_LOCKED_OTHER_IMAGE
- STAT_STOPPED_IMAGE
- STAT_UNLOCKED
- STAT_UNLOCKED_FAILED_IMAGE
- TEAM_TYPE

Consult the standard for more information.

Appendix E
Text extracts, English, Latin and coded

English and Latin

```
YET IF HE SHOULD GIVE UP WHAT
HE HAS BEGUN, AND AGREE TO MAKE US OR
OUR KINGDOM SUBJECT TO THE KING OF ENGLAND
OR THE ENGLISH, WE SHOULD
EXERT OURSELVES AT ONCE TO DRIVE HIM OUT AS
OUR ENEMY AND A SUBVERTER
OF HIS OWN RIGHTS AND OURS, AND MAKE SOME
OTHER MAN WHO WAS ABLE TO
DEFEND US OUR KING; FOR, AS LONG AS BUT A
HUNDRED OF US REMAIN ALIVE,
NEVER WILL WE ON ANY CONDITIONS BE BROUGHT
UNDER ENGLISH RULE. IT
IS IN TRUTH NOT FOR GLORY, NOR RICHES, NOR
HONOURS THAT WE ARE FIGHTING,
BUT FOR FREEDOM - FOR THAT ALONE, WHICH NO
HONEST MAN GIVES UP BUT
WITH LIFE ITSELF.


QUEM SI AB INCEPTIS
DIESISTERET, REGI ANGLORUM AUT ANGLICIS NOS
AUT
REGNUM NOSTRUM VOLENS SUBICERE, TANQUAM
INIMICUM NOSTRUM ET SUI NOSTRIQUE
JURIS SUBUERSOREM STATIM EXPELLERE NITEREMUR
ET ALIUM REGEM NOSTRUM
QUI AD DEFENSIONEM NOSTRAM SUFFICERET
FACEREMUS. QUIA QUANDIU CENTUM
EX NOBIS VIUI REMANSERINT, NUCQUAM ANGLORUM
```

```
DOMINIO ALIQUATENUS VOLUMUS
SUBIUGARI. NON ENIM PROPTER GLORIAM,
DIUICIAS AUT HONORES PUGNAMUS
SET PROPTER LIBERATEM SOLUMMODO QUAM NEMO
BONUS NISI SIMUL CUM VITA
AMITTIT.
```

```
from'The Declaration of Arbroath'
c.1320. The English translation is by
Sir James Fergusson.
```

Coded

```
OH YABY NSFOUN, YAN DUBZY LZ DBUYLTUBFAJ
BYYBOHNX GPDA FNUZNDYOLH
YABY YAN SBF LZ B GOHTMN FULWOHDN DLWNUNX
YAN GFBDN LZ BH NHYOUN DOYJ,
BHX YAN SBF LZ YAN NSFOUN OYGNMZ BH NHYOUN
FULWOHDN. OH YAN DLPUGN
LZ YOSN, YANGN NKYNHGOWN SBFG VNUN ZLPHX
GLSNALV VBHYOHT, BHX GL YAN
DLMMNTN LZ DBUYLTUBFANUG NWLMWNX B SBF LZ
YAN NSFOUN YABY VBG YAN
GBSN GDBMN BG YAN NSFOUN BHX YABY DLOHDOXNX
VOYA OY FLOHY ZLU FLOHY.
MNGG BYYNHYOWN YL YAN GYPXJ LZ DBUYLTUBFAJ,
GPDDNNXOHT TNHNUBYOLHG
DBSN YL RPXTN B SBF LZ GPDA SBTHOYPXN
DPSENUGLSN, BHX, HLY VOYALPY
OUUNWNUNHDN, YANJ BEBHXLHNX OY YL YAN
UOTLPUG LZ GPH BHX UBOH. OH
YAN VNGYNUH XNGNUYG, YBYYNUNX ZUBTSNHYG LZ
YAN SBF BUN GYOMM YL EN
ZLPHX, GANMYNUOHT BH LDDBGOLHBM ENBGY LU
ENTTBU; OH YAN VALMN HBYOLH,
HL LYANU UNMOD OG MNZY LZ YAN XOGDOFMOHN LZ
TNLTUBFAJ.
```

Appendix F
Formal syntax

Statement Ordering

Format statements may appear anywhere between the use statement and the contains statement.

The following table summarises the usage of the various statements within individual scoping units.

Kind of scoping unit	Main program	Module	External sub program	Module sub program	Internal sub program	Interface body
use	Y	Y	Y	Y	Y	Y
format	Y	N	Y	Y	Y	N
misc dec.	Y	Y	Y	Y	Y	Y
derived type definition	Y	Y	Y	Y	Y	Y
interface block	Y	Y	Y	Y	Y	Y
executable statement	Y	N	Y	Y	Y	N
contains	Y	Y	Y	Y	N	N

misc dec. (miscellaneous declaration) are parameter statements, implicit statements, type declaration statements and specification statements.

Syntax Summary of Some Frequently Used Fortran Constructs

The following provides simple syntactical definitions of some of the more frequently used parts of Fortran.

Main Program

```
program [ program-name ]
[ specification-construct ] ...
[ executable-construct ] ...
[contains
[ internal procedure ] ... ]
end [ program [ program-name ] ]
```

© Springer International Publishing AG, part of Springer Nature 2018
I. Chivers and J. Sleightholme, *Introduction to Programming with Fortran*,
https://doi.org/10.1007/978-3-319-75502-1

Subprogram

    procedure heading

    [specification-construct] ...

    [executable-construct] ...

    [contains

    [internal procedure] ...]

    procedure ending

Module

    module name

    [specification-construct] ...

    [contains

    subprogram

    [subprogram] ...]

    end [module [module-name]

Internal Procedure

    procedure heading

    [specification construct] ...

    [executable construct] ...

    procedure ending

Procedure Heading

    [recursive] [type specification] function function-name

    ([dummy argument list]) [result (result name)]

    [recursive] subroutine subroutine name

    [([dummy argument list])]

Procedure Ending

    end [function [function name]]

    end [subroutine [subroutine name]]

Specification Construct

    derived type definition

    interface block

    specification statement

Derived Type Definition

    type [[, access specification] ::] type name

    [private]

    [sequence]

    [type specification [[, pointer] ::] component specification list]

    ...

    end type [type name]

Interface Block

    interface [generic specification]

    [procedure heading

    [specification construct] ...

    procedure ending] ...

    [module procedure module procedure name list] ...

    end interface

Specification Statement

 allocatable [::] allocatable array list
 dimension array dimension list
 external external name list
 format ([format specification list])
 implicit implicit specification
 intent (intent specification) :: dummy argument name list
 intrinsic intrinsic procedure name list
 optional [::] optional object list
 parameter (named constant definition list)
 pointer [::] pointer name list
 public [[::] module entity name list]
 private[[::] module entity name list]
 save[[::] saved object list]
 target [::] target name list
 use module name [, rename list]
 use module name , only : [access list]
 type specification [[, attribute specification] ... :: object declaration list

Type Specification

 integer [([kind=] kind parameter)]
 real[([kind=] kind parameter)]
 complex[([kind=] kind parameter)]
 character[([kind=] kind parameter)]
 character[([kind=] kind parameter)]
 [len=] length parameter)
 logical[([kind=] kind parameter)]
 type (type name)

Attribute Specification

 allocatable
 dimension (array specification)
 external
 intent (intent specification)
 intrinsic
 optional
 parameter
 pointer
 private
 public
 save
 target

Executable Construct

 action statement
 case construct
 do construct
 if construct
 where construct

Action Statement

    allocate (allocation list) [,stat= scalar integer variable])

    call subroutinename [([actual argument specification list])]

    close (close specification list)

    cycle [do construct name]

    deallocate(name list) [, stat= scalar integer variable])

    endfile external file unit

    exit [do construct name]

    goto label

    if (scalar logical expression) action statement

    inquire (inquire specification list) [output item list]

    nullify (pointer object list)

    open [and close] (connect specification list)

    print format [, output item list]

    read (i/o control specification list) [input item list]

    read format [, output item list]

    return [scalar integer expression]

    rewind (position specification list)

    stop [access code]

    where (array logical expression) array assignment expression

    write (i/o control specification list) [output item list]

    pointer variable => target expression

    variable = expression

Appendix G
Compiler Options

In this appendix we look at some of compiler options we have used during the development of the programs in the book.

Simplistically there are two kinds of compile or build.

- A debug build - used when developing code
- A production build - used when executing or running code

We provide debug and production build options for each compiler.

There are also extracts from the help files on what the various options mean.

G.1 Cray

G.1.1 Debug

```
-G Debug level
-R run time checks
```

G.1.2 Production

We used the default compiler options.

© Springer International Publishing AG, part of Springer Nature 2018

I. Chivers and J. Sleightholme, *Introduction to Programming with Fortran*,

https://doi.org/10.1007/978-3-319-75502-1

G.2   gfortran

G.2.1   Debug

```
gfortran
-fbacktrace
-fcheck=all
-ffpe-trap=zero,overflow,underflow
-g
-O
-pedantic-errors
-std=f2008
-Wall
-Wunderflow
```

G.2.2   Production

```
gfortran
-ffast-math
-funroll-loops
-O3
```

Here are some extracts from the help files.

```
debug
```

```
-fbacktrace
   trace back in the event of a run time
   error, i.e. the Fortran runtime library
   tries to output a backtrace of the error
```

```
-fcheck
   Enable the generation of run-time checks;
   the argument shall be a comma-delimited
   list of the following keywords.
   all Enable all run-time test of -fcheck
```

```
-ffpe-trap=list
   Specify a list of floating point exception
   traps to enable
```

```
-pedantic
  Issue warnings for uses of extensions to
  Fortran 95

-std
  standard conformance

-Wall
  Enables commonly used warning options
  pertaining to usage that we
  recommend avoiding and that we believe
  are easy to avoid.  This
  currently includes -Waliasing,
  -Wampersand, -Wconversion,
  -Wsurprising, -Wc-binding-type,
  -Wintrinsics-std, -Wtabs,
  -Wintrinsic-shadow, -Wline-truncation,
  -Wtarget-lifetime,
  -Wreal-q-constant and -Wunused.

-Wunderflow
  Produce a warning when numerical constant
  expressions are    encountered, which
  yield an UNDERFLOW during compilation.
  Enabled by default

-Wrealloc-lhs
  Warn when the compiler might insert code
  to for allocation or    reallocation of
  an allocatable array variable of intrinsic
  type in intrinsic assignments

production

-fcoarray
  none
    Disable coarray support; using coarray
    declarations and image-
    control statements will produce a
    compile-time error. (Default)
  single
    Single-image mode, i.e. "num_images()"
    is always one.
  lib Library-based coarray parallelization; a
    suitable GNU Fortran
```

```
        coarray library needs to be linked
```

```
-fopenmp
   Enable the OpenMP extensions
```

G.3   Intel

G.3.1   Debug

```
ifort
/check:all
/debug:all
/fpe:0
/gen-interfaces
/standard-semantics
/traceback
/warn:all
```

You will also need

```
/Qcoarray
/Qopenmp
```

when compiling the coarray and openmp examples.
   Here is an extract from the help files.

```
/check:all
```

```
enables the following
```

```
check arg_temp_created
```

```
    Enables run-time checking on whether actual arguments are
    copied into temporary storage before routine calls. If a
    copy is made at run-time, an informative message is
    displayed.
```

```
check assume
```

```
    Enables run-time checking on whether the
    scalar-Boolean-expression in the ASSUME directive is true
    and that the addresses in the ASSUME_ALIGNED directive are
```

aligned on the specified byte boundaries. If the test is
.FALSE., a run-time error is reported and the execution
terminates.

check bounds

Enables compile-time and run-time checking for array
subscript and character substring expressions. An error is
reported if the expression is outside the dimension of the
array or the length of the string.
For array bounds, each individual dimension is checked. For
arrays that are dummy arguments, only the lower bound is
checked for a dimension whose upper bound is specified as *
or where the upper and lower bounds are both 1.
For some intrinsics that specify a DIM= dimension argument,
such as LBOUND, an error is reported if the specified
dimension is outside the declared rank of the array being
operated upon.
Once the program is debugged, omit this option to reduce
executable program size and slightly improve run-time
performance.
It is recommended that you do bounds checking on
unoptimized code. If you use option check bounds on
optimized code, it may produce misleading messages because
registers (not memory locations) are used for bounds values.

check contiguous

Tells the compiler to check pointer contiguity at
pointer-assignment time. This will help prevent programming
errors such as assigning contiguous pointers to
non-contiguous objects.

check format

Issues the run-time FORVARMIS fatal error when the data
type of an item being formatted for output does not match
the format descriptor being used (for example, a REAL*4
item formatted with an I edit descriptor).
With check noformat, the data item is formatted using the
specified descriptor unless the length of the item cannot
accommodate the descriptor (for example, it is still an
error to pass an INTEGER*2 item to an E edit descriptor).

check output_conversion

Issues the run-time OUTCONERR continuable error message
when a data item is too large to fit in a designated format
descriptor field without loss of significant digits. Format
truncation occurs, the field is filled with asterisks (*),
and execution continues.

check pointers

Enables run-time checking for disassociated or
uninitialized Fortran pointers, unallocated allocatable
objects, and integer pointers that are uninitialized.

check stack

Enables checking on the stack frame. The stack is checked
for buffer overruns and buffer underruns. This option also
enforces local variables initialization and stack pointer
verification.
This option disables optimization and overrides any
optimization level set by option O.

check uninit

Enables run-time checking for uninitialized variables. If a
variable is read before it is written, a run-time error
routine will be called. Only local scalar variables of
intrinsic type INTEGER, REAL, COMPLEX, and LOGICAL without
the SAVE attribute are checked.
To detect uninitialized arrays or array elements, please
see option [Q]init or see the article titled: Detection of
Uninitialized Floating-point Variables in Intel Fortran,
which is located in
https://software.intel.com/articles/detection-of-uninitializ
ed-floating-point-variables-in-intel-fortran

/debug:all

Generates complete debugging information. It produces
symbol table information needed for full symbolic debugging
of unoptimized code and global symbol information needed
for linking. It is the same as specifying /debug with no
keyword. If you specify /debug:full for an application that
makes calls to C library routines and you need to debug
calls into the C library, you should also specify /dbglibs

to request that the appropriate C debug library be linked
against.

/fpe:0

Floating-point invalid, divide-by-zero, and
overflow exceptions are enabled throughout the application
when the main program is compiled with this value.
If any such exceptions occur, execution is aborted.
This option causes denormalized floating-point
results to be set to zero.

/gen_interfaces

Tells the compiler to generate an interface block for each
routine in a source file.

/standard_semantics

Determines whether the current Fortran Standard behaviour of
the compiler is fully implemented.

/traceback

Tells the compiler to generate extra information in the
object file to provide source file traceback information
when a severe error occurs at run time.

/warn:all

alignments

Warnings are issued about data that is not naturally
aligned.

general

All information-level and warning-level messages are
enabled.

nodeclarations

No warnings are issued for undeclared names.

noerrors

Warning-level messages are not changed to error-level messages.

`noignore_loc`

No warnings are issued when %LOC is stripped from an argument.

`nointerfaces`

The compiler does not check interfaces of SUBROUTINEs called and FUNCTIONs invoked in your compilation against an external set of interface blocks.

`nostderrors`

Warning-level messages about Fortran standards violations are not changed to error-level messages.

`notruncated_source`

No warnings are issued when source exceeds the maximum column width in fixed-format files.

`nouncalled`

No warnings are issued when a statement function is not called.

`nounused`

No warnings are issued for variables that are declared but never used.

`usage`

Warnings are issued for questionable programming practices.

G.3.2   Production

Intel (autoparallel)

```
ifort
/fast
  enables
  /QxHOST /O3 /Qipo /Qprec-div
/fp:fast=2
/heap-arrays
/Qopenmp
/Qparallel
```

Here are some extracts from the compiler documentation.

/QxHost	generate instructions for the highest instruction set and processor available on the compilation host machine
/O3	optimize for maximum speed and enable more aggressive optimizations that may not improve performance on some programs
/Qipo	Interprocedural Optimization (IPO) enable multi-file IP between files
/Qprec-div	improve precision of FP divides (some speed impact) /Qprec-div- goes for speed over precision
/fp:<name>	enable <name> floating point model variation
except[-]	- enable/disable floating point exception semantics
fast[=1|2]	- enables more aggressive floating point optimizations
precise	- allows value-safe optimizations
source	- enables intermediates in source precision sets
	/assume:protect_parens for Fortran
strict	- enables /fp:precise /fp:except, disables contractions and enables pragma stdc fenv_access
consistent	- enables consistent,
reproducible	
	results for different optimization levels or between

```
                         different processors of the
                         same architecture
/heap-arrays    temporary arrays are allocated
                         in heap memory rather than on the
                         stack.
/Qparallel      enable the auto-parallelizer to
                         generate multi-threaded code for
                         loops that can be safely executed
                         in parallel
```

G.4   Nag

G.4.1   Debug

```
nagfor
-C=all
-C=undefined
-f2008
-g
-gline
-ieee=stop
-info
-mtrace=verbose
-thread_safe
```

Here are extracts from the compiler documentation.

```
-C=check
```

```
   Compile checking code according to
   the value of check, which must be one of:

   all        (perform all checks except for
               -C=undefined),
   array      (check array bounds),
   bits       (check bit intrinsic arguments),
   calls      (check procedure references),
   dangling   (check for dangling pointers),
   do         (check DO loops for zero step values),
   intovf     (check for integer overflow),
   none       (do no checking: this is the default),
   present    (check OPTIONAL references),
```

```
pointer    (check POINTER references),
recursion (check for invalid recursion) or
undefined (check for undefined variables).
```

-f2008

```
Specify that the base language is Fortran 2008.
This is the default.
```

-g

```
Produce information for interactive debugging
by the host system debugger.
```

-gline

```
Compile code to produce a traceback when a

runtime error message is generated.
```

-ieee=mode

```
Set the mode of IEEE arithmetic operation
according to mode, which must be one of
full, nonstd or stop.
full
```

```
   enables all IEEE arithmetic
   facilities including
   non-stop arithmetic.
```

nonstd

```
   Disables non-stop arithmetic, terminating
   execution on floating overflow, division
   by zero or invalid operand. If the
   hardware supports it, this also disables
   IEEE gradual underflow, producing
   zero instead of a denormalised number;
   this can improve performance on some systems.
```

stop

```
   enables all IEEE arithmetic facilities
```

except for non-stop arithmetic;
execution will be terminated on

floating overflow, division by zero
or invalid
operand.

The -ieee option must be specified when

compiling the main program unit, and its
effect is global.

The default mode is -ieee=stop. For more

details see the
IEEE 754 Arithmetic Support section.

-info

  Request output of information messages. The

  default is to suppress these messages.

-mtrace=trace_opt_list

  Trace memory allocation and deallocation
  according to the value of trace_opt_list,
  which must be a comma separated
  list of one or more of:

```
address  (display addresses),
all      (all options except for off),
line     (display file/line info if known),
off      (disable tracing output),
on       (enable tracing output),
paranoia (protect memory allocator data structures
         against the user program),
size     (display size in bytes) or
verbose  (all options except for off and paranoia ).
```

-thread_safe

  Compile code for safe execution in a
  multi-threaded environment.

```
This must be specified when compiling
and also during the link phase.
   It is incompatible with the -gc and -gline
options.
```

G.4.2   Production

```
nagfor
-O4
-openmp
-thread_safe
```

Here are some extracts from the compiler documentation.

```
-ON
```

```
Set the optimisation level to N. The
optimisation
 levels are:
```

```
-O0
```

```
No optimisation. This is the default, and
is recommended when debugging.
```

```
-O1
```

```
Minimal quick optimisation.
```

```
-O2
```

```
Normal optimisation.
```

```
-O3
```

```
Further optimisation.
```

```
-O4
```

```
Maximal optimisation.
```

G.4.3   Nag Polish

The Nag compiler has a *polish* option. Here are some of the options used in the reformatting of the examples in the book. The examples in the book were set with a line length of 48 to fit the printed page. The examples on the web site were set with a line length of 132.

```
nagfor =polish -alter_comments
-noblank_cmt_to_blank_line
-blank_line_after_decls -break_long_comment_word
-format_start=100  -format_step=10   -idcase=L
-indent=2 -indent_continuation=2   -indent_max=16
-keep_blank_lines -keep_comments  -kwcase=L
-leave_formats_in_place -margin=0
-noindent_comment_marker
-noseparate_format_numbering -relational=F90+
-renumber -renumber_start=100 -renumber_step=10
-separate_format_numbering
-terminate_do_with_enddo  -width=48
```

G.5   Oracle

G.5.1   Debug

```
sunf90
-ansi
-w4
-xcheck=all
-C
-ftrap=common,overflow,underflow
```

G.5.2   Production

```
sunf90 -fast ch2502.f90 -V -v
```

maps into

```
-xO5
-xtarget=native
```

```
-xchip=pentium
-xcache=generic
-xarch=sse3
-xdepend=yes
-aligncommon=dalign
-fma=fused
-fsimple=2
-fns=yes
-ftrap=division,invalid,overflow
-xlibmil
-xlibmopt
-nofstore
-xregs=frameptr
-y-fsimple=2
-a dalign
-m3
-ev
-xall
-xivdep=loop
-H
```

Here are some extracts from the help files.

```
-C
  Enable runtime subscript range checking
-O
  Use default optimization level (-xO3)
-O<n>
  Same as -xO<n>
-aligncommon[=<a>]
  Align common block elements to the
  specified boundary requirement;
  <a>={1|2|4|8|16|dalign}
-ansi
  Report non-ANSI extensions
-autopar
  Enable automatic loop parallelization
-dalign
  Expands to -aligncommon=dalign
-fma=<a>
  Enable floating-point multiply-add
  instruction; <a>={none|fused}
-fns[={yes|no}]
  Select non-standard floating point mode
-fopenmp
```

```
    Equivalent to -xopenmp=parallel
-fprecision=<a>
    Set FP rounding precision mode;
    <a>={single|double|extended}
-fstore
    Force floating pt. values to target
    precision on assignment
-ftrap=<t>
    Select floating-point trapping mode in
    effect at startup
-g
    Compile for debugging
-xO<n>
    Generate optimized code; <n>={1|2|3|4|5}
-xarch=<a>
    Specify target architecture instruction set
-xcache=<t>
    Define cache properties for use by optimizer
-xchip=<a>
    Specify the target processor for use by the
    optimizer
-xdepend[={yes|no}]
    Analyze loops for data dependencies
-xivdep[=<a>]
    Ignore loop-carried dependences on array
    references in a loop;
    <a>={loop|loop_any|back|back_any|none}
-xlibmil
    Inline selected libm math routines for
    optimization
-xlibmopt
    Link with optimized math library
-xregs=<a>[,<a>]
    Specify the usage of optional registers;
    <a>={frameptr}
-xtarget=<a>
    Specify target system for optimization
```

Index

Printed in the United States
by Baker & Taylor Publisher Services